THE RECONSTRUCTION OF PALESTINE: ISSUES, OPTIONS, POLICIES AND STRATEGIES

Edited by
A.B. Zahlan

Kegan Paul International
London and New York

First published in 1997 by
Kegan Paul International
UK: P.O. Box 256, London WC1B 3SW, England
Tel: (0171) 580 5511   Fax: (0171) 436 0899
E-mail: books@keganpau.demon.co.uk
Internet: http://www.demon.co.uk/keganpaul/
USA: 562 West 113th Street, New York, NY 10025, USA
Tel: (212) 666 1000   Fax: (212) 316 3100

Distributed by

John Wiley & Sons Ltd
Southern Cross Trading Estate
1 Oldlands Way, Bognor Regis
West Sussex, PO22 9SA, England
Tel: (01243) 779 777   Fax: (01243) 820 250

Columbia University Press
562 West 113th Street
New York, NY 10025, USA
Tel: (212) 666 1000   Fax: (212) 316 3100

© A. B. Zahlan 1997

Set in Baskerville 10 on 12pt
by Intype London Ltd
Printed in Great Britain by TJ Press, Padstow, Cornwall

British Library Cataloguing in Publication Data
The reconstruction of Palestine: urban and rural development
1. City planning – Palestine   2. Rural development – Palestine
3. Palestine – Economic conditions   4. Palestine – Social policy
I. Zahlan, A. B. (Antoine Benjamin), 1928–
307.1'2'095694

ISBN 0–7103–0557–5

Library of Congress Cataloging-in-Publication Data
The Reconstruction of Palestine: urban and rural development/edited
by A. B. Zahlan
p. cm.
Includes bibliographical references (p. 18–19).
ISBN 0–7103–0557–5 (pbk. ; alk. paper)
1. Urbanization—West Bank.   2. Urbanization—Gaza Strip.
3. Rural development—West Bank.   4. Rural development—Gaza Strip.
5. Housing—West Bank.   6. Housing—Gaza Strip,   7. Real estate
development—West Bank.   8. Real estate development—Gaza Strip.
I. Zahlan, A. B. (Antoine Benjamin), 1928–   .
HT384.W47R43   1996
307.7'6'095694—dc20   96–16434
CIP

THE RECONSTRUCTION OF PALESTINE

CONTENTS

v

THEME FOUR: HOUSING ALTERNATIVES AND OPTIONS FOR CONSERVATION AND RENEWAL

THEME FIVE: FINANCIAL SERVICES FOR HOUSING AND URBAN DEVELOPMENT

THEME SIX: THE CONSTRUCTION INDUSTRY

FOREWORD

This Monograph is the outcome of a Conference on the Urban and Rural Reconstruction of Palestine held in Amman, 24–27 November 1995. It provided Palestinians and other interested parties with an opportunity to discuss issues, options, policies and strategies. It was attended by 170 participants, including architects, contractors, consultants, planners, construction engineers, economists, mayors and representatives of municipalities and NGOs, finance officers, bankers, investors and others. They represented a cross-section of Palestinian, regional and international organisations.

Two approaches were adopted to increase participation and encourage interaction with local institutions. First, participants met in six theme-oriented parallel sessions, as well as in plenary sessions at the beginning and end of the Conference. Second, informal meetings were organised with six Jordanian institutions to encourage personal and institutional contacts.

The discussions which took place were viewed as a vital accompaniment to the urbanisation programme that is presently underway. A principal objective was to initiate a sequence of similar informal conferences. One of the first to take place will be a conference on affordable housing at Birzeit University in November 1996 as a direct sequel to this initial step.

INSTITUTIONAL FOUNDATIONS OF RECONSTRUCTION

Urban and rural reconstruction is one of the most far-reaching activities which Palestinians will undertake during the next few decades. The long historical process of national self-expression and development is reflected in the present revival of construction activity in many forms.

Palestinians are late-comers to development and could benefit from the experiences of other societies. The challenges of reconstruction have already been faced by many developing societies, although none would have faced similar political conditions. By the same token, Palestinians could provide other developing countries with the benefits of their unique experiences.

The reconstruction of Palestine cannot take place without the reconstruction of Palestinian institutions. The establishment of an institutional infrastructure to support reconstruction activities is vital. Engineers will ask what, how and where to build. Sensible answers to these questions

ix

can only be found within the context of the emerging cultural, economic, technological and social structures of Palestine.

Like any other economic activity, reconstruction involves many different costs which are institution-dependent. There are three major sources of cost: (i) the cost of searching for and acquiring information; (ii) the cost of decision-making, which is often related to measuring and/or assessing what is exchanged; and (iii) the cost of implementing and enforcing decisions once they have been made or the contract has been signed.

The institutions related to these three critical activities are still in the early phases of formation and require much support. The challenge is to construct institutions to: generate statistics and diffuse information; establish standards and codes; standardise measurements and norms; introduce safety procedures and regulations; adopt relevant accounting practices; establish a modern land tenure and legal system.

An operative system has to exist to facilitate and enforce exchanges between economic stakeholders and organisations. Without the appropriate legal and policing systems, the enforcement of contracts cannot be effective. This is particularly important in the case of property rights.

The importance of institutions in development has been confirmed empirically [1]. Institutions are of vital economic importance because they provide cost-minimising arrangements and rules which have been changing and evolving with the changes in the nature of these costs.

One of the many negative consequences of the past 28 years has been the stunting and dismantling of Palestinian institutions. Institutional development requires considerable national and international assistance to overcome this legacy.

The shortage of housing and the rush for quick fixes are already leading to the adoption of construction projects that are poorly designed and ill advised. Construction is being conducted without proper town planning, without any regard to architectural content, with inadequate consideration to transport and parking requirements, and without due allowance to safety and security measures.

THE CONTRIBUTIONS TO THIS MONOGRAPH

The papers presented in this Monograph emphasise the institutional and multi-disciplinary aspects of rural and urban reconstruction. The papers have been organised around six main themes:

1 Institutional and Planning Structures and Housing Policies;
2 Land Use and Tenure;
3 Regulatory Framework: Building Codes, Standards and Regulations;
4 Housing Alternatives and Options for Conservation and Renewal;
5 Financial Services for Housing and Urban Development; and

6 The Construction Industry.

Institutional and Planning Structures and Housing Policies:

This is a complex theme which receives a considerable amount of attention. The quality of new institutions and organisations created by Palestinians to deal with their challenges will set the pace of reconstruction. The paucity of experience in institution building and limited political imagination could easily stunt the development of appropriate structures.

Attention is drawn to the importance of developing the institutional structures of municipalities which are crucial components in any effective urban and rural programme of reconstruction.

Palestinian towns and villages have been frozen in time. They now have to overcome the vestiges of the past and anticipate the 21st century. One way to do so would be to utilise the advantages of the revolution in telecommunications to improve the Palestinian world of work. Changes in the management of the environment and in transportation systems could be planned for; and new measures in the organisations of towns, cities and rural areas could also be implemented.

Land Use and Tenure:

This theme highlights some of the most difficult challenges facing Palestinians. Enormous research and public discussions will be required before a suitable system can be developed to replace the old one. The medium and long term requirements for construction should be considered in the legislation of planning and zoning laws.

The Regulatory Framework: Codes, Standards and Regulations:

This section discusses the enormous amount of preparation needed to establish a comprehensive regulatory framework in Palestine. A great deal may be learned from international experience. Jordan has adapted and Arabised international systems. Thus, Palestine need not start from zero. Palestinians could adopt the Jordanian codes and regulations, and work to improve them. The process of improving and developing these codes could be shared with other Arab countries to accelerate the process and reduce the cost.

Housing Alternatives and Options for Conservation and Renewal:

Palestinians in the West Bank and Gaza are in dire need of housing. The economic study for 1994–2000, commissioned by the PLO Department of Economic Affairs and Planning [2], estimates that more than 60 per cent of total investments should be devoted to housing and related infrastructure.

The provision of urgently needed shelter will require the construction of around 300,000 homes (some observers set demand at 500,000) during the next decade. Construction activity is ceaseless: peace and prosperity will call for more and better buildings and facilities.

The construction needs of Palestinians also involve massive infrastructural development, and an improvement in community services, such as universities, schools, medical services, recreational facilities, transport, and so on.

Construction projects need to be carried out within a regulated framework which directs planning and building activity. It is also necessary to ensure that the development of new urban communities reflects the traditions and social organisation which best serve the needs and wishes of Palestinians.

Thus, architectural styles and town planning are issues which need to be addressed and emphasised in housing policies. Although an enormous amount of new construction is required in Palestine, this should not marginalise the importance of restoring and renovating historical buildings.

Palestine is one of the oldest continuously inhabited countries in the world. Our historic and cultural heritage is extensive, including many precious architectural treasures. Conservation is of prime importance also as a potential touristic resource.

Financial Services for Housing and Urban Development:

Arab banks were shut down during the first 27 years of occupation. Furthermore, appropriate financial services for housing, and the consulting and contracting services have not been available. Modern financial services have yet to emerge: this is a challenge commensurate with all the others facing Palestinians.

The estimated requirements of housing in Palestine are around $15 billion. Various international agencies have provided a few hundred million dollars to finance construction projects. International assistance cannot make a significant contribution to resolving the housing crisis unless it contributes to releasing the $15 billion from private investors. Without risk cover to encourage the emergence of mortgage and financial services, investors will be unwilling to release their own funds. This is obstructing the flow of investments.

The Construction Industry:

The construction industry is the locomotive of any economy; it is the instrument through which many socio-economic needs are met. Recent international developments in construction have: reduced cost; improved the safety and energy-efficiency of buildings; and reduced the negative environmental impact of human settlements. Palestinians could benefit considerably from these and other contemporary advances.

The establishment of support systems is vital to enabling the consumer, the contractor, the consultant, and the producer of materials and services to meet the housing needs. Such support systems should aim to reduce cost, improve quality and increase labour productivity. This is a formidable list of challenges.

In 1994 there were more than 54,000 Palestinians engineers, of whom only 4,000 are in Palestine. This rich supply of engineers has still to be deployed at home.

Palestinians have established a considerable track record regionally and internationally in the construction industry, but considerable effort is required to reap the benefits of this expertise for the reconstruction of Palestine.

The Recommendations made during this Conference address this and other issues.

A.B. Zahlan
Director, PECDAR Planning Unit
London, April 1997

ENDNOTES

1) North, Douglas, 1990, **Institutions, Instititutional Change and Economic Performance**, Cambridge University Press, Cambridge, UK.
2) For an empirical study, see Liedhom and Mead, *Small Scale Industries in Developing Countries: Empirical Evidence and Policy Implications*, Michigan State University International Development Papers, Paper No.9, 1987, pp. 100–1115.
3) See *Pathways to Change: Improving the Quality of Education in Developing Countries*, World Bank Discussion Paper 53, 1989.
4) Department of Economic Affairs and Planning, Palestine Liberation Organization, 'Programme for Development of the Palestinian National Economy for the Years 1994–2000', Tunis, July 1993.

ACKNOWLEDGEMENTS

My sincere thanks go to all the authors of these papers who dedicated their time and expertise into making this Monograph a unique and timely publication.

My thanks go to all those individuals and institutions who have helped in the organisation of the Conference and in the preparation of this volume.

A number of organisations have provided financial support. This work was carried out with the aid of a grant from the International Development Research Centre (IDRC), Ottawa, Canada, which provided the initial support for the programme to be launched; it also contributed funds towards the publication of the Arabic text. Special thanks go to Eglal Rashid, Fawzi Kishk and Geoff Oldham of the IDRC.

The Economic Development Institute of the World Bank (EDI) provided funding for: the Conference Planning Committee and a Working Group of Experts meeting in London, 28–30 June 1995; the Conference in Amman, 24–27 November 1995; and, printing the documents which were distributed to Conference participants. The EDI also contributed funds towards the preparation for publication of the Proceedings in English and Arabic. We are especially grateful to Manuel Sevilla for sharing his extensive expertise in housing issues with us and for his unswerving support. We are also grateful to all members of the World Bank staff who participated in this programme, especially Lawrence Hannah and Abdul-Karim Sadik.

The European Commission (EC) provided funding for the Conference, and for publication of the Proceedings in English and Arabic; we are especially grateful to Jean Paul Jesse, Gavin Evans and Mundeep Hothi.

We wish to thank Farouk Kaddumi, Chairman of the Board of Governors of PECDAR, and Ahmad Qurai, Managing Director of PECDAR, for supporting the programme which could not have taken place without their active support.

Thanks are also due to Adnan Stetieh, Secretary to the Board of Governors of PECDAR, who provided valuable technical assistance and support throughout the many phases of this programme.

The tasks of organising and designing the final preparations of this programme were greatly facilitated by the efforts and contributions of the members of the Conference Planning Committee who met in London in June 1995: Samih Abed, Ministry of Planning, Gaza; Ishaq Al-Qutub, Palestinian Housing Council, Jerusalem; Manuel Sevilla, EDI, World Bank;

Konstantinos Vryzakis, European Commission; and Mohamad Ziara, Ministry of Housing, Gaza.

I am also grateful to the group of experts who met in London at the same time and provided valuable advice regarding the organisation of the Conference: Johnny Astrand, Centre for Habitat Studies, Lund University; Anthony Coon, Centre for Planning, University of Strathclyde; Nabeel Hamdi, Centre for Development and Emergency Planning, Oxford Brookes University; Stephen Mayo, World Bank; Seyfeddin Muaz, Building Research Centre, Royal Scientific Society, Amman; Kamal Naser, Cardiff Business School, University of Wales; and Patrick Wakely, Development Planning Unit, London. Thanks are also due to Jan Söderburg of Lund University for presenting a Theme Paper for the Conference.

Sultan Barakat, Kamal Naser and Shadia Touqan contributed to the development of the programme and assisted in reviewing some of the papers. To all three, I extend warm thanks.

Thanks are also due to the many people who gave generously of their time to discuss the programme, to provide useful information and/or support:
Rami Abdul-Hadi, Centre for Engineering and Planning, Ramallah; Shawki Armaleh, PLO Ambassador in Brussels; John Britten, Building Research Establishment, UK; Charles Cockburn, Post-War Development and Reconstruction Unit, University of York; Ibrahim Daqqaq, Jerusalem; Barbro Ek, Aga Khan Program at MIT, Cambridge, USA; John Gault, Geneva; Jette Jensen, UNIDO, Vienna; Raja Khalidi, UNCTAD, Geneva; Terry Lacey, Cooperation for Development, UK; Jose Ospina, CHISEL, London; Zainab Othman, Architect, London; Adel Al-Sayed, Technical Department, World Bank; Mohammad Shadid, Palestinian Housing Council; Mubadda Suidan, USA and UAE; John Warren, UK; John Worthington, Institute of Advanced Architectural Studies, University of York.

I would like to thank the UN-ESCWA in Amman for their support of the Conference. In particular, Hazem Biblawi, Executive Secretary; Thoraya Obaid, Deputy Executive Secretary; Nabil Zohairy, Antoine Matta, Abeer Fahoum and their team provided enormous help before, during and after the Conference.

Many thanks are due to Hani al-Mulki, Director of the Royal Scientific Society, for his help in the preparation of the Conference and for hosting a meeting for the participants.

I owe my friend Antoine Soussa a lasting debt of gratitude for the operational help which he provided so willingly and graciously at the time of the Conference.

Seyfeddin Muaz, of the Royal Scientific Society, helped to organise informal meetings between the staff of Palestinian and Jordanian organisations. Six Jordanian organisations were invited to organise small informal sessions during which their staff could meet with interested participants. These meetings were with the staff of: ESCWA's Department of Human Settlements (thanks to Riadh Tappuni); the Housing Bank (thanks to Zohair Khoury); the staff of the Building Research Centre at the Royal Scientific Society (thanks to Seyfeddin Muaz); the staff of the School of Engineering of Jordan University (thanks to Fawzi Al-Gharaybeh); the members of the Association of Jordanian Contractors (thanks to Mohamad Murad); the Association of Jordanian Engineers (thanks to Leith Shubeilat).

I would like to extend my thanks to John Carswell, Director of Islamic Department, Sotheby's, London, for taking the time to provide a photograph for the cover of this volume from his private collection.

This programme would not have reached completion without the dedication and hard work of the staff of the PECDAR Planning Unit in London. Warm and very special thanks to: Joumana Lababidi for her total commitment to the project and her assiduous follow-up of authors and others to meet deadlines; Tareq Naqib for his creative contributions to the management of the software to unify the 37 different papers of this Monograph into World Bank standard form; and Ranya Sihweil for her valuable and priceless assistance, and for her willingness to join the team at the eleventh hour. We would also like to thank Richard El-Charif for managing the various accounts related to the project.

The papers were written by a multinational group of experts, and required strong editing which would at the same time preserve the original flavour of the papers. Thanks are due to Pamela Ann Smith who devoted many weeks to this assignment. Edited papers were exchanged with authors to make sure that the editorial work did not alter their content. Ranya Sihweil assisted in the editorial work, mediated with the authors, formatted the documents and prepared them for publication. She did so with great efficiency and expertise, for which I am very grateful.

The translations were in the capable hands of Ghada Dallal, Amman; Gamil Mattar, Arab Centre for Development and Futuristic Research, Cairo; and Reem Nusseibeh, Washington, D.C. Jeanine Albina undertook the task of comparing the translations to the original texts. My thanks to all of them.

As always, I am grateful to Rosemarie Said Zahlan for her generous help in the development of the conceptual framework, for her advice at decisive points in the evolution of the programme and for her organisational and editorial contributions.

The opinions expressed in the papers of this book are those of their respective authors and do not necessarily reflect the views of PECDAR, the EC, the IDRC or the World Bank.

A. B. Zahlan
Director, PECDAR Planning Unit
London, April 1997

LIST OF PARTICIPANTS AND CONTRIBUTORS

Abbasi, Ahlam	Orient House, Jerusalem
Abdel Rahman, Hasan	PLO, 1730 K Street. NW, Washington, DC
Abdel-Hamid, Nadira	President's Office, Gaza
Abdelmoumene, Mohammed	UNRWA, Amman
Abdul-Hadi, Ayman*	Arab Bank plc, Park Lane, London
Abdul-Hameed, Marwan*	Ministry of Housing, Gaza
Abdulhadi, Rami	Centre for Engineering and Planning, PO Box 301, Ramallah
Abdulhak, Mohammed	Bir-Zeit University, PO Box 71 Bir-Zeit
Abdullah, Samir	PECDAR, PO Box 506, Ramallah
Abed, Samih*	Ministry of Planning and International Cooperation, Jerusalem
Abu Ayyash, Ibrahim	Arabtech-Jardaneh, Amman
Abu Ghazaleh, Nizar	Palestinian National Fund
Abu Ghouch, Omran	Housing Bank, PO Box 7693, Amman, 11118
Abu Obaid, Jamal	Housing Bank, PO Box 7693, Amman, 11118
Abu Rahma, Maged	Municipality of Gaza, PO Box 16, Gaza
Abu Znaid, Jihad	Women and Housing Rights Movement (PHRIC), PO Box 51090, Jerusalem
Abu-Dagga, Issam El-Din	Municipality of Khan Younis, Khan Younis, Gaza
Abu-Eisheh, Sameer*	Al-Najah National University, PO Box 1466, Nablus
Abu-Shokor, Abdelfattah*	Al-Najah National University, PO Box 7, Nablus
Abughatas, Khalil	MAG Engineering, PO Box 9246, Amman
Al-Amad, Mohammed	Private Developer (Sector), Amman
Al-Horani, Abdalla	Ministry of Social Affairs, PO Box 3693 Al-Biereh
Al-Momani, Shawkat	Housing Corporation, PO Box 2100, Amman

Al-Nashashibi, Mohamad	Ministry of Finance, Palestine
Al-Qutub, Ishaq*	Palestinian Housing Council, PO Box 17128 Jerusalem
Al-Saad, Mahmoud	AITEC, 21 rue Voltaire, 75011 Paris
Al-Salaymah, Mansour	Jericho Chamber of Commerce, Jericho
Al-Samadi, Hassan Dawood	Palestinian Housing Council, Amman
Al-Sayyed, Ahmad	Ramallah Municipality, PO Box 782, Ramallah
Al-Taher, Taher	Amman Chamber of Commerce, PO Box 3277, Amman
Al-Taher, Thabet	Jordan International Consulting Group, PO Box 830155, Amman
Al-Zoubi, Salti	Jordan Construction Association, Amman
Alaraj, Abdel Aziz	Ministry of Economy, Jericho
Amer, Ahmed*	Ministry of Housing, Gaza
Amiry, Suad	Ministry of Culture, PO Box 212, Ramallah
Amr, Ibrahim	Palestinian Housing Council, Hebron
Arnott, Jane	W.S. Atkins, Woodcote Grove, Ashley Road, Epsom, Surrey
Ashor, Abed Al-Hadi	Rafah Municipality, Rafah, Gaza
Ashqar, Simon	Progress Water Projects, PO Box 70012, Antelias, Lebanon
Assadi, Bashar	Sadat Associates, 116 Village Boulevard, Princeton, NJ 08525
Audeh, Abeer	PADCO, 1025 Thomas Jefferson St., NW, Washington, DC 20007
Awadallah, Faisal	Bir-Zeit University, Bir-Zeit
Awwad, Nicola	Chamber of Commerce, Bethlehem
Ayoub, Walid	Ministry of Housing,
Azzam, Mohamed	GTZ/PECDAR, PO Box 931, Jerusalem 91008
Barakat, Ali	Ministry Local Government, Jericho
Barakat, Sultan*	University of York, The Kings Manor, York Y01 2EP
Barghouthi, Abdul-Hamid	PECDAR, Jerusalem
Beseiso, Fouad	Palestinian Monetary Authority, PO Box 4026, Gaza
Biau, Daniel	HABITAT, Nairobi, PO Box 30030, Nairobi, Kenya
Bizri, Omar	ESCWA, PO Box 927124, Amman
Bouakouir, Cherif	Construction Participation Fund, 12 Amirouche Boulevard, Algiers

Brown, Dennis	UNRWA, Amman
Bustami, Leila	Jordan University for Women, PO Box 922016, Amman, 11192
Chakkour, Lamia	ESCWA, Amman
Clement, Fernand	European Commission, PO Box 22207, Jerusalem
Coon, Anthony*	Centre for Planning, University of Strathclyde, Glasgow
Corneil, Jeanne*	Harvard University, 48 Quincy Street, Cambridge, Massachusetts
Dajani Khairi, Hidaya	Housing Corporation, PO Box 2100, Amman
Dajani, Shukri	International Labour Office, 4 Route des Morillons, 1211 Geneva 22
Dakkak, Ibrahim	PECDAR, PO Box 19502, Jerusalem 91194
Davis, Ian*	Oxford Centre for Disaster Studies, PO Box 137, Oxford OX4 1BB
Drummond, Wayne	University of Florida, 331 Arch Building, Gainesville, Florida 32611
El-Agha, Anwar	Ministry of Housing, Gaza
El-Agha, Zakaria*	Ministry of Housing, Gaza
El-Aloul, Hussam	Save the Children Federation, Gaza
El-Amad, Adnan	PECDAR, Al Ram, Jerusalem
El-Bayya, Majed*	Ministry of Housing, Gaza
El-Hindi, Nagi	Ministry of Housing, Gaza
El-Khoudary, Riyad	Al-Azhar University, Gaza
Elhaj, Riad	Consolidated Contractors Company, Gaza, 82546
Enshassi, Adnan*	Islamic University, PO Box 223, Gaza
Erbach, Gerald	PADCO, 1025 Thomas Jefferson Street, NW, Washington, DC
Fakhri, Yousef	Jordan Contractors Association, PO Box 5140 Amman
Faramand, Ghassan	Bir-Zeit University, Bir-Zeit
Fethi, Ihsan*	Jordan University of Women, PO Box 961343, Amman
Friesen, Daniel	Federation of Canadian Municipalities, 24 Clarence Street, Ottawa
Gattoni, George	World Bank, 1818 H Street, NW, Washington, DC, 20433
Ghawi, Nabil	Dar Al-Handasah, PO Box 2292, Amman
Ghnaim, Maher	PECDAR, Jerusalem

Ghoreeb, Michel	Ghoreeb Investment, 23 Rue du Depart 95015, Paris
Habash, Sakher	
Haddad, Antoine	ESCWA, PO Box 927115, Amman
Hamdi, Nabeel*	Oxford Brookes University, Gypsy Cove, Oxford OX3 0BP
Hammadeh, Ali	Housing Bank, PO Box 7693, Amman, 11118
Hammoud, Mai A.	Union of Arab Chambers, PO Box 7029, Amman, 11118
Hannah, Lawrence	World Bank, 1818 H Street, NW, Washington, DC, 20433
Hararah, Jamil	Ministry of Economy Trade and Industry, Gaza
Hasna, Walid	UNDP, Jerusalem
Hassouna, Asaad Faris	Chamber of Commerce, Ramallah, West Bank
Hijazi, Basel	Municipality of Jericho, Jericho
Ismail, Mohamad	PRE. Company, Amman
Jabr, Falah	AFFI, PO Box 13025, Baghdad
Jadallah, Ahmed	PO Box 21914, Salt Lake City, Utah 84171
Jensen, Rolf H.*	Ministry of Planning, Ramallah, West Bank
Jweinat, Nabih	Housing Bank, PO Box 7693, Amman, 11118
Kahiri, Dana	PECDAR, Jerusalem
Kanaan, Taher	World Bank, PO Box 950499, Amman
Kassim, Anis	PO Box 961919, Amman
Khalifa, Abdalla	Jordan Contractors Association, PO Box 2713 Amman
Khamaisi, Rassem*	Centre for Strategic Planning, PO Box 1460, Kaffer Canna
Kharma, Saad	Engineers Syndicate, Gaza, 21246
Khatib, Hisham*	PO Box 925387, Amman
Khoury, Munir	Consolidated Contractors Company, PO Box 830392, Amman, 11183
Khoury, Nabil	International Labour Office, 4 Route des Morillons, 1211 Geneva 22
Kilani, Mohammed	Palestinian Housing Council, PO Box 140106, Albayader, Amman
Kishk, Fawzy	IDRC, PO Box 14 Orman Street, Giza, Cairo
Kutteineh, Rania	PECDAR, Jerusalem

Lababidi, Joumana	PECDAR, 58–60 Kensington Church Street, London W8 4DB, UK
Lea, Michael	Consulatant, World Bank, 2207 Via Tiempo, Cardiff, California, 92007
Maayah, Tareq	Ministry of Communications, Ramallah, West Bank
Madanat, Suheil	UNCHS – HABITAT, Makitorpantie 40 E 45, 00640 Helsinki 64 ???
Makdah, Jad	CJC, PO Box 457 Amman
Malhotra, Romessh Kumar	BBC, PO Box 911315 Jabal Lweibdeh, Amman
Mashal, Ahmad	Palestinian Monetary Authority, PO Box 4026, Gaza
Mayo, Stephen K.*	World Bank, 1818 H Street, NW, Washington, DC, 20433
Mihyar, Sana'a	Housing Corporation, PO Box 2100, Amman
Mikdashi, Mohammed	Team International, 4 Al-Ahram St. Makattam, Cairo
Milort, Gerard*	VNG (Association of Netherlands Municipalities), Nassalilaan 12
Muaz, Seyfeddin*	Building Research Centre, RSS, PO Box 925819, Amman, 11110
Muenis, Fares	Municipality of Gaza, PO Box 16, Gaza
Mughrabi, Jawad	Jordan Contractors Association, PO Box 5140, Amman
Muhanna, Ibrahim	Palestine Liberation Organisation, PO Box 182819 Amman, 11118
Mukhtar, Naji*	Cardiff Business School, University of Wales, Cardiff, Wales, UK
Mumtaz, Babar*	University College London, 9 Endsleigh Gardens, London WC1, UK
Naji, Jawad	Ministry of Industry, Jerusalem
Naser, Kamal*	Cardiff Business School, University of Wales, Cardiff, Wales, UK
Nigim, Hani	Bir-Zeit University, PO Box 14, Bir Zeit, West Bank
O'Dell, Alan*	Government Service, Building Research Establishment, UK
Obaid, Thoraya	ESCWA, PO Box 927115, Amman
Petro, Joseph	Housing Bank, PO Box 7693, Amman, 11118
Qaqish, Nidal	Housing and Urban Development Corporation, PO Box 2110, Amman

Rabbani, Mouin	VNG (Association of Netherlands Municipalities), Nassalilaan 12, The Hague
Rustom, Rifat*	Islamic University, PO Box 223, Gaza
Sabri, Nidal Rashid*	Bir-Zeit University, Bir Zeit, West Bank
Sadik, Abdul-Karim	World Bank, 1818 H Street, NW, Washington, DC, 20433
Sakr, Mohamed	Islamic University, PO Box 13015, Gaza,
Salam, Yusef	Team International, PO Box 145303, Beirut
Saleh, Abdul-Rahman	Housing Bank, PO Box 1473, Ramallah, West Bank
Saleh, Selim	Ministry of Public Works, Gaza
Samara, Adnan	Ministry of Economy Trade and Industry, Ramallah, West Bank
Sansur, Ramzi*	Bir-Zeit University, PO Box 14, Bir Zeit, West Bank
Saqer, Matar	UNRWA, Amman
Sarraf, Falak Halim*	Royal Scientific Society, PO Box 925819, Amman
Serageldin, Mona*	Harvard University, 48 Quincy Street, Cambridge, Massachusetts
Sevilla, Manuel	World Bank, 1818 H Street, NW, Washington DC, 20433
Shaaban, Ibrahim*	Palestinian Housing Council, PO Box 20724, Jerusalem
Shabou, Ali	HABITAT, PO Box 35286, Amman
Shadid, Mohammed*	Palestinian Housing Council, Jerusalem
Shadid, Raouf	Contracting Association, Amman
Shakah, Ghassan	Nablus Municipality
Sharaf, Firas	Constructions Research Centre
Shawa, Ala'edeen	Development Resource Centre (DRC), PO Box 23, Gaza
Shawwa, Hashem	Palestine Real Estate Company, Gaza
Sihweil, Ranya	PECDAR, 58–60 Kensington Church Street, London W8 4DB
Soussa, Antoine	Printing and Packaging Company, PO Box 2888 Amman
Steitieh, Adnan	PECDAR, 58 Avenue Bilal, El Menzah, Tunis
Sulieman, Adeeb	Engineers Association, Jerusalem
Söderberg, Jan*	Construction Management, Lund University, PO Box 118, Lund

Tahboub, Nashaat	Palestinian Housing Council, PO Box 17128, West Bank
Talab, Jamal*	Director, Land Research Committee, Arab Studies Society, Jerusalem
Tappuni, Riadh*	ESCWA, PO Box 927115, Amman
Tarazi, Nabil	Palestinian Housing Council, Gaza
Tarazi, Sami	PECDAR, PO Box 1008, Gaza
Tbaileh, Mohammad Sameh	Nablus Chamber of Commerce
Tellefsen, Ulf*	Ministry of Planning and International Cooperation, Jerusalem
Tewfik, Magdy*	Jordan University for Women, PO Box 961343, Amman
Thaher, Sameer*	Head of Legal Department, Ministry of Housing, Gaza
Toivanen, Minna	SIDA, Stockholm, 10525 Sweden
Touqan, Shadia*	UNESCO, c/o UNDP, PO Box 1188, Aden
Troche, Jean-Pierre	AITEC, 21 rue Voltaire, 75011 Paris
Wakely, Patrick*	University of London, 9 Endsleigh Gardens, London WC1, UK
Wiggers, Arthur*	VNG (Association of Netherlands Municipalities), Nassalilaan 12, The Hauge
Williams, Angela	UNRWA, PO Box 140157, Amman, 11814
Yaish, Emad	Palestinian Housing Council, Jerusalem
Yousof, Mohammad Ata*	Al-Najah National University, PO Box 1370 Nablus, West Bank
Youssef, Riad Farid	Palestine Human Rights Info. Centre (PHRIC), PO Box 20479, Jerusalem
Zahlan, A.B.*	PECDAR, 58–60 Kensington Church Street, London W8 4DB
Ziara, Mohammed*	Ministry of Housing, Gaza

* *Contributors to this volume.*

RECOMMENDATIONS

The participants of the Conference discussed the issues and challenges confronting Palestinians in the reconstruction of Palestine. It was obvious to all that the way forward is subject to severe constraints, and it was considered necessary to focus on vital and high priority objectives to overcome the most restrictive.

The participants divided their recommendations into two categories: urgent and immediate measures; and long term measures. They recognised that the efficient and effective utilisation of the limited available resources would require considerable and serious effort.

The overwhelming focus of the recommendations was on institution building. It was acknowledged that Palestinians would not be able to cope with the many challenges that they face without the necessary legal, policy-making and financial institutions.

URGENT AND IMMEDIATE MEASURES

The participants identified 11 measures which need to be urgently adopted by the appropriate authorities. These are grouped into four categories below.

1. Measures to be Taken by Public Organisations

It is recommended that measures be adopted to promote data collection, analysis, policy making, consultation and co-ordination among concerned parties. These measures should co-ordinate efforts on the national, international and local levels.

Inter-ministerial co-ordination

It is recommended that inter-ministerial co-ordination be achieved through the High Planning Committee (HPC). The HPC is to be responsible for the design and management of policy concerned with housing and urban planning. It is also recommended that the HPC be concerned with defining the roles and co-ordinating the work of public agencies active in housing and urban planning.

Housing strategies

It is recommended that the PNA establish specialised departments in appropriate public organisations to: survey existing housing conditions on a regular basis, develop long term perspectives and housing strategies in the light of economic and social conditions.

Promotion of consultation between all stakeholders

It is clear that there are many parties who are concerned with urban planning and housing and they should be involved in a systematic manner in the formation of public policies and local planning. It is recommended that the HPC establish suitable mechanisms through which all parties are involved in deliberations on these issues.

Co-ordination of national and international planning

Social housing will depend on the availability of international assistance; furthermore, the development of national financial services will also depend on the provision of risk cover. It is recommended that the HPC co-ordinate the efforts of public organisations concerned with securing international assistance with those of private and public organisations concerned with the local planning.

2. Measures to be Taken by Public Organisations Concerned with Land Legislation and Municipal Affairs:

Protection of cultural heritage

Palestine has a very rich cultural heritage embodied in buildings. A large number of archaeological sites have still to be excavated and/or studied. Palestinians are custodians of the oldest inhabited part of the world. This inheritance entails great responsibility and calls for the adoption of conservation and protection policies. It is recommended that the HPC invite all the parties involved (private and public) to develop a national programme for the conservation, renovation and permanent protection of the cultural heritage. Such a programme should be the basis for urban planning and housing development.

Modernisation of the land registration system

It is recommended that the HPC establish a National Committee of experts and responsible officials to study and revise existing land registration laws and procedures. Priority should be given to: property rights, zoning regulations, landlord-tenant relationships, construction regulations and the management of space and buildings classified under cultural heritage.

Upgrading of neighbourhoods

It is recommended that the PNA adopt policies which focus on the upgrading of existing built-up areas within a neighbourhood framework.

Support of private initiatives

The private sector is essential for the development of housing. It is recommended that close co-operation between the public and private sectors be established through the provision of land with suitable infrastructure.

3. Measures to be Taken to Support the Development of a National Construction Industry

Adoption of codes and standards

It is recommended that the appropriate authorities adopt suitable codes, standards, regulations and quality controls as soon as possible; and that they adopt the necessary measures to implement such a policy throughout the country.

Availability of construction materials

The severe delays and losses imposed on all construction projects are well known. It is recommended that the PNA establish a Task Force to facilitate and expedite the movement of all construction materials and equipment.

4. Follow-up

It is recommended that a Committee be established to follow-up and facilitate the adoption and implementation of the recommendations made at this Conference.

MEDIUM- AND LONG-TERM MEASURES:

Several recommendations were presented under this heading. These fall into the four following categories.

1. Enabling Institutions

The most critical enabling institutions at this time are those concerned with the provision of financial services and the management capabilities of municipalities and village councils.

Develop property tax system

It is recommended that a property tax system be developed in order to strengthen the housing finance system. Ultimately, this will promote the efficiency in both land markets and equity, as well as create a second mortgage facility and mobilise private sector funding.

Strengthen municipality and village councils

The current state of municipal and village councils in Palestine is inadequate. It is recommended that their capabilities and jurisdiction be increased to provide them with the additional power necessary to perform their responsibilities.

Provide support for the private sector and non-governmental organisations

It is recommended that the field work be conducted to develop and implement effective policies to promote full private sector and participation by non-governmental organisations in the reconstruction of Palestine.

Establish a national authority for the protection of cultural heritage

It is recommended that the PNA establish a National Authority for the Protection of Cultural Heritage with responsibility for establishing regulations, supervision and monitoring of the management of buildings and historic sites.

2. Land and Housing Management

Rent control

It is recommended that detailed studies be conducted to determine the most equitable ways to progressively remove rent controls to stimulate the provision of housing for rent. This is necessary because low rents prevent investments in new housing.

Management of public land

Physical space in Palestine is very limited and considerable effort should be made to make the best use of what is available. It is recommended that the agency responsible for the management of public lands be strengthened to enable it to develop effective policies and procedures.

Development of a land registry and information system

Proper management of the available limited land resources is essential. It is recommended that a suitable land registry and information system be established.

3. Support for the Construction Industry

Enforcement of codes and standards

It is recommended that every effort should be made to develop and enforce suitable codes, standards, regulations and quality control.

Support for research

It is recommended that all the relevant Ministries support research, training and technology transfer in relation to the construction industry, conservation of cultural heritage, and environmental conservation.

Promotion of new technology

It is recommended that the Ministries of Public Works, Housing, Education and the Economy support efforts to identify relevant construction technologies and promote their absorption by Palestinian consulting and contracting firms.

4. Follow-up

It is recommended that an institution be established to maintain the analytical efforts, exchange of ideas, and policy dialogue which were initiated at this Conference and that this institution would follow-up and guide the adoption and implementation of policy.

ACRONYMS AND ABBREVIATIONS

AASHTO	American Association of State Highways and Transportation Officials
ACI	American Concrete Institute
AID	(See USAID)
ASTM	American Standard Testing Materials
ADA	Americans with Disabilities Act
BCD	Beirut Central District
BOD	biochemical oxygen demand
BS	British Standards
CBO	Community Based Organisation
CBS	Central Bureau of Statistics
CDC	Centre for Development Consultancy
CEP	Centre for Engineering and Planning – Ramallah
CRED	Centre for Research in the Epidemiology of Disasters
CSR	codes of practice, standards and regulations
CSS	Codes, Standards and Specifications
dB	decibels
DPU	Development Planning Unit, University College, London
EC	European Commission, Brussels
EDI	Economic Development Institute
EIA	environmental impact assessment
ESCWA	Economic and Social Commission for Western Asia
EU	European Union
GDP	Gross Domestic Product
GIS	Geographic Information System
GNCR	Gaza National Committee for Rehabilitation
GNP	Gross National Product
HABITAT	(See UNCHS)
ICB	Israeli Central Bureau of Statistics
IEEE	Institute of Electrical and Electronics Engineers
JD	Jordanian dinars
JMCC	Jerusalem Media and Communication Centre
KWH	kilowatt-hour
LP	liquefied petroleum gas
mg/L	milligrams per litre
MM	millimetres
MPS	marginal propensity to save

NBCJ	National Building Council of Jordan
NGO	non-governmental organisation
NIS	New Israeli Shekels
OECD	Organisation for Economic Co-operation and Development
PECDAR	Palestinian Economic Council for Reconstruction and Development
PHC	Palestinian Housing Council, Jerusalem
PLO	Palestine Liberation Organisation
PNA	Palestinian National Authority
PRDU	Post-War Reconstruction and Development Unit
RSS	Royal Scientific Society, Jordan
SII	Standards Institute of Israel
SOLIDERE	Lebanese Company for the Development and Reconstruction of Beirut Central District
TDS	total dissolved solids
TOE	one ton of oil equivalent
UEPM	urban and rural environmental planning and management
UNCHS	United Nations Centre for Human Settlements
UNDP	United Nations Development Programme
UNDRO	United Nations Disaster Relief Organisation
UNICEF	United Nations Children's Fund
UNRWA	United Nations Relief and Works Agency
USAID	United States Agency for International Development
VAT	value added tax

NOTE ON STATISTICS

Studies of Palestine, its geography, people, culture, economy and society, are all hampered by the almost complete lack of reliable, up-to-date statistics. The division of Mandate Palestine, ruled by Britain, into territories occupied by Israel, Jordan and Egypt after 1948 precluded any unified approach to the gathering of data and the compilation and interpretation of statistical material.

After 1967, the occupation of the West Bank (formerly ruled by Jordan) and of Gaza (which had come under Egyptian control in 1948) by Israel added to the complexity and discontinuities. For example, although Israel conducted a census of the occupied territories in 1967, it excluded Jerusalem and the related areas which it had itself annexed. The inability of Palestinian researchers to conduct their own surveys meant, in addition, that any figures provided by the occupying powers lacked authority, as well as accuracy, given the understandable reluctance of large parts of the Palestinian population to co-operate with their occupiers even at times of relative civil peace.

Until recently, information on the West Bank and Gaza has often had to rely on the West Bank Data Base Project carried out by Israeli researchers in the mid-1980s (Benvenisti, M., and Khayat, S., 1988; Roy, S., 1986), even though this material, like much of the data published by Israel's Central Bureau of Statistics, is no longer up to date. Figures produced by the United Nations Relief and Works Agency (UNRWA) for both territories have also been used as a basic reference, even though these generally refer only to the refugee population. Other studies, and statistical estimates for Palestinian-related topics provided by the Amman-based Economic and Social Commission for West Asia (ESCWA), the United Nations Commission on Trade and Development (UNCTAD) in Geneva, the United Nations Industrial Development Organisation (UNIDO) in Vienna, the United Nations Development Programme (UNDP) and the United Nations Centre for Human Settlements (Habitat) have been used by contributors for this work.

Since the advent of the peace negotiations, the signature of the Declaration of Principles in September, 1993 and subsequent Israeli withdrawals from parts of the Palestinian Territories(PT), Palestinian researchers and academics have been freer to conduct surveys of their own, although many constraints remain, not the least the lack of the required funding, technology and access to specialised skills. As a result, the body of data produced by Palestinians themselves is growing rapidly, although fully-up-to-date, comprehensive and accurate figures will still be difficult to obtain failing a complete Israeli withdrawal from the PT and the installation of a sovereign Palestinian government.

Nevertheless, a number of important studies are now available which provide data and statistics relevant to urban and rural reconstruction in Palestine. These include the pioneering report written by Palestinian, Scandinavian and other authors on *Palestinian Society in Gaza, West Bank and Arab Jerusalem: A Survey of Living Conditions* produced in 1993 by the Fagbevegelsens senter for forskning (FAFO) in OSLO.[1]

The *Programme for Development of the Palestinian National Economy for the Years 1994–2000* produced by the Palestine Liberation Organisation's Department of Economic Affairs and Planning in July, 1993 is a basic reference for data and statistics on the Palestinian economy and on future plans.[2] The *Passia* handbook for 1995 published by the Palestinian Academic Society for the Study of International Affairs (Passia) in Jerusalem in 1995 provides a wealth of up-to-date figures and estimates on the geography, population, economy and society of the PT and Jerusalem based on Palestinian, Israeli and international sources.[3]

The Editor

---

1 Fabevegelsens senter for forskning (FAFO), 1993, **Palestinian Society in Gaza, West Bank and Arab Jerusalem: A Survey of Living Conditions**, FAFO Report 151, Oslo.
2 Palestine Liberation Organisation, 1993, **The Program for Development of the Palestinian National Economy for the Years 1994–2000**, Department of Economic Affairs and Planning, July, Tunis.
3 Palestinian Academic Society for the Study of International Affairs, 1995, **Passia 1995**, Jerusalem.

INTRODUCTION

A NATIONAL OUTLOOK FOR HOUSING IN PALESTINE*

Zakaria El Agha
PALESTINIAN MINISTER OF HOUSING

The Palestinian National Authority (PNA) seeks to build a Palestinian homeland as a culmination of the journey that we have recently begun. It also aspires to continue its efforts toward establishing an independent Palestinian state. In shouldering the burdens of this arduous and intricate process, the PNA is fully aware of the tremendous challenges that lie ahead. This includes erasing the effects of the Israeli occupation as well as dealing with the burdens it has left behind.

In order to understand the nature of these tremendous challenges, it is necessary to define and comprehend the legacy that Palestinians are facing; namely, a state of affairs that is unprecedented in the history of foreign occupations. The Israeli authorities have completely neglected the developmental needs of the West Bank and Gaza, just as they have failed to maintain and preserve the structures that existed prior to their occupation. The Palestinian people and the PNA find themselves having to begin the process of reconstruction from point zero, and therefore they have to double their efforts to compensate for the years which were lost under the Israeli occupation.

The Israeli authorities implemented a policy that sought to make Palestinians' lives as difficult as possible in an attempt to force them to leave. This policy manifested itself in the housing sector by restricting new construction and making it difficult to maintain existing buildings. Consequently, many residential buildings were abandoned. The net result was a marked deterioration of the housing sector, which was further exacerbated by a lack of opportunities to meet the increased demand for housing caused by the growth of the population, continued repression and the demolition of buildings.

The PNA realises both the depth and scope of these challenges. We

---

* This paper is a revised and expanded version of the Opening Address at the Conference.

are attempting to deal with these challenges realistically and objectively. We have endeavoured to mobilise Palestinian resources both from the inside and outside. We opened channels of dialogue and participation among the various institutions and attempted to benefit from international experience that is most relevant to our situation. We are also in the process of developing tools and mechanisms to ensure continuity, co-operation and co-ordination among these institutions, so that we can effect a qualitative change in construction and development.

We hope to arrive at a scientific and methodological analysis of existing problems, to establish priorities, to review expertise from both industrial and developing countries in development and construction, and to discuss their relevance to the situation in Palestine. We also aim to review the alternatives and, through dialogue, to arrive at recommendations and suggestions.

Our institutions have been suppressed during the occupation. The restrictions have been imposed forcibly. We have been denied financial, technical and human resources, and have lacked support for development and training. The situation has been further aggravated by the degenerate state of the legal system in Palestine and the unjust Israeli military orders that served the occupier's objectives. The occupation authorities neither developed nor modernised existing laws and regulations to serve Palestinian needs and meet the requirements of a changing world.

Today, we are in the process of establishing our Palestinian state. We are beginning to build, develop and reorganise our national institutions, as well as train staff. We are also working on providing our institutions with the means and mechanisms to build modern organisational structures.

POLICIES AND GOALS

The PNA has also embarked on a comprehensive plan to revise and evaluate existing legislation, especially concerning development, planning and construction. The PNA is also examining production regulations developed in Arab and industrial countries for environmental protection, energy conservation, the promotion of sound construction, technology, improved building materials and quality control, as well as measures to safeguard the safety of the individual.

The Ministry of Housing seeks to enable each citizen to live in permanent and appropriate housing, and to encourage scientific research in the area of housing. It also aims to develop a domestic construction industry, control the quality of existing housing, and to draft measures regulating the construction industry, as well as to incorporate principles of Arab Islamic architecture.

The preparation of a carefully studied national strategy for housing is a time consuming process; it would take many years to complete, especially given the lack of reliable statistics, scant financial resources and comprehensive expertise. In addition, there are the pressures of daily operations and the urgent and incessant need to address acute housing problems we face in Palestine. Despite this, the Ministry of Housing has been able to prepare an initial policy that conforms to the wider objectives of the national strategy for housing.

The housing system aims to provide housing for all citizens, including those who cannot afford it without government subsidies. The Ministry is attempting to strike a balance between all the factors that play an important role in housing. Among these are the contractors, financial institutions, municipalities, financial policies and financial resources. The Ministry supports a financial policy that is self-reliant and which encourages the private and public sectors to provide loans on competitive terms. The private sector is to play the dominant role in solving existing housing problems. At the same time, the Ministry recognises that there is a huge gap between what the private sector can provide and what the population can afford.

Increasing the national stock of existing housing rapidly requires intervention by the public sector. The provision of long-term mortgages to facilitate construction and to improve existing housing are primary objectives that the Ministry seeks to achieve through specialised commercial banks. The PNA has decided to establish the Palestine Housing Bank as a co-operative venture between the public and private sectors.

In addition, the Ministry seeks to achieve the following objectives:

- A reduction in land prices;
- An increase in land suitable for construction;
- An increase in the housing stock;
- Encouragement of investment in housing;
- The use of local building materials;
- The provision of long-term mortgages;
- Priority for self-sustaining commercial projects; and
- The provision of suitable conditions for housing through the enforcement of controls and regulations.

Foremost among the conditions that have aggravated the housing problem is severe over-crowding, both inside and outside the refugee camps. This is in addition to the intense growth of the population, which is rising by 5 per cent a year; the return of Palestinian expatriates; and the needs of those employed by the PNA. The demolition of houses by the Israelis, their policies of restricting construction and of withholding building permits, as well as their actions limiting the size of the existing municipalities and villages are still other factors contributing to the problem.

More research is required in order to identify the scale of the existing problem of the lack of resources for research; there are differences of opinion regarding the number of housing units that will be required. However, there is no doubt that Palestine suffers from a shortage of housing in both quantity and quality. Initial statistics indicate that 200,000 housing units will be needed by the year 2000.

All these factors suggest that an estimated 34,000 new housing units will be needed each year, 14,000 of which are to meet the natural growth of the population and 6,000 to replace deteriorating and run-down buildings. Moreover, 4,000 units are required for other reasons, and 10,000 units to alleviate over-crowding in existing housing. Some 6,000 existing housing units need to be rehabilitated.

Construction in Palestinian cities, given the preference for multi-storey construction due to the high price of land, is more suitable than horizontal construction which is practised in refugee camps. The Ministry of Housing, in co-operation with various parties, has implemented a new regulatory system governing multi-storey buildings in a way that serves the public interest and enables the private sector to invest in the housing sector.

Despite the economic and financial obstacles, we are taking measures to prevent multi-storey buildings causing adverse environmental and social effects. This is being done through considering the design of these buildings and the experience of industrial and developing countries in this regard. We are seeking to learn from the experience of these countries regarding the choice of sites, the height, building materials, and the social mix of future residents, as well as the means required to maintain and manage such buildings.

These are examples of what our policies seek to achieve. There are various, and sometimes conflicting, needs in our society. Governments cannot direct investment nor the activities of individual or private institutions; nor can it interfere directly to make housing and other services available to all. Nevertheless, by drawing up and enforcing laws, regulations and controls and by making resources, materials and tax breaks available, it can encourage and support certain trends to serve the whole population.

The special economic and political situation in Palestine requires professionals and experts to devise particular and original solutions to address the current problems. We have to learn from all proposals and existing development paradigms available and examine their appropriateness to Palestinian conditions.

In the past few years, several countries have sought to encourage the renovation, rather than the demolition, of old buildings so that they can eventually be used for housing. This is also seen as helping to minimise the adverse environmental side effects that the expansion of cities and new transport networks can create. This orientation has proved quite effective at the economic, environmental and social levels, as well as in preserving the national heritage.

PRESERVING THE ARCHITECTURAL HERITAGE

While Palestine today urgently needs to design and build new housing projects, we are aware of the need to consider the deteriorating conditions of existing residential buildings and the need to renovate and develop them in a way that responds to the social, health and environmental needs of the population. Statistics available to the Ministry indicate that almost 12 per cent of housing units in urban areas have been abandoned, compared to only 8 per cent in rural areas. We must consider using these buildings to help satisfy housing needs and encourage owners to renovate and develop them.

The Ministry will continue in its efforts to prepare a strategy which has the primary objective of encouraging citizens and housing co-operatives to improve and develop existing buildings and housing. Private investors will also be encouraged to develop and renew used and abandoned housing units.

Worldwide in the midst of the rush to develop new construction, many historic buildings and sites have been demolished. Planners and engineers have realised the gravity of this mistake, and as a result, construction trends have changed so that most development and construction policies today recognise the need to preserve precious historical sites and to revive historic centres.

The Ministry is aware of the need to maintain the spirit of our distinctive local architectural heritage in Palestine. Although technological advances have provided us with the modern techniques and materials, new designs should be inspired by our national heritage which has always been, and continues to be, one of the richest in the world. We have a responsibility to preserve our legacy of historical and religious sites and should spare no effort to renovate, revive, and renew these sites for use by the coming generations. We also must respect the various methods used by our forefathers so that the new designs harmonise with the older structures.

We hope that our construction policies will include suitable regulations required to guarantee the preservation of Palestinian heritage and encourage planners, consumers and investors to renovate and re-use historic buildings. At the same time, the policy we have in mind will need to take measures to prevent such regulations becoming obstacles to innovation, creativity and the use of the most modern methods and technical systems. It will also need to ensure that measures to preserve old historic buildings and cities do not simply turn these structures into mere museums and tourist sites but rather centres for social, religious,

7

educational, entertainment and commercial activities in addition to housing.

We also have to build the society of the next century, satisfy its needs and meet the expectations of our own people. Therefore, we need to help society plan its development in line with the latest available scientific and technological advances. We have to benefit from the scientific advances in communications and transport, as well as in the organisation of rural and urban areas.

We hope that our architects, many of whom enjoy varied and rich expertise, will be able to create designs that are both innovative and original and which are an expression of the era we live in, rather than replicating the past or simply drawing on imported designs. The reconstruction of Palestine gives architects and technicians a golden opportunity to design and build projects that reflect our national identity and social cohesion and which express our determination and persistence to establish a state worthy of all the sacrifice and suffering that the Palestinian people have endured on the road to freedom and independence.

The Palestinian Ministry of Planning and International Co-operation, in co-operation with other ministries, is responsible for the preparation of a comprehensive physical development plan for the Palestinian state and its cities. These plans will need to respond to the social and cultural needs of our people and define the means to achieve them. It will also have to address the requirements for building the infrastructure, including water, electric, sewage, communications and transport. The team working on preparing this plan will be conducting discussions and consultations with the various ministries and with central and local governmental bodies in order to incorporate their needs into the national plan. It will also work with popular organisations and voluntary associations to ensure that the national plan sincerely reflect the needs and aspirations of all sectors of the Palestinian people.

THE CONSTRUCTION INDUSTRY

Like other economic sectors in the Palestinian Territories (PT), the construction industry has suffered from a severe shortage of financial, technical and natural resources, as well as from the lack of any subsidies provided by a national government or outside sources. Restrictions were imposed on imports and there were no financial institutions to support investment nor were there laws, regulations and standards to control the quality of materials and methods used.

Contractors operated, until recently, without the benefit of standards and codes or any scientific specifications or professional supervision. Contractors also suffered from difficulties in obtaining the tools, machinery and building materials necessary for the proper implementation of their projects. This has resulted in poor quality construction, delays in the implementation of contracts, rises in costs and the exacerbation of environmental problems.

With the advent of the PNA, an appropriate environment was established to enable contractors to re-organise themselves. Legislation governing their activities to guarantee that they function properly and to give them the ability to evaluate their financial, technical, training and educational needs is being drafted. Today, a consensus exists that the right path can only be achieved if the obstacles that the current political situation dictates are removed so that the necessary natural resources, materials, tools and labour can be obtained.

Palestine is rich in the primary components needed for producing building materials. Any future plan to develop the building materials industry and the construction sector in general will require a comprehensive training programme covering institutes, technical colleges and universities. The Ministry of Housing has established research centres that operate in co-ordination with governmental bodies and appropriate scientific institutions. Their objective is to promote scientific inquiry, while benefiting from the expertise available in the neighbouring Arab countries and from the experience of the industrialised countries.

We at the PNA have embarked on a project to develop systems to control the quality of manufactured products to ensure their conformity with known international standards and regulations. We are also seeking the technical support and training that will be required in all these areas. In addition, we are trying to learn from the experience Arab and other countries concerning technical and legal methods in the field of contracting and tenders to guarantee the proper and effective implementation of construction projects.

We realise that our aspirations in this area may exceed the capabilities available to us. Yet while we strive to achieve the highest standards in the long-term, we have to take into consideration the importance of beginning reconstruction based on the methods, tools and expertise currently available to us. We must balance our urgent needs against our limited capabilities in the short-term. Despite important limitations, many low-income housing projects are being built in the developing countries using simple and cheap methods. We have to encourage such possibilities at the same time as providing technical supervision and the necessary support.

HOUSING FINANCE

Because of the absence of investment and financial institutions under the occupation, the Palestinian financial sector has not been able to play a significant role in development. Today, it is in its formative stages for serving the housing sector. In addition to establishing the Palestine Housing Bank, the PNA has been also attempting to encourage the growth of a Palestinian financial sector to support housing and to provide the necessary training for financial institutions.

Efforts are underway to draft laws to protect both lenders and borrowers. In addition, incentives are planned through a simplified taxation system to alleviate the burden of debt and to attract investors to the housing sector. A Palestinian Currency Authority has also been established and new financial regulations are being drafted to incorporate a policy on lending.

In addition to providing appropriate housing and contributing to urban and rural development, the housing and construction sectors play a vital role in reviving and improving the economy, including the provision of job opportunities. Our people are the greatest source of our national wealth, and the available enormous human resources, determination, and commitment to serious work and sacrifice remain a source of great pride and confidence, in addition to demonstrating that we possess the abilities needed to build our country.

SUMMARY AND CONCLUSION

I can summarise the battle for long-term reconstruction in three stages:

1) The evaluation stage;
2) The planning stage; and
3) The implementation stage.

Our particular political situation dictates that we proceed with the three stages simultaneously, for there are urgent needs that we cannot afford to ignore. We are forced to proceed to the implementation phase before finishing the stages of evaluation and planning. Similarly, planning requires short-term, immediate and long-term measures. The evaluation process that we have begun needs to be revised constantly, including both a qualitative and quantitative evaluation of the existing stock of buildings, services and construction techniques, as well as an appropriate assessment of the various phases of planning and implementation.

The PNA realises that it will need to provide the various support programmes to enable the consumer, the contractor, the engineer and those producing materials and services to confront the challenges aimed at improving the quality of production, decreasing costs and increasing labour productivity.

Our motto is co-operation with, and among, the various participating sectors in construction including professional institutions and labour unions, investors, municipalities, financial institutions, co-operatives and non-governmental institutions. The aim is to build a common homeland that satisfies the aspirations of all.

The PNA's budget suffers from a severe lack of revenues at the same time that there are sizeable expenditures. Despite this fact, we have set aside what we can to launch our housing reconstruction campaign. We hope that the private sector and local contractors, in whose efforts we take pride, as well as foreign investors, will make considerable areas of land available for construction. We have provided, and will continue to provide, flexible regulations that would attract investment to support development and to secure the necessary guarantees.

We have endeavoured to secure peace for our people and have contributed to the achievement of peace for all the peoples of the region and all over the world. We realise that everything we are building today is nothing other than a building block for the peace that we hope will become permanent and comprehensive. This peace is neither a slogan that we chant, nor simply an agreement. Instead, it forms the edifice we are erecting, and which we are determined to erect, on sound foundations.

THE PALESTINIAN MINISTRY OF HOUSING: CHALLENGES AND OPPORTUNITIES

Mohammed M. Ziara

ABSTRACT

Housing is the one of the most difficult problems facing the Palestinian National Authority (PNA). In addition to highly populated Gaza, there are thousands of Palestinians who are returning home as a result of the peace accords.

During the Israeli occupation, only scant resources were devoted to the housing sector, and thousands of Palestinian houses were demolished by the Israeli army. There is an immediate shortage of more than 40,000 housing units and it is estimated that 200,000 housing units will be needed by the year 2000. Moreover, housing requirements are expected to increase significantly in subsequent years due to the high natural birth rate, the return of expatriates, the needs of the police force and other demands.

This paper includes a critical analysis of the housing situation in the West Bank and Gaza and an account of the policies, both short- and long-term, of the Ministry of Housing, as well as the activities of related institutions. The role of the various housing institutions is identified. The challenges and opportunities facing Palestinians in dealing with housing and urbanisation are also discussed. Recommendations regarding the co-ordination of all sectors are provided.

INTRODUCTION

Housing plays a major role in government strategies to improve the social, economic and environmental quality of human settlements and in general economical development. It alleviates poverty and generates employment, in addition to providing shelter for people. Towns and cities are the centres of economic growth and the focus of human activity and

12

progress. However, the successful planning and management of human settlements requires financial and technical resources as well as capacity for positive change through institutional improvements. Undoubtedly, resources play a key role in providing housing; however, imagination, vigour, courage and commitment are also major factors.

The government of Israel and the Palestinian Liberation Organisation (PLO) signed the Declaration of Principles on Interim Self-government Arrangements on 13 September 1993, and the Implementation Agreement on Gaza and Jericho on 4 May 1994. As a result, the political, economic and social realities in the area have changed tremendously. Providing shelter for Palestinians will consolidate the peace process and raise the development level of the Palestinian people.

Given present harsh economic realities, housing is one of the most difficult problems facing the PNA, especially in highly populated Gaza. In addition to the present population of Gaza, there are thousands of Palestinians who are returning home as a result of the peace accords. As usual, in hard times, it is the poor and disenfranchised who suffer the most. It is the responsibility of the PNA to ensure that Palestinians are provided houses, jobs, food and quality of life without harming the environment.

Developed Palestinian areas should be used to maximum effect and their attractiveness as places to live and work should be improved. Patterns of development which help to sustain urbanisation and those who minimise energy consumption through more compact urban development should be promoted. Recent world-wide experience has clearly shown that human settlement is becoming predominantly urban. Planning and managing this change is becoming vitally important. As for Palestinians, learning from what has been done in other countries, including examples which have failed as well as those which have been successful, will contribute to Palestinian success.

ISSUES: THE HOUSING PROBLEM

Population and Demographic Trends

The most recent population census for the Occupied Territories (OT) was conducted by Israel in 1967 (Central Bureau of Statistics, 1967). No independent Palestinian estimates of the population exist, although the Palestinian Central Bureau of Statistics is planning to conduct such a census. Meanwhile, a wide variety of population estimates are available (Israel, Central Bureau of Statistics, 1992 and The Co-operative Housing Foundation, 1993).

However, the 1967 census is regarded as acceptable for evaluating the current housing situation in Gaza and the West Bank according to

13

Table 1 Estimated Population of West Bank and Gaza (in thousands).

Year	West Bank	Gaza	Total
1992	1207.0	716.8	1923.8
1993	1253.7	752.6	2006.3
1994	1302.3	790.2	2092.5
1995	1352.7	829.7	2182.4
1996	1405.2	874.2	2279.4
1997	1459.6	914.8	2374.4
1998	1516.2	960.5	2476.6
2000	1655.0	1040.0	2695.0

the United Nations Commission on Human Settlements, even though this in effect double counts Palestinians living outside the OT (1995).

According to UNCHS, the population in the West Bank at the end of May 1967, was estimated to total 845,000; in September 1967, after the Israeli occupation, this figure had fallen to 585,000. The corresponding estimates for Gaza were 442,100 and 380,860 respectively. Until the end of 1986, the population of the west Bank stood at approximately the same level as in May, 1967.

In contrast, the population of Gaza had increased by 27.8 per cent during same period. The average growth rate of the OT population was estimated at 2.6 per cent during the period between 1968 and 1992. The natural average increase of Palestinians in the same period was 3.24 per cent and 3.79 per cent in the West Bank and Gaza respectively.

This percentage went up from 2.18 in 1968 to 5.03 in 1992 and from 2.22 to 4 for Gaza and the West Bank respectively, according to Israeli figures (Central Bureau of Statistics, 1992) The growth of the population is expected to reach the rate of natural increase in the near future, i.e. 4 and 5 per cent in the West Bank and Gaza respectively.

Based on this estimate, Table 1 shows the projected total population, according to the UNCHS report (1995). The total population is expected to reach 2,695,000 by the year 2,000.

About 50 per cent of the population is under age 14 and only 10 per cent is over 45. In addition, it is reasonable to assume that, for strategic planning purposes, approximately one million Palestinians, out of a total of some 4 million living in the diaspora will return home by 2,000 (the majority are in the Arab states: about 42 per cent in Jordan, 14.2 per cent in Lebanon, and 8.86 per cent in Syria). The refugee camps accommodate more than 10 per cent and 35 per cent of the population in the West Bank and Gaza respectively.

The distribution of the Palestinian refugees who have been registered and issued identification cards by the United Nations Relief and Works Agency (UNRWA) in refugee camps in June, 1990 was estimated by UNRWA as shown in Table 2. The total refugee population should be

Table 2 Refugee Population in the West Bank and Gaza in 1990 (in thousands).

Area	Total Population	No. of Camps	Camp Population	Population not in Camps	Percentage not in Camps
West Bank	414.3	20	110.0	304.3	73
Gaza	496.4	8	271.9	224.5	45
Total	910.7	28	381.9	528.8	58

Table 3 Number of Housing Units in the West Bank and Gaza in 1990 by Category (in thousands).

Area	Urban	Rural	Refugee Camps	Total
West Bank	92 (53%)	67 (38%)	16 (9%)	175
Gaza	58 (54%)	10 (9%)	39 (36%)	107
Total	150 (53%)	77 (27%)	55 (19%)	282

increased by an estimated 6 per cent to account for Palestinians not registered as refugees.

Existing Conditions

The housing industry in Palestine presents many challenges and opportunities and should be considered the top priority in the general reconstruction of Palestine. Current housing need is far greater than any available public sector resources can fulfil. During the period of Israeli occupation, not only scant resources were devoted to the housing sector, but thousands of Palestinian houses were demolished by the Israeli army. This has aggravated the problem. In 1990, the total number of housing units in West Bank and Gaza was estimated to be 282,000. This included units located in urban and rural areas, as well as in the refugee camps (see Table 3).

Given the lack of independent Palestinian estimates, verification of the data concerning the number of houses, identification of building materials, access to water, sewer, electricity and other facilities is usually estimated from information gathered during visits made by different missions to Palestine. These estimates indicate that 80 per cent of the housing units in urban areas can be considered acceptable; 15 per cent need upgrading to meet the minimal acceptable standard for a dwelling unit, i.e. 50 square metres with basic services; and 5 per cent of the units are non-upgradable. Table 4 shows the housing conditions for urban and rural units and for the refugee camps.

Estimates based on available data for 1985 indicate that in urban areas in the West Bank 7 per cent of the units did not have a kitchen, 9 per cent did not have running water, and 2 per cent did not have electricity

Table 4 Conditions and Number of Housing Units by Category in 1990 (in thousands).

Category	Acceptable	Need Upgrading	Non Upgradable	Total	Over-crowding
Urban	120 (80%)	22 (15%)	8 (5%)	150	45 (30%)
Rural	42 (55%)	31 (40%)	4 (5%)	77	27 (35%)
Refugee Camps	8 (15%)	14 (25%)	33 (60%)	55	22 (40%)
Total	170	67	45	282	94

(The Co-operative Housing Foundation, 1993). The corresponding figures for Gaza are 4 per cent, 17 per cent and 6 per cent respectively.

In the rural areas of the West Bank, 24 per cent of the units did not have a kitchen, 15 per cent did not have a toilet, 50 per cent did not have running water, and 54 per cent did not have electricity. Corresponding values for Gaza are not available.

In the refugee camps in Gaza, 6 per cent of the units did not have a kitchen, 3 per cent did not have a toilet, 32 per cent did not have running water, and 6 per cent did not have electricity. The corresponding values for the West Bank are not available.

Housing Needs

Based on available information regarding population and housing stoke, the Co-operative Housing Foundation estimated that approximately 34,000 new units would be required per year for the period from 1990 to 1995. Of these, 14,000 were for new households, 6,000 for the replacement of housing stock that has decayed, 4,000 for the replacement of non-upgradable housing stock, and 10,000 to relieve overcrowding. Another 6,000 units were to be upgraded annually. The distribution of housing needs for urban areas was to require an estimated 20,000 new units per year.

According to the estimates, rural areas would require 13,000 units, with no new construction inside refugee camps. Upgrading of existing units was projected at the rate of 6,000 per year during the period 1990 to 1995. For the next five years from 1995 to 2000, approximately 25 per cent more housing would be required, of which 43,500 would be new units and 7,780 upgraded.

Other fact finding missions have estimated that there is an immediate shortage of more than 40,000 housing units (Palestinian–Norwegian Fact Finding Mission, 1995). Moreover, housing requirements are expected to increase significantly in subsequent years. An estimated 200,000 housing units will be needed by the year 2000.

Current trends are leading toward the construction of multi-story buildings because of the high price of land. Typically, each floor contains four

Table 5 Existing Dwellings, end 1992.

Rooms per dwellings	West Bank (total dwellings = 173,515) percentage of dwellings	number of rooms	Gaza (total dwellings = 11,698) percentage of dwellings	number of rooms
1	10.1	17525	20.0	24340
2	29.2	101332	34.7	84458
3	31.9	166054	30.0	109528
4	19.8	137424	12.4	60362
6	8.9	92656	2.8	20445
Total rooms	100.0	514991	100.0	299133
Average rooms per dwelling	2.96		2.45	
Average number of persons per room	2.04		2.39	
Average persons per household	6.06		5.89	

apartments with an area of about 140 square metres. The large size of apartments is attributed to the large size of Palestinian families. The housing density per room is high with an estimated average of 2.03 in 1992. In addition, it is estimated that more than one-third of Palestinians are living in overcrowded conditions with more than three persons per room.

Rents for new apartments in the major cities rose to more than $500 for an average-sized unit per month. Table 5 shows the estimated average room per dwelling, and the average size of households for the West Bank and Gaza in 1992 (UNCHS, 1995).

The large average size of households is explained by extended families occupying a single house, as well as by the shortage of housing for low-income people. For purposes of comparison, the average household size for Israeli Jews is 3.38 persons, while the average of number of persons per room is 1.03. The building industry, especially in Gaza, is characterised by an inadequate supply of local building materials. It is almost entirely dependent on products imported from Israel, including cement, reinforcing steel, wood, glass, electrical and mechanical materials. In addition to these difficulties, there are no formal financial institutions to deal with the construction and management of houses.

Most houses, with the exception of those in the refugee camps and in informal areas, are built of permanent materials, i.e. cut stone, concrete blocks or concrete. In the refugee camps, the houses are built with concrete block exterior walls and roofs of asbestos-cement or zinc corrugated sheets. UNRWA is responsible for the refugee camps where they were built more than 45 years ago as temporary places to shelter the refugees.

At present, UNRWA has a limited programme to improve existing living conditions in the camps by installing water and sanitation systems. These efforts are co-ordinated with the Ministry of Housing. The quality of housing in urban and rural areas improved between 1961 and 1985 due to the desire of Palestinians to improve their living conditions and to expand their presence in Palestine despite the constraints imposed by Israelis.

HOUSING INSTITUTIONS AND PERFORMANCE

No Palestinian housing institutions existed until a Palestinian Housing Council (PHC) was founded in 1991. The work of the municipalities regarding housing was limited to issuing permits within their boundaries, and these were subject to Israeli approval.

The Palestinian Housing Council

The Palestinian Housing Council (PHC) was established as a non-profit organisation to reduce housing problems. Although it is not organised as a public institution, it has certain links with the PNA. The main office of the PHC is in Jerusalem and it has offices in most major cities in the West Bank and Gaza. The Council has been responsible for several new housing projects totalling 800 housing units approximately. The projects were financed by the European Union (EU), USAID, and the Japanese government.

The Ministry of Housing

In May, 1994, the PNA created the Ministry of Housing. It consists of five directorates: research, planning and development; policy and urban planning; projects; administrative affairs and financial affairs. The institutional structure is shown in Figure 1 and in Table 6.

The aims of the Ministry of Housing are:

- To enable every resident to live in a durable, suitable house;
- To encourage scientific research in the field of housing;
- To develop the local housing industry, quality control, codes, standards and regulations;
- Regarding construction and urbanisation; and
- To revive Islamic/Arabic architecture.

The policy of the Ministry of Housing is to support the activities of the private sector while making critical public interventions to promote national objectives. The housing system will aim to serve all residents, including those who cannot afford housing without some form of subsidy.

18

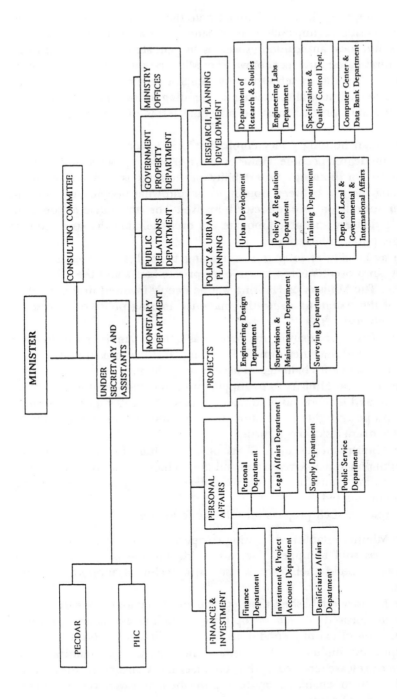

Figure 1 The Institutional Structure of the Ministry of Housing

Eventually, the Ministry will co-ordinate the activities of all participants in the housing sector, including consumers, developers, financial institutions and local authorities, as well as the impact of fiscal measures on the entire Palestinian economy. The Ministry will support a housing finance system that is self-sustaining. Such a system will permit private, public and institutional borrowing and lending for housing at competitive rates. Housing finance must be on equal terms with all sectors of the economy.

Palestinian housing policy emphasises private sector financing to the maximum degree possible. However, there is wide gap between the supply and need for housing. Affordability of housing is a major obstacle. Reducing the gap between housing costs and what people can afford to pay cannot rely on private sector initiatives. The imperative to speed up housing delivery and accommodate the overwhelming demand requires strategic public intervention.

The availability of long term financing to facilitate the construction and site improvements is a key role for private banks and the Ministry of Finance. The Ministry of Housing will be deeply involved in the development of the system to assure that national housing policy objectives are adequately met.

Under Israeli occupation, the policy was to deny families rights to build homes on land that they owned. Resolving land tenure issues for private property is a major challenge to accelerating the production of housing. The goal of the Ministry is to support and update a legal environment in which land is more easily sold and bought. A greater sense of security about property rights in relation to these transactions would help to reduce current risks and returns.

The Ministry hopes to fulfil its objectives fully in the near future, depending on available resources and the political situation in the region. Measures and plans for projects to achieve these objectives have already been implemented.

Examples of such projects include the following:

- The Ministry established housing co-operative projects in which public land was sold to upper, low and middle-income people at nominal prices to build their own houses with technical support from the Ministry.
- The Ministry established the Department of Scientific Research which started research projects of top priority, such as evaluation and documentation of existing conditions of the public land in Gaza.
- Despite the limited available funds, the Ministry has financially supported researchers from the Engineering College in the Islamic University to enable them to report their research on housing at international conferences.

Table 6 Present Employment in the Ministry.

Directorate	Department	Total Staff			Employed Staff		
		Senior	Junior	Total	Senior	Junior	Total
Research,	Research	7	8	15	1	4	5
Planning	Labs	5	27	32	2	–	2
and	Quality Control	3	18	21	2	2	4
Development	Data Bank	4	16	20	1	1	2
Sub-Total		19	69	88	6	7	13
Policy	Urbanisation	5	22	27	1	7	8
and	Policies	3	5	8	1	–	1
Urban	Local Affairs	4	8	12	1	–	1
Planning	Training	3	10	13	2	–	2
Sub-Total		15	45	60	5	7	12
	Design	5	18	23	3	3	6
Projects	Supervision	4	26	30	1	20	21
	Survey	4	28	32	2	24	26
Sub-Total		13	72	85	6	47	53
	Employment	3	7	10	2	4	6
Administration	Supply	3	10	13	1	3	4
Affairs	Services	3	22	25	1	7	8
	Legal	3	7	10	2	1	3
Sub-Total		12	46	58	6	15	21
Financial	Finance	5	8	13	2	3	5
Affairs	Investment	3	9	12	1	1	2
	Beneficiaries	4	10	14	1	6	7
Sub-Total		12	27	39	4	10	14
TOTAL		71	259	330	27	86	113

- The Ministry has established building regulations for multi-story buildings. Also, technical help and supervision are given to concrete batching plants, and engineering material labs to improve their quality controls.
- All the housing projects which are implemented jointly by private investors with the Ministry must be approved by the Ministry regarding their architectural style.

So far, key staff members have been employed by the Ministry, including senior staff members (heads of sub-departments, directors, and director general) and junior staff members. Table 6 presents the present status of employment in the Ministry's various departments.

In addition to the staff members of the five directorates, there are the Minister and his deputies and their supporting staff. The total number of employees in the Ministry was expected to amount to 428. Special independent committees were formed from universities, industry and the Ministry to hire staff. However, although qualified Palestinian candidates were available, some of them had little practical experience in working in the housing sector.

Currently, the Ministry has limited resources. The cost of building the Ministry's headquarters, which is located in Gaza, is being paid by using public land. Furniture and equipment such as computers, printers and photocopying machines, have been obtained using grants from Japan and other donor countries with the assistance of the World Bank. No budget has been allocated for housing projects, whether by the donor countries or the PNA. Most existing housing projects are implemented utilising public land.

The Ministry is being administered with trust and monitoring activities, rather than through controls. Clear tasks and responsibilities, flow of information, decentralisation, team work, flexibility, effective dynamic administration, continuous evaluation and review of mission and goals, co-operation between departments, belonging and motivation, as well as investment in human resources have also been among the main characteristics of the Ministry of Housing. Some of the difficulties facing the administration of the Ministry are the lack of practical experience in establishing and running such a large institution, in addition to the lack of facilities and resources.

POLICIES AND STRATEGIES OF THE MINISTRY

Policy Overview

The housing problem will be solved with civic engagement, sustainability and equity and will involve shareholders at all levels; the role of government is to provide the enabling environment. The emphasis will be on getting the right policy framework and on guiding socio-economic development.

At present, the existing housing institutions, which include the PHC, local authorities, engineering unions, housing co-operatives and other organisations, are not very well established and have limited resources and experience. Co-ordination between these institutions including defining responsibilities is not satisfactory, but is being improved.

Because of this, although effective participation of the entire population will be recognised as an important element in shaping the human settlement policy, the emphasis will be on a 'top-down' approach. In other words, although the implementation of any human settlement programme requires a participatory process centred on the recipients, the process of policy-making, implementation, monitoring, evaluation, consultation and review will continue to be carried out by the government.

The shelters to be provided must be adequate, affordable, safe, and hygienic and located in both the urban and rural area of the West Bank and Gaza. The focus will be on low-cost, environmentally-sound and appropriate products and technologies in housing construction and in the human settlement sector in general.

The role of planning is aimed to be comprehensive and to treat fairly the problems of urban and rural settlements as integral parts of the development of sustainable human settlements. In Palestine, especially in Gaza, there is a lack of access to land. In addition, unplanned settlements exist alongside environmental deterioration.

For Palestinians, access by the poor to land and finance are important issues. Market forces may have a role in urban development and in the provision of housing for people with adequate incomes, but it is the role of government and public agencies to provide shelter for those affected by poverty and for those in special conditions, such as the families of the police forces and those whose houses have been demolished by the Israeli forces.

The Ministry of Housing, in an attempt to help the poorest sections of the population, has taken measures to bridge the gap between the formal and informal sectors. For this reason a set of remedial measures have been taken, including the establishment of housing co-operatives in which public land is given to poor people at nominal cost.

Strategies for Solving the Housing Problem

Given the limited resources and the size of the problem, the Ministry has adopted two approaches towards dealing with the housing issue. The first involves a research programme, while the second concentrates on remedial action to solve urgent problems.

The Department of Research and Development, jointly with the World Bank, is finalising the terms of reference for a research programme to draft a long-term plan and proper housing strategy to solve the housing problem. The aim of this approach is to arrest the deterioration in human settlements in Palestine and ultimately to create the conditions for achieving improvements in the living environment in these settlements which are sustainable. The research and development programme will use a system of indicators to identify housing requirements and to formulate and monitor strategies for housing, including a plan of action.

The implementation is to be characterised by participation, consultation and enhancement of partnerships which contribute to the basic objectives: ennoblement, empowerment and co-ordinated governance. Also, new theoretical and methodological frameworks dealing with human settlement are to be integrated with scientific analysis and policy-making.

The second approach seeks to provide remedial measures to resolve urgent problems. These include firstly, the development of a housing co-operative system to enable those in low- and medium-income brackets to secure public land at a nominal price to build their own homes. Loans for this programme should be provided through a housing bank.

The work for this programme has begun, but loans cannot be provided at this stage due to the lack of financial institutions and funds. A survey conducted by the Ministry indicated that about 500 housing co-operatives, with some 8,000 beneficiaries, could be established soon in West Bank and Gaza. The housing co-operative section in the Department of Local Affairs is responsible for this programme in co-operation with other departments in the Ministry.

The second urgent problem concerns the development of an investment policy to allow investors to buy public land in order to build housing units, hotels, factories, recreation facilities and other facilities. In return, the investors are to build housing units and hand them over to the PNA for renting and selling. More than 100 projects have been started based on this investment policy, of which the PNA's share is to reach 4,000 housing units. The Department of Investment is responsible for this programme, in co-operation with other departments in the Ministry.

Small villages are also being planned on public land. These villages will be provided with the requisite infrastructural works, including water networks, sewer systems, telephone and electricity networks, roads, primary schools, health centres, and other service facilities. The land will then be given to investors, co-operatives and individuals for construction.

This programme has been discussed with the World Bank, which has shown considerable interest. A complete proposal is being finalised, jointly between the Ministry and the World Bank, to be submitted to donor countries to obtain funds. The Department of Urbanisation is responsible for this programme, in co-operation with other departments in the Ministry.

Another problem relates to the fact that most existing new buildings, especially in Gaza, have been designed to be multi-storey. However, because of lacking of funds and other factors often only a few stories have been actually built.

In addition, the problem of unemployment is becoming very severe following the repeated closure of Gaza and of the West Bank by Israel. In an attempt to solve both problems, i.e. the housing shortage and unemployment, independent technical, legal, economical and social committees have been formed to tackle this problem. They have studied the idea of helping people to complete their buildings. The results of the study confirmed that the idea is feasible, and a number of recommendations were suggested for implementation of the project.

However, among the difficulties which will be encountered are the lack of funding, technical staff and specialists in the field of housing market. Although the intention is to encourage the private sector to take part, public funding is necessary in order to start such a programme. The technical committee estimated that about $50 million will be required to launch a pilot project to build 5,000 housing units in the first year; in other words, 1,250 units every three months.

Of course, the project could be launched if any significant amount of money becomes available. The funds will be lent in the form of loans, credits or in other forms. After collecting the money, another phase of the project will be started. Success will not only contribute to solving the problem of housing and unemployment, but also would affect positively supporting industries such as factories producing bricks, tiles and other building materials. A housing bank will be established to implement this project. The World Bank will be approached, via the donor countries, for funding.

The establishment of a housing bank with a capital of $100 million is aimed at providing financial services for those who work in the housing sector, as well as for people of limited income. The by-laws of the bank have been drafted, and the bank is expected to begin operations in the next few months.

A Joint Programme with the World Bank

Currently the World Bank is showing interest in supporting the housing sector. A comprehensive housing programme is being finalised jointly by the World Bank and the Ministry of Housing. The programme will be designed as a market-oriented programme, providing a range of housing choices for buyers. It will rely mainly on the private sector for land development, construction of housing units and a substantial portion of funding through the commercial banks.

The government role would be to manage the programme, arrange competitive access to building land, set and monitor building codes and construction standards, mobilise donor funds, monitor construction and design and mange the low income subsidy programme. The programme would start with a number of demonstration or pilot projects in geographically dispersed urban and rural locations in Gaza and the West Bank. This is aimed at testing the market for the model units, designed with the participation of the communities at the internal target sites. Being modular, it would be flexible to expand or contract to meet demand. The units themselves would be relatively low in cost to provide immediate access to some shelter, yet capable of being developed more later.

The housing projects could include different developments, such as:

1) New communities, including:
   • Land development;
   • Shell buildings;

- Complete buildings; and
- Supported core units.
2) Neighbourhood developments, including:
    - Infrastructure;
    - House improvement and infrastructure; and the
    - Completion of existing buildings.
3) Off-site infrastructure and services.

The programme will include other activities related to housing, such as the following:

• Data collection and analysis

At present, there is a lack of data and information which are necessary for the development of short- and long-term housing strategies. A data system is to be established including hardware and software, in co-ordination with the computer centre in the Ministry. A reporting system, including publications and other access, will be developed. Facilities would be established and equipment would be furnished to allow the PNA to manage and update the Geographic Information System (GIS) data base. A training programme for the staff of the Ministry of Housing also needs to be established.

• International-Palestinian centres

International-Palestinian centres will be set up to promote peace in the region by supporting Palestinian efforts to solve the housing problem. A draft joint project between the Ministry of Housing and the University of Florida in the USA is being finalised.

• Land and housing regulations

Standards, codes of practice, regulations and specifications need to be issued immediately in Palestine because the area is now under active development. Property rights and ownership, land titling, and condominium law constitute the most pressing regulatory issues that need urgent action if a legal environment in which land is more easily sold and bought is to be created.

• Technical assistance and training

One of the main objectives of the Ministry of Housing is to build and strengthen human capacities and to improve both institutional and individual performance, by designing a set of training courses and workshops.

26

These training programmes will provide administrative, technical, and policy making assistance to the Ministry's staff, and at a latter stage to the Palestinian institutions and organisations involved in housing.

• The role of government

The Ministry encourages the private sector to take a major part in solving the problem of housing. However, the direct involvement of the PNA can not be avoided in some cases such as providing houses for police forces and their families as well as for poor. The funds available for this purpose are few. The donor countries have promised to contribute financially to such projects, but the actual help received is still nominal.

• The role of the private sector

Previously, most of the effort and resources of the private sector in Palestine have been directed towards investment in luxury houses and in commercial buildings. There is a need to direct the private sector to play a stronger leadership role in investment in affordable houses and to overcome social, economic and environmental problems. In order to implement the enabling policy, the Ministry has encouraged the private sector by giving investors public land, at reduced cost, to build affordable houses.

• The role of local authorities

The problems of human settlements are first and most directly perceived at local authority level. Participation and co-operation of local authorities will be a determining factor in fulfilling the strategies of housing. Local authorities must be empowered to act effectively for their communities. They need to be associated with the regional planning process and engage jointly with the national government regarding the economic and social factors which affect human settlements.

However, past experience related to the work of Palestinian local authorities, such the municipalities and village councils, has shown the need to improve their capacity and performance in dealing with the problems of urbanisation and shelter. In an attempt to set an adequate framework for the development of this partnership approach and to enhance performance, joint committees from the Ministry of Housing, the Ministry of Local Government, and the Ministry of Planning in the PNA have been formed. The main purpose of these committees has been to act jointly in dealing with both urgent problems as well as long-term planning regarding urbanisation and economical development.

RECOMMENDATIONS

The Role of the Ministry

The challenges facing Palestinians dealing with the housing sector are tremendous. These include limited public resources, lack of experience, shortage of houses and a lack of time required for planning. However, imagination, motivation, new ideas, learning from other people experience and utilising the wisdom and resources of private sector are factors which could represent opportunities to solve the housing problems and to plan sustainable human settlements. This needs a great deal of co-ordination and teamwork.

At present, the number of institutions that deal with the housing sector and with human settlement is limited. Moreover, the responsibility and the role of each institution is not very well understood. In addition, other institutions involving housing are expected to be established. The need for co-ordination between all of these institutions is obvious if time, effort and resources are not to be wasted. The Ministry of Housing, as an official representative of the PNA, should play the role of co-ordinator. This should not adversely affect the policy of decentralisation nor preclude the participation of all key parties in developing and implementing housing strategies, but should ensure that the national policy is being implemented and that any duplication of work is avoided.

HOUSING FINANCE INSTITUTIONS

A housing finance system which conforms to housing policies aiming to supply affordable and sustainable housing is required. This should be co-ordinated with institutional development which fosters the upgrading of new governmental and financial institutions for fund management as well. Such a system is necessary because of its essential role in promoting the supply of funds. Also, the financial sector must be reformed through the establishment of effective governmental institutions to encourage a supply of funds.

Once it is established and operating, the Palestinian Monetary Authority (PMA) will have a vital role in securing good financial management and performance. At present, little affordable housing is being provided for low- and limited-income people because private investors are directing their efforts and resources to highly profitable housing projects. In addition, the resources available to the Ministry of Housing and the public sector in general are limited.

The components of the housing finance system include financial institutions such as a housing bank, mortgage system, housing funds, lending and saving programmes, private intermediaries, the private sector, PMA and donor countries, as well as other participants.

A Housing Bank

This will support and promote housing projects. It could serve as an effective tool in receiving and directing funds toward investments in low-cost housing. Such a bank would need to take into consideration the fact that three currencies are used in Gaza and the West Bank; namely, US dollars, Jordanian dinars and Israeli shekels.

A Housing Fund

Various methods of supplementing financing are necessary. A public housing finance agency can be a partial answer to this problem. It would operate under the supervision of the Ministry of Housing, but as an independent entity. Potential sources of money for the Housing Fund include existing capital grants from the donor nations, potential new donor allocations and soft loans from the World Bank.

The proposed design could have three linked parts: a government subsidy, personal savings, and a commercial loan. The concept is to encourage personal savings among families to afford a down payment for their housing. The saving account would be matched with a relatively low subsidy to create sufficient buyer equity. The remaining amount would be from a commercial loan. This approach is targeted at moderate income families.

Housing Associations

The associations would receive enough funds to balance the shortage in financing low-cost housing in co-ordination with other financial institutions.

Mortgage Finance

The sources of funds for housing will come from household savings, private mortgage lending, and government subsidies. The potential of private sector contributions remains unclear. Outside investors have a perception of high risks and political uncertainties. Donor funds to under-write or guarantee their investments will be a necessary financial incentive to begin the process. The Authority's capacity to generate funds for subsidies is limited. As the development of Palestine continues, workers will find jobs, pay taxes, and be able to afford housing with less help from the government.

29

Financial Guarantee Programmes

The success of these programmes can only be achieved by co-operation between the private housing institutions and other governmental bodies, whether local or international bodies.

Loan Programmes

These would be especially designed to suite specific housing projects, especially those intended for low-income people.

An Emergency Housing Fund

For those families in most distress, the above alternatives may not work. In a typical case, it would take many years to qualify for a minimum standard house. Other more direct and immediate methods to assist them will be necessary. The first step is to identify precisely how many families are experiencing serious distress and how they coping today. Developing cost estimates about how much is needed to carry out such a programme, and securing the necessary money is a top priority of the Ministry.

The Palestinian Monetary Authority (PMA)

The PMA would use its authority to determine the discount rate and to control interest rates, liquidity, credit and deposits, in addition to analysing the private banks and balance sheets according to international standards, as well as organising financial operations in general. All the above mentioned will lead to good administration for the financial sector which in turn would encourage investment in the housing sector. In addition, good financial management will address the risks of interest rates changes, inflation, and currency market fluctuations.

BIBLIOGRAPHY

Atari, Bassam M., 1994, **Gaza Housing Project Technical Assistance: Market-Based Affordable Housing Finance Loan Terms** (Project, 254–0006), August, 1994, Report prepared for the US Agency for International Development, Document No. G/PRE/H PCE–1008–I–00–2066–00.

The Co-operative Housing Foundation, May, 1993, **Housing Needs Assessment for the West Bank and Gaza**, Report prepared for the US Agency for International Development, Revised edition, Washington, D.C.

Government of Israel, Central Bureau of Statistics, **Census of Population in the Administered Area, 1967**, 5 vols, Jerusalem.

Government of Israel, Central Bureau of Statistics, Department of Statistics, Central Administration, 1992, *Interim Report*, **Israel Statistical Abstract**, Jerusalem.

Government of Israel, Central Bureau of Statistics, n.d., **Census of Population and Housing in East Jerusalem, 1967,** 2 vols, Jerusalem.

Palestinian–Norwegian Fact Finding Mission, March 1995, *Housing and Building Material Sector.* Paper prepared for the Norway Representative Office in Palestine.

United Nations Centre on Human Settlements, 14 February 1995, Document No. HS/C/15/2/Add.4, Geneva.

A HOUSING STRATEGY FOR THE PALESTINIAN TERRITORIES

Mohammed Shadid

ABSTRACT

The housing shortage in the West Bank and Gaza is presently estimated at approximately 250,000 housing units; this shortage is projected to grow by a further 185,000 units over the next five years. This paper is a comprehensive study of the housing crisis in the West Bank and Gaza. It analyses the housing sector generally in the past 50 years, and provides a projection of immediate needs for the next five years. It also suggests a strategy for coping with the current crisis.

Major objectives of a Palestinian housing strategy include providing adequate and affordable housing for all income groups, providing public housing for the lowest income groups, making the required planning and infrastructure available, establishing housing credit institutions and encouraging merchant banks to provide credit for housing projects.

Housing co-operatives, the Palestinian Higher Council and the Ministry of Housing will play a major role in achieving these objectives. The housing sector urgently requires the skilled necessary labour to implement plans. There is also a need to develop the planning schemes of cities, towns and villages, and to plan for rural and community development to prevent internal migration. All these activities require the establishment of the appropriate legal framework.

INTRODUCTION

The housing problem is one of the most serious aspects of the many and varied dimensions of the Palestinian problem. The various phases of dislocation affected the Palestinian people and their entire socio—economic and political structure. During the period of the British Mandate, Jewish immigration, which was accompanied by the establish-

32

ment of settlements, was the first measure to have affected the structure of Palestinian housing resources.

The creation of Israel brought about the first major dislocation of the Palestinian people, a large number of whom moved to the West Bank, Gaza and neighbouring Arab countries to escape Zionist terror. Another major displacement took place immediately after the June, 1967 war. A systematic process of indirect displacement has been taking place ever since. Land confiscation, the creation of settlements and political and economical pressures have been the major tools of that process.

Palestinians hope that the peace process will be another major point of change in the socio–economic fabric of their society, and hundreds of thousands of Palestinians are expected to return to the West Bank and Gaza.

It is very clear that there is a great and urgent need for a Palestinian housing strategy. Such a strategy should take into account the tragedies of the past and the hopes and expectations of the future.

ISSUES: THE HOUSING CRISIS

The establishment of Israel in 1948 resulted in hundreds of thousands of Palestinians leaving their homes for the West Bank, Gaza and Arab countries. By 1951, there were approximately 880,000 Palestinian refugees living in the various regions and registered with the United Nations Relief and Works Agency (UNRWA; UNCTAD/ESCD/SEU 14, 1994). Israel occupied more than 77 per cent of Palestine. Of the remainder, the West Bank was placed under Jordanian rule, and Gaza under Egypt's.

Before 1967, planning and socio–economic development in the West Bank and Gaza was very limited. Housing comprised single-unit dwellings, which were occupied by extended families; the housing density was thus relatively high.

Outline plans were prepared and approved for 60 per cent of the municipalities of the West Bank. The plans were similar to those made during the Mandate period: they concentrated on roads and their set-backs, and tended to preserve current building trends (UNCTAD/ECDC/SEU 14, 1994). New buildings required special permits either from municipality councils or from the district committees in towns and villages which had no councils.

In the early 1950s, UNRWA carried out a massive construction pro-gramme to provide shelter for the refugees in the West Bank and Gaza: 18 camps were built in the West Bank and eight in Gaza. Although the construction in the camps was overseen by UNRWA, it was carried out mostly by the residents themselves. Lots were assigned to families and plans were drawn. The buildings were generally simple: concrete walls and tin roofing.

There was a boom in housing construction in the West Bank and Gaza during the late 1950s and early 1960s. This was a direct result of the wealth created by new employment opportunities which Palestinians found in Kuwait, Saudi Arabia, North and South America.

Studies of the period show that 60 per cent of houses accommodated single households and that 25 per cent housed two or more households. Only 13 per cent had running water and 7 per cent bathtubs (Jordanian Department of Statistics, 1961).

The construction sector during this period contributed an average of 15 per cent to the gross domestic product (GDP) of the West Bank and 6 per cent to the GDP of Gaza. These figures do not include activities by UNRWA in the two regions. The sector employed approximately 20,555 workers in the West Bank and approximately 4,000 workers in Gaza (Bahiri, 1989).

Most houses were built as a result of individual efforts. Housing co-operatives existed, but had little impact on the overall housing situation. In Gaza, no housing co-operatives existed until 1993.

There were 12 housing co-operatives in the West Bank in 1966. They comprised 5 per cent of the total number of co-operatives (Zaghmouri, 1991). Several housing co-operatives implemented projects; the co-operative of the Jerusalem Post Office Workers built 40 units in addition to a club and a shop. The Jericho Housing Co-operative built 72 units in 1960 (O'beidat, 1992).

In 1967, Israel occupied the remainder of Palestine and applied military rule to the West Bank and Gaza. Hundreds of thousands of Palestinians left the West Bank and Gaza for Jordan and other countries; most of them were 1948 refugees, especially from the Jordan Valley around Jericho. The Israeli military occupation destroyed all aspects of Palestinian life. The construction sector has been probably the most affected by Israeli policies and military orders.

There are two major elements of the housing crisis: the first is external and results from Israel's military occupation and its policies; the second is internal and relates to Palestinian obstacles, especially in the construction sector. Each of these factors is discussed briefly here.

External Factors

External factors refer to the Israeli occupation and the policies which affected the Palestinian economy in general and the housing sector in particular. The impact of these factors will be clarified in the section on internal factors which follows.

Here it is important to emphasise that Israeli policies have been aimed at distorting the Palestinian construction sector in order to make way for the settlement of Israelis. Israeli authorities have allowed the production of building materials in the West Bank to be developed only when they serve the interests of Israel's construction industries. This includes building-stone production and the quarry business. Israeli policies towards the housing sector are as follows.

Israel expropriated and confiscated vast areas of Palestinian land. This resulted in the reduction of a major and vital resource for the development of the construction sector. More than 60 per cent of the West Bank and Gaza were expropriated, confiscated or closed for a variety of reasons.

The Israeli authorities imposed severe restrictions on the use of the remaining lands owned by the Palestinians. These restrictions prevented the construction sector from developing and providing housing and other necessary infrastructure. Construction in villages and towns requires permits from central authorities. District committees were immediately eliminated by the occupying forces. In municipalities, building work needs local approval from the councils, but this is restricted to municipal boundaries which have not been allowed to expand.

The establishment of industrial units has required the approval of Israeli military authorities. Permits have been granted in accordance with Israeli policies whose objective have been to achieve total Palestinian dependence on the Israeli economy. Thus, industries which reduce dependence have not been permitted. Israel has refused to issue permits for cement and steel factories, and the establishment of new quarries has faced many obstacles.

The occupation authorities have hampered the establishment of Palestinian national institutions or co-operatives that could administer housing strategy.

Israeli punishment to Palestinians involved in resistance activities included demolishing their homes. Approximately 1,000 houses have been demolished and sealed off since December 1987 (PHRIC, 1995).

The Israeli authorities closed all Arab and Palestinian banks immediately after the occupation, but sanctioned the opening of branches of Israeli banks. This has deprived the Palestinian economy as a whole and the construction sector in particular of credit sources. Most housing finance has been made available through personal savings. Israeli banks concentrated on facilitating trade with Israel.

Israeli laws concerning the so-called 'absentee' property have discouraged Palestinians living abroad from building at home. Instead, most of those who had financial resources built their homes in Jordan.

The continued application of previous rent laws discouraged the emergence of corporate housing projects and apartment buildings.

Internal Factors

Internal factors refer to Palestinian obstacles and problems facing the construction sector. They include the absence of a national strategy, lack of finance sources, lack of planning and managerial skills, and problems related to the availability of building raw materials.

A National Strategy

The Israeli occupation has been accompanied by the absence of Palestinian sovereignty, with the result that there was no national agency responsible for the planning, financing and development of housing. In most countries, housing strategies are directly influenced by economic plans and policies. The absence of a Palestinian economic authority resulted in the ad hoc growth of the various sectors. Moreover, Israeli policies were directed to serve the Israel economy.

As with other sectors, housing relied on support from the PLO, Jordan and the Arab League. In 1978, the Arab Summit established the Joint Jordanian–Palestinian Committee to oversee the spending of the funds appropriated by Arab countries to support economic development in Palestine. In the early 1980s, the Committee initiated a programme to support housing development in the Palestinian Territories (PT). The programme provided approximately $70 million in loans to individuals and housing co-operatives.

Later, the housing sector was given high priority in the Programme for Economic and Social Development in the Occupied Territories (1986–1990), which was prepared by the Jordanian government in November, 1986. This programme estimated that the residential construction sector in the PT required an investment of around 96 million to 164 million Jordanian dinars (JD), equivalent to approximately $280 million to $475 million). This figure covered the projected increase of housing units, over and above private sector construction (Jordan Ministry of Planning, 1986).

The Programme for the Development of the Palestinian National Economy for the Period 1994–2000 which was prepared by the PLO and published in July 1993, gave high priority to the housing sector, as one that would lead the development of the Palestinian economy. The programme estimated a total need of around 185,000 housing units during the period under study; each of these units could house 6 persons. These were to accommodate the expected increase in the Palestinian population due both to natural increase and the Palestinians returning home. In addition, these units would replace poorly built, unsafe and overcrowded houses, including those in refugee camps (PLO, Programme for the

Development of the Palestinian National Economy for the Period 1994–2000, 1993).

In 1992, in response to the European Union's express intention to support Palestinian housing, the Palestinian Housing Council (PHC) was established and endorsed by the PLO. The Council has also been recognised as the agency responsible for planning and implementing housing policy in the PT. On 8 July, 1992, the PHC and the European Commission signed an agreement to grant ECU29 million ($36 million) to the PHC (PHC, 1995).

The PHC started planning and implementing a Palestinian housing strategy which is the first in Palestinian history. The PHC will be presented in more detail below.

Following the establishment of the Palestinian National Authority (PNA) in Gaza/Jericho, a Ministry of Housing was established in 1994. This Ministry is to assume responsibility for planning and implementing a Palestinian housing strategy and policy. The Ministry is still in the establishment phase, however, and cannot start to implement its infrastructural and development plans until financing is made available.

Lack of Financial Sources

One of the first military orders issued by the Israeli occupation forces closed all banks and branches of banks working in the PT. Branches of Israeli banks were allowed to open. It was not until 1986, that Arab banks were opened in the PT. Israeli banks concentrated on attracting deposits and on facilitating trade with Israel.

This absence of credit facilities in the occupied PT was a major constraint on the development of the economy in general, and housing in particular. The Joint Committee tried to minimally address this problem but had little effect, as described above. The banks which have started operations in the West Bank and Gaza since 1986 have not been able to extend credit or mortgage facilities. Israeli banks in East Jerusalem offer prohibitive credit programmes to Palestinians.

The establishment of the Palestinian Monetary Authority (the Central Bank of Palestine) provides an opportunity for the Palestinian Authority to establish a Palestinian housing bank. This bank is greatly needed to provide the bridge to finance credit gaps, from which the Palestinian construction sector suffers.

Lack of Planning and Managerial Skill

The construction sector in the West Bank and Gaza suffers from inadequate skills at the planning and implementation levels. The absence of a national code of standards and specifications is a major obstacle . The absence of a national authority contributed to the inability to enact such a code. The Engineering Association in the West Bank attempted to do so, but was unsuccessful.

Palestinian professionals in construction have graduated from universities all over the world. The wide variety of institutions which trained them has contributed to a lack of uniformity in methods and structures. Together with a lack of coherent national plans and codes, this has led to only a minimal focus on a comprehensive outlook on construction.

The limited nature of the local markets did not provide opportunities for engineers and architects to acquire experience in designing and building complex large-scale projects, when they did exist, they were mostly designed manually and supervised either by expatriate Arab firms (e.g., in the case of the campuses of Birzeit and An-Najah Universities) or by Israeli firms.

Only a few engineering offices capable of comprehensive planning and designing large-scale construction projects have been established. In most housing projects (residential), the planning, design and supervision are carried out by individual engineers.

Building Materials Restrictions

As with most activities in the PT, the building materials industry suffers from restrictions on expansion, from heavy taxation and from Israeli competition. In addition, the Israeli refusal to grant permits for major factories, e.g. cement, placed a heavy constraint on the sector and made it dependent on imports from and through Israel.

The Palestinian construction industry produces building materials, including stone, marble, concrete, gravel cement blocks, terrazzo floor tiles, plastics, PVC pipes, electrical control boards, steel water tanks and solar heating equipment. These products use local and imported materials.

However, Palestinians import a large proportion of items, such as Portland cement, steel, aluminium and glass, which are imported from or through Israel.

Quarrying and stone-cutting industries are scattered throughout the West Bank. Major quarry sites are located near Jenin, Nablus, Tulkarem, Ramallah, Bethlehem, and Hebron.

Marble, grave, tile and cement blocks factories are widespread in the West Bank and are sold in the local markets and exported to Israel, Jordan and other Arab countries.

THE MAGNITUDE OF THE CRISIS

The political and socio–economic environment that shaped Palestinian life after 1967 resulted in a distorted housing sector, especially with regard to the quality of housing, high room occupancy densities, and inadequate housing facilities.

Housing laws and characteristics differ according to the degree of urbanisation. Housing in the PT is usually divided into three types of residences: urban, rural, and the camps. But before presenting characteristics of Palestinian housing, it is necessary to discuss population distribution and housing development.

Housing Activity since 1967

Most of the housing development activities in the West Bank and Gaza since 1967 were undertaken by the private sector. Public expenditure accounted for an average of only 1 per cent over the period 1980–1987. It was higher in Gaza, reaching an average of 2.1 per cent a year over the same period (CBS, Statistical Abstract of Israel, 1980–87).

Housing development in the PT increased rapidly between 1970 and 1976 at a rate of about 43 per cent a year. The average growth rate of housing development in the West Bank was about 37 per cent and in Gaza, the rate reached 79 per cent for the same period. After that, housing development slowed down in both regions. It reached 8 per cent for 1978 and 3 per cent for 1980. Then it declined until 1985 when implementation of the projects of the Joint Committee began. It increased at moderate rates for the period 1985–1987. However, housing declined in 1985 in Gaza by 11 per cent and by 0.4 per cent in 1987 (CBS, Statistical Abstract of Israel 1980–87).

The early 1970s witnessed the highest growth in per-capita income in the PT. This was the result of extensive Palestinian employment in Israel and the Gulf countries (Abdel-Razeq, O., 1991). In addition, the housing market suffered from shortages during the early years of Israeli occupation.

Available data indicate that most of the construction undertaken in the West Bank and Gaza was for residential purposes. Its proportion of the total was over 80 per cent for every year since 1970, except for 1987 when it was 76 per cent in the West Bank.

On average, 3,508 buildings which comprised about 4,170 dwellings, were built in the West Bank annually for the period 1980–84. The figures for Gaza for the same period were 1,641 and 1,838 respectively. The next period witnessed an increase in the figures to an annual average of approximately 4,084 buildings and about 5,161 dwellings in the West Bank; but declined to 1,053 buildings and 1,291 dwellings a year in Gaza.

On average, the per centage of buildings in cities and towns (urban and semi urban) was about 40 per cent in the West Bank and 80 per cent in Gaza.

Israeli statistics show that in 1970 about 24,000 Palestinians worked in construction: of these, about 8,400 of them (35 per cent) worked in the West Bank and 4,100 (17 per cent) worked in Gaza. The remaining 11,500 (48 per cent) worked in Israel.

In 1993, about 56,000 Palestinians worked in construction in Israel; 21,500 worked in construction in the West Bank and 13,000 in Gaza.

The Jordanian–Palestinian Committee spent JD24.5 million ($70 million) on housing projects, of which JD9.5 million was allocated to housing co-operatives (O'beidat, 1992). The Committee concentrated on housing, education, health, water, energy, tourism and public works.

But the programme of the Committee faced many problems. One major problem was the minimum control allowed for implementation of the projects. As a result, in some cases, some loans were totally spent before completion of construction. Moreover, it was found that in some housing co-operative programmes the loans covered only 15 per cent of the cost of structure, when they were supposed to cover between 30 and 50 per cent of total cost.

After 1987, the activities of the Palestinian Intifada and Israeli measures to counter-act them resulted in a large drop in per-capita income and GDP in the PT. This adversely affected the construction sector and its contribution to the economy.

Population Distribution and Density

The last population census in the West Bank and Gaza was conducted in 1967. Recently, there have been attempts to estimate population in the West Bank and Gaza using statistical models (UNCTAD, 1994; and Benvenisti and Khayat, 1988). Our concern here is with population distribution, rather than figures. Housing demand will be estimated before a discussion of population figures takes place.

Generally, Palestinian population is distributed between a large number of communities with relatively small populations. There are few relatively large cities; Jerusalem, Nablus, Hebron and Gaza.

In addition, a significant proportion of Gaza population lives in refugee camps. Table 1 gives an approximate population distribution in the West Bank and Gaza.

However, urbanisation in the PT has not witnessed any noticeable trends since 1967. Different estimates of distribution over urban, rural, and refugee camps are found in the literature depending on the models used to estimate Palestinian population.

Table 1 Approximate Distribution of Palestinian Population.

Size of Locality (persons)	Number of Location	Per cent of total population
> 70,000	4	25
20,000–70,000	9	14
5,000–20,000	50	19
2,500–5,000	70	10
> 2,500	376	15
1,000–60,000*	28**	17

* This represents the range of size of refugee camps in the OT.
** (28) camps; (8) of them in Gaza.
Source: Master Planning the State of Palestine, Center for Engineering and Planning, March 1992.

Israeli statistics show that in 1967, approximately 61.2 per cent of Palestinians lived in rural areas and 38.8 per cent lived in urban areas. But the West Bank Data Project shows that in 1987 the rural population accounted for 59.1 per cent and urban population was 40.9 per cent (Benvenisti, M, and Khayat, S, 1988). The UNCTAD report, Construction and Housing in the West Bank and Gaza, provides a special classification for urbanisation status and divides the West Bank and Gaza into four types: urban, semi-urban, rural, and refugee camps (ECDC/SEU/4; 1994).

Urban communities include all localities with populations exceeding 10,000. These clearly have a definite urban role, and perform administrative, commercial, and services functions. Under this category fall the cities of Jerusalem, Jenin, Tulkarem, Nablus, Ramallah, El-Bireh, Bethlehem and Hebron in the West Bank, and the cities of Gaza, Khan Yunis, Deir el-Balah and Rafah in Gaza. The 1990 population distribution shows the urban population in the West Bank was 41.6 per cent. Together with the urban population of Gaza, the average for both regions amounted to 31 per cent.

Semi-urban communities include all those with a population between 5,000 and 10,000, in addition to other communities which have municipal or village councils and perform some administrative, commercial, or services functions. Examples include Qalqilia, Anabta, Tubas, Al-Ram, Yatta, Dura, Bir Zeit, Bani Zeid, Salfit, and Jabalia. The 1990 population distribution show that this category accounts for 22.3 per cent of the total West Bank population and about 7.7 per cent of that in Gaza. For both regions, the average is about 17 per cent.

Rural communities include all localities with population less than 5,000 people, and which perform no administrative, commercial or services functions, but have a population active in agriculture. It covers all communities which are not urban, semi-urban or refugee camps. The 1990 population distribution shows that this category accounts for 46 per cent

41

of the West Bank population and 20.3 per cent of Gaza population. An average of 37 per cent of both regions.

There are 28 refugee camps in the West Bank including, Jerusalem and Gaza. Eight of the camps are in Gaza. The 1990 distribution shows that this category accounts for about 6.7 per cent of the West Bank population and 30.4 per cent of that of Gaza. For both regions, the average is about 15 per cent.

In 1990, the average national population density was 367 persons per square kilometre. The highest density was in Gaza at around 2,100 persons/square kilometre, followed by Jerusalem district at 277. Much higher densities occur in the major urban centres: 21,000 persons/square kilometre in Jerusalem, 13,900 in Gaza, 11,900 in Nablus, 11,700 in Tulkarem, 8,100 in Hebron and 7,500 in Ramallah.

Population Growth

In 1961, the total population of the West Bank and Gaza was 1.5 million. By the end of 1967, the total de facto population, according to the Israeli census, was only 1 million, excluding Jerusalem and the annexed areas.

Assuming an average annual net growth of 3 per cent in the West Bank and 3.5 per cent for Gaza, the total population in 1994 is estimated at approximately 2.5 million. According to these estimates, the approximate population in 2000 for the West Bank is expected to be 1.8 million, and 1.1 million for Gaza, giving an approximate total population of 2.9 million.

THE MAIN CHARACTERISTICS OF HOUSING

Studies have shown that housing in the PT has been characterised by a high density of occupancy and a lack of adequate facilities and utilities. These are discussed in detail as follows.

Occupancy Density

Available data show that on average 83 per cent of all dwellings in the West Bank and 87 per cent of all dwellings in Gaza have three or more rooms. A relatively large proportion (36 per cent) of dwellings in Gaza have five or more rooms; the corresponding proportion in the West Bank is 16 per cent (CBS, Statistical Abstract).

A field survey financed by The Welfare Association in 1991 gave totally different results. The proportion of dwellings with two sleeping rooms or less reached 60 per cent However, the draft report of the survey does not describe how the sample was chosen.

According to Israeli statistics, dwellings have generally become larger over the years.

Regarding occupancy and overcrowding, available data show that in 1975, approximately 77 per cent of all West Bank households and 76 per cent of those in Gaza lived in housing units with two or more persons per room.

The data also show that 53 per cent of West Bank households and 47 per cent of those in Gaza lived in housing units of three or more persons per room.

In 1989, approximately 30 per cent of all West Bank households and 34 per cent of those of Gaza lived in houses with densities of three or more persons per room. This an indication of an improvement in densities over the years. It is believed that three or more persons per room causes serious overcrowding.

The Welfare Association field survey shows different results. It estimates the proportion of families living in houses with densities of four or more persons per room at 79 per cent.

Availability of Facilities

Table 2 shows the status of houses in the PT according to Israeli statistics. Considerable improvements in the availability of facilities have clearly taken place.

Table 2 Availability of Facilities in Palestinian Houses (per cent).

	West Bank 1974	West Bank 1985	Gaza* 1974	Gaza* 1985
Kitchen	64	90	86	96
Bathroom	24	53	26	79
Continuous Electricity	46	63	57	94
Running water	24	62	26	83

*Does not include camps.
Source: CBS, Statistical Abstract of Israel, various years.

Tenure

Israeli statistics show that ownership of housing units in West Bank urban communities accounted for 48 per cent of total dwelling units in 1974 and increased to 68 per cent in 1985. It is significantly higher in rural areas, increasing from 86 per cent in 1974 to 91 per cent in 1985. Rentals decreased from 44 per cent in 1974 to 30 per cent in 1985 in urban communities, but remained at 7 per cent in rural areas.

With regard to refugee camps, no clear definition of ownership exists;

however for practical purposes, one can consider the residents of houses as owners, as long as the camp exists (UNCTAD/ECDC/SEU 14;1994).

The situation in Gaza is not very different. Ownership of housing units increased from 72 per cent in 1974 to 89 per cent in 1985. The percentage of rentals decreased from 19 per cent to 8 per cent.

Housing Co-operatives

With regard to co-operative housing development, the period after 1967 can be divided into three phases: 1967 to 1978, the period prior to the establishment of the Jordanian–Palestinian Joint Committee; 1978 to 1986, the period of the Joint Committee; the period since 1986.

1967 to 1978

Co-operative housing remained stagnant due to a lack of finances. There were a number of political reasons which prevented its development. Israeli authorities refused to grant building permits for the establishment of new co-operatives, thus preventing them from functioning properly.

Three housing co-operatives were active during this period (O'beidat, 1992). They were the following:

- In 1975, the Hebron Housing Co-operative was re activated. It was able to get a loan from the Housing Bank in Jordan (JD300,000) and built its housing project which was completed by 1978.
- The Beireh Domestic Housing Co-operative was established. Twenty eight members joined it and purchased the necessary land. The Co-operative obtained financial help from the Joint Committee after it was established.
- The Jerusalem Teacher Housing Co-operative obtained a loan from the Housing Bank in Jordan and got the necessary permits to build its project. However, in 1979 the Israeli authorities prohibited the Co-operative form completing the buildings, and later withdrew the building permits.

1978 to 1986

During the period when the Joint Committee was active, it provided the housing sector with JD24.5 million ($70 million dollars). The share of co-operative housing reached JD9.5 million, or 39 per cent, The aid was granted in the form of long-term interest free loans to be repaid over 15 years with a two-year's grace period.

The records show that 98 housing co-operatives were registered in Jordan and applied for loans from the Joint Committee. The total number

44

of housing co-operatives which received loans from the Joint Committee was only 43. The total number of houses which were built by housing co-operatives in this period was 1,415 units. However, only 400 of these units were completed and occupied (UNCTAD/ECDC/SEU/14; 1994).

It should be noted that the Joint Committee also extended individual housing loans totalling about JD16.6 million: the West Bank received about JD14.9 million and JD1.74 million went to Gaza.

Housing Demand

It is difficult to estimate housing demand, because it depends on a variety of social and economic assumptions. In the Palestinian case, it also depends on the outcome of the political process especially with regard to Israeli settlements and Palestinian refugees.

In 1980, it was estimated that in 1990 the total number of housing units required in the occupied PT, excluding those already available, would be around 41,792 for a housing density of 3.03 persons and 165,774 for housing densities of 1.4 persons. These estimates were based on Israeli official population figures for the period 1967–1976. The density figure of 3.03 was the estimated figure in the PT at the time and that of 1.4 was the declared Israeli goal for density in Israel (Abu Kishk and Ghurani, 1980 in UNCTAD/ECDC/SEU/14:1994).

However, Bahiri calculated the demand for housing units in the PT in 1989. It was found to range between 215,300 and 233,300 units, based on the Israeli population estimate of 1.4 million in 1987 (excluding Jerusalem). Moreover, when population estimates of the West Bank Data Project were used (1.72 million for 1987), the demand for housing units ranged between 264,600 and 286,700 units. Among other assumptions, Bahiri assumed that 6.5 people would live in a housing unit and about 2.4 persons per room.

Estimates of housing demand depends on the national housing strategy, costs, income and availability of credit and finance in addition to social measures. Thus, it is quite difficult to estimate demand except by assuming different scenarios which is not within the scope of this paper.

The Cost of Housing

The total cost of a building is the sum of the cost of land, construction materials, labour, infrastructural arrangements, size, planning and management.

Land

The cost of land varies a great deal from one place to another. It depends on urbanisation status and on the position of the site relative to locality. The price of land ranges from a few hundred dollars per dunum in some rural areas to several hundreds of thousands of dollars per dunum in urban centres. Multiple storey buildings reduce the share of land of total cost.

Construction Materials

Most materials are imported from and through Israel. Some have local substitutes such as tiles, marble, and some plastic products; but others do not, such as cement, steel, glass and aluminium. The prices of such materials often fluctuate. They depend on local and Israeli market conditions. It is possible to reduce the tendency for these prices to increase by establishing factories for materials which are not currently produced, as well as by encouraging investment in the production of local materials. It is estimated that the cost of building materials accounted for 40–50 per cent of the total cost and for as much as 80 per cent of the direct cost of housing construction.

Labour

Working in Israel and other labour markets has affected wages in all sectors of the economy. One of the sectors most affected was skilled workers in construction. This is due to the high Israeli demand for these workers over the years. Training programmes to strengthen available skilled construction workers should help to stabilise labour costs in the sector.

Infrastructural Requirements

The extent and type of available infrastructures vary considerably within the PT. The main elements include roads, electricity, water supply and distribution, and sewage collection and disposal. In urban communities, most of these structures are largely available. Sewage treatment may be available to a lesser extent, but it is increasing. In semi-urban and rural towns and villages, the extent and quality of such structures are lower than in urban areas. In refugee camps, the situation is even worse, especially with regard to sewage treatment and quality of roads. The cost of infrastructure varies from one location to another.

THE SPECIAL CASE OF JERUSALEM

Jerusalem has been central in the Arab Israeli struggle. For Arabs and Muslims, no solution to the struggle is acceptable without regaining control over East Jerusalem. It has been the central issue of the agenda of Muslims all over the world. To Israelis, there is the claim of their right to have control of the Holy City because of the Temple, as well as other claimed sites.

On the ground, the race for Jerusalem has not been fair. Israel took control of the city in 1967 and since then has been executing plans and policies in pursuance of its goal of eternal control of the city. It has also been restricting Arab activities which might hinder Israeli policies and plans.

The Oslo Agreement signed between the PLO and Israel, left the issue of Jerusalem to the final stage negotiations. However, Israel continued with its plans to strengthen its control over Jerusalem. Israeli settlement activities are stronger than before Oslo; Israeli harassment of Palestinian institutions in Jerusalem is at its peak; and the closure of Jerusalem and its separation from the rest of the PT appear to have a strategic rather than a security objective.

Immediately after the 1967 occupation, the Israeli authorities annexed more than 70,000 dunums of East Jerusalem to the municipality of West Jerusalem. On 27 June, 1967, Israeli laws, jurisdiction, and administration were imposed on that area. This clearly violates Regulation 43 of the Hague Regulations of 1907, which require an occupying force to continue to apply the legal principles that existed at the time of occupation.

Since then, Israeli governments have treated East Jerusalem in a different manner from the remainder of the PT. The reason for this is that successive Israeli governments have regarded the future of the PT as an open question, but have persisted in considering unified Jerusalem as the eternal capital of Israel.

The Palestinians of East Jerusalem have a special status. They have permanent residency, i.e. they are not citizens and are not like Palestinians of the rest of the PT. The status of permanent residence means that they are citizens of another country (Jordan), and this status is temporary; it is up to the Israeli Interior Minister to grant, renew, or cancel the permanent residence. Rules have been devised to limit the granting of permanent residence to the smallest number possible of Palestinians, and policies have been implemented to withdraw it from as many Palestinians as possible.

The central criterion which was applied at the time of planning the unification of Jerusalem, was to 'include as much land, and as few Palestinians as possible, in "unified" Jerusalem' (Krystall, N.; 1993). Israeli plans exist to expand the administrative area of Jerusalem northward past

Ramallah eastward toward the Jordan Valley and southward toward Hebron. This would expand greater Jerusalem to 27 per cent–28 per cent of the total area of the West Bank.

The Housing Situation

No accurate data about housing conditions in East Jerusalem are available. Some studies have attempted to analyse the housing problem in Jerusalem but they included to cities like Ramallah, El-Bireh, Bethlehem, Beit Sahour, Beit Jala and their surrounding villages as in East Jerusalem district (Khoury, J. et al., 1985). Thus, the figures available do not give an accurate picture of the situation in East Jerusalem, the city central to struggle and negotiations.

Some figures estimate the number of persons per room in Jerusalem to have ranged between 2.55 in 1967 to 3.2 in 1976, and to 2.2 in 1993 (B'tselem, 1995 and Khoury, J. et al., 1985). An extremely serious housing shortage among Palestinians in Jerusalem is noted in the B'tselem report. This shortage is estimated to exceed 20,000 residential units.

By the end of 1989, the total number of residential units inhabited by Arabs in Jerusalem was only 16,000, compared with more than 26,000 units constructed for Israeli settlers in East Jerusalem. Figures indicate that the average number of Arabs per residential unit is 8.9, while the average number of Jews per unit does not exceed 4.7 persons (Abu Arafeh, 1992).

When comparing the housing situation between Palestinians and Jews in Jerusalem, we see that the gap in housing conditions between Jews and Palestinians has become more and more profound since the annexation of East Jerusalem in 1967 and as a result of the policies of the Israeli governments. Jerusalem has undergone a wave of residential housing construction greater than at any previous time. As of February 1995, more than 76,150 residential units had been built an increase of 109 per cent of the number of residential units that existed in 1967. This rapid development and massive construction, however, was almost exclusively for the Jewish population. Between November 1967 and February 1995, the division of residential units between the two groups was as follows:

- Some 64,870 housing units, or about 88 per cent of all units, were built in Jewish neighbourhoods. Only 8,890 housing units, or about 12 per cent of all units, were built in Palestinian neighbourhoods. The gap widened in the last few years, there were 9,070 residential units built between 1990 and 1993, but only 463 units (about 5 per cent of total) were built in Palestinian neighbourhoods.
- Most construction in Jerusalem since 1967 occurred in the Jewish neighbourhoods of East Jerusalem. In February 1995, the number of

residential units in the Jewish neighbourhoods in East Jerusalem was about twice those in Palestinian neighbourhoods. The number of units in Palestinian neighbourhoods was 20,900, whereas the number in Jewish neighbourhoods reached 38,500 units.

Moreover, the average residential area for each Jewish resident of Jerusalem is more than twice as high as that of a Palestinian resident. As of December 1993, the built up area per Israeli resident reached 17.8 m2, but the built up area per Palestinian was only 8.7 m2. Furthermore, the gap in the per room density of the two groups grew wider over the years. In 1967, on the average, 1.6 Israelis lived in a room and 2.55 Palestinians lived in one; in 1993, the figures became 1.1 Israelis per room, and 2.2 Palestinians per room.

The Housing Crisis

The housing crisis in Jerusalem has many similarities with that of the West Bank and Gaza. However, the housing crisis in Jerusalem differs from that in the rest of the PT. This is because Israeli authorities have had a declared goal to change the demographic situation in Jerusalem in favour of the Jewish population. Israeli governments have implemented policies to achieve such a goal.

This means that the housing problems faced by Palestinians in Jerusalem are the cumulative result of the deliberate and systematic discrimination of Israeli government policy since 1967 with regard to planning, development and housing in Jerusalem. Publicly known stands of Jerusalem officials (of all Israeli political affiliations) show that

Jerusalem's urban development was dictated, above all, by national— political considerations intended to strengthen Israeli control in every part of the city. Throughout the years, the planning authorities in Jerusalem have set their sights on one central goal: creating a demographic and geographic reality that will pre-empt any future attempt to question Israeli sovereignty over East Jerusalem. (B'tselem; 1995)

In 1990, Israeli officials hoped that the massive waves of Jewish immigration from the Soviet Union would change the demographic situation in Jerusalem in favour of a Jewish majority. An internal working paper of Jerusalem municipality stated that 'for the first time since 1967, a possibility exists to alter the demographic balance in the city, and not only to preserve it.' (B'tselem; 1995) This makes it very clear that the intentions of Israeli governments have been to achieve an absolute Jewish majority in Jerusalem, and to make it impossible to re-separate the Holy City and return East Jerusalem to Arab control.

Israeli Policies

In order to ensure Israeli control over East Jerusalem, Israeli policy had three dimensions:

- Confiscation of Palestinian land for Israeli settlements.
- Using development and planning schemes to further Israeli aims.
- Using the permanent residency status of Jerusalem Palestinians, and the laws concerning it, to reduce the growth of Palestinians as much as possible.

Confiscation of Land

Immediately after 1967 occupation, the Israeli government started the land confiscation process in Jerusalem. Jewish settlements started popping up in all directions. A total of more than 50,000 dunums of Palestinian land have been confiscated in Jerusalem since 1967. The expropriation policy in East Jerusalem has been exclusively for the welfare of the Jewish population. The housing shortage and the basic urban needs of the city's Palestinian population have been blatantly ignored.

By February 1995, about 38,500 residential units had been built for approximately 160,000 Israelis on expropriated land. Not one housing unit was built on those lands for the Palestinian population. Senior officials of the municipality told the municipal council that the policy underlying the expropriations was to build Jewish neighbourhoods. Many of the areas expropriated in the initial period of annexation were not put to use until many years later. It is clear that expropriations were intended to deprive the Palestinian population of the possibility of building on those lands. Israeli governments held these lands on reserve for future Jewish settlements.

An examination of the policy of so-called land expropriation for public purposes in Jerusalem since 1967, reveals that it is nothing but land confiscation, as that carried out in the rest of the PT. The difference between the two is that in Jerusalem it is carried out in the name of development planning of the 'unified eternal capital' of the Jewish—Zionist State. It is also clear that this policy is based mainly on political and national considerations that only serve the Jewish population.

The purpose is, as B'tselem observed:

> to entrench Jewish rule in East Jerusalem and create a 'fait accompli' that will thwart any effort at partitioning the city. This policy is a flagrant violation of property rights and is a striking example of discrimination on grounds of nationality. When the same population group always benefits from the land expropriations, the claim that

they were done for 'public purposes' becomes a cloak for a consistent pattern of discrimination. (B'tselem; 1995)

By 1989, ten Israeli settlements had been set up in the eastern part of Jerusalem. More settlements were set up in the early 1990s to accommodate the new waves of Soviet immigrants.

Development and Planning Schemes

Planning policy for Palestinian neighbourhoods in Jerusalem is an important element in the overall policy of the Israeli government, which aims to consolidate its territorial control over all parts of the city, and to preserve the demographic primacy of the Jewish population. To achieve these goals, the government has, for years, utilised three measures regarding planning schemes:

- No town planning schemes were drawn up for most Palestinian neighbourhoods.
- Approval for existing plans is delayed, seemingly for ever.
- When approval is granted, the planning schemes serve as additional means in the hands of government to limit development, reduce the areas designated for building, and strengthen Jewish control in every part of the city.

Municipal officials have not granted building permits to Palestinians in Jerusalem because of their claims that town planning schemes are not available. This excuse has prohibited building on most of the remaining Palestinian land in East Jerusalem. In 1974, the local building and planning committee in Jerusalem issued a decree declaring post-1967 Jerusalem a regional planning area.

According to Israeli law, such a decree requires the local committee to submit a town planning scheme for the entire municipal area within 3 years of the decree being issued. Until May 1995, 21 years later, no planning scheme for all East Jerusalem had been submitted. In the absence of an approved plan, it is impossible to obtain a building permit. As a result, tens of thousands of Palestinians do not have the legal possibility to build, and may have built illegally and thus face heavy fines and possible demolition of property.

An examination of the planning and approval procedures for the local town planning schemes in Palestinian neighbourhoods shows that it frequently drags on for a long period of time. The procedures for the approval of a planning scheme for the Beit Safafa neighbourhood, for example, took more than 13 years (from November 1977 until December 1990). It is clear that the delay was deliberate. For example in the Beit Hanina and Shuafat case, the deputy mayor and chairman of the local committee at the time (1987, Mr. A. Kahillah) stated: 'Today, this again a framework plan and not detailed specifications. When the original plan spoke of 18,000 housing units, there were some who thought that the building would be immediate, whereas the plan spoke about planning for the next 50 to 100 years.' (B'tselem; 1995).

An examination of the town planning schemes that have been prepared for Palestinians shows that they ignore the population growth among the Palestinians and that their purpose is to prevent the Palestinians from making use of the little land that is left available for them.

The city engineer stated in February 1993, in a discussion of the planning schemes for Sur Baher and Umm Touba: 'There is a government decision to maintain the proportion between the Arab and Jewish populations in the city at 28 per cent Arabs and 72 per cent Jews. The only way to cope with that ratio is through the housing potential. On this basis, the growth potential is defined, and the capacity is a function of that here as well.' (B'tselem, 1995)

The stated goals are achieved through several measures:

1. Reducing the number of housing units allowed in the planning scheme. This low capacity of housing sites can be clearly seen when comparing with Israeli capacity in plans. The area for the plans of Sur Baher and Umm Touba, which is not yet approved, is 3,600 dunums. The capacity of housing in the plan is fixed at 2,350 units.

This gives a planned average density of 0.6 housing units per dunum. By contrast, the nearby Jewish settlement of Har Homah is planned to cover an area of 1,850 dunums, and the potential capacity of housing sites is fixed at 6,500 units, giving a planned average density of 3.5 units per dunum. In order to reduce the capacity of housing sites in Palestinian neighbourhoods, the planning authorities reduce as much as possible the area designated for Palestinian building and the permitted building per centages there.

Reducing the boundaries of the plans. Research has shown that planners used the concept of green areas where building is prohibited. Municipality documents show the use of these green areas over the years, and these green areas have been exploited as a means of achieved political and national goals regarding Jerusalem. It is in fact intended to deprive Palestinians from the right to build on their land and to keep these areas in reserve for building earmarked for the Jewish population.

Reducing building per centages in addition to substantially reducing the area available for building. Building per centages for Palestinians are set much lower than for Israeli neighbourhoods. A plan for building an Israeli neighbourhood in the heart of Palestinian Ras Al-Amud neighbourhood, allows for a building per centage of 112 per cent and four storeys. The plan for Palestinians in Ras Al-Amud allows only 50 per cent and two storeys.

Residency Status of Jerusalem Palestinians

International lawyers maintain that peoples of annexed territories should be given citizenship automatically by the annexing state. It is not the obligation of an annexed people to request citizenship. The Israeli government however, had no intention of registering tens of thousands of Palestinians as citizens of Israel. This would contradict the aims of all Israeli governments, and those of the Zionist leadership, which is to increase the number and proportion of Jews in Israel, and to reduce the number and proportion of Palestinians who have Israeli citizenship.

Therefore, the Israeli government left the citizenship issue up to the Palestinians of Jerusalem, knowing that most of them would refuse it. Requesting Israeli citizenship would mean accepting annexation and occupation. The Israeli government considered all Palestinians present in Jerusalem at the 1967 census as permanent residents according to the laws governing 'Entry to Israel'.

Any Palestinians who were not present at the time of the census, and any Palestinian who is not classified by the Israeli government as a permanent resident of Jerusalem (including spouses, children, and other relatives of East Jerusalem permanent residents) must apply for family reunification to legally reside there. The decision to grant or deny these reunifications is that of the Israeli Interior Minister, who is not required to justify refusals.

This means that Palestinians residing in their homes and lands in Jerusalem were considered by the Israeli government as citizens of other countries, but are permanently permitted to reside in Israel if they continue to fulfil certain conditions. This arrangement suits the interests of Israeli governments and Jewish national goals of limiting Palestinian population in Jerusalem to the proportion recorded in the 1967 census, that is 24 per cent.

Palestinians living in Jerusalem face many problems because of their permanent residency status:

- Tens of thousands of Palestinians and their families who were separated from East Jerusalem as a result of the 1967 occupation and are still being denied the right to return and live in their homes.
- The Israeli government has used Regulation 11 of the Law of Entry to Israel, to prevent thousands of Palestinians from Jerusalem from living in their homes. Regulation 11 states that:

- If a permanent resident
- Lives outside of Israel (including Jerusalem) for more than 7 years (for these purposes the West Bank and Gaza are not considered parts of Israel)
- Becomes a permanent resident of another country or applies for citi-

zenship in another country, he/she is liable to lose his/her status as a permanent resident of Israel.

- Travels abroad. Travel for East Jerusalem Palestinians is restricted,. They require an exit permit any time they want to travel abroad. Travel through Jordan requires special permits which last for 3 years, renewable each year for 3 more years. Travel through Israeli airports requires obtaining the travel document called 'Laisser–Passer'. This procedure goes through intelligence agencies, which have the right to deny issuance of the documents.
- Has a husband who are is not a permanent resident. He is usually refused that status and thus not allowed to join his wife to live in Jerusalem. As a result of this unwritten policy, many Palestinian women have had no choice but to leave Jerusalem.
- Has a child whose father is not a permanent resident. In such cases, the children usually have great difficulties in being registered as permanent residents. Moreover, children born outside Israel (including the West Bank and Gaza) are not entitled to permanent residence, even if both parents are permanent residents. In such cases, parents must apply for family reunification.

It has been made clear that Israeli goals for East Jerusalem include achieving Jewish control over every part of it, and pressuring Palestinians to move beyond the city limits. A wide range of policies have been used to attain such goals. The efforts have been highly successful: more than 50,000 Palestinians from East Jerusalem are now living in the West Bank (Krystall, N.; 1993). The tools of Israeli policies are varied, but rely mostly on: housing shortages, neglecting Palestinian neighbourhoods, and problems relating to permanent residency status.

Other measures have been used over the years, including the following.

1) Municipality tax (Arnona); Palestinians pay 26 per cent of the cost of municipal services but receive only 5 per cent of those services. More than 55 per cent of Palestinians in Jerusalem are behind in their Arnona payments. Many Palestinians have left Jerusalem because of it. New settlers, by contrast, are encouraged to live in Jerusalem by exempting them from the Arnona for 5 years.

National Insurance; Palestinians living in Jerusalem are entitled to national insurance payments. In 1973, a law was passed that guaranteed national insurance payments to all those who received Israeli identity cards, even if they lived outside Jerusalem so long as they consistently paid their national insurance dues. This ended up as another form of encouragement to leave Jerusalem. In 1984, the national insurance office began to change its policy; children born after their parents moved from Jerusalem did not get national insurance payments. Soon afterwards, all Jerusalem residents and their families who moved to surrounding villages stopped receiving payments. Recently, it was decided that national insurance payments will resume.

Refusal to renew Jerusalem identity cards (I.D.s); many Jerusalem Palestinians were not given new I.D.s because they were living outside Jerusalem. These actions and policies are usually not announced and people only know of them when want to renew their I.D.s. because of any reason, e.g. its destruction, loss, or confiscation by soldiers at check points. Sometimes, Israeli authorities announce the necessity to renew I.D.s.

The Israeli Government has increasingly filed the income tax returns of Jerusalem permanent residents who moved to the West Bank in offices of the West Bank, instead of East Jerusalem. This has gradually led to the relocation of Jerusalem Palestinians.

During the Gulf war in 1991, Israel imposed a military closure on the West Bank and Gaza. This prevented Palestinians from outside Jerusalem from entering the city. In March 1993, the Israeli government imposed another military closure, and, until now, people wanting to enter Jerusalem need a permit from the Civil Administration offices. Jerusalem residents are separated from their relatives . Spouses were given 3 month permits, but have to leave Jerusalem at sunset.

THE FUTURE

The Palestinian Programme for the Development of the Palestinian National Economy expected the construction sector to lead the development programme, and emphasised the role of the private sector in such a programme. World experience seems to support such a vision. The public sector should play a supportive role to ensure the appropriate development of the private sector.

In this sense, Palestinian housing strategy must concentrate on facilitating competitive housing as a main mechanism to achieve national housing goals. It should be noted that housing strategies cannot be implemented in isolation. They must be co-ordinated in overall economic and social strategies and plans. In this section, we will present housing strategy objectives, and the suggested mechanism for achieving them. This will be followed by a brief description of existing housing institutions will be given.

Housing Objectives

The broad goal of housing development in Palestine is to provide appropriate housing at an affordable cost to all citizens, taking political, social, economical, and geographical considerations into account. Achieving this will be facilitated through short-term and long-term policies and measures.

It is clear that a work force with the adequate skills in planning, engineering, management, technology, construction, and maintenance is necessary to achieve the stated housing goal. In addition, it is necessary to create the full range of institutions which are capable of carrying out the planning, managing, and financing the operational activities required for the proper, timely and economic implementation of housing programmes and projects.

The objectives of the Palestinian housing strategy should take into consideration the wide range of national inter-sectoral and sectoral development achievement to be tested during implementation period.

The major strategy objectives include:

- To provide adequate and affordable housing for all income groups.
- To provide a public housing programme to meet the needs of the lowest income group.
- To facilitate the improvement of housing conditions in existing structures.
- To facilitate adequate supply to meet the increasing demands of newlywed couples, rising population, and Palestinian returnees.
- To facilitate the needed infrastructure for housing development.
- To facilitate the legal framework necessary to encourage the private sector to invest in housing.
- To expand the land markets of all major towns and urban centres in order to make land affordable.
- To encourage the efficient use and production of local building materials.
- To help establish the necessary credit institutions to serve all income groups through a variety of finance programmes.
- To revitalise the communal and co-operative spirit in housing.
- To preserve Palestinian architectural heritage.
- To restructure city and town boundaries and outline plans and zones in order to allow for the horizontal and vertical expansion of housing.
- To encourage effective and cost reducing industrialisation of the construction sector.
- To provide the sector with the necessary skilled labour.

Mechanisms and Actions

It is clear that the job at hand is enormous, particularly in view of the high expectations of Palestinians. Moreover, the expected return of thousands of people is will exert enormous pressure on housing, particularly in urban centres. Furthermore, it is unlikely that the present capacity of the construction industry would be able to respond effectively to the excessive increase in demand for housing. Emergency measures to accommodate these returnees are required.

The mechanisms used should emphasise the role of the private sector and give the public sector supportive role. These mechanisms should depend on specialised public, private and NGO institutions like co-operatives and the PHC. Municipalities and district committees should be given a major role in planning and implementation. Much attention should be given to co-ordinating housing institutions with other economic and social ones. Suggested actions are classified below into short-term and long-term measures.

Short-term Actions

- It is vital and necessary for an accurate assessment of housing needs and the capacity and potential of the construction sector to be made. This should include availability of sufficient water and energy supplies.
- It is necessary to adopt a clear rural development strategy in order to avoid massive migration to urban centres.
- It is necessary to immediately establish a Palestinian housing bank and to encourage existing merchant banks to engage in financing housing.
- It is essential to establish the necessary legal framework to organise property rights and ownership, building rules, and rental contracts.
- It is necessary to improve existing infrastructure and develop whatever is missing.
- It is necessary to provide some subsidies to housing projects for needy groups and to compensate those whose houses were demolished by Israeli authorities.
- It is necessary to encourage co-operative housing, local municipal and village councils and district committees to assume leading roles in planning and managing projects.

Long-term Action

- A programme of formal vocational education related to construction should be implemented.
- A comprehensive plan should be drawn up for the development of the construction industry and the production of building materials. Such a plan should include the establishment of cement and steel factories.
- Structural plans and boundaries of cities, towns, and villages should be reviewed and improved to accommodate the housing needs and the new political and development conditions.

- A policy for low income family housing must be adopted. This should adhere to equity and minimal cost standards.
- The required public buildings and facilities must be established to enable the proper implementation of housing strategy to take place.
- A programme to preserve and protect Palestinian architectural heritage should be implemented This should be carried out in co-ordination with Waqf and tourist institutions.

Housing Institutions

The period since 1967 (i.e. since the Israeli occupation) has been characterised by the almost total absence of housing institutions; the only organised institutional form was housing co-operatives, whose activities and role were discussed earlier. The Joint Committee represented the first serious attempt to provide planning and financing for Palestinian development activities.

The institution which has existed ever since 1948 is UNRWA which has been responsible for refugee life in camps. It has planned and controlled housing projects in the camps. Until the refugee problem is resolved, UNRWA is expected to continue to play the major role in meeting refugee needs, including housing. These UNRWA activities must be co-ordinated with the Palestinian authority to ensure their integration into a national housing strategy.

In 1991, the Palestinian Housing Council was formed as a Palestinian non-governmental organisation; and in 1994 the first Palestinian Ministry of Housing was established as part of the first Palestinian authority in Gaza/Jericho

The Palestinian Housing Council

The PHC was established in 1991 as a non-profit corporation governed by 26 members. The general assembly elect the board of directors who lay down policies and designs for short and long-term housing development strategy.

In July 1992, representatives of the PHC and the European Commission (EC) signed an agreement to grant ECU29 million ($36 million) to the PHC. This enabled the first Palestinian drive toward the construction of 'public' housing in the West Bank and Gaza to be launched.

The main goal of the PHC is find a practical solution to the housing problem. Detailed objectives include studying all aspects of the housing problem to know its exact extent; proposing a national housing strategy; utilising modern planning and construction techniques; helping in the establishment of a Palestinian housing bank; lobbying the international community to fund housing projects in Palestinian territories; and developing and encouraging the private sector.

As of June 1995, the PHC had signed several aid agreements with various countries. These included the following.

European Union Aid

Two agreements have been signed with the EC; the first (see above) granted ECU 29 million ($36 million) for the construction of 1,200 units, divided equally between the West Bank and Gaza; the second was signed on 28 November 1994 and granted ECU 1 ($11.5 million) to the PHC to support and enhance the housing programme.

United States Aid

Total US aid to housing in the Palestinian territories has been set at $25.5 million. The grant has been divided into five programmes to be implemented by the PHC.

Japanese Aid

The Japanese government contributed $10 million for the construction of 256 housing units in Gaza for the Palestinian police. The agreement was signed by the Japanese government and the Palestinian authority in Gaza on 1 August 1994. The PHC is supervising the implementation of the project in co-operation with the United Nations Development Programme (UNDP).

There are six housing projects for 606 apartments underway in Gaza. Another 160 apartments are planned for Gaza and are awaiting finance. In the West Bank, there are 227 units under construction in different areas. The total is expected to increase in 1995 to 594 units; two thirds of this total are planned for rural areas. The PHC has not been able to build in Jerusalem because of prevailing Israeli policy. Other alternatives are being considered by the PHC.

The Ministry of Housing

It is hoped that the Ministry will be supportive of the private sector by facilitating legal and structural frameworks, supporting finance and credit institutions, and financing housing programmes for the most needy groups. The Ministry is expected to co-ordinate the work of the PHC, the housing co-operatives, UNRWA and the private sector.

Housing Co-operatives

The Palestinian housing co-operative movement is the oldest institutional framework to have helped in developing the housing sector. There are at present more than 100 registered housing co-operatives in the West Bank and Gaza. During the past 2 years, housing co-operatives have started to be established in Gaza.

The experience of such institutions since 1967 has not been encouraging because of various reasons. However, the principles underlying co-operatives, which depend on community work in a collective manner, are considered an intrinsic part of Palestinian culture and society. In many developing countries, such social practices have been encouraged by international agencies such as HABITAT. Therefore, the role of the Palestinian housing co-operatives could be very important if its leaders and members adopted a new outlook which focuses on development rather than charity.

CONCLUSION AND RECOMMENDATIONS

This study shows that the major cause for the Palestinian housing crisis started almost 100 years ago with Zionist immigration to Palestine which resulted in the establishment of Israel. Its occupation in 1948 of 77 per cent of Palestine resulted in the relocation of more than 800,000 Palestinians who. moved to tent camps in the West bank and Gaza, Jordan, Lebanon, and Syria. This started the housing crisis in the West Bank and Gaza.

In 1967, Israel occupied the remainder of Palestine. Hundreds of thousands of Palestinians fled to Jordan. Israeli policy after occupation destroyed all aspects of Palestinian life; the housing sector was greatly affected. Israeli policies had a major impact on housing and construction. These included:

- land confiscation;
- restricting use of remaining lands;
- preventing the establishment of factories related to construction;
- demolishing homes of Palestinians who participated in national resistance; and,
- closing banks and credit institutions.

Internal factors which contributed to the housing crisis include the absence of a national housing strategy, lack of finance sources, lack of planning and managerial skills, and problems associated with building materials.

Housing in the West Bank and Gaza is characterised by high room occupation densities and inadequate housing facilities. Available data show that on average 83 per cent of all dwellings in the West Bank and 87 per cent of all dwellings in Gaza have 3 or more rooms. Dwellings are becoming generally larger over the years.

As for occupancy and over crowding, available data show that in 1975 approximately 77 per cent of all households in the West Bank and 76 per cent in Gaza lived in housing units with 2 or more persons per room. In 1989, approximately 30 per cent of all households in the West Bank and 34 per cent in Gaza lived in houses with densities of three or more persons per room. It is noted that considerable improvements on availability of facilities have taken place.

It is estimated that total demand for housing units in the West Bank and Gaza is approximately 250,000 units. However, due to expected population growth, the expected return of thousands of Palestinians due to the peace process and the expected solution to the refugee problem; the estimated future demand for housing units is approximately 180,000 units over the next five years.

The broad goal of housing development in Palestine is to provide appropriate housing at an affordable cost to all citizens, taking into account political, social, economical and geographical considerations. Achieving this will be facilitated through short-term and long-term policies. The objectives of the Palestinian housing strategy should take the wide range of national inter-sectoral and sectoral developments requirements into consideration. These objectives should be defined to allow their achievements to be tested during implementation.

BIBLIOGRAPHY

Abed, Alrazq and Shehadeh, Omer and Odeh, 1992, **Palestinian Agricultural Economics, 1967–1992**, Ma'an Development Center, Jerusalem.

Abu Arafah, Abed Elruhman, 1992, **The Judaisation of Jerusalem**, Arab Thought Forum, Jerusalem.

B'tselem, 1995, **A Policy of Discrimination: Land Expropriation, Planning, and Building in East Jerusalem**, May, Jerusalem.

Bahiri, S., 1989, **Construction and Housing in the West Bank and Gaza**, WBDBP, The Jerusalem Post, Jerusalem, pp. 11 and 14.

Israel, Central Bureau of Statistics, 1980 to 1987, Israeli Statistical Abstract, Jerusalem.

United Nations Commission on Trade and Development, 1994, Construction and Housing in the West Bank and Gaza, ESCD/SEU/14, Geneva.

Jordan, Department of Statistics, 1960, First Census of Population and Housing, Housing and Household Characteristics, vol 3, November, Amman.

Jordan, Ministry of Planning, 1986, A Programme for Economic and Social Development in the Occupied Territories, 1986 to 1990, November, Amman.

Khouri, J. et al, 1985, **Housing in the West Bank and Gaza**, Engineering Association, Jerusalem.

O'bidat, Adnan, 1992, **A Practical Experience in the Co-operative Housing Pro-**

jects in the Occupied PT, Shu'un Tanmawiyyeh, Arab Thought Forum, Jerusalem.

PHRIC, 1994, **Human Rights Update**, June, Jerusalem.

Zaghmouri, Odeh S., 1991, **Role of Co-operatives in the Development of the West Bank and Gaza**, Ma'an Development Center, Jerusalem.

Theme One

INSTITUTIONAL AND PLANNING STRUCTURES AND HOUSING POLICIES

LOCAL GOVERNMENT, INSTITUTIONAL DEVELOPMENT AND MANAGEMENT OF THE HOUSING SECTOR

Patrick Wakely

ABSTRACT

This theme paper takes as its premise the words of Mohammed Ziara, Director General of Palestine's Ministry of Housing: 'The solution to the housing problem (of Palestine) will be characterised by civic engagement, sustainability and equity approaches. While civic engagement involves stakeholders at all levels, the role of government is to provide the enabling environment.'

It reviews the issues and summarises the themes presented by the contributors to the first section on *Institutional and Planning Structures and Housing Policies* in this monograph, namely: institution building (Rolf Jensen, Samih Abed and Ulf Tellefsen); national housing policies and strategies (Babar Mumtaz, Rolf Jensen and Patrick Wakely); the role and function of local authorities (Arthur Wiggers) and the institutional fabric of urban development (A.B. Zahlan). In addition, it draws on the introductory article by Mohammed Ziara on the Palestinian Ministry of Housing and on the paper by Stephen Mayo concerning housing performance and strategies in the West Bank and Gaza.

POLICY CONTEXT

Throughout the world there is a move to base public housing policies on the principles of *enabling*. This demands a shift from the central provision of housing, infrastructure and services by national governments to the provision of supports that empower and enable local government, the private sector, communities and individual households to play the

65

leading roles in the production, maintenance and management of settlements.

The theme of enablement is the main issue debated at the *City Summit*, the United Nations Conference on Human Settlements (Habit II) in Istanbul in June 1996. It underpins Agenda 21, the programme for environmental sustainability which emerged from *Earth Summit*, the United Nations Conference on the Environment held in Rio de Janeiro in 1992. It also formed a major component of the discussions which took place at the United Nations *Social Summit* held in Copenhagen in March, 1995.

In most countries, the adoption of the new paradigm entails the abandonment of many well entrenched traditions and procedures of central control. It requires the de-regulation and liberalisation of many aspects of business, finance and environmental development. It calls for the redefinition of public sector roles, the reform of bureaucracies and the retraining of professional, technical and administrative officers. Such structural changes and retooling is an uphill, and often demoralising, task which the Palestinian National Authority (PNA) has the opportunity to short circuit: a point made by many of the papers prepared on this theme.

There are many arguments for the pursuit of an enabling strategy for housing and municipal management in Palestine. They are made both in the light of international experience and in response to the particular circumstances of the West Bank and Gaza. Underpinning them all is the understanding of housing as a real and direct contributor to both the local and national economy (Wakely) and the importance of treating housing as a single market, albeit one embracing a range of submarkets (Mayo), as well as the importance of housing to social stability, to the reinforcement of cultural values and to sustainable community development (Zahlan).

There is still a tendency to view housing merely as domestic shelter that is not economically productive, and government intervention in low-income housing as a welfare function with no economic return. However, houses in Palestine, particularly those of the lowest income groups, are not just dwellings; they are centres for the production of goods and services which are important to a wide range of consumers both in, and beyond, the immediate community.

The impact of adequate housing on family health is becoming well understood, and the impact of good health on individual and collective productivity is now clearly demonstrable. The importance of secure housing and its users' identity with it, and responsibility for it, can be linked to social well-being and stability that directly contributes to economic productivity.

The lower end of the domestic building business provides an entry into the construction sector across a broad spectrum: from the apprentice-ship of artisans and tradesmen to the setting up of small construction and contracting companies and the employment of women.

The difference between the use value and exchange value of housing has been understood for some time. However, only relatively recently has the extent to which they exist together throughout the housing sector been appreciated. Whilst recognising the importance of the domestic property market amongst the urban upper income groups, there has been a tendency to perceive low-income housing, and particularly that in informal settlements, as providing shelter, but not an exchangeable commodity. This assumption has led to many public sector frustrations, particularly in connection with the perceived abuse of public subsidies.

It is important to regard housing as a commodity tradable in a range of submarkets, embracing high cost, highly serviced central city apart-ments and suburban villas; ageing traditional urban and village housing which often embraces premises for commerce and/or manufacturing; refugee camps run by the United Nations Relief and Works Agency (UNRWA); and basic dwellings in informal settlements with minimal access to services. However, in policy terms, it is also important to under-stand the connections between these submarkets and the extent to which they impinge upon each other; how they respond to changes in demand occasioned by demographic and economic change; and how they are affected by changes in the supply of land, credit and building materials, as well as by regulatory controls.

The foundations of a sustainable enabling strategy for the production of housing and the management of settlement development is the identi-fication and recognition of roles and the actors who play them most effectively. Individual households as the end-users inevitably play the prin-cipal role in an enabling strategy. However, there is a wide range of agencies and institutions, the roles of which are to *enable* or support them. They fall into four broad categories, each embracing two subcateg-ories. Each has very different characteristics and abilities and, in some cases, needs enabling support itself (Wakely).

They are:

- **International aid agencies:**
  Multilaterals (United Nations, World Bank, etc.); and
  Bilaterals (individual country aid programmes);
- **Public sector:**
  Central government (PNA, Ministry of Housing); and
  Local government (municipalities, village councils);
- **Private sector:**
  Formal sector industry and commerce; and
  Informal sector enterprise;

- **Community sector:**
  International and national non-governmental organisations (NGOs); and
  Community groups and organisations (CBOs).

To ensure the optimum effectiveness and economic efficiency of a housing and settlement development strategy, it is essential that each of these actors plays the support role to which it is most suited. Many of the problems and diseconomies that characterise public housing policies all over the world stem from decisions concerning the use of resources being made at the wrong level, i.e. at too high a level.

Identifying the right level of decision-making and ensuring that there are appropriate institutions at that level and that they are adequately equipped and/or supported to make the decisions for which they are responsible, is the essence of the task facing the PNA and the Ministry of Housing.

RESOURCES AND CONSTRAINTS

The principal resource available to Palestine is its people, amongst whom is a small cadre of highly skilled professionals and entrepreneurs. A significant, though probably short-term, resource of direct significance to investment in housing and settlement development is remittances from overseas Palestinians. These have been important in the past (Mayo) and are likely to increase with the continuation of the peace process. The rise of international aid and technical assistance following the signing of the peace accords is a substantial short-term resource that needs to be used with care to ensure a longer term benefit.

There has not been a reliable census in the West Bank and Gaza since 1967 when the population totalled 845,000 in the West Bank and 442,000 in Gaza. The best estimate is that the present total population amounts to 2,180,000. By the turn of the century, i.e. in four years' time, this is expected to have risen to about 2.7 million due to the natural increase of the population. To this figure should be added between one and four million Palestinians who may have returned from the neighbouring states (Ziara).

The estimate that 45 per cent of the population is under 14 years old, and less than 10 per cent over 45, is of considerable significance (Ziara). Within ten years, almost half the national population will be in the process of creating new households, demanding jobs and incomes with which to support them. This will require land, services, credit and technical assistance for the construction of new dwellings and pose a major challenge that must be anticipated simultaneously with addressing the current shortage of acceptable housing which, in addition, will be seriously aggravated by the return of Palestinians living in the diaspora.

However, offset against this is the evidence given by Mayo that argues that the current combined formal and informal sector rates of construction represent an annual housing production rate of about ten new units per 1,000 existing dwellings. This is more than adequate to cope with the current and short-term future projections of demand, although he does go on to question the extent to which this rate of investment in housing can be sustained.

The principal constraint facing the PNA and Ministry of Housing is the weakness or absence of effective institutions as a result of 28 years of neglect, obstruction and dismantlement. For instance, Zahlan points out because of institutional incapacity, two years after the signing of the Oslo Agreement only about $58.5 million of construction contracts had been awarded. This situation has been aggravated by the shortage of developed land, the high price of construction, inadequate infrastructure and the lack of affordable finance for house building and environmental development. Whilst these issues are dealt with in greater depth in other theme papers, each is worth a cursory comment here as they are central to the examination of the strategic proposals that follow.

Access to appropriate and approved land for housing is currently a major constraint to settlement development, particularly in Gaza where, according to Jensen, Abed and Tellefsen, 'there is virtually no unused land.' Nevertheless, 27 per cent of land is owned by government, more than half of which is within municipal boundaries. Stringent development controls in the form of planning and building restrictions imposed by the Israeli civil administration, together with bureaucratic delays in their administration, further frustrate land development and, to a large extent, account for the inordinately high cost of land which can be developed. This has resulted in the informal (or 'illegal') construction of housing which is estimated to account for more than 80 per cent of all new construction in Gaza and about 65 per cent in the West Bank (Jensen, Abed and Tellefsen).

The high cost of construction, stemming from the price of building materials which is estimated to be 50 per cent above the average of international prices (Jensen), is another major constraint to housing production. The root cause of this is the high import content, estimated to be some 70 per cent of the building materials and components consumed.

Access to domestic infrastructure and services throughout the Palestinian Territories (PT) is relatively good by comparison with other countries in the region. However, Mayo suggests that even with expenditure by UNRWA of about $20 per capita per year on infrastructure giving a total of $55 per capita per year, almost twice the amount should be invested to ensure an adequate level of infrastructure. Moreover, such calculations do not take into account the expansion of the system which will be required to cope with the anticipated growth of the population.

The fourth major constraint has been the virtual absence of any access to finance for housing and settlement development. The Palestinian banking sector has been severely restricted by the Israeli civil administration. Whilst Jordanian and Egyptian banks with branches in the PT have served as conduits for the deposit of savings, they have not had access to sufficient guarantees to enter into any of the long-term lending arrangements which are usually necessary to build housing.

Strategies for the development of legislation, procedures and institutions must address these principal constraints to the development of an effective housing sector in Palestine, in addition to the myriad of problems facing the PNA and the Ministry of Housing regarding urban and rural reconstruction.

STRATEGIC OBJECTIVES

The development of local government and the management of housing in the context of *enabling* is not just a question of establishing new procedures but also of designing, staffing and equipping new institutions. This will be easier than in many countries because of the absence of effective institutions in the PT and the widely recognised need to replace the confusion of traditions inherited from the Ottoman, British, Jordanian and Israeli administrative structures and legislation (Jensen). At the same time, the development and installation of the new order will not be easy because of the lack of institutional capacity.

Mayo outlines with unquestionable clarity the characteristics of a well functioning housing sector from the point of view of each of the five principal actors: 1) the consumers/users of housing; 2) the (private sector) producers of housing; 3) (private sector) housing finance institutions; 4) local government; and 5) central government. His list describes the conditions under which each of the actors performs most effectively and achieves the greatest satisfaction. It sets the objectives for policy making and strategy design and is worth close scrutiny by everyone engaged in both. However, as he points out, several of the objectives are not mutually consistent. Some of the aims of some actors are in direct conflict with those of others. Resolving these issues is the political process of setting priorities.

Central to this list of objectives, and the strategic observations and proposals presented by many of the other authors, is the need to ease the operation of the formal private sector housing market in Palestine, and to do so in a way that is contributory to national economic development. Mayo, having reviewed the housing situation as best as he could given the shortage of reliable data, makes international comparisons with neighbouring countries in the region and draws some tentative, but significant strategic objectives for policy action.

In general, these are to reduce the current distortion in housing prices by reducing the cost of house purchase and increasing the level of rents. This will entail a reduction in the cost of construction and increases in spending on infrastructure which in turn will be reflected in lower premiums for serviced land and which should bring the level of investment down to a more sustainable level. It will also mean repealing rent control legislation or reducing its restrictiveness without creating disadvantages for the most needy. Considerable reductions should be made in the amount of unauthorised housing which exists by awarding secure tenure to land and giving recognition to the structures on it.

Regularisation of the camps is, of course, a major and urgent priority. In addition, a mortgage market should be established to provide easy and affordable access to long-term credit for housing.

Less attention has been given to those excluded access to the formal private sector housing market through poverty or alienation, and to the social and managerial attributes of housing production and maintenance that are not directly market responsive, for instance processes of collective or representational decision making. These issues will require a careful examination of the different levels of local governance and the relationships between them and their relationships with central government (Wakely).

Ziara points out that the nature of local government and administration is of key importance in Palestine. Municipal and village councils have a pivotal position in the management of housing and the delivery of services, coming between the policy directives of the PNA and Ministries and their implantation 'on the ground' by private sector institutions and communities. However, amongst all the participants in the game, local authorities are arguably the weakest and the most demoralised after a quarter of a century of Israeli civil administration. Thus, one of the most important and urgent needs in the field of institutional capacity building is the re-definition of the role of local government and administration (Zahlan) and of the style of operation needed to play that role.

It is essential that local government is both responsive to changing local needs (i.e. flexible) and that, at the same time, it is the principal vehicle for the local implementation of national policy (i.e. regulatory). These two roles may, at first sight, seem contradictory. However, in the context of the enabling paradigm, which depends upon the devolution of authority to the lowest effective level of decision-making, the responsiveness of local authorities becomes central to national policy (Wakely).

The conceptual shift that is needed to embrace the difference between a traditional policy based on providing and controlling and a policy based on enabling and supporting, depends upon understanding the difference between *top-down* and *top-supported, bottom-up* development. Top-down development measures success in terms of centrally established targets and professional competence and technical efficiency; the goals of the organisation, not the demands of the client; and in terms of ability to meet expenditure targets. Top-down development tends to be exclusive and non-participatory, and often produces an inability to cope with crisis situations or a scarcity of resources. Officials hide their inadequacies behind the exercise of procedures, statutory standards and codes of practice.

In contrast, bottom-up development measures success in terms of the ability to meet demands and respond to opportunities; effectiveness in the solution of problems; and the extent of the population supported and served. Decisions are reached by negotiation. It means decentralising and/or delegating responsibility further down the ladder to NGOs and communities. This may be regarded as a loss of power and an exposure to risk, leading to loss of status and creating personal insecurity. It entails entering contractual arrangements with the private sector that lay authorities and individual officers even more open to corruption. It calls for a new degree of accountability and transparency.

The effective implementation of such an approach to local development requires that local authorities, as well as central government agencies, adopt organisational structures with 'flatter' hierarchies, i.e. which give easier access to the top and greater autonomy of decision-making at the bottom. It entails local authorities' acceptance and encouragement of NGO and community group participation in the development and management of settlements as partners. It necessitates their recognition as a new tier of local government, coming between the local authority and individual households, and also their involvement in planning processes as well as in those of implementation and management.

There is no room for the traditional hierarchical separation between the making of plans and carrying them out, either at the level between central government and local government or between local government and community organisations. A new meaning is given to participation and consultation.

Such operational and organisational criteria demand a very different approach to local administration from that to which Palestinians are accustomed. This in turn requires a new type of local government officer with a different kind of training than that which is commonly on offer.

IMPLEMENTATION PROCESSES

The PNA has established the Ministry of Housing to co-ordinate central government support for the housing sector as a whole. In order to foster close collaboration between the Ministries of Housing, Local Government and Planning, the PNA has also established a series of joint committees (Ziara). Despite these measures, the Ministry of Housing is seriously constrained in the process of policy formulation and the development of a strategic framework for its implementation due to the lack of both financial and human resources (Ziara).

To cope in these circumstances, Mumtaz makes a case for the appointment of an intersectoral, multidisciplinary Housing Strategy Task Force with a mandate to develop a national housing strategy and make proposals for the implementation of each of its components. To be effective, the Task Force must have the patronage of the highest levels of the PNA and ideally should be officially chaired by the Minister for Housing. Without the support of such authority and identity, it is unlikely that the Task Force would be able to make the sort of far-reaching and radical innovations which are required with any certainty of their being implemented.

As its name implies, such a body should have a limited lifespan. Its job is to 'get things going' in the present situation of change and scarcity, not to replace the functions of the office of the Minister.

An Information and Monitoring Unit should be set up in the Ministry (or contracted by it) at the same time as the Housing Strategy Task Force. Logically it should be linked to the Task Force, if not actually part of it. However, unlike the Task Force, it should be permanent. Once a reliable basic set of macro-level housing indicators (Mayo) has been established and a mechanism to monitor them has been put in place, the Information and Monitoring Unit should apply itself to the development of procedures to monitor more complex and sensitive aspects of housing production, management and maintenance aimed at keeping the Ministry informed on the process and progress of the national strategy at all levels (Mumtaz). Ultimately, this process should be delegated to each of the executive levels of local government (community, village council or municipality), rendering the task of the Information and Monitoring Unit relatively mechanical.

Of equal importance and urgency to that of establishing a national housing strategy and identifying the principal participants and actors who will implement it, is the development of an approach to institutional and professional capacity building. The need for a radical and widespread regeneration of local government has been outlined above, as has the shortage staff available to the Ministry of Housing, as well as other ministries, including that of Local Government (Zahlan and Ziara).

Zahlan points out that Palestinians both in the PT and in exile possess a relatively high level of managerial and professional skills. However, there is little chance of attracting any but the most idealistic professionals to public service, particularly in local government, unless there are clear and attractive career opportunities and salary scales that are competitive with those in the private sector. The diseconomy and damage caused by underpaid and over-protected public appointments cannot be over-emphasised. They are major contributors to the collapse of government administration and even national economies. Public sector institutional capacity building makes it essential that the high expectations of those in the new Palestinian administration are met, i.e. that they are rewarded with good salaries and career opportunities.

The Ministry of Housing has given a high priority to managerial, professional and technical training for the Ministry staff and, at a later stage, the personnel of related agencies (Ziara). Mumtaz identifies three tiers of training needs and describes a potentially very powerful approach to the management of a strategy for the formulation, dissemination and skilling of the public and community sectors for the implementation of a national housing strategy. This is a spiral of policy workshops for senior executives and administrative officers, management training for middle level managerial and professional personnel, and technical and supervisory training for field level staff. To be effective it must involve all the public sector actors in the housing and settlement development process, from any ministry, department or branch of local government. It must also involve the staff of NGOs and community leaders. The essence of the programme is the sequence of procedure design, testing, implementation and refining that combines training and practice. It is a process of learning-by-doing and doing-by-learning through which the early stages of the enabling strategy are implemented as part of the process of developing the strategy itself and, at the same time, training the actors in their new roles.

Concurrent with this public sector process, support must be given to communities, particularly amongst the lowest income groups, to assist them to form strong representative organisations for the management of their neighbourhoods and housing. This will have to be accompanied by access to constitutional and management training in order to equip them to play the important role that they will inherit as part of the strategy. It has been found that this range of tasks is most effectively undertaken by voluntary sector organisations, NGOs, etc. However, they in turn will need government support in the form of appropriate recognition, legislation and political patronage, if not financial support.

Enhancing the capacity of the private sector for its role in the national housing and shelter development process is basically a process of ensuring the optimum conditions for it to function in the market, at the same time protecting the poorest households and disadvantaged groups from commercial exploitation. This entails a careful examination of the minimum degree of regulation that is needed to ensure equity without constraining initiative and investment. It may also entail a review of possible affordable incentives that government could provide to induce

74

the private sector into sections of the market that would not otherwise be sufficiently profitable or free of risk.

The most obvious and important of these are the supports that are needed to enable the banking sector to enter the housing market with affordable and manageable mortgage finance (Mayo). Another is the development of the local building materials and construction sector (Zahlan).

Several imaginative and important recommendations for specific actions and projects and were made in the papers presented in this theme and they should be studied carefully. However, at this stage, they should not distract attention from the principal issues facing the PNA and the Ministry of Housing, i.e. those regarding local government, institutional development and the management of the housing sector which have been summarised above.

INSTITUTION BUILDING FOR SUSTAINABLE PHYSICAL PLANNING IN PALESTINE

Rolf H. Jensen, Samih Abed and Ulf Tellefsen

ABSTRACT

The occupation of Palestine has led to significant changes in land, use with the result that Palestinian interests have been adversely affected. The Palestine National Authority (PNA) must now find a way to organise development for sustainable growth, taking advantage of both theory and practice elsewhere.

In this paper, we present a set of guiding principles for institution building. We have concentrated on pilot studies in order to help to solve critical needs and, at the same time, to help gain valuable experience locally.

The different situations which prevail in Gaza, Jericho and the remainder of the West Bank have been taken into consideration. Because of the lack of reliable data, scenarios are used to examine possible effects over the long term, in addition to projecting short-term effects resulting from incremental, initial 'emergency' measures. A brief practical experience is given from Gaza for both Gaza City and the Gaza Strip.

Recommendations are made concerning the legal setting and the physical planning processes. Public awareness and active participation are highlighted in a combination of both the *bottom up* and *top down* approaches. Finally, the importance of sound organisational solutions, as well as the quality of products to be delivered, is emphasised as a prerequisite to sustainability.

INTRODUCTION

Institutions in Palestine have been prevented from functioning properly for almost 28 years. A Civil Administration which was set up in their place by the occupying forces, is to a large extent, a military administration.

76

This has had a detrimental impact on physical planning, which has been used as an effective tool to limit economic development (JMCC, 1994).

Physical planning under Israeli control is best portrayed by the creation of numerous settlements which are restricted for the use of Jewish citizens only. They are a symbol of the physical changes and oppression. Large areas have been designated as military secret zones to which the public is forbidden access. The new highways being built to serve the new Jewish settlements are also breaking up Palestinian residential areas and agricultural fields, creating very tight constraints and preventing the expansion of Palestinian towns and villages. One could also highlight the situations where requests for building permits have encountered special restrictions and extremely delayed handling, with years of waiting. This has led to houses being built in despair by the Palestinians and to the demolition of these by the Israeli authorities (Coon, 1992; JMCC, 1994).

The institutional set-up for this is unique and has proven extremely effective in practice for the occupying power. Most of these changes are not carried out according to prescribed, formal procedures for physical planning in Israel, but rather by military orders (JMCC, 1995) and the special Israeli use of *streamlining*, the informal planning which is used under special circumstances (JMCC, 1995; Gertel and Law-Yone, 1991; Law-Yone and Lipshitz, 1990). Traditional tools for physical planning, such as zoning, are used in a manipulative way, by zoning the land for either security reasons or as a reserve, and then expropriating it. Shortly afterwards, its use is changed to allow settlements or the construction of connecting links between settlements, thereby making a mockery of conventional planning procedures.

The institutional consequences of these actions are many and include the breakdown of Palestinian professionalism and capacity. The entire field of physical planning is disrupted, encouraging an attitude of disrespect towards physical planning, especially on the private level, regarding building permits and controls.

The peace process has opened up new opportunities and a new start for Gaza and Jericho; but hopefully also for the West Bank (PLO, 1994). A new nation with limited land and natural resources and with a rapidly growing population needs strategic regulations covering land use, transportation and the physical consequences of economic and social development (PLO, 1993). The preparation of such measures and/or guidelines is a prerequisite for institution building, professionally, administratively and politically. This in turn requires clear organisational solutions from the national to the local level. The necessary agencies must be established and their responsibilities documented within a concise legal framework.

ORGANISATIONAL ISSUES AND PRINCIPLES

During the period of occupation, Palestinian influence on physical planning was, to say the least, very limited. However in municipalities and villages, local authorities were allowed to function within a specified framework. Some international organisations, like the United Nations Relief and Works Agency (UNRWA) and the United Nations Development Programme (UNDP), carried out their tasks and a variety of non-governmental organisations (NGOs), some of which were established by the PLO, could also assist the Palestinian people. Nevertheless, physical planning was essentially controlled and carried out by the Israeli Civil Administration (Coon, 1992).

As changes were brought about and the Palestinian authorities were allowed to take on a more prominent, practical role, a transition period began. UNRWA's responsibility for the refugee camps did not lead to any *external planning* of, for example, new residential areas; rather it was limited to general improvement inside the camps, linked to infrastructure and housing. UNDP had different projects which were specifically concerned with the rural dimension. It also started a preliminary study regarding micro-regions (UNDP, 1995). Other NGOs continue to operate in areas where new governmental structures eventually must find their own role.

The creation of the Palestinian Economic Council for Reconstruction and Development (PECDAR) as an organisation in charge of utilising World Bank and donor money in systematic development and reconstruction constituted another step towards Palestinian institution building. Infrastructure projects are vital tools in the creation of an efficient and well functioning society. As ministries evolve and develop as organisations with their own professional and administrative capacities in place, the expectation is that the ad hoc organisations will be less needed. However, PECDAR will still have its place as a co-ordinating and implementing organisation until other permanent solutions can be found and are operational.

Regarding development, there are three different types of related characteristics which need to be identified (Baster, 1972; Conyers, 1982; Conyers and Hill, 1984). First is the multi-dimensional character of development, including its economic, social and political dimensions. These are intertwined and cannot be separated from one another. The economic perspective reflects a concern with production, commercial and monetary issues. The social perspective reflects a concern with the more general well-being of individuals or groups of people. And the political perspective is concerned with the distribution of power between different groups or individuals to control, or make decisions about the use of resources.

The second characteristic of development is the need to take into account *structural* and *institutional* changes as well as growth. *Structural* refers to the changes in the occupational structure of the population, changes in the social structure and pattern of distribution. *Institutional* refers to organisational changes.

The third characteristic is concerned with the position of a country within the international system. These characteristics, when examined (Abed, 1987), shed valuable light on the Palestinian situation.

Physical planning and the organisational and legal challenges linked to it (which constitute an overriding problem for the PNA) give rise to certain basic principles and practical experiences which surface constantly, irrespective of the cultural setting. These are the following:

- There must be a clear definition of the organisational goals; for example, the central functions of the ministries;
- Organisations expected to work together must develop a clear understanding of their respective roles, central functions and marginal areas;
- There must be agreement in principle about divisions of responsibility and authority between ministerial, local and intermediate levels;
- There must be a determined, leading idea regarding centralisation and decentralisation to achieve organisational solutions. In general, decentralisation should be applied as far as possible, especially for a well-educated society;
- There is always a danger when too much power is concentrated in closed circles;
- Transparent structures and public involvement are to be encouraged; and
- Finally, every organisation needs to be alert regarding budgeting and the establishment of effective routines, serving their planning and monitoring.

The achievement of organisational solutions in Gaza, Jericho and the rest of the West Bank requires a variety of legal measures given the mixed heritage of the Ottomans, the British Mandate and of Egyptian and/or Jordanian rule, not to mention Israeli military orders still in place. The effect of each needs to be thoroughly studied. Physical planning is expected to be modernised through a new *Planning and Building Act,* drawn on international experience (Alexander, Alterman and Law-Yone, 1983).

STRATEGIES FOR PARTICIPATION AND AWARENESS

The reconstruction of Palestine requires an overriding policy of active public involvement. The Palestinians have resources both inside Palestine and in the diaspora. Institution building needs to utilise this from the very start by ensuring a fair and open recruitment in all public offices, so that the best qualified person is able to do his or her share. There exists an eagerness among the young, as well as the experienced, to take part in the starting of a new future.

This sentiment and attitude should be rewarded by allowing professionals to have the chance to do so. However, it should also be borne in mind that that economy is a fact of life, also on the personal level. Economic compensation should be set at a level which allows public employees to contribute devoted service.

It is also important to attract expertise from the diaspora to obtain professional talent which is not available locally. Secondly, it is important to obtain local experience which can ensure the relevance and local understanding of issues. Creativity will be required of all, regardless of background. There will be many questions to address; answers will not easily be found.

Problem solving should take place as close to the roots of the problem as possible. Professionalism will play a vital role in providing a constructive arena for this. Viable new roots will have to be established politically, administratively and professionally.

Questions regarding authority and responsibility must be seriously addressed between sectors as well as between political and administrative levels. A general experience in developing, as well as developed, nations is that a high degree of decentralisation should be a goal for institution building and for physical planning in particular.

The reasons for this are as follows:

- Problems are best defined as close to their source as possible;
- The relevance of problems taken up is most typically defined locally; and
- Priorities must echo people's needs.

In addition, it is important to realise that for plans to be viable in everyday life, rather than decorations in bookshelves, people at the local level need to feel that the plans are theirs, not something which intrudes upon their daily life or privacy. It should also be remembered that:

- Implementation is much more probable in practice with a high degree of local involvement;
- Monitoring and adjustments are easier when local experience can lead immediately to adjustments in the plan;
- The whole idea of physical planning becomes more rooted in people when they participate and can see and use the results;
- Decentralisation boosts a belief in local resources as well as faith in higher authorities who show their reliance and trust in people; and

- It feeds the best information to the higher levels for conceiving overall strategic policies and for planning.

Nevertheless, in a time of reconstruction, it is necessary to centralise some important decisions. Scarce resources and national goals and priorities, (say for economic development for public housing, or for environmental protection, etc.) will bring about a national framework for local planning which must be adhered to. Monitoring such progress is essential. Often, intermediate levels, i.e. some form of regional levels, are used for this. Hence, the physical planning, as indeed most planning, will be a combination of both the *top down and bottom up* approaches, towards which empirical studies, as well as new theory, are converging (Abed, 1987).

In addition to this, both practical experience and some new theory for physical planning are placing emphasis on the creation of arenas for dialogue, negotiations and mediation. The blending of traditional trades and professions within physical planning with these new characteristics has yielded encouraging results (Jensen, 1990), especially for difficult tasks such as conflict resolution regarding transportation, water rights, solid and hazardous waste, heavy industry, the debate concerning environmental protection versus economic development and other issues.

Finally, international experience also appears to support the realisation that professional skills (and organisational specialisation) ought to be utilised in a model based on linkages, rather than pushing everything into one supposed coherent conglomeration. Planners' general ideas about large-scale master plans with integrated comprehensives remain an illusion and can be dangerous in their ability to foster inertia (Alexander, Alterman and Law-Yone, 1983).

PRODUCTS, OUTPUTS AND QUALITATIVE RESULTS

Long-term and Short-term Options

In many developed countries, like the Nordic countries for example, it can be seen retrospectively that when compulsory physical planning was enacted, the expectations and the believed importance were far above actual possibilities. One has to be aware of this from the start, in order to place expectations and results more in accordance with realities. This is stated as a caution and as advice with the very best of intentions.

Physical planning has to keep in mind what in the end will be seen from, and gained by, the general public's side. Included in this is the openness and the participatory character of the planning process, and the organisational solutions with the responsibility and authority entrusted at the local level, as well as the quality and the timing of the practical results. At the same time, broad participatory approaches often lead to unrealistic expectations of delivery from higher levels. Unfortunately, this in turn can lead to disappointment and dissatisfaction, which might jeopardise the whole intention of planning, unless deliberately avoided from the very beginning.

Physical planning in Palestine faces some basic obstacles not only in the political situation, but also in the lack of reliable data and information about the actual situation in almost every field (PCBS, 1995). This must be kept in mind, since the general experience of *garbage* in *garbage out* quite easily can be the case, unless particular care is taken.

In fact, creating *scenarios* based on assumed, but controlled, conditions might yield more information when relative differences and characteristics are examined. The art and skill of using scientific judgement for designing models or scenarios is well developed for physical planning. A variety of long-term perspectives say to the year 2010 or 2020 can be analysed and examined for sustainability and functional aspects. Based on such relative characteristics found in alternative long-term development patterns, more incremental and flexible policies and solutions can be advocated, according to needs, preferences, resources required and the possible long-term consequences.

In the short-term, the *festival planning* principle may also be used. We may recognise it in operation when nations and cities compete for, and are 'rewarded' with, events such as world trade exhibitions or the Olympic Games. Nations and cities may also celebrate jubilees to mark their founding charters, or some important person's birth or death, etc.

The clue lies in the fact that such events mobilise efforts and resources far beyond the usual in both the private and public sectors. Such planning opens up a willingness to try new solutions and to create more lasting monuments by focusing on larger investments which may otherwise be prohibited. One might also argue that donors and 'gifts' often follow the same procedure, i.e. by saying in effect: 'Look what tangible results my money gave Palestine.'

If such short-term views fall within a reasonably well prepared framework, there is nothing wrong in adjusting to such a human approach. This approach also enables a proper framework to be kept and comprehensive perspectives maintained regarding defined goals.

A Brief Illustration From Gaza

In the agreement between the PNA and Norway regarding assistance to institution building for physical planning capacity in Palestine, Gaza is, of course, one important geographical area. Its small size (just 365 square kilometers; 40 kilometers in length and between six and 12 kilometers wide) and heavy concentration of population (approximately 950,000 living at densities of between 29,000 to 100,000 persons per square kilometer) with a large portion living inside crowded refugee camps (approximately 40 per cent) make Gaza a challenge on all accounts. Added to this is its very young and growing population (54 per cent under the age of 15, and a growth rate of 4 per cent a year).

A planning unit (consisting of about 10 planners and professionals) has been established. It is closely related to the Ministry of Planning and International Co-operation. The problems to be addressed are so many that an *emergency approach* has been taken to the planning, working at two levels simultaneously. Pilot projects are under way for the city of Gaza at the local level, and for the Gaza Strip as a whole at the regional level.

Some of the challenges to be faced are as follows:

- *Human resources and its needs.* Although different scenarios can be constructed, the bottom line is still that the population will double within 15 to 20 years.
- *The refugee situation,* where UNRWA has no long-term strategy, requires that the PNA take more responsibility for this.
- *Employment and sustainable growth* are paramount for Gaza. Agriculture needs to be changed and improved, and new industrial zones need to be created in close co-operation with the private and public sectors.
- *New housing and urban rehabilitation* are also demanded within the economical reach of the population. Both financial solutions and new land for development are issues to be solved.
- *Good and effective infrastructure* is a prerequisite for urban upgrading and development. According to actual needs, Gaza lacks most of this.
- *The scarcity of land and land-use conflicts* must be solved in light of the substantial population growth.
- *The environmental degradation* constitutes a very serious challenge for water, agriculture, coastal zone management, landscape and cultural heritage (Palestinian Environmental Protection Authority, 1994, 1995).
- *The institutional constraints* are many and difficult. There is a lack of legal and political authority, with the consequence that presently 70 to 80 per cent of all building in Gaza is illegal. The lack of planning capacity applies to all sectors and levels, and this again leads to lack of co-ordination and priorities.
- *The sense of identity* and people's positive views for the future are being strained given the difficult situation in Gaza.

Physical planning can only play one of the many roles needed to find solutions. For Phase I (the first eight months) of our project, we have, at the regional level, concentrated on environmental issues as tools for suitability studies regarding water, agriculture, historical heritage and potential recreational sites.

At the local level, we have assisted Gaza City in finding an emergency approach to the handling of high-rise buildings and other important tasks for an action plan lasting from one to five years. All of this is within a framework for a structural plan.

Through the studies and the planning conducted so far in our project, it has become clear that new or modified planning tools are needed in order to meet both the urgency of the situation and the comprehensiveness demanded for sustainability. However, it has also become clear beyond any doubt that the legal system, organisational solutions and staffing and enforcement in practice in short, the institutional building need tremendous efforts to alter existing practices and to prepare for a better future.

SUMMARY AND RECOMMENDATIONS

Sustainability is an important goal for physical planning. Institution building must be designed in such a way that it ensures a continuous and lasting concern for sustainability. This is done in principle by, on the one hand, utilising the information and the organisational side of professional knowledge in the field to create the quality content of the planning, and on the other hand, by incorporating in the planning process as much as possible an awareness, and openness toward, environmental issues and concerns.

In this paper, we have not dealt in detail with other professional issues of importance, such as nature and ecology; culture, both as heritage and in the present; human experience of classes and creeds; development for enduring values, etc. Instead, we have emphasised the understanding and importance of institution building through sound organisational solutions, processes in, and between, organisations, and the quality of products to be delivered.

Unfortunately, these questions are often omitted or downplayed when sustainable physical planning is discussed. However, proper attention to, and the efforts placed on the questions discussed here, are prerequisites for sustainable development and reconstruction.

Our project is addressing this with full vigour in its second phase, entering into discussions with municipalities and villages, creating a professional body for the two large regions and setting up a central unit for national policies and planning. All of this is within the framework of proposals for a modernised legal system which can help turn plans into reality through effective implementation.

BIBLIOGRAPHY

Abed, Samih Hussein, 1987, **Rural Development Planning: The Formulation of Planning Policies for Development Planning Areas (DPAs), With Special Refer-**

ence to the District of Jenin, West Bank; Ph.D. diss., University of Liverpool, UK.

Alexander E.R., R. Alterman and H. Law-Yone, 1983, *Evaluating Plan Implementation: The National Statuary Planning System in Israel*, **Progress in Planning**, ed. Diamond D. McLoughlin.

Baster, N., 1972, **Measuring Development**, Fray Gass, London.

Conyers, D., 1982, *Bridging the Gap Between the North and South*, **Third World Planning Review**, 6:4.

Conyers, D. and P. Hill, 1984, **An Introduction to Development Planning in the Third World**, John Wiley & Sons, Bath, Avon, UK.

Coon, A., 1992, *Urban Planning in the West Bank Under Military Occupation: An Examination of the Law and Practice of Town Planning in the Occupied West Bank*, **Al-Haq**, Dartmouth Publishing Company, UK.

Gertal, S. and H. Law-Yone, 1991, *Participation Ideologies in Israeli Planning: Environment and Planning*, **Government and Policy**, IX.

Jensen, Rolf H., 1990, **Bifocal, Negotiative Planning**, Paper, Stockholm.

Jerusalem Media and Communication Centre (JMCC), 1994, **Israeli Obstacles to Economic Development in the Occupied Palestinian Territories**, 2d edition, Jerusalem.

Jerusalem Media and Communication Centre (JMCC), 1995, **Israeli Military Orders in the Occupied Palestinian West Bank 1967 to 1992**, Jerusalem.

Law-Yone, H. and G. Lipshitz, 1990, **Goal Ambiguity and Ad Hocism: The New Settlement Program in the Galilee**, Paper, July.

Palestine Liberation Organisation (PLO), Department of Economic Affairs and Planning, 1993, **Programme for Development of the Palestinian National Economy for the Years 1994 to 2000, Executive Summary**, Tunis.

Palestine National Authority, 1994, **Agreement on the Gaza Strip and the Jericho Area**, Cairo.

Palestinian Central Bureau of Statistics, 1995, **Developing Palestine Official Statistics. The Master Plan for Palestine Official Statistics**.

Palestinian Environmental Protection Authority, 1994 to 1995, *Part One; Inventory of Resources* (1994); *Part Two; Interactions between Man and Environment* (1995); *Part Three; Towards a Sustainable Use of Resources* (1995), **Gaza Environmental Profile**.

United Nations Development Programme (UNDP), 1995, **Integrated Rural Development Planning in Palestine**, Forthcoming, Autumn.

HOUSING STRATEGIES IN PALESTINE: A POINT OF VIEW FROM GAZA

*Rolf H. Jensen**

ABSTRACT

The issue of housing, especially for low-income people, is briefly presented with comments and viewpoints based on the situation in Gaza. With a population already close to one million, with a density for built-up areas which is among the highest in the world, and with very limited land available, the consequences of the doubling of the population within the next 15 to 20 years are alarming indeed!

Varying scenarios provide little difference in expected housing needs. Costs and financing are a major challenge for affordable housing, whether on new land or as rehabilitation within the built-up areas. Alternative strategies for public and private involvement are discussed, as are also strategies for rehabilitation. The conclusion calls for a national housing policy with attention to the main concerns.

INTRODUCTION

Housing is one of the most important challenges in Palestine. Many partial approaches have been taken to analyse issues and propose solutions. Both needs and demands, as well as the importance for economic development have been taken up and deliberated upon (PLO, 1993). So far, very little has led to practical results and above all, a national policy is not yet established.

The situations in the West Bank and in Gaza are quite different. Without question, there is a great need for housing also in the West Bank, especially in areas like East Jerusalem where Palestinian building

* This paper is to a large extent based on an internal preliminary report 'Housing Development Strategy' prepared for the Palestinian–Norwegian project for Institution Building for Physical Planning Capacity in Palestine, dated April 1995 and written by Espen Rude.

permits are extremely restricted ('Israeli settlers are issued permits at 120 times the rate they are issued to Palestinians.' (JMCC, 1994)) and in the refugee camps, as well as for those areas that are experiencing 'development-pressure.' Nevertheless, it appears that a combination of market forces, family networks and more available land will alleviate the situation (Svendsen and Skattum, 1995). Also, the Palestinian Housing Council (PHC) has several projects totalling about 600 apartments. More projects are ready to start if funding can be arranged.

THE EXISTING SITUATION

In Gaza, there is virtually no unused land. Of the total area, more than 30 per cent is either Israeli settlements, restricted zones, or yellow areas (The Cairo Agreement, PNA, 1994). About 10 per cent can be classified as built-up areas, i.e. where densities are above 0.2 housing units per dunum. New areas for housing will have to be weighed against agricultural needs.

The ownership of the land often shows that land is subdivided into small units as a consequence of cultural tradition and heritage, creating difficulties for larger housing schemes. Land is also co-owned, which might make the situation even more complicated. At the same time, however, if one looks at the whole of Gaza, the government owns about 27 per cent of the land (98,000 dunums). About 16 per cent of this or 16,000 dunums lies within municipal boundaries. This should at least theoretically open up for possible large scale housing development.

When looking at the housing standards, one needs first of all to distinguish between the refugee camps with an average of 6m^2 per person and towns and villages with 8m^2 per person (Heiberg and Ovensen, 1993). Both are far below the normal standard of 12 m^2. Utilities are surprisingly well connected to housing units, but the standard of the water and sewerage systems (where it exists) is very poor.

The complex legal setting regarding planning as well as building permits constitutes a major challenge both professionally and for the general public. This leads to many illegal situations where one estimates that perhaps as much as 80 to 90 per cent of the building activity is informal (illegal). Such conditions are also found to be prevailing in portions of Cairo (Mayo and Katz, 1982).

In addition to the private sector, the Palestinian Housing Council (PHC) is presently the only major participant within the housing sector. Its role, however, is still a minor one in comparison with the need for low-cost housing.

The United Nations Relief and Works Agency (UNRWA) is, of course, a major factor; they are responsible for more than half the population in Gaza refugee camps. It is a challenge to find a more permanent, long-term solution to the problems of the camps, envisioning a gradual transformation into regular urban areas and providing new areas for population overflow.

Finally, the financial situation is a major obstacle to practical solutions for affordable housing. There exists no long-term financing, and today's interest rates (11 to 13 per cent a year), combined with speculative high land values (up to $1 million for one dunum), make it impossible for the many who have low incomes to enter the housing market. Nevertheless, efforts are under way to create new economic mechanisms for improvements (USAID, 1994; World Bank, 1993).

DEMANDS AND NEEDS

The project (Rude, 1995) has developed several scenarios and used two of them for further studies: one being *status quo* and the other *realistic best case*. The first assumes few changes in the present situation, whereas the second is based on a continuation of the peace process. The assumed population growth varies between 4 and 3.5 per cent per year. This would yield a population of 1.7 million to 1.6 million in the year 2010.

Although the decrease in population growth alone is not impressive, and the need for housing units is not reduced significantly for the period 2000 to 2010 (106,000 housing units are required in Gaza), the calculated need for housing development investments are decreasing as household capital increases.

For the present situation, the building costs are too high for affordable housing. A closer look at the costs show that about 70 per cent consist of expenditure for material, the rest is for labour (in the Nordic countries, by the way, the percentages are just the opposite: 70 per cent labour and 30 per cent materials). The costs for materials are much higher than international prices (a preliminary estimate indicates about 50 per cent higher).

In addition, the use of materials could be easily reduced by more modern building design and construction, which would give at least a cost reduction of 10 to 15 per cent. Still, new policies for housing financing are needed to overcome the gap for low income people. Most countries have some form of subsidies (national or locally) for affordable housing, either by directly entering the market as a housing supplier or landlord, or by using 'market mechanisms', such as special low-interest loans, grants; or other economic incentives such as free, or low priced, rental land directed towards the needy.

Housing is, of course, not only new development on open land. It is also very much a question of rehabilitation and improved conditions within already existing built-up areas. Just by looking at densities alone, we have found that according to a 'standard' of 4.5 to 5 housing units per dunum, 17 per cent of the built-up area needs improvement. On the other hand, with such an average density, we gain capacity for new housing units within low density areas.

Our theoretical calculations show further that a need for 80,000 housing units outside the built-up areas require about 20,000 dunums of new land, when the needs for kindergartens, schools, public services, infrastructure and recreation areas are included. These concerns require, in fact, about 50 per cent of the land (hence, actual net housing density is eight units per dunum). Transferred into 'neighbourhood units' or villages, we are talking about approximately 100 new pieces. Land needed for the main road system is not included.

ALTERNATIVE STRATEGIES

Three principal strategies can be presented for housing:

1) Public responsibility;
2) Private responsibility; and
3) Co-operative responsibility.

When full *public responsibility* is devoted, it is a major commitment from the authorities. A national programme has to be developed, and financing, should be facilitated for example, through a *Palestinian Housing Bank* and targeted towards those who need special treatment. Land use plans and legal foundations must be prepared for practical solutions, and organisations built up for planning, implementation and monitoring.

Public authorities themselves might, in special cases, take on the role as landlords. Although tempting at first glance, experiences often show that the forces of bureaucratism, unfortunately set in, leading to the very inefficient handling of problems.

When the complete trust is placed in the market, *private responsibility* is at its peak. Low-income groups will have to rely on family, social programmes, or philanthropic efforts. The public involvement is minimal.

A *co-operative strategy* tries to bridge the two previous ones by assuming public responsibility for national programmes, where many actors can play, and limit the public involvement to creating financial frameworks, so that others, like private banks or insurance companies, co-operative housing movements, etc. can take part. The main emphasis for the public concern will be directed towards those who need it the most, where as market forces handle the rest. This strategy can give rapid results and it seems to fit Palestinian tradition the most. It requires few investments in institution building.

For urban areas in need of redevelopment, several strategies can be combined, depending on the actual situation. A complete *renewal strategy* with radical demolition and development of new residential areas within the urban structure, can be applied where conditions are beyond repair, and alternative housing can be offered to the inhabitants involved. This requires usually a strong public involvement with plans and organisations to implement the programmes, plus a legal basis for the actions.

Conservation strategy can be described as the rehabilitation and technical upgrading of built-up areas, including the technical infrastructure and rehabilitation of housing stock. Density is not increased, and the overall space available inside housing units will be unaltered. Institution building in all respects is also needed here.

A third strategy aiming at long term changes in the city fabric is called *transformation strategy*. Areas with too high densities will gradually be reduced, and an increase in low density areas might be encouraged. In addition, new areas for urban expansion are required. When implementing this strategy, more effort is placed on incentives and voluntary participation through consensus building. Never the less, public involvement is needed for all elements of the strategy.

In principle, all three strategies could also be applied to the refugee camps. It is our impression, however, that UNRWA adheres to the conservation strategy.

CONCLUSION AND RECOMMENDATIONS

To pinpoint and define the bottlenecks for effective housing strategies in a decisive way is not easy, since most of the information available is insufficient. This, in turn, gives us a precarious feeling.

There is a lack of reliable, basic data on population, family characteristics, housing conditions, income, financial possibilities, taxation, building costs, land uses, organisational build up and responsibility, a legal base, social obedience, implementation possibilities, monitoring capacities, etc. The list could almost be infinite. Nevertheless, if anything is going to be regarded as a public responsibility and it is impossible to think otherwise regarding housing due to both the actual situation and to the tremendous population growth at hand even without immigration from the diaspora then the institutional clarification and build up is paramount.

Housing must be thoroughly placed on the agenda (Mayo, 1995). In fact, the housing issue requires the same attention as the employment issue, keeping in mind that a conscious housing policy has a great impact directly on employment (PLO, 1993). Investments in housing development will also have a lower risk than investments in trade, tourism and industrial developments.

For Gaza, the existing feasibility studies for infrastructure, lay the ground for actions and implementation with good improvement characteristics also for housing. Some restrictions must be presented and enforced, in order to protect single buildings and areas of great architectural and historic value. The same is the case for land of environmental importance, and also due to the need for efficient use of scarce resources. Some housing projects are almost ready to be started with small extra efforts; this should be done. And finally, the building costs, including taxation, have to be inspected closely with an eye for social consequences.

Finally, we recommend a Housing Development Policy be established with a practical programme. The Policy must deal with land use planning, rehabilitation efforts, and economical considerations. Also, institution building in its broadest sense must be addressed, catering for active public participation, and co-operation between the public and private sectors.

BIBLIOGRAPHY

Heiberg, M. and G. Ovensen, 1993, **Palestinian Society in Gaza, West Bank and Arab Jerusalem: A Survey of Living Conditions**, FAFO (A Norwegian Institute for Applied Social Science, Oslo).

Jerusalem Media and Communication Centre (JMCC), 1994, **Israeli Obstacles to Economic Development in the Occupied Palestinian Territories**, 2d edition, Jerusalem.

Mayo, S.K., 1995, **Housing Sector Performance and Housing Strategy in Gaza and the West Bank**, Unpublished draft paper, World Bank, Washington D.C., June.

Mayo, S.K. and J.L. Katz, 1982, **Informal Housing in Egypt**, Abt Associates, Inc. and Dames and Moore Inc. for the United States Agency for International Development, January.

Palestine Liberation Organisation, Department of Economic Affairs and Planning, 1993, *Executive Summary*, **Programme for the Development of the Palestinian National Economy for the Years 1994–2000**, Tunis.

Palestine Liberation Organisation, 1994, **Agreement on the Gaza Strip and the Jericho Area**. Published by the Palestinian National Authority, Cairo.

Rude, E., 1995, **Housing Development Strategy**, Internal project report for The Ministry of Planning and International Co-operation, Institution Building for Physical Planning Capacity in Palestine, April.

Svendsen, S.E. and H.P. Skattum, 1995, **Housing and Building Material Sector**, Palestinian–Norwegian Fact Finding Mission, March. (Unpublished report delivered to the Norwegian Agency for Development Co-operation (NORAD), Oslo).

United States Agency for International Development, 1994, **The Gaza Home Improvement Loan Program**, A proposal from the Co-operative Housing Foundation. Report obtainable from USAID, Tel Aviv.

World Bank, 1993, *Housing: Enabling Markets to Work*, **Housing Policy Paper**, Washington, D.C.

A NATIONAL HOUSING POLICY: ACTION AND IMPLEMENTATION

Babar Mumtaz

ABSTRACT

Housing policy today is no longer an amalgam of the programmes and projects being undertaken in a nation; rather, it states how all the households in the country shall have access to housing. Moreover, the households are viewed as partners in providing access, rather than simply as beneficiaries.

This paper defines a national housing policy in terms of a question: '*How* will *who* have access to *what* form of housing?' Formulation of a policy, in turn, depends on the response to another question: 'How *does* who have access to what form of housing *currently*?' This response, and a subsequent stage the development of options and alternatives are the primary subjects of discussion.

Other topics covered include the role of the government and of the housing task force, as well as consultants and external agencies in instituting a national housing policy. The implementation of policy, through the Ministry of Housing and other government departments, the private sector, communities and households are also examined, as is the importance of monitoring, evaluation, feedback and refinement. A final section looks at the pivotal role that training and re-training of existing staff, along with newly recruited graduates and professionals, will play in decision making.

INTRODUCTION

A housing policy used to be a statement of what was (or was going) to be done to provide housing. Increasingly, with the shift in emphasis towards more participatory approaches that aim to explicitly shift the role of governments from that of being direct providers or producers of housing to one of facilitating and supporting the initiatives and actions

92

of the private, community and household sectors, there is a need to match this with a shift in policy statements. Today, we would expect a housing policy to state how households are expected to have access to housing. Therefore, by extension, a national housing policy is a statement by the national government relating to housing access for all the households in the nation.

The change is significant. Under the previous paradigm, a housing policy was an amalgam of the different programmes and projects being undertaken in the national territory and included the various measures and actions under land and land development, building materials and technology, finance and funding, as well as actual construction, development and refurbishment of housing. Under the old paradigm, it was enough for a government to have the housing institutions, schemes and proposals. Thus, governments established housing cooperatives, building societies, and housing banks; they subsidised houses, construction activity and housing finance; they built blocks of flats and set up pre-fabrication plants; they cleared squatter settlements and set up sites and services schemes. By and large, measures of effectiveness and efficiency applied to these institutions and the projects rather than to assess the extent to which they were meeting the needs of the population.

Thus, it was not unusual to find that public sector housing programmes rarely provided housing for more than 10 per cent of the households that needed housing, and often less than 2 per cent of the housing was produced by these programmes. For example, in Sri Lanka, the government was only able to claim success for its housing programme which aimed to provide 100,000 housing units between 1979 and 1983 by including some 50,000 units built by individual households.

In Pakistan, the Karachi Development Authority developed and allocated some 120,000 plots from 1974 to 1980. However, while these remained unused for building purposes, squatter settlements grew by over 200,000 households during the same period.

Surveys in most developing countries have shown that less than 20 per cent of the housing finance came from formal sector sources. In India the figure was 12 per cent, in Nigeria around 5 per cent. In Tunisia, the figure is 17 per cent (including 5 per cent in the form of direct subsidies); in Pakistan, 12 per cent. In most cases, the actual number of units is far less because houses with formal financing tend to be at least ten times more expensive than those built without recourse to formal financing mechanisms.

Under the new paradigm, the relative role of policy instruments vis-a-vis 'beneficiaries' has been reversed. A housing policy statement has to state first and foremost what the policy maker's intentions are for the households whose needs it is meant to address: the programmes and projects are the means by which their needs will be met.

93

Under the new paradigm, the households are no longer viewed as (more or less passive) recipients or beneficiaries of public action. Rather, they are more likely to be partners, acting in concert with public agencies, or even as clients, paying for the services being offered. This change alters the way housing policy is conceived and developed.

ISSUES: HOW, WHO AND WHAT

Defining a Policy

A simple, working definition of a national housing policy may be provided by responding to the following question:

How will who have access to what form of housing?

HOW means the particular processes that households must undergo in order to access housing. These processes will include those for saving and for accessing housing finance; for acquiring land; for obtaining on-site and on-plot infrastructure; and for building and constructing the house, including obtaining the necessary connections, approvals and permissions.

By access, whether to housing or to a particular process, is meant the possibility, if not the right, to acquire or obtain the ownership or use rights to housing or one of its components. It is not assumed that every household will necessarily purchase or own its housing, but that if it wants to, it will have the right to acquire the rights to own or use it under one of a variety of options that may be available to it. Obviously, access is not provided if the terms or conditions set are such that no one in that particular group could meet them; for example, if the price asked is beyond their means, or if accessing a housing loan requires title to land in a context where this does not exist as a legal entity (though there may be well established traditional rights to the use of the land).

WHO means the different household groups, categorised on the basis of their needs and demands. Thus it is likely that the households will be categorised on the basis of their incomes, their geographical location and perhaps their ethnic or cultural identity.

Income categories should be based not merely on the level of earning, but may also include the type and nature of employment (full or part time; regular or intermittent; public or private sector; employee or self-employed), since each of these impact on the capability and capacity of the household to access different forms of housing.

Similarly, the categorisation based on geographical locations should distinguish between rural and urban households (and whether they are temporarily or permanently resident there; whether they are nomadic), as well as any climatic or terrain classifications that may be pertinent, since these will also affect demand.

Cultural groupings may be necessary in situations of diversity to ensure that the type of housing designs being considered respond to any particular spatial, orientation or configuration needs that might apply to each grouping. The intention being to ensure that the particular needs of every households can and are being met by ensuring that their particular demands and preferences are being catered for.

The categorisations are not meant to act as criteria for eligibility of a particular household for a particular type or category of housing. This should be true of all categories, including, for example income-based affordability criteria.

WHAT means the type and form of housing that is available to households. This means both in terms of the physical type of housing, whether single story detached housing units or maisonettes, or sites and services, as well as the form in which the housing is made available, ranging from outright ownership, through various forms of hire-purchase, to rental housing.

By type or form of housing, it is not ordinarily necessary to indicate the precise design and detail of the housing, but rather the generic type or form. However, in some cases it might be necessary to specify more precisely what is on offer, in terms of size (two-roomed units, core-houses, 100m² built-up area) where this makes a substantial, qualitative difference and variation in the housing units on offer.

What housing is made available also includes how and by whom it is provided. This is the supply side equivalent of the *HOW*, in that it specifies what is on offer, as opposed to indicating *HOW* the demand is being met, and for *WHOM*.

In order to develop a meaningful response to the question that should be asked when formulating a national housing policy, it will be necessary first to answer the question:

How does who have access to what form of housing currently?

In other words, the development of a *future* policy should be based upon an assessment of the current situation, both to identify the shortcomings and opportunities in the present situation, and also to act as a yardstick with which to measure the proposed policy.

In the case of the development of a national housing policy for Palestine, the current exercise (which includes the production of this volume and the subsequent discussions based upon it) should provide all the material necessary not only for this stage but also for the next stage: the development of alternatives.

95

Options and Alternatives

A forum such as the one intended to be provided as part of the current exercise is the right place to initiate a debate on the alternatives and options that are available. Judging by the outlines of the papers, the new paradigm seems to have found acceptance amongst most of the contributors. Certainly since the *International Year of Shelter for the Homeless* (IYSH) 1987 and the subsequent declaration by the United Nations of its global shelter strategies programme, *Shelter for All by the Year 2000*, most governments have undertaken to adopt a more enabling and support-based response to housing.

However, even if we take for granted, or presume the acceptance of the new paradigm, its particular application in the context of Palestine leaves considerable room for debate and discussion. The substance of the options and alternatives are likely to be provided by the other papers in this volume, and it is not the intention of this paper to second guess the outcome of the debate itself. However, it is likely that although there may be broad consensus on the approach, on some of the particular strategies, and even on projects and programmes as well as instruments and modalities to be deployed, it is unlikely that the general session will be able to draft a housing policy.

Therefore, it is suggested that a small (perhaps five to ten persons) working group or *Task Force* on housing policy be constituted with the purpose of drafting the national housing policy. Much of the content will of course be derived from the deliberations and recommendations of the general plenary sessions and the specialist working groups. The document will need to draw these together as well as to produce a coherent, workable policy. Within that document, there is also likely to be a number of instances where alternative means and measures are developed. The task of the group would be to develop viable alternatives for presentation to the political decision-takers: the government of Palestine, which will be responsible for the national housing policy.

In the development of alternatives and the overall policy document, the Task Force would do well to look at the *Guidelines for the Preparation of Shelter Programmes* prepared by the United Nations Centre for Human Settlements (Habitat) and the accompanying *Shelter Model* developed by the Ministry of the Environment of the government of Finland. The former provides a step-by-step guide to the formulation of policies, while the latter is a spreadsheet-based model for calculating the costs and quantities of inputs required and, therefore, for assessing the availability of finance, manpower, land and materials required to implement the policy.

Popular Participation

As part of the process of developing the document and of identifying priorities and selecting alternatives and options, the Task Force should institute a process of popular participation. The preparation of papers for this volume will have included a considerable amount of data collection and surveys of all kinds. While the data so collected may not be statistically accurate given the lack of a census and the problems associated with data collection and information generation during the occupation, many of the researchers have been ideally placed to act as informed participant sources themselves, and deficiencies in the numerical accuracy of the data are likely to be overcome by the qualitative strengths.

Therefore, the emphasis of the Task Force's interactions with communities and households as well as the private sector should be on attempting to carry out a market research exercise and arrive at a consensus rather than carrying out a census type survey. The purpose of the market research exercise will be to explain through small group discussion sessions the main thrust of the proposed policy and of eliciting preferences regarding some of the instruments and mechanisms for implementing the policy.

Therefore, the policy document that emerges will need to have had both formal political backing and popular acceptance. To the extent possible, it should also be made into a statutory instrument, but that is not altogether necessary. However, many of the components will require legislative support. Therefore, a housing policy that is publicly declared or legally constituted will obviously be easier to implement.

INSTITUTING THE NATIONAL HOUSING POLICY

The Role of Government

In instituting the national housing policy, therefore, the role of the national government is critical, not least because the policy will need to be the policy of the government. Since it is likely that the Ministry of Housing will be responsible for introducing the policy to the government and obtaining its approval, and once approved, for its implementation, there should be a strong (though not necessarily large) presence of the Ministry on the Task Force. Indeed, the Task Force should be a task force of the Ministry of Housing.

The Ministry will also have to ensure that the policy is acceptable to, and has the support of, the various associated Ministries and Departments. Prominent amongst these are likely to be those responsible for finance, land and local government.

While a support approach will end up developing more housing at a faster rate, the need to involve the community and participate in the processes of the people is likely to mean a slower start-up procedure and an initial period where little seems to be happening. Indeed the greatest draw-back of a support policy, at least from a politician's point of view, or that of a government in a hurry, is that little of the visible action can be claimed by the government to be its doing. There is also less of an opportunity to have opening ceremonies of large housing projects. However, by reaching a larger proportion of the population than would be possible with a conventional policy, there is considerable political capital to be made while assisting households with their housing needs.

The Task Force

The Task Force will act as the secretariat of the housing policy and will have to oversee the development of the initial stages of the policy. This will mean commissioning studies and programmes, and also spreading the notion of a support approach to the rest of the Ministry and municipal departments.

In a similar situation, the Task Force requested and obtained a year's transitional period. During this year, the policy was initiated in part of the country and covered only some subjects. During this period the modalities of implementing the policy were developed, tried and tested. Valuable insights and experience was gained from the feedback. This was used to refine and even redesign practical, procedural matters.

Though small, it is important that the Task Force be made up of persons who have links to or experience in a variety of different aspects of housing, and if possible of government, administration and management. Although a competence in housing per se is essential for at least some members of the Task Force, administrative and managerial experience and an open mind willing to tackle new problems is more important.

The Task Force should be chaired by a high-ranking and influential member of the government. Ideally, the Minister would be the chair. That way the recommendations and operations of the Task Force would have the greatest effect. If that is not the case, it is likely that political and commercial pressures from within the government and outside it will mean that the Ministry will likely implement and initiate other programmes and projects that are not in conformity with the policy. One most obvious case would be the demand by big contractors to be given the go-ahead to embark on 'public housing projects'. Similar pressure is also likely to come from donor and other external aid and assistance agencies looking for quick ways to disburse funds.

Consultants and External Agencies

Whereas it is important that the housing policy be managed and operated by a national team, it is likely that in the initial stages consultants and external aid and technical agencies can play a useful role. First of all, consultants can provide instant skills and expertise that may not be immediately available amongst the national professionals. However, it is important that any such involvement of consultants is done under the direction and control of the Task Force, and that the role of the consultants is more of support and training (see below) than of implementors.

Sometimes consultants can also provide a useful interface between different departments and agencies. This is particularly the case where there are inter-agency or personality clashes, or where a national professional from one agency is considered too junior to be taken seriously, despite having good, workable ideas. In that context, an external consultant can help bring people and institutions together, and by listening to disparate voices can often come up with a consensus that would not otherwise have been possible.

On the other hand, consultants have their own agenda. For many consultants, their loyalties are not with the client government department or agency, for whom they may never work again in any case, but to their funding agency who is more likely to be in the position of future consultancies. As such, consultants will often stick to the Terms of Reference they have been provided with, especially if they see these as being the criteria by which the funding agency will judge their work, rather than on-the-ground realities. It is not unheard of to find that consultants have carried out a phase or aspect of their assignment when clearly the government's counterpart staff is not yet in place, or where other complementary tasks have not yet been implemented.

Aid and technical assistance agencies exhibit many of the same characteristics as the consultants, except that their agenda may also be dictated by their own political and institutional considerations. For instance, an agency will be as eager to enter into an agreement in order to respond to its own constituency as to the needs on the ground. In this it is likely to impose conditions and require reports and other information to the extent that it begins to take officials away from their own work in order to chaperone visiting dignitaries and the agency's senior officials around.

While some of this is essential public relations work, it must not be allowed to detract from the task at hand. Ironically, the more successful the programme, the more external agencies will want to jump on the bandwagon to take credit. This will also result in more funds and assistance being made available than the recipient can comfortably cope with. An important point to keep in mind is that as far as the *project officer* is concerned, the signature of, or agreement to, a project is just as, if not more, vital to them as it is for the recipient government. Therefore, it is possible for the recipient to stand firm and insist on being accommodated without the fear that in doing so the external assistance or funding will not be forthcoming.

The other important role for consultants and external agencies is in acting as a conduit for information exchange. By having easier access to other situations that may be experiencing similar problems or by dealing with similar issues, they can provide opportunities for a lateral exchange between professionals or even communities, indirectly if not directly. On the other hand, there is a temptation to read each programme with the vision acquired in the previous project, with the result that it is as easy to misinterpret the situation as it is to provide insights into it.

IMPLEMENTING THE NATIONAL HOUSING POLICY

The Ministry of Housing

As the lead agency, the Ministry will obviously have a pivotal role to play in the implementation of the housing policy. However, it is important to bear in mind that the Ministry, and indeed the government, is but one actor amongst others in a support-based policy. The temptation to literally bulldoze communities into action must be avoided, and the Ministry must learn from its actions and be prepared to be flexible in its implementation.

The most important role of the Ministry, once it has initiated and instituted the national housing policy is in listening to the feedback from the communities and the households. In any situation, especially one where a policy is being tried out for the first time, there are bound to be teething troubles. Things will go wrong. The answer is not to apportion blame or to look for scapegoats, but to find ways of learning from experience.

The most important trap the Ministry should avoid is any resort to direct intervention, or to the creation of a dependency relationship with the communities. Numerical targets are a case in point. While officials are accustomed to meeting targets even if it means abandoning the principles upon which the policy is founded, once a household or a community has been excused from meeting, or fulfilling, its part of the bargain, it is likely to do so on other occasions. This is also likely to encourage other communities to do the same. Everyone is after a cheap meal, if not a free lunch.

The other important role for the Ministry is to act as an intermediary between the communities and other government departments and agencies, and as a bridge and conduit to external agencies. This is particularly important since much of the work required of the Ministry in its support role will be to do with administrative and legislative actions which will require co-operation from other departments. To the extent that the Ministry is able to implement a successful programme and is seen to be doing so, other ministries and departments will be happy to be associated with that success.

Other Government Ministries and Departments

The essential role of other ministries and departments has been indicated above. Foremost amongst these is likely to be the Treasury and the Ministry of Finance, the ministries of Lands and of Municipalities. The likely legislative and administrative changes required are also going to require assistance from those Ministries.

These ministries and departments are more likely to provide the required assistance if they are kept well and properly informed not only about what is being done, but also why it is being done the way it is. As well as building formal co-ordination channels and means of communications through liaison officers and co-ordinating committees, it is also important for the Ministry and particularly the Task Force to develop informal contacts.

Another way that the process can be furthered is by involving officials from these departments to participate in ceremonies and visits. They should also be invited to training programmes or other similar capacity enhancing occasions. The presence of officials from other departments will not only make for a better learning opportunity, but will also help build informal networks. This is particularly so if their members can be included in visits or missions to other countries.

The Private Sector

The private sector has a key role to play in the production and development of housing. As was indicated earlier, the private sector is in any case likely to have been involved in the bulk of the housing provision previously. However, the new paradigm not only recognises this contribution, but by making the private sector an integral partner in the process, accords it a more interested role.

In a situation where the government may control few of the essential resources such as land or capital, it will be the private sector that will take on the major role in making these available for housing. It is important in this context that wherever possible, the government does not interfere, but provides opportunities for collaborative workings.

For example in the provision and development of land, it is not necessary for the government to go about expensively purchasing or acquiring

101

land only to sell it back to the private sector once it has been developed. Most governments have neither the resources nor the expertise to undertake the assembly of land at the rate and scale required to meet the needs of the population. By working together with the private sector, the government can obtain a return in the form of land that will be accessible to the lower income groups.

The main temptation to avoid is to involve the private sector in a way that replaces a large government bureaucracy for a private monopoly or oligopoly. Though it may mean greater administrative inputs in the first instance, it will be more beneficial if a large number of small enterprises, contractors and firms can be involved than if the programme limits itself to a few large 'experienced' firms.

Communities

As with the private sector, communities and households should be seen as collaborators and partners to be incorporated into the policy. The role of the communities is to act as a bridge between the government and the individual households. Without this, it would be nearly impossible for the government or even the private sector to deal with issues that affect more than one household, such as the provision of infrastructure.

Communities should not be confused with localities. It is often presumed that because a group of households occupy a common area of the city, they make up a community. Nor is a locality necessarily united or homogeneous in its aspirations or capabilities. A community is made up of a group of people or households that have something in common. This means that for different purposes households may join and belong to a community, whereas for other purposes, the same households would be unwilling to come together as a community.

A housing programme that is based on decentralising decision-making to the lowest level can in fact create communities by giving households a common purpose and a shared objective. However, there is always the likelihood that if a representative route is taken, many of the benefits and decision-making will be hijacked by the more powerful members of the community. Therefore, for a community to be able to participate effectively, it is also necessary to use participatory methods of decision making and collaboration.

An important guiding principle of the policy should be to start with the lowest possible level for all decision-making processes, and to move up only when it is absolutely clear that the level is incapable or inappropriate for the particular purpose even if adequate support were to be provided.

Households

Households are the objective and the prime purpose of a support-based enabling housing strategy. They are the ultimate clients and users of the products of the policy. As such, their involvement in all stages is absolutely vital. For this it is important that all households are treated as clients and the ultimate paymasters of any policy, and not as recipients or beneficiaries.

It should be kept in mind that given adequate information, households are more likely to make the right decisions for themselves than any professional can. This is especially true where the professional is poorly informed about the circumstances of the household. It is unlikely that the professional can be adequately informed about the circumstances of every household. Therefore, when it comes to deciding on affordabiltiy levels or space standards or service provision, it is better to inform and equip the households to take their own decisions and for the policy to provide the support that may be needed to do so, than for a professional or technical decision to be taken that will impose long term burdens on the household.

For households to be fully involved, they must be fully informed, and their views and participation built into the programme from an early stage. However, as with communities, it is important to recognise that all households are not the same. Therefore, generalisations should be avoided. To the extent possible, the policy should aim at making alternative choices and options available to households that can then decide which they want.

CONSOLIDATING THE NATIONAL HOUSING POLICY

Monitoring and Evaluation

For the sort of responsive policy that is being envisaged, it is essential that it be based on the principles of 'learning by doing'. This means that a system of monitoring and evaluation should be built into all aspects of the programme from the beginning. The first step in that process is to be clear and implicit in stating the objectives of each and every action. Without a clear set of objectives, it will be impossible to derive a set of criteria for measuring progress or success.

It goes without saying that this also means having a clear understanding of the conditions prevailing previous to any intervention. However, this need not mean a gigantic survey aimed at measuring and recording everything. If the community and the households have been fully briefed and are fully involved, they can undertake much of the on-the-ground monitoring and even evaluation. After all they know what is there now, and they will be the ones who can best testify as to what changes have taken place: the best evaluation can only rely on their testimony.

For a proper monitoring and evaluation system to be in place requires not only that it be thought about from the beginning, but that it be implemented at virtually the same time as the rest of the programme. As well as establishing base-line data, objectives and measurement criteria, it is important to establish recording and documenting processes, instruments, methods and routines. As well as the households themselves, it would be possible to enlist the services of educational establishments, from primary schools through to universities to help in the process by incorporating monitoring and evaluation into their curriculum: children love counting, measuring, drawing and recording.

Feedback and Refinement

Monitoring and evaluating is one essential part of the programme, but it is only half as useful if feedback mechanisms are not built into the process. It is one thing to be able to set up procedures for recording and measurement. It is also important to establish from the very start what will be done with the information that is so gathered. Where there are particular benchmarks, levels of performance, etc. that are critical either to the current programme, or in influencing its future direction, or choices that need to be exercised, these must be made explicit and instituted as part of the management and operational procedures of the policy.

Feedback from the field, the reporting back of the results of particular actions, is absolutely critical in helping determine whether a particular action or way of executing it ought to be strengthened, altered or replicated elsewhere.

Training and Support

Training has a particularly central role in a support-based process. Obviously training is necessary to ensure that all the actors are aware of the role that they play in the policy and its implementation. Training is also necessary to provide the skills and technical know-how that may be required, and to generally build the capacity and the capability of the various institutions and individuals so that they can be effective and efficient participants in the process.

A switch to a support approach will entail a major, radical shift in the way people, particularly housing officials, perceive and perform their functions. This necessitates an extensive training operation to help bring about the transition efficiently and effectively. The training style and methodology required for a support approach has to be at least as respon-

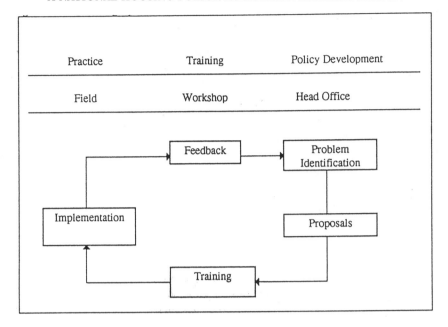

Figure 1 Training Cycle.

sive and evolutionary as the policy itself. As with the policy, the training has to be based upon learning-by-doing.

As soon as the initial preparatory stage begins, a training core team should be established to assist in formulating policy by introducing policy-makers to the support approach and identifying areas of skills and expertise that are needed, or that need strengthening in order for a housing policy based on a support approach to be formulated. Thereafter, the training team should assist in the 'learning by doing' process by both making the learning more efficient and by ensuring that the doing is 'by learning'.

This would involve the establishment of an implementation-training-implementation cycle that would both assess and evaluate implementation in practice, identify shortcomings in both practice and procedure, advise on policy response and then help in changing practice by introducing and initiating modified procedures (See Figure 1).

This cycle, repeated over time and covering new territory both spatially and in terms of aspects of housing, becomes an expanding spiral. Sup-plementing this policy-development and policy-translation work of the training core team would be a series of training teams to help in the dissemination of policy and procedures to different areas and dif-ferent groups involved in the housing process. The core team would also act as the initial trainer of trainers of these secondary training teams.

To some extent this interactive role of training would be appropriate to the introduction and implementation of any housing policy in any country. However, it is essential for a support approach. We will assume for this paper that we are looking at the training needs for a country that has, or is about to adopt, a support approach in its housing policy. There will be three distinct phases, with differing training needs:

1) The *preparatory* phase when the decision to switch is being considered but not yet made policy;
2) The *introductory* phase when the policy is first put in to practice; and
3) The *consolidation* phase once the policy has been put into place and has been in operation for some time.

For each of these phases, we shall look briefly at who needs to be trained in what and then consider how such training may best be done.

The preparatory phase

In the preparatory stage, the primary need is to make sure that the policy makers themselves understand what a support approach is and what it entails. They will need not just to understand but to be convinced that it is indeed a viable alternative and also to comprehend the implications of adopting it. Among the more difficult aspects of the approach is the necessity to decentralise and relinquish decision-making powers not just away from themselves at the centre but right down to the households. At this stage we are talking about reaching a very small group – perhaps less than a dozen people who are crucial to the whole approach and whether it gets adopted. Some of these people will already have been convinced and converted and may, therefore, be willing to opt for the support approach. Others will, perhaps, never be fully convinced, but they must be made to give it a try and to go along with the proposals.

The training needs of this group at this stage are to do with changing attitudes rather than adding skills. They are more in the nature of education than of training per se. Here we make the distinction between the two, with 'education' being the acquisition of knowledge and ideas that cover a whole range of skills, and 'training' focusing on the provision of specific information relating to particular functions. While using training in the sense of subject specific information provision – i.e. related to a particular approach to housing – we will be talking of the need to provide both general 'education' (in the sense just introduced) and specific 'training' in different combinations to different audiences.

In the preparatory phase, then, the need is more to educate than to train. Some of the target group will already have been educated through attendance at various courses, symposia and exchange visits or through the literature. This process should be extended and intensified. It is at this stage that external assistance is perhaps most useful since such ideas are best understood and assimilated when observed in practice. (In a situation like Palestine, which has yet to adopt a support approach, it will have to look at work in other countries.)

It is this same group that will in this phase be responsible for drawing up the details of the support policy. Whereas it would be possible, and has often been the traditional practice for the policy to be developed by consultants (whether local or foreign), this is counter-productive. The development of the policy is perhaps the best education/training opportunity and every support must be given to utilise it as such.

The introductory phase

In any new policy, there is a period at the start when it is necessary to orient and familiarise those concerned with the new policy and there is an inevitable period of adjustment until the policy is institutionalised. To that extent we can distinguish between an *introductory* phase and the later, ongoing *consolidation* phase in any housing policy. However, with the support approach there is a further, more fundamental difference and distinction between the two phases.

By its very nature the support approach is responsive to the actions and demands of households and communities the users of housing in a way that previous approaches have not been. Therefore, once the policy is in place, new developments will flow upwards from the household and community level; in the introductory phase, these will of necessity ensue from the national policy level.

Whereas the general frameworks can be identified and installed, what takes place within them is very much a matter dictated by local circumstance and local experience. Therefore, the structure established for implementing and managing the policy has to be responsive and dependent on the feedback it gets from implementation.

Putting the administrative structure in place is perhaps the primary aspect of the second stage.

At all levels, from the national through the regional/provincial, down to neighbourhoods, who is to be responsible for doing what will have to be spelt out. Usually, the personnel, and often the institutions that will be incorporated into the scheme, will have been in existence before the support policy, and many of them will have been involved with housing. However, they will now be expected to perform a different role particularly *vis-a-vis* the users of housing. Housing officials at almost any level are by and large concerned with policing and upholding laws and regulations of various sorts: building and planning regulations during the design and construction phases and rent or repayment collections afterwards.

Under a support approach, they will be expected to perform not so much as law enforcement officers but as law easement officers seeking ways to assist households to attain their objectives, changing legislation in the process if need be. During this phase, then, each of the various organisations and individuals instituted to interact in the housing process will need training. On the one hand, they will need to be educated regarding the approach itself, and become familiar with the overall intentions and orientation of the policy. On the other, they will need to be familiar with the procedures and processes of the policy, particularly as it applies to them.

Since the policy involves the users of housing, the above applies to them as well. Indeed, a part of the training programme will need to be devoted to educating and informing the public about the support policy, how they are affected by it, and how they can participate in it. Some of this general public education and awareness will have to be done through the mass media, but it is important that it is supplemented by sessions at the neighbourhood and community levels, particularly in those areas which are targeted for early involvement in the process.

The consolidation phase

During the third phase, when the policy has been in place for some time and most of the teething troubles have been sorted out, the need for training will shift from educating to informing. As more communities are brought into the scheme, they will need to be informed how to operate. In this they will be considerably helped by having around them examples of successful operation by other households and communities.

With time, improvements will be made in all aspects of housing provision, and this experience will need to be transferred across to others in similar situations, as well as upwards to influence policy changes at the national level. During this phase it will also be possible to introduce changes in the training of professionals and technicians to reflect their new responsibilities under the support approach (See Figure 2).

Whereas in the first two phases most of the personnel will require retraining or reorientation since they will mostly be officials already in postion, during the third phase new staff will have to be recruited from the universities, colleges and other institutions of learning. To the extent that a support approach requires a different perspective regarding the role that users of housing play in relation to the producers, this will require modifications in the basic training of prospective professionals. The most fundamental change here is that professionals, rather than taking decisions on the basis of a presumed technical superiority or exclusive information, will have to work towards enabling users to take

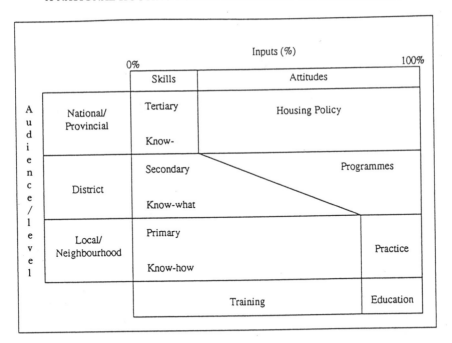

Figure 2 Who Needs What Training.

decisions on the basis of informed assessments of the implications of various alternatives.

HOUSING NEEDS AND PROVISION IN PALESTINE: THE SCOPE OF HOUSING SURVEYS

Alan O'Dell

ABSTRACT

This paper considers the use of surveys for the collection of information to develop strategies and policies for housing. It deals with the assessment of housing need and the assessment of the existing housing stock. It also provides a description of the process by which data requirements may be defined in a cost-effective way. Drawing upon the experience of the United Kingdom in conducting housing surveys, it considers lessons which may be applicable to Palestine.

Significantly, this paper is also concerned with technical matters; i.e. the procedures for data collection and the tools of analysis, rather than with the setting up of institutions or administrative frameworks for a new housing system. This is better dealt with by those intimately acquainted with the country.

The paper begins by considering the planning of housing in the wider context, and argues the need for a cautious, phased approach to ensure co-ordination between all the related aspects of a national plan. But it also argues for the introduction of a development control system, and a system of technical building regulations at an early stage.

It goes on to consider in greater detail the development of a housing strategy, and the use of housing needs and housing stock assessments for this. The intention is to give practical guidance derived from experience. An analytical framework for a variety of surveys is examined, and options regarding the precision and detail are suggested, as is the possibility of using samples instead of a comprehensive survey.

INTRODUCTION

In a paper prepared for the United Nations Commission on Human Settlements on *Housing Requirements of the Palestinian People*, Dr. Rami Abdul Hadi reviewed the situation as it existed in the early 1990s and looked forward to the coming decade or so (UNCHS, 1992). He concluded by recommending three areas for action:

- The development of a national housing strategy;
- The establishment of a housing finance system; and
- The enhancement of the institutional capacity with respect to housing finance and production.

Abdul Hadi found that each of these areas is intimately connected with the other, and advocated that efforts should proceed simultaneously in each. In particular, he examined the main themes which could form the basis of a housing strategy.

He also pointed out the inadequacy of existing data and made a number of suggestions for collecting information, such as the preparation of a housing needs assessment to identify the size and condition of the existing housing stock and effective demand. This would generate the essential starting point for a housing strategy, and provide the groundwork to determine how an international perspective could help.

There may be particular approaches or technical solutions to problems developed elsewhere which could be implemented without change in Palestine. More often, the methods or institutions adopted in one country at a particular stage of development, with a given level of wealth and with a particular cultural background, will not be transferable to Palestine without considerable adaptation. Of course, adaptation of existing methods is likely to be more cost-effective than re-inventing them.

What may well be more easily transferred than working methods is the experience of tackling and solving problems within a certain field. The description of practices and achievements in other countries serves then as a demonstration of the ability to tackle the problems, rather than as a blueprint of what should happen in Palestine. It is in this spirit that this paper is written.

HOUSING STRATEGIES

Housing is an important topic, but it is only one of many interacting areas which have to be grappled with simultaneously. The planning framework as a whole might be seen as a pyramid: at the apex sits the controlling strategy for economic development and land use: this feeds down to the next level at which are situated the strategic areas of industry, employment, public utilities, transportation, housing and so on: at the next level might come health, education, etc. How the different areas are delineated and their precise position in the hierarchy might be the subject of debate, but the general view would be accepted by most. The broad plan for each of these aspects determines the priorities and the policies for achieving the objectives, but these are influenced and constrained by the requirements and assumptions built into the plans for other areas.

Although the development of this framework is normally represented as a logical and ordered procedure, in reality, for most developed countries it is the outcome of a continuing historical process of organic change relying heavily on the institutions, customs, and conventions established in the past. Rethinking strategy usually comes down to cutting out a part of the overall structure and replacing it with something else, often not radically different from the original because it is constrained by the various connections which are already in place.

Countries like Palestine which are facing a new start, have the luxury not afforded to others, of starting with a relatively clean sheet, and being able to think things through from first principles. On the other hand, because all strategic areas are at the same level of development, they face the vital but difficult task of co-ordinating planning over a very wide field. This affects not just the organisational framework under which the planning has to be conducted, but also the nature of the plans themselves and the processes which are gone through to arrive at them. The plans must be particularly robust against changes in connected areas, and this requires the use of sensitivity testing to determine what would be the likely outcome if a particular assumption or condition were to break down.

Priorities for Strategy and Planning

This extreme need for co-ordination does suggest a rather cautious step-wise approach since changes of direction are likely to be required during the initial stages. The lack of a strategy is unlikely to be a problem for housing in Palestine in the immediate future. The rate of planned housing development in recent years has increased but is still relatively slow; and the need for new housing is so great that anything which is built now will be adequately accommodated within a future strategy. If the rate of development should increase, as it will certainly need to if significant progress is to be made over the next decade, then the need for a comprehensive strategy will be felt. So there is a strong argument for beginning the process now, even though it may be some time before it is firmly established.

However, it may be desirable to consider some more immediate measures. In certain locations there are signs that privately initiated unplanned housing development is beginning to take place, the sort of development which in other countries has been found difficult to control without strong zoning measures. Without some action such building could undermine future local plans on a number of fronts (environmental, utility provision, etc.), as well as prejudicing national and regional plans for economic development, for the hierarchy of commercial and industrial centres and for the disposition of population. So there is an argument for developing policies and introducing a control system in this area even without the guiding framework of a wider housing strategy.

It would also perhaps be wise to act to ensure that current building practices will not prejudice future standards, that the construction methods, sizes of buildings, their internal layout, the arrangement of groups of dwellings and the space around them will not limit changes which will be demanded in the future. A range of considerations fall under this umbrella. These are:

- Technical: the strength and durability of materials and structures, and the safety of buildings;
- Public health: the provision and maintenance of adequate drinking water supplies and sewage systems; occupation densities;
- Personal: space standards; the provision of food preparation, bathing and heating facilities; space outside the home;
- Environmental: provision for motor transport and car ownership; and
- Social: possible future changes in household composition, family size and disposable incomes.

While many of these factors come within the ambit of a general housing strategy, there is a need to consider at an early stage the sort of regulation system which will provide the necessary control. Some of this regulation could form part of the development control system, but there would need to be a further system which for simplicity we might call technical building control.

Information for Strategic Planning

We now turn to the housing strategy itself, and to the information needed in its generation. What follows below attempts to spell out the relationship between, on the one hand, the data to be collected and, on the other, the content of the strategy and the procedures in its development.

The collection of information is costly and it is important to make sure that what is collected is what is needed. This general principle can be expressed as rules for obtaining the best value for money from the enterprise. It is perhaps worth listing these at the outset, to provide a backdrop for the more detailed discussion to follow.

Balancing thinking and data collection

The well known American planning researcher, John Quigley, was asked during a lecture about the need for data. He replied, 'If I were given $1 million tomorrow, none of it would go on data collection: it would all go on thinking'. This may have been an exaggeration, but it made a profound point: that it is ideas, not data, which drive the planning process.

Information already available

In his paper referred to above, Dr Rami Abdulhadi called for more information. But he also showed what can be achieved with what he regarded as limited and out-of-date data: he was able to set down and explore most of the themes of a housing strategy. Whenever a data collection exercise is proposed, it is always worth trying to address the questions involved with the aid of whatever data are already available not just to identify the data needed, but actually to attempt to obtain answers to the questions. Sometimes this demonstrates that there is no need for further data collection. More often, the need remains, but any gaps in existing data can be more precisely defined.

The analytical framework

It is important, if at all possible, to identify at the outset the precise questions which are to be answered with the aid of the data, and the precise policy decisions which are to be taken. It is then possible to establish in advance the framework for analysis, which will include not just the plan for data processing, but also the quantitative criteria against which the policy decisions are to be taken. Going through this process using information already available, or hypothetical data, helps to ensure that the data collected are precisely those needed for the decisions.

Survey complexity and the scope of the data collection

The information which already exists should be used to help in the design of a survey. If a good deal of information already exists then a fairly sophisticated approach is likely to be needed to increase understanding. If very little is known in advance, a *broad-brush* approach will probably be sufficient; it could well be wasteful to try to be too sophisticated when the basic understanding is in doubt. When little is known but detailed information is required, it often makes sense to use a two-stage process, the first stage *broad-brush* and the second more detailed.

Data quality and adequacy

Experience has shown that housing surveys can be notoriously unreliable if precautions are not taken to ensure data quality. This is particular true when subjective assessments (such as the quality and state of disrepair of a building) are being recorded, or when sensitive data (such as household income, financial resources, or social attitudes) are requested. It is important to pay attention to data definitions, to surveyor or interviewer training, to the testing of questionnaires and survey schedules, and to fieldwork control procedures. It is also necessary to avoid (or measure and correct for) bias in sampling procedures or in survey non-response. Again the requirement is to match the data quality to the demands of the particular data collection exercise. Newcomers to housing surveys can learn from the experience of others.

Validation of methods and procedures

Before committing resources to a comprehensive collection of data, it is important to run small-scale, pilot exercises which employ all the methods, questionnaires and procedures in just the way they are to be used in final study to ensure that these behave in the expected way. *Do not collect data which 'might' be useful.* They seldom are!

ASSESSING HOUSING NEEDS AND STOCKS: AN ANALYTICAL FRAMEWORK

One of the key rules listed above is to *set up the analytical framework in advance.* This framework has to relate to the purpose and objectives of the study, and it has to spell out the operations in which the data are to be used. The aim is to be able to say about any particular data item, 'this will be used to inform such and such a decision, and in order to do this effectively it should have these characteristics', or perhaps, 'this serves no useful purpose, and should not be collected'.

No general framework can be given; the choice will depend on the particular task in hand. But perhaps the following might serve as an example of the process of thinking through the task to arrive at a specification for the information to be collected.

Objectives

The main objective for housing policy in any country must be to improve living standards and the quality of accommodation available to the general population. There will be subsidiary objectives, often expressing particular constraints. For example, in the particular circumstances of

115

Palestine today, these might include social factors such as the need to maintain and enhance cultural identity and traditions; economic ones, to make the best possible use of very limited resources, and to support the broad economic and land use strategy, and demographic ones, to handle the influx of returning population.

A strategy to accomplish these objectives is likely to attempt to do the following:

- To conserve and build on what already exists;
- To establish a balance between new building and repair and improvement of the old;
- To co-ordinate investment in infrastructure of all types so that the different programmes support one another;
- To identify priorities and to plan phased development (acknowledging that it is impossible to achieve everything immediately);
- To maintain and develop existing communities while accommodating the incoming population;
- To establish new communities in accordance with wider plans;
- To develop the economic and physical infrastructure and the financial institutions to best achieve the necessary changes; and
- To establish the regulatory and development control systems to manage the changes.

Process

The planning process is normally an iterative one. The following steps are usually involved.

- The starting point is generally an initial attempt to establish the quantitative picture, the numbers of households and the accommodation which will be needed for them in order to determine the scale and speed of change to be planned for.
- Then a consideration is needed of the means by which the changes are to be achieved, together with the constraints which limit the scale or speed of change. The constraining factors are likely to include the financial resources available and the institutions to manage these; the capacity, and the technical and skill base of the construction industry; the availability of building materials; and the availability and quality of the infrastructure.
- Where constraints are significant, consideration has to be given to the possibility of alleviating their effects (for example by a retraining programme to improve the skill base of the construction industry, or the establishment of a housing finance bank).
- The constraints are likely to place some limitation on the scale of change (the household population which can accommodated at a

116

given standard) or the timescale under which the changes can be introduced.

- This then requires a re-examination of the initial assumptions on which the initial quantitative picture is based, and of the mechanisms which determine the number of households to be provided for.
- Finally, the process returns to the starting point for another iteration.

A DWELLING-HOUSEHOLD BALANCE SHEET

The overall objective is to ensure that all households are adequately housed. The quantitative description of this state of affairs is the household-dwelling balance sheet. The first requirement is that the number of households and dwellings match; more detailed enquiry demands some consideration of the quality of the housing (the condition of the fabric and the services offered) and of the match between the particular needs of individual households and the accommodation offered.

In diagrammatic terms, the balance sheet might look something like Figure 1. This is intended to show the situation at some short time (five or ten years) into the future. The situation at the start of the period is indicated by the heavily outlined boxes. The arrowed lines indicate the *direction* of the calculations required to determine the household and dwelling numbers for which a balance is being sought.

A separate sheet is needed for each geographical region since people are constrained by work places and social interactions to look for accommodation over a limited area. There can however be movement of population over time from one area to another, indicated on the diagram by the box labelled *Internal migration,* and movement from outside the country, indicated by the *Immigration box.*

The boxes to the left-hand (household or demand) side of the balance sheet and outlined in double lines, represent processes which determine changes in the numbers of households. At the start of the planning period something may be known or discovered about these processes, and this information will be required to make the first tentative calculations. However as time goes on these processes may change, as a result of changes in the aspirations or resources of the population, or of changes in market condition determined by the supply of accommodation. It is these changes which introduce uncertainty into the balance sheet calculations, and which demand that calculations are performed under a range of different assumptions about the processes.

The equivalent boxes at the right-hand (dwellings or supply) side of the balance sheet relate to the standard of accommodation available. Again the situation at the outset is determined by the existing stock of dwellings and by the way in which they are occupied. Changes in standards may be demanded by rising aspirations of people or by the regulatory systems for development control and zoning, public health and building safety. Of course standards will always (to a considerable extent) be constrained by the availability of resources. Also acting on the supply side are constraints set by the availability of infrastructure, land use zoning, and the capacity of the construction industry. These appear in a shaded box because information about these cannot be obtained from housing or household surveys, the main topic of this paper. They are nevertheless of vital importance and their impact on the household-dwelling balance must be considered.

Another factor which has to be taken into account is the option of government to intervene in the market. This might be done by providing publicly owned or controlled housing for rent to selected groups (low income households, 'key' workers, etc.); by offering financial subsidies or grants to households buying or renting in the private sector; by directly limiting the operation of the market in some way; or by rather more all-embracing measures such as migration control. Such actions affect directly housing demand, or the process by which households are matched to dwellings, and where they exist have to be taken account of in the balance sheet. Where there appear to be failures in the market in ensuring equitable access to housing, consideration has to be given to proposing intervention measures.

The Phasing of Programmes

In reality processes are in a continual state of flux. However, for practical reasons, the diagram of Figure 1 is taken as relating to a single time period during which changes proceed uniformly. In practice it is usual to develop plans in a number of phases, and reconsider the diagram for each of the phases. This has three main advantages, which are as follows.

- The action programme may be implemented gradually, with standards being increased over time to match the prevailing circumstances and to use resources as they become available. Priorities may be established for each phase. These may be based on the principle of treating the worst conditions first, or concentrating on key household groups, or on chosen local areas.
- The level of detail in the planning can match the reliability of information. Knowledge of current circumstances will always be more complete and more reliable than information about the future, so plans drawn up for different time periods serve different functions. Those for the immediate future may be regarded as *blueprints* for action: those for 15 years ahead are intended to set the general direction for change and to identify the nature and scale of any problems on the horizon.

118

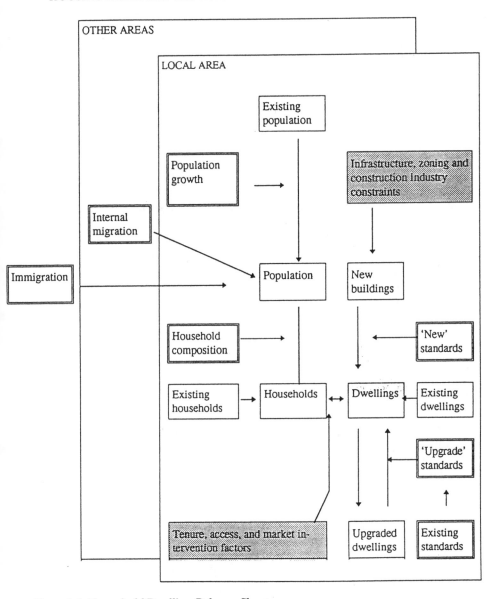

Figure 1 A Household-Dwelling Balance Sheet.

- A plan is always likely to be thrown off course by events. It is important therefore that progress is monitored from time to time. The end of a particular phase in a plan marks a sensible point for this monitoring to take place.

119

The Framework's Use

The above is intended to show how a framework for defining information needs and for analysing and making use of the information might be developed. It is not intended to be complete or comprehensive, and indeed, although there are elements in this discussion which would be relevant in most situations, each individual plan has its own peculiar needs.

It is also useful to recognise that the process of thinking through and recording how the task may be approached is probably as useful as the framework itself.

INFORMATION FROM SURVEYS

Considerable attention has been given above to the household/dwelling balance sheet. This is because it gives a convenient summary of the information required for the development of a housing strategy. Some of the data needed are indicated explicitly in the balance sheet, but in addition the various processes are represented so that the role of particular information in addressing the objective of the strategy is apparent. The balance sheet can therefore provide the starting point for group discussion which ultimately leads to a description of the information to be collected.

Some of the information relates to the physical characteristics of the dwelling, and some to the people occupying the building.

The former is best obtained by surveys in which individual dwellings are inspected by surveyors with some professional experience of construction or with special training, since a technical expertise is required. Ideally, the latter requires interview surveys in which households or knowledgeable members of households are questioned by trained interviewers; an alternative is the use of a *self-completion* questionnaire, distributed and returned by post, but this approach has a number of problems and is best avoided if possible. Information about the dwelling which can only be gained by the experience of living in it is obviously best collected during an interview survey. There are considerable advantages to carrying out both types of survey at the same address, since this allows the two sorts of information to be directly linked.

Normally *sample* surveys are used, since a total coverage of all households and dwellings would be unmanageable. As long as the sample is carefully drawn and the rules of statistics observed this approach gives perfectly acceptable results.

Some information required in the development of a housing strategy (for example the annual house building capacity of the construction industry) cannot be collected in this manner, and requires a different approach. However it is often possible to obtain related information from a house or household survey (for example, the quality of repair and improvement work carried out by the industry).

Information is required for the stock as a whole and for the household population taken in its entirety, but also for particular sub-sets of dwellings and households. The greatest flexibility is obtained if the data are collected and stored at the level of the individual dwelling or household, to be aggregated when this is needed.

Under the heading *primary data* is listed the information available from the particular type of survey which is needed to feed into the household-dwelling balance sheet. This includes information used to describe the current situation and also information which will provide indications or clues to likely future changes (in for example household sizes or standards of accommodation demanded).

Under the heading *derived data* is listed various measures or quantities obtained from the *primary data* but which have a more direct use in the setting of policies and priorities. Some of these measures may be constructed during the survey itself, or they may be assembled during the analysis stage when all of the data have been collected. If the latter, then it will have been necessary to determine in advance the procedures to be employed to ensure that the primary data are adequate for the purpose.

The assumption is that the household-dwellings balance sheet may need to be looked at from three distinct viewpoints; namely:

- In terms of crude overall numbers, to show the shortfalls or surpluses in different local areas;
- In terms of *housing need*, to provide information on the number of households who are inadequately housed and how far their conditions fall below the desirable standard; and
- In market terms, to show the degree to which the purchasing power of some household groups falls short of what would be required to acquire adequate housing, or the degree to which some groups are limited in their access to appropriate housing.

A Survey of Dwellings

Primary data

- The size of dwelling, its design, layout and form of construction, and the facilities and services it offers;
- The defects in the buildings, the state of repair, and the likely costs of bringing it up to standard;
- The ease with which the building could be upgraded, and any problems of the building itself or of its surroundings which might constrain this;

- Whether the building has particular architectural, historical or cultural merit; and
- The quality of the infrastructure and environment of the building, and the proximity of community facilities and employment.

Derived data

- Categorise the dwelling against a range of accommodation standards.
  In advance, it would be necessary to devise standards for housing services in relation to health, safety, privacy, space, and convenience, taking into consideration arrangements for cooking, bathing, toilet facilities, living and sleeping. Ideally a range of standards (from the *basic* to *high quality*) should be defined, to allow the development of action programmes which take into consideration, for example, the projected future lifetimes of individual dwellings or the priorities in a phased programme.
- Categorise the dwelling against construction standards.
  The standards are likely to be based on the seriousness and urgency of any repairs needed, the estimated cost of putting the dwelling in good repair, and the expected future life of the dwelling (which in turn will depend on its present condition, its structural strength and durability of the building materials).
- Categorise the dwelling in terms of its priority for action.
  This will depend on the dwelling's ranking on both accommodation and construction standards as well as such factors as architectural merit, etc.
  A suitable categorisation might identify dwellings to be (i) saved and conserved, (ii) accepted as they are, (iii) repaired/upgraded for a limited life, (iv) accepted in poor condition for a limited life, (v) demolished and replaced, or (vi) demolished and not replaced.

A Survey of Households

Primary data

- The size and composition of the household; the ages and sexes of and relationships between its members; the composition in terms of the separate family units;
- Any problems of health or disability which might affect accommodation requirements;
- The particular accommodation needs and aspirations of the household;
- The income and the financial capability of the household to pay the basic housing costs, and to support repair and improvement work;

122

- The human resources (physical capacity and skills) for self-help and for some contribution to community help;
- Recent history of moving and any intentions or plans for future moves; and
- Future intentions or aspirations for independent living by the separate family units which make up the household.

Derived data

- Categorise households according to their accommodation needs.
  This will take into account the space and privacy requirements of the household, and any special requirements relating to health or disability problems.
- Categorise households according to their ability to 'help themselves.'
  This process will take into account their current financial position, their future likely earning power, their creditworthiness and ability to finance a loan, their capacity for self-help (building and organisational skills), the degree of family support.
  An important measure within the overall categorisation system will be the monthly financial sum which could be allocated for housing.

A Joint Survey

A joint survey would investigate both the dwelling and its occupants. In addition to that listed above, it would include:

Primary data

- The occupation density in the dwelling (crudely persons per room) and the impact this has on the sharing of facilities, privacy and space availability; and
- The costs of the dwelling to the occupants, the rent or the market value, and any other incidental costs.

Derived data

- Categorise households according to the match or mismatch between their current housing, and their needs determined in relation to the range of accommodation standards.
  This will take into account the occupation density, the availability and degree of sharing of the basic housing facilities and services, and any special needs dictated by health or disability problems.

123

- Categorise households according to their purchasing power within the market.

This will take into account both the finance available to the households, and the costs of housing in the particular local area.

OPTIONS: PRECISION AND SAMPLING

Precision Goals

An important consideration in any survey is the precision and level of detail to be aimed for. The earlier discussion may have given the impression that a very comprehensive and detailed analysis is always required, but this is not the case.

There will often be aspects of knowledge, particularly about future conditions, and particularly when large changes are expected, which are very incomplete or uncertain. If these aspects are key to the plan, then a major part of the effort ought to go into attempting to improve the state of knowledge in these areas or to devising plans which limit the impact of the uncertainty. One of the first jobs in devising a strategy is therefore to attempt to identify these critical factors.

In the Palestinian context (ignoring political issues) the biggest unknown factors are probably those relating to the size, makeup, and geographic disposition of the population. These include the following.

Rural/urban movement

In most countries, economic development has been associated with large-scale movements of people from rural areas to towns, resulting in accelerated (often uncontrolled) urban development. So far this has not happened in Palestine. Will it happen in the foreseeable future? Presumably this will depend on broader land use and economic policies which have yet to be formulated, but within an interview survey of households it might be possible to obtain some indications of a propensity to move from a rural to an urban location.

Return of the exiled population

Potentially the exiled population who might wish to return to Palestine could constitute up to one third of the total population. Whether or not they do so will depends upon the rules to be applied by the Palestinian administration, and on the availability of jobs and accommodation.

124

Changing household composition

Currently, there tends to be a high occupation density associated with large household size. This pattern presumably derives from the traditional social structures and from a shortage of housing. In most developing countries a fall in household size tends to occur due to a fall in the birthrate and an increase in independent living by basic family units. It is likely that in Palestine there would be a desire and a propensity for this to happen if housing is available. Again something might be learnt about the likely dynamics of such a process through an interview survey of households.

Market impact of the incoming population

It is not immediately clear what impact returning population will have on the market. If they are households with relatively large financial resources then they may be able to outbid existing the population and in certain areas drive prices up. If they have relatively little, then they may not be able to compete within the local market and will be prevented from returning. It is not possible, by means of surveys within the country, to obtain information on this topic.

Where information is lacking in areas likely to be critical, and there is no way of obtaining the necessary information, it is important to consider whether it is possible to set up procedures to monitor future developments, and to warn of any unexpected changes.

Samples and Procedures

Sample surveys

In general, it is unnecessary and too costly to carry out a survey of a complete housing stock or a whole population of households. The exception to this is a population census in which the aim is merely to count the population so that very little information needs to be collected.

Generally, for housing purposes, a sampling procedure is used. If the procedure is carefully controlled and the characteristics of the stock from which the sample is drawn is reasonably well-known, then a sample which is representative of the whole stock is obtained, from which reliable conclusions may be derived. The errors associated with such a survey are then dependent only on the size of the sample. Typically in the UK samples of from a few hundred to a few thousand are used.

Where specific problems, or specific types of buildings or geographic locations, are the focus of the study, it is often possible to sample preferentially from selected parts of the stock, to enhance the efficiency by ensuring a larger sample size among the properties of interest.

As indicated earlier, the more that is known about a stock, the more detailed will subsequent investigations need to be, and hence the bigger the sample required. To get a broad general picture a relatively small sample is adequate, and for some purposes in the Palestinian context a small sample may be all that is required.

However, to use sample surveys effectively it is necessary to have access to a reliable *sampling frame*, a list of the complete stock or of a well defined part of the full stock from which the sample might be drawn. It is unclear whether such sources are available. A recent population census (collecting the basic data on household characteristics and addresses) would provide an ideal starting point.

If formal lists of addresses cannot be found to be used as a sampling frame, all is not lost. In a local survey it may be possible to count the number of addresses in each street, to estimate the number which would be needed in a sample, and to select by some randomising procedure specific addresses for survey. Such a process of course requires careful control on the ground.

Local or national surveys

Even if a nation-wide survey is wanted, it is often sensible to base this on a series of local surveys. Economies may be achieved, for example, by restricting the number of local areas included in the exercise. This can be done by excluding certain towns or villages which are known to be similar in their characteristics to others already included.

If the local areas are programmed to be surveyed sequentially, it becomes possible to validate the methods employed at an early stage in the overall survey so that modifications can be made before progressing on to other areas. It can also happen that the first areas surveyed throw up unexpected or interesting results which warrant a shift of emphasis in the topics addressed in subsequent areas.

Data quality

Experience with one the United Kingdom's national surveys, the *English House Condition Survey*, has shown that nothing can be left to chance if adequate data quality is to be ensured. The planning and preparation for a survey, as well as the control during its execution, have to be very carefully managed. And this applies to both dwelling and household surveys. Some aspects of this task are considered below.

Data definitions and questionnaire design

It is important that all tasks required of surveyors or interviewers are clearly understood. This means that all procedures to be used, all measurements to be taken and all questions to be asked of households are precisely specified in advance and described in a document which is made available to surveyors and interviewers. All terms used in the document, and particularly those which have a broad meaning in natural language but a precise and specific meaning within the survey, should be defined. Examples should be given to illustrate what is required, and to highlight potential pitfalls.

Piloting methods

All the procedures and questionnaires should be tested in small-scale *pilot* surveys. It is important that these pilots reproduce the circumstances to be met in the main survey (in terms of the types and condition of the dwellings, the types of households, and the level of training and experience of the surveyors and interviewers). Ideally the data collected in pilots should be processed through the procedures to be used later for the main surveys, to validate all aspects of the survey.

Training surveyors and interviewers

Normally it will be expected that surveyors and interviewers will already have relevant experience. However they will need specific training or briefing in the tools to be used because some of the procedures or definitions may not accord with what they have used in the past. The training should include practical exercise in using the tools (in inspecting real dwellings, or interviewing people).

Reducing surveyor and interviewer variability

It cannot be assumed that two surveyors or two interviewers confronted by the same dwelling or the same household, and nominally employing the same tools will obtain precisely the same results. This is particularly the case when fairly *subjective* information is being collected. In the *English House Condition Survey*, it has been found that surveyors agree reasonably well when describing what they observe in a defective building; they disagree a little more in describing the underlying reasons for what they observe; and disagree considerably when describing the work needed to remedy the defect. Therefore, it is necessary during the training of surveyors to devise methods to reduce the variability of their responses. Opportunity has to be given for the discussion of the results of fieldwork exercises, for surveyors to compare their own results with those of others and to make corrections in their approaches where this is necessary.

Testing surveyors and interviewers

Before surveyors or interviewers are allowed into the field for the main survey they should be tested to ensure that they conform which the general standards required.

Fieldwork control

It is necessary to ensure that standards are maintained during the course of the fieldwork. This is best achieved by conducting repeat surveys for a proportion of addresses selected randomly. This has the dual benefit of ensuring that surveyors or interviewers know that there is a possibility they will be checked upon, as well as providing information on the variability of data within the main survey.

Measuring and counteracting bias

Not all addresses selected for a survey will yield useful data. Sometimes it will not be possible to contact the occupant, or perhaps the occupant will refuse to co-operate. It is important to ensure that the addresses missed in this way are not predominantly of one type or another. Should this be the case, there is a chance that the bias introduced will distort the results. Some means has to be devised to investigate this phenomenon, and if necessary to implement measures to counteract the bias.

Treatment of uncertainty

All the above indicates the opportunity for error to be introduced into survey results from inadequacies of the tools employed. There is also the error which arises naturally from the use of a sample to draw conclusions about a larger population of dwellings or households. This implies that there is bound to be some level of uncertainty in the quantitative results. It is advisable to recognise this fact by attempting to make estimates of the magnitude of uncertainty, and by quoting results in the form of ranges rather than single numbers which give a false impression of precision.

This list of potential problems is not intended to be exhaustive; nor is it suggested that they will all be significant in all surveys. The intention is rather to show the sort of consideration which needs to be given to the detailed planning of a survey, and the advantage to be gained from making use of experience already available in the field.

CONCLUSION AND RECOMMENDATIONS

Most developed countries employ regular population censuses, collecting data to monitor and predict demographic change. Many have produced predictive models to estimate future need or demand for housing (see the *Bibliography*). Municipalities often conduct local surveys to assess housing need.

Many countries also undertake housing surveys (routinely or as 'one-off' exercises) to examine both the state of the housing stock and the housing conditions experienced by the population. These are carried out at local as well as national level, and are intended to feed information into policy development and programmes for practical implementation at these levels.

While these tools may require changes to be used in a Palestinian context, it is likely that some could be adapted effectively. More importantly, a wealth of technical expertise and experience underlies the methods which have been used in surveys in other countries. This could be invaluable in assisting in the development of tools specifically directed towards the needs of the new Palestine.

BIBLIOGRAPHY

Corner, Ian, 1993, **From Population Censuses and Surveys to Housing Demand Projections at Regional and Local Level: Evolving Methodologies in England**, Paper presented to the EAPS/BIB conference on Population-Relevant Policies in Europe, Wiesbaden, Germany; United Kingdom Building Research Establishment, London.

O'Dell, Alan, 1991, *The Changing Condition of the English Housing Stock: Measuring Modelling and Managing It*, **Management, Quality and Economics in Building**, E. & F.N. Spon, London.

United Kingdom, Department of Environment, 1988, **English House Condition Survey, 1986**; Her Majesty's Stationery Office (HMSO), London.

United Kingdom, Department of Environment, 1993, **English House Condition Survey, 1991**, Her Majesty's Stationery Office (HMSO), London.

United Kingdom, Department of Environment, 1993, **Local House Condition Surveys: A Guidance Manual**, Her Majesty's Stationery Office (HMSO), London.

NATIONAL HOUSING POLICIES AND STRATEGIES: THE NEW PARADIGM

Patrick Wakely

ABSTRACT

This paper starts from the position that urban areas in developing countries, as the centres of manufacturing, government, trade and communications, are fundamental to the process of national economic development. Effective rural development is to a very large extent dependent upon the effectiveness of the commercial, administrative and economic support that is provided by cities.

The most obvious of these supports are: the provision and control of markets, both national and international; the dissemination of technical and commercial information; the management of transport and distribution networks; the provision of credit, banking and insurance systems; and, above all, the processing of primary products. In addition, towns and cities are centres for the industrial production of the exportable goods upon which the economic development of many countries depends (Harris, 1990).

This paper goes on to argue that housing (which in many developing countries constitutes as much as half of the fixed capital formation of cities and which covers 70 per cent or more of the developed land area) is a major contributor to the economic development of cities and therefore, by extension, to national economic growth. However, the effectiveness of this contribution is often constrained by inappropriate government intervention.

It is argued that governments must develop a new set of relationships with the private and community sectors to enable them to operate more effectively and equitably in the production, maintenance and management of shelter. This approach is completely consistent with programmes aimed at the alleviation of poverty, the enhancement of urban productivity and the promotion of economically and socially sustainable development that characterise the agendas of the World Bank and of the United Nations Development Programme (UNDP) for the 1990s.

THE SHELTER SECTOR IN URBAN DEVELOPMENT

During the past decade, there has been a major shift in the understanding of how important the production, maintenance and management of housing is to urban economic development.

Until recently, apart from its contribution to the construction and building materials industries, housing has generally not been seen as part of the productive sector of the economy. Nevertheless, for political reasons, most governments have recognised that the public sector does have a role in the production of housing for lower income groups which, through poverty and lack of access to land and credit, are denied admission to the formal private sector urban housing market. Thus, public housing programmes have been on the agendas of national development plans and in government budgets for a long time, but cast as a social overhead cost rather than a productive investment.

To a very large extent, this attitude stemmed from the approach which governments adopted when intervening in urban housing provision. This approach developed from the 'colonial' public works tradition of providing quarters for civil and military employees. When translated into the production of housing for ordinary low income households, this resulted in programmes for the construction of high standard (though small), fully serviced dwellings for rent or hire-purchase at highly subsidised rates.

These were built on land zoned as 'residential', thereby officially excluding any other use, such as commerce, trade or industry. Clearly, such public housing was not directly productive and it often did not fulfil its welfare functions either, as the low income beneficiaries for whom it was intended almost invariably sold it to wealthier households either to benefit directly from the public subsidy or because they could not afford to maintain the rent or hire-purchase payments.

The high cost, and high risk, of government inputs to public housing was reduced with the introduction of sites and services projects and slum and squatter upgrading programmes in the 1970s. However, these are still usually treated as discrete public sector projects for the provision or improvement of physical infrastructure (such as water, sewerage, drainage, access ways and solid waste disposal) with little, if any, understanding of their potential to serve as catalysts for a much wider range of development initiatives.

Now, however, there are signs that this approach is changing, as is the understanding of the nature and importance of housing production by urban low-income groups. The role of housing as a social and economic activity is being distinguished from the products of construction: dwellings and utilities.

The production of a dwelling is being understood to be a long (and often never-ending) process of intermittent investment of time, energy and resources in response to individual households' changing needs, priorities and fortunes rather than a programmable project that can be planned and budgeted. This process is being recognised as a component of individual social and economic development by which low income households gain access to basic construction and management skills that, with the right opportunities, can become marketable.

Informal sector low-income neighbourhoods are being recognised as being much more than just residential areas. Houses are not just dwellings; they are centres for the production of an enormous variety of goods and services which are important not only to the immediate community but also to the city at large. Such informal 'mixed development' – to coin a phrase from the formal lexicon of town planners – is of particular significance to the productivity of women who have to maintain a dual role: that of manager of the home at the same time as contributor (or often the only contributor) to household income.

Although the initiatives and goals of informal sector development are essentially those of individuals and families, they frequently involve some degree of collective or community participation, particularly in the provision of basic services and the allocation and control of land development by 'new-comers'. Where there is particularly strong local leadership or community cohesion, such communal action can run to the installation, maintenance and management of a wide range of infrastructure and services, including those that are normally provided by local authorities.

However, there are few such urban communities, particularly among the lowest income inhabitants of new informal settlements, that have achieved such cohesion without outside stimulation and support. More commonly, such neighbourhoods, while providing flexible and affordable accommodation and centres of informal commerce and industry, also present some of the more hazardous urban environmental conditions that not only impinge upon their own inhabitants but also on those of the better serviced areas of the city that surrounds them.

This is most dramatic in extreme situations such as the outbreak of environmentally aggravated epidemics like cholera (which is alarmingly but perhaps predictably increasing in Latin America and Africa). However, it also has a more low-key but equally devastating impact on urban economies and societies. For example, it has been estimated that in Third World cities an average of one-tenth of each person's productive time is sacrificed to disease that results directly from lack of access to safe water and sewage disposal (Hardoy and Satterthwaite, 1989).

Support and Enablement

The new paradigm for public sector intervention in the urban housing market in developing countries is that of 'support and enablement'. This goes beyond the sites and services approach to the provision of land and utilities for households to develop on their own, and the upgrading of infrastructure in un-serviced slums. It entails the provision of appropriate packages of legislative, managerial and financial supports (which include advice and training) which enable households, communities and enterprises to be more effective in the initiatives that they take and the investments that they make. It is to do with enhancing productivity, economic efficiency and sustainability.

The paradigm is absolutely consistent with the aims of two important documents which were published in 1991: the World Bank policy paper, **Urban Policy and Economic Development: an Agenda for the 1990s**; and the United Nations Development Programme (UNDP) strategy paper, **Cities, People and Poverty: Urban Development Co-operation for the 1990s**, as well as with the aims of the United Nations Urban Management Programme which entered its second phase in the same year.

The World Bank's agenda embraces four issues which are regarded to be fundamental to the effectiveness of urban and national economic development. These are urban productivity, poverty, the environment, and the need for research.

The UNDP strategy covers basically identical concerns though giving greater emphasis to social problems and human development. These include poverty alleviation; infrastructure, shelter and services for the very poor; environmental improvement; strengthening local government; and the promotion of the private sector and NGOs.

The joint United Nations Centre for Human Settlements (UNCHS)/ World Bank/UNDP Urban Management Programme, the second phase (1992–97) of which is concerned with dissemination and the provision of support through a system of country consultations, has five interrelated components: land policy and management, finance and administration, infrastructure, the environment, and poverty.

However, none of these programmes mentions housing. The subject has been subsumed in the wider issues of urban management, sectoral partnerships and supports.

The Nature of Enablement

In discussing the concept of 'enablement,' there is still a tendency for governments and international agencies to think in terms of the traditional public/private, two-sector model of national institutions. However, recognition of the third, or community, sector as more than just a subsidiary of the private (commercial) sector is essential to the effective implementation of an 'enabling' strategy for urban housing.

The aims, style of operation and need for support of the private and community sectors differ considerably. The private sector is in business to make a profit and the basic supports that it needs are commercial incentives and trading advantages. The community sector exists to achieve clearly defined goals and is specifically non-profit making. The supports that it needs are institutional and managerial.

In discussing the nature of the 'enabling' support needed to implement an effective housing strategy, it is useful to break each sector into its 'major' and 'minor' components. These are:

- Public sector:
  Central or national government.
  Local government (metropolitan, municipal, district).
- Private sector:
  Formal sector industry and commerce.
  Informal sector enterprise.
- Community sector:
  International and national level non-governmental organisations (NGOs).
  Community-based groups and organisations (CBOs).

Although enablement is generally taken to mean the provision of public sector support to the private and community sectors, this degree of aggregation is often unhelpfully simplistic. In many countries, one of the most basic needs for support to enable the production of secure and healthy urban housing is central government backing to municipal authorities; that is, support which comes entirely from within the public sector.

Increasingly, communities and households are being enabled by both technical and financial assistance from national and international NGOs with no intervention by the public sector. During the past decade, both in response to, and as a result of, this, there has been a substantial increase in the attention given to improving the performance of the community sector, principally by international NGOs, bilateral and multi-lateral aid agencies, such as UNICEF.

It is important that this support by both the international and local organisations continues to increase. Nevertheless, the most urgent and important need for reappraisal remains the roles and responsibilities of governmental institutions and their procedures and practices (UNCHS, 1990).

The Categories of Support

However, before getting into the nature of the institutional changes that are needed, it is necessary to examine the principal components of support that are likely to be demanded from public sector agencies. These fall into four broad categories:

1) Access to suitable land;
2) Affordable and manageable finance;
3) Environmentally sound infrastructure and sustainable services; and
4) Technical and managerial assistance.

Whatever the political or legislative system, a market in the rights to the use of urban land exists everywhere, be it formally recognised or pushed by legislation or custom into the informal sector. The competition for access to land that is appropriately located and serviced, puts it beyond the reach of vast numbers of low-income urban households throughout the Third World. Thus they are forced into situations of insecurity which have resulted, for example, in illegal squatting or renting in overcrowded, under-serviced slums. This has prohibited any sustained investment in their housing (Turner [ed.], 1988 and Hardoy and Satterthwaite, 1989).

The most obvious and, in a strict sense the only, form of support to enable low-income households to gain secure tenure to appropriate land for housing is for governments to enter the land market on their behalf. In market, i.e. cash, terms, this is rarely possible in the short- and medium-term, as opposed to long-term 'land banking' policies, for the reason that it inevitably entails extensive subsidies which few governments can afford.

However, there is a growing catalogue of legislative and administrative strategies made possible by the adoption of 'enabling' strategies for housing. These can be applied by governments without the exchange of cash. These include approaches such as the rationalisation of the use of existing public land; the introduction of various forms of tied tenure to protect public investment; land-sharing development deals with the private sector; and the simplification of procedures for land subdivision, titling, transfer and registration (Angel, Archer, Tanphipat and Wegelin [eds], 1983 and McAuslan, 1985).

A substantial proportion of lower income urban households are denied access to credit with which to develop their own housing, not because they cannot afford it, but because of their inability to provide acceptable security against default in repayment. For instance, it is common for mortgage banks to insist that borrowers have regular employment in the formal sector and the freehold ownership of land on which to build. Thus, it is impossible to get a loan to purchase land and the self-employed, and those employed in the informal sector, are denied access to credit which many of them could afford and would be willing to repay.

Consequently, a wide range of informal credit mechanisms, based on savings and loans associations and other forms of revolving funds have developed. However, although these are reliable and accessible, they tend to be limited by a lack of capital backing and efficient management. Provision of this would stimulate a substantial increase in investment in adequate housing by urban low-income families.

In many situations, this could be extended by the provision of government guarantees to underwrite formal private sector lending for lower- and middle-income housing, thereby obviating the need for stringent and restrictive collateral. Contrary to conventional wisdom, there is a growing body of evidence which shows that such action carries a surprisingly low risk (Mumtaz, 1991 and Jorgensen, 1977).

In most of the world, urban infrastructure and public services are provided and maintained by the public sector out of locally generated revenue. However, the inability of both local and central authorities to be able to meet the dramatic increase in demand for utilities or to adequately maintain existing networks at the standards to which they aspire, has led to serious environmental degradation and social deprivation for many urban low-income communities.

In response, community-based organisations, usually with the support of national or internationally backed NGOs, are beginning to take over the provision and management of urban services in low-income neighbourhoods. However, they are rarely able to meet the official engineering standards deemed necessary to minimise the burden on recurrent maintenance that, out of tradition, remains the responsibility of local government.

This has led to technical proposals for the provision of incrementally upgradable infrastructure and strategic recommendations for various forms of commercial privatisation of service delivery and, in a few interesting cases, to the formal devolution of authority to community groups. Such support strategies go well beyond the modification of technical specifications and the transfer of responsibility. They involve the reappraisal of well entrenched by-laws and official standards as well as changes in long established procedures of local administration (Cotton and Franceys, 1991 and UNCHS, 1990).

The provision of technical, professional and managerial assistance to communities and individual households is at the centre of the management of enabling strategies for housing. To a large extent, this is becoming the domain of NGOs which, as they are in direct contact, and often in partnership, with community groups, are in a position to understand needs, respond to demands and initiate action with a degree of sensitivity that is difficult, if not impossible, for most public sector agencies. Nevertheless, NGOs must have at least a measure of political and legislative support to be able to operate effectively.

Moreover, although the basic premises of an enabling strategy are decentralisation, deregulation and the devolution of authority, governments must take care to minimise the chances of some people slipping through the net, either because the NGO system does not embrace them, or as a result of the ephemeral nature of voluntary organisations that are at liberty to withdraw their support at any time.

The Management of Shelter

Identifying and responding to the lowest effective level of decision-making and authority lies at the centre of designing and managing enabling strategies for the production, maintenance and management of urban housing. There are four levels at which shelter-related decisions are made. In ascending order, these are: household, community or neighbourhood, local authority (urban or municipal council), national or state government.

In simplistic terms, it is argued that decisions concerning the effective investment of financial and technical resources in dwellings can only be made at the level of the household, i.e. by those whose resources they are. Decisions that determine the type of infrastructure, standard of servicing and the provision of amenities to a neighbourhood should be devolved to the community, i.e. the users of the neighbourhood. Those to do with the distribution of trunk infrastructure and the delivery of social services clearly cannot be taken below the level of the municipality. And so on.

The most important and radical need for innovation in existing procedures for the development of appropriate housing and domestic infrastructure is at the level of the community. Effectively community organisations or neighbourhood councils are beginning to constitute a new tier of local government. They are filling the wide gap which has always existed between individual householders and established local authorities (urban or municipal councils). The range of responsibilities which should be devolved to this level is, perhaps, best illustrated by the role of the urban Community Development Councils (CDC) in the implementation of the Sri Lanka Million Houses Programme in the mid-1980s.

Strategies: The Example of Community Development Councils

These were neighbourhood councils that were elected or generally recognised and accepted by the community to manage local affairs and to represent it in negotiation with government and other authorities. Typically, they represented some 40 to 60 households and had a pivotal role in the development, improvement and management of housing and domestic infrastructure. In the case of the development of new housing areas in which the National Housing Development Authority and/or local council allocated land to a group of householders, the CDC was officially responsible for the demarcation of plots and the allocation of sites to individual households.

This entailed reaching a consensus on the extent and location of public open space and obtaining the agreement of all households on the distribution of individual sites. In slum and shanty upgrading projects, the CDC was responsible for the redistribution of land to allow for the provision of infrastructure, access and open space and for the recording and registration of land titles.

Through the CDC, the standard of infrastructure provision to the neighbourhood was established by debating the trade-off between the cost and level of amenity; for example, through the installation of communal water standpipes and latrines as opposed to individual facilities.

The pros and cons of relatively low initial capital investment in infrastructure which, in turn, required relatively higher maintenance efforts and costs to the community were also debated.

Investment in this kind of infrastructure, such as in polythene water distribution pipes, unlined storm water drains and unsurfaced access ways, was compared with the more conventional, higher-cost infrastructure that met official engineering standards.

The CDC was also officially responsible for the determination, by consensus, of planning standards and norms covering issues such as plot coverage and building set-backs from site boundaries. It was required to maintain public infrastructure; collect mortgage repayments, water tariffs and other service charges; manage public amenities like the local community centre (and even some its services such as classes, skill training, etc.).

In those communities where the Sri Lanka Million Houses Programme operated well, the Council served both as the local government and the administration, in the most immediate and democratic of senses. Low-income urban communities were directly in control of the management of their domestic environment and able to exercise their own priorities for the investment of their time, energy and resources in it.

In doing so, they relieved the urban and municipal councils of a major administrative burden which, in practice, few were staffed or equipped to exercise. However, a new responsibility was placed on government: that of providing the educational, training and advisory supports which enabled low-income households and CDCs to responsibly, and effectively, take decisions and exercise authority (UNCHS, 1987 and DPU/WEDC, 1989).

As indicated above, the adoption of an enabling strategy for housing and local development does not imply a reduction in the activities of municipal authorities, even where there is a well developed community sector and a strong NGO tradition. Inevitably, it entails a restructuring of local administrative responsibilities and acquisition of the kind of skills needed to provide appropriate support to low-income communities and households. For example, line officers become advisers and trainers.

It also requires a reappraisal of the processes for the administration of development controls and of the control legislation itself. For example, building by-laws and planning codes become performance specifications and guidelines for safe practice and sustainable development. For many budget lines, it means new units of account and possibly new accounting procedures, such as collective and community accounts instead of accounts and rolling budgets for individual household units.

RECOMMENDATIONS

Academic Assistance to the Shelter Sector

Institutions of higher education and research have an important contribution to make to initiating and helping to sustain the institutional change which is needed to support enabling shelter strategies. This contribution is not limited to the traditions of research and the education of new professionals but, perhaps more importantly, includes the application of research and learning to the provision of training and advice.

Whatever their policy intentions, and however desirable is their improved performance, most shelter-sector bureaucracies at the levels of both central and local government are so understaffed and hard pressed that senior management has little time in which to reflect on alternative strategic approaches, let alone design institutional changes for their implementation. External technical assistance that provides specialist professional and technical advisers to work at the level of policy and strategy formulation is welcome and can make a substantial impact.

Technical assistance can also be highly effective and is urgently needed for help with institutional development, capacity building and training for the design and implementation of new approaches and procedures for the provision of support to the production, maintenance and management of housing and environmental infrastructure. Such assistance may, or should, operate at a variety of different levels and in several different modes. These include:

- The training of trainers for local level capacity building on an extended scale;
- In-country programme/project related training for middle-level personnel of both public and non-governmental sectors;

139

- Policy workshops, conferences and carefully prepared and conducted study tours to expose senior decision makers to alternative approaches;
- Degree and diploma level education (i.e. overseas) and support for reforming and strengthening local education and training establishments; and
- The production and distribution of training materials and teaching aids.

In addition, such assistance often lends status and therefore acceptability to innovation and institutional change which in turn can be used to generate local political support (or patronage) that might not otherwise be forthcoming.

Increasing, it is being recognised that capital aid and cash subsidies generally are not the most effective way of supporting the shelter sector, even for the lowest income groups. The provision of technical co-operation to support institutional change and capacity building can clearly be very productive. Support for the devolution of responsibility and the deregulation of authority in the development and management of the domestic environment contributes directly to the enhancement of public sector productivity and indirectly to a reduction of some of the social costs of economic adjustment.

For example, giving security of tenure to land for housing and deregulating restrictive development controls, savings and surpluses are diverted into house building and improvement, creating jobs for the lowest-paid in both the formal- and the informal-sector construction industries. The devolution of responsibility for the maintenance and management of neighbourhood infrastructure and local services also creates some employment at no cost to the public sector. More importantly, it also enhances community cohesion and the development of informal local welfare support mechanisms which the public sector is unable to provide.

In summary, we are still talking about public participation. However, under the new paradigm it takes on a very different and much more complex meaning to what we understood by it in the 1960s and 1970s. In the days of aided-self-help and advocacy planning, community participation meant the participation of people in government programmes and projects. Now it means the participation of government in people's programmes. And although there has been a substantial increase in support to community groups in the organisation and management of their part of the process during the past few years, virtually no attention has been given to the restructuring of local government or to the retraining of public sector officials and professionals.

BIBLIOGRAPHY

Angel, S., R. Archer, S. Tanphipat, and E. Wegelin, eds., 1983, **Land for Housing the Urban Poor**, Select Books, Singapore.

Cotton, A. and R. Franceys, 1991, **Services for Shelter**, Liverpool University Press, Liverpool, UK.

Development Planning Unit (DPU), University College London, 1989, **DPU/ WEDC Galle Urban Project Manual**, Mimeo, London.

Hardoy, J. and D. Satterthwaite, 1989, **Squatter Citizen: Life in the Urban Third World**, Earthscan, London.

Harris, N., 1990, **Urbanisation, Economic Development and Policy in Developing Countries**, Development Planning Unit (DPU), University College London, DPU Working Paper No. 19, London.

Jorgensen, N., 1977, **Housing Finance for Low Income Groups**, HRDU, Nairobi.

McAuslan, P., 1985, **Urban Land and Shelter for the Poor**, Earthscan, London.

Mumtaz, B., 1991, **Housing Finance Manual for Developing Countries: A Methodology for Designing Housing Finance Institutions**, Development Planning Unit (DPU), London.

Turner, B., ed., 1988, **Building Community: A Third World Case Book**, BCB, London.

United Nations Centre for Human Settlements (Habitat), 1987, **Supporting Community Based Housing: Sri Lanka Demonstration Project**, Nairobi.

United Nations Centre for Human Settlements (Habitat), 1990, **People, Settlements, Environment and Development**, Nairobi.

United Nations Centre for Human Settlements (Habitat), 1990, **Roles, Responsibilities and Capabilities for the Management of Human Settlements**, Nairobi.

A NATIONAL ASSOCIATION OF LOCAL AUTHORITIES: ITS ROLE AND FUNCTIONS

Arthur Wiggers

ABSTRACT

The need for rapid growth in the social housing sector in Palestine requires concerted action. The commitment and close collaboration of all parties involved is a necessary prerequisite to achieve quantitative objectives and their even distribution socially and geographically. Not only are complementary activities needed between the public and the private sectors, but also between the various levels within the public sector.

Legislation and planning at the national level, and regulation and planning at the regional and local levels, must complement each other if success is to be achieved. Based on the experience of the Netherlands, this paper describes how a national association of local authorities can play a key role in achieving co-ordination between the central and local levels. It also describes the services such an association can provide to its members to help them in the process of urban development. Some basic organisational aspects will also be discussed.

THE ASSOCIATION OF NETHERLANDS MUNICIPALITIES (VNG)

The VNG was founded in 1912, at a time when municipalities in the Netherlands were assuming increasingly larger responsibilities in various fields such as housing, health care, transport, garbage collection, education and law enforcement. Its foundation therefore responded to a real need for better information, improved communication, and institutionalised consultations between municipalities and the central government on the one hand, and between the municipalities themselves on the other.

The association also brought financial advantages for the members, as purchasing activities were combined.

When it was founded, 26 municipalities became members. In the beginning, the office was small and the number of staff was limited. The advantages for the membership, both financially and in terms of services, soon became obvious. As time went by, more and more local authorities joined the association, and since 1950, all Dutch municipalities have become members. Membership, however, has always been on a voluntary basis.

Today, the association employs approximately 500 people and is renowned for its high level of expertise in local government affairs. It has become, on behalf of its members, an established partner for other tiers of government.

MAIN FUNCTIONS

The main functions of the VNG (or indeed of most national municipal associations) can be summarised as follows:

- It acts as an intermediary between central and local governments (including the collective representation of member municipalities);
- It provides services and advice to member municipalities (whether on an individual or collective basis); and
- It provides a forum for members to exchange both experience and know-how.

How these functions are performed, and which priorities are set, is determined by the specific needs of the members. At all times however, the guiding principle is the promotion of good quality within local government in order to allow the decentralised local authorities to act in the best possible interests of the people.

INTERMEDIARY ROLE

Many national laws must be implemented at the local level. Many of the needs defined at the local level demand policy changes at the national level. The public administration can function well only if the different tiers of government appreciate and understand each other's role. This presupposes, of course, that open communication between these tiers exist. A national association of local authorities can therefore be instrumental in creating the conditions in which the central government and local authorities can effectively complement each other. Provided that the association has a broad-based membership, it can act as a valuable channel of communication between the central and local levels of authority.

The VNG has regular consultations with the Minister of Home Affairs. The VNG advises and comments on proposed legislation and on bills that have been presented to Parliament. The policy makers maintain a high level of consultation with almost all central government departments, much of it through informal contacts such as the telephone. Negotiations in departmental working groups are, of course, common practice and furthermore, the VNG has representatives in a large number of advisory bodies throughout central government.

Representation is one of the pillars of VNG's legitimacy. With all the local authorities as members, the association obviously wants to take into account the overall interests of good (local) government, and not just the particular interests of certain local authorities. It must also be strictly neutral in party politics. With an eye to this, the VNG strongly involves the members in the preparation of its positions. The points of view of the VNG are carefully prepared in committees of local administrators. The composition of these committees reflects the variety of political parties in the councils as well as the variety of large and small, urban and rural, wealthy and poor municipalities. There are committees for all fields of municipal activity.

After preparatory discussions within the committees, the Board of Directors and the Executive Committee, or the Governing Board, decide on the views to be expressed on behalf of all municipalities. In the case of very important subjects, special meetings are sometimes held before the VNG adopts a definite viewpoint.

Dissenting opinions are not heard very often. Specific groups of municipalities do plead, however, for the attention of central government to their specific problems. This applies in particular to the four largest municipalities (Amsterdam, Rotterdam, The Hague and Utrecht), whose size and complexity gives their administrative problems an extra dimension.

In the discussions between the Big Four and the central government, the VNG takes part with the aim of representing the interests of all other municipalities.

In order to perform its intermediary role well, the VNG has to take into account an important factor: the quality of its argument. Continual contact with members, both through the association's bodies and in daily work, ensures that the ideas and proposals put forward to central government reflect the reality as well as the needs and possibilities of local government. A highly qualified staff ensures that these ideas and proposals are compatible with legislation, taxation requirements, etc.

SERVICES AND ADVICE

A substantial part of the activities of the VNG is the provision of services and advice to its members. Municipalities have a wide range of tasks and responsibilities, for which they receive financial support and for which they employ staff. To do their jobs well, both the staff and the administrators sometimes need professional advice. The VNG's staff collectively possess a body of expertise that an individual municipality could never afford to acquire on its own. The VNG's expertise is accessible to all member-municipalities on an equal basis, i.e. without extra charges.

In many cases, the provision of services (information) and advice to municipal administrators and officers is related to:

- The right application of laws and regulations with a relevance for municipalities;
- The policy development of the central government insofar as it is important to municipalities;
- The financial aspects of the municipal administration; and
- The experiences of other local authorities in their policy development.

Services and advice are provided in different ways, such as the following:

- Individually over the telephone, in writing or in direct consultation. Most of the time this is done by officers of the different specialised policy departments.
- By making available publications, documents, professional literature including jurisprudence, through the specialised library and document-ation services department.
- Collectively, through different means such as:

  * circular letters to all members;
  * newsletters on specific issues;
  * model by-laws;
  * loose-leaf publications and handbooks on specific fields of local government;
  * brochures, books and a weekly magazine;
  * seminars, information-meetings and courses (most often on payment).

Among the VNG's most widely used resources are its model by-laws. For example, all municipalities are required by law to have separate by-laws controlling the quality of construction, prescribing building and safety codes, and regulating the distribution of available housing. Model by-laws on these subjects developed by the VNG and provided to all its members save them much effort and considerable expense. Crucially, such model by-laws are written so that they can be easily adapted by an individual municipality to its own specific circumstances.

Model by-laws and other published materials are edited and distributed through VNG's own publishing house. All the members receive one copy of all publications free of charge. Extra copies can be obtained upon payment.

INSTITUTIONALISED EXCHANGE AMONG MEMBERS

In situations where local authorities are confronted with either new challenges or rapidly changing circumstances, meetings with colleagues can be both fruitful and productive. If common problems exist, common solutions can be discussed and formulated. Additionally, less experienced or less equipped local authorities can profit from the know-how of their more experienced counterparts.

Through the regular organisation of conferences, training seminars, and similar events, a national association can provide an institutional forum in which information, experiences, and know-how are shared and exchanged among members, often with tangible results. Through the compilation and distribution of relevant documentation and databases, the VNG is also able to increase the utility of such meetings.

In 1994, the VNG organised 190 conferences and similar events, with the number of participants totalling almost 20,000. Approximately half the events were organised on the initiative of the VNG itself, while the other half were organised as a result of the initiative of various ministries, municipalities and/or professional associations of municipal officers.

Local administrators have the opportunity to meet colleagues in both the VNG committees and in the meetings of the provincial branches of the association. The function of the forum is particularly evident during the annual two-day congress; it provides great opportunities for both mutual contact and discussions about current policies. Usually, the congress is attended by approximately 2,000 municipal administrators.

In 1996, the congress theme will be related to the management of human settlements. Long-term developments such as population growth, the increased mobility of people, increased criminality, etc. will have an important impact on people's lives. The congress is expected to discuss the consequences of these developments for municipal policy-making. Issues surrounding such long-term developments will be raised, i.e. how local authorities can either influence or affect such developments and how and where such new settlements should be built.

ORGANISATIONAL ASPECTS

As the above demonstrates, an association of local authorities is generally more effective if it has a broad base membership. The more representative it is of all local authorities, the more important it becomes as an effective channel for communication, both as a platform for discussion as well as a consultation partner for national government. To be fully representative, the association must maintain an interest in involving member authorities in the formulation of its policies.

The VNG's General Assembly, which meets once a year during the annual congress, approves the association's accounts, considers amendments to its constitution and sets membership fees. It also elects the Governing Board, taking into account that the composition of the Board should reflect the existence of large and small municipalities and that the members should be representatives from all geographical parts of the country.

The president of the VNG is elected by the General Assembly on the recommendation of the Governing Board. An Executive Committee is formed from within the Governing Board.

The Governing Board is in charge of the management of the association. It meets once every two months. It approves the budget and appoints the members of the VNG committees. The Executive Committee meets at least once a month. It prepares the agenda for the Governing Board and supervises the execution of its decisions. Furthermore, it handles matters that require immediate attention. VNG delegations consulting the Government or Parliament mostly consist of members of the Governing Board and the Board of Directors.

Another important and more permanent way for members to be involved in the development of the association's policy development is through its standing committees, composed of elected representatives. A key criterion in the composition of these committees is that the various categories of municipalities have a well-balanced representation. Equally, all regions of the country are proportionately represented. And most importantly, such considerations are not permitted to interfere with the quality of the committees; their members must also be experts in the subjects their committee addresses.

It will become obvious that the daily activities of the association, such as the provision of services and advice to the members, the preparation of policy and points of view, are assumed by VNG staff in The Hague, led by the Board of Directors.

An important issue to raise is obtaining the funding for many of the activities of this national association. In the Netherlands, the members of the VNG pay an annual subscription fee according to a sliding scale (determined according to population). In exchange for this fee, they receive a package of basic services. For certain additional services, they are required to pay supplementary fees. Other sources of income are the profits of the VNG's Central Purchasing Agency (which also supplies many of its members) and of the VNG's publishing section. Additionally, the VNG is reimbursed by the central government (and at times by other institutions as well) for work on special projects.

THE INSTITUTIONAL FABRIC OF URBAN DEVELOPMENT

A.B. Zahlan

ABSTRACT

Urban development is a long-term, complex and difficult activity. It is synonymous with the management of national space with a view to meeting cultural, social and economic needs. The process calls for vision, policies and institutions.

The Arabs have considerable historical experience in urban planning. Of particular interest is the fact that the institutional fabric was always central to the planning and functioning of the Islamic city (Amirahmdi and El-Shakhs, 1993; Rivlin and Helmer, 1980 which contains an extensive and useful bibliography; Panzac, 1991; Robinson, 1992; Serjeant, 1976).

This paper aims to highlight the institutional dimension. Reconciling the many demands on urban space and urban services calls for a diligent understanding of the interactions of these demands in the context of current and emerging technologies. Becker and Steele (1994) have examined the constraints that a traditional environment places on modern business, and the ways and means to transform the workplace into an instrument for the promotion of organisational efficiency.

Urban development encompasses many and diverse elements: community life, work and employment, financial policies, the construction industry and infrastructure. Public policies concerning physical planning, property rights, telecommunications, education and public health determine the type of development that is possible.

Unless urban development is consciously and actively pursued, chaos will prevail. The management of personal and public needs must be mediated by institutions, government, non-governmental organisations (NGOs), municipalities, chambers of commerce, financial bodies, centres of research and development (R&D) if these needs are to be met in an equitable fashion.

This paper dwells on this aspect of the challenge and aims to draw attention to the importance of institutional involvement in the formation of urban policies.

The Significance of the Institutional Fabric

As a result of the past 100 years of dispossession and dispersal, Palestinian institutions have been weakened and marginalised: the dispossession of Palestinians included being stripped of their institutions which could provide identity and sustain continuity. Consequently, they find themselves with weak institutions in a truncated country fragmented by Israeli settlements and continuing military occupation.

During the last 50 years, Palestinians have sought with great determination to recreate the institutions which have been destroyed. The best known of these efforts at institution building have already received attention (Brand, 1985; Robinson, 1992). But the relentless pressure of the occupying power has stripped the Palestinians of their land and property and has gone a long way towards reducing Palestinian control over many aspects of urban life and policies.

Two years after the signing of the Oslo Agreement and the accompanying international meetings to organise pledges of assistance, economic conditions are worse than ever. An indication of the extent of the calamity is provided by the fact that by the end of June 1995, *only* 112 construction contracts had been awarded with a total committed value of just $58.5 million (PECDAR, 1995). Contrast this small sum with the multi-billion dollar promises of international assistance.

Two major causes for this lack of performance are: the inadequacy of Palestinian institutions; and the lack of assistance in redressing this inadequacy.

World Trends

A number of technological and managerial developments over the last 50 years have had a considerable impact on the use and planning of urban areas. The major revolutions have been in information technology, energy efficiency, environmental management (water, waste disposal and air quality), transport systems, adapting built space to the needs of the physically disabled and disaster management.

The revolution in information technology has had, and continues to have, a massive impact on all aspects of urban life and organisation. Its secondary effects have been the restructuring of governments, municipalities and companies. We shall return to this aspect later.

Technological change has had a considerable impact on the cohesiveness of all societies: the nature of work, the transformation of jobs

150

brought about by the computer, the transformation of commercial and financial organisations brought about by the combined effects of tele-working, globalisation and intensive competition have had a marked impact on human relations.

Telecommunications have also made world knowledge accessible to anyone with a modern telecommunications system and a computer. Tele-communications are now enabling remote medical centres to access information to obtain detailed and low-cost diagnoses and advisory services. These services are influencing the size and design of hospitals and will have an impact on choice of location.

In business, where access to information has become vital, telecom-munications have been playing a greater role in providing partners in any transaction with immediate access to vast databases.

There are many social, bureaucratic and cultural consequences of these changes. Heckscher (1995) finds that rigid staff loyalty has become a liability to a firm; the traditional association of members of the same family, neighbourhood and village/town results in rigidities which could become counter-productive in a social, cultural and economic sense. He considers that the predominant trends are toward greater mobility of staff, a higher rate of change in the membership of functional groups in firms and openness to ideas and information originating outside the firm. All these changes have implications for urban planning, because they call for greater mobility and connectivity of the population.

Palestinians must incorporate these and other current advances into the design of urban areas in order both to respond to technological changes and to sustain their own cultural traditions.

The opportunity to benefit from achievements taking place in the rest of the world have a price: they call for strong institutions and collective behaviour. We have a tendency to operate on an individual level, rather than to work through consensus and in a participatory fashion. The development of institutions would be instrumental in overcoming these old habits.

URBAN POLICIES, TECHNOLOGY, NATIONAL UNITY AND SOCIAL COHESION

The management of urban development calls for a balance between conflicting demands. These demands are associated with work and resi-dential areas, cultural and educational infrastructure, physical infrastructure, protection from natural and man-made hazards, the needs of the physically disabled, the enhancement of the aesthetic quality of the environment, the cost and economic efficiency of the system, pol-lution, waste disposal and health standards.

Optimally, a society must provide for the needs of its community at

Table 1 Population distribution in the West Bank and Gaza, 1990.

Zone	Total	Urban		Semi-Urban		Rural		Refugee camps	
		Number	%	Number	%	Number	%	Number	%
West Bank	1,604,810	401,792	25.0	357,105	22.3	737,932	46.0	107,980	6.7
Gaza Strip	894,984	372,572	41.6	69,211	7.7	181,263	20.3	271,930	30.4

Source: Abdul-Hadi, Rami (Centre for Engineering and Planning, Ramallah) 1994. 'Construction and Housing in the West Bank and Gaza Strip', United Nations Conference on Trade And Development, UNCTAD/ECDC/SEU/4.

various levels of gross national product (GNP). Without strong institutions, it is impossible to cope with such a high level of complexity. The task is extremely difficult and calls for intensive community participation in decision-making.

In an industrial society, each of the above requirements is dealt with by a different organisation: municipalities; ministries of housing, public works, finance, justice, tourism, health; the courts, schools and universities, private companies, NGOs, professional associations of engineers, and others. The harmonious collaboration of these different organisations cannot be induced and managed without institutions.

Rapid urban development provides an opportunity to redress past mutilations and put in place new institutional machinery to cope with them. Hence the opportunity and challenge.

What Kind of Urbanisation?

Palestine is one of the Arab countries whose population has been traditionally dispersed uniformly. More than 50 per cent of the population still lives in small towns which have a population of less than 5,000. Table 1 summarises the available information on Palestinian human geography. The data leaves much to be desired; it is hoped that the new Palestine Bureau of Statistics will soon be able to supply more detailed and reliable data.

The present geographic distribution may be changed with relative ease during the next ten years because some 200,000 new housing units will be built during this period. What, where and how these new housing units will be built will determine the urban future of Palestine.

Will Palestinians choose to build in the rural areas to reduce the cost of land, and to retain the present social fabric of Palestine? Or, will they choose to concentrate on a few urban centres and restructure the human geography of Palestine?

These decisions are of immense importance at all levels: strategic, economic, social and cultural. It is thus vital that any decision be taken after full and active debate among civil and public organisations. This is why a number of papers are presented in this monograph on this subject.

Many Third World capitals have grown through rural migration, with the result that cities have been ruralised. As a result, basic urban institutional infrastructure failed to emerge.

A modern city is expected to provide its inhabitants with a vast range of services: medical, educational (schools, universities and R&D centres), cultural (museums, theatres), financial and business support and information. It is this large array of institutions that distinguishes a city from a ruralised settlement. The objective of urban planning is to identify those policies which encourage the evolution of critical urban institutions.

Furthermore, at present, the nature of work worldwide is undergoing massive and rapid change: teleworking and outsourcing are revolutionising modern industrial organisations and management systems; it is no longer necessary for people to work in the same building. Swissair, for example, sub-contracts its accounting to a company in India. Many companies allow their staff to work from home; major industrial firms sub-contract the manufacturing of 70 per cent or more of their components to small firms. All these changes have had a massive influence on international trade and the development of cities.

The public debate concerning urban policies is of the highest importance and urgency. This debate cannot be conducted piece-meal; it must involve all the key actors in society.

National Unity

Despite an acute sense of personal commitment to their cause, Palestinians have undergone far-reaching and divergent development. Naturally, their experiences have resulted in a diversification of their patterns of social, political, economic and cultural behaviour. These differences could become sources of strength or weakness, depending on how they are viewed.

The consequences of 50 years of enforced separation between the West Bank and Gaza has resulted in some alienation between them, as the recent studies by Shikaki demonstrate (Shikaki, 1994). The separate development of Palestinian communities in various parts of the world has already produced differing attitudes regarding common problems.

Palestinians have accumulated a vast and rich experience: they have lived and worked in many countries and this could enrich their culture. Diversity could enhance creativity; but it could also lead to dysfunctional behaviour and fragmentation.

Therefore, planners must give considerable attention to the social dimensions of urban planning: the relationships between camp refugees and city residents; the relationships between residents of different areas;

153

and the many-faceted relationships between diaspora and homebased Palestinians.

First, urban planners have to undo the effects of many years of Israeli attempts at fragmentation. Second, Palestinians have to develop powerful national and international methods to recover expropriated lands and property. Third, planners have to work with the consequences of having separate communities in the diaspora.

Sensitive and serious consideration of all these aspects cannot be the result of hasty and superficial planning: extensive sociological fieldwork is needed to identify intelligent and creative solutions.

Universities, NGOs, independent scholars and consulting firms should undertake extensive social studies. The results of such studies have to be debated and discussed and then incorporated into urban planning.

Social Cohesion

The structure of a village and a town has serious implications to social cohesion. In traditional Arab towns, for example, houses are built very close to one another and inhabitants have no choice but to interact; by contrast, the California-style model which has been blindly adopted in many Arab cities encourages distances between neighbours and makes the car essential to daily life.

Distances between houses obviously reduce the chances of informal encounters between neighbours; they also increase the cost of housing and infrastructure enormously. The adoption of California-style urban methods by societies where per capita income is at best 10 per cent of the California level inevitably results in an increase in the slum areas which are created to meet the high cost of well-to-do areas of the city.

Urban Policies

During the next 20 years, a combination of mobility, the return of diaspora Palestinians and the natural doubling of the population are bound to increase the population in the West Bank and Gaza from the present level of some 3 million to 9 million or more. This high rate of population change will be accompanied by the massive construction of some 1,000,000 housing units and a large number of hotels, offices, industrial plants, hospitals, schools and universities.

In other words, an opportunity exists for the radical transformation of the urban character of Palestine. Therefore, it is important to initiate a far-reaching debate among Palestinians about what type of urban environment to choose. The search for useful answers cannot be conducted without stable and dedicated institutions.

Obviously, the urban character of a society is decided as a result of a large number of micro- and macro-decisions over a number of years. Urban policies result from the process of reconciling a wide variety of views, including those held by developers and local government, with the tastes and wishes of the people.

Palestine is a relatively small country. Physical distances are not great. The restrictions imposed by years of occupation have made short distances appear further than they are, but urban policies cannot be decided on the basis of this unnatural experience.

During the last 50 years, many developments have taken place worldwide; the car and the computer have transformed distance and the nature of work; and outsourcing and subcontracting have reduced the importance of large agglomerations of population.

Sound urban policies have to consider the geography of work, and the location of schools and medical facilities. Obviously, small villages with a population of less than 5,000 cannot expect to have all the necessary social services. However, it is relatively easy for a constellation of five or more villages to co-operate to conveniently locate all required services. Given intelligent planning, it is possible for a small community to develop its own local industrial or agricultural interests.

Environmental Considerations

The high density of urban populations and the expectations for a long and quality life have caused people everywhere to focus increasingly on their interactions with the environment. Palestine covers a very small area of land and is densely populated. This can only increase. Thus Palestinians have to be very concerned with environmental issues.

The lack of serious attention to these problems during the last 50 years means that the Palestinians today are faced with an accumulated load of environmental problems. The most pressing issues now are concerned with the provision of sewerage, clean water and refuse disposal facilities. Fortunately, the technical aspects of such issues have been solved elsewhere. The challenge is to select the best and most economical solutions, and implement them in ways that can guarantee high quality and low cost.

Industrial pollution is still at a low level. But this could increase very rapidly if the effects of industry are ignored. Power plants, cement production and the intensive use of agricultural fertilisers and agro-chemicals have immediate and substantial polluting effects, as do most industries.

The process of integrating industrial and urban development with sensible environmental policies calls for institutional development. First, there has to be extensive social and cultural awareness of all these matters; second, widespread public debate and discussion must take place to familiarise people with the costs and benefits of various alternatives.

155

The alternative to sound environmental planning is severe damage to the health and economy of the population. The Arab countries have a very poor record in this domain. In December, 1994, the World Bank presented a report on the serious environmental situation in the Arab region to the Sixth Session of the Council of Arab Ministers Responsible for the Environment. In it, the annual cost of the consequences of the present environmental conditions were estimated at $10 billion a year, or 3 per cent of gross domestic product (GDP).

Ultimately, people will question the performance of government and accuse it of incompetence and an abuse of power. In an interesting paper, Ahmed Shawky (1994) discusses the legal accountability of the Arab state in the environmental field.

Municipal Government

Municipal government is central to sound urban development. It plays a decisive role in all key areas of urbanisation: implementing national standards, adopting local policies to promote affordable housing, providing infrastructure and setting architectural standards.

Palestinians have to leapfrog and adopt the most suitable and relevant local government systems for the 21st Century. To catch up with 1967 or 1990 is insufficient.

A major challenge is to initiate participatory processes to evolve common objectives within each local authority; and then to explore the optimal ways to implement these objectives. In short, we need to develop powerful procedures and institutions that could undertake such planning.

An examination of international experience here could prove helpful. The Association of Netherlands Municipalities (VNG) was established by Dutch municipalities to share the cost of sound, high quality, and effective planning and to develop the tools to assist themselves. We are fortunate to have included a paper on the VNG experience in this Monograph.

In addition to the Dutch experience, another concept is now being widely adopted in the main industrial (OECD) countries: that the management of local authorities is a science and a business, and that it is possible to separate their political functions from their management functions. The elected officers serve on a municipal board, while the day-to-day technical affairs are run by professional managers and technicians.

Many Palestinian cities are the custodians of a rich cultural heritage which includes living museums. The full flowering of these historical resources is an important responsibility of municipalities; they are also major landmarks which could provide focal points for a prosperous tourism sector.

It is clear from the above that municipalities will require a considerable institutional structure to enable them to play their full role in local development.

URBANISATION AND TELECOMMUNICATIONS

The development of telecommunications in Palestine will have a direct and profound impact on urbanisation. An efficient, high-capacity telecommunications system with low operating costs is essential. The development of joint urban and telecommunications policies is vital: the two have an immediate and direct influence on cultural, political and economic life.

The PNA is presently deciding its telecommunications policy. Telecommunications could liberate Palestinians from the confining structures imposed on them, and provide them with worldwide links.

Information-based Services

The computer has transformed modern life. Palestinians must design their cities for the future and focus on the integral relationships that exist between urban and information policies. This section provides examples of these relationships and discusses access to international knowledge, teleworking, outsourcing, industry-related services and teleshopping.

Office Building, Employment and Teleworking

Teleworking is already a major activity in industrial countries, and will no doubt grow rapidly in Palestine. Its impact on office space, transport facilities and the nature (size and location) of towns and cities is far reaching. For example, IBM reduced its requirement for office space in the UK from 4 million square feet to 2 million square feet in the short span of three years. The company saved £60 million ($95 million) a year in operating costs (London, 1995). IBM is not unique in this respect: almost all major organisations have opted for teleworking.

Teleworking has many other positive consequences, apart from the savings in office space. These include reduced costs for transport and commuting time, and an impressive improvement in labour productivity, which is estimated at 25 per cent (Wheelwright, 1995).

The telewired society also has negative aspects: loneliness and isolation. But this could be avoided: sound urban planning could easily compensate for such developments through the juxtaposition of houses and public recreational areas where people can meet. Here, the model of an Arab and/or Islamic city could provide good examples of what can be done in this respect.

Outsourcing and Industry-Related Services

Many large firms and organisations in industrial countries have adopted a policy of outsourcing. It is more profitable to outsource a great deal of their routine office work (such as personnel management and accounting, editing and publishing, printing and computing) as well the manufacture of many components and parts.

The extent of outsourcing is formidable. Some organisations encourage their staff to resign and re-organise in order to provide their former employers with the requisite services. Others outsource in a foreign country; e.g. Swissair outsources its management services in India while a Swedish pharmaceutical firm outsources some of its R&D requirements to an Indian firm which it helped to establish.

Palestinians have excelled in consulting, contracting, finance, insurance, accounting and management. It is very likely that the economy of Palestine will move towards the export of these and other similar services, but this will depend on high quality telecommunications.

One of the fastest areas of outsourcing is in computer services. Electronic Data Services (EDS), for example, is a US company which employs 85,000 workers to provide all the computer needs of certain organisations, these include Xerox (worldwide), the Inland Revenue (UK) and the Dutch rail system (Jackson, 1995; van de Krol, 1995). The annual turnover of EDS is around $9 billion in a market that is worth some $19 billion in all.

Tele-education

Telecommunication technologies have brought educational institutions to students. Distance learning technologies are currently being incorporated into traditional learning systems. These technologies, which are based on efficient telecommunications systems, could become enormously important for the development of Palestinian education.

Teleshopping and Telebanking

Teleshopping is a fast growing business in many industrial countries. Telecommunication technologies have made it possible for shoppers to view goods on their home screens, place orders and pay for them, all from the comfort of their own homes. Telebanking is already advanced and such services are being rapidly diffused already. These services promise to change the shape of shopping and transport systems.

Changes in social customs are slow, and it will take at least 25 years for a substantial transformation to take place. But it is important to take these possible changes into consideration because of their obvious and considerable implications for urban planning.

THE ECONOMICS OF URBANISATION

The construction industry is the instrument through which urbanisation is undertaken. Because it is generally recognised as the major locomotive, the construction industry sets the tone for the national economy.

When, as at present, the local contents of construction (minus the cost of land) are about 30 per cent of construction costs, urbanisation becomes a drain on the economy and has to be permanently subsidised. In order for construction to become the locomotive of the economy, local contents have to be increased to more than 80 per cent of construction costs.

The cost of land constitutes an important proportion; this is much higher in cities than in villages. Furthermore, cities require more roads, parking facilities and infrastructure per inhabitant for the same quality of life than do small towns. Therefore, unless there is a good reason to do otherwise, it is more economical, and often healthier, to live in small towns.

Palestinians will need to promote considerable public discussion, research and planning before they optimise their limited land resources. Furthermore, they will need to develop suitable and effective methods to manage decision-making in this complex area.

Housing: Social And Normal

A variety of financial services are required to facilitate social (i.e. subsidised) and normal (i.e. self-financed) housing. Social housing calls for various amounts of subsidies depending on the ultimate owner. These subsidies have to be raised through taxation or international assistance. The availability of subsidies is always limited and in short supply, so the process has to be carefully regulated to ensure that only *bona fide* candidates receive them.

Normal housing should depend on well-regulated and efficient financial markets. All parties in these transactions should be protected. The provision of a secure environment for the lender and the borrower calls for powerful economic and legal institutions.

Sale of Public Land

There is considerable pressure on the PNA to release public land for private use. Various arrangements are being considered. This is an issue of considerable importance and calls for extensive public debate on how to undertake it in an equitable manner.

The Ministry of Planning is undertaking the development of a programme in physical planning. The sale of land should be co-ordinated with a long-term view of land use. Land is scarce, and will become scarcer as the population increases. It is vital that whatever policy is adopted, it takes into consideration the long-term view of urban requirements.

Fiscal and Financial Policies

A critical challenge is how to develop effective and modern financial services to enable citizens to plan and build affordable homes for themselves. A number of articles in this book cover this from a wide variety of angles.

Financial instruments could be utilised to promote the concentration and/or dispersal of population. Suitable taxation policies could be developed, together with the introduction of various financial services to promote desirable urban development. For example, developers and contractors prefer cities to rural areas. In order to encourage them to address the needs of small villages, sufficient tax incentives could ultimately redress the balance in favour of the rural areas; the consequent reduction in the need for heavy city infrastructure would pay for these incentives.

The Economy, Employment and Urban Policies

Employment and urban policies are interdependent, and therefore the integration of medium and long-term economic planning with urban planning is vital. It is essential that suitable mechanisms between local governments and the relevant ministries and organisations be developed in order to integrate future economic activities with the local urban fabric.

THE INTERFACE BETWEEN NGOS, PRIVATE AND PUBLIC SECTORS

Palestinian urban development involves a large number of institutions other than those of central government; for example, some 14 to 16 per cent of Palestine is the property of Muslim and Christian *awqaf.* These are the custodians of our architectural and physical inheritance. The organisations of the *awqaf* should have a say regarding the formation of our cities and towns. The development of harmonious relationships between the *awqaf* and the public and private sectors is central to the prosperity, and efficient development, of Palestinian urban centres.

160

SCIENCE AND TECHNOLOGY

Urban development refers to the maintenance, renovation and construction of a wide variety of structures. The construction industry is one of the largest sectors of the economy in all developing countries; in the Arab world, it is the largest economic activity. Few people realise that the total Arab expenditure on all types of construction is larger than its oil income!

In Palestine, the construction industry is by far the largest economic activity, and it plays a vital role in both the domestic and export markets. We have already noted that diaspora Palestinians have excelled in the provision of construction services. For this reason, the science and technology of construction should occupy an important place in planning.

Research work on all activities connected with construction has been taking place around the world for a long time. Palestinians could benefit immediately from this vast experience. But to do so, we need to establish and develop the basic institutional infrastructure of an adequate science and technology system.

Such a system should aim to integrate activities in construction with standards and codes, professional organisations, bureaux of statistics, municipal government, R&D activities, access to information (hence telecommunications), financial services, higher education and technical training, industrial production and data bases on products and services.

The Construction Industry

The construction industry is the physical tool through which architectural plans are translated into fixed assets. Therefore, it is essential for the achievement of national goals.

Diaspora Palestinians have excelled in the establishment and development of world-class consulting and contracting firms. The annual turnover of these contracting firms may be around $2 to 4 billion. According to Marwan Abdel Hameed, more than 56,000 Palestinians have earned degrees in various engineering fields. Thus the real problem is not to educate more engineers, but how to make profitable and constructive use of the available expertise.

If the process of urbanisation is carefully managed, it should provide unparalleled opportunities for the development of holistic and comprehensive skills in all aspects of urbanisation.

It would not be sensible to seek to compete in those heavy industries which provide building materials and supplies such as cement, iron bars, paint, and industrial ceramics. Instead, Palestinians should aim to complement Arab expertise.

Palestinians should apply their expertise to the production of items

161

where there is considerable value added, such as the manufacture of kitchen furniture, specialised ergonomic furniture for offices and hospitals, high quality furniture for hotels and schools, central air conditioning systems, energy-efficient heating systems, elevators, devices for modern intelligent buildings, safety and security systems, and so on.

One of the most common Third World problems is how to provide shelter at affordable prices to all members of society. Despite much thought and deliberation on how to respond to this challenge, most people in the Third World, including Palestine, still do not have access to suitable homes. This poses a major R&D challenge in Palestine.

WAYS FORWARD

Palestinians face grave uncertainties. The most fundamental are those involving land and property, transport and security. Thus the challenge is how to build a future under conditions of maximum distress and constraints. Here, post-industrial technology could offer real and practical solutions.

The Palestinian community is young with a high level of investment in education. With some effort and a modern telecommunications system, Palestinians could be transformed by steadfastly seeking to enter the new world of the 21st Century.

Mitchell (1995) examines the changes that are taking place in the real world today as a consequence of the revolution in telecommunications and information technology. He discusses their implications to urban space, architecture, city planning, occupations and human relations. The author provides a glimpse of a new world in the making where the old concepts of property, identity, movement and expression will no longer apply in old, familiar ways.

Palestinians have been deprived of a great deal, including access to space and transport facilities, and they have been immersed in a hostile environment for many decades. The only way out is through cyberspace, i.e. through a modern telecommunications system and a computer literate society. The acquisition of information technology would allow Palestinians to work in a foreign country while remaining at home. It would also allow them to access any museum and library in the world without having to travel or order a book, to shop without leaving home, and countless other possibilities. In this way, they could avoid the hostilities surrounding them.

To free themselves from the shackles of the present, Palestinians need to travel rapidly towards the 21st Century and join the cyberworld. They have little choice: they could either endure continued repression and economic terrorism, or seek liberation through cyberspace.

BIBLIOGRAPHY

Amirahmadi, Hooshang and Salah El-Shakhs, eds., 1993, **Urban Development in the Muslim World**, Centre for Urban Policy Research, New Jersey.

Becker, Franklin and Fritz Steele, 1994, **Workplace by Design: Mapping the High-Performance Workspace**, Jossey-Bass Publishers, San Francisco.

Brand, Laurie A., 1985, **Building the Bridge of Return: Palestinian Corporate Mobilisation in Egypt, Kuwait and Jordan**, vols. 1 and 2, Ph.D. Dissertation, Columbia University, New York.

Heckscher, Charles, 1995, **White Collar Blues: Management Loyalties in an Age of Corporate Restructuring**, Harper Collins, New York.

Hourani, A.H. and S.M. Stern, eds., 1970, **The Islamic City**, Bruno Cassirer Limited, Oxford.

Jackson, Tony, 1995, 'EDS Is Getting To Know All About You,' **Financial Times**, 18 April.

Jacobs, Jane, 1984, **Cities and the Wealth of Nations**, Penguin Books Limited, Middlesex, UK.

London, Simon, 1995, 'The Mobile Office,' **Financial Times**, 10 March.

Mitchell, William J., 1995, **City of Bits: Space, Place, and the Infobahn**, The MIT Press, Cambridge, Massachusetts.

Panzac, Daniel, 1991, **Les Villes dans L'Empire Ottoman: Activites et Societes**, CNRS, Paris.

PECDAR, 1995, **PECDAR Emergency Rehabilitation Project**, Progress Report Inception Through June 30, 1995, Jerusalem.

Rivlin, Helen Anne B. and Katherine Helmer, eds., 1980, **The Changing Middle Eastern City**, Centre for Social Analysis and the Program in Southwest Asian and North African Studies of the State University of New York at Binghamton, New York.

Robinson, Glenn Edward, 1992, **Creating Space: Organisation, Ideology, and Leadership in the Palestinian Intifada**, Ph.D. diss., University of California, Berkeley.

Roy, Sarah Mae, 1988, **Development Under Occupation: A Study of United States Government Economic Development Assistance to the Palestinian People in the West Bank and Gaza Strip**, 1975–1985. Ph.D. diss., Harvard University, Cambridge, Massachusetts.

Sergeant, R.B., ed., 1976, **The Islamic City**, Selected papers from the Colloquium held at the Middle East Centre, Faculty of Oriental Studies, Cambridge, UK, 19–23 July.

Shawky, Ahmed, 1994, 'The State Accountability for Harmful Impacts on Health Caused by Industrial Pollution in Egypt,' **Third World Legal Studies**, 1993; Law, Accountability and Development: Challenges and Response; Legal Methodologies of Accountability, pp 135–160, International Third World Legal Studies Association and The Valparaiso University School of Law, Valparaiso, Indiana.

Shikaki, Khalil, 1994, **The Future Political and Administrative Relations between the West Bank and the Gaza Strip**, PASSIA, Jerusalem.

Troin, Jean-François, ed., 1993, **Urban Research on the Middle East Comparative Approaches by German, British and French Geographers**, Urbama, Tours.

van de Krol, Ronald, 1995, 'EDS Wins Dutch Rail Contract,' **Financial Times**, 14 June.

Wheelwright, Geoffrey, 1995, 'Teleworkers Gain More Flexibility,' **Financial Times**, 7 June.

Theme Two
LAND USE AND TENURE

LAND USE AND TENURE

Anthony Coon

ABSTRACT

This paper covers one of the six themes in this Monograph – *Land Use and Tenure*. Within the scope of this theme are questions relating to the most desirable way in which the physical development of Palestine should proceed in the future, the organisational mechanisms which would be most appropriate to ensure that the desired form of physical development does in fact occur, and questions relating to the ownership of land which will affect the planning of future development.

After a brief outline of the contextual framework, including the effects of military occupation, the scale of future development and national development objectives, the paper deals with organisational issues, such as government institutions, legislation, the planning system and planning controls. Physical planning options for development are dealt with in a subsequent section, including urban development location, new towns, transport, conservation and the refugee camps. The final section covers issues of land ownership, notably current problems and the provision of land for future development.

The purpose of the paper is to stimulate discussion about the best way in which to tackle the reconstruction of Palestine. The issues identified here appear to be among the most crucial – either because early decisions will have to be made, or because they seem likely to affect the overall success of the re-development task. However, the issues discussed in this paper are not the only ones that can be raised; nor are the options outlined here the only ones available. The primary purpose is to create an awareness of the choices to be made, and to provoke further discussion among the experts and interested parties who will help to formulate and implement plans for Palestinian reconstruction.

THE CONTEXT

The Effects of Military Occupation

The Israeli military occupation has had a dire impact on all issues dealt with in this paper – government institutions, development patterns and land ownership. These impacts have been quite extensively reported elsewhere, and those contributing to this Monograph are only too painfully aware of them. For these reasons, this paper does not dwell on the problems of the past, but instead focuses on the future. It seems likely that the organisational and policy framework which has been applied under the occupation will have to be almost completely replaced. Moreover, this will have to be done rapidly and in line with the emerging Palestinian government structures.

The Scale of Future Development

There is great uncertainty about the scale of future development. This will depend primarily on the rate at which Palestinians from the diaspora return to live in Palestine, and on the resources available to provide adequate accommodation for the existing inhabitants. Both of these in turn will depend largely on the economic prosperity of the country.

It does, however, seem very likely that it will be necessary to plan for an extremely rapid rate of development in the next few years – rapid in comparison with past rates of growth, with adjacent countries, and with international trends.

For the sake of illustration, we could make the following assumptions:

- That 1.5 million Palestinians from abroad will return over a ten-year period;
- That the refugee camps are to be transformed;
- That a significant improvement is to be made to other housing; and
- That current demographic trends continue.

Under these assumptions, there will need to be some 600,000 housing units built over a ten-year period, or an average of 60,000 a year. This is about *six times* the rate of house construction in recent years.

In terms of land needed for new urban development over the same ten-year time period, perhaps 630 square kilometres will be required. This is about *three times* the size of all the existing urban areas in Palestine, and would cover an area 50 times the size of the existing municipal area of Nablus, housing a population *30 times* as great.

Huge physical changes in Palestine are likely. Therefore, there is a the need for plans which are decisive yet flexible, for government administration which is sensitive to needs and opportunities, for a planning system which has strong legislation and efficient procedures, and for an adequate supply of land to be available to developers.

National Development Objectives

Questions of national spatial strategy which are largely determined by political priorities will inevitably arise. Two such issues which arise in planning elsewhere, and which will apply to Palestine are the relative growth of the different regions, and the growth of the capital city.

The Relative Growth of the Different Regions

Are there reasons why the different regions are likely to grow at different rates, or why national policy should encourage different rates of growth? Such reasons might include:

- Strategic/military considerations;
- Varying opportunities in the regions concerning, for example, land availability (which is lowest in Gaza, and most plentiful in the Jordan Valley), or the presence of exploitable natural resources; and
- Varying levels of attractiveness to Palestinian returnees.

Location of Capital City Functions

It will be necessary to make an early decision on where the major capital city functions are to be located, both for the immediate future and in the medium-term. Regardless of the precise choice of location for the main edifices which are symbolic of the State, consideration will also have to be given to the degree to which the main offices of the ministries should be concentrated or dispersed.

Concentration in the capital city. This is traditional practice in most countries, but can be criticised because of the unbalanced form of development which results.

Dispersal of ministry employment and government agencies to selected locations. This becomes ever more feasible with improvements in telecommunications.

ORGANISATIONAL ISSUES

Institutions

The planning system in Palestine (as in most other countries) has always been organised in a hierarchical system, with the decisions of each tier being subordinate to the one above. In the West Bank, three tiers were established under Jordanian law: the national government, the regional authorities and the local authorities [1]. The local authority tier is the municipality (for areas where a municipality exists). The three regional authorities are Nablus, Jerusalem and Hebron. The agency representing the national government is the Higher Planning Council (HPC), which consists of:

- The Minister of the Interior (who also serves as Chairman);
- The Mayor of the capital city;
- The Undersecretary of the Ministry of Public Works;
- The Undersecretary of the Ministry of Public Health;
- The head of the Construction Council;
- The head of the Housing Council;
- The head of the Central Planning Department; and
- The Chief Prosecutor.

Among the issues which need to be considered in relation to the future administration of planning in Palestine are the following.

Composition of the Higher Planning Council

The problem is to devise a body which can represent government opinion across the wide range of ministries concerned, and which has the necessary powers of co-ordination and implementation. It will be necessary to decide which ministries (or other government agencies) are represented on the HPC, and whether the members should be politicians or civil servants. Should the subsidiary tiers be represented on the HPC, and by whom? On the other hand, the HPC could be comprised of members of one ministry with a dominant role in the development process.

Responsibilities of the Higher Planning Council

The HPC must be able to co-ordinate the implementation of development with the planning of development. For this purpose, it may be necessary to give the HPC powers to influence the investment programmes of ministries, and responsibilities for allocating finance to private developers and development agencies. The HPC could also have responsibilities for designating and extending municipalities, and for designating and co-ordinating development agencies. If the HPC does not itself have these responsibilities, it will be necessary to ensure the necessary close co-ordination.

Establishing Development Agencies

The scale of the envisaged development task is such that consideration needs to be given to establishing agencies with specific tasks. These could be for certain types of development, such as housing or industry, or for the development of designated areas such as new towns, rundown inner city districts or urban conservation areas. Which agencies should be established, and to whom should they be responsible? How can overlaps and conflicts between them be minimised? How would they relate to the municipalities?

The Regional Tier

Is there a need for a regional tier of authority? If regional authorities are to be established to provide other services anyway, then there is no problem in giving them certain planning powers. The main scope for decision-making at the regional level appears to be in the areas outside the municipalities. On the other hand, the powers of the regions under the Jordanian system were not extensive, and a two-tier system (omitting the regional tier) would be simpler to understand.

The boundaries of the regional authorities could correspond to those which already exist (i.e. Gaza, and the areas centred on Nablus, Jerusalem and Hebron). Alternatively, the Nablus region could be sub-divided (i.e. into regions for Nablus, Tulkarem and Jenine), or an additional *Jordan Valley* region could be created.

The Local Tier

Questions to be considered here include criteria for the designation of additional municipalities, and the need for extending municipal boundaries. Outside the municipalities, are the village councils to have any planning powers? If not, are the local planning functions in these areas to be carried out by the regional authority, or by joint village councils, covering a population of, say, 25,000?

The Central Planning Department

There will, as envisaged in Jordanian law, need to be a technical body to advise the HPC (see *Composition of the HPC* above). If the responsibilities of the HPC are to include aspects of implementation, then any Central Planning Department (CPD) which is established will need to have skills in this field as well. The whole question of how to make the best use of the available technical expertise needs to be considered. Perhaps the CPD should (in addition to its function of advising the HPC) serve as a central pool of expertise available to municipalities to assist in carrying out their planning functions.

Legislation

Planning Legislation

Planning legislation in the West Bank is Jordanian law *No. 79* of 1966, and in Gaza the planning ordinance of 1936 enacted during the British Mandate (which is rather similar). These laws need to be standardised for the entire Palestinian territory, brought up to date to meet current best international practice, and adapted to meet current needs (i.e. to cope with very rapid growth). Two options are available.

1) *New legislation.* Preparation of new legislative proposals would be time consuming and appears therefore to be less appropriate than revising existing laws.
2) *Revised legislation.* Jordanian Law *No. 79* could continue as the basis of future planning, but with revisions to take account of the agencies to be designated responsible for planning. In addition, it appears desirable to review the following aspects of the law:

   - Procedures for considering objections to plans and approving plans;
   - Procedures for appealing against the refusal of a building permit;
   - The relationship between granting permission for a building permit and for subdivision (or parcellation);
   - The difference between *detailed plans* and *outline plans*, and whether detailed plans are really necessary; [2] and
   - The relationship of agencies such as housing co-operatives and new town development corporations to the planning system.

The Planning System

Very few parts of Palestine are covered by an adequate development plan. Taken as a whole, the plans provide nothing like the opportunities for current development pressures, let alone those likely to arise in the future. Hence, the most urgent need is to provide an adequate development plan covering the entire territory.

Such plans should ideally be up-to-date; approved; compatible with each other and with national objectives; clear; comprehensive in their scope; sufficiently precise to provide confidence for investors and local communities; and sufficiently flexible to cater for unexpected demands. Such conditions would be difficult to achieve anywhere, but they will be especially difficult to achieve in Palestine in the short term.

Producing and Approving Plans Rapidly

Three options are available, as follows:

1) *Preparation of plans by consulting firms*, operating in some cases in conjunction with the staff of municipalities;
2) *Preparation of plans by a central agency* (such as a Central Planning Department); and
3) *Preparation of plans by (or on behalf of) developers.*

Developers could be allowed or encouraged to prepare plans for the development they propose, on the land they own. There would need to be safeguards to ensure no adverse affects occurred on adjacent land, and the legislation would need to provide for the publicity and approval of such plans, and their compatibility with other plans. Such procedures might be particularly suited to housing co-operatives.

Simplifying Plan Production

Here, three options arise.

1) *Interim plans.* The full planning process almost inevitably takes a long time. If a lot of development is to take place, then it is better that there should be an interim plan to guide it than no plan at all. Perhaps an abbreviated process of plan production, publicity and approval could be formalised. Such a plan should have legal power pending production of the full plan.
2) *Standardisation of plan content.* Rapid production of plans will be assisted by guidelines which specify the appropriate scope of each tier of plan, the format and categories to be used on the proposals map, the assumptions to be used in forecasting, and the scope of the regulations which form part of the plan. Indeed, it may be possible to standardise the regulations.
3) *Regional plans* to provide guidance for village development. Preparation of plans for each of the 500 villages would be a huge task. On the other hand, regional plans could swiftly specify the broad principles to which development should conform, pending production of village plans.

Controls

Planning controls are, not surprisingly, associated in the minds of many Palestinians with Israeli occupation. This will make enforcement of controls by the Palestinian National Authority particularly challenging. However many opportunities are made available for development in the future, it will always be necessary to have a strict code of planning control and to ensure the adherence of all citizens to these controls. If development is allowed to take place in contradiction to planning policy, then it will be difficult to return to a situation in which the rule of planning law is respected.

Ensuring Adherence to Planning Controls

The following measures may help, although other options will need to be considered as well:

- *Publicity for plans.* Full, convenient and permanent publicity should be given to all plans (and any other statements of policy), so that people are in no doubt as to what sort of development is allowed and not allowed.
- *Publicity for applications for building permits.* Permit applications and decisions, and the reasons for the decisions could be available for public inspection. Site notices could be required to be displayed when applying for permits and when they are issued
- *Monitoring development.* The scale of unauthorised development should be monitored and reported by a central authority (and/or by the municipalities). In the light of the findings, it may be felt necessary to relax controls or to increase penalties.
- *Increasing penalties.* In principle, penalties should not be less than the benefit accruing to the developer.

Reducing Pressure on Development Control Staff

It may be possible to designate areas within which building permits are not required, subject to basic requirements regarding safety, etc. One option is:

> *Simplified planning zones.* These would be areas where building permits are not required. They could apply to some industrial areas, or to major landowners such as universities, or they could apply to some or all of the operations of registered housing (or other) co-operatives (see also *Preparation of Plans by Developers* above).

PHYSICAL PLANNING OPTIONS

Theoretical Options for Locating Urban Development

The scale and distribution of development in Palestine is likely to be transformed in the next ten years (see *Location of Capital City Functions* above). What, in principle, are the options available for locating this new development in relation to an existing urban area?

Theoretical Models for Urban Development

The options can be summarised as follows: (a) peripheral expansion of existing towns and villages; (b) intensification of existing development (i.e. increasing the density of areas already partly developed); (c) the establishment of new settlements; and (d) linear development, i.e. development along a chosen *corridor.*

International experience suggests that each of these has a range of advantages and disadvantages. The most favoured urban strategy is almost certain to be a combination of these options.

Of the four theoretical options noted above, two are rather consistent with current trends: peripheral expansion and intensification. The other two – new towns and linear development – imply a much more deliberate strategy of steering development into particular locations.

Peripheral development. The outward development of towns in all directions is the most prevalent form of urban expansion. Advantages may include proximity of new development to existing development, which allows economic and convenient provision of services and infrastructure for the new development. Peripheral development may also allow natural expansion of the various social and kinship communities.

On the other hand, two problems with peripheral expansion need to be born in mind. First, the town's services and infrastructure may have little spare capacity, and their expansion may be impractical, costly or disruptive. Second, continued outward expansion of nearby towns may result in the towns merging, and hence loosing their particular identity.

Intensification. Intensification can take place through the infilling of vacant plots in areas which have been subject to sporadic development or where the development process is incomplete. It also is achieved by increasing building densities. This could be accomplished by allowing new buildings to be higher, or to cover a larger proportion of the plot, or by replacing existing development with buildings which are higher or cover a greater proportion of the plot.

Intensification, like peripheral development, is taking place already in the larger Palestinian towns, and it seems almost inevitable that it will continue. Pressures for intensification will be increased if alternative opportunities for development are not provided (i.e. if land is not released at the appropriate rate) with a consequential increase in land prices (see *Land Release* below). The potential problems of intensifying development include:

- The loss of land for public open space (and other public needs) to housing;
- The loss of amenity to adjacent areas (i.e. overlooking, disturbance during construction);

175

- The inappropriateness of multi-storey living to traditional norms and social needs; and
- The harmful impact of high or dense development on the visual character of the town and its natural setting.

New Towns. Internationally, countries such as the United States, the former Soviet Union, France, Britain, Germany and Egypt have experience in building new towns. The reasons for establishing them included a desire to relieve congestion; to develop under-populated areas, to exploit natural resources, to establish economic *growth poles*, to curb the growth of existing cities, and to reduce pressures to develop agricultural land. The scale of future development in Palestine is such that it seems almost inevitable that at least part of future growth will have to be accommodated in new settlements.

The advantages of new towns include the potential for:

- An efficient structure, with appropriate location and phasing of the main activities;
- A balanced structure (i.e. between the workforce and the number of jobs);
- A harmonious environment (i.e. by establishing strict development guidelines, or by providing a distinctive architectural form);
- Efficient use of roads and infrastructure planned and phased to meet future needs;
- Minimisation of energy needs and pollution; and
- The provision of land and facilities to match specific industrial needs, thereby promoting economic competitiveness.

The main difficulty in establishing new towns is that they require a substantial initial investment, probably by government, in advance of any economic or social return. Thus there is a risk in a new towns strategy that the initial investment may not be successful. Also, in order to implement a new town it may be necessary to create a specific agency to organise the project.

A major priority for any new towns programme is to focus on opportunities to develop the Palestinian economy, i.e. to promote opportunities for production (both for export and for goods which can substitute for imports). In many cases, this means that the new towns should be located and designed to attract the private sector initiators of industrial development, much of which will be high technology requiring high standards of infrastructure and environment.

Among the issues which will need to be considered are the extent to which reliance should be placed on the free market, the degree to which a new town programme should be concentrated or dispersed, and the distance of the new towns from existing settlements. These issues and options are summarised in the special section on *Planning for New Towns* below.

Linear development. Unplanned (or at least unintended) linear development already characterises parts of the West Bank. Such linear development is usually a response to topographic constraints or to the uncoordinated clustering of developments along major roads, often with harmful consequences for the traffic flow along those roads.

Planned linear developments can have the advantages of:

• Convenient transport (particularly public transport) throughout the town, based on a simple linear system; and
• Almost limitless opportunity for progressive expansion.

Some of the advantages of linear development may be combined with those of peripheral development, by selecting the preferred direction(s) for the outward growth of a town; this will allow for the *organic* development of the town, while providing flexible opportunities to meet the scale of external demand.

The Planning of New Towns

Three issues are worth mentioning regarding the planning of new towns.

Free Market versus Planned Location

To what extent should an overall programme of new towns be centrally planned? Could new towns be initiated and developed by private enterprise?

Centrally planned programme. Prepare a phased, comprehensive programme for new town development. This would require a thorough understanding of market demand, a substantial element of state finance, and a strategy to ensure that the land is made available to developers. An agency to co-ordinate the new towns programme would be needed, as well as an agency to implement each new town.

Private initiative. Encourage private enterprise to identify opportunities and to develop new towns in response to market demands.

Mixed strategy. This would include elements of both of the foregoing options. For example, private sector bids could be sought for elements within the centrally planned programme, or private initiative could be encouraged to conform to national policy either by restrictions (for environmental or other reasons), or by different rates of subsidy for different locations or types of development.

177

Concentration or Dispersal?

Concentration. This involves a small number of large new towns in carefully selected locations and has the advantage that this would probably be the most efficient use of technical and financial resources.

Dispersal. This involves a large number of smaller new towns and could provide greater opportunities for local participation and a wider range of potential development locations. Taken to an extreme, this might imply a *rural* emphasis to development.

Distance from Existing Settlements

Separation from existing towns. New towns could be designed and located to be relatively self-contained and independent of existing towns, although in practice Palestine is so densely developed that, except for the Jordan Valley, almost no location would be far from existing towns or villages.

Twin towns. An alternative concept is that new towns could be established in close proximity to some of the existing towns. Such new towns would be satellites, and the potential advantages are that initial start-up costs would be less. Facilities and social provision (and possibly the municipal organisation) would support the initial growth of the new town.

Combining elements from the three main issues discussed under new town planning above provides a strategy which appears to have considerable advantages. It would involve the development of a small number of sites for major new towns in the first phase. There are likely to be accelerating trends of population movement to the major towns, so these sites could all be adjacent to the major Palestinian towns of Nablus, Jerusalem, Hebron and Gaza.

Possible sites would be east of Nablus, north of Ramallah, between Ramallah and Jerusalem, north of Hebron, and at Gaza. The second phase might include new towns at Jenine, Tulkarem, Khan Younis and Rafah. In the third phase, selected groups of villages could form the nucleus of new towns, and new towns could also be established at more remote locations having high development potential, i.e. at the entry points to Jordan.

Transport

Planning policy in Palestine (as throughout the world until recently) proceeds on the basis that full use of the private car is to be provided for and encouraged. There has been little attempt to provide for public transport in plans. Congestion in larger towns is increasing and will almost inevitably increase much more.

Should Public Transport be Encouraged?

Most people have no access to a car. There are increasing possibilities of providing efficient and competitive means of public transport. Increasing car use depletes resources and damages the environment. Among the options available are the following:

- *Guidance to municipalities.* The central authority could advise municipalities on how public transport should be provided for in plans, and how public transport priorities can be provided in congested areas; and
- *Land use patterns to foster public transport use.* Linear development along major bus routes could be encouraged. Certain types of development could be required to locate only where public transport is available.

Conservation

The resources of Palestine include natural and man-made features of great beauty and distinction. These include:

- *Landscape:* dramatic topography and rock formations and sky-lines; coastline; ecologically valuable areas (plants and wild life);
- *Built heritage:* fine individual buildings of historic or architectural interest; the historic *cores* of many towns and villages, exemplifying a long tradition of building and a way of life; the separate cultural and spatial identity of the villages; and archaeological remains of great number and variety; and
- *Agricultural land* is itself an economic resource and it also forms part of the beauty of the landscape. Farming is fundamental to cultural heritage.

Almost all of the above features are under threat, or could be threatened, by future development on the scale expected.

There are two views which can be taken on this. On the one hand, it might be felt that, in the case of Palestine, the years of subjugation and tribulation make it impractical to consider restricting development opportunities and individual freedom in the interests of conserving such features as the above. On the on the other hand, it might be claimed that these tribulations make it all the more important to conserve the essential beauty of the land, and to hang on to the cultural heritage of the Palestinian people.

179

The historic *cores* (almost all of which are in a sad state of dilapidation) are a particular case in point. On the one hand, they represent an opportunity for development and a potential source of wealth for their owners. On the other hand, they represent the survival – and potentially a continuation – of a way of life which has existed for centuries and which can inform and enrich the environment of all Palestinians in years to come.

Is Conservation a High Priority?

Is a high priority to be placed on identifying and conserving elements of the landscape or of cultural value in the plans for Palestinian reconstruction? If the answer is *yes*, then the following implications arise:

- Inventories will have to be prepared;
- Landowners may need to be compensated;
- The resources will need to be managed and restored as well as preserved and advice on this will need to be given to owners and municipalities;
- Development plans and development control procedures will need to respect conservation requirements; and
- Areas may need to be designated where special procedures apply, i.e. national parks and urban conservation sites.

Refugee Camps

The camps are the main concentrations of unacceptable living conditions. It will be an urgent priority to improve these.

The Future of the Refugee Camps

A choice between the following two alternatives will need to take into account local conditions, the availability of finance, the views of the inhabitants, community structure within the camps, and arrangements for transfer of responsibility from the United Nations Relief and Works Agency (UNRWA). There are only two options:

1) *Clearance.* The land could then be developed. Replacement housing could attempt to retain the previous community structures; and
2) *Improvement.* This could be gradual or comprehensive. It would include housing, infrastructure, roads and facilities. Land ownership issues would need to be resolved. Nearby opportunities will need to be provided for development requirements which cannot be met on site.

Development Location

A number of factors will need to be taken into account in selecting the areas where intense urban development is to take place.

Factors Affecting Choice of Land for Development

What factors should be taken into account and where are the areas affected? The following is a partial list of factors which may be considered to preclude development:

- Land needed for military use, or precluded for military reasons;
- Very steep land;
- Land subject to flooding;
- Agricultural land, or land with mineral potential;
- Land of landscape/ecological value; and
- *Green belt* land: i.e. land around selected towns and villages kept free of development in order to preserve the character and setting of the town or village.

On the other hand, what factors are favourable to development besides proximity to other development? Is land in public ownership to be favoured?

LAND OWNERSHIP

There are significant problems relating to land ownership which have a bearing on the national development effort. All except the first two of the problems listed below are found in other countries. In the case of Palestine, most of them have been made worse by military occupation. Some of these problems are the following:

- The seizure by the Israelis of more than two-thirds of the land, and the denial to Palestinians of the benefit, use and/or access to this land;
- Land ownership patterns are uncertain. Less than half the land has been formally registered. Moreover, the land registry is not available to Palestinians;
- The categories of land ownership established under Ottoman administration are confusing and inappropriate to present needs;
- The pattern of ownership is very complex and highly fragmented. Also, much land is under multiple ownership;
- There is little or no market in land. This, together with the previous point, constrains the rate of urban development and the manner in which it takes place;
- Very little land is in public (i.e. Palestinian) ownership; and
- Land prices are rising due to speculation and some of the factors

181

noted above. In some areas, a near monopoly of land ownership may exist.

As a result, the following issues arise:

The Return of Seized Land

Pending final resolution of the status of the Jewish settlements, what assumptions should be made about the eventual use and development of these areas? Of more immediate concern, what about the use and development of seized land not forming part of the settlements?

Land Registration

Assuming the land registers are made available to the PNA, how can the information in them be analysed and used to facilitate the process of national reconstruction? How can the process of registration be completed and updated for the whole of Palestine?

Land Release

How can land be provided to developers at the right time and the right place and in suitably sized plots to meet the huge urbanisation needs of the future? The following suggestions may be of use:

- *Government land acquisition.* The government (or municipalities) could acquire extensive tracts (or selected sites) of land scheduled for future development. This would preferably be at existing use value, and could be either by voluntary agreement or through compulsory purchase powers. Such land could then be developed by public bodies, or auctioned to developers;
- *Pre-emption.* As a variation on the above, the government (or municipalities) could have powers to buy designated lands when they are next sold. Such land would remain in the present owner's hands until he wished to sell, when he would be required to sell to the government;
- *Reparcellation.* The present law allows voluntary or compulsory reparcellation of land to take place. Under this process awkwardly shaped plots can be combined and reparcelled suitable for development. Advice needs to be given to municipalities (and to landowners) on how this complex but highly beneficial process can be used to best effect;
- *Public share of land.* The present law allows the planning authority to claim a proportion of a developer's land for public use. The proportion appropriate to different circumstances needs to be reconsidered, and the law should then be applied in all cases in the interests of fairness;

- *Betterment tax.* Taxes on any increase in the value of land arising from zoning decisions or from the grant of a building permit should be imposed; and
- *Improvement of the land market.* There may be steps that the government can take to improve the market in land, i.e. by encouraging owners who do not wish to develop their land to sell to those who do. Opening up of the land register, and the licensing of professional estate agencies, would help this.

SUMMARY

While the scale of future development in Palestine is uncertain, it seems very likely that an extremely rapid rate of development can be expected in the next few years. Some 600,000 housing units alone may be needed in the coming decade. The relative growth of the different regions and the growth of the capital city will depend on political priorities and the national strategy regarding space.

The future administration of planning in Palestine necessitates a consideration of issues such as the composition of the Higher Planning Council (HPC) and its responsibilities; the establishment of development agencies, the question of whether a regional tier of authority is needed and whether additional municipalities need to be created or existing boundaries expanded. In addition, the establishment of a Central Planning Department may be considered.

New and/or revised legislation will be required, along with the provision of adequate, up-to-date development plans for the entire country. Consideration needs to be given to how these can be rapidly produced and approved and how the planning process can be simplified. Adherence to planning controls is another important organisational issue.

Questions also arise as to the options available for locating new urban development, including the peripheral expansion of existing towns and villages, the intensification of existing development, the establishment of new settlements and/or linear developments. Transport, and particularly the role of public transport, is a major issue, as is the importance and advisability of conservation. Refugee camps will need to be cleared or improved, and the factors affecting the choice of land for development decided.

Finally, land ownership has a significant bearing on national re-development. Issues arising in this regard include the return of seized land, land registration and land release.

ENDNOTES

1) The word 'region' is used in the same sense as 'district' or 'province'.
2) The law specifies four types of plan: regional, outline, detailed and parcellation.

LAND AND BUILDING USE IN RELATION TO URBAN POLICIES

Anthony Coon

ABSTRACT

Land resources for urban development are determined both by land ownership and land availability. Urban land needs depend on demographic and economic growth, as well as the density at which development takes place. On the assumptions and examples given in this paper, the urban area to be developed over the next ten years could be about three times the size of existing urban areas in Palestine.

New development will need to take into consideration the current pressures and trends of development; the options for spatial locations of the new projects; Palestine's social structure and the implications which the present pattern of development will have on future patterns of growth.

The unbalanced nature of investment under the Israeli occupation means that a proportionately larger amount of development will need to take place in the non-residential sector. Studies will also need to be taken on the needs and preferences of returning Palestinians as well as the specific needs and locations of the refugee camps.

Any attempt to base the redevelopment of Palestine on a single comprehensive plan is likely to fail. Instead, a regional balance of growth should be sought, and regional planning should help to regulate the scale of development in addition to helping to identify infrastructure, industry and priorities for conservation. Both peripheral expansion and intensification may be appropriate policies in certain circumstances.

Plans drafted for the local scale could serve a variety of purposes and will be necessary wherever development or change is likely to take place. In any case, intervention by the government in the development process is desirable. The quality of national redevelopment will depend not only, or even primarily, on the plans themselves, but rather on the way they are implemented.

Table 1 Demographic Assumptions For Land Need Estimates.

	West Bank	*Gaza*	*Palestine*
1990 Population (Thousands)	1,492	773	2,265
Natural Population Increase (Per Cent per Annum)	3.0	3.5	
Average Household Size for Years 1990,1995 for Year 2005	6.5 6.0	7.0 6.0	
Population in Refugee Camps (Per Cent)	7	35	
Net Increase by Migration for 1995–2005 (Thousands)			1,500

LAND RESOURCES

Land Needs

Land needs for the future urban development of Palestine will depend on demographic and economic growth and on the density at which development takes place. Obviously, there is great uncertainty about the future trend of demographic and economic growth. The question of density is subject to policy choices.

Uncertainties about demographic growth relate mainly to uncertainties about the rate at which Palestinians from outside the country will settle within the newly independent Palestinian state. Economic prospects will affect the need for industrial land, and also the rate at which problems of overcrowding, substandard housing and deficient social provision can be remedied.

For the purpose of a broad illustrative assessment of land needs during the next ten years, Table 1 sets out some possible assumptions.

Of these, by far the most problematic is the number of returning Palestinians. Here, it is assumed that 1.5 million will return over a ten-year period. To allow for the land needed to ease overcrowding, it is assumed that additional land would have to be found outside the existing urban areas for 50 per cent of the refugee camp population and 10 per cent of the rest of the population.

The consequent need for land in terms of housing units is shown in Table 2.

Natural increase in population as well as a progressive decrease in family size are together likely to require 206,000 units, while land for an additional 67,000 units might be needed to re-house the population at present inadequately housed. The (admittedly, highly arbitrary) assumption about the scale of incoming migration would imply a need for some 250,000 units, i.e. of a similar magnitude to the housing needs of the

Table 2 Housing Needs (Households in Thousands).

	West Bank	Gaza	Palestine
(a) Due to Natural Increase and Household Size			
Population 2005	2324	1295	3619
Household 2005	387	216	603
Household 1995	266	131	397
Inc. In Households 1995–2005	121	85	206
(b) Due to Redevelopment			
Refugee Camp Population	20	46	66
Non-Camp Population	50	18	68
Total	70	64	134
Total of above	191	149	340
(c) Due to Migration			
Net Population Increase 1995–2005			1500
Increase in Households			250
Total of all above			590

existing population [(a) and (b) in Table 2]. All these figures relate to a ten-year period, i.e. a total of 590,000 units, averaging some 59,000 units per year.

As far as past trends are concerned, data for the rate of house construction in the West Bank and Gaza is given in official Israeli sources. This data, which is of doubtful accuracy and is probably an underestimate, suggests that up to 1987 about 3,000 units of housing were completed each year in West Bank villages and a similar number in municipalities. This would represent, perhaps, a total of some 10,000 units in both the West Bank and Gaza.

Consequently, the required production of housing under the assumptions made above would be some six times greater than levels recently achieved. This confirms that the formidable scale of planning and construction implied by this scenario would require a radical overhaul of all the assumptions and procedures which prevail at present. Of course, this overall average rate of development could only be achieved by a progressive increase from present levels to a rate very much higher than the average at the end of the ten-year period.

The land provided for this amount of housing and for the other necessary components of urban development will depend to some extent on public policy. It might, for instance, be decided to explicitly encourage low or high densities, or indirectly to affect densities by land release policies. Furthermore, public policy may affect the efficiency with which land is used and hence the amount of land needed. Efficiency in this

Table 3 Urban Densities in Palestine.

	Year	Area (square kilometres)	Population (millions)	Density persons/ square kilometre
Gaza And West Bank Palestinian Built-Up Areas. Existing[1]	1990	200	2.27	11,325
West Bank And Gaza Jewish Colonies. Existing[2]	1990	70	0.24	3,428
West Bank Palestinian 'Urban Areas'. Existing[3]	1987	0.437	1,950	
Gaza Palestinian 'Built-Up Areas'. Existing[4]	1986	57	0.634	11,213
Nabulus Municipality. Existing[5]	1987	12.800	0.107	8,360
Bir Nabala Village Outline Plan Proposed[6]	About 2006	2.170	0.0007	3,226

Sources: [1]CEP, 1992. Pp 16 and 18; [2]CEP, 1992. P16; [3]Benvenisti and Khayat, 1988. P52; [4]Benvenisti and Khayat, 1988. P112; [5] Benvenisti and Khayat, 1988. P134; [6]CEP, 1988. P7.

regard is likely to be promoted by adherence to a plan in which the various needs are carefully forecast, and development proceeds in an appropriate sequence.

Some broad estimates of gross densities of urban development (i.e. including all non-residential uses as well as housing) are set out in Table 3. In practice, development is likely to take place at a wide range of densities. If, for the sake of illustration, we assume an overall gross density for new Palestinian development of 5,000 persons per square kilometre (or 833 dwelling units per square kilometre), then the required area for the urban development, including the housing projected in Table 2, is set out in Table 4.

On the assumptions made, the urban area to be developed during the next ten-year period would be about three times the size of all the existing urban areas in Palestine. An alternative way of considering this is that the projected urban development would cover an area about 50 times the size of the present municipal area of Nablus and house a population 30 times as large.

Land Availability

A judgement on whether land is available for urban development is by no means as straightforward as may at first be supposed. In practice, a level of judgement and a degree of uncertainty are involved (Barrett et al., 1978), and issues of suitability, market demand, alternative use, economic cost and land conservation arise inevitably. While few, if any, of

Table 4 Land Requirements for Urban Development (1995–2005).

	Housing Units (Thousands)			Land Need (Square Kilometre)		
	West Bank	Gaza	Palestine	West Bank	Gaza	Palestine
(a) Natural Increase	121	85	206	145	102	247
(b) Redevelopment	35	32	67	42	38	80
Total of (a) and (b)	156	117	273	187	140	327
(c) Migration			250			300
Total			523			627

the following factors would preclude development absolutely, they may discourage development to a greater or less degree.

Political and Military Factors

At present, more than two-thirds of land in the West Bank and Gaza has been seized by Israel (Halabi et al., 1985). Leaving aside the obvious political implications, the significance of this land seizure for Palestinian development lies in Israel's policy permitting the use of this 'state land' solely by Jews, and the consequent prohibition on its use by Arabs. Of course, a reversal of this policy is a fundamental requirement for the provision of sufficient development opportunities for Palestinians, including seized land in general, and the particular case of the land adjacent to the newly built road system serving the Jewish settlements; the land around and within these settlements; and even the buildings within these settlements.

Issues of a more direct military nature will also arise, including the constraints which may arise as a result of any international agreement to protect Israel's interests, and constraints which the Palestine National Authority may place on development for its own defence.

Military restrictions have a considerable impact in constraining opportunities for urban development in developing countries, and it is to be hoped that the needs of urban development can be taken into account before any such restrictions are imposed in the new Palestinian state.

Development Costs

Development costs in various places may differ due to ground conditions such as steep slopes and unstable soils, the cost of providing infrastructure (especially roads, sewerage and water), and the cost of building materials (i.e. as a result of the distance from the source of supply). These factors (apart from the last mentioned) may vary locally as well as over the state as a whole. However, none of these factors would preclude development – development may go ahead despite these factors, as indeed has often been the case in Palestine in recent years. The most obvious and widespread consideration is steep slopes, which are widespread, especially near many of the larger towns.

Certain land uses, such as for heavy industry, may require particularly flat areas, and extremely few of these exist in the West Bank. This consideration could well be decisive in selecting locations for such land uses and other associated development.

Resource Conservation

Use of land for development may conflict with alternative uses of that land – either existing or contemplated. The most obvious and widespread use is agriculture, particularly cultivation, and most particularly areas which are irrigated or capable of irrigation. Other uses include extraction of minerals (especially stone for building or aggregate), and possibly water gathering areas. To some extent, the market value of the land for these present or potential uses reflects the value of these resources and will deter urban development. However, governments elsewhere widely practice a policy of preventing development which would conflict with the conservation of resources, such as those considered to have a long term value to the nation, with varying degrees of success. The case of cultivated land is particularly significant since much of this land in Palestine (as elsewhere) is close to existing development – and indeed was the principal economic stimulus for the urban development in the first place.

Landscape Conservation

Policies to prevent, or restrict, development to encourage landscape conservation are widespread in international practice, and are provided for to some extent in the present town planning legislation of the West Bank and Gaza. Such policies apply particularly to land in its natural state (e.g. the Jordan Valley), although in many countries (and this may include Palestine) land subject to the impact of man's traditional activities is thought worthy of conservation. Important elements of landscape include unusual, dramatic or varied topography and rock formations, and skylines. Particular concern is reserved for areas which are visible from significant viewpoints or roads.

A further consideration which also could apply to Palestine is to protect landscapes (and particularly sky-lines) viewed from within urban areas. Another consideration is the possibility of conserving land for its ecological value, i.e. to protect and perhaps restore the wildlife and vegetation. Some of these areas may overlap with landscape areas, and satisfactory protection of these will depend not just on preventing development but also on positive management and restorative measures.

Finally, one should note the scope for conserving the archaeological and built heritage of Palestine, which expresses the nation's history and which could offer inspiration to future builders and citizens. The areas are mostly very small in extent but they tend to be very strategically situated near the centres of towns and villages, and are therefore highly vulnerable to pressures for redevelopment.

Economically, the conservation of landscape, the ecology and urban areas could promote international tourism and provide income and jobs for Palestinians. Where conservation can not be justified in these terms, it will be necessary to make judgements at a political level (based on the necessary surveys and assessments) on whether conservation interests should be taken into account in assessing the availability of land for urban development.

On the one hand, it might be felt that in the case of Palestine the years of subjugation and tribulation make it impractical to consider restricting development in the interests of conservation; on the other hand, it might be claimed that these tribulations make it all the more important to conserve the essential beauty of the land.

OPTIONS: LOCATION AND FORM OF NEW DEVELOPMENT

There are four main considerations when deciding the form which future development in Palestine should take: firstly, the current pressures and trends of development; secondly, the theoretical options for spatial location of new development; thirdly, the particular requirements posed by Palestinian social structure; and, fourthly, the implications of the present pattern of development for future patterns of growth. In the following paragraphs, the current trends, ideal models, social needs and geographical realities for each of these considerations will be discussed briefly.

Current Trends

In many ways, it would be desirable to dismiss the relevance of past and current trends in development. After all, there is much that is regrettable about the form of development which has taken place in recent years, and developers will be faced with a very different range of constraints and opportunities with the end of Israeli rule.

However, there is a substantial momentum for development which exists now and which will have an inevitable impact on the overall form of development in the next few years. Development under construction will need to be completed; development for which permits have been granted will, in most cases, go ahead; land for which infrastructure has been provided may be developed, and so also may the extensive tracts of adjacent land for which the owners have high expectations of realising the profits from urban development.

It is not possible to predict how much development of this kind will take place. Much of it will undoubtedly be contrary to the public interest. It will be possible – and indeed necessary – to curb much of this development pressure, and to divert it to more efficient and harmonious patterns of growth once these have been agreed. Experience elsewhere suggests it is not possible to abruptly terminate such long standing trends and expectations and to provide immediate alternative spatial provision which accords with national strategy.

Consequently, there will be a need to (a) assess the nature and scale of this 'unpreventable' development, (b) assess the extent of any conflict between this development and national development objectives, and (c) determine the means of curtailing or mitigating such conflicting development. These means would include the imposition of controls, the provision of incentives and the acquisition of land by public agencies.

In practice, the prospect of a major co-ordinated planning and development programme in Palestine is likely to *increase* the very pressures which might conflict with planning objectives. In changing course from the present to more desirable modes of development, a compromise will need to be reached which will incorporate selected locations, or characteristics, of these trends in future policies while hopefully securing conformity to more desirable locations or modes of development elsewhere.

Theoretical Options

The options for geographically locating the substantial development expected in the next ten years are:

a) Peripheral expansion of existing towns and villages;
b) Intensification of existing development, i.e. increasing the density, of areas already partly developed;
c) The establishment of new settlements in open country; and
d) Linear development, i.e. development along a chosen 'corridor.'

All these options are essentially 'urban', and a choice between them ideally should be made within the context of selected national and sub-regional strategies. The options differ markedly in terms of their compatibility with current trends, although elements of all four of these models are discernible, in varying degrees, in Palestinian development during the years of occupation.

International experience suggests that each has a range of advantages and disadvantages, and that the desired urban strategy (and to an even greater extent the ensuing pattern of development) is likely to be a compromise between the four options. We also need to guard against too easy an assumption that it is possible for the state to opt for, or choose, a development pattern: such a choice is only realistic if the state has the legislative, financial and administrative means to implement a specific option, and if a consensus exists about the assumptions and values of the chosen option.

Social Structure

The need for a thorough understanding of social structures has long been accepted internationally as a desirable prerequisite to the formulation of physical plans, particularly in the often traumatic circumstances of rapid industrialisation and urban growth. Present social structures and their spatial implications need to be understood so that the envisaged pattern of development – which will be very different from what exists at present if only because of its scale – offers scope for the accommodation and enrichment of family and community support systems, and for the development of the often varied and potentially conflicting individual and community aspirations.

However, the potential difficulties of collecting the necessary data and using it in the process of plan formulation are considerable. Likewise, an agreed social policy is sometimes considered to be an essential input to the redevelopment process, although the lack of a clear social policy in other countries is perhaps more the rule than the exception. In any case, this has not always precluded the emergence of a physical strategy.

The difficulties of analysing social conditions and formulating a social strategy will be no less in the case of redevelopment in Palestine. The impact of the Israeli occupation in distorting and complicating patterns of social behaviour and in inhibiting the study of social structures will add to the difficulties of identifying the crucial characteristics of Palestinian society which should influence the form of future urban development.

Social factors are considered in more detail elsewhere in this volume. It certainly seems that, though it will be even more difficult than elsewhere to foresee the appropriate relation between present social structure and the future pattern of economic and physical development, it will be even more important to attempt to do so.

The most obvious factors which will need to be taken into account follow.

- Firstly, the deep-rooted attachment of Palestinians to their own villages and to their own landholdings. To many, if not most, Palestinians, the crucial issue will not be which of the four options mentioned above is to be chosen, but whether their particular village is provided with appropriate opportunities to continue the advancement of the activities of individual households on their landholdings. There is a need to understand the nature and spatial configuration of present community and family structures in order to maximise, where possible, the scope for providing appropriate development opportunities not only *in* each village but also *within* each village.

- Secondly, there will be the need to minimise the extent of disruption which may be caused to existing patterns of activity and community structures. Any plan for radical economic change and physical improvement in a densely populated country is bound to have some disturbing social impacts. Land may be needed for new roads and infrastructure may damage existing communities; redevelopment of existing urban areas may take place in a form or at a pace which is against the interests of the inhabitants; new housing areas may be located and designed without taking into account existing community structures; development may take place in a form so unrelated to the traditions of Palestine that changes in behaviour patterns are forced on the community; the requirements of a technological age may dictate development out of human scale and inconsistent with past forms; the plan (or more probably, the way the plan is implemented) may enrich a few rather than the community as a whole, and hence be a source of social discord and mistrust.

These are all difficulties which have faced cities throughout the Arab world in the second half of the Twentieth Century. The search for an urban form which respects Arab traditions, values and social structures has intensified in recent years (Al-Olet, 1991). The insights of specialists in social structure and social planning will be particularly valuable in Palestine where reconstruction needs to address not only the ravages of time and the demands of technology but also social and community rehabilitation after the years of occupation.

Inadequate Existing Developments

One of the principal objectives of future development strategy should be to remedy the inadequacies of existing urban developments, many of which have been caused, or aggravated by, Israeli policies under the occupation.

Firstly, the economic conditions and restrictive policies under the Israeli occupation mean that there is a pent-up demand for housing. Much of this will appropriately be located close to existing towns and villages. Because of the very large number of small villages (and the fact that development has been more strongly suppressed in the villages than in the municipalities), development is likely to be much more dispersed than would normally be the case in a developing country. Consequently, development pressures may threaten the conservation of agricultural land adjacent to the villages and towns. The preferred location of new housing will need to be the subject of social surveys. So too will the nature of desired housing, particularly regarding density and the split between houses and flats. Finally, social surveys will be needed to determine the amount (probably very substantial) of required low-cost housing.

Some of the housing provided in recent years has been sporadic and dispersed, partly because of the opportunistic nature of the development process in the face of Israeli restrictions, with consequent economic, social and environmental disadvantages. Significant opportunity exists for infill development in these areas.

However, the unbalanced nature of investment under the occupation (Jerusalem Media and Communications Centre, 1992) means that a proportionately greater need exists for development in the non-residential sector. This includes the need for industrial areas (e.g. in the northern and southern areas of the West Bank), public open space within and adjacent to towns throughout Palestine (the provision of which will probably require public acquisition as well as zoning), and commercial areas. The latter will no doubt expand significantly with economic improvement, and early consideration will need to be given to radical replanning, reconstruction and the possible relocation of many existing commercial areas to meet modern urban standards.

Significant deficiencies of the road system will have to be met, including not only the construction of new roads – particularly to provide relief to town centres from through traffic, but also the improvement of existing roads and the management of traffic to secure satisfactory access, safety and environmental conditions in the face of almost certainly worsening congestion. For the same reason, public transport will need to be planned, and strategies for this may well influence not only the planning of existing urban areas but also the location and form of new areas for development.

Finally, there is the question of the historic 'cores' which still exist in many towns and villages, mainly in a sad state of dilapidation. On the one hand, they represent an opportunity for development and a potential source of wealth for their owners. On the other hand, they represent the survival – and potentially a continuation – of a way of life which has existed for centuries and which can inform and enrich the environment of all Palestinians in years to come. A vitally important decision on this point of principle must be made – not only on the zoning of any such areas, but also on the means by which they are to be conserved and enhanced.

Returnees

The above discussion relates primarily to the existing residents of Palestine. But there is also the question, 'Where should the potentially substantial returning population live?'

Studies will need to be undertaken regarding the requirements and preferences of returnees, and potential returnees, to establish their wishes, and the strength of their ties (socially, financially and in terms of their landholdings) to particular communities within Palestine. In principle, it would seem that there are advantages in establishing new settlements intended (at least in part) to satisfy the specific needs of returnees.

The housing of returnees will raise political as well as social questions; for example, a national decision on the relative growth stimulus to be applied to each region would imply appropriate inducements to returnees to settle in the various regions. At a more local level, it may be necessary to consider not only whether the development of specific areas particularly for returnees is to be encouraged, but also whether the means of implementation, i.e. through the provision of finance, may unintentionally result in the spatial segregation of returnees, and whether this would be consistent with national objectives.

The Refugee Camps

The main question here is whether, and how, future policies for urban development outside the refugee camps need to take into account the specific needs and locations of these camps.

For example, land may need to be allocated and implementation mechanisms specifically provided for the needs of the camp populations. Some or all of this may have to be provided outside the camps and preferably adjacent to the camps.

Within the camps, development policies will depend on the future status of the camps and of the refugees. There is a small but growing body of information and experience on the physical improvement of conditions in the camps (Llewelyn-Davies, 1989). Any study of living conditions in Palestine would undoubtedly identify the camps as the areas in most urgent need of improvement. However, policies regarding the camps should be coupled with policies to limit, or reduce, the already unbearably high density of population.

Decision-making

The orthodox view is that when planning all at once, the issues which arise are too numerous and too many things can go wrong. As a result, hierarchical decision-making has been adopted. In this concept, extensive areas are first planned looking a long way ahead but in broad outline only, followed by plans for progressively smaller areas in progressively finer detail. The main priority is areas for early development. Each plan should conform to the one further up in the hierarchy.

Planning legislation in both the West bank and Gaza has always been based on a sequence of regional plans, town plans, and plans for the development of local areas. The system has administrative as well as technical advantages, as it facilitates the official approval process by distinguishing broad principles from details, concentrating initially on the former.

However, it is important to be aware of some of the practical problems of the hierarchical 'top-down' approach. These are:

a) The overall process will probably take a long time, especially if there are several stages in the hierarchy;
b) Subsequent review and modification of the plans will have knock-on effects on other plans in the sequence;
c) There is scope for public confusion, inconsistency and repetition; and
d) Local insights may in practice suggest the need to modify policies in plans further up the hierarchy, i.e. a 'bottom up' approach.

All these considerations apply in Palestine, and perhaps especially (a) in view of the scale of expected change and the deficiency of current plan coverage.

POLICIES: PLANNING PRINCIPLES AND GEOGRAPHICAL SCALE

While bearing in mind the practical difficulties, it is important to consider the planning principles for Palestine in hierarchical sequence. In the following paragraphs, we deal with these principles on the national, regional, and local scales.

The National Scale

Any attempt to base the redevelopment of Palestine on a single comprehensive national document would certainly be in vain: it would be difficult or impossible to secure agreement to it, and it would quickly become out of date. Instead, it will be necessary to identify the crucial issues which will need to be determined at national level, to prepare sectoral policies for these, and to seek to co-ordinate these. The following paragraphs identify some of these crucial issues for national planning in Palestine at the present time.

It will be necessary to determine the desired balance of development between the different regions of the state. For example, the very much higher density in Gaza at present suggests that Gaza's migrational growth in future should be much less than that of the West Bank. National policies on directing (or more probably, influencing) the settlement of returnees will be the main tool to achieve a desired regional balance, but this will need to be used in conjunction with an industrial policy to affect the location of jobs in both the public and private sectors.

There may also be considerations of a more directly political nature, such as: (a) national objectives on equalising opportunities and incomes in the regions, or for the settlement of more remote land for strategic purposes; (b) the form and location of 'capital city' functions (where significance is symbolic as well as practical and, in the case of Palestine, of the profoundest political significance). The possibility exists to exploit modern telecommunications and the dispersed population pattern of Palestine to avoid the over-concentration in capital cities which is characteristic of many developing countries.

The location of certain major state-funded investment projects will need to be centrally determined at an early stage, including (a) transport facilities, particularly seaport, airport and arterial road systems; (b) energy facilities, particularly electrical generation and distribution; (c) water extraction and storage (as well as pricing and allocation policies).

It is likely that water conservation policies will have an impact on the location of urban development in general as well as on water treatment facilities. National priorities will also need to be determined in relation to the conservation of the natural and built heritage. This will include reaching a consensus on the significance of this issue; the criteria, agencies and procedures of site designation and approval; and the legislative and compensation implications.

National objectives and standards will need to be established for (a) the provision of community facilities, i.e. education, and (b) the provision of low-cost housing. The standards could cover land and building space needs, the type and form of construction, locational needs and frequency of provision. The aim should be to avoid unnecessary prescription by ensuring that national funds are used equitably, while leaving maximum freedom of local choice.

Central government will need to pass town planning legislation which would be appropriate and applicable throughout the new state. Existing legislation in the West Bank and Gaza, although grossly abused under the occupation, covers both development plans and development control, and could form a suitable basis for new legislation to meet current conditions.

However, legislation needs to be improved in the following areas:

a) Specification of the purpose and avoidance of duplication of function between the different types of plan;
b) Clear procedures for consideration of objections to plans and for plan approval;
c) Specification of the form of plans to strike a satisfactory balance between the needs for certainty and flexibility (more emphasis on written material and less on the map);
d) Linkage between provision of government development funds and up-to-date development plans;
e) Satisfactory integration of the process of development and land subdivision control;
f) The means of controlling land and building uses as well as construction;
g) Rights of appeal (against refusal, etc.);
h) Procedures for giving publicity to plans (and to draft plans and development proposals) and for soliciting and considering citizens' views;
i) Conservation of the natural and built heritage; and, finally
j) Special regimes.

This last need arises from the likelihood that it may be necessary to allow specific legislation to apply to particular zones in order to allow the expected rapid development to take place in an orderly fashion; for example, development agencies may be given powers and responsibilities within designated areas, or registered housing co-operatives may assume a planning function within their land.

Other legislative needs to be addressed by central government include the powers of municipality, district and village councils, and the designation and review of their boundaries; the powers of development agencies; land registration; provision of information and guidance.

The latter two of these are particularly important in the Palestinian situation. The need to open up the Land Registry, to allow public access and to complete the process of formal land registration throughout Palestine (which was halted by the Israeli government in 1967) is a prerequisite to a resolution of the land seizure and Jewish settlement problem, and will assist in opening up the land market, in addition to providing a basis for local taxation.

The role of the state in providing information tends to be forgotten. National objectives can be achieved not only by legislative edict but also by providing advice. This includes advice to municipalities, to landowners, and to potential developers regarding procedures, opportunities and design.

199

The Regional Scale

The primary aims of regional planning are to regulate the massive development which is expected; to identify the locations of the main infrastructural and industrial projects, as well as urban developments and their implementation mechanisms; and to identify the main priorities for conservation.

The second of these is particularly important. Politically difficult choices will have to be made in the case of areas designated for future development. For reasons of economy and resource conservation, it is preferable that a strong distinction should be established and maintained between such areas and other areas of open countryside. The regional plan is the appropriate vehicle to explore and demonstrate the options and to provide a context for town and village development.

Given the scale of future developments, consideration will need to be given to enlarging municipal boundaries and to designating development agencies to implement the regional proposals. What has happened in the past (and this has also been the pattern elsewhere in the Middle East) is that areas have been selected for urban development because they are within municipal boundaries, rather than because they are the most suitable for development.

Boundaries

Planning regions may be chosen because of the *character* (of activities, etc.) or because of their *focus* on a particular urban centre. In terms of the latter criterion, suitable planning regions might be Gaza, Hebron, Jerusalem and Nablus. The latter region might also be sub-divided into Nablus, Tulkarem and Jenin. Smaller regions than these would not be appropriate.

As a further variation, the particular characteristics of the Jordan Valley area might suggest this as a region. The boundaries selected will need to take local perceptions and historic patterns into account, especially if regional (or district) councils are to be elected.

Urban expansion and new towns

Of the four theoretical options noted above, two are consistent with current trends: (a) peripheral expansion and (b) intensification. The other two, (c) new towns and (d) linear development, imply a much more deliberate strategy of steering development into new forms.

Both peripheral expansion and intensification will be appropriate policies in certain circumstances. A strategic decision (at regional scale) will need to be taken on whether the social, visual, administrative and historic separation between adjacent towns or villages should be maintained, or whether they should be allowed to merge and eventually to become one conurbation in which the identity of the original towns is largely lost. This is already happening in several cases, and where it is likely to happen anyway, it is better that it proceeds on a planned basis, possibly including designation of a new centre. A case in point is the area of the three towns of Bethlehem, Beit Sahur and Beit Jala, which have a present population of some 70,000 located within a radius of 5 kilometres.

It would be regrettable if the distinctive pattern of towns and villages, each in their own distinctive setting, were to be entirely, or largely, lost. A policy of keeping selected land undeveloped, i.e. by designating green belts, may be adopted following an assessment of the capacity of a town to absorb further peripheral expansion.

Intensification should take place by infilling of areas already partly developed, according to a plan which should seek to provide the necessary community and open space facilities. There have been trends also towards increasing densities, and pressure for increased densities will undoubtedly increase (as elsewhere in the Arab world) especially where land is not available for development in sufficient quantity, and where land prices consequently rise. Ideally, decisions on permissible density levels (and on maximum building height) should be made on the basis of social needs and urban design principles rather than, as has happened in the past, in response to speculative building pressures.

The main difficulty in establishing new towns is that they require a substantial initial investment, probably by government, in advance of any economic or social return. Thus there is a risk in a new towns strategy. Also, there are problems in establishing a development agency and ensuring that it is publicly accountable. Questions of land ownership and betterment are also difficult. However, many of these problems will arise with other models of development. The scale of future development, even if substantially below the levels discussed above, is such that it seems inevitable that new towns will form a significant element of the Palestinian reconstruction strategy.

The advantages of new towns include the potential for:

a) A balanced structure (i.e. as between the workforce and the number of jobs;
b) A harmonious environment (i.e. by establishing strict development guidelines, or providing a distinctive architectural form);
c) Efficient use of roads and infrastructure planned to meet future needs;
d) Minimisation of energy needs and pollution; and
e) The provision of land and facilities to match specific industrial needs, hence promoting economic competitiveness.

All these advantages are potentially available from a new towns strategy, although in practice compromises would be necessary. Moreover, while a balance – in the sense used above – would be desirable, it would be unrealistic to expect these new towns to be 'self-contained: there would inevitably be substantial commuter flows in and out of them because of the almost inevitable near proximity of other towns, the increasingly specialised occupations and activities which will characterise future Palestinian industrial growth, and the fact that these new towns will be suitable locations for major new facilities having a national role and influence.

It would be premature to suggest locations for new towns. Some small new towns might be located to exploit a local resource or employment opportunity (i.e. intensive agriculture, mining, new airport). Most of the new town population should however be located in a relatively small number of potentially large towns. The main consideration in drawing up detailed plans for these towns is that they should be flexible in terms of ultimate population. Thus the initial development could comprise one or more neighbourhoods and neighbourhood centre(s), with the town centre being developed in a subsequent stage and in a manner which would allow further expansion.

The criteria for site selection will include:

a) Freedom from topographic and other constraints;
b) Relative ease of land acquisition, or possibly land owner interest in development;
c) Freedom from adverse impact on conservation interests and agricultural land; and
d) Maintenance of a national balance of development opportunity as between the regions.

Linear development concepts have, in theory, the advantage that they provide (a) convenient transport throughout the town based on a simple linear system, and (b) almost limitless opportunity for progressive expansion. Unplanned, or at least unintended, linear development already characterises parts of the West Bank – as in Nablus where topographic constraints have largely determined the shape of the town, or in cases where development has proceeded along or close to an important transport route, particularly between towns. There are many examples of the latter, but the most striking is the emerging linear metropolis between Ramallah and Bethlehem (including Jerusalem) – a distance of some 30 kilometres. In addition, it may soon extend another 30 kilometres to Halhul and Hebron.

This example is by no means a model of what should happen in the future, given that it involves a great waste of land, with little account taken of environmental factors. A major consideration in planning future linear forms of development is the question of mode of travel. Up to now planning, including the planning by the Israelis of the new road system, has proceeded on the basis that car travel has to be provided for, with buses of course having access to the road system but not significantly influencing its design.

In developed countries, where this mode of thinking has also prevailed in the past, there is increasing emphasis on giving primary consideration to public transport in the interests of ensuring a satisfactory living environment and reducing pollution and energy use. Hence, the main concern in planning linear developments could be the maximising of potential patronage of public transport systems.

Some of the advantages of linear development may be combined with those of peripheral development. This could be achieved by selecting preferred direction(s) for outward growth, which would allow a more organic development of an existing town while providing a comprehensive planning opportunity to meet the pace of market demand.

The Local Scale

The form and coverage of plans at the 'local' scale will depend on the purposes which such plans are expected to serve. These could include the following:

a) Providing the basis for deciding applications for building permits;
b) Guidance on opportunities for development, and on the preferred modes of development;
c) Identification of priorities and means of resource conservation and environmental enhancement;
d) Provision of opportunity for community participation in plan making;
e) The identification of land for (compulsory) purchase by a public authority or for (compulsory) reparcellation;
f) Establishing the parameters to which subsequent reparcellation should conform;
g) Defining priority areas for physical upgrading or for the provision of facilities or infrastructure; and
h) Defining the phasing or order in which development is to take place.

These planning purposes are compatible with one another and could in principle be encompassed within the same plan. In the past, the intention and actual practice of planning in the West Bank and Gaza has focused on (a), i.e. the plan as the means of deciding whether or not a development permit should be issued (although the legislation makes some mention of urban conservation (c) and compulsory purchase (e)). A separate plan is intended to be approved for reparcellation (f).

Local plans will be necessary wherever development or change is likely. This certainly includes all existing urban areas, and other areas proposed in regional plans for new urban development: in other words, a substantial part of Palestine. In addition, guidance should be available on intentions toward allowing, encouraging or discouraging change else-where – i.e. potentially the whole of the rest of Palestine. In view of the grossly deficient coverage of plans at present, the strong development pressures, and manpower shortages – it is clearly going to be necessary to mount a very large-scale plan making effort, to determine the most efficient means of plan approval, and to concentrate initial efforts where they are most needed.

Policies for less pressured (mostly rural) areas could, at least in the first instance, be set out in regional plans. More emphasis could usefully be placed on providing a degree of flexibility in the plans about what is to be allowed, while not loosing sight of the need to protect environ-mental conditions and the interests of adjacent owners. The local plans need to be more explicit about objectives than they have been in the past.

Many of the policies and zoning categories could be defined by central government in the form of advice to municipalities and other planning agencies, which could adopt, or adapt, these and incorporate them into their plans. This would speed plan production and approval, and facilitate public understanding of the plans, provided that this advice is used flexibly and with sensitivity to the needs of the local situation.

It is particularly important in this regard to reconsider the categories to be depicted on the zoning map, which have changed little in 60 years – for example, the practice of defining three density categories for housing. Any categories used in these local plans should be plausibly related to social needs, market demands, and environmental impact.

RECOMMENDATIONS

Land Ownership and Availability

Patterns of existing land ownership, and the ambitions of landowners are a significant influence on land availability. A wide range of views on the proper role of the state in influencing urban development exists, but the World Bank concluded as long ago as 1972 that it is 'abundantly clear that market values are usually not an efficient allocator of urban land' (World Bank, 1972). In view of the problems in Palestine noted above, and the unprecedented scale of development likely in the near future, the advantages of intervention by government in the development process are considerable.

The possibilities include the following. Firstly, the acquisition by govern-ment of extensive tracts (or selected sites) of land scheduled for future development, preferably at existing use value, either by voluntary agree-ment or with compulsory purchase powers. The land could then be developed or serviced by the government, released to specific users or allocated for certain types of development by sale or lease to public or private agencies, at a rate which would reduce land speculation elsewhere.

Secondly, much more use could be made of existing legislation which allows the compulsory reparcellation of land, i.e. the consolidation of existing ownerships, and redistribution to the original owners in parcels suitable for development. A portion could be retained for public use. The government has a role in advising municipalities on 'best practice,' based on past examples with a view to improving design standards, increasing public confidence and reducing the time taken for this process.

Thirdly, substantially increased land taxes could be imposed on vacant land which is zoned for development in order to discourage land speculation.

Fourthly, some means of securing betterment for the benefit of the general public needs to be devised. At present, increases in land values arising from a general increase in demand for land, or because of public development projects in the vicinity, all accrue to the landowner. Existing planning legislation allows for the recoupment of betterment, but apparently has never been used effectively.

Fifthly, government should give encouragement to the establishment of an efficient market in land. Registration of all land, public accessibility to this register, and the regulation of estate agencies as professions will help.

Implementing the Plan

The quality of the national redevelopment of Palestine will depend not only, or even primarily, on the plans themselves, but rather on the way they are implemented. Some guidelines for the future follow.

a) Clear responsibilities need to be allocated to local government, together with the resources to carry out their tasks effectively and to budget ahead. Central government priorities and requirements should be made as clear as possible, but within these constraints, maximum freedom of action should be given to municipalities and other local agencies.

b) Consideration should be given to the need for public acquisition of land in advance of urban development, and to the imposition of a betterment tax on increased land values.

c) Town planning legislation needs to be reviewed to bring it in line with current needs. Greater emphasis could be placed on public consultation as a means to improve the quality of the plans, to secure the support of the public and to reduce the scope for corruption among officials or elected representatives.

d) Controls on development should be imposed and enforced. Planning controls are, not surprisingly, associated in the public mind with Israeli occupation. An end to occupation should not mean the end of controls; on the contrary, controls should be seen as necessary in the public interest, and the means of enforcing the controls should be strengthened.

e) Fast, but fair, means of formally considering, consulting on, approving and publicising development plans need to be introduced.

f) Central government can itself set an example by ensuring the co-ordination of its development projects, and the conformity of these projects with agreed development plans and policies.

g) Agencies such as redevelopment or new town corporations charged with particular development projects should be established by central government. Planning legislation could provide for these, e.g. in plan making or development control, in designated localities. The role of housing associations should be strengthened as one means of securing the participation of the general public and of decentralising decision-making in the formidable redevelopment effort that lies ahead.

BIBLIOGRAPHY

Al-Olet, Ahmed S., 1991, **Cultural Issues as an Approach to Forming and Managing Future Neighbourhoods**, Ph.D Thesis., University of Strathclyde, Glasgow.

Benvenisti, M. and S. Khayat, 1988, **West Bank and Gaza Atlas**, West Bank Data Base Project, Jerusalem.

C.E.P. (Centre for Engineering and Planning), 1988, **Master Plan for the Village of Bir Nabala**, Ramallah.

C.E.P., 1992, **Master Planning the State of Palestine**, Ramallah.

Coon, Anthony, 1992, **Town Planning Under Military Occupation**, Dartmouth, Aldershot.

Government of Jordan, 1966, **Law of Cities, Villages and Buildings**, Number 79, Amman.

J.M.C.C. (Jerusalem Media and Communications Centre), 1992, **Israeli Obstacles to Economic Development in the Occupied Palestinian Territories**, Jerusalem.

Halabi, Usamah, Aron Turner, Maron Benvenisti, 1985, **Land Alienation in the West Bank**, West Bank Data Base Project, Jerusalem.

Llewelyn-Davies Planning, 1989, **Refugee Shelter and Services in the West Bank and Gaza Pre-Feasibility Study**, UNRWA, Vienna.

World Bank, 1972, **Urbanisation Sector Working Paper**, Washington, D.C.

INSTITUTIONALISED PLANNING IN PALESTINE

Rassem Khamaisi

ABSTRACT

The present study deals with the development of legislation for planning, construction and the planning authority now operational in Palestine. It covers the origin of laws, their objectives and the type of structural plans they have produced.

Jordanian law *No. 79* of 1966 concerning the planning of towns, villages and buildings is considered the legal basis for the planning process and for the establishment of the planning authority in the West Bank. In Gaza, planning depends on decrees promulgated by the Egyptian administration. In both these parts of Palestine, the *Town Planning Act* of 1936 is also considered to govern planning.

Following the Israeli occupation in 1967, these laws were amended and the planning authority was changed to serve Israeli policies which sought to control all resources and facilitate the establishment of Israeli settlements while, at the same time, hindering the development of Palestinians and preventing their active participation in the planning process and in the planning authority. These amendments concentrated on the physical aspects of planning, rather than on the establishment of planning institutions to suit the real needs of the Palestinians.

This paper attempts to show the importance of the planning authority in Palestine, and proposes that all prevailing laws and systems be reconsidered and that the present planning authorities be restructured. At the same time, the important role of management in the planning process is highlighted.

Guiding principles should be established for the use of land in Palestine by preparing alternative structural plans in keeping with Palestinian interests. The need for new planning authorities and for a legal system which can deal with strategic planning in addition to physical planning is also discussed. The importance of each planning stage and level and the need to delegate responsibilities and determine prerogatives so as to avoid any duplication which would lead to a waste of limited resources or hinder the development process is emphasised.

The study gives a brief explanation of the principles and foundations of a Palestinian Planning Authority from the point of view of the planner, affirming the need to set up a multi-disciplinary team of specialists to translate these principles into a system, law or guiding principle to be applied in Palestine as in other states. The importance of drawing lessons from others and of benefitting from experience which could suit Palestine is stressed.

INTRODUCTION

During more than 28 years of occupation, the Israelis have imposed restrictions and obstacles, making use of construction laws and planning mechanisms to limit Palestinian urban development, while allowing every opportunity for the development of Jewish settlements in the occupied territories. Despite this, Palestinian towns and villages did develop, their populations increased and their built-up areas have expanded, mostly without previous planning.

With the beginnings of a political solution accompanied by Palestinian sovereignty over the occupied territories, a great urban expansion is to be expected, particularly when more resources become available and when new projects are developed within the Palestinian entity. This expected urban and economic boom will coincide with the return of Palestinians to their state. The leadership of this state is responsible for finding housing, for creating job opportunities, and for providing infrastructure and services. This means an increasing demand on resources, especially land, a fact which requires rational organisation and planning of land use.

The limited surface of the Palestinian entity, its physiographic and climatic characteristics, along with the population growth, make it essential for decision-makers in the field of spatial development to establish plans for urban development and to set up the planning institutions that would guide and rationalise land use, bearing in mind the objective Palestinian reality.

The question which arises is whether the present organising authority is ready and willing to deal with Palestinian needs and requirements and whether the present structures can make up for the shortcomings of the new state in such a way as not to hamper the required development. The present planning authority was amended by military orders to serve the purposes of Jewish occupation and settlements in Palestine. It is, consequently, difficult to imagine that such structures and organisational authorities can respond to present and future needs of the Palestinian state.

This study will first review the development of planning in Palestine, the setting up of planning authorities, and the advantages of land use planning as conceived during the Mandate, then the Jordanian amendments to the planning institution and the changes brought by Israeli occupation. Such a review will enable us to judge their adequacy for the future, and how we can benefit from our own past experience and from other experiences all over the world in setting up a structure for the planning authority in the state of Palestine.

The study will include principles for structural planning at different levels, bearing in mind local government as an additional mechanism for urban planning. By planning, we mean legalised area planning, but this does not preclude the economic and social dimensions of planning.

LEGALISED AREA PLANNING

The legislation for town planning in Palestine started towards the end of the Ottoman era with the promulgation of the 1877 law for regional *welayat* and towns. A system of building permits for towns was set up as well as rules for the appropriation of land for building roads and for regional development. The law also provided for taxes to be collected from those whose lands appreciated as a result of the building of new roads. Some aspects of this law are still applied in the PT to the present day, although the lack of institutions has limited its proper implementation and allowed it to be used as a means of obtaining financial revenues for the central and local authorities (McLean, 1930). Planning under the Ottomans stressed the physical aspects: roads and buildings, particularly in the towns, disregarding the economic and social aspects.

With the arrival of British troops in Jerusalem, the British issued a military proclamation on 9/12/1917 prohibiting building in an area covering 75 metres all around Jerusalem. Any construction within the walls was also prohibited in order to preserve the character of the city. In the course of the first two years of British occupation, structural plans were set up for the towns of Jaffa and Jerusalem (Hyman, 1994). The British occupying authorities were preparing new legislation for town planning based on the British experience during the first decade of the twentieth century when the term 'town planning' first appeared in 1906 (Gordon, 1974: 31).

Town planning was established as a system in Britain in 1909 to plan space and areas to solve urban, environmental and social problems created by the industrial revolution and the structural changes in British society. The British carried town planning to the territories under their Mandate, such as India, Nigeria and Malaysia (McGoubrey, 1988; Home,

1993); Palestine was also included. When British military rule became civilian in 1922, town planning laws were adopted, but they were to be implemented only in towns. Building plans and space planning were established for the Palestinian towns of Jerusalem, Jaffa, Haifa, Nablus, Bir Al-Sab', Gaza and others; construction plans, building permits and roads were organised at both the local and central organisational levels.

This town planning proclamation remained operative until 1936 when a new system was approved, adding the regional level to the local and central ones. Since the British Mandate extended over Palestine and Jordan, the 1932 town planning system in Britain was changed into the 1936 planning system in Palestine through the *Town Planning Order* of 1936. This was then adopted as the legal basis for the establishment of related institutions until law *No. 31* of 1955 was issued for town planning and construction in the West Bank.

The 1936 Town Planning Order divided Palestine into six regions, each of which proceeded to prepare regional plans in 1937; in 1942, the town planning consultant and the High Commissioner began to ratify the plans.

The planning institution set up by virtue of the 1936 *Town Planning Order* was composed of three levels: local committees in the towns, regional committees in charge of planning and approving the plans for the whole area and the central level which included the town planning consultant and the High Commissioner in his capacity as the supreme authority for the British Mandate. The office of the town planning consultant (headed by architect Henry Kendal between 1935 and 1948) prepared and approved regional and local plans.

The planning institutions, at the time, may have been dispersed in terms of their locations, but were centralised in regard to performance. The town planning consultant had considerable authority to plan, approve and amend. Regional plans were set up for all Palestinian provinces at the time, the plans for most Palestinian towns were approved and construction plans were prepared for 25 out of 900 Palestinian villages (Lipidott, 1977).

A close examination of the aims and substance of the structural, provincial and local plans prepared during the Mandate, some of which are still in force in Palestine, show that they were particularly intended to control and restrict Arab construction, in addition to controlling the development process in general. These aims can be summarised as follows:

1) To establish the legal basis for town and village organisation throughout Palestine;
2) To prevent unplanned land use and construction, and to prohibit linear construction along the main roads in villages and outside the

town areas, as well as to prevent excessive construction along the roads leading to towns;

3) To safeguard historical and natural sites and special landscapes (including coastal areas);
4) To preserve agricultural land and to limit the expansion of building areas; and, finally,
5) To raise the standard of environmental space by organising the use of land into secondary areas and establishing rules, systems and criteria for each building area.

Land use in each region was divided into four types of usage: construction and development areas, agricultural areas, coastal areas and natural reserves. The planning included the organisation and orders for issuing building permits concerning the surface of the site, the percentage of the building area, the height of the building, and the recession line. All this affected the construction and development areas and the agricultural areas where different concentrations of construction were allowed.

The plans were established on the basis of imported concepts orchestrated by the town planning consultant, i.e. concepts developed in an industrial society like Britain. The British Mandate in Palestine transposed and implemented them through its control over space and the issuing of building permits, because Palestinian society was mostly an agricultural and village society, developing at a relatively slow pace, functioning on the basis of rural concepts stemming from their own values and customs. This limited the effect of regional planning on the villages, with the exception of roads. As for the towns, local plans were prepared and approved; they were implemented through municipal authorities which became local organising committees, responsible for issuing permits, for planning and control as well as for space development within the area of the town.

The provincial structural planning and the 1936 Town Planning Order established the basis for the planning process, for land use and for the planning authority in Palestine despite their limited implementation. The nature and style of the planning process, which was aimed at organising and controlling the use of land, the instructions for implementation and the institutions set up to implement plans and laws could only lead to centralisation.

When the British Mandate came to an end in 1948, Palestine was divided and Israel was created in one part of it. The other part, the West Bank, was annexed to Jordan, while Gaza was placed under Egyptian administration. As for the planning process, the structural plans established under the Mandate remained in force. During the Jordanian Mandate, law *No. 31* of 1955, which was not much different from the 1936 order, was adopted for town and village planning and construction.

211

Subsequently, law *No. 79* of 1966 was adopted entrusting the Kingdom of Jordan with full planning authority for the West Bank. The British system remained in force in Gaza.

The Jordanian authorities did nothing to amend the planning system established by the British Mandate. They only devised structural plans for some towns and supervised construction. They did not prepare plans for the villages, except in a few cases such as El Taiba, near Ramallah.

The Jordanian structural plans for some of the towns in the West Bank disregarded demographic development and needs as well as the future economic and social requirements of the population (Al-Gerbawy and Abdelhadi, 1990). They were established along the same lines as under the British Mandate and further restricted urban development in the towns. They also failed to assign sufficient land for public buildings and economic activities, thus limiting economic and industrial developments in the towns. Moreover, the planned network of roads disregarded future needs and the increasing number of vehicles, thereby encouraging a network of roads incompatible with the needs of the population. This has resulted in the traffic crises plaguing Palestinian town centres today, despite their relatively small size and the relatively low standard of living.

As far as town planning authorities and institutions are concerned, law *No. 79* of 1966 established three levels of authority: a national level represented by a Supreme Planning Council (SPD) and a central town and village planning department in Amman. On the level of the region, district town, village and construction committees were set up and on the district level, the local committees were formed to organise towns and areas to be decided by the minister and approved by the central department as a local committee. The law also allowed for joint local and regional committees (The Hashemite Kingdom of Jordan, 1980), and gave the minister the possibility of granting some village councils the prerogatives of local planning committees.

The law stipulated that the committees represent public authorities, political and professional, with a hierarchy of responsibilities and prerogatives. The law tended to concentrate authority in the hands of the minister. This had a particular effect on planning and development in the PT following the Israeli occupation in 1967.

The Jordanian period brought no noticeable development in the field of planning and construction, perhaps due to the limited development of Palestinian society as a result of the massive emigration of Palestinians from villages and towns. Moreover, the development of the East Bank of Jordan was the priority rather than the West Bank. Awareness of the importance of planning was poor, among both the public and the authorities. The State did not develop any regional plans, nor structural provincial plans. As a result, the plans established under the Mandate remained operational, a fact exploited by the Israeli authorities after occupation, when deciding building permits.

Throughout the Jordanian era, the *Town Planning and Villages and Building Law No. 79* of 1966, which was authorised through the *Town Planning Order* of 1936, was in effect. Under this law, the municipalities began to prepare town planning schemes for towns like Ramallah, El-Bireh, Nablus, Jenin and Tulkarem. These plans replaced and changed the town planning schemes that were prepared during the Mandate.

PLANNING UNDER ISRAELI OCCUPATION

At the time of the Israeli occupation of the West Bank and Gaza, most villages and many towns lacked approved structural plans. Moreover, the Israeli occupation came one year after the approval of the amended Jordanian law *No. 79* of 1966. No institutionalised planning authorities with long traditions existed, and this meant that the PT were 'uncovered' regarding town planning. Consequently, it was easy for the Israeli authorities to amend the relevant laws and regulations to serve their interests, taking advantage of the legal and central changes in the Jordanian law to gain a free hand in controlling land use and in granting building permits to Palestinians.

Until 1971, the process of granting building permits continued in accordance with Jordanian laws and the plans established by the Mandate. Perhaps the Israeli decision-makers did not expect the occupation to last, hence their limited interference with the legal basis and mechanisms for planning. The Israeli authorities concentrated on security aspects and control of building processes through the army. The big change came in 1971 with the issuance of military order *No. 418* which established the basis for the planning authorities under Israeli occupation. This order came to be known as the *Decree concerning the Organisation of Towns, Villages and Buildings in the West Bank (No. 418* for the Hebrew year 5731, i.e. 1971 A.D).

The decree abolished the district level of planning and building, transferring authority to a Supreme Planning Council established for each part of Palestine, i.e. the West Bank and Gaza. The comprehensive powers granted by the Jordanian law to the minister passed to the hands of what was called *the responsible*, who was appointed by the military leader of the area. The same military order also dissolved the planning committees in village councils, later establishing six regional and village committees in the West Bank and two in Gaza.

The same decree granted the military leader of the area the authority to appoint the members of the SPC and the regional and village committees; the Council would also set up subsidiary or ad hoc committees as it deemed necessary. Once the military order had been issued and

213

implemented, the Palestinians were robbed of all authority and responsibility for their own organising and planning institutions. Their presence in the province and village committees, or in the committees emanating from the Council, was simply formal. *The responsible* set up the Council and appointed Jewish members, with no Palestinian representation, thus going against law, customs and international laws.

Military order *No. 418* re-established a central and a local level for planning institutions, bringing the situation back to what it was before the town planning regulations issued in 1936. The planning institution became essentially centralised, the local village and town levels being quite weak and directly under the control of the Council or the director of the Central Planning Department (CPD) and his assistants, all of whom were Jewish employees. The latter fully controlled planning authorities and the building process, later also determining the policy for land use and the initiative for the preparation of structural plans.

This total control transformed the law in force into an efficient mechanism to restrict Palestinian urban growth, limiting construction by refusing building permits and by reducing the land earmarked for industrial and economic projects, thereby depriving both towns and villages a functioning economy. Planning became a tool for the military government to prevent the expansion of construction by Palestinians; instead, it allowed them to set aside vast areas of land for Jewish settlements in the PT and to annex these areas (Shehada, 1990).

What increased the negative effect of such planning is the fact that the Israeli occupation authorities used the Mandate's structural plans and the Jordanian system in a selective manner, concomitant with Israeli interests. *Article 7* of military order *No. 418* granted special authority to *the responsible* appointed by the area commander; he was given 'absolute' authority since the law stated that, despite the contents of *Article 5*, the Council could enact the following measures:

1) Amend, cancel or suspend any design or permit for a given period;
2) Take over any of the prerogatives of any committee mentioned in *Articles 2* and *5* (regional or village committees or municipalities);
3) Issue any permit normally granted by any of the committees mentioned in *Articles 2, 3* and *5*; and (through the area commander) amend or cancel any permit; and
4) Exempt any person from the need to obtain a permit in accordance with the law (see military order *No. 418*, 1971).

The area commander appoints the members of the Council in contravention to the Jordanian law of 1966 which has remained in force despite the occupation and which was recognised by 'military order *No. 418*' in *Articles 1* and *5* regarding the authority of local organising committees in the municipalities. In this way, the planning institutions were set up to suit Israeli interests.

The composition of the Council and its subsidiary committees made it a pliant tool and a means to implement Israeli policy aiming at dominating the PT, restricting Palestinian urban expansion and development and increasing the dependency of the Palestinian economy on Israel. Palestinians were prevented from participating in decisions concerning the development of their own spaces (Al-Arbawy and Abdelhadi 1990; Khamaisi 1989, Coon 1992).

In contrast, the door was wide open for developing, planning and guiding Jewish settlements in the PT. Settlements were even sometimes exempted from the need to obtain a building permit or to prepare a structural project, since *the responsible* in charge, by virtue of military order *No. 418*, was entitled to grant such a dispensation. It became very difficult and costly for Palestinians to obtain a building permit; the process went through many stages and required authorisation from several institutions and departments (Antiquities, the Custodian of Absentee Property, the Military Governor, the information committee, taxation authorities, internal revenue officials, and others.) (Khamaisi 1990, Coon 1992). The difficulty in obtaining building permits led some Palestinians to build without them and, in many such cases, the building was later pulled down. This difficulty also forced other Palestinians to forego having a house altogether.

Among the reasons which contributed to the limitation of building permits was the absence of local structural plans for Palestinian towns and villages. The legal basis used for the granting of permits centred on the regional planning regulations set up during the Mandate, which were not in keeping with the needs of the Palestinians even by the 1940s (when the need for development and construction was far less), let alone the 1970s.

The absence of structural plans for some cities, and the lack of allowance for urban expansion in others, gave the organising authorities, dominated by Jews, a practical means of withholding permits on the pretext that there were no structural plans to allow for the granting of permits to build houses, roads or schools (see Jordanian law *No. 79, Chapter 4, Article 34*). Yet the Palestinian population was increasing and so was their need for housing, services, economic activities and infrastructure, but planning and building permits were used technically to prevent the fulfilment of these essential needs.

An examination of the Jordanian law, still used as the basis for organisation in the PT, shows that the responsibility for preparing regional and local structural plans lay with the local committees and the provincial committee; in the absence of the latter, it became the responsibility of the Council (see *Chapter 3, Articles 14 to 23* of Jordanian law *No. 79*

215

of 1966). This means that the occupying authorities did not fulfil their duty towards the citizens of the PT in accordance with international covenants (Greenwood, 1988) since they established local structural plans designed to reduce Palestinian expansion to a minimum, while maintaining several buildings outside the established structural plans.

The Israeli occupying authorities rejected the provincial and regional levels of the planning institution, perhaps considering Gaza and the West Bank as Israeli provinces even though they are merely occupied, and considering the Council in each to be a provincial committee with full authority and responsibility for organisation and construction.

As for the local level, the Israeli occupying authorities did not transform any village council into a municipality so that it could assume the authority and responsibility of a local committee; nor did they appoint a new village council other than what was proclaimed under Jordanian rule. Thus they froze the expansion of local government, reduced its responsibilities and deprived it of its authority as regards organisation and construction. The Israeli occupying authorities, however, set up bodies, known as *village planning committees*, for each region, with authority over areas outside the city limits.

Thus the Nablus area was considered a local organisational region under one village regional committee. Bethlehem and Jericho came under another, and the whole West Bank was divided into six village local committees, directly subject to the authority of the SPC, issuing permits on instructions from the director of the CPD and the information committee emanating from the Council which, in turn, was headed by the person responsible for regional planning. This post, like all executive and decision-taking posts, was headed by a Jew.

The occupying authorities divided the West Bank and Gaza into Jewish provincial councils and set up local councils such as Maalia Adomim and Arenel, in charge of preparing structural plans, approving them and submitting them to the Council even though these settlements fell within areas which should have been under the village planning committees (Benvenisti and Khayat, 1988). The application of different yardsticks, one for the Palestinians and another for Jewish settlers, created a duality in the planning and organisational activities covered by the Council which was based on racial and ethnic considerations.

The organisational authorities working in the settlements have clear responsibilities and a distinct hierarchy: covering the local, district and national levels. The planning authorities in the Palestinian areas have all the responsibility but no authority at either the local or central levels. The regional level does not exist, even though the Jordanian law and the Mandate had recognised its importance for efficient organisation in Palestine. The presence of such a level may have obstructed the realisation of Israeli objectives. That is the Israelis changed it, while maintaining the normal hierarchy within Israel and in the Jewish settlements in the PT.

STRUCTURAL PLANS TODAY

As previously explained, structural plans for cities started with the British Mandate in Palestine. The villages remained without any structural planning, all building permits and development in them being done in accordance with the Mandate's regional structural plans which remained in force during the Jordanian administration and during the first period of Israeli occupation.

The significant change in the preparation of the structural plans of cities and villages came in 1979, following the political take-over of power in Israel by the right-wing Likud party, under the leadership of Menahem Begin. The Likud sought to establish the domination of the State of Israel over what was considered to be historical Israeli territory, including the Palestinian territories occupied in 1967. Begin strove to restrict Palestinian urban expansion while rationalising and deepening Jewish settlements in the PT, particularly after the first ten years of occupation.

During that period, the number of Palestinian inhabitants in towns and villages had greatly increased and so had their needs. It became necessary to prepare structural plans that would safeguard Israeli interests and control and limit Palestinian progress and development while establishing the legal basis for issuing permits.

The SPC and the CPD worked on three levels. The first was to prepare alternative regional plans, which began with the centre, around Jerusalem. The aim of the plan was to establish a legal basis for issuing permits and organising the use of land as a substitute for *RJ-5*, the regional plan established by the Mandate. The new plan earmarked territories for the present and future expansion of Jewish settlements, while limiting the space available for construction by Arabs (Abdulhadi, 1990). The plan was subject to objections and has not been executed to date, even though it is being applied by organisational departments.

In Gaza, a regional plan was prepared to replace the one from the Mandate, and to guide the process of establishing local structural plans which, in accordance with Jordanian law *No. 79* of 1966, *Article 15-1*, were to be established on the basis of provincial plans. The regional plans for Gaza were approved by the planning authorities. With the exception of these two plans, no global regional plans were prepared for the PT.

The second level of planning focused on the preparation of a partial provincial plan for road building, military order *No. 50*, indicating the highways, the national, regional and local roads. Instructions were issued for the implementation of these plans which did not include any other kind of land use and which formed part of the national plan for roads

217

(*T-M-A-3*) within the green line approved by the Israeli government in 1973; it did not include the PT and was thus a partial provincial road plan to strengthen the link between the PT and the settlements within Israel.

The third level concerns local structural plans; the CPD proceeded to prepare such plans for the villages based on the plans of the Mandate. Those plans did include the need to set up local plans for towns and villages as a basis for issuing permits and setting rules for development. Nevertheless, they were not carried out until 1979, forty years after their approval, when the Department proceeded to prepare local structural plans which included a network of main roads, three residential areas of various population densities, building instructions and sites for some public buildings.

A close examination of these plans shows them to be repetitive and unprofessionally prepared. Palestinian protests and the fact that the Department itself did not find them convincing led the latter to put a freeze on their preparation, even though 183 village plans had been drafted. Yet they continued to be a reference for granting permits since the director of the CPD maintained, contrary to the fact, that there was no other option.

In 1985, the operation of preparing local village plans was resumed, this time allowing the participation of Palestinian planners, whereas only Jewish planners had been involved before. However, the contradiction between the policy and instructions of the Department and the professionally prepared plans drawn up by Palestinian planners and which aimed to develop Palestinian villages was too great. They could only be approved after being radically altered.

Meanwhile, most Palestinian planners became convinced that it was impossible to work, given such contradictions. In fact, seventy plans prepared by Palestinian planners for towns and villages were rejected by the Council.

During the *Intifada*, the Department began to prepare special local structural plans with the help of its employees, pursuing the same aim of limiting Palestinian urban expansion. So far, such plans have been devised for two-thirds of the Palestinian villages and towns. They form the basis for granting building permits, even though they have not been prepared in accordance with accepted professional rules concerning the allocation of sufficient land for housing, the distribution of land ownership, the earmarking of sufficient land for public buildings, and other matters regarding industrial and commercial areas, etc. This has resulted in the housing crisis and the added pressure on the already brittle infrastructure in Palestinian towns and villages, not to mention traffic bottlenecks, rising land prices, insufficient land for public buildings and expensive housing.

In most towns and villages, there are no industrial areas to act as an economic basis to generate income (Khamaisi, 1994).

All the above goes to show that the existing structural plans at the local level are contrary to Palestinian needs and only increase their dependence in terms of development. On the regional level, the structural plans of the Mandate are still in force, along with the amendments made by the Israeli occupying authorities to serve their purposes.

No such plans exist on the national level, because the Palestinian territories intended to become sovereign are part of the Palestine that was under the Mandate before 1948 and part of the Hashemite Kingdom of Jordan between 1948 and 1967, which was then occupied by Israel after 1967; i.e. it was never an independent territory as such, and no plans were set up for it. Moreover, under the Mandate no landscaping was developed and the plans only concentrated on the regional level. National institutions had been set up under the Jordanians but they prepared no overall plans to guide regional and local planning. During the Israeli occupation, national plans were designed for Israel, but they did not directly include the PT. The situation remained vague and this helped to open up opportunities for Israeli Jews to settle in the PT and to control land and resources.

There was little participation by Palestinians in planning; all initiatives came from the central authority. The Palestinians' refused to normalise relations with the occupying authorities and to deal with them on a daily basis; moreover, there was always hope that the long occupation would come to an end. There was little awareness of the importance of planning, since Palestinian society is mostly rural with a low economic standard of living, and a relatively slow pace of development. Foreign occupation for more than two decades deprived Palestinians of any sovereignty in running their business and planning for it. They looked upon planning as a tool at the service of 'alien' authority.

Local government was weak in most towns and absent in the villages, producing a lack of planning initiative. Only in the last decade, when Israelis started to use planning as an effective technical tool for controlling their land and expanding Jewish settlements, has structural planning become very important for Palestinians.

ALTERNATIVE STRUCTURAL PLANS

As the process of transferring authority and responsibilities from the occupying authorities to the national Palestinian authority progresses, it expected that, sooner or later, authority for planning and building will be transferred to the Palestinians. Therefore, the question arises, 'Should we keep the planning institutions as they are, or does their form, their substance, their aims, and their concepts as well as the people in charge

All members of the levels shaded in grey are Jewish

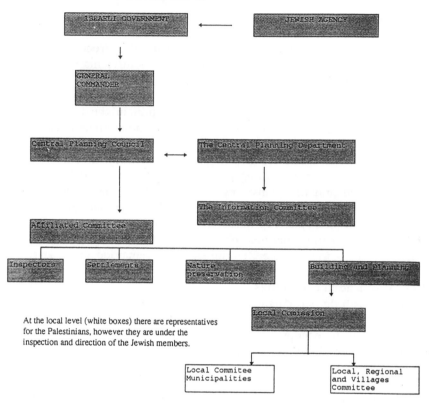

Figure 1 The Structures of the Planning System in the Palestinian Territory (Jordanian *Law No. 79*) 1966 and the adjustments pertaining to Military Order *No. 418*).

need to be changed?' There is, undoubtedly, a great need for new structural plans for most Palestinian towns and villages to be prepared on a legal and professional basis to serve the aims of the Palestinians. The PNA should prepare these on three levels – national, regional and local.

Because the Palestinian entity has become a political unit with a national authority, there needs to be a national structural plan including the Palestinian coastal area, Gaza and the West Bank. Such plans should reflect Palestinian strategies and aims regarding land use, the economy, construction, parks, agricultural land, airports, and other topics. The main plan would form a basis for regional plans.

The PT should be divided into four districts or departments: Gaza, Hebron, Jerusalem and Nablus. A regional structural plan, including land use in the province, should be designed for each. They should reflect the national plan in detail and replace the ones that had been used so far.

As for the local level, general local plans should be made for each town, village or village complex. They need to reflect the regional plan and determine the needs of the town or village, in relation to local, regional and national objectives. Each plan would serve as the legal basis for granting building permits in small villages, and for the preparation of detailed plans in large towns.

All such plans are to be entrusted to multidisciplinary, professional teams so that all future needs may be catered for in services, infrastructure, housing and economic structure. These structural plans should form the rules to guide sectoral or regional planning in line with the comprehensive planning.

The expected urban and economic activity that will follow the establishment of the State of Palestine requires appropriate planning with regard to needs and priorities. At the same time, it must reflect the limited resources and emphasise the importance of citizens' participation in planning decisions yet avoid the duplication and obstacles that can result from excessive citizen representation. This is essential to begin the developmental process in Palestine.

THE PLANNING INSTITUTIONS

Official national planning institutions should be established, along with local ones, to implement the law and guide the planning and development process. A Central Planning and Construction Authority, similar to a Supreme Council, should be established to take charge of planning. This authority or council should be headed either by the Minister of Interior or the Minister of Local Government. It should be composed of representatives of all the ministries, at the level of general directors, to avoid duplication and contradictions at the national, regional and local levels.

Provincial planning committees should be set up for four districts: a coastal province with Gaza as its centre; a southern district with Hebron as its centre; a central district with Jerusalem as its centre; and a northern province with Nablus as its centre. The district planning committee should be headed by the governor or director of the province in the Ministry of the Interior or the Ministry of Local Government. The provincial committee should be composed of representatives from the various ministries, as well as representatives of towns and villages to be elected from among the heads of local government. The head of the town municipality should also be a member.

As for the local level, independent local planning committees should be established in all the municipalities and villages which have more than

10,000 inhabitants. All the members of the local authority would be members of the local organising committee, together with a representative from the provincial committee. Joint local planning committees should be set up for each village complex having 25,000 or more inhabitants. The members of the local planning committee would represent the local authorities of the villages, one for each 2,000 to 2,500 inhabitants. The head of the largest village in the complex should preside over the local committee. The committees should also include representatives from the architects' union.

Each local authority should include at least one architect planner whose task would be to approve any construction or development plan before its approval by the local committee. In small villages where there is no local authority, a regional authority to serve several villages should be established. The architect planner of the provincial local authority would be responsible for approving plans to make sure they are in keeping with the overall structural plans (see Figure 2).

In addition to active and efficient planning institutions, strategic planning units including the architect planner assigned to the municipality and to the engineering department need to be set up. The task of these units would be to design future strategies for the development of towns, translating needs into global and comprehensive working plans that would include economic, social and cultural planning, as well as physical planning. Those units should co-operate with the local planning committees to integrate development with a long-term view and without neglecting the activities to be undertaken in the short-term.

The proposed institutional structure is meant to accompany the proposed structural plans, while delegating powers and responsibilities to those active in the field. The institutional structure should allow streamlined information flows and avoid contradictions and duplications. They should facilitate building permits and rationalise the development process.

It should be an uncomplicated institution, allowing sufficient freedom for local government without excess. A link should be established between the planning institution and the type of plans, with clear conditions regarding the qualifications of planners and administrators to ensure a professional level of work. All these principles should be incorporated into a Palestinian law of organisations which needs to be drafted and adopted.

CONCLUSION AND RECOMMENDATIONS

This study proposes a Palestinian planning institution or authority based on a hierarchy of responsibilities. The development of planning and its institutions in the Palestinian entity has been reviewed. In the past,

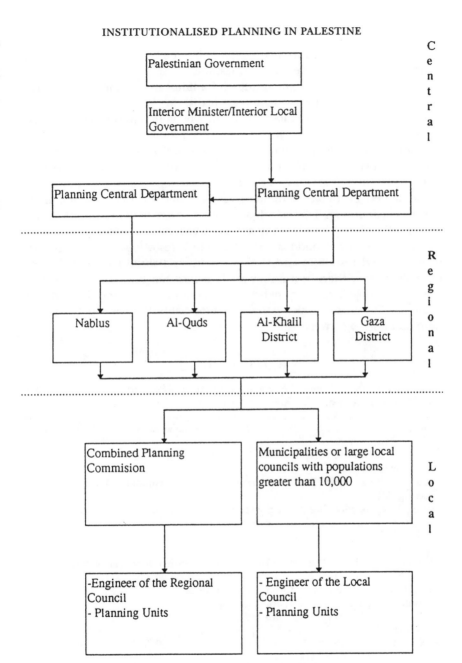

Figure 2 Structure for Suggested Planning System in Palestine.

changes were made in these institutions in response to the needs of each authority dominating the area and in keeping with their respective interests. This occurred regardless of the needs and interests of Palestinian citizens. The importance of planning in controlling the land, a method used by the Israeli authorities, was emphasised.

The study showed that any change in political power and in the overall aims necessitates a series of structural plans.

Updating the Jordanian law *No. 79* of 1966 is important, because most Palestinians are familiar with its details. Moreover, this law allowed decision-makers a degree of flexibility while, at the same time, expressing the British experience in regulating a planning institution and process.

The planning institution and the preparation of plans should be accompanied by the development of local and district government to ensure streamlining. The fact that political power now lies in Palestinian hands will ensure that planning serves Palestinian society.

Planning is of tremendous importance in Palestine, particularly in view of the limited resources and the economic and social situation. Experience shows that there is a direct relation between the state's capacity to achieve its objectives and between its administrative and institutional strength. The stronger the latter, the more able the state is to achieve development objectives.

BIBLIOGRAPHY

Abdulhadi, R., 1990, *Land Use Planning in the Occupied Palestinian Territories,* **Journal of Palestine Studies**, vol. 76, No. 9 pp. 46–60, 4 (Summer).

Al-Gerbawy and R. Abdulhadi, 1990, *Israeli Organisation Plans, the Perfect Tool for Incorporating the Occupied Territories in Israel,* **Majallat al-Dirasat al-Filastiniyah**, 2 (Spring), pp. 22–58.

Benvenisti, M. and S. Khayat., 1988, *The West Bank and Gaza Atlas,* **The Jerusalem Post**, Jerusalem.

Coon, A., 1992, **Town Planning Under Military Occupation**, Dartmouth Publishing, UK.

Drure, D., 1988, **Planning Authority in Judea and Samaria**, M.A. Research paper, Department of Law, Hebrew University, Jerusalem (Hebrew).

Gordon, E.C., 1974, **The Evolution of British Town Planning**, Leighton Buzzard: L. Hill, London.

Greenwood, C., 1988, **The Administration of Occupied Territory in International Law**, Al-Haq, Ramallah.

The Hashemite Kingdom of Jordan, 1980, **Interim Law No. 79 for 1966, Law for Town, Villages and Construction Planning**, Amman.

Home, R, 1993, *Transferring British Planning Law to the Colonies,* **Third World Planning Review**, vol. 15, No. 4, pp. 397–410.

Hyman, B., 1994, **British Planners in Palestine, 1918–1936**, Ph.D. Thesis, London School of Economics, London.

Judah and Samaria, **Military Order Number 418, Planning of Town and Village and Building Law**, 1971.

Khamaisi, R., 1989, **The Israeli Policy for Planning and Destruction of Buildings in the West Bank**, Palestinian Academic Society for International Affairs, Jerusalem.

Khamaisi, R., 1990, **The Israeli Policy for Planning and Destruction of Buildings** in the West Bank during the Intifada, Centre for Planning and Studies, Kafar Kanna.

Khamaisi, R., 1994, *Structural Plans as a Means of Local Development for Palestinian Government*, Al-Syasah al-filastiniyah, Palestinian Studies and Research Centre, Nos. I and II, Nablus, pp. 65–91 (Arabic).

Lipidott A., 1977, **The Regional Planning Schemes in the British Mandate as a Window for the Planning Process in Eretz Israel**, M.A. research paper, Geography Department, Hebrew University, Jerusalem (Hebrew).

Mc Coulrey, H., 1988, *The English Model of Planning Legislation in Developing Countries*, **Third World Planning Review**, vol. 10, No. 4, pp. 371–387.

Mc Lean, W.H., 1930, **Regional and Town Planning in Principle and Practice**, London.

Shehadeh, A. et al., 1984, **Regional Road Planning Order Number 50**, Al-Haq, Ramallah.

Shehadeh, R., 1990, **The Occupier's Law, Israel and West Bank**, Institute of Palestine Studies, Beirut (Arabic).

NEW TOWNS IN THE
PALESTINIAN STATE

Rassem Khamaisi

ABSTRACT

This study addresses the pattern of new town building in Palestine by drawing on the experience of various countries in building new towns. The example of England, which was the first country to enact legislation on the subject through its *New Town Act* of 1946, is examined.

The study provides an overview of actual Palestinian settlement and notes that most of the Palestinian towns are in fact big villages with access to small urban centres. In the overview, the principles of planning and building these towns, in addition to their relationship with the existing towns, is considered.

The study also discusses the expected needs assessment to provide an appropriate house and its components, taking into consideration that neither the existing private sector in Palestine, nor the Palestinian villages and towns, are able to fulfil the enormous housing demand.

By reviewing the experience of various countries, the objectives, strategies and mechanisms applied by those countries to build their new towns can be perceived. The study concludes by drawing lessons from these countries' experience, given their different surface areas, population and urbanisation problems. Within the framework of these lessons, the study reviews Palestinian realities, addressing the need to build new towns, the issue of building techniques and the suggested sites. These lessons can be used as a guide when developing policies for the building of new towns in Palestine.

In view of the Palestinian realities indicated in this study, a strategy to build a settlements network in Palestine is recommended. The paper concludes by asserting that building new towns will be fulfilled by developing existing towns, and by building parallel new towns which, in the first phase, need to be integrated in developmental urban centres. In the second phase, it is suggested that building new towns in strategic axial sites would help to meet the urgent need for housing and the reconstruction and building of the Palestinian settlement network.

The pattern of new towns, arising from the nature of the Palestinian reality, fulfils strategic development by launching housing solutions and creating employment opportunities. New towns also help to maintain a balanced Palestinian settlement network without wasting limited resources and by benefitting regional economic relations. Finally, this study evaluates various alternatives to develop the Palestinian settlement network. The recommended alternative does not neglect the existing towns and villages, but places different emphasis on the suggested sites in the first phase.

INTRODUCTION

Establishing a Palestinian state in the West Bank and Gaza requires a strategy for developing Palestinian towns and villages, and for providing solutions to housing and labour problems. The new strategy includes the need to explore the possibility of building new Palestinian towns, in addition to developing the existing towns and villages which were built and developed without any central planning. A central planning authority to provide resources and investments to build new districts or even to develop the existing districts was lacking during Jordanian rule in the West Bank and Egyptian rule in Gaza. After the Israeli occupation in 1967, immeasurable obstacles and restraints limited the development of these towns and villages, while the Israeli authorities built new towns and more than 160 Jewish settlements in the Palestinian West Bank and Gaza.

The change in political authority from the Israeli authorities to the Palestinian National Authority (PNA) should be accompanied by necessary developmental policies to provide housing solutions and to develop the rural and urban environment, enabling them to absorb the Palestinian people. The question is whether new towns should be built as part of an urban strategy to absorb returning Palestinians. Alternatively, should development concentrate on the existing towns and villages in the first phase and then consider the possibility of building new towns later?

This paper aims to review the international experience in new town building, explains the motives involved and draw lessons. It then recommend a developmental urban strategy based on the Palestinian reality and addressing its needs. The paper will also present a strategy, suggesting a planning concept, and indicating that the best solution in the first phase is to build new districts as twins to the existing Palestinian towns which possess a long cultural history, in order to support these towns and enhance their developmental role.

In the long term, we suggest the possibility of building new towns in specific areas which need to be served by towns, in addition to turning some villages into towns.

THE INTERNATIONAL EXPERIENCE

The creation of new towns did not start in the 20th Century. Since early history, towns have been built without any planning initiatives, while other towns were built where ancient cultures were established through the planned initiatives of rulers and leaders. The importance of building new towns in the last century was a direct result of using these towns as tools to implement a territorial developmental policy, to induce changes in the network of towns and villages to achieve a population balance, or to solve high population density problems in certain areas, in addition to utilising available economic resources.

The term new town has different meanings in the countries using it. This difference is related to the definition of the term town in various countries, because each group of population starting to settle in a certain site is new; hence, a part of the new towns terminology is philosophical rather than descriptive (Clapp, 1971). New towns were built in different countries to accomplish objectives which varied by type, size and epoch. The different definitions reflected the development of the concept of new towns as a large worldwide urbanisation phenomenon in the last century (Golany, 1978).

However, there were efforts to develop a typological concept of new towns. A group of researchers have issued criteria for defining new towns depending on the size, population and site (Phillips and Yeh, 1987). Golany's typology depended on the degree of self-containment as a central factor. According to him, new towns may be classified in two groups: the first consists of new towns of relative economic independence and which have obtained a special identity. This group includes new towns, new societies and developmental centres. The second group includes the economically dependent satellite towns (Golany, 1978).

The new towns typology can be correlated to the towns' objectives, as some towns were built as service centres with an agricultural ambience, and other towns were built to reduce the population density of a metropolitan centre. Other towns, such as in Brazil or Australia, were built as new capitals. Another group of new towns were established as industrial towns to exploit economic resources, to accomplish geopolitical objectives, or to achieve a balanced population distribution in some parts of the state, as those built in Israel (Efrat, 1989).

Further typological development may be applied depending on the state's development level, considering the distinctions between the developed and developing countries. Distinctions can be made between big countries having wide surface areas and receiving immigrants, such as the USA, Australia and the former Soviet Union, and relatively small industrial countries such as England, Denmark or Germany.

Consequently, the definition and development principles of new towns are related to state needs and conditions, taking into consideration the obstacles and motives and benefitting from other countries' experience in order to build successful new towns without jeopardising the overall development of the country. The assessment of the need to build new towns in Palestine should be preceded by a brief review of the experience of a number of countries, concentrating mainly on Britain, which is considered a pioneer in this field.

The British experience started accidentally while building the Garden Cities initiated by Ebenezer Howard at the beginning of this century, then adopted by the British government in 1946 as a national project. The *New Town Act* was enacted in 1946 to specify the regulations and rules for new town building, their responsibilities and competence, funding and decision-making process, and their relationships with the existing local authorities.

The adoption of the New Town Act in 1946 was preceded by the work of official committees, e.g. the Scot Commission in 1942 and the Uthwatt Committee also in 1942. These committees explored the urban problems in London's peripheral areas, and building new towns in them.

Assessing the new towns project in Britain reveals that the main purpose was to reduce the population density in London and to transfer inhabitants to areas of low density, in addition to using the economic and natural resources, as well as encouraging emigration to these new towns. The planners expected to reduce the pressure on the centre of London and eliminate slums. These new towns were based on the objectives of economic autonomy, social balance and integration of the different emigrating sectors to create a homogenous and planned social fabric.

To facilitate implementation of the Act, the Labour government issued the *Town Planning Act* in 1947 to specify the expropriation of land and the related compensation process, as well as to identify the relationship between a new towns development company which was set up by the Act, and the local authorities and planning agencies.

These regulations and rules took into consideration the fact that the project for building new towns in Britain was to be implemented within the context of a national strategy, for which public resources were mobilised, and various agencies and regulations were developed. By 1991, a total of 29 towns had been built, accommodating a total of 2,245,000 citizens. The number of inhabitants previously amounted to only 945,000. The planners expected the total to rise to 2,753,000 in the target years.

Hence, it is estimated that these new towns contain 80 per cent of the target population, representing 4 per cent of the total population of Britain in 1991. Land equivalent to 418,000 dunums (1 dunum = 1,000 square metres) was allocated to the new towns. There were around 1,100,000 employment opportunities in the new towns in 1991, an increase of 145 per cent. In 1970, £737 million was allocated by the public sector for new town infrastructure (Ward, 1993; Schaffer, 1972).

Because building the new towns took place within the framework of a national strategy, the central government played an key role in the initiation and selection of the towns' sites, land expropriation, financing, planning, monitoring and construction (Corder, 1977). Most of the new towns are located in the peripheral areas of a metropolitan city, while some of the new towns were built to make use of natural resources. Until 1975, most were built in populated areas near small villages; the new towns built after that date were expansions of the main towns.

There are different opinions concerning the evaluation of the British experience in new town building. Some researchers consider it to have been successful in achieving its objections, while others consider it unsuccessful compared to its costs. Although it was a national project, it has been implemented in various areas, and its objectives have changed over time to building developmental poles instead of building new towns.

In comparison to the British experience, the purpose of building new towns in the USA concentrated mainly on developing regions and using natural resources. This was implemented with private initiative, rather than through government, in the financial as well as planning aspects.

In contrast, the central government in the Soviet Union initiated and provided funds for building new towns after the October, 1917 revolution to reduce the expansion of the main cities, to support satellite towns, and to increase the number of small and moderate towns in under-populated areas. The number of new towns in the Soviet Union was about 1,200. In 1990, 65 per cent of the towns in East Siberia were new ones (Underhill, 1990).

In France, the new towns experience began after World War II, when Paris suffered from enormously high population density and the centralis-ation of activities and services. The first step involved the withholding of licences for industrial establishments in the capital. This was followed by a decision to build a chain of new satellites around Paris, similar to the British pattern. Each of the new towns absorbed around 60,000 citizens.

Nine new towns were built in France, five of them within a distance of 19 to 33 kilometres from Paris, two in Marseilles, one near Lille and one near Rouen. The new towns movement was directed by the central agency for new towns established especially for the purpose of new town building. The French government has encouraged and supported people to settle in these priority towns. The French government has also built houses and encouraged developers to participate in the developmental effort (Kinsey, 1969).

The German experience of building new towns is different from either the British or French experiences. New towns in Germany are identified as any big development under a specific authority's control. The urbanisation law in Germany, issued in 1971, covers the renewal and developmental process, and includes the building of new towns and districts. The objectives were to halt the growth of big cities and counties; to transfer people to agricultural areas, thereby forming a peasant class; to build new towns to implement industrial projects; and to build satellite towns, twin towns, administrative towns, villages and industrial cities.

In Egypt, which has drawn on the British, French and German experiences, new town building is part of an urbanisation development strategy and not a replication of the previously mentioned efforts. In this context, the urbanisation development strategy includes two components. The first is to build a chain of new towns and villages for subsequent generations surrounding the regions of the Delta and Valley which can be considered regional economic developmental poles to help reduce population density in the existing towns and governorates and to form new urbanisation centres so that the remaining areas of cultivated land can be maintained.

The second component involves exploring new under-populated areas rich in natural resources. This aims to select depopulated areas suitable for living, and may be used as attraction sites to reverse the trend of population density in Egypt. This component of the urbanisation growth is connected to the strategy of solving the population problem in Egypt.

It is worth noting that the term *new towns* or *new communities* in Egypt refers not only to the construction of housing units or the reconstruction of towns – such as the reconstruction of the Canal zone after the October 1973 War – but also to the structure of new communities. This is based on the principle of building developmental poles to spread economic progress, to implement services, create employment opportunities, and to achieve maximum profits (Hatem, 1992:84).

An independent authority called The New Communities Authority has been established as an autonomous legal entity. Its responsibilities and powers include offering loans, facilities and support to investors in these communities.

The new communities can be categorised in three main groups. The first is a group of satellite cities having access to the main cities and benefitting from existing economies of scale. These satellites are the 15th of May City, the 6th of October City, Badr City, and El-Obor City, in addition to the ten urbanisation sites around greater Cairo.

The second group involves twin towns, consisting of an expansion of housing in the existing desert towns, subject to the existence of an economic base to facilitate building these towns, but which have access to the services delivered by the main city. In others words, they are a group of towns depending on the services supplied by the mother city.

These expansions, based on the existing cities' support, avoid the problems and mistakes of the existing cities. Examples of these twin towns include New Beni Suef, New Minya and New Assiut.

The third group consists of self-contained cities which reflect the long-term policy of building new cities on an independent economic base. These self-contained cities are built in distant locations to achieve economic and social autonomy, and are located in the desert far from the Nile Delta, e.g. Sadat City and the 10th of Ramadan City. Egyptian development policy encompasses these three groups to modify the population map through a central supporting drive for private investment in these new communities.

The experience of other countries in building new town, such as Malaysia, Japan, Singapore (Phillips and Yeh, 1987) and Saudi Arabia (Hugh and Robert, 1979), could be described in detail. All these countries benefitted from the previously mentioned experience.

Various countries have selected one of the three main forms of new town building: satellite cities, urbanisation self-contained centres and twin towns. Each country takes into consideration its objectives, its social and economic conditions and its need to determine a long-term or short-term policy for building new towns.

THE ACTUAL SITUATION IN PALESTINE

About 2.5 million people are currently living in Palestine. One-third of them live in Gaza, which has a surface area of around 365 square kilometres. The average population density is around 2,082 per square kilometre. About 1.7 million people live in the West Bank, including Jerusalem (The Palestinian Statistics Centre, 1994), which has an area of nearly 5.690 square kilometres and an average population density of 300 per square kilometre.

Obviously, the area of Palestine is relatively small and has a high population density. It is divided into two geographic units of longitudinal shape: Gaza is 52 kilometres long and six to 13 kilometres wide, while the West Bank is 150 kilometres long and 51 to 58 kilometres wide. One-third of the West Bank (i.e. the eastern part along the JordanValley) has a low population density and a desert climate.

This physiographic reality has an impact on the present and future population distribution, insofar as the Palestinians are centred alongside the Zahr El-Gabal line dividing the old Palestinian towns from Jenin in the north, passing through Nablus, Jerusalem and Hebron (Al-Khalil) in the south. This urbanisation settlement axis is in the middle of the West Bank where most Palestinians live in small towns and villages, with a maximum of 170,000 population in each central town. However, there is an urban expansion between the central towns and their rural background, such as Nablus which expands from Beit Wazn to the west to Howara and Rogayeb in the east, or in Jerusalem which has an urban expansion from Bethlehem in the south to Ramallah in the north, where 500,000 people live.

Rural domination is one of the characteristics of the Palestinian settlement network. The Palestinians are spread among 537 towns, villages and refugees camps (excluding the Bedouin camps and small hamlets). This includes four towns of more than 70,000 people each. In about 70 per cent of Palestinian villages, the number of inhabitants is less than 2,500 people. (The Centre for Engineering and Planning, 1992).

Despite their rural orientation, the population has expanded around a large number of these villages and towns situated near each other, forming population groups living in villages with low population density, and lacking an essential economic or social base. Another feature of the Palestinian settlement network is the existence of refugees camps outside the main cities, consisting of districts with special living patterns in view of their high population density, different structures and various levels of social and economic services.

The building style and development of the Palestinian settlement network depends on local private initiative. The central authority did not interfere in development or provide housing solutions that changed the general pattern of Palestinian towns and villages. Under the Israeli occupation after 1967, many obstacles limited the development of Palestinian urbanisation.

The occupation forces did not encourage the construction of new towns supported by both economic and housing infrastructure. On the contrary, the Israeli occupation destroyed the housing infrastructure by controlling planning and building processes and by failing to provide financial resources or the human resources capable of changing the actual situation. Economically, the Israeli occupation did not enhance the economy of Palestinian towns and the Israeli authorities refused to build industrial zones in most Palestinian towns. This increased economic dependence on the Israeli economy.

In contrast, the Israeli authorities built Jewish settlements and new towns in the West Bank as satellite towns. In the case of Jerusalem, this included Maaliat Adomim, Gilo and Besghat Zaaif and in the case of Tel Aviv the towns of Arael and Emanoul. Twin towns like Keryat Arbaa in Hebron (Al-Khalil) were also built, regardless of the racial and political differences between the original and the new towns.

The purpose of building these towns was to reduce Palestinian urbanisation and to isolate cities and towns, preventing them from dominating wide geographic areas and forming an ethnic urbanised group. In addition, such building aimed to increase the number of Jewish inhabitants as a preliminary step to annexation. In other words, Israeli settlements are new towns built in the Palestinian territories, and this limits the resources for building new Palestinian towns.

FUTURE NEEDS

There are several reasons why new town building is needed. The first is to meet the expected high demand for housing. This involves providing housing in line with the natural increase of the population and for nuclear families requesting housing separate from their extended kin.

A second reason is that families are expected to want to improve their housing conditions, which have deteriorated as a result of the high population density, the lack of elementary services, and the small size of the housing units. In the West Bank, 57.7 per cent of Palestinian families have three persons sharing one room. This percentage rises to 68 per cent in Gaza (Central Statistics Bureau, 1995).

Thirdly, refugees living in the PT will expect to improve their housing conditions, as will those Palestinians returning from abroad to settle in the PT. In addition, emigration from the villages to the towns is expected to increase as people seek employment and housing.

All these groups have a crucial need for short-term housing, and the question is how to find solutions for this enormous demand.

In addition to housing, there will also be a crucial need in the future to raise economic standards by providing employment opportunities and to attract those with initiative, as well as others who can help develop Palestine. In 1992, the percentage of Palestinians in the labour force was 38 per cent; for females, the figure was 6.9 per cent. Of the total labour force, 20 per cent works in agriculture, 12.1 per cent in industry, 34 per cent in construction and 33.9 per cent in other economic sectors (Central Statistics Bureau, 1994).

In 1992, 36.2 per cent of the work force was employed in Israel despite restrictions against Palestinian labour in Israel. Only 53.2 per cent of the Palestinian labour force worked near their homes, and this indicates how limited adequate employment opportunities are in the existing Palestinian towns, given their weak economic base. The limited employment opportunities in various advanced services and industrial sectors has also adversely affected the skills and quality of Palestinian labour. Yet there are many individuals who possess theoretical knowledge and abilities and only need the opportunity to practice their professions or skills.

In conclusion, the lack of economically structured towns, and the reliance of the Palestinian economy on foreign economic sectors, has led to the present economic situation. Consequently, building new towns, or expanding and developing the existing towns, should focus on developing the Palestinian economy without increasing consumption or reducing production. This means that any housing strategy, including the development of the settlement network, should be implemented within the framework of a wider strategy for developing the Palestinian economy by attracting people with initiative and by providing employment opportunities in advanced economic sectors.

The deteriorating economic situation, along with the pressures and restrictions imposed by the Israeli occupying authorities, has delayed the emergence and development of local government (Shahwan, 1993). As a result, an independent local government capable to playing a significant role in the development process is lacking. Although some large towns such as Nablus, Hebron (Al-Khalil) and Gaza have self-government, they are still incapable of implementing a drive for development. Nor can they provide the essential services needed to accelerate the developmental process.

There is a crucial need to re-build and renew the structure of Palestinian towns and villages. Most of these lack essential facilities, such as roads and sewage systems. This which means that any additional population and housing will increase the pressure on the existing infrastructure and services, and will create urban and environmental problems that will hinder the development process in the future. The existing Palestinian towns share the urban problems of the big cities despite their small areas and low population densities because of the hasty housing process and the lack of planning, infrastructure and basic services.

This situation also has a bearing on determining the pattern for new town building in Palestine, and implies that building new towns should be part of an integrated expansion of the existing towns. The review of the actual situation should be preceded by an overview of the political situation. The newly established Palestinian state has great responsibilities in the political, administrative, services and economic domains, and is trying to face these challenges. The actual situation, as well as the needs assessment for new town building, should be taken into consideration when determining the appropriate pattern for building new towns in Palestine.

THE PROPOSED PATTERN FOR NEW TOWNS

Before describing the proposed pattern for new towns, it is necessary to specify the objectives of the PNA and of society, as well as the new town's role in fulfilling these objectives. These objectives are as follows:

- To raise the economic level of the present Palestinian inhabitants, and the Palestinian people returning from abroad, by providing employment opportunities in all industrial and services sectors;
- To provide the appropriate infrastructure necessary for development in the Palestinian towns and villages;

- To maintain a progressive Palestinian settlement network appropriate to the size of towns and villages, in addition to making use of the relative advantages of each town and village;
- To maintain a balance of population distribution and of employment opportunities to avoid their being concentrated in certain locations;
- To set up urban development centres to help create employment opportunities and to enhance economic initiatives; and, finally,
- To provide housing solutions to meet the expected population increase.

The spatial character of Palestinian society is similar to that of other countries, including factors such as internal emigration from rural areas to central cities, the gap between the centre and periphery, the greater employment opportunities, economic facilities and contacts available in central cities, as well as the centralisation of services in the central cities which attracts a large number of people.

These spatial characteristics are of recent origin in Palestine. Jerusalem and Ramallah are Palestinian urban centres where most of the administrative, economic and cultural facilities are centred, and internal emigration has begun to take place from nearby small towns and village. Were it not for the Israeli restrictions that have limited Palestinian expansion in Jerusalem and its surrounding areas, the number of people would have increased greatly. This is also true for infrastructure and services.

Several proposals to build new towns, to establish a Palestinian settlement network strategy, and to accomplish the previously mentioned Palestinian goals may be discussed. One of these proposals focuses on developing Palestinian rural areas by providing essential resources, and allowing the law of supply and demand to govern individual developers in the existing towns.

The other alternative is to concentrate mainly on the development of a central city, at least in the first stage, by providing resources for the infrastructure, essential services and central administrative facilities. Jerusalem could be taken as an example. This process would encourage Palestinian emigration to the central city.

The third proposal involves measures to encourage competition among towns and villages and their reliance on private initiatives and local governance by mobilising interested investors and by providing essential facilities.

Other proposals may be developed to establish new central independent towns, irrespective of the new town building process. The proposed pattern deemed appropriate to Palestinian realities will focus mainly on building twin towns as satellites to the existing towns and not just on building new self-contained towns to compete with the existing ones.

This is because of the expense of new town building, the lack of adequate locations and the possibility of providing short-term identities.

The proposed pattern adopts the satellite pattern taken from the British, Egyptian and Danish experience but is combined with the new town pattern of Egypt. New towns are proposed for areas near the main towns of Nablus, Jerusalem, Hebron (Al-Khalil) and Gaza, as a first stage. In the second stage, a medium- and long-term strategy should be developed to transform a group of villages and to maintain an urban access to the new towns. In addition, new towns should be built in areas of relative priority, i.e. north of the Jordan Valley in the Geftalk region and at the main crossroads situated alongside the bridge connecting Palestine and Jordan.

In the first stage, new twin towns should be located at the main central towns east of Nablus, north of Ramallah and between Ramallah and Jerusalem, as well as north of Hebron and Gaza. In the next stage, new twin towns should be located near the Palestinian central towns of Jenin, Tulkarem, Khan Younis and Rafah.

The Advantages of the Proposed Pattern

No doubt any planning solution has its positive and negative aspects; however, the proposed planning solution should involve more positive aspects in the short- and long- term. Building new twin towns near the central towns will help to re-distribute the population and will enhance the urban core of existing cities in order to attract people with initiative who are willing to settle in urban centres. Big cities offer better employment and housing opportunities.

The existing small- or medium-sized Palestinian towns have a limited capacity to absorb emigrants or those Palestinians expected to return from abroad. They also have limited opportunities to expand employment.

Building new towns near existing towns will reduce their environmental and urban problems, by reducing the load on the mother town's infrastructure. Moreover, because the new towns will both absorb Palestinians returning back from abroad and be able to provide a housing solution for current inhabitants, social solidarity should be enhanced.

The new twin towns pattern will promote the future centralisation and the developmental role played by the existing towns. The proposed pattern is also compatible with the spatial characteristics emerging in Palestine, including the emigration to the main cities, especially Ramallah.

Implementing New Towns Construction

The experience of the British and Egyptian patterns points to the need to establish a special agency to implement the national projects. In the first stage, an official government steering agency concerned with the new town building should be established. The Palestinian government would nominate the members of this agency and would provide the necessary resources.

On the local level, a local authority should be responsible for planning and implementation in the new towns. Co-ordination between the local authority in the new towns and the local government in the main cities would ensure that the planning, implementation and development of the infrastructural network and services is complementary.

The role of central and local authorities is mainly to establish the essential infrastructure, to establish regulations and laws and to attract individuals with initiative and private sector companies to participate in the planning and implementation process, as well as to build the towns. Most importantly, new town planning should involve both the mother town and the new town, and should include designating land which can be used for economic purposes to develop industrial, trading and services activities.

CONCLUSION AND RECOMMENDATIONS

In conclusion, this study reveals that the Palestinian reality, together with the international experience in new town building, suggests that the appropriate strategy is to strengthen the existing Palestinian towns by establishing new twin towns. In addition, the formation of an integrated urbanisation centre and the dissemination of development to rural satellites is to be recommended.

This pattern for new town building in Palestine will save land, money and energy which is urgently needed by the Palestinian State to solve the present problems of housing and population. Such savings will also help to promote economic development.

BIBLIOGRAPHY

Centre for Engineering and Planning, 1992, **The Principles of the Palestinian State Main Planning**, Ramallah.

Clapp, J.A., 1971, **New Towns and Urban Policy**, Danellen, New York.

Corder, C., 1977, **Planning Cities: New Towns in Britain and America**, Sage Library of Social Research, 55, London.

Efrat, E., 1989, **The New Towns of Israel** (1948–1988), Minerva Publishing, Tel Aviv.

Golany, G., ed., 1978, **International Urban Growth Policies: New Towns Contributions**, John Wiley and Sons, New York.

Hatem, S.A., 1992, **The New Societies, the Route for Economic Development,** The Egyptian Lebanese Printing Press, Cairo (Arabic).

Israel, Central Statistics Bureau, 1994, **Judea, Samaria and Gaza Strip Statistics,** Parts K and B, Jerusalem (in Hebrew).

Israel, Central Statistics Bureau, 1995, **Israeli Statistical Yearbook,** 45, Jerusalem.

Khamaisi, R., 1996, *The Strategy for Urbanisation Civil Development in the Palestinian State,* **Majallaal-Dirasat al-Filastiniyah,** 25 pp. 97–122 (Arabic).

Kinsey, D.N., 1969, *The French Z.U.P. Technique of Development,* **Journal of the American Institute of Planning,** November, p. 370.

The Palestinian Statistics Centre, 1994, **The Palestinian Settlement Population in the West Bank, Gaza Strip,** Ramallah, (Arabic).

Phillips, D. R. and A. Yeh, eds., 1987, **New Towns in East and South East Asia,** Oxford University Press, Oxford.

Roberts, M. and Hugh, P., 1979, **An Urban Profile of the Middle East,** Croom Helm, London.

Schaffer, F., 1970, **The New Town Story,** MacGibbon and Kee, London.

Shahwan A., 1993, *The Local Administration in the Occupied Lands,* **Shu'un Filistiniyya,** 3, pp 2–37 (Arabic).

Underhill, J. A., 1990, *Soviet New Towns, Planning and National Urban Policy,* **Town Planning Review,** vol. 61, 3, pp. 263–285.

Ward, C., 1993, **New Towns, Home Towns: The Lessons of Experience,** Calouste Gulbenkian Foundation, London.

LAW AND HOUSING IN PALESTINE*

Ibrahim Shaaban

ABSTRACT

The legal status in Palestine has evolved over the last century in a particular way. Various and even contradictory legal systems have successively governed the country. When Palestine was part of the Ottoman Empire, it was subject to all the applicable systems until the Empire collapsed. However, some Ottoman laws are still being applied in Palestine today. The most important of these are *Al-Ahkam Al-Adleya* (the Civil Law), the Law of Land and the system of profit sharing.

After Ottoman rule, Palestine came under the British Mandate. Britain established a new legal system and strengthened it by establishing a system of courts and introducing many British laws. The laws covering planning, registration and the transfer of immovable property represented important landmarks at that time.

During the Jordanian era, a legislative revolution took place, and most of the laws were replaced by new ones, including the Constitution. This was followed by laws concerning trade, banking, municipalities and investment.

When Palestine was occupied by Israel, legal distortions occurred. The Israeli Military Governor issued more than 1,300 military orders which amended or abolished most of the previous laws, with questions related to land receiving first priority.

The Oslo Declaration and Cairo Agreement introduced a new and more complex legislative situation. *Article 7* of the Cairo Agreement allows laws to be promulgated to an extent which almost annuls the power of legislation. In addition, parts of the West Bank are still under occupation.

The legal situation will not be discussed here except in relation to housing. Proposals will be made to help eliminate legal obstacles at all

---

* All the references for this paper are in Arabic and are published in the Arabic edition
   of this book (Centre for Arab Unity Studies, Beirut, 1997).

levels. New laws appropriate to the era and consistent with developments in the fields of planning, construction, housing and financing will be suggested as well.

INTRODUCTION

The most important Ottoman laws in the field of housing still applied in the Palestinian Territories (PT) are *Al-Ahkam Al-Adleya* [1] the Law of Land [2] and its appendices, the law concerning the transfer of immovable property, and others regarding the *Tabo* System [3] and profit sharing [4].

During the British Mandate, which lasted more than three decades, major changes were introduced to Palestinian laws, especially those related to housing, land [5], the sale of land owned by minors [6], successive *Tabo* systems [7], prohibitions on selling, occupancy disputes [8], construction [9] and property taxes [10].

The legislative revolution which took place in Palestine under Jordanian rule covered many legal fields. This affected the Constitution [11], *Law No. 40* of 1952 concerning the settlement of land and water disputes [12], *Law No. 2* of 1953 on ownership [13] and *Law No. 79* of 1966 on organising cities and villages [14], as well as general laws such as the Law of Commerce, the Penal Law and the Banking Law.

In 1967, after the Israeli occupation of the West Bank and Gaza, the Military Governor enacted more than 1,300 military orders. The most important were those relating to the separation of powers, which were put into one authority [15]; the application of Emergency Regulations; and the amendment to the Land Laws and Regulations [16].

In 1987, the Palestinian *Intifada* began, and this led to two extremely important developments which added to the complexity of the legal status of the PT. The first of these dissolved the legal and administrative links between Jordan and the West Bank. In 1988, King Hussein announced the severance of these links and this was followed by exclusive Jordanian elections in the East Bank. A Council of Deputies was formed, composed solely of the inhabitants of that Bank.

The other development was the meeting of the National Council in Algeria which declared the establishment of the State of Palestine on 15 November, 1988. This declaration necessitated the enactment of unified Palestinian laws.

The development of the international law on human rights affected the Palestinian legal system. The provisions of The Hague and Geneva agreements, which form the substance of the law governing military occupation, should apply at a time of military occupation [17].

The era which started after the Second World War and began with the United Nations Charter witnessed an international world-wide movement for recognising human rights. This has led to the conclusion of various international treaties, conventions and declarations to protect and guarantee human rights, all of which affect the PT and the people of Palestine [18].

The Oslo Declaration and Cairo Agreement increased the legal complexity of Palestine. According to *Article VII* of the Cairo Agreement, Palestinian legislative powers were restricted and the military orders which were in force in the West Bank and Gaza as of 4 May, 1994 were made legitimate [19].

This, together with the anticipated delivery to the PNA of sovereign powers will make the legal system in Palestine more complex and diverse. The question of housing comes under the general legal framework and the power of legislation. It is connected with the applicable laws, notwithstanding the time of their issuance or the nationality of the entity which issued them, so long that they remain in force. It is also closely connected with immovable property, financing, administration, sale, investment, banking, leasing and the like. Furthermore, it is connected with the desired legislative system and the radical legal reforms that can be introduced in this context.

For these reasons, the question is very wide and comprehensive, and it is not advisable to deal with details or particulars, which would also deviate from the substance of the subject. Here, the general lines, together with proposals and solutions, will be emphasised.

THE SUBSTANCE OF LAW

Laws are the set of social rules which an individual is obliged to obey, even by force when necessary. This definition is comprehensive. It comprises the constitutional rules, laws of emergency, laws of necessity, ordinary laws, sub-legislation, customs and principles of equity. This is so, whether the law embodies several, or even one, rule [20].

Compulsion is a fundamental element of law; without this, it would became only advice or a recommendation. It makes no difference whether the law is ratified by a legislative authority or by the executive authority. It should be noted that the judicial authority does not establish laws, it just interprets and applies laws [21].

The type of the political regime in a country does affect the law, nor is the form of the legislative authority relevant. Such authority may be formed through elections, by appointment or by both. The legislative council may be formed by direct election or by indirect election. Elections may also be bound by qualifications or property conditions or by other conditions. Election may be effected by simple majority, by specific majority or by proportionate representation. The country may have one or two councils. It may be a parliamentary or presidential regime. All these factors have no role in establishing the law. They are merely tools to form the legislative authority which creates a law [22].

Any rule which organises the social behaviour and which is general and abstract, i.e. not addressed to specific persons but to people in general and does not cover specific facts but facts in general, and if such rule is compulsory by all ways and forms of compulsion, provided that it is enforced by the public authority; such would become a legal rule notwithstanding its form, the way it was established, nor the difference between the political regimes, taking into consideration the territorial or temporal restrictions of law [23].

The force of law is not diminished if it is addressed to a specific group or sector of the society. In general, a law should be addressed to the majority of the people, but the nature of a law would not be changed if it is addressed only to some sector of the society, even to one person only, so long as this rule is general and abstract. Accordingly, rules related to contractors, architects or beneficiaries are valid and compulsory legal rules and must be applied even though they are addressed to a small sector of society.

To be more precise, laws follow a hierarchical arrangement; this does not contradict the law but conforms to it. The constitution exists above them, followed by emergency legislation, then the ordinary legislation and at the end, the sub-legislation (regulations and decrees). The lower laws should not contradict with one of a higher tier. If any such contradiction occurs, primacy should be given to the higher law. For this reason, ensuring the constitutionality of laws necessitates the enforcement of the higher law, not the lower law [24].

It should be noted that the law does not differentiate between the branches of law nor does it give preference to one over the other. Since Roman days, jurists have divided the science of law into general law and private law, but this division is only formal and academic and is of no practical use. Civil, penal, financial, commercial, labour, maritime, taxation and military rules are all legal, whether they are mandatory or complementary, because both are legal as long as they contain the main constituents of the law [25].

For these reasons, the law remains valid, compulsory and in force so long as it has not been abolished. In the event that a law is abolished, its compulsory effect shall apply to the events that occurred during its existence. Pursuant to the principle of non-retroactivity of laws, a new law shall not apply to the events that occurred before its promulgation. It should also be noted that some laws are temporary, others are connected with economic or social conditions and still others are more permanent. However, this does not affect the validity of law, because such validity depends only on whether a law has been abolished [26].

THE RIGHT TO A DOMICILE

The right to have a suitable house is the basis for the international strategy for having a habitat and is considered one of the most important human needs. Internationally, it has one of the principal human rights. Jurists relate it to human dignity, to mental and physical health and to the quality of life in general. Safe water and suitable sanitation facilities are considered basic needs that must be made available in every house. A suitable dwelling is defined as providing 'a reasonable degree of intimacy, sufficient space, security, lighting and ventilation, adequate infrastructure and a suitable position in respect of the place of work and the basic facilities. All this at a reasonable cost' [27].

The right to have a suitable dwelling is the right of every man, woman and child anywhere. This is stipulated in the *International Declaration of Human Rights* (Section 1, Article 25). It is also stipulated in the first paragraph of *Article 11* of the *Covenant of Economic, Social and Cultural Rights* of 1966. Following the adoption of two basic texts, the right to have a suitable dwelling has been included in at least 12 international statutes.

The right to have a dwelling means that the original inhabitants should have the right to identify, plan and execute all housing plans and other related social and economic programmes. The original inhabitants must also have some autonomy in respect of their internal and local concerns, including housing. Governments should translate these legal rights into objective facts for the benefit of those eligible. The question is not only financial, legislative, local, municipal or organisational, but also comprehensive and general and is connected to many economic, social and cultural issues.

Accordingly, governments must review their legislation in respect of housing in all its aspects by evaluating existing legislation, amending what should be amended and cancelling laws which create problems. National laws should be adopted appropriate to the size of the problem and in conformity with general policies. The PA must enact this legislation urgently, and adopt measures to identify the present housing situation and to develop policies and establish priorities. Hopefully, such measures would conform to international covenants [28].

If the citizen's right to have a dwelling is accepted as a fundamental duty of governments, governments should recognise this right and should not diminish its legal importance. Such recognition should take the form of legislation, policies and laws to protect this right. Governments should provide subsidies to those who are eligible to receive a dwelling, give legal protection to those who possess houses and make building materials available at low, affordable prices [29].

THE PRESENT AND FUTURE LEGAL SITUATION

In view of the anticipated delivery of full civil competence in the West Bank to the PA, and in the light of what was agreed in the Cairo Agreement concerning legal and legislative powers, it is correct to take the Cairo Agreement as a basis for this study in order to determine the legal position in the transitional period. This conforms with the general principles of law, although strong reservations must be made concerning the provisions of the Agreement.

The legal situation in Palestine is neither favourable nor miserable. The real problem is that there are deficiencies in laws which should be corrected. Laws originate from the prevailing social, economic, political and moral conditions. These conditions are in continuous change and, accordingly, the legal conditions must be changed as well. For example, before the year 1967 the construction of flats for sale was rare and extraordinary; today it is the prevailing system. Therefore, a law must be enacted to organise the ownership of floors and flats which conforms with the developments that have taken place.

The problem concerns the tool or mechanisms for overcoming these deficiencies, especially in the absence of a legislative authority. The question is, to what extent does the PA have power to legislate, in which ways and on which issues? Other questions concern the extent to which the previous laws remain valid and whether the military orders are applicable [30].

We must first admit that all laws which were in force in the West Bank and Gaza before the 5th of June 1967 are valid and applicable, and therefore all Ottoman, British, Jordanian or Egyptian laws remain effective within these jurisdictions regardless of the subject of the law or its legislative rank.

MILITARY ORDERS

The amendments made by the occupying forces to these laws through the issuance of military orders constitute a major problem. The Cairo Agreement in *Article 7, Paragraph 9* stipulates that 'Laws and military orders in force in Gaza and the Ariha area before signing this Agreement and which have not been amended or abolished pursuant to this Agreement remain valid'.

However, the judicial authority has a heavy responsibility to examine the legality of the military orders. Although the Cairo Agreement restricted the powers of the PNA in respect of the laws and military orders, the judiciary may refuse to apply the military orders on the grounds that they are illegal and contradict international laws on military occupation and human rights.

This competence of the Palestinian courts is established and inalienable. The courts have the right to examine any military order and to decide on its legality. If a court decides that an order is illegal, it can refrain from applying it. In other words, although a court cannot abolish an illegal order, it has the right to abstain from applying it. On the other hand, if a court concludes that a military order is legal, it would enforce it.

The question of the legality of military orders should be raised through a plea brought before the ordinary courts, which could bring the matter to the High Court or the Constitutional Court. The High Court would render a final judgement on the matter, to be published in the *Official Gazette*. In this way, contradictions between decisions should be avoided in the event that such powers are given to all courts, while guaranteeing the courts central control.

Obviously, the High Court should be guided by the provisions of The Hague and Geneva Agreements and the restrictions they place on the power of a Military Governor in an occupied territory; especially in view of the fact these two Agreements do not contradict each other.

LEGISLATIVE POWERS

At a first glance, it would appear that the Cairo Agreement conferred legislative powers on the PNA. But a more careful examination reveals that what was given with one hand was taken away by the other. *Article 7, Paragraph 1* gives full power to the Authority to promulgate legislation, including fundamental laws and regulations and other legislative acts. At the same time, *Paragraph 2* of the same article stipulates that the legislative acts of the PNA should conform with the provisions of the Agreement. In other words, the legislative acts of the PNA are to be approved by the Israelis, whether by a legislative subcommittee, control council or the Liaison Committee, and such acts should not concern security issues. No laws have been issued by the PNA and so the Israelis neither approved nor rejected any laws.

It is obvious that legislation involves the exercise of sovereignty. Normally, laws are applicable within the boundaries of a state, i.e. up to the point where territorial sovereignty ends. The principle of the territoriality of law has been established [31]. Because Israel does not refer to a Palestinian state and denies Palestinians the right of sovereignty, the Israelis have restricted the legislative powers of the Palestinians.

Under these conditions, the question is whether the PNA has the power to legislate or not. If it does, there should be no limitations or restrictions on it. If such power is subject to the approval of Israel, the position is completely different; particularly because the PNA has not issued any law to test Israeli's reaction. Consequently, the situation remains vague and open to different interpretations. However, the answer inevitably depends upon the Israeli reaction.

Some people may feel that Palestinian sovereignty is an established fact and that the right of the Palestinians to make laws is undeniable. They would argue that once Palestinians begin legislating, the matter would be settled. However, although Palestinian sovereignty is established, inalienable and belongs to the Palestinian people, and a sovereign power has the right to legislate, the Cairo Agreement is an international agreement which is obligatory according to the *Vienna Convention on International Treaties* of 1969, which is binding on both the Palestinian and Israeli parties to it [32].

For legal and political considerations, the Palestinians cannot abstain from applying the Cairo Agreement. Palestinians are eager not to issue laws subject to Israel's approval, and concerned not to establish this as a precedent that would acknowledge restrictions on Palestinian sovereignty. This is the reason for not promulgating any laws until now. However, failing to promulgate laws does not solve the problem, and the Palestinians should find solutions to resolve the ambiguity in the Cairo Agreement on the issue of legislative powers.

Article 4, Paragraph 2 concerning the competence of the PNA to decide its own 'internal procedures' is completely different from *Article 7, Paragraph 2* which refers to 'basic laws, laws, regulations and other legislative acts.' Furthermore, as to the form, the internal procedures comes under the title *The Structure of the Authority and its Administrative Systems* while *Regulations – General Administrative Decisions* comes under the title *Legislative Powers of the Palestinian Authority*, and this weakens our legal position.

The question remains: What should the Palestinian legislator do? If Palestinian elections take place, the elected council should be solely legislative and should not accept any administrative functions. The President should appoint ministers from outside the Legislative Council, and they should form the executive branch. Thus, the principle of separation of powers would be realised and each authority would have its own functions.

Furthermore, the PNA's Council may, in applying the Constitution in force in both areas, issue so-called *emergency laws* or *transitional laws* for public safety, public order and public security without Israeli approval, because such laws are not subject to delay or adjournment.

Another option would be for the PNA to draft laws and present them to the Israelis for approval. In the event that the Israelis disapprove of them, the Authority should appeal against the decision within the procedures set out in *Article 7*.

Nevertheless, *Article 7* of the Cairo Agreement be amended or abolished altogether because prevents the promulgation of all Palestinian laws. *Article 7* prohibits the enforcement of any law related to an Israeli security matter or which seriously threatens Israeli interests, or which may cause irreversible damage to, or prejudice of, Israeli interests. Moreover, the term used, 'Israeli interest,' is too wide, because it was not defined, limited or restricted.

Clearly, the extent of the PNA's legislative power needs more study, research and diligence in order to lay down legal rules for the public policy actions it adopts. The legal rules reflect the mandatory nature of public policies; without such rules, policies would become mere advice and guidance, which may or may not be applied.

PROPOSED LAWS

In view of this heterogeneous legal structure, recent international developments in the field of law and successive political events, legislative action must be taken to update old laws. Many social and economic events have also taken place which necessitate the promulgation of new laws, or the amendment of existing ones. Hopefully, the Authority will acquire the power to legislate and then effect a legislative revolution for the benefit of all citizens and their security and for justice and human values.

Consequently, the following is recommended.

Enactment of a Palestinian Constitution

Britain issued a Constitution for Palestine in 1922 [33], Gaza had a constitutional system in 1962 [34] and Jordan promulgated a Constitution in 1952 [35]. However, all these are addressed to persons who have a practical existence no longer. Furthermore, the principles were incomplete, the conditions were different, the authority structure has changed, responsibilities have been modified and new functions have emerged. A modern constitution should be adopted after holding a popular referendum. Currently, a projected Palestinian Constitution prepared by Professor Anis El Kassem is being discussed and debated [36].

The Palestinian Constitution must define the competence of the legislative, executive and judicial authorities and establish general principles such as equality, non-discrimination, the right to resort to courts, ownership rights, freedom of residence and of movement and other basic rights such as non-immunity for administrative decisions and ensuring the courts have control over all administrative acts. If the Constitution contains guarantees for individuals, in combination with other political conditions, investment would be encouraged and stability would prevail, and this would have a favourable effect on construction and housing.

Annulment of Emergency Laws

No doubt that the Palestinian people live under difficult conditions, but such conditions do not necessitate emergency laws or military orders. If investors feels that the authority may enforce exceptional laws, they will hesitate to invest or may not invest at all. Naturally, the ordinary laws are the rule, and emergency laws are the exception. The ordinary law contains rules sufficient for the ordinary courts to judge any accused person. The use of exceptional conditions as a pretext to justify the actions of the executive power is inadmissible. The pretexts may never end, and because the executive is often reluctant to have its actions controlled by ordinary courts composed of civilians, such power may resort to the military or to the military courts [37].

Emergency laws may be used to the detriment of the interests of common people, companies or investors under several pretexts. Such pretexts are endless, and therefore these laws and their serious implications should be abolished. People, investors and builders should feel that their money and the future of their projects is secure.

Modernisation of the Civil Law

The civil law is the main reference for all other laws. It is not possible to have modern legislation when our civil law, *Al-Ahkam Al-Adleya*, was issued at the time of the Ottoman Empire. This law must be modernised since it is the origin of all private law legislation. All the Arab countries which formerly applied legislation governed by *Al Ahkam Al Adleya* have abolished it and replaced it with a new civil law [38].

No legislation should be enacted until a new civil which conforms to modern juridical trends and matches the developed social and economic conditions is adopted. It should specifically expand on the rules of contracts, clarify ownership rights, the ownership of flats and floors, the rights derived from ownership of housing such as *Al-Taker*, leasing, mortgages and liens and the registration thereof.

Law on Organising Towns, Villages and Buildings [39]

Law No. 79 concerning the organisation of towns, villages and buildings was enacted in 1966. According to it, committees were established. It also specified licence regulations, property rights, expropriation in the public interest and how to control all these matters.

Article 67 of the above-mentioned law entitles the Council of Ministers, pursuant to the recommendation of the Higher Organisational Council, to give instructions for the application of the said law. This Article specifies 27 areas where the law can be applied, including construction, licensing, public safety, public meetings, roads, building materials, debris and removing them, preparing for projects, selection of materials, organising neighbours' rights, delineation of borders, amount of indemnity, construction of shelters, demolishing and removal of old neighbourhoods and abandoned buildings, survey of lands, and the construction of low-cost houses. In addition, each municipality established local regulations concerning construction.

Consequently, the PNA may issue, scores of regulations and orders organising matters related to housing based on this law. The question remains whether the PNA has the power of legislation according to *Article 7* of the Cairo Agreement. The other problem is the Israeli amendments made by military orders, especially insofar as these orders remain valid from a 'legal' point of view because the Israeli occupation of the West Bank and Gaza continues.

There also remains the problem of the implications of the Oslo Agreement. The Protocol dealing with civil affairs (*Appendix 2* of the Cairo Agreement) includes serious issues raised in *Clause 2*, which deals with planning and organisation. They are as follows:

a) The powers, capacities and responsibilities related to settlements and military zones shall not be transferred to the PNA;
b) Planning projects, laws and regulations in force before signing the Cairo Agreement shall remain valid unless amended or annulled;
c) Palestinian planning projects shall be published in the form of law and Israelis may object to them; and
d) The PNA can elect to amend, annul or issue planning projects, issue licences and give exemptions, only in accordance with the Agreement.

This brings us back to the question of legislative powers. It is abnormal that planning projects should be raised to the level of laws, thereby giving the Israelis the opportunity to refuse them, especially as this implies that Palestinians are deprived of the right to deal with their own land.

It would appear that the issue of land and planning is central to the negotiations about the transitional period. If the situation remains as it is, the whole question would simply require an administrative decision by the Chairman of the PNA to appoint a Higher Organisational Council and other bodies, such as town organising committees, local organising committees and joint organising committees, in addition to co-ordinating administrative measures in conformity with the law.

Ottoman Land Law

The Ottoman Land Law was established in conformity with the conditions existing during the Ottoman Empire. Land was divided into owned, *amereya*, *waqf*, abandoned and waste land. Owned land was divided into areas within towns and villages, and *amereya* land into land granted on a proprietary basis, tithe and *kharaj*.

This law deals with issues which no longer exist, such as tithe, *kharaj* and abandoned land. Furthermore, the concept of certain kinds of land, such as *amereya*, has changed altogether. The Khalifal Ottoman regime and Ottoman Empire no longer exist and several of the rights which were vested in the Ottoman Sultan by virtue of the Land Law are no longer applicable. The general concept of abandoned land has also changed. The word wasteland does not conform with the definition used in *Article 6* of the Land Law. Moreover, current concepts of nation and public interest contradict the Land Law legislation, insofar as the Law restricted rights to special categories of people, i.e. the inhabitants of certain villages who were allowed by the Law to fell trees and use them.

Many legal rules contained in the Ottoman Land Law helped Israel to plunder Palestinian lands; particularly because *amereya* land was considered to be public land. Therefore, a law must be enacted to match the current social and economic conditions, remove complications and categories of land which no longer exist, as well as provisions that do not conform with new developments. For example, it is unreasonable that land should be considered wasteland if it is away from a village to the point that a loud cry of a person would not be heard, i.e. which was estimated be one-and-a-half miles or half an hour's walk. The law should be streamlined, along with its procedures, registration, *tabo* and sorting, so that acquired rights can be preserved and equity upheld.

Land and Water Adjustment Law [40]

Given that only about 38 per cent of Palestinian land had been subject to adjustment, adjustment was often incomplete and in other cases, no adjustment had been carried at all. Given the importance of adjustment in establishing rights, in building roads and in settling disputes about common properties, the adjustment law is particularly significant.

Land is not a renewable resource and therefore its sale, exchange, donation and/or division, as well as the determination of its boundaries must be effected in a formal way at the land department. Every related matter must be registered. For this reason, the PNA must adopt a project of land and registration, to prevent any illegal transfer of ownership, particularly because Palestinian land has been subject to false, crooked and/or invalid sales. Moreover, the practice of successive proxies, instead of official registration, gave rise to forgery, fraud and deceit.

As in other cases, the problem is related to the military orders made in respect of land and water adjustment, the extent to which these orders are legal and whether their application can be avoided. This relates to the legislative powers of the PNA in general.

Laws on Immovable Property

There are many laws related to immovable property, such as the following:

- Expropriation of Land for Public Projects Law (2/1953 [41]);
- Lease and Sale of Immovables to Foreigners Law (40/1953 [42]);
- Transfer Property of Land From *Amereya* to Private Ownership Law (41/1953 [43]);
- Land Delineation and Survey Law (42/1953 [44]);
- Mortgage of Immovables Law (46/1953 [45]);
- Division of Common Immovables Law (48/1953 [46]);
- Disposition of Immovables Law (49/1953 [47]);
- Disposition of Immovables by Juridical Persons Law (61/1953 [48]);
- Law Amending Provisions Related to Immovables Law (51/1964 [49]);
- Law of Registration of Immovables Not Previously Registered (6/1984 [50]);
- Land Tax Law (30/1955 [51]); and
- Law of Land Registration Fees (26/1958 [52]).

All these and other laws related to immovables need to be modernised and streamlined, especially because registration and other procedures have been made lengthy and complicated under Israeli rule. The PNA should enact laws or amend the existing laws in order to facilitate matters. It should also accelerate the administrative procedures to prevent fraud, as well as the levying of new taxes which might also be reduced.

Flat and Floors Law

Before 1967, it was common to build houses in a horizontal direction; Palestinians were not used to building multiple floors and flats. Consequently, there was no law governing flats and floors at that time.

After 1967, the construction of multi-storey buildings became more widespread, especially in Gaza and in city centres. This created a problem related to the ownership of flats and floors and the issue of whether a flat or floor is jointly owned, owned by a housing co-operative, or has another form of ownership.

The enactment of a law to regulate the ownership of flats and floors is vital. The right to own a flat or a floor should be defined, specifying what such ownership includes and does not include, what the common matters between owners of different units in a building are, how to maintain and manage the proprietor's share and how it should be registered in the land department, as well as the action needed to insure the building against fire and risks and to provide for common charges and expenses.

Landlords and Tenants Law

Jordan enacted *Law No. 62* of 1953 [53] for landlords and tenants. This law gave wide protection to the tenant, who was considered the weaker party. Soon tenants made use of this protection to the detriment of the interests of landlords, and their relationship was distorted.

Consequently, a new law for landlords and tenants was issued in 1982 amending the provisions of the previous law. Subsequently, the Military Governor of the occupied territories issued Military Order *No.* 1271, effective 1/4/1989; however, most lawyers in the West Bank refused to recognise it.

The situation in Gaza is the same as in the West Bank; both were originally subject to *Al-Ahkam Al-Adleya* insofar as general rules are concerned. From a practical point of view, the *Law on Defining Rent for Houses* of 1940 and the *Law on Defining Rent for Buildings used for Business* (No. 6) of 1941 are applied. Both give protection to the tenant. In any case, a new law for landlords and tenants is needed which takes into consideration social solidarity, human relations, inflation, the encouragement of investment, currency depreciation, the taxes imposed on properties and income and present and future salaries.

Other Laws

Conditions favourable for local and foreign investors should exist. These conditions cannot be realised without laws to attract capital from abroad. Many of these laws are in place, but they need to be activated, rather than being left ineffective. Laws exist regarding the establishment, competence and autonomy of courts, the hierarchy of legal rules, ways to appeal decisions, judicial authority, the non-immunity of administrative decisions and the separation of authorities. The problem is how to put mechanisms and instruments in place to activate all these laws, so that investors can be assured that all decisions are legal and not based on political influence.

In addition, the body of financial laws needs to be completed by establishing an investment law and by annulling the law concerning absentee ownership, issuing a law for a Housing Bank to issue credits for housing, amending the property and tax laws on incomes accruing from construction, reducing licence fees, establishing general saving funds guaranteed by the state and by amending the Ottoman legislation on *murabaha*.

Building Regulations

When Palestine was under its own authority, each municipality developed its own building regulations according to its particular situation. The regulations inside towns and villages were also different from those outside them. However, the situation changed completely after 1967 because Palestinians no longer controlled their own land. It is not clear to what extent the PNA will have control over the land in the future, especially the areas lying outside the towns and villages.

In any case, the current property regulations need to be changed radically regarding classification, planning, division and licensing. Building regulations need to be developed taking into consideration the limited areas in which building is permitted, floor areas and the number of flats in each building. Likewise, reclassification of land use, the height of buildings, population density, land improvement and removal of debris should be dealt with. An architectural, social, economic and legal committee should develop a concept for various housing issues aimed at expanding building activity. This could help extend construction possibilities to low – and medium – as well as high-income groups.

CONCLUSION AND RECOMMENDATIONS

Housing did not develop in Palestine, especially after 1967, for many reasons. These include the loss of control over the land because of the Israeli occupation; the expropriation of Palestinian land for Israeli settlements and road building; the closure of areas for Israeli military training; the prohibition of building along public roads within 150 metres and the demolition of houses for organisational considerations, on the grounds of security or as a punitive measure. The fact that there are no banks except Israeli ones, few savings and a lack of saving instruments has compounded the problems. Moreover, the situation has been made still worse because of high birth rates, high licensing fees, difficulties in transferring immovables, a lack of infrastructure outside the towns and the existence of Palestinian refugee camps.

The Palestinian Housing Council (PHC), which was formed to solve the problem of housing in the Territories, did not receive adequate financing to solve these overwhelming problems. When the Ministry of Housing was formed after the Oslo Agreement, it could not engage in actual building for the same reason.

The issue of housing is multifaceted and needs financial, architectural, social and administrative solutions. The real problem is that none of the agencies in the PT has expertise or previous experience in the field of housing. Many laws must be amended, others must be implemented and, in some cases, new laws should be enacted along with the relevant regulations and decrees.

The real problem is *Article 7* of the Cairo Agreement which practically prevents the PNA from exercising legislative power except with the approval of the Israelis. In contrast, the Agreement has given legitimacy to the military orders which existed on the eve of the signature of the Cairo Agreement.

The PNA is eager to legislate on many issues, but so far it has failed to enact any new laws. The issue is how any new laws should be applied in the absence of legislative power. Therefore, the Cairo Agreement should be amended regarding this power, whether by agreement or in practice.

In addition, if the PNA wishes to co-ordinate its work with the international strategy for the habitat and with the United Nations Centre for Human Settlements, it should continue its legislative efforts on all levels to eliminate any obstacles.

Finally, we would emphasise the role of the courts, which must be given wide-ranging competence, or rather should acquire it practically, by considering military orders illegal, thus removing an important obstacle impeding housing activities. The PNA, and particularly the Ministry of Housing, should regulate and co-ordinate all matters related to housing and should propose solutions to facilitate the adoption of the proposals set forth in this paper.

THE DEVELOPMENT AND RECONSTRUCTION OF REMOTE AND OUTLYING AREAS OF PALESTINE

Jamal Talab

ABSTRACT

Practices undertaken by the Israeli occupying forces pose the greatest obstacle to the planning process in the rural areas of Palestine. This paper reviews these practices, looking first at Israeli settlement activity, the construction of new settlements, roads and bypasses to and between them, as well as other areas where the aim is to limit the expansion of the Palestinian population and its access to agricultural land.

This paper also examines Israeli plans for the construction of new quarries in the West Bank, the conversion of forests and natural resources belonging to Palestinians, the lease of state land as private property for settlement, land prices and the problem of land ownership. Recommendations are made regarding the incorporation of villages and small populated areas in Palestine into administrative districts and the use of land within these districts.

This paper is not comprehensive; instead, it incorporates the findings of field research that can be used as a basis for additional research by specialised researchers in planning.

OBSTACLES TO STRUCTURAL PLANNING

Israeli occupation practices in the West Bank and Gaza constitute the biggest obstacle facing structural planning in Palestinian rural areas. Here we will review the practices that have both threatened and prevented urban and rural development in the Palestinian Territories (PT).

Table 1 Israeli Occupation Measures During the Peace Process: Land Confiscation for Settlement Purposes and Uprooting of Trees.

Phase	Time Period	Monthly Average: Dunums and Trees		
		Land confiscation (dunums)	Settlement	Trees Uprooted
Before Madrid	before 30/Oct./1991	4,766	233	2,971
Madrid–Oslo	30/Oct./1991–13/Sept./1993	2,400	873	3,908
Oslo–Cairo	4/May/1994–31/Sept./1996	6.624	638	1,613
Post–Cairo	4/May/1994–1/March/1995	834	389	1,616

Source: Statistical Interference from Data in following Tables.

Israeli Settlements

The accelerating horizontal expansion of Israeli settlements on Palestinian land in the West Bank (including Arab East Jerusalem) has been deliberately designed to fragment the Palestinian population and to disrupt the growth of Palestinian housing. This is especially true insofar as Israeli settlements encircle the areas where there is a concentration of Palestinians, turning them into ghettos with no land in which they can expand.

In contrast, the incessant and rapid expansion of Israeli settlement activity following the commencement of the peace process demonstrates conclusively that Israel's policy of constricting the structural development of the Palestinian population is both premeditated and intentional.

Despite the Oslo Declaration, the signature of the Cairo agreements and the transfer of Gaza to the Palestinian National Authority (PNA) in 1994, the Israeli authorities have persisted in their policies of land confiscation and settlement construction, road construction, the changing of the landscape of the Green Line at the expense of Palestinian agriculture and other provocative, illegal measures. Palestinians affected by the settlement projects launched by the Israeli Civil Administration and the Higher Land Council were given two-months notice to examine the plans and to protest through the subsidiary offices of the project architects located inside settlements.

This procedure bypasses the land offices in West Bank cities which are run by Arab employees. Yet it is virtually impossible for Palestinians to obtain admission into Israeli settlements, let alone deal with these offices. This confirms the suspicion that the whole process aims to create a legal cover for the seizure of Palestinian land for Israeli settlers.

The peace agreement between Palestinians and Israelis called for the postponement of negotiations over existing settlements until a later stage. In effect, this implies a freeze on the expansion and construction of new settlements given that the legality of the settlements remains questionable

Table 2 Size and Numbers of Confiscated Land, Settlement, Trees Uprooting throughout the Phases of the Peace Process.

Phase	Time Period	Confiscation (dunums)	Settlement (dunums)	Trees Uprooted (number)
Madrid–Oslo	30/Oct./1991–13/Sept./1993	54,000	19,206	85,976
Oslo–Cairo	13/Sept./1993–4/May/1994	53,000	5,102	12,902
Cairo–Present	4/May/1994–1/March/1995	8,333	3,891	16,159

Source: Field Research, Land Research Center, Arab Studies Society, Jerusalem.

even by the Israeli authorities. The only logical conclusion regarding settlement activities advertised in local newspapers is that this settlement activity is illegal and contradictory to the peace process.

Forests and Natural Reserves

The total area of Palestinian land closed off as forests and natural reserves amounts to about half a million dunums. At present, the Israeli occupation authorities are converting areas of Palestinian agricultural lands and those suited for construction to forests and natural reserves on the pretext of protecting or improving the quality of the environment. They are seizing these lands from their rightful Palestinian owners for alleged public use.

Later, these lands are to be utilised for the construction of Israeli settlements. The land (forests and wildlife reserves) will be leased to settlers to cut down the forests and to build Jewish neighbourhoods and settlements instead. This practice already has occurred in more than one area, such as in the settlement of Rekhes Shufat in Shufat (1973) and the housing of Jewish immigrants in Mount Abu Ghneim, south of Jerusalem.

Obviously, the forests created, or being created, by the Israeli authorities on Palestinian land are part of land reserved for Israeli settlements.

Bypasses to Israeli Settlements

The network of roads constructed by the Israeli authorities does not serve future Palestinian planning. Rather, Israeli road construction designs prevent Palestinian planning in the future because they fail to take into account the needs and movement of the Palestinian population, its growth and agricultural, touristic, environmental, industrial and commercial activity. Through its road networks, Israel seeks to achieve the following:

1) To connect and surround Israeli settlements with special secure roads that link these settlement concentrations to the areas inside the Green

Line. This aims to strengthen Israeli domination on the pretext of protecting Israeli settlers. This amounts to total Israeli military hegemony over Palestinian land.

2) To limit the expansion of the Palestinian population. Israeli authorities follow a deliberate policy of building new roads on land adjacent to Palestinian concentrations. This is in addition to imposing restrictions on Palestinian planning and construction, such as stipulating that it be carried out at least 150 metres away from main roads and that there be a street width of 80 metres where Palestinian homes are built.

3) To break up Palestinian agricultural land. The Israeli authorities made no attempt to avoid agricultural land when building new roads and, as a result, these lands and the activities on them have been destroyed.

The large number of new main and side roads being built and/or expanded throughout the West Bank before the full redeployment of the Israeli army confirms the suspicion that these roads serve a political objective: the prevention of Palestinian planning for a future Palestinian state. These new roads are disproportionate to the size and population of the West Bank, Palestinian and Jewish alike.

Quarries

The Israeli occupation authorities are currently preparing for the construction of seven new quarries to be exploited by Israeli investors in the West Bank on the fringes of the Green Line. These plans are certain to create tremendous difficulties for the PNA in the future. The planned quarries, which are to be built on Palestinian agricultural land adjacent to populated areas, violate norms for the protection of the environment and are certain to hinder Palestinian structural planning.

Land Ownership and Sovereignty

The Oslo Accords have deferred the issue of sovereignty over land and borders to the final status negotiations. Meanwhile, the Israeli authorities have exploited this delay by allowing themselves a free hand in determining the future of state-owned land.

Most threatening among their practices is the lease of vast areas of these lands to Israeli settlements for settlement activity. Worse than that, the Israeli authorities have permitted the registration of these lands as the legal private property of settlers, while denying Palestinians this right by confiscating their land.

If Palestinians do not enjoy full control of the land now considered Israeli state property after the final status negotiations, then the Palesti-

Table 3 Land Prices in the West Bank.

Area	Utilisation	Approximate Price ($)	Observations
Hebron Villages	Agricultural Housing	3,000–7,000 15,000–20,000	This applies to most villages in the Bethlehem, Ramallah, Nablus and Jenin areas, except those adjacent to cities
City of Hebron	Housing Commercial	30,000–50,000 100,000–150,000	
Cities of the Bethlehem area and adjacent villages	Housing Commercial Cultivated	80,000–120,000 100,000–150,000 30,000–60,000	
Cities of Ramallah and Al-Bireh	Housing Commercial	80,000–120,000 200,000–1,000,000	

nian government is likely to clash with the settlers and users of this land on the one hand, and with the Palestinian owners who do not recognise the seizure of their land by the Israeli authorities, on the other. Consequently, there is a vital need to re-register these lands in a methodical fashion that addresses the accumulating chronic problems associated with their status.

The Israeli settlement activity in the midst of Palestinian population concentrations in cities such as Jerusalem and Hebron, and its consequent security problems, presents additional obstacles and problems for planning for Palestinian housing in these areas.

LAND PRICES

The question of land prices is a complex problem that one can only venture to address. The observations discussed above play an important role in determining the price of land suitable for construction. Over and above these factors, one could add the following:

- The location of these lands inside or outside village and/or city limits;
- The proximity of these lands to Jewish settlements or to other Arab villages and cities;
- Proximity to main streets. Palestine represents an exception in that land close to main streets outside urban areas is of low value, as construction on these lands is prohibited by the Israeli authorities for security reasons. A distance of 75 metres away from the main street should be observed on each side;
- The issue of land sales has assumed a national dimension as Jewish

organisations played a big role in the purchase of Palestinian land, resulting in an unusual rise in the price of land sold to non-Palestinians. Sale of land to non-Palestinians has traditionally been viewed with suspicion, amounting to a virtual taboo;

- A tribal rationale that gives neighbours priority over outsiders in purwchasing land. This makes it extremely difficult for outsiders to purchase land, especially in villages; and
- Members of different religions exhibit great sensitivity and reservations about selling to, and buying land from, members of other faiths. This applies even to Muslims and Christians who, despite their common national bond, continue to demonstrate such reservations.

THE PROBLEM OF LAND OWNERSHIP

The PNA should take into account the pride Palestinians have in land ownership when drafting a land ownership policy for the purposes of development. It should be able to balance this policy against Palestinian national feelings toward land by taking control of all the land that the Israeli authorities have regarded as state or public land, even though in most cases this land was privately owned by Palestinians. The PNA should balance this fact against its need to utilise some of these lands for public purposes and for the fulfilment of pressing Palestinian development needs.

Furthermore, a future Palestinian land ownership and housing policy should take into account the fact that the majority of private housing projects are likely to be concentrated in areas which yield the greatest benefit, i.e. in major cities. This could aggravate existing overcrowding and environmental problems in the cities and encourage the neglect of more remote areas, leading to their degeneration and the aggravation of the problems of poverty.

The PNA is hard pressed to develop legislation that would set a ceiling on land prices which takes the location of the land into consideration and which could be applied across the board for the public good. Unlimited freedom for individuals to determine land prices might lead to a sharp hike in these prices and constrain the ability of the public housing sector and of housing co-operatives to purchase land suitable for housing projects. This problem is further aggravated by the multiple ownership of the majority of Palestinian land, a fact which complicates the process of co-ordination among the various owners for the purpose of establishing big projects.

Table 4 Land Area Confiscated in the West Bank and Gaza from
13/Sept./1993 to 1/March/1995.

Phase	Public Confiscation	Settlement Activity	For Military Purposes	Roads	Adjustment of Green Line Borders	Total
From Oslo–Cairo 13/Sept./1993–4/May/1994	32,634	5,102	4,478	8,149.6	2,624	52,987.6
Cairo–Present 13/Sept./1994–1/March/1995	538	3,891	620	3,284.4	–	8,333.4
Total	33,172	8,993	5,098	11,434	2,624	61,321

Source: Field Research, The Land Research Centre, Arab Studies Society, Jerusalem.

RECOMMENDATIONS FOR VILLAGES AND OUTLYING RURAL AREAS

In the light of the fact that Palestine consists of a large number of Palestinian villages and small populated areas, the following recommendations can be made.

Each set of adjacent villages and quasi-villages which are geographically and socially similar should be incorporated into an administrative district. A joint administrative council should be set up for the purpose of planning and policy implementation at the level of the entire district in a uniformed manner. The proposed district would be involved in the areas of planning main and side roads, public and private transportation, public sewage and water collection, electricity, water and telecommunication networks, schools and kindergartens, rehabilitation and training centres, clubs and social, women and sport activities, central health clinics, hospitals, central shopping areas and public parks.

The size of agricultural land, which is generally privately owned, should be determined within the framework of a central agricultural planning policy that balances the nature of the climate and soil against the need for a centrally planned agricultural policy on a national scale. Agricultural activity should be centrally administered. Produce should be brought to a central agricultural market for the district, but ties to larger markets at the regional level should be maintained as well.

Such planning would be likely to keep the largest possible number of workers in the agricultural sector, thus preserving the traditional rural social lifestyle while improving the level of income both at the individual and national levels.

A piece of land that is appropriate both in terms of location and the environment should be dedicated as an industrial zone to serve the entire district. It should be based on a central plan for the whole district. The industrial zone should be able to absorb excess labour and to activate public and private industrial production based on central planning.

Land within the limits of the district appropriate for construction should be allocated for the construction of housing units. The land should be centrally divided by the administration of the district in accordance with a building code that is in line with Palestinian rural tradition.

This would encourage investment by the private and public sectors for the building of housing sufficient to absorb the families of expatriates and to provide housing for newly-weds and the families of agriculture and service labourers working in the district.

OWNERSHIP, URBAN PLANNING AND THE LEGAL SYSTEM

Samir Thaher

ABSTRACT

Ownership laws and regulations in the West Bank and Gaza have been affected by various occupations over a long period of time and by Zionist immigration and the imposition of British mandatory rule. These laws and regulations served the interests of the occupying powers, rather than the Palestinian people.

This paper looks at the laws and regulations governing urban areas and urban planning; in particular, *Law No. 28* of 1936 and its various amendments and *Law No. 527* of 1957. Procedures established by these legislative acts to obtain building licences are examined as well.

The paper also outlines property rights under the *Ottoman Land Law*. The four types of privately owned land are discussed, as are *waqf*, abandoned land, wasteland and *ameriya* land. The role of the Palestinian National Authority (PNA) in protecting state land and government-owned property is examined. The paper concludes with a discussion of Palestinian law and the transfer of ownership, including the preparation of new regulations by the PNA.

INTRODUCTION

The political reality of the Palestinian people acted negatively on the organisation of social life and the building of civil society. Various powers occupied Palestine over a long period and enacted legislation to support their interests. The laws they decreed reflected only their aims of controlling the destiny of the Palestinian people, occupying their land and paralysing their resistance.

The laws currently applied in the areas under the PNA and in other parts of the occupied territories are a legacy of the Turkish, British, Egyptian and Jordanian legal systems. This has led to a distorted legal reality which provides little benefit. Zionist immigration to Palestine led to enacting laws and regulations with the purpose of giving the new immigrants ownership of Palestinian land.

The instability of private ownership, conflict of interests between citizens and diverse occupying forces and explicit or implicit political interests, caused discrepancies between ownership laws and organisational laws and regulations. In the urban centres, a relationship of opposition prevailed between local authorities and citizens. Every project or structural chart was received with scepticism. For this reason, laws on property, urban development and structures were not up to the required standards.

British laws applied in Palestine, including the Balfour Declaration, the Mandate instruments and related laws, facilitated the acquisition of land by Jews by adding a sixth category to the classification of land stipulated by the *Ottoman Land Law. Article 8* of the Palestine Constitution issued on in 1922 stipulates that 'Public lands are those Palestinian lands under the control of the Palestinian Government by virtue of treaties and agreements and also all land owned for public interest or for other reasons.'

Articles 12 and *13* gave the British High Commissioner the right to donate, lease or to dispose of public lands. This resulted *ameriya* land (managed for the interest of the Palestinian people irrespective of the existing governing system) being considered state property which was disposable at the discretion of the High Commissioner, notwithstanding the interests of the Palestinian people.

Sir Herbert Samuel, the first High Commissioner in Palestine, allocated most of the land to the Zionist movement and its institutions. This included the land of Kabbara, Atleit and Kaysariya. *Article 16* of the Constitution also authorised the High Commissioner to change the classification of land from public to private ownership and abandoned land to other ownership categories.

ORGANISING TOWNS AND URBAN PLANNING

Law No. 28 of 1936 on organising towns and its amendments, Nos. *58* of 1936, *8* of 1938, *5* of 1939, *30* of 1941 and *Order 527* of 1957, regulate the competence of the central committees and local committees for organising towns. Both of these committees were required to report to the British High Commissioner. Thereafter, such authority was inherited by whoever managed or occupied the West Bank and Gaza.

Order No. 527 of 1957 specified the competence of the central committees. *Article 3* provided that membership of the central committee for building and town organisation should include the manager of town and village affairs as chairman, with the following as well:

1) A representative of the public works manager;
2) A representative of the legal affairs manager;
3) A representative of the health affairs manager;
4) The administrator; and
5) The manager of the town organisation and survey department.

The situation changed under the Israeli occupation following the issuance of *Order No. 125*. It stipulated in *Article 3 [1]* that the members of the committee be appointed from among military officers of the departments, in addition to security officers, and that they should report to the military chief officer of the region.

The competence of the organisation committee includes the power to issue from time to time internal regulations for all towns located within its area of competence, conditions for and restrictions on giving licences, construction conditions for the licence, object of the licence, licence fees, required charts and regulations related to the preparation or the execution of any project proposed by a local agency.

The law provided for the formation of local committees and their competence. It stipulated in *Article 6* that if the British High Commissioner issues an order or a decree specifying that a certain area is a town, and such area had its own municipality, the board of that municipality shall itself be the local committee.

Article 8 defined the relations between the central and local committees. The local committee is required to inform, from time to time, the central committee of all details about the needs of expansion or building of new roads or public squares.

Article 9 specified the competence of the local committee which is authorised to regulate the construction and demolition of buildings and expansion and improvement of roads. The Israeli occupying authorities made use of the wide powers provided for by the *Organising Towns Law* and its amendments, and prepared new structural charts without taking into consideration the economic and social conditions of the people.

Due to the fact that 70 per cent of Palestinian land is composed of rural regions, the competence of organising these lies within the powers of central committees. These committees used to refuse plans presented to them by Palestinian local committees for defining the structural charts of villages or to expand their area. Such refusals aimed to maintain large areas of land for colonisation purposes.

PROCEDURES TO OBTAIN A BUILDING LICENCE

Law No. 28 of 1936 and its amendments lay down the procedures to obtain building licences. The local committees receive the applications of citizens wishing to erect buildings, accompanied with structural charts in order to receive approval. A delay may be given to allow for objections by interested persons. The authority to give licences lies with the central committees, and is outside the scope of competence of the local committees. The central committees follow bureaucratic procedures; they ask for sorting documents and charts; and they adopt various formalities which discourage people from applying for licences.

When the PNA took power pursuant to the Cairo Agreement, the powers of the central committees were transferred to a Local Government Ministry. This Ministry forms these committees composed of representatives of various ministries of the PNA. However, due to the presence of settlements and the so-called *yellow* and *white* areas – which means that joint competence is exercised in overlapping areas, the current effect of the work of these committees might be restricted.

The Agreement subjected many aspects of planning and construction to security arrangements which are revised every six months. Such arrangements allow the construction of buildings within 500 metres beyond the security areas and in the *yellow* areas, provided that only one building is erected on a plot of land, the area of which should not be less than 25 dunums. In addition, the building should not exceed two storeys in height and its area should not exceed 180 square metres. The Agreement also stipulates that Palestinians should not erect buildings or constructions within 75 metres of main roads.

PROPERTY RIGHTS

Palestinian legislation regulated the rights of property. Provisions dealing with landed property are included in the *Ottoman Land Law* which classified such property as follows.

Privately-Owned Land

Pursuant to *Article 2* of the *Ottoman Land Law*, owned land is of four types:

1) Areas within villages and their surroundings up to half a dunum which can be considered part of the dwelling;
2) Lands sorted out of *Ameriya* land;
3) *Ashriya* land, which was delivered on an ownership basis at the time of the Islamic conquest; and
4) *Kharaj* land which was left to its original non-Muslim owners.

The owner is entitled to dispose of his or her land and to carry out all legal transactions. However, this right is subject to some restrictions, such as those specified by the law regulating disposition by persons of immovables, ownership of fields surrounding villages or in military camps or ports, and those related to neighbourhood rights.

Waqf Lands

The *waqf* lands, pursuant to *Article 1* of the *Ottoman Land Law*, are classified in the third rank of land ownership. *Waqf* means that the land may not be given to any person as private property; its returns are to be used to benefit poor people or for a charitable purpose.

Abandoned Land

Abandoned land is regarded as land near inhabited areas left to the public for use as pasture or for wood gathering (*Article 1271, Al-Ahkam Al-Adliya*). This category of land is divided land left to a specific village or a group of villages and land left to the general public, e.g. public roads. *Articles 19* to *102* of the *Ottoman Land Law* lay down the provisions related to abandoned land and conclude by stipulation that no buildings may be erected, nor trees planted on such land, and that it may not be sold, bought or cultivated. The rule of prescription does not apply to this land.

Wasteland

Wasteland is land which is not owned by any person and is neither pasture nor available for wood gathering (i.e. it is not abandoned land). It should be far from the inhabited areas. The use of wasteland takes place by reclamation, and the right to dispose of this land is vested in the person who reclaims it. However, the ownership of land remains with the government, i.e. ownership of the person who reclaimed the land is incomplete.

Ameriya Land

This is land whose ownership is deemed to be held by the 'Treasury' of the Muslim people. Usufruct of this land is granted by the ruler, or his authorised representative according to certain conditions and in consideration of a fixed sum of money paid to the Treasury. The right to dispose of this land is acquired by the same rules according to which the right of ownership is acquired, i.e. acquisition by appropriation, accession, preemption, acquisitive prescription, inheritance and legal action by way of contract or making will.

Ownership Rights and Protection

The Palestinian Constitution and laws protect ownership rights. The Constitution issued by the Legislative Council of Gaza stipulates that 'private ownership is inviolable'. *Al-Ahkam Al-Adliya* and land laws also specify ways of transferring ownership and its protection against illegal extortion. Laws of 1927 and 1928 included provisions concerning the right of ownership. Legal writings on the transfer of ownership, whether by inheritance, will or donation, refer to the provisions which protect ownership rights.

Ownership: Law and Reality

In spite of the provisions regarding the right, practice and guarantees of ownership, the conditions in which the Palestinian people live, their subjugation to successive occupying forces and the violation of their legislative and judicial powers has resulted in a state of chaos. Some people have made use of the this instability and the fact that the executive power was not keen on defending ownership rights and that violation of these rights became widespread as a result.

Demographic Conditions and Ownership Rights

Because the Palestinian people were forced to immigrate after 1948, many of them had to settle in the West Bank and Gaza where they were placed in refugee camps without any ownership rights. This is evident in Gaza, where more than 60 per cent of the inhabitants live in refugee camps.

Another aspect of this arrangement is that ownership rights are concentrated in a few families who inherited such rights for long periods. This situation was an obstacle to all planning, development and preparation of structural maps because of the influence of these families.

THE ROLE OF THE PNA IN PROTECTING GOVERNMENT PROPERTY

Government property continued to be subject to confiscation by the Israeli occupying forces. Israeli settlements were erected on most of the land registered as government property. The Israelis also gave some individuals legal rights on the property of the government. These acquired rights may not be easily annulled in the future.

Moreover, many military orders govern the use of such land and the Cairo Agreement does not contain an explicit provision which specifies the powers of the PNA in respect of such land. However, the PNA needs to take action to protect government ownership and to ensure its optimum use. Relevant measures include:

- Registration, adjustment and the survey of all government land;
- Examination of all dealings made in respect of this land during the Israeli occupation and the annulment of those which were originally illegal;
- Preparing a general and comprehensive plan for all land pertaining to the PNA and determining priorities of its use; and
- Encouragement of investment in government property.

TRANSFER OF OWNERSHIP

It is well known that ownership is established by actions which transfer it, such as its sale, donation, will, inheritance and other actions arising from occupancy and the like. Ownership, according to Palestinian law, is transferred after taking the requisite action and registering the ownership in the *Tabo* (registration book).

Many problems arise at the time of the transfer of ownership, because as it becomes apparent that the property has been subjected to many transactions simultaneously, such as occupancy and the like. However, the PNA is preparing new regulations which would lead to the stability of ownership, such as a flat and floors project law, survey project law and the project of defining and examining actions taken in respect of government property.

The flats and floors project law regulates ownership of flats and floors located in multi-floor buildings and their use and management. Such ownership is not known under the present Palestinian law and the law project is consistent with the efforts of the PNA to encourage the vertical expansion in construction activities and to solve the housing problem.

Theme Three

REGULATORY FRAMEWORK: BUILDING CODES, STANDARDS AND REGULATIONS

THE REGULATORY FRAMEWORK: BUILDING CODES, STANDARDS AND REGULATIONS

Seyfeddin Muaz

ABSTRACT

This theme paper will synthesise the various contributions made by several authors on the following subjects: *Codes, Standards and Specifications*, by Seyfeddin Muaz; *Codes, Standards and Regulations in Palestine*, by Mohamed Ziara, Rifat Rustom, Majed El-Bayya and Ahmed Amer; *Energy Conservation and Efficiency*, by Hisham Khatib; *Planning for Accessibility for the Disabled in Palestine*, by Riadh Tappuni; and *Disaster Preparedness For Palestine*, by Sultan Barakat and Ian Davis.

The various issues, options and strategies presented in these papers will be summarised and discussed within the regulatory framework of building codes, standards and regulations.

CODES, STANDARDS AND REGULATIONS

The paper by Seyfeddin Muaz deals with the importance of establishing codes, standards and specifications (CSS) before launching a reconstruction programme in Palestine. Recognising the similarity in both natural and human resources between Jordan and Palestine, it advocates drawing on the Jordanian experience for issuing and implementing CSS by the Palestine National Authority (PNA).

The paper gives a complete list of codes of practice, relevant practical manuals, standard specifications and technical specifications available in Jordan. It proposes a simple process of issuing a new national CSS based on currently available CSS in other countries which are tailor-made to suit Palestinian requirements. This process necessitates the formation of technical committees and working groups to carry out the required work. The mechanism to activate these committees and working groups is described in detail.

The paper emphasises the fact that CSS should always be revised and updated in a dynamic and continuous process, because of new techniques and developments in both materials and methods of construction. It proposes a revision period of five years for codes and ten years for technical specifications and allows for more frequent revision and updating of standards whenever it is necessary.

The paper also focuses on the implementation of CSS. It states that enforcing CSS during the design stage alone does not ensure good buildings and infrastructure. It should be followed by proper control and supervision on site as well.

It recommends that for the implementation of codes, the relevant ministries and government offices should, at the beginning, assume responsibility for building control. At a later stage, when local authorities are formed and acquire the required technical staff and expertise, this responsibility could be transferred to local municipalities.

It adds that the ultimate goal should aim to establish private engineering offices which are able to check designs, drawings and contract documents and which could issue a certificate or a licence of compliance stating that these documents are 'deemed-to-satisfy' the building regulations. However, the paper suggests that small buildings of an area less than 150 square meters may be exempted from building controls at the initial stage of implementation.

For the implementation of standards, the paper suggests that existing laboratories at the universities be employed for the quality control of both local and imported construction materials. Private laboratories can also be accredited to act as the technical arm of government authorities for testing materials. It is indicated that beside the preventive measures taken by government agencies, actual control must be carried out on site, according to specifications and whenever it is deemed necessary. As for the technical specifications, the paper notes that they form an important part of the contract documents. They are implemented through the contract and during the construction by the site engineer.

The paper sets priorities for CSS requirements. It gives a list of CSS documents which are needed immediately. In order of priority, they cover the following subjects:

Codes

a) Structural safety and stability;
b) Public health and safety;
c) Conservation of resources;
d) Safety against natural hazards;
e) Economy and efficiency;
f) Protection of the environment;

g) Convenience;
h) Amenity; and
i) Others.

Standards

a) Cementitious materials;
b) Aggregates and natural stones;
c) Metals;
d) Building materials;
e) Asphaltic materials; and
f) Electrical installations.

Specifications

For buildings:

a) Civil and architectural works;
b) Mechanical installation and services; and
c) Electrical installation and services.

For highways and bridges:

a) Earthworks;
b) Pavement, base and sub-base constructions;
c) Culverts, bridges and super structures;
d) Landscaping; and
e) Lighting, traffic signals and electrical installations.

The paper concludes with the following recommended actions which are to be carried out immediately:

a) The PNA must form a National Building Council to be responsible for initiating immediately needed CSS;
b) Available Jordanian CSS should be adopted for immediate use until national CSS are developed;
c) Building control should be assigned to the Ministry of Housing or to the Ministry of Public Works initially. After the establishment of municipal authorities, this assignment could be transferred easily to them; and
d) Extensive training programmes should be initiated on CSS development and implementation. Other programmes on: testing of building materials, quality control, and methods of practical design, construction and building control should also be commenced.

The paper, *Codes, Standards and Regulations in Urban and Rural Construction in Palestine*, by Ziara, Rustom, El-Bayya and Amer identifies the codes, standards and regulations (CSR) which are most used in Palestine. It focuses on those related to structural concrete which is the common building material used in local construction. It provides two examples of building permits: the first is given by municipalities for low-rise buildings; the second is supervised by the Ministry of Housing and is for high-rise buildings.

The paper states that different international codes are currently used for the design and construction of housing projects, such as the El-Karama and El-Nusierat projects. In smaller projects, design codes are rarely followed and construction is not supervised. Even those buildings which are designed according to available codes do not satisfy all the requirements of the code for earthquakes, winds and for soil investigation.

The standard specifications used in the construction of buildings, roads and bridges are based on experience gained by Palestinian engineers who graduated from universities, or worked, in Jordan, Egypt and other Middle Eastern countries. There are several projects which do not follow standards nor carry quality control.

The paper differentiates between the building regulations which are followed in the West Bank and in Gaza. The building regulations in the West Bank are influenced by the Jordanian regulations while those in Gaza are influenced by the Egyptian regulations. Two cases are presented as examples. The first one is based on the old regulations, which are still in use, for low-rise buildings in Gaza. These are divided into two categories: the first is applied to buildings in the city and the second to buildings outside it.

Because of the high density of buildings within the city limits of Gaza, strict regulations are applied by the municipality. They include, among other things, the minimum area of a lot, the maximum percentage of built-up area and the minimum setback of the building lines. There is no restriction on building height outside the city limits. Instead, the floor area, the number of floors and the number of buildings on every 25,000 square meters of land are regulated.

The second example illustrates the regulations for high-rise buildings. These were prepared in an attempt to control safety and serviceability and cover the following major areas of concern:

a) Planning requirements;
b) Structural and architectural requirements;
c) Services requirements;
d) Fire safety requirements; and
e) Electrical requirements.

The paper states that due to the rapidly increasing number of high-rise buildings which have been built in Gaza, an emergency plan was prepared to draw up *High-Rise Building Regulations* (HRBR) to control the design and construction of such buildings. A steering committee was formed as well, representing the Ministry of Housing, the Ministry of Justice, the Gaza and Rafah municipalities, the Engineers Association and other organisations. The draft of HRBR was prepared by the steering committee and then distributed to relevant ministries, organisations and institutions for review and comments.

It was initially approved by the Legal Department of the Ministry of Justice and finally approved by the PNA. Another committee, named the *High-Rise Building Committee* (HRBC), was formed to control the implementation of HRBR. It is responsible for reviewing and approving documents, drawings and designs according to HRBR requirements.

The process of issuing a high-rise building permit involves two stages of control. In the first one, the municipality gives its initial approval for the preliminary drawings. This allows the owner to proceed toward developing the full documents. In the second phase, the documents are checked by the Engineers Association and the HRBC before receiving final approval and the permit issued by the municipality.

The paper concludes with a recommendation, among other options, to adopt regionally or internationally available CSR and to modify them to suit local needs. The paper also calls for the establishment of a Building Research Institute to develop and implement those CSR which are adopted. It promotes a quality control system to enhance the building industry.

ENERGY EFFICIENCY AND CONSERVATION

The paper written by Hisham Khatib maintains that energy consumption per capita depends on the economic activity of a country, the availability of indigenous energy resources, energy pricing and conservation policies and, finally, on the country's prevailing weather patterns.

The West Bank and Gaza have a southern Mediterranean climate of hot summers and cold winters. In most parts of the country, it is necessary to have heating in winter and desirable to have cooling (air conditioning) in summer. There are no local energy sources which means that fossil fuels will be imported at international prices and with limited foreign currency resources.

Therefore, energy consumption must be managed very efficiently. For this, the paper calls for action on three fronts: the first concerns fiscal measures regarding the pricing of energy products, and duties and customs on appliances which use energy.

The second action is technical and deals with the development and utilisation of energy efficient engineering practices, the encouragement

277

of energy efficiency and conservation measures, and the promotion of public education and awareness. The third action is regulatory and involves the issuance of laws, regulations and codes of practice to regulate the ways and means that energy is utilised and its relationship with the environment.

The proposed three actions are inter-related and form integrated parts of the energy management policy. The paper then explains in detail the implications of each action as follows.

Energy Pricing

All energy products, such as fuels and electricity, are imported in the Palestinian Territories (PT) and are expected to be so for many years to come. Building refineries and power stations are expensive and not recommended at the early stages of urban and rural development. Therefore, energy products and electricity are considered costly and very valuable. They have to be conserved and utilised efficiently.

The main tool to achieve this is a proper pricing policy. It involves establishing prices in a way that excludes subsidies, discourages misuse and waste and reflects the real cost of these imported products. Price subsidies for energy products are not recommended for the following reasons:

a) It causes misallocation of resources and encourages overuse;
b) It encourages excessive imports of consumer goods;
c) It benefits the rich more than it helps the poor; and
d) It contributes to pollution and has a detrimental impact on the local environment.

Subsidies, if any, must be provided for those activities which lead to improving the productivity of the economy and the maximisation of public and individual welfare.

Technological Aspects

It is not enough to set a correct pricing system in order to achieve proper energy management in the urban and rural housing sector. It is also necessary to introduce energy efficient technologies, to prepare and enforce building codes and regulations, and to educate and assist the public in conserving energy.

Energy efficient technologies are available for consumers. They include household apparatus, electrical appliances, heating and air-conditioning installations and after-use maintenance standards. Energy consumption in housing can be reduced by proper architectural design, making use of the principles of physics in buildings.

Energy requirements for heating and air-conditioning can also be reduced in buildings by using thermal insulation and solar equipment. If doors and windows do not comply with the standard specifications and are not properly installed, they can be a main source of low thermal efficiency of buildings.

Due to the solar intensity in the region, the PT are one of the best places in the world for the adoption and application of Passive Solar (PS) technologies in new construction. PS utilises the interaction of solar radiation with the building itself and is affected by the orientation of the building, its location and construction methods. S also is affected by the design and orientation of doors and windows that can help to reduce the need for heating in winter and cooling in summer. With minimum, or no, investment, PS can help to reduce the costly expense of weather conditioning in buildings.

Solar water heating is another useful technology. It can ensure a constant flow of hot water in a house for more than 330 days of the year, while saving an enormous amount of energy and paying for itself in less than three years.

To achieve the dual purpose of energy conservation and energy efficiency, it is not enough to have the right pricing policies and legislation, consumers and energy users must be helped and educated regarding technologies and techniques that can aid energy conservation and its efficient utilisation. One of the most effective ways of doing this is to establish Energy Consumers Centres. The concept of such centres is explained in detail in Khatib's paper.

Regulations and Legislation

Laws and regulations should encourage energy efficient technologies and inhibit the introduction of energy intensive industries and products. They would also include fiscal measures and standards regarding production and the importation of energy efficient machinery, appliances and transport vehicles. They would also involve making insulation mandatory in building construction and solar heating obligatory in new buildings.

However, regulations alone can not achieve energy efficiency and conservation. They should be a part of an integrated strategy that includes pricing policies, assistance and guidance to the public.

The paper concludes with highlights on the environmental problems that may be caused by utilising energy in transportation and heating. In this regard, it focuses on the importance of the concept of *life cycle cost* as a way to encourage investment in energy conservation techniques in new constructions.

ACCESSIBILITY FOR THE DISABLED

Tappuni presents a strategy for accessibility in Palestine through his paper which is entitled *Planning for Accessibility for the Disabled in Palestine*. The paper begins by examining the extent of disability in the PT, the kinds of disability and their frequency.

The two major causes for disability among Palestinians are presented as endogenous marriage and civil unrest. The first is described as a common phenomenon in Arab countries and in all sectors of society. It results in all forms of impairment.

Disability due to civil unrest is assumed to have a more prominent dimension as a result of the *Intifada*. The accompanying suppression results mainly in physical disabilities among the younger age groups.

The United Nations Relief and Works Agency for Palestine Refugees in the Near East (UNRWA) reported, in December 1990, that over a period of less than three years, live rounds, beating, plastic coated metal bullets, rubber bullets, tear gas and other forms of attack resulted in 58,000 casualties. Thirty per cent of the victims were children under 15. As a consequence, 10 per cent of the victims suffered permanent disability.

The figure before the outbreak of the *Intifada* for disability in the West Bank and Gaza was 60,000. Data on disability in Bureij and Al-Shati' camps in Gaza and in Palestinian villages in the Jenin area are used to give a definition of the extent of disability among Palestinians.

The paper maintains that designing for the disabled can result in accessible environments for the majority of people. One important objective of accessible design is the integration of the disabled into the community and enabling them to lead fulfilling lives.

In order to achieve this, the paper maintains that a disabled person should have the benefit of freedom of movement between home, work, recreation and services and should have access to the same facilities available to his or her fellow citizens. For this reason, it calls for the design of a barrier-free environment, and asserts that the application of standards in planning and design will help to make newly designed environments accessible.

The rehabilitation of existing buildings towards overcoming barriers is also regarded as an important issue for consideration. The paper reviews cases from international experience on how to plan for accessibility on an urban scale. At the regional level, reference is made to the current Lebanese experiment in providing a barrier-free central district of Beirut, which later is to be expanded to the entire country.

On a policy level, the paper recommends that the provision of a barrier-free environment should be supported through legislation. A national strategy in this field would be incomplete without the formulation of regulations that enforce the application of essential parts of the standards on accessibility. The paper concludes by suggesting a strategy on how to handle accessibility in the case of Palestine.

DISASTER PREPAREDNESS FOR PALESTINE

The paper by Barakat and Davis identifies two types of disasters. The first is natural, such as earthquakes and floods, while the second is man-made, such as those which occur in industry, transport or because of conflict. Both types can cause massive casualties and a great deal of disruption to normal life in a large number of countries around the world.

Palestine is not an exception, and both natural and man-made disasters are possible. Due to the lack of data on the levels of hazard and vulnerability in Palestinian settlements, the authors based their discussion on comparative studies and findings from Jordan and Israel.

The paper describes the seismicity of Palestine as being well established and studied by several investigators who have compiled maps and historical records. It states that strong and devastating earthquakes struck Palestine in the past. The 1927 earthquake was one of the most devastating earthquakes of this century in the region. The epicentre of that earthquake is believed to have been within the immediate surrounding of Jericho. It resulted in great damage on both sides of the Jordan valley, leaving 500 persons killed and more than 700 badly injured, with thousands made homeless. Thousands of houses were destroyed as well.

The paper adds that concentration of people and industry in any large town or city poses a range of risks as well as opportunities for the population. These threats can include a range of technological hazards such as fires, explosions or seepage of toxic gas or liquids from industrial plants, environmental health risks, pollution, etc. In addition, many cities, such as Jerusalem and Jericho, are sited in hazard-prone areas. Therefore, codes of practice, standards and land use planning controls are developed to design and maintain a safe urban environment, and to prevent loss of life and minimise property losses.

A mitigation strategy based on the principle of 'risk spreading' is suggested for urban safety. This principle calls for adopting a number of strategies in parallel, on the basis that if one fails, others may succeed. A typical strategy could include the following elements.

Education and Training

Introducing public awareness programmes for school children and regular training in disaster preparedness and mitigation for architects, planners, engineers, decision makers, etc.

Legislation

Laws are needed to establish a system of building codes and land-use planning control to make certain that future buildings and developments are constructed and sited to minimise risk of damage or destruction on a future disaster.

Planning tools

A six-staged sequence of actions for disaster planning is outlined as follows:

1) Inception of disaster management;
2) Risk assessment;
3) Define levels of acceptable risk;
4) Preparedness and mitigation planning;
5) Testing the plan; and
6) Feedback from lessons learned.

Insurance

Insurance can be used as a tool to promote safety. House builders wishing to reduce their insurance premiums must build in accordance with the hazard-resistant building code.

Urban Management Tools

Authorities managing a major urban centre must be selective as regarding what they can protect and what they must ignore. The *lifelines* – buildings, monuments and infrastructure – that may be given special protection include:

a) Buildings that have multiple occupancy (i.e. mosques, cinemas and schools);
b) Buildings that house children;
c) Buildings that are historic monuments, or which house vital historical or cultural artefacts (i.e. museums, art galleries and libraries);
d) Buildings which house vital functions which must continue after a disaster (i.e. television stations, airport control facilities, hospitals, police stations and schools for use as emergency shelters); and, finally,
e) Critical services or infrastructure, such as electrical power, telephone services, water, drainage, radio, road, rail and air links.

Building such new structures and infrastructure to high safety standards is easier than dealing with the existing building stock and existing infra-structure. The later requires a very expensive strengthening process, *retrofitting*. Whilst it will never be possible to strengthen all buildings and infrastructure, it is normally feasible to achieve this with all designated lifelines.

The paper concludes by stating that disaster mitigation and preparedness are vital elements in the protection of lives and property in any country or urban area that is prone to natural and technological hazards and outbreaks of civil strife. Protective planning is not an isolated process, but an integral part of national development planning.

ISSUES, OPTIONS AND STRATEGIES

After 27 years of occupation, repression and destruction, the PT suffer from a lack of proper housing, schools, clinics, roads, sewerage systems and other infrastructural facilities. One of the main challenges facing the PNA is to undertake a large reconstruction and development programme that will meet the expectations and aspirations of Palestinians in the PT.

It is estimated that 300,000 to 500,000 houses will need to be built in the West Bank and Gaza in the next ten years. Schools, government buildings, roads and many other facilities are also urgently needed. In the meantime, the PNA faces many constraints and has only limited resources to meet this challenge.

Natural resources are scarce. Energy and some of the required building materials are yet to be imported. Like many countries around the world, Palestine is vulnerable to both natural and man-made disasters. The long years of repression and torture produced a high percentage of disability in the younger generation.

However, the situation is not all gloomy. There are many bright points on the road to meeting the challenge. Palestine is rich in human resources. According to Marwan Abdul-Hameed, there are 56,000 Palestinian engineers in the world. Moreover, a class of skilled labourers who gained experience by working in Israel in the construction field has emerged during the 27 years of occupation. Palestinians can learn from the mistakes of others and find shortcuts to achieve their objectives. Above all, the will and determination of both people and government can play an important role in making dreams come true.

Positive measures through proper planning and correct decision-making must be taken, otherwise chaos, wastage of natural resources and aggravation of social and economic problems will not be avoided. One step in this direction is to adopt the CSS available in neighbouring Arab countries which suit Palestinian requirements. The other option for the PNA is either to start preparing its own national CSS or to adopt more known international CSS. The first option is time consuming and very expensive. The second option, however, may not be suitable for local building materials, common practices in design and construction and prevailing environmental conditions.

Jordan for example, spent more than 12 years preparing its own CSS documents, following the second option above. Reconstruction and development in Palestine cannot wait that long.

Another step forward is to start an extensive training programme for engineers and technicians on subjects such as construction management, testing of building materials, quality control, methods of practical design, construction and building control, energy conservation and utilisation, disaster preparedness and mitigation and design methods for a barrier-free environment.

In his paper, *Delays in Construction Projects in Gaza Strip*, Adnan Enshassi cited five reasons which cause delays. Two of these reasons can be eliminated by providing proper training and adopting suitable CSS.

None of the papers in this book addressed the issue of up-grading the refugee camps. Anthony Coon estimated that 7 per cent of the population in the West Bank, and 35 per cent of the population in Gaza, live in refugee camps. Development of these camps should be given due attention.

CONCLUSIONS AND RECOMMENDATIONS

All five papers presented under this theme stress the importance of having codes, standards and regulations. The reconstruction programme in Palestine cannot be achieved without the implementation of CSR. The actions proposed by Hisham Khatib to manage energy properly are incomplete without enforcing codes and regulations.

The precautions and safety measures required to minimise risk of damage or destruction by both natural and man-made disasters are priority subjects in the list of codes recommended by Seyfeddin Muaz. Buildings will not be accessible for the disabled voluntarily; accessibility must be enforced by law.

In conclusion, the following points are worth noting.

a) Implementation of codes grows with their continual use, preparation of manuals for the practical application of codes, and through training programmes for engineers and technicians.

b) Affordability of implementing CSR should be looked at when considering low-cost housing for limited income groups. Small houses with an area less than 150 square meters may be exempted from the requirements of certain codes and regulations. This exemption should not lead, in any case, to the construction of low quality houses.

c) The procedure given by Ziara et al, to issue a building permit for high-rise buildings is complicated and lengthy. A simpler procedure is proposed by Muaz.

d) Khatib proposed that Energy Consumer Centres be established to educate people, to help them conserve energy and to solve their problems regarding energy utilisation. The same concept could be used by the building inspectors. They should help people to solve their construction problems in addition to inspecting buildings.

e) Palestine has a unique opportunity to reward those who fought against occupation and suffered from repression and torture by offering them a barrier-free environment.

f) In areas prone to hazards, it is more economical to build new structures and infrastructure to high safety standards than to deal with the aftermath of destruction and reconstruction.

The following actions are recommended to be carried out before the urban and rural reconstruction in Palestine takes place:

a) The PNA must form a National Building Council to be responsible for initiating immediately needed CSS;

b) Available Jordanian CSS should be adopted for immediate use until national CSS are developed;

c) Building control should be assigned to local governments in the PT;

d) A proper energy pricing policy should be adopted by the PNA. Such a policy should exclude subsidies, discourage misuse and waste and reflect the real cost of imported products;

e) Passive solar technologies and solar water heating should be introduced in new construction;

f) Energy Consumer Centres should be established to assist people in the conservation and utilisation of energy, to help people employ good practices in construction and to help them solve technical problems during construction;

g) A barrier-free environment should be provided from the outset of the reconstruction programme in Palestine;

h) A mitigation strategy to spread risk should be adopted for urban safety;

i) New structures and infrastructure should be designed to high safety standards to protect against natural and technological hazards; and

j) Extensive training programmes should be initiated. Such programmes may include the following:

- CSS development and implementation;
- testing of building materials;
- methods of practical design, construction, quality control and building control;
- construction management;

- energy conservation and utilisation;
- disaster preparedness and mitigation; and
- design methods to create barrier-free environments.

Finally, it is recommended that:

k) Schemes for upgrading refugee camps be prepared.

DISASTER PREPAREDNESS FOR PALESTINE

Sultan Barakat and Ian Davis

ABSTRACT

Although it is impossible to prevent disasters from happening, human and material losses can be reduced through careful disaster preparedness and mitigation planning. We identify two dimensions that must come together to constitute a disaster: a natural hazard which triggers the disaster; and a vulnerable environment, or context, which allows the natural hazard to develop into a disaster.

Comparative studies and findings from Jordan and Israel have been used in lieu of the necessary basic data required for Palestine. Toxic and hazardous materials and wastes, floods, drought and forest fires are hazards with high probability and relatively low impact. These are discussed, along with earthquakes and war, two major hazards with low probability in Palestine, but high impact.

Disaster is often referred to as a cycle, incorporating actions both before and after an event occurs. While attention is often focused on the immediate response to a disaster, i.e. the stages of relief and rehabilitation, we explain why we believe that preparedness and, particularly mitigation, are far more important in curtailing loss in the long-term.

This paper examines the benefits of disaster preparedness and strategies of mitigation, including education and training, legislation and planning, insurance and management. Prerequisites for effective disaster preparedness planning are out-lined, and a staged sequence of the required measures is recommended.

INTRODUCTION

Disasters, whether natural (e.g. earthquakes, floods, volcanoes, etc.) or man-made (industrial, transport, conflict, etc.), cause massive casualties and a great deal of disruption to normal life in a wide number of countries around the world. Their effects are particularly severe on developing countries, as they place extra stress on already overstretched economies.

Disasters can no longer be regarded as isolated events that have little or no relationship to the political or economic development of a country. International experience has proven the strong inter-relationship between disasters and development. Disasters are major contributors to underdevelopment, in the same way as underdevelopment is one of the major contributors to disasters.

Palestine is not an exception, the possibilities of natural and man-made disasters exist. Although it is impossible to prevent disasters from happening, their effects can be mitigated and reduced in the level of their intensity by reducing the level of vulnerability. Human and material losses can be reduced through careful disaster preparedness and mitigation planning. Otherwise, many years of progress can be wiped out and chances for further progress set back as a result of a disaster that is not prepared for.

Thus, it is extremely important that Palestinian reconstruction decision makers and planners become fully aware of the potential impact of disasters and the role that reconstruction and development programmes can play in mitigating them and in reducing vulnerability.

Disaster preparedness brings a number of tangible benefits to any society undertaking this task:

1) It is a well proven way to reduce casualties and damage;
2) It reduces the cost of relief and recovery measures in a future disaster;
3) It provides governmental officials with a degree of confidence that their society will act in a well planned manner in the event of an emergency;
4) It can assist in creating a safe environment for the introduction of development projects (this is likely to be particularly important in Palestine in the coming five years); and
5) It brings many side benefits, such as better resource management, the development of community solidarity, the strengthening of local institutions and the development of leadership at all levels.

ISSUES: THE PALESTINIAN CONTEXT

Due to the lack of basic data on the levels of hazard and vulnerability in Palestinian settlements, we have had to base our discussion on comparative studies and findings from Jordan and Israel [1].

According to Afif Al-Ghoul, Director-General of the Jordanian Civil Defence, the most frequent hazards encountered daily are: 1) urban, industrial and transport hazards; 2) extreme temperature causing wildfire in forests; 3) drought; 4) locusts; 5) flash floods in valleys and low ground during winter accompanied by snow in the high ground [2]. In general, these can be categorised as hazards with high probability and relatively low impact. On the other hand, earthquake and war can be counted as two major hazards with low probability but high impact. In fact, for the last few decades conflict in its different forms has always been on the top of hazards facing human settlements in the Middle East in general and in Jordan and Palestine in particular.

There is a danger however, that authorities could become preoccupied with relatively high probability yet low impact emergencies and neglect the assessment, preparation and planning for low probability, high impact disasters. This pattern has been observed in many countries.

The seismicity of Palestine is well established and has been studied by several investigators who have compiled maps and historical records such as Amiran (1951) and Amnon (1974).

Although prior to 1954, no instrumental observations were made, data have mainly been collected from witnesses and historic records. A survey of historic documents for earthquakes during the last 2000 years in the eastern Mediterranean shows that throughout this span several tremors have been recorded, some of which, according to descriptions, had a considerable intensity. However, strong and devastating earthquakes struck Palestine in the years 551, 748, 808, 1202, 1837, 1903 and on 11 July 1927. The frequency of medium to strong earthquakes in this region, however, is one every 100 to 200 years (Harowitz, 1979).

The 1927 earthquake was one of the most devastating of this century in the region, the effects of which are still vivid in people's memories as well as in their recorded folklore. The epicentre of that earthquake is believed to have been within the immediate surroundings of Jericho. It has resulted in great damage on both sides of the Jordan valley, leaving 500 persons killed and more than 700 badly injured, with thousands made homeless. Thousands of houses were destroyed as well, 600 in Nablus alone (Al-Nimr, 1975).

DISASTERS AS A PROCESS

The magnitude of man's involvement in all kinds of disasters needs to be emphasised, even in the so-called natural disasters. Although disasters are referred to by the events that cause them, a disaster is not the event itself. For example, an earthquake is a natural phenomenon; if it does not strike a populated area with weak buildings, it is not likely to be a disaster. Thus, in our definition of disasters we identify two dimensions that have to come together in order to constitute a disaster: a natural hazard which triggers the disaster and a vulnerable environment

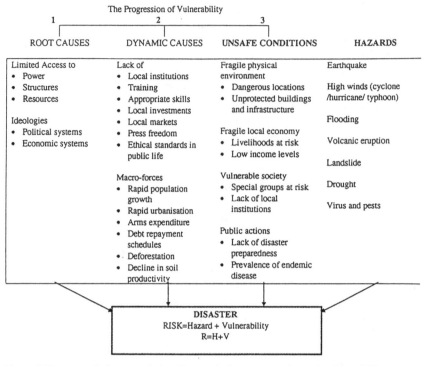

The Progression of Vulnerability

1 ROOT CAUSES	2 DYNAMIC CAUSES	3 UNSAFE CONDITIONS	HAZARDS
Limited Access to • Power • Structures • Resources	Lack of • Local institutions • Training • Appropriate skills • Local investments • Local markets • Press freedom • Ethical standards in public life	Fragile physical environment • Dangerous locations • Unprotected buildings and infrastructure	Earthquake High winds (cyclone /hurricane/ typhoon)
Ideologies • Political systems • Economic systems		Fragile local economy • Livelihoods at risk • Low income levels	Flooding Volcanic eruption Landslide
	Macro-forces • Rapid population growth • Rapid urbanisation • Arms expenditure • Debt repayment schedules • Deforestation • Decline in soil productivity	Vulnerable society • Special groups at risk • Lack of local institutions Public actions • Lack of disaster preparedness • Prevalence of endemic disease	Drought Virus and pests

DISASTER
RISK=Hazard + Vulnerability
R=H+V

Figure 1 'Pressures' that result in disasters: the progression of vulnerability.

(context), which allows the natural hazard to develop into a disaster (see Figure 1).

No matter how significant the role played by man in natural disasters is, it is limited to the vulnerability dimension and never to the source of hazards. However, there are some exceptions to this role: in certain hazards it is possible to take action to affect the hazard itself (i.e. flood control measures, such as building overflow channels or reforestation and soil conservation in drought prone areas). Thus, our role is basically in reducing the level of vulnerability by taking measures for improvement, mitigation and preparedness.

Even the so-called man-made disasters are mainly triggered by accidents occurring in the manufacture, transport, or distribution of hazardous substances such as fuel, chemicals, explosives, etc. During recent decades rapid development and industrialisation have resulted in a number of technological disasters, which by their nature have been more severe when occurring in cities lacking effective preparedness. The catastrophic gas leak at the pesticide plant in Bhopal, India, in 1984 is an example. It has to be emphasised that in such urban environments the likelihood of accidents occurring and the potential damage is greater than it is in

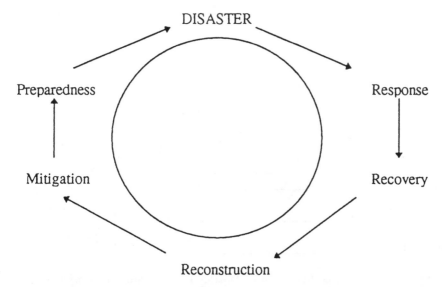

Figure 2 The Cycle of Disaster Management.

cities that are well prepared. In addition, it is often observed that in developing countries the death tolls from industrial accidents are magnified because industries are often encircled by shanty towns and slums filled with migrants from the surrounding countryside.

The process of a disaster is often referred to as a cycle, incorporating actions both before and after an event occurs (Figure 2). Within this process, attention is often focused on the immediate response to a disaster, i.e. the stages of relief and rehabilitation. However, we believe that preparedness and, particularly mitigation are far more important in curtailing loss in the long-term. Ideally the impact of disaster should be represented in a spiral, as the aim is to reduce the impact each time disaster strikes through gaining experience and achieving goals of mitigation and preparedness. These processes can be incorporated into recovery actions but ideally they will become pre-disaster, normal acceptable practice (Figure 3).

DISASTER MITIGATION AND URBAN PLANNING

The concentration of people and industry in any large town or city poses a range of risks as well as opportunities for the population. As we have indicated earlier, these threats can include a range of technological hazards such as fires, explosions or seepage of toxic gas or liquids from industrial plants, environmental health risks, pollution, etc. In addition,

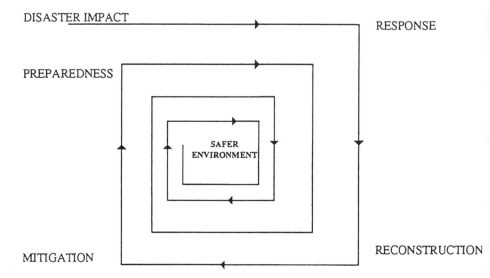

Figure 3 The Gradual Reduction of Disaster Impact Through Incorporation of Mitigation and Preparedness Measures.

many cities, such as Jerusalem and Jericho, are sited in hazard-prone areas.

Therefore, to prevent loss of life and minimise property losses, responsible civic leaders and their technical staff develop codes of practice and standards as well as land use planning controls to design and maintain a safe urban environment.

It is inevitable that during the process of urban planning, policy-makers and planners often find themselves faced with conflicting situations and demands, as well as conflicts of interests between various social and economic groups. Thus, reaching the most appropriate solution for a given urban problem, will often be based on some kind of compromise and on trade-offs.

This is particularly true when it comes to planning in disaster prone-areas, where planners must introduce into their physical development schemes the necessary measures at their disposal to make a safer urban environment. Some protective measures in the area of physical development will create additional cost. However, the question we should always ask ourselves is how far is it possible to diminish the potential risk and for what additional cost.

However, achieving a safer urban environment is a far harder task than is often assumed, since safety will inevitably require the support of all sections of society. It also requires the sustained commitment of political leaders, that once introduced becomes a continuous feature of urban management, funded as a permanent concern. Wise authorities tend to use a well balanced mixture of *carrots and sticks* (or incentives and regulations) to achieve a safe environment.

Whilst both are needed it is probably true that incentives, such as financial grants and tax relief, are more effective tools than draconian laws to punish those who violate a planning control or a building by-law. Experience suggests that regulations tend to be observed by the middle classes and above but poorer families tend to ignore them since they can pose a threat to their economic survival. Furthermore, enforcement of regulations is always a severe problem, particularly within the informal sector where unsafe conditions are most likely to prevail.

MITIGATION STRATEGIES

A sensible approach to urban safety is to apply a principle of *risk spreading* by adopting a number of strategies in parallel, on the basis that if one fails, others may succeed. A typical strategy could include the following elements:

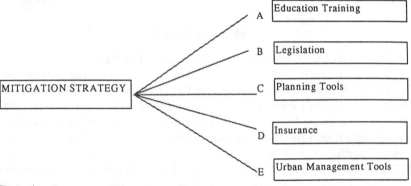

Figure 4

Education and Training

This consists of several measures, such as:

1) *Public awareness programmes* for school children such as road safety, public health, earthquake awareness, fire prevention and crime prevention;

2) Inclusion of *relevant safety elements* in the curriculum of key professions such as architects, planners, urban designers, engineers, housing officials and by-law enforcement officers;

3) *Regular training courses* in disaster preparedness for decision-makers working in governmental as well as in non-governmental organisations (NGOs); and

4) Enrolling *the media* to raise awareness, education and opinion forming in order to increase recognition of the potential for disaster reduction to save human lives and protect property [3].

Legislation

Laws are needed for a number of purposes:

1) They are very useful public-awareness tools;
2) To establish national, provincial and local preparedness planning with legal provision for the designated officials to be able to requisition goods and allocate cash resources in the event of an emergency; and
3) To establish a system of building codes and land-use planning controls to make certain that future buildings and developments are constructed and sighted to minimise risk of damage or destruction in a future disaster.

As already noted the ways to succeed in implementing these controls could be through a system of punishments or a range of incentives.

Planning Tools

The next section of this paper outlines a six stage sequence of actions for disaster planning which includes assessment, planning, testing and feedback of lessons. However, as part of the process of planning for reconstruction, and when undertaking *environmental impact analysis* (EIA) prior to embarking on major new initiatives it will be possible to include *hazard impact analysis* (HIA) in areas subject to seismic movement, landslides, flooding, etc.

Furthermore, in granting approval for the development of an industrial plant which handles hazardous materials, authorities will need to insist on the provision of two plans: firstly, an *off-site safety plan* which will cover such matters as warning systems and evacuation plans in the *high risk zone* that will surround the plant, and; secondly, an *on-site safety plan* that will include required emergency preparedness plans and a range of appropriate technical measures, such as safety cutoff valves, local fire fighting provisions, etc.

Insurance

In many countries useful alliances have been made between governments and insurance companies to promote safety. For example in Fiji, in the South Pacific, which is subject to earthquakes and high winds, house builders wishing to reduce their insurance premiums must build in accordance with the governments hazard-resistant building code. They then have the completed property inspected and approved by a government building inspector. At this stage they can take the certificate to the insurance company who will insure the property for approximately fifty per cent of a normal premium. This is a good example of an incentive being used to good effect.

Urban Management Tools

A very effective policy is for governments to set a good example of safe practice in the manner in which they build and site their own buildings (such as schools, medical dispensaries and hospitals, police stations and guest houses). This has two benefits: it gradually builds up a range of key *lifeline buildings* into the urban fabric and it provides a useful environment where builders learn the techniques of safe construction.

Authorities managing a major urban centre have to be selective as to what they can protect and what they must ignore. Resource limitations require that cash and expertise must be applied to buildings and infrastructure which is particularly critical.

Therefore the concept of *lifelines* has been adopted. Buildings, monuments and infrastructure selected for special protection are often based on the following criteria:

1) Buildings that have multiple occupancy (i.e. mosques, cinemas, schools, etc.);
2) Buildings that house children, as the future of any community (i.e. schools, mosques, etc.);
3) Buildings that are historic monuments, or house vital historical or cultural artefacts (i.e. museums, art galleries, libraries);
4) Buildings that house vital functions that must continue after a disaster (i.e. TV stations, airport control facilities, hospitals, police stations, schools (for use as emergency shelters); and
5) Critical services and infrastructure, such as electrical power, telephone services, water, drainage, radio, road, rail and air links.

It will be comparatively easy to build such new structures and infrastructure to high safety standards. However the problem is to deal with the existing building stock and existing infrastructure. This can require a very expensive strengthening process, normally termed *retrofitting*. Whilst it will never be possible to strengthen all buildings and infrastructure, it is normally feasible to achieve this with all designated lifelines.

An innovative, and relatively inexpensive approach to disaster mitigation has been adopted in Mexico City where the planning authorities have experimented with a policy to switch building functions in order to reduce risks. For example if a building that houses a *lifeline function* (such as a school) is found to have a poor seismic resistance and another building, (such as a warehouse), has a very high anticipated seismic resistance then there may be merit in swapping the school into the warehouse and vice versa. The principle of this transaction was based on the level of exposure to the threat. In the case of the warehouse only a few people worked in the building at any time (an acceptable risk), whilst the school had a high density of occupation (an unacceptable risk).

Disaster mitigation and preparedness are vital elements in the protection of lives and property in any country or urban area that is prone to natural and technological hazards and outbreaks of civil strife. However, protective planning is not an isolated process, it is best regarded as an integral part of general resource on national development planning. It is also one vital stage in a six part cycle of disaster planning which will be described within this paper.

RECOMMENDATIONS

Prerequisites for Effective Disaster Preparedness Planning

A major disaster can affect all sectors of a society which include political, social, cultural, environmental, physical, technological and economical aspects. Therefore, attempts to reduce risks through effective protective planning and efficient emergency management are dependent on a number of key factors being in place. These are as follows:

- *Political commitment* to disaster planning being available and maintained at all levels of national and local government;
- *A governmental* structure being in place with clearly defined authority. Ideally this will be through a central co-ordinating body such as a National Disaster Co-ordination Council (NDCC) being placed in the Prime Minister's or Cabinet office that will draw together representatives from key line ministries or departments. An example is the Jordanian Supreme Council for Civil Defence, which has the overall responsibilities of planning and management of governmental response in times of disasters, emergencies and war [4];
- An appropriate *budgetary commitment* to maintain effective disaster planning;
- Adequate *emergency resources*: cash, skills, goods, etc. being available within the affected country;
- A *mitigation plan* being adopted with a wide diversity of structural and non-structural measures being in place; and
- An *up-to-date, well rehearsed preparedness plan* that is comprehensive in scope, operational at all levels (central, provincial and community), understood and fully accepted by the relevant authorities and the public they serve.

To serve a preparedness plan, accurate information is a vital key and this will need to flow from a diversity of sources. The basis of this information system is the identification, acquisition, verification, storage, maintenance, synthesis, analysis and application of data. All of these requirements will be needed at some stage in the planning process.

The Sequence of Disaster Planning [5]

Disaster management is split into pre and post disaster contexts, and the flow chart (in Figure 4) represents the ideal sequence of actions. This sequence embraces pre-disaster actions which are concerned with the six stages of inception of disaster planning, risk assessment, defining levels of acceptable risk, preparedness and mitigation planning, testing the plan and feedback from lessons learned. Expressed another way there is a sequence that moves from assessment (or diagnosis), to planning, to implementation. The essence of such planning is therefore represented as a cycle to represent the need for continual development as opposed to a non-recurring linear process.

Stage One: Inception of Disaster Management

The normal process is for disaster planning to begin after a major event. It is also clear that further disasters can act as a powerful stimulus to maintain the planning process.

Stage Two: Risk Assessment

Physical and social baseline data is needed to provide a solid 'chess board' on which all subsequent hazard, vulnerability and resource data has to stand. This has to include topographical maps at appropriate scales, census data, etc.

The aim of this diagnostic process is to balance known risks against available resources. This process starts with the assessment of potential disaster risks through a combination of hazard mapping and vulnerability analysis.

Measures to reduce risks begin with accurate assessment, yet this vital process is often omitted, or tackled half-heatedly so that authorities may be planning their economy or infrastructure to resist threats that may not be serious, or conversely that may well exceed expectations.

Risk assessment is ideally a three part process that has to be undertaken in the following sequence:

- *Hazard mapping*
  Hazard mapping reveals the areas which are particularly susceptible to

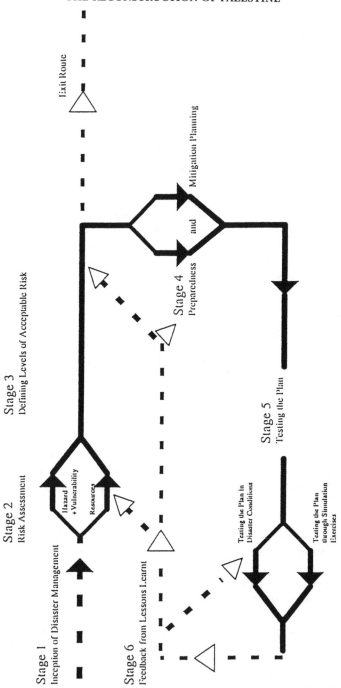

Figure 5 The Sequence of Disaster Planning in Six Stages.

seismic, volcanic, flood, drought, avalanche and high wind forces. Hazard information is needed in spatial and temporal terms on such matters as location, frequency, duration and severity (i.e. wind speeds, water flow data, etc.). The data is obtained through local scientific analysis as well as historical investigation of past hazard incidence. With this information it will be possible to develop contours that indicate the severity of risk. For example, a map that indicates a 200, 100, 50, 20 and 10-year return period for a flood event.

- *Vulnerability assessment*
  The next stage is to assess the vulnerability of persons or property to the hazard which has been mapped. This is another complex data collection process to determine elements 'at risk'. These include social, economic, natural and physical environmental factors. Vulnerability analysis is always a site-specific process with a concern for unique characteristics of a local situation.

- *Resource assessment*
  Assessment of hazards and vulnerabilities will reveal a range of critical problems which precedes the final analysis, that of available resources, often termed an 'assessment of capacities'. These local strengths can cover a wide diversity of elements: community coping mechanisms that help them to survive under hazard conditions, local leaders and institutions that can fulfil a vital role in times of acute need, community facilities, cash, credit, the location and quantity of goods that may be needed in an emergency, etc.

Undertaking a resource assessment after analysing hazards and vulnerability is a therapeutic process that looks for solutions to all the risks that have been identified.

It is also a useful activity with benefits that extend far beyond the disaster context, since it can provide a community with an audit of a wide diversity of strengths which may lie unrecognised.

Stage 3: Defining Levels of Acceptable Risk

The information gathered through the various processes in Stage 2 is then passed to political leaders in a suitable format to enable them to decide on a responsible course of action. Typical questions include the following.

- Should they initiate risk reduction measures to protect their citizens or are there other more pressing risks to address such as road safety public information programmes?
- If they decide to proceed with risk reduction against natural hazards, then what level of protection is required? For example, should infra-

structure be planned or upgraded to resist a flood that recurs every 20, 100 or even 200 years?
- Should certain critical elements such as schools and hospitals be given extra levels of safety than say individual dwellings?
- What is the 'perception of risk of the affected community'?

Such decisions are always difficult judgements concerning what is essential, acceptable, affordable or politically expedient.

In the cycle, an exit route has been included in Stage 3. This is to recognise that the elected leaders of some countries may decide that in the light of the diagnostic data on potential risks presented through Stage 3, as well as other pressing demands on the public purse, that it will not be realistic to undertake protective planning.

Stage 4: Preparedness and Mitigation Planning

These processes include measures that are aimed to reduce the impact of disasters in three ways:

1) Through methods to reduce hazard impact;
2) Through preparedness measures that emphasise short term activities. These can prepare officials for all the stages of recovery; and
3) Through longer term mitigation measures.

- *Hazard reduction measures*
  Certain hazards can be reduced through the development of protective infrastructure. For example, dams or levees can be built to control flood waters. Diversion channels can be constructed and areas can be designated to store excess flood water. An example of a measure to reduce bush fire damage is controlled burning off prior to high-risk season. In the case of tropical cyclones, the planting of shelter breaks in coastal zones can reduce wind forces to provide localised protection. Similarly, the planting of mangroves can reduce wave forces in flood surge conditions. However there are no hazard reduction measures currently available to reduce the impact of earthquakes.

- *Preparedness*
  This involves measures which enable governments, communities and individuals to respond rapidly to disaster situations and to cope with them effectively. Such measures include the formulation of viable disaster plans, the development of warning systems, and the maintenance of inventories and the training of personnel. These include relief measures to satisfy the basic needs of survivors for shelter, water, food, medical care and psychological support. They may also embrace search and rescue measures as well as evacuation plans to vacate areas that may be *at risk* from a recurring disaster.

300

Preparedness will need to cover the assessment of damage, and emergency repairs to critical facilities. To summarise, preparedness measures are aimed towards saving lives and protecting property. They range from ways of coping with the immediate impact as well as indirect effects of a disaster. Preparedness planning needs to be supported by appropriate legislation in the form of a national disaster law, often leading to a disaster plan.

- *Mitigation* [6]
This refers to actions taken to reduce the effects of a disaster on a nation or community. The term normally implies that while it may be possible to prevent the effects of some disasters, other effects will persist and can be moderated or reduced if appropriate action is taken. For example the development and application of building codes can reduce damage and loss in the event of earthquakes and cyclones.

- *Rehabilitation*
This involves interventions taken after a disaster to restore the stricken community to its normal living conditions. In many ways, the rehabilitation period is the most difficult for the victims. The most appropriate type of aid during the rehabilitation phase is cash and credit, job-producing activities and construction projects. Such inputs can all be incorporated into a comprehensive preparedness plan.

- *Recovery* [7]
This refers to the actions taken to re-establish a community after a period of rehabilitation subsequent to a disaster.During this period, people reconstruct housing and other buildings, and repair roads and other community facilities. Agriculture returns to normal during this phase. Mitigation measures can effectively be incorporated into reconstruction.

Stage 5: Testing the Plan

In the representation of Stage 5, two ways are indicated to test the plans that were developed in Stage 4. One way is through simulation exercises and public drills. This approach is obviously a rather inadequate method to determine whether a preparedness plan will work or not, and such plans do not begin to address the effectiveness of structural mitigation measures.

The acid test of protective measures will be an actual disaster situation. Following such events, there is a requirement for accurate information on the impact of the event in terms of deaths, injuries and damage to property as well as the specific needs of the surviving population. Such impact data must include knowledge of the developing disaster event,

301

including any new threats that may be emerging as a secondary impact such as earthquake aftershocks.

Data is also needed on the character, scale, location, timing and impact of assistance. Such information has to be given in precise spatial terms as well as severity of impact (i.e. scale of injury, level of building damage, etc.). In the past, there has been much confusion concerning the value in using such vague classifications as 'injured', 'affected', 'homeless', etc. and a valuable attempt has recently been made by the Federation of Red Cross and Red Crescent Societies and the Centre for Research in the Epidemiology of Disasters (CRED) to provide a set of much more precise definitions that replace such vague terms.

Stage 6: Feedback from Lessons Learned

Information on changes needed in preparedness and mitigation planning as well as on risk assessment will need to be passed back to an appropriate stage in the cyclical planning process.

ENDNOTES

1) At this early stage of development in Palestine, it is vital that careful risk assessment for all natural and technological hazards is carried out throughout the country. This data needs to be systematically documented, stored and disseminated to build up a vital planning tool.
2) Personal conversation with Sultan Barakat in April, 1995 at the Civil Defence Headquarters in Amman.
3) Quoted from the Yokohama Strategy and Plan of Action for a Safer World; Guidelines for Natural Disaster Prevention, Preparedness and Mitigation, IDNDR, Yokohama, Japan, 23–27 May 1994.
4) The Jordanian Supreme Council is made up of: 1) the Minister of Interior as a President; 2) the Head of Police as vice-president; 3) Representative Members of the Secretary-Generals of the Ministries of Interior, Public Works, Social Development, Health, Finance, Trade and Industry, Education as well as the Cabinet; 4) the Director-General of Civil Defence; and 5) a high ranking General from the armed forces.
5) The following text is abridged from the article, *Disaster Management for Disaster Planning* by Ian Davis and David Bickmore, in Natural Disasters: Protecting Vulnerable Communities, Merriman and Browitt, London, 1993.
6) The United Nations Disaster Relief Organisation (UNDRO) has used mitigation in a broader sense, encompassing allocations taken prior to the occurrence of a disaster.
7) Recovery, a term used by some authors and institutions, includes both rehabilitation and reconstruction.

BIBLIOGRAPHY

Al-Nimr, Ihsan, 1975, **Tarikh Jabal Nablus wa al-Balqa** (The History of Jabal Nablus and Balqa), Nablus (Arabic).

Amiran, A., 1950, *A Revised Earthquake Catalogue of Palestine,* **Israel Exploration Journal,** 1, pp. 223–246.

Amnon, Shinar, 1974, **Judea and Samaria: Studies in Settlement Geography,** Jerusalem (Hebrew).

Aysan, Yasmen, Ian Davis, Andrew Clayton and Alistar Cory, 1993, **Building for Safety Compendium, An Annotated Bibliography and Information Directory for Safe Building Programmes in Disaster-Prone Areas,** Intermediate Technology Publications, London.

Bay Area Regional Earthquake Preparedness Project, 1989, **Earthquake Vulnerability Analysis for Local Governments,** San Francisco.

Blaikie, Cannon, Davis and Wisner, 1994, **At Risk, Natural Hazards, People's Vulnerability and Disasters,** Routledge, London.

Coburn, Andrew and Robin Spence, 1992, **Earthquake Protection,** John Wiley & Sons, New York.

Coburn, Andrew, Robin Spence, Antonios Pomonis and Richard Hughes, 1993, **Technical Principles of Building for Safety,** Intermediate Technology Publications, London.

Dudley, Eric and Anne Haaland, 1993, **Communicating Building for Safety,** Intermediate Technology Publications, London.

Harowitz, A., 1979, **The Quaternary of Israel,** New York.

International Federation of Red Cross and Red Crescent Societies, 1995, **World Disasters Report,** Geneva.

Organisation for Economic Co-operation and Development, OECD Development Assistance Committee, 1994, *Guidelines for Aid Agencies on Disaster Mitigation,* **Guidelines on Aid and Environment,** 7, Paris.

Rarrot, Andre, 1968, **Land of Christ: Archaeology, History and Geography** (trans. by James H. Farley), Fortress Press, Philadelphia.

Shinar, Amnon, 1974, **Judea and Samaria: Studies in Settlement Geography,** Jerusalem (Hebrew).

Spangle, William et al, 1991, **Rebuilding after Earthquakes; Lessons from Planners,** Stanford University, Portola Valley, California.

Toft, Brian and Simon Reynolds, 1994, **Learning from Disasters,** Butterworth Heinemann, Oxford.

ENERGY CONSERVATION AND EFFICIENCY IN RURAL AND URBAN CONSTRUCTION

Hisham Khatib

ABSTRACT

Country energy consumption depends on economic activity, availability of local energy resources and on the weather. Although both the West Bank and Gaza have relatively mild weather, most population centres need heating during the four months of winter and, to a lesser extent, for air-conditioning and cooling in long summers. A lack of local energy resources generally necessitates the importation of energy products at international prices, often with limited foreign currency resources.

Energy requirements can be reduced drastically through energy management. This calls for proper pricing, energy efficiency and conservation, utilisation of energy efficient technologies and public awareness. Energy prices must reflect the real cost to the economy and should be set at a level that inhibits waste and overuse.

Such prices encourage the introduction of energy efficient technologies, regulations and codes of practice which aid energy conservation. The public also needs to be educated and helped to achieve the objectives of energy management.

Buildings and new construction in the West Bank and Gaza must adopt energy efficiency and conservation techniques to reduce the burden of energy costs on the economy. Transport in urban and rural areas must also conserve energy for the same purpose, and to ensure a healthy environment in population centres.

INTRODUCTION

In any country, energy consumption per capita depends on the extent of economic activity, energy pricing and conservation policies and also on weather patterns. The West Bank and Gaza have a southern Mediterranean climate of hot summers and cold winters. In almost all parts, it is necessary to have heating in winter and desirable to have cooling (air conditioning) in the summer. Although the geographical area is small, the diversity of weather conditions between the mountainous areas (some 800 meters above sea-level) and the Jordan Valley (less than 200 meters below sea-level) is great. In summer, the coastal areas are hot and humid and the mountainous parts pleasant and quite dry. Therefore, it is impossible to determine a single weather pattern for the West Bank and Gaza that would dictate a common weather conditioning strategy.

There are very few indigenous energy sources in these areas, and only very small oil deposits have been discovered. Commercial, although not very large, natural gas reserves have been discovered in Jordan and are currently being exploited. No important hydro-energy sources are available. Solar intensity and potential is high; however, because of solar's diffusion and its low efficiency, the prospect of utilising it on a large commercial scale is limited. Therefore, the West Bank and Gaza, as well as Jordan, are expected to continue to depend on imported fossil fuels for many years to come.

At present, fossil fuels provide almost 97 per cent of the energy supplies in these regions, compared with a world average of about 90 per cent. Most of the fossil fuels are imported, and their excessive cost strains the limited amount of foreign currency reserves available.

Present annual energy consumption in Jordan is almost one ton of oil equivalent (TOE) per capita. It is utilised as follows: 30 per cent in transport; 35 per cent for electricity production; 13 per cent in industry; 11 per cent domestic; and about 11 per cent other uses (mostly pumping water). These proportions are expected to be the same in the West Bank and Gaza where similar social and other standards prevail. As a result, high standards of energy conservation and efficiency in energy use will be required in urban and rural construction and in energy utilisation.

ENERGY MANAGEMENT

Energy management calls for action on three fronts. One of them is fiscal; the second is technical; and the third is regulative. Fiscal measures dictate the price of energy products and also duties and customs on energy utilising apparatus.

Technical measures relate to policies that encourage the development and utilisation of energy efficient engineering practices as well as energy efficiency and conservation measures, including public education and awareness. Energy regulation involves laws, regulations and codes of practice which, in many cases, regulate the way energy is utilised and determine its relationship with the environment, particularly in new construction and housing.

The three measures are inter-related and they are integrated parts of the practice of energy management, the aim of which is the rational and economical utilisation of energy sources in the energy consuming sectors. It is not possible to encourage efficient energy use in the economy without fiscal (pricing) measures. Equally, it is not possible to achieve rational energy use with fiscal measures only.

Technical measures and regulations that foster energy efficient engineering practices and conservation are also very essential to rationalise usage. The following sections of the paper will deal with these issues and their importance in achieving proper energy management in housing and other building works in the West Bank and Gaza.

ENERGY PRICING

Energy pricing covers the pricing of refined energy products: gas oil (benzene), diesel oil, containers of liquefied petroleum gas bottles (LPG), kerosene and also electricity. Gas oil (benzene) is extensively used in private and public transport; diesel oil (light fuel) is utilised in public transport, by trucks (which also use kerosene) and as a fuel to heat homes. LPG is mainly used for cooking, but also for heating in some cases. Electricity is used mainly for lighting and home appliances. Increasingly, it is used for air conditioning as well as for heating.

At present, the West Bank and Gaza import all their energy products, fuels and electricity. This is expected to continue for a few years. Building refineries and power stations are highly capital intensive projects and it is not wise to embark on investing in them in the early stages of urban and rural development as long as there are alternative sources of supply for these products. However, energy products and electricity, whether processed locally or imported, are costly and must be paid for in hard currency. Correspondingly, they are valuable and must be conserved, utilised efficiently and with care. Proper pricing can help to achieve this.

Indeed, it is impossible to attain efficient energy utilisation without a rational pricing policy. This means setting prices in a way that excludes subsidies, discourages misuse and waste and reflects the real cost to the economy of these imported products.

Price subsidies cause a misallocation of resources and encourage overuse. Reduced prices for resources do not necessarily lessen the burden on the citizen; sometimes, if accompanied by capital expenditure, they can have the opposite effect. Energy subsidies often benefit the rich more than the poor. Besides causing a misallocation of resources, they encourage excessive imports of consumer goods (such as cars, over-sized air conditioners, etc.) and contribute to pollution and detrimental effects on the local environment.

The citizen's welfare is optimised by pricing products and services at their real cost to the economy; subsidies, if any, should be directed to those sectors which improve the productivity of the economy and maximise public and individual welfare, such as education, health, the environment, etc.

The cost to the economy of oil products involves not only the cost of oil imports, refining and distribution, but also other, more expensive complimentary public expenditure and infrastructure. The cost of transporting fuels must cover the cost of the transportation infrastructure: roads, traffic facilities, pollution hazards. In the case of countries with limited foreign exchange, the cost to the economy must also include the economic burden of imported cars purchased with foreign exchange that may also have to be used for more pressing needs such as food imports.

Similarly, the price of electricity must also reflect the cost of investment in generation and distribution facilities. A subsidised price will lead to over-use and wastage, and will, in turn, require over-investment in very expensive power stations, transmission and distribution facilities. All of these are extremely costly and greatly exceed the cost of fuel.

The marginal cost for producing each kilowatt-hour (KWH) of electricity is now no less than six (US) cents; of this, four cents represent the cost of the facilities (the hardware) and only two cents (or less) the cost of the fuels. Moreover, most water consumption in the region has now become linked to energy use (through desalination and/or pumping). Subsidising water prices beyond what is required to meet basic needs usually leads to overuse of both water and energy.

Generally, the main beneficiary of subsidised energy products and electricity is not the citizen but the foreign exporter of cars, power stations and expensive energy-intensive consumer goods. The national economy and its citizens pay dearly for this. That part of the population which have limited incomes can be allowed to pay a subsidised price for electricity to meet their essential needs, but consumption above this should be priced at the full cost.

Energy and transport systems, particularly electricity networks, are highly capital intensive and demand a lot of investment. In many developing countries, investment in electrical power amounts to almost one-fourth gross capital formation. Reducing inefficiencies and waste in this sector will greatly reduce pressures on the national economy.

Another aspect of pricing involves the need to streamline prices so that substitution of one energy product by another is only encouraged by national economical policy. For example, a low subsidised price for electricity simply shifts the burden of heating costs into heating with electricity instead of with gas-oil heaters. Of course, this overloads the electric system and necessitates heavy investment and other costs.

TECHNOLOGY IN ENERGY MANAGEMENT IN HOUSING CONSTRUCTION

Establishing a correct pricing system is insufficient to achieve proper energy management in urban and rural housing. It is also necessary to: 1) introduce the energy efficient technologies; 2) prepare and enforce building codes of practice and regulations that assist in conserving energy use; and 3) assist the public in achieving these objectives.

Energy Efficient Technologies and Apparatus

Households generally use many energy consuming appliances at home. In addition to lighting, there are electrical appliances and heat conditioning installations (including both heating and air conditioning). Since the oil adjustment prices at the end of 1973, great attention was given by manufacturers of electrical appliances into producing energy efficient products. Many of the electrical appliances in the West Bank and Gaza are either post-1973 vintage or still to be purchased. Therefore, their electrical products are likely to be efficient.

With the proliferation of local manufacturing, some of the local energy utilising appliances are not as efficient as their imported counter parts. It is essential to overcome this by establishing suitable manufacturing standards and regulations. However, efficiency does not depend solely on the manufacturer; the user is also important.

The energy consumption of an electrical washing machine, for example, depends to a great extent on its work load, utilisation factor, water temperature and method of use as much as on the efficiency of the washing machine itself. The amount of heating (or cooling) of a house is more dependant on the construction of the house (insulation and materials), its planning and orientation (to utilise solar parameters) than on the efficiency of the boiler (or air conditioner).

Increasingly, it has become common practice for regulators to insist that manufacturers specify the energy consumption of their products and life-time cycle costs (i.e. the capital cost of the appliance plus the cost of operating it during its useful service years). This allows consumers a choice, and trade-off between capital and life-time operating costs.

The efficiency of most of the equipment utilised for weather conditioning, particularly boilers for heating and air conditioners, is influenced by maintenance standards. Boilers in particular need annual and periodic maintenance. Their efficiency depends to a very large extent on the maintenance and periodic tuning of certain parts.

Unfortunately, periodic maintenance in most developing countries leaves much to be desired, taking place only after breakdowns or after the efficiency has completely deteriorated.

Insulation of Buildings

As already explained, most buildings in the West Bank and Gaza require heating in winter and, to a lesser extent, air conditioning in summer. The amount of heating and air-conditioning which is needed can be greatly reduced by effective building design and execution. Thermal insulation and the use of solar parameters are two examples.

The installation of thermal insulation, which uses simple building methods, in all new buildings has become mandatory practice in many countries, including Jordan. Unfortunately, most building materials used in the West Bank and Gaza and in Jordan, such as limestone, are not good insulating materials. Without additional insulation, such buildings would demand a lot of energy for weather conditioning.

Walls can be insulated by having air spaces between outside walls and the interior walls, or by filling these spaces with insulating materials such as fibreglass or synthetic materials. Plastic painting of exterior walls greatly helps in preventing moisture intrusion. Similar arrangements on the top ceiling can reduce heat penetration and also prevent any penetration of moisture.

Doors and windows can be a main cause of low thermal efficiency in buildings in the West Bank and Gaza, particularly in winter. A lot of heat escapes from windows and doors because of their poor execution, particularly in the case of aluminium frames. A lot of attention should be devoted to manufacturing good sealed windows and doors. Training must also be provided to ensure efficient installation.

Double glazing of windows is being introduced into some expensive and prestigious buildings and apartments. It is expensive and is only needed in very cold areas. However, its efficiency and usefulness also depend on proper installation.

Passive Solar in New Construction

Passive Solar (PS) uses solar parameters to obtain maximum solar warmth in winter and minimum solar heat in summer. Due to the solar intensity in the region, the West Bank and Gaza are one of the best places in the world for the adoption and application of PS technologies in new construction.

PS utilises the interaction of solar radiation with the building itself, its location and construction methods. Passive solar also applies to the design and orientation of doors and windows and includes the provision of as much daylight as possible, thus saving energy for lighting. Measures regarding the height of buildings and the planting of trees to shield them as much as possible from the effect of gusts and wind are also involved in PS.

With a minimal level of investment, or even no investment at all, the need for costly outgoings to weather condition buildings can be eliminated with PS. Thus, it is a cheap way of achieving significant and lasting results in protecting, to a great extent, the building and its occupants from extreme weather conditions. What is essential is intelligent architecture, including landscape architecture.

PS, in a crude way, has been known in our part of the world for centuries. Unfortunately, this knowledge has not been applied extensively. Recently, PS technologies have been developed world wide, particularly in Europe, to reduce the need for energy in heating and cooling.

Solar Water Heating

As mentioned earlier, the West Bank and Gaza enjoy levels of solar activity and intensity which, to some extent, can compensate for the lack of commercial energy sources in the area. Although solar energy has low intensity, it can be collected for some of the applications which may be used in existing houses and new construction. The most important of these is solar water heating utilising solar collectors which are generally referred to as 'flat-plate' collectors of the thermosyphon type.

If used efficiently and wisely, solar water heating will ensure a constant flow of hot water in a house for some 330 to 360 days of the year, depending on the location. It can save enormous amounts of energy and pay for itself in only three years. Solar panel technology is very easily understood and applied. Most of the manufacturing, as well as assembly and erection, can be done in the West Bank and Gaza, thereby also providing a source for employment.

Utilisation of solar panels is widespread in Israel, where almost one million units are in existence, as well as in Jordan and Cyprus. The technology is well proven and benefits have been demonstrated for years. Their application can be made mandatory in all new construction (except high rise buildings), thus ensuring the energy savings that result.

A major problem occurs in high rising buildings, i.e. those over 24 meters, in which the roof area cannot provide enough space for housing the large number of panels needed. However, this type of construction in the West Bank and Gaza is rare.

There have also been attempts to utilise solar panels for space heating in new construction. However, the technology has not been well developed yet.

Public Energy Conservation

Having set pricing policies which inhibit waste and encourage conservation, it is necessary to protect the population and shield it from the burden of high energy prices by helping them to conserve energy and to utilise it efficiently. Energy conservation means using energy only to the extent that it is needed. Energy efficiency means using less amounts of energy for carrying out certain tasks. To achieve the dual purpose of energy conservation and energy efficiency, it is not enough to have the right pricing policies and legislation. Energy users and consumers must also be aided and informed about technologies and techniques that can enhance energy conservation and its efficient utilisation.

LEGISLATION AND REGULATIONS

Laws and regulations can affect a wide spectrum of energy activities, including fiscal measures, which have already been explained. In addition, they can affect the application of efficiency standards in the production and importation of energy efficient machinery, appliances and transport vehicles. The insulation of walls in new construction can also be made mandatory. The same applies to regulation which makes installation of solar heating obligatory in new construction.

Laws and regulations (including prices) can also affect general planning insofar as they encourage energy efficient technologies and inhibit the introduction of energy intensive industries and products. Both prices and legislation should give the right messages to planners of new construction in the West Bank and Gaza.

Although very important in achieving energy efficiency and conservation, legislation and regulation can only be successful as part of an integrated strategy which includes programmes to assist and guide the public in ways to reduce energy consumption, as well as the correct pricing policies. The introduction of modern energy conserving technology is also essential.

OTHER CONSIDERATIONS

Urban and Rural Energy Use and the Environment

Urban construction in the West Bank and Gaza is not yet congested. However, urban centres in the West Bank and Gaza are gradually going to become congested and over-populated. Utilisation of energy in transport and heating can cause serious environmental problems in urban centres, mainly through air pollution. The exhaust from cars and central heating chimneys can cause fumes, acids and solid particles that can affect health and also harm buildings, particularly ancient buildings and antiquities.

Future environmental problems in the West Bank and Gaza, emanating from energy use, can be reduced in many ways: (i) by reducing congestion

311

in urban zones; (ii) by limiting cars and traffic congestion in highly populated zones; and (iii) by ensuring the quality of fuels utilised in cars and in central heating through the provision of low sulphur, low lead fuels with less other harmful contents such as nitrogen oxides and carbon dioxides. The same applies to the inhibition of polluting fuels such as fuelwood, coal, charcoal and heavy fuels.

The availability of natural gas for heating and for public transport and of liquefied petroleum gas (LPG) for cooking has greatly helped to reduce urban pollution in many areas of the world. It is not expected that natural gas will become available in the West Bank and Gaza soon. However, LPG is readily available and its use should be encouraged, especially for cooking instead of less efficient fuels such as wood and charcoal. Kerosene can also be used. The practice of used lubricating oil in furnaces (i.e. in bakeries) or of mixing it with other fuels should be strictly forbidden in urban areas because of the detrimental effect this has on health.

Energy Use in Transport

Transport is a major user of energy in the West Bank and Gaza and will continue to be so for many years to come, mainly because of the lack of efficient public transport and the proliferation of housing and urban construction across large areas. Excessive utilisation of oil products – mainly benzene (gas oil) and diesel oil – will not only hurt the economy of the West Bank and Gaza but can also have detrimental environmental effects (see the section above on Energy and the Environment).

Pricing policies are insufficient to limit energy use in transport, not least because price elasticity is very limited (at least in the short term) due to the lack of alternatives. Other methods include encouraging the use of small fuel-thrift cars, encouraging public transport and also utilising fuel-saving techniques in bulk transporters like trucks and lorries. Energy use is also reduced by good maintenance.

Encouraging the use of petrol-economic small cars can be done through legislation and fiscal policies, including pricing, taxation, registration fees, etc. The more fuel thirsty large cars can be penalised in the same way, thus reducing the prospect of purchasing them. Public transport greatly reduces the need for private transport, thus contributing towards less energy use in the economy.

Efficient use of fuel in trucks and lorries (as well as other vehicles) can be improved by many small techniques such as: wind deflectors, choice of right type of tyres and maintaining their correct pressure, speed limits and ensuring proper maintenance and fuel efficient driving techniques.

Life Cycle Costs

The life cycle cost of any building, machine or appliance which uses energy is the sum of the capital cost plus the discounted present worth of its energy consumption (plus maintenance and other costs) over its useful life. Life cycle cost should dictate construction plans and the purchasing policies for new equipment. Price and investment costs are not the only indicators.

Normally, many builders and purchasers opt for cheaper prices. They are concerned with today's cost rather than the future. Although this is a short-sighted policy, it is widespread. It can only be changed by educating planners and the public to the importance of future economies when making decisions today.

In the case of construction, many important decisions involving life cycle costing need to be taken. The most important concerns building insulation and lighting. Heating, cooling and lighting are the main users of energy in new construction in the West Bank and Gaza. Although it involves capital expenditure, including insulation in new buildings saves a lot of future energy costs and more than compensates for the cost in terms of comfort. New, very efficient lighting, such as the compact fluorescent kind, is already available in local markets. However, it is expensive. The price of energy, i.e. of electricity, is crucial in this regard, but so too is information.

Decisions must be made regarding tradeoffs between present and future costs. Life cycle costing is not easy, but designers and purchasers can be helped with information and calculations undertaken by specialists which try to give an idea of future operational costs, particularly for energy, and which combine it with current investment costs. Life cycle costs should be a primary consideration when investment decisions for new construction in the West Bank and Gaza are made in the future.

RECOMMENDATIONS

It is not enough to impose measures, through pricing and legislation, that force consumers to conserve energy and improve efficiency of use. What is also important is to educate people to conserve energy with as little as possible disturbance to their welfare and productivity.

The establishment of Energy Consumer Centres (ECCs) in the West Bank and Gaza could help to achieve this. They would also help to reduce the need for investment in energy infrastructure and capital projects such as refineries and power stations. In addition, ECCs could help to lower the impact which energy utilisation has on the local, regional and global environment.

Requirements

Normally, ECCs would not require heavy capital investment. What is most crucially needed is capable and motivated manpower.

Technical assistance and training are needed more than equipment. Rent and salaries are local expenses. Manufacturers and producers of energy efficiency and conservation equipment could provide the necessary equipment, as well as services.

Activities of the Centres

The ECCs would provide their services free. Their activities should include the following.

1) Displays and invitations to consumers (individuals as well as large industrial and construction firms) to visit the Centre to review available equipment and facilities and to discuss their problems over with the Centre experts.
2) Holding specialised seminars for major users on efficient insulation in buildings, reducing fuel consumption of large transport trucks, efficient lighting, application of solar parameters in buildings, solar water heaters, etc.
3) Offering free energy audits to important installations such as certain factories, hospitals, commercial centres, large energy consumers, etc.
4) Assistance in finding solutions for local energy problems, as well as assistance to government institutions in energy legislation, standards and regulations.
5) Education of the public, particularly school children, regarding the culture of energy conservation and the encouragement of school groups to visit the Centre for education in the ethics and values of conservation.
6) Dissemination of information and knowledge that assists in conservation through posters, mail, television, press announcements, etc.
7) Education and dissemination of energy audit consultants. (Once there are trained staff, they will be inclined to leave the Centre and start their own consulting firms that may compete with the Centre in some of its work, such as energy audits and the provision of advice. This actually serves the Centre's strategy of spreading information and services for energy efficiency and conservation).

BIBLIOGRAPHY

Khatib, Hisham, 1995, *Financial and Economic Evaluation of Projects*, **IEE Power Engineering Journal**, (October).

Ministry for Public Works and Housing, 1989 and later, **Codes for Buildings**, Amman (in Arabic).

Organisation of Arab Petroleum Exporting Countries, Kuwait, 1995, **Proceedings of the Arab Energy Conference, Cairo, April 1994**.

United Nations Development Programme, Bureau for Arab States, New York, 1993, **Proceedings of the Seminar on Domestic Energy Policies and Management in the Arab Countries, Cairo, October 1992**.

CODES, STANDARDS AND SPECIFICATIONS

Seyfeddin Muaz

ABSTRACT

Neither the 300,000 homes needed for Palestinians nor the substantial infrastructure required for both small and large towns can be built adequately without the development and implementation of codes, standards and specifications (CSS) for construction. Because the development of CSS needs a long time and extensive expertise, it is recommended that the Palestinian National Authority (PNA), before launching its reconstruction programme in West Bank and Gaza, adopt CSS suitable for the prevailing conditions in these territories.

The most suitable CSS documents are available in Jordan. Environmental conditions, local building materials, methods of construction and other factors are similar to those of Palestine. This justifies the adoption of Jordanian CSS for immediate use by Palestinian officials.

This paper describes the process which will be required for the successful adoption of CSS and proposes a method of implementation as well. A list of the CSS which will be needed immediately is also provided, as are the measures which the PNA will need to take to enforce building controls.

It is also recommended that an extensive training programme concerning CSS development and implementation be initiated, in addition to training on the testing of building materials, methods of design and construction, quality controls and methods of building control.

INTRODUCTION

The huge demand for housing, schools, clinics, roads and other facilities is one of the major problems facing the PNA. In the case of housing, an estimated 300,000 units are needed immediately.

For any government, proper planning and correct decision-making

316

are required to avoid chaos, the wastage of national resources and the aggravation of social and economic problems. Without CSS, the construction of the large number of homes which will be needed in Palestine could create many problems that would be difficult to resolve later. Moreover, the implementation of CSS could help to safeguard the interests of consumers, consultants, contractors and the building industry. It would also help to develop the industrial and engineering sectors of the Palestinian economy.

The absence of CSS in some of the Arab countries during the construction boom in the 1970s was the reason behind the current situation which can be seen in some cities. This can be described as follows:

- Many structures suffer from improper design;
- Many structures are unable to resist unexpected natural disasters;
- An architectural style reflecting the national heritage is absent;
- Existing structures are poorly maintained;
- Conventional methods of construction are expensive; and
- Building materials have been wasted unjustifiably.

Therefore, it is recommended that the PNA, before launching the reconstruction programme in the West Bank and Gaza, adopt CSS which are appropriate for these territories. The Jordanian Codes of Practice, Standards and Specifications are the most suitable for adaptation in the West Bank and Gaza for the following reasons:

- The environmental conditions between the two regions are similar;
- The available local building materials and methods of construction are similar;
- The architectural style is common in both countries;
- Palestinian and Jordanian engineers have similar backgrounds;
- Jordan is the only Arab country which has a complete set of CSS which has been in use for some ten years;
- Jordan has a dynamic process for updating its CSS;
- Jordan has practical manuals to apply easily the major codes in use; and
- The Council of Arab Ministers of Housing and Reconstruction has adopted more than 20 Jordanian building codes as the basic ones for the preparation of the unified 'Pan-Arab Building Codes.'

DEFINITION OF CODES, STANDARDS AND SPECIFICATIONS

It is important to differentiate between codes and specifications on the one hand, and standards and technical specifications on the other. The important distinctions are as follows.

- *The Standard Specification* is a listing of minimum requirements for

Table 1 Available Codes and Standards in Neighbouring Countries.

Country	Codes	Number of Codes and Standards Available Standard Specifications	Technical Specifications
Jordan	32	Available	4
Egypt	10	Available	4
Iraq	2	Available	–
Syria	–	Available	–

materials of construction, construction products, dimensions of elements, test methods and/or test conditions. The standard specification states the basis for evaluating the test results of these materials or products. Examples of such standards are the ASTM and BS Standards.

- *The Technical Specification* is a quantitative description of the required characteristics of a structure, structural element or method of construction. The technical specification includes the conditions that should be satisfied by a certain project, and specifies the requirements of the standard specifications and the codes of practice. It also includes, among others, methods of measurements, quantities, composition of products to be produced on site and specific requirements.

- *The Code of Practice* is a collection of rules and regulations scientifically acceptable for the design of structure, structural elements or a system. It specifies the design characteristics and conditions to secure safety, proper performance and durability of the structure, the structural elements or the system.

CODES AND STANDARDS AVAILABLE FOR POSSIBLE USE

Table 1 shows a comparison of available codes and standards in four neighbouring countries: Jordan, Egypt, Iraq and Syria (Second Committee, 1989). Of the Arab countries, Jordan has a complete set of CSS for highway and building construction which has been implemented for a long period of time.

Due to the similarity in environmental conditions, cultural background and building materials between Jordan and Palestine, this paper will emphasise the codes and standards in Jordan which are available for immediate application in Palestine.

Codes of Practice

The National Building Council of Jordan (NBCJ) has issued 32 codes to be used by designers, consultants and others. These codes cover all design aspects for reinforced concrete, prestressed concrete and steel structures. They include architectural requirements, as well as electrical and mechan-

Table 2 List of Codes of Practice in Jordan.

Volume No.	Title	Date of Issue
1	Generalities.	1993
2	Loads and Forces.	1990
3	Site Investigations.	1990
4	Bases, Foundations and Retaining Walls.	1992
5	Plain and Reinforced Concrete.	1993
6	Prestressed Concrete.	1994
7	Steel Structures.	1988
8	Formworks.	1993
9	Scaffolding.	1988
10	Masonry and Walling.	1990
11	Building Materials and Their Usage in Building Industry.	1988
12	Space Requirements for Buildings.	1993
13	Thermal Insulation.	1990
14	Acoustics.	1988
15	Fire Protection.	1990
16	Natural Ventilation.	1992
17	Natural Lighting.	1992
18	Water Supply for Buildings.	1988
19	Drainage and Sewerage in Buildings.	1988
20	Urban Aesthetics.	1990
21	Refuse Disposal.	1988
22	Public Safety in Construction Sites.	1988
23	Electric Wiring and Installations.	1988
24	Interior Illumination.	1988
25	Earthing.	1988
26	Lightening Protection.	1988
27	Fire Alarm Systems.	1988
28	Lifts.	1990
29	Central Heating.	1990
30	Mechanical Ventilation and Air Conditioning.	1988
31	Shelters.	1993
32	Building Requirements for Disabled.	1993

ical installations and devices. Formworks, scaffolding, thermal insulation, fire protection and refuse disposal are other subjects mentioned.

Table 2 shows the complete set of codes issued to date. Some of these codes have been revised recently while others will be revised soon. Four practical manuals have been drafted to help engineers apply the codes easily and efficiently. These manuals cover the following topics:

- Plain and reinforced concrete;
- Electrical installations in buildings;
- Central heating in buildings; and
- Architectural design for buildings.

The draft of the first three manuals is complete; the fourth is still under

Table 3 Number of Standards for Major Sectors in Jordan.

Serial No.	Major Sector	Number of Available Standards
1	Measurement, testing and Instruments	57
2	Environmental and safety engineering	25
3	Energy Technology	13
4	Electrotechnology	50
5	Mechanical Engineering	30
6	Transport Engineering	12
7	Construction	69
8	Materials	17
9	Metallurgy	19

preparation. It is expected that the four manuals will be issued and printed in 1996.

NBCJ has recently decided to draft a manual for the design of steel structures based on the code for steel structures; however, it is not expected to be issued before 1997. The Royal Scientific Society (RSS) of Jordan is currently working on a manual for earthquake-resistant structures. It is due to be completed in 1997.

Standard Specifications

The Jordanian Directorate of Standards (Ministry of Industry and Trade, 1995) has issued some 1,000 standards for different materials. Among these, more than 200 standards deal directly with building materials.

Table 3, shows a number of available Jordanian standards for sectors related to building and highway construction.

Technical Specifications

Jordan's Ministry of Public Works and Housing has issued four volumes of technical specifications for the construction of highways and buildings. They include the following:

- Volume 1, civil and architectural works;
- Volume 2, mechanical services for buildings; and
- Volume 3, electrical services for buildings.

They were issued in Arabic in 1985 and are used extensively by engineers, designers and contractors. A comprehensive committee has been formed recently to review and update the three volumes on building construction. The committee has contacted all the sectors involved and received many comments from designers, contractors and other users. These comments have been reviewed carefully for possible consideration in the new edition. It is expected that this updated and expanded version will be issued by the end of 1996.

The fourth volume, which is entitled *Specifications for Highway and Bridge Construction*, was issued in 1991 in English, in the form of an updated version of the original work which was issued in 1974. The content of this volume consists of eight parts:

1) Ggeneral provisions;
2) Earthworks;
3) Subbase and base courses;
4) Bituminous construction;
5) Concrete, steel and structures;
6) Lighting, traffic signals and electrical installations;
7) Landscaping and irrigation;
8) Incidental construction.

This volume is extensively used by consultants, contractors and the relevant ministries.

ISSUING A NEW CSS

The process of issuing new CSS is a long one which requires a great deal of expertise and group effort. The process differs from one country to another.

There are two methods of issuing CSS. The first depends on carrying actual research and extensive testing of local materials and products, methods of design and common practices and/or methods of construction and installations. This method reflects the proper characteristics of available materials and the local practices in construction. It is a costly process, which Palestinians cannot afford, and consumes a lot of time which Palestinians should not waste.

The second method adopts currently available CSS which are tailor-made to suit Palestinian requirements. This is a quicker process, and costs less than the first method. The philosophy of this method is to adopt one, or several, available CSS which are the most suitable to meet the needs and requirements of the construction industry in Palestine. Then the adopted CSS can be modified to comply with local materials, common practices and methods of design and construction specifically applied in Palestine. It is recommended that the second method be used for issuing new CSS by the PNA.

The Second Method: Drafting New Codes

It is imperative beforehand to designate an authority to be responsible for formally issuing codes. This authority could be the Ministry of Public

Works, any related council or corporate within the jurisdiction of the PNA. Committees at three different levels should also be formed to monitor and promote the issuing process for the new codes. These should include:

1) *The level of decision makers.* At this level, a committee representing ministries, corporations and institutes that are related to the construction industry must be formed as the Higher Committee (HC). This committee should be responsible for approving the new codes submitted by lower level committees. The members of this committee must be at the level of ministers, general directors or heads of institutes;

2) *The level of experts.* At this level, a committee representing ministries, corporations, institutes, municipalities and private companies and institutions of related work must be formed as the Technical Committee (TC). This committee should be responsible for reviewing the final draft of new codes submitted by lower level committees. Members of this committee should be experts in their respective field with minimum 15 years experience. They should include experts from different related disciplines; and

3) *The level of specific expertise.* Here, experts in a specific field or discipline where all members have experience from 10 to 15 years in the same field should form the Technical Sub-Committee (TSC). This committee should be technically responsible for drafting a new code. The sub-committee should be assisted by a Draft Working Group (DWG) which should collect the information and write the first draft.

Mechanisms for action

The mechanism to activate these committees and working groups could be as follows:

1) Each DWG should be assigned to draft one particular code;
2) Each DWG should review different available codes for one particular subject and collect the necessary information, then write the first draft of that particular code. The approximate time for this work would be about six months;
3) The first draft would then be submitted to the TSC which would carefully review the draft and make the necessary alterations within a two-month time period. After making all necessary changes, the draft should be edited and then submitted as the second draft to the TC;
4) The TC should review the second draft and make any necessary remarks, comments or alterations. It may request the addition or subtraction of items and return it to the TSC to make the requested

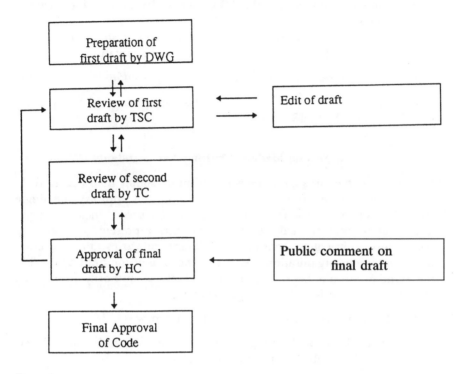

Figure 1

changes and prepare the final draft. The time needed for this would be about two months; and

5) The TC should review and approve the final draft and submit it to the HC for final approval. At this stage, the HC may approve or reject the code, stating the reasons for its action. This action should be decided within one month's time.

Options for action

Four options could arise. They are as follows:

1) In case of rejection, the final draft should return to the TSC through the TC to fulfil the requirements of the HC and the process mentioned in steps c to e should be repeated again;
2) If the HC approves the final draft, it must be made public for a period of three months for the engineers, consultants, contractors, academicians and relevant individuals to comment on the code. The

purpose of this step is to get the public awareness and concession of the new code;

3) If comments are received, the TC should review and decide on these comments; and

4) If no comments are received, then the code is submitted to the responsible authority for formal approval and adaptation.

Figure 1 summarises the drafting process of a new code.

The total period of time required for the completion of this process would be about 15 to 18 months.

The Second Method: Drafting New Standards

Drafting new standards could be achieved more simply than codes. Technical committees are usually formed to review and approve one single standard prepared by the DWG. Such a committee should include experts in the field of that particular standard and must represent governmental institutions, universities, consultants, relevant industries and interested non-government organisations. After the approval of the draft by the TC, the standard would be submitted to the official authority for official approval and then issued by the government.

Figure 2 summarises the drafting process for a new standard.

The time required for drafting, reviewing, approving and issuing a new standard would be about three to five months.

The Second Method: Drafting New Specifications

The process of issuing new technical specifications is very similar to the issuing process for a new code. There must be an official authority to issue the specifications. It could be the same authority that will issue new codes. Similarly, a Higher Committee, Technical Committee and several Sub-Committees, as well as several Draft Working Groups, would be needed for the process of drafting specifications.

Figure 3 shows the suggested process, which differs from that for drafting a new code in the following ways:

- Each DWG would deal with one or more chapters of a relevant subject, while in drafting codes one DWG would deal with the whole code. This is because the technical specifications, usually deal with various subjects of different disciplines;
- Each TSC would review the drafts from several DWG instead of reviewing all the content of the technical specification, as would be the case in drafting codes; and

324

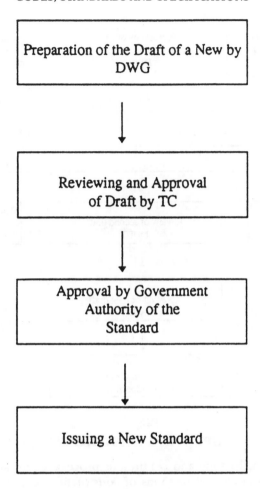

```
┌─────────────────────────────────┐
│  Preparation of the Draft of a New by │
│              DWG                 │
└─────────────────────────────────┘
                │
                ▼
┌─────────────────────────────────┐
│      Reviewing and Approval      │
│         of Draft by TC           │
└─────────────────────────────────┘
                │
                ▼
┌─────────────────────────────────┐
│      Approval by Government      │
│          Authority of the        │
│             Standard             │
└─────────────────────────────────┘
                │
                ▼
┌─────────────────────────────────┐
│      Issuing a New Standard      │
└─────────────────────────────────┘
```

Figure 2

- The TC would review, approve and submit the final draft of the specifications to the HC. It also would receive and edit the comments from who are not members of any of the committees. This is different from the process in drafting codes because of the variety of the technical subjects contained in the technical specifications.

Furthermore, because the codes would deal with rules and regulations, their approval would be similar to that for government laws and regulations. This is not applicable in the case of technical specifications. Some specifications might be relaxed, or even disregarded, if this were to be specified in the job contract.

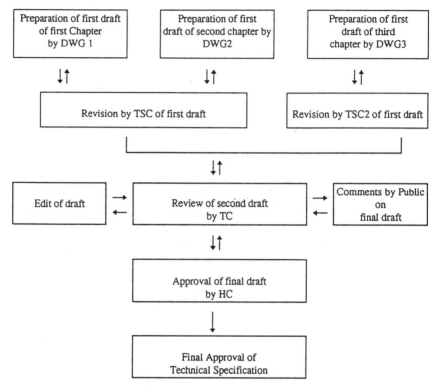

Figure 3

UPDATING EXISTING CSS

Issuing CSS is a dynamic and continuous process. There are always new techniques, materials and methods of construction. CSS are not permanent documents; once drafted, they cannot be used forever without taking new developments into consideration.

Therefore, CSS should always be revised and updated. The introduction of new techniques and cancellation of previous methods of testing and construction is part of the overall development process of the construction industry. The codes are usually reviewed and updated every five years, while the technical specifications may be updated every ten years. Because standards deal with one specific material or product, they are reviewed and updated more often, i.e. whenever necessity dictates.

The request for change is usually initiated, in the case of standards, by manufacturers, research institutes or consumers. Codes are usually updated upon the request of consultants and due to technological developments, while specifications are usually reviewed and updated as a result of accumulated comments and suggestions by the practising engineers.

It is recommended that the updating process should follow the same procedure in the drafting process. Any approved revisions, omissions or additions should be issued in the form of addendum for codes and specifications, and in the form of a new version of the original standards.

STRATEGIES FOR IMPLEMENTING CSS

Shelter is one of the basic needs for people, and securing proper infra-structure is a basic necessity for development. The construction of both shelter and infrastructure requires large investments. Natural law implies that people should obtain proper products and services for their money.

Therefore, it is natural to set up laws and regulations to protect the consumer and the producer, and to control the industry in order to protect public health and to preserve natural resources. Building control, for example, provides safety and economic use of local materials.

National authorities are usually responsible for making the laws and regulations, but their implementation can be delegated to other qualified local agencies. For the purpose of building control, for example, CSS are the fundamental laws and regulations, and their implementation can be carried out by agencies which acquire certain qualifications such as the following:

- They should have a cohesive team of experts in building regulations;
- They should be consistent in the level of enforcement and quality of judgement;
- They should have the ability to respond and act immediately on critical issues; and
- They should have easy access to accredited laboratories for testing of materials.

However, while codes and standards are usually implemented by a variety of agencies using varied procedures, technical specifications are implemented through the contract document and within the construction process itself. In the following paragraphs, the implementation of CSS will be dealt with by category.

A final note is that enforcing codes during the design stage alone does not ensure good buildings. It should be followed by proper control and supervision on site as well.

Implementation of Codes

Building regulations specify where and how building control is practised. For example, the National Building Law of Jordan (Ministry of Public Works and Housing, 1993), states that:

'All Ministries, Government Offices and Corporations, Municipalities and Local Councils, and Public Stock Companies are required to observe the codes in construction [projects] undertaken by them.'

In another paragraph, it also states that:

'All Consulting Companies and Offices, as well as Construction Contractors are required to observe the codes in the work they design, supervise or construct.'

These are the obligations by law. The questions are, 'How will they be enforced', and 'Who will actually carry out the control?' One or more of the following agencies could assume responsibility for control:

- Ministries and government departments, such as the Ministry of Public Works;
- Local authorities, such as municipalities;
- Specialised private agencies, such as engineering consultant offices; and
- Non-governmental organisations (NGOs), such as engineering associations and research institutes.

As far as Palestine is concerned, it is recommended that the relevant ministries and government offices should, at the beginning, assume responsibility for building control. At a later stage, when local authorities are formed and acquire the required technical staff and expertise, this responsibility could be transferred to local municipalities.

However, the ultimate goal should aim to establish private engineering offices which are able to check designs, drawings and contract documents and which could issue a certificate or a licence of compliance stating that these documents are 'deemed-to-satisfy' the building regulations. However, in no case, should this exempt the design and/or site engineer from his or her responsibility to comply with building regulations to ensure safety, serviceability and durability of the structure.

Nevertheless, building controls cannot be imposed immediately on every single structure to be built. There must be some exceptions, such as small buildings of less than 150 square meters.

The overall scenario for the implementation of codes would be as follows:

- Architectural, structural and electro-mechanical designs should be performed according to specified codes and specifications;
- A set of engineering drawings should be produced according to the designs which have been executed;
- A contract document with technical specifications should be prepared;
- All the above-mentioned designs, drawings and documents should be submitted to local authorities for a check on their compliance with the land-use and building regulations. If approved, a certificate of

compliance stating that they are 'deemed-to-satisfy' the building regulations would be issued;

- A team of supervisors, or the chief engineer (site engineer, superintendent, surveyor, etc.), should be assigned to control the work during construction;
- A qualified contractor should be chosen to carry out the construction work according to the approved contract documents and under the supervision of the chief engineer; and
- Upon completion of the contract, a committee of qualified engineers should issue a certificate of compliance and completion of the work.

Implementation of Standards

Standards are issued and implemented by separate laws and regulations. In Jordan, the Directorate of Standards is the office responsible for implementation. They carry out testing in their laboratories whenever possible.

Otherwise, they make use of the laboratories at the RSS. A similar arrangement is possible for the Palestinian authorities. At this stage, existing laboratories at the universities can be employed for this purpose. Private laboratories can also be accredited to act as the technical arm of government authorities for testing materials.

It is proposed that any building material, whether locally produced or imported, should conform to the national standards. This can be accomplished by the following procedures:

For local materials:

1) Samples, randomly chosen in time and space, must be collected and tested according to standards;
2) Samples which do not conform to standards must be rejected, and a note must be sent to the producer informing him of the results and requesting him to improve his products; and
3) In the case of repeated failure to comply with the standards, the authorities must take measures provided in the law to enforce an end to the production of such products.

For imported materials:

1) Random samples from the materials to be imported must be checked and tested for compliance with standards; and
2) If test samples fail to comply with the standards, the materials must be rejected and should not be imported.

The above are preventive measures; actual control is carried out on site, according to specifications and whenever it is deemed necessary. Quality control of materials and products must be continuously applied before, and during, the building work.

Implementation of Specifications

The technical specifications form an important part of the contract documents. They are implemented through the contract and during the construction by the site engineer. The technical specifications are the reference and last resort for any dispute or judgement on technical issues encountered during the construction phase of any contract. The construction engineer and the supervising engineer must be well informed of the content and application of the technical specifications.

POLICIES AND RECOMMENDATIONS

Priorities for CSS Requirements

Building regulations in the Palestinian Territories have not been upgraded or revised since 1966. To fill this gap, a large amount of CSS documentation is needed, and painstaking work must be carried out in a short period of time. Therefore, priorities must be established to save time and effort. Immediate CSS requirements include the following:

Codes

The following, in order of priority, are required:

A. Structural safety and stability:

1) Plain and reinforced concrete;
2) Steel structures;
3) Loads and forces; and
4) Site investigation.

B. Public health and safety:

1) Public safety in construction sites;
2) Drainage and sewerage;
3) Electric wiring and installations;
4) Fire protection; and
5) Earthing.

C. Conservation of resources:

1) Water supply;
2) Thermal insulation; and
3) Solar water heaters.

D. Safety against natural hazards:

1) Seismic design of structures; and
2) Lightening protection.

E. Economy and efficiency:

1) Foundations and retaining walls;
2) Formworks and scaffolding; and
3) Lifts.

F. Protection of the environment:

1) Refuse disposal;
2) Natural ventilation;
3) Natural lighting; and
4) Acoustics.

G. Convenience:

1) Space requirements;
2) Central heating;
3) Building requirements for disabled; and
4) Mechanical ventilation and air conditioning.

H. Amenity:

1) Urban aesthetics; and
2) Interior illumination.

I. Others:

1) Prestressed concrete;
2) Precast concrete;
3) Masonry and walling; and
4) Fire alarm systems.

Standards

The following, in the order of priority, are required:

A. Cementitious materials:

1) Cement:
   portland cement; portland pozzolana cement; sulphate-resistance port-land cement; and white portland cement; and
2) Concrete:
   methods of sampling fresh concrete; ready mix concrete; concrete admixtures; concrete blocks; and kerbstones.

B. Aggregates and natural stones:

1) Aggregates:
   aggregates for concrete; light weight aggregates for structural con-crete; and light weight aggregates for thermal insulation; and
2) Natural building stones (limestone).

C. Metals:

1) Steel:
   steel bars; structural steel; and wires;
2) Aluminium:
   doors, windows and curtain walls; and aluminium profiles; and
3) Portable water tanks.

D. Building materials:

1) Tiles:
   cement tiles; ceramic tiles; terrazzo tiles; and roof tiles;
2) Bricks:
   clay bricks; burnt clay bricks; and sand lime bricks;
3) Pipes:
   asbestos-cement pipes; precast concrete pipes; low and high density polyethylene pipes; p.v.c. pipes; steel pipes; thermoplastic pipes; and fittings; and
4) Others:
   paints and varnishes; wood; gypsum; marble; and insulating materials.

E. Asphaltic materials:

1) Hot asphaltic mixes for pavements; and
2) Asphalt used in roofing.

F. Electrical installations:

1) Electrical cables; and
2) Electrical fittings.

The above mentioned list is of broad subjects. Under each heading, there may be more than one standard specification required.

Specifications

Technical specifications for buildings, highways and bridge construction are required immediately. The specifications for buildings should cover the following:

- Civil and architectural works;
- Mechanical installation and services; and
- Electrical installation and services.

The specifications for highways and bridges should cover the following:

- Earthworks;
- Pavement, base and subbase construction;
- Culverts, bridges and superstructures;
- Landscaping; and
- Lighting, traffic signals and electrical installations.

POLICY RECOMMENDATIONS

The construction of the 300,000 homes and substantial infrastructure required for small and large towns in Palestine cannot be achieved without the development and implementation of CSS. Therefore, it is recommended that the following actions be carried out immediately.

- The PNA must form a National Building Council to be responsible for initiating immediately needed CSS.
- Available Jordanian CSS should be adopted for immediate use until national CSS are developed.
- Building control should be assigned to the Ministry of Housing or to the Ministry of Public Works initially. After the establishment of municipal authorities, this assignment could be transferred easily to them.
- Extensive training programmes should be initiated on CSS develop-

ment and implementation, as well as programmes to test building materials. Quality control and methods of practical design, construction and building control should also be taught.

BIBLIOGRAPHY

Daghestani, Fakhruddin et al, 1983, **Building Codes and Specifications for the Arab World**, The Macmillan Press Ltd., London.

Ministry of Industry and Trade, 1995, **Jordanian Standards Catalogue**, Jordanian Directorate of Standards, Amman.

Ministry of Public Works and Housing, 1985, *Civil and Architectural Works, Mechanical Services for Buildings, Electrical Services for Buildings*, **General Technical Specifications for Buildings**, 3 vols., Ministry of Public Works and Housing, Amman.

Ministry of Public Works and Housing, 1991, **Specifications for Highway and Bridge Construction**, Ministry of Public Works and Housing, Amman.

Ministry of Public Works and Housing, 1993, **National Building Law of Jordan**, Ministry of Public Works and Housing, Amman.

Second Committee, 1989, **Agreement of Co-operation Between Member States of the Arab Co-operative Council in the Field of Housing and Reconstruction**, Second Committee Report on Unification of Standards and Codes for Buildings, Cairo [in Arabic].

PLANNING FOR ACCESSIBILITY FOR THE DISABLED IN PALESTINE

Riadh R. Tappuni

ABSTRACT

The two major causes of disability in Palestine are endogamous marriage and civil unrest. The first is a common phenomena in all Arab countries and in all sectors of society, and results in all types of impairment. Disability due to civil unrest assumed a more prominent dimension with the outgrowth of the *Intifada* and the accompanying suppression, resulting in mainly physical disabilities among the younger age groups.

This paper starts with a general discussion about the extent of disability in the West Bank and Gaza, with a general overview of the types of disabilities and their frequencies. Data on disability in Bureij and Al-Shati' camps in Gaza and Palestinian villages in the Jenin area are used to give a definition of the extent of disability among Palestinians.

A truly barrier-free environment should provide accessibility at all components of the environment, including building interiors, entry into buildings and external spaces. Access requirements vary according to the type of disability. People on wheelchairs can only move over level pavements with sufficient circulation space. They should be able to reach lift buttons, door knobs and electrical switches.

The blind or partially sighted need routes that are clear of obstructions and acoustic information to supplement visually displayed information, as well as tactile pavements on even surfaces. A segregation of vehicular and pedestrian traffic is essential for the hearing impaired, together with clearly visible and well lit signs. The disabled have a right to access all public areas, and provision should be made for transportation aids. Some urban elements must be especially designed.

The application of standards in planning and design can only help to make newly designed environments accessible. A more important issue is the rehabilitation of existing buildings to overcome barriers. This will require concerted efforts involving non-governmental and local organisations, together with the promotion of public awareness.

This paper reviews cases from international experience on how to plan for accessibility on an urban scale. At the regional level, reference is made to the current Lebanese experiment in providing a barrier-free central district for Beirut, and later for the whole country.

On a policy level, the provision of a barrier-free environment should be supported through legislation. A national strategy in this field would be incomplete without the formulation of regulations that enforce the application of essential parts of the accessibility standards.

The paper concludes by suggesting a strategy on how to handle these issues in the case of Palestine. Finally, recommendations are made concerning the necessary requirements for the built environment.

INTRODUCTION

The conventional approach to the design of buildings is usually structured around the needs and capabilities of the adult person. Design standards like height of steps, position of electrical and control switches and furniture dimensions are developed to cater for the 5th, 50th or 95th percentile data, rather than the majority of the population whose anthropometric data do not fall into these percentiles.

The capabilities of people also vary to a great extent. For example, a considerable proportion of the population does not have perfect vision or hearing, nor can they speak distinctly. The deviations in the capabilities of people from the assumed average person are numerous and wide. Kidd and Clark (1982) called for the consideration of abnormality as the prevailing human condition.

Planning and design carried out according to commonly adopted standards often produces handicapping environments. The variety of walking aids a person may use gives an idea of the scope of the issue in question. These can vary from canes, crutches, walkers, and wheelchairs to guide animals. Designing for the disabled can result in accessible environments for the majority of people.

One important objective of accessible design is the integration of the disabled into the community and enabling them to lead a fulfilling life. To achieve this, a disabled person should have the benefit of freedom of movement between home, work, recreation and services, and should have access to all facilities available to his fellow citizens. Hence the call for the design of a barrier-free environment.

Every person is the product of three overlapping and inseparable spheres. A physical disability in a person will most likely have consequences for his or her life mentally and socially.

In general terms, the disabled can be divided into two categories: the

Table 1 Demography Of Bureij And Al-Shati' Camps.

	Bureij	Al-Shati'
Total Households	2,035	3,465
Households with at least one disabled member (%)	682	861
Households with at least one disabled member	26	25
Total number of disabled	820	1,185
Estimated population	18,000	27,720
Rate of disability(%)	4.5	4.3

Source: The Gaza National Committee for Rehabilitation (GNCR); Diakonia (1993).

ambulatory disabled and wheelchair users. Planning for each of these categories constitutes the basis of barrier-free design. Disability is generally understood as a permanent condition, yet most people suffer from disability at some point in their lives. Everyone is exposed to certain causes of disability, such as accidents, temporary illness and old age. Design for wheelchair users and persons with walking aids, the visually impaired and the hearing impaired usually benefits other categories such as the mentally disabled.

DISABILITY IN PALESTINE

The two major causes of disability among Palestinians are endogamous marriage and civil unrest. The first is a common phenomena in all Arab countries and in all sectors of society, and results in all types of impairment. Disability due to civil unrest assumed a more prominent dimension with the onset of the *Intifada* and the accompanying suppression, resulting in mainly physical disabilities among younger age groups.

The United Nations Relief and Works Agency for Palestine Refugees in the Near East (UNRWA) (December, 1990) reported that during a period of less than three years (from December, 1987 to October, 1990), live rounds, beatings, plastic coated metal bullets, rubber bullets, tear gas and other forms of attack resulted in 58,000 casualties. Thirty per cent of the victims were children under 15. As a consequence, 10 per cent of the victims suffered permanent disability. The pre-*Intifada* figure for disability in the West Bank and Gaza was 60,000.

A survey of the Bureij camp, conducted between 1991 and 1993, revealed that the rate of disability is 4.5 per cent in a population of 18,000. This is distributed among 2,254 households. The average size of families with disabled individuals is 9.95 persons. In Al-Shati' camp, the rate of disability was found to be 4.3 per cent in a population of 27,720 (see Table 1).

The male section of the disabled population is higher than the female section, forming 58 per cent of the total disabled population in Bureij and 55 per cent in Al-Shati'. The higher percentages of males can be

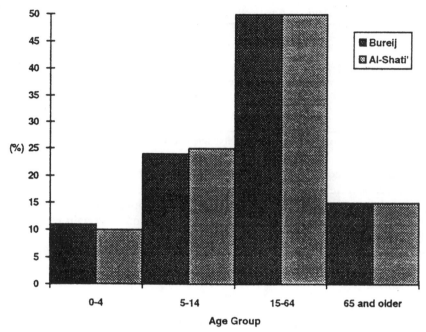

Figure 1 Disabled By Age Group in Bureij And Al-Shati' Camps.
Source: The Gaza National Committee for Rehabilitation (GNCR) and Diakonia, 1993.

attributed to the fact that disabled females in this society are sheltered and not exposed and therefore are more difficult to detect than disabled males. Figure 1 indicates that about 50 per cent of the disabled population are in the active age group of 15 to 64 years.

It is clear from Figure 2 that the most prevalent disability among Palestinians in Bureij and Al-Shati' camps is that of movement, followed by visual impairment. It is worth noting here that disabilities like speech, learning difficulties and strange behaviour can be inter-related because a mentally retarded person can suffer from all of these.

Among young people, the most significant cause of disability is the ruthless suppression of the *Intifada*. In a study of those reported wounded or injured up to September 1988, UNRWA found that beating was the major cause. As a result of the suppression, various forms of disability increased significantly. In the category of physical disabilities, the cases of artificial limbs increased 76 per cent (See Dajani, 1992).

A survey of 22 Palestinian villages in the Jenin District, conducted in the end of 1992 and published by the Northern Regional Committee for Rehabilitation (1994), reported 893 persons with disabilities living in 864 households. The disabled constituted 1.9 per cent of the surveyed population.

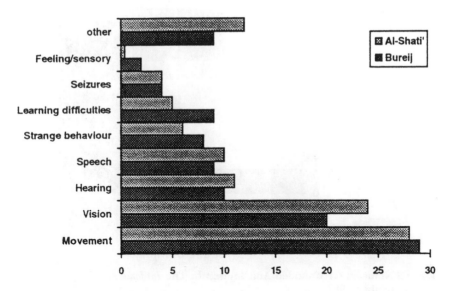

Figure 2 Disabilities By Type in Bureij And Al-Shati' Camps.
Source: The Gaza National Committee for Rehabilitation (GNCR) and Diakonia, 1993.

Twelve per cent of the surveyed households had one or more disabled persons. The highest percentage of disabled persons in any given community was found to be 3.9 per cent. As in Bureij and Al-Shati' camps, a higher percentage of male disabled persons was reported. Males constituted 60 per cent of the disabled population. As for age groups, it was found that 35 per cent of the disabled are between 15 and 49 years old (see Figure 5).

The survey also confirmed the findings of the Bureij and Al-Shati' study that the highest percentage of disability type was related to movement. This amounted to 27 per cent of the total, followed by multiple disabilities at 20 per cent and sight at 17 per cent (see Figure 6).

Studies carried out by the Economics Department of the Palestine Liberation Organisation (1984–1985) on Palestinians in Al-Yarmouk camp in Syria concluded that young people aged between 15 and 19 constituted the highest percentage among the disabled. This can be explained by the fact that this group is the most visible in comparison to other age groups, where there is a general tendency to conceal disability (see Figure 7).

The same study categorised the disabled into the blind, the deaf and dumb, those with loss of upper limb, those with loss of upper limbs, those with loss of lower limb, those with loss of lower limbs, the paralysed and the mentally handicapped. Paralysis accounted for the highest percentage of the disabilities in this community, followed by mental

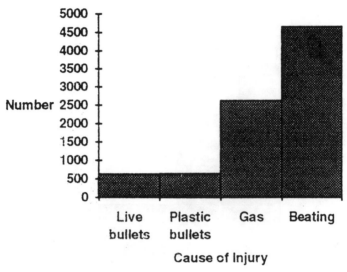

Figure 3 Numbers Of Wounded And Injured In The *Intifada**.
*To September, 1988.

handicap. The blind and the deaf and dumb accounted for slightly less than 10 per cent each.

Estimates made by Giacaman et al, (1994) indicate that about 40 per cent of *Intifada*-related injuries in the inland region during 1988–89 resulted in permanent disability. Ninety-two per cent of the injured were male adolescents and young adults; 69 per cent were between 15 and 24 years of age.

Hearing and speech disabilities were estimated to account for 25 per cent of the total disabilities. Since 1987, up to 1,000 young Palestinians per year have been permanently or semi-permanently rendered in need of rehabilitation services. The same author makes a conservative estimate, based on a 2 to 3 per cent rate of disability in society at large, placing 30,000 to 37,000 persons in the West Bank and 16,000 to 25,000 persons in Gaza in need of rehabilitation services, probably for life.

As no comprehensive statistics covering the whole area of the West Bank and Gaza are available, some assumptions are usually made. Diakonia (1995) assumes that 3 per cent of the population are disabled, with 30 to 35 per cent of these having physical disability. Assuming a population of two million, an estimated 60,000 individuals are disabled; of these, 20,000 have physical disability.

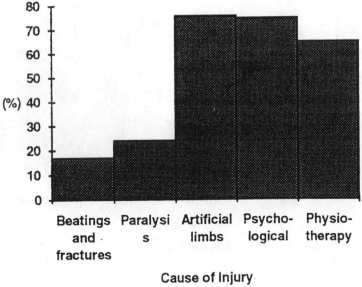

Figure 4 Increases in Disability Cases in the *Intifada.*

OPTIONS: INTERNATIONAL EXAMPLES OF ACCESSIBILITY

The United States of America

The Americans with Disabilities Act (ADA) became a law in 1990. It 'prohibits discrimination on the basis of disability in employment, state and local government services, transportation provided by public and private entities, places of public accommodation and commercial facilities, and telephone services available to the public.' The definition adopted by the ADA is so broad that it insures that practically all components of the private sector are covered by the law.

Relevant ADA regulations contain 'requirements and standards governing the new construction and alteration of both commercial facilities and places of public accommodation.' As for existing buildings, the regulations require the removal of barriers from places of public accommodation, when that is 'readily achievable.' According to the ADA, it is the duty of public accommodation to eliminate such barriers.

The Netherlands

North European countries pioneered efforts in the field of disability, and there are many lessons to be learnt from their experience. With the support of the Department of Transport and Public Works of the Nether-

341

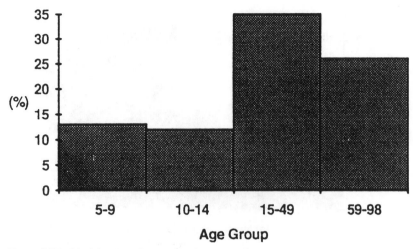

Figure 5 Disabled by Age Group in the Jenin District*.
*For 22 villages.

lands, the city of Gouda produced a report in 1982 entitled 'Route Plan for People with a Handicap.'

One aim of the report was to demonstrate methods of eliminating barriers in open circulation areas and ways of increasing safe movement to other local councils in the Netherlands. Implementation of the plan was to be carried out over three stages covering the city centre and the areas outside it.

As a start, an identification was made of the most frequently used routes in the city. These were later adapted to meet the immediate needs of the disabled, with a view to the provision of full accessibility for all in later stages. These measures were then evaluated by monitoring movements of the disabled and the reaction of the general public towards the alterations. The scheme divided the disabled into four target groups and identified the necessary provisions for each (see Table 2).

Denmark

Tappuni (1992) cited another demonstration project that was undertaken in Fredericia, Denmark, which has a population of 46,000. It was selected as a result of a national competition among 16 cities. Five main groups were set up, each including a representative of the target group. Co-ordination of their work was carried out by a steering committee.

The formation of the groups reflected the various aspects of accessibility in the urban environment. Two important features were included in the

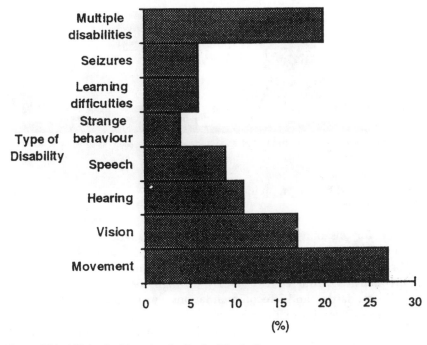

Figure 6 Disabilities by Type in the Jenin District*.
*For 22 villages.

project: an obstacle-free pedestrian route and a special service bus route for general use by everyone, including the disabled, the elderly, children and mothers with prams. The bus route was chosen to serve transport terminals, public service buildings, parks, hospitals and special buildings for the elderly and the handicapped as well as to provide connections with the obstacle-free pedestrian route.

Lebanon

One of the most important experiments in post-war reconstruction in the Arab region is presently underway in Lebanon. Because particular importance is attached to the reconstruction of the capital, Beirut, a special company has been set up for this purpose. Tappuni (1994) reported on a joint effort by ESCWA and the Lebanese Company for the Development and Reconstruction of Beirut Central District (SOLIDERE).

After meetings with representatives of non-governmental organisations concerned with disability, officials of the Ministry of Social Affairs and some members of the National Council for Disability, a national

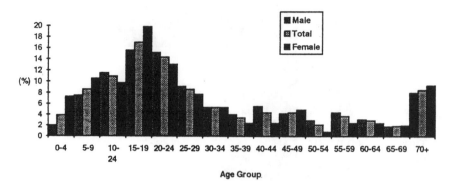

Figure 7 Disabled by Age group in Al-Yarmouk Camp.
*For 22 Villages.

strategy for disability was formulated. This called for a dual track approach.

The first track aimed to influence the development and reconstruction of the Beirut Central District (BCD) through the application of established standards and recommendations with appropriate review procedures. The aim of the second track was to provide accessibility at the national level through the development and legal enforcement of standards and regulations.

It was envisaged that implementation of the first track would make the BCD a good demonstration case on the national and regional levels. Reconstruction of the BCD involves the renovation of old, but retained buildings and the construction of new ones. A manual is being prepared by SOLIDERE and ESCWA for publication in 1995, aiming to guide all those involved in the reconstruction process on how to provide for a barrier-free environment.

The manual divides the subject into four parts: urban design considerations, architectural design considerations, building types, and emergency and fire safety. 'Implementation checklists' are also devised in order to make systematic the identification of handicapping elements and to suggest solutions (see sample, Table 3).

The manual is also supported by a troubleshooting reference for the major disabled categories. Problems are identified and measures suggested, with cross-references to the relevant chapters (see Table 4).

Building on the experience to be gained from applying the manual, legislation should be established to guarantee accessibility for the disabled in Lebanon in general.

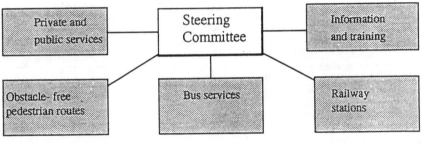

Figure 8

RECOMMENDATIONS

A National Strategy for Palestine

The recent drive towards reconstruction and institution building in Palestine represents a window of opportunity which should be utilised to institutionalise the provision of a barrier-free environment. Universal accessibility can be assured if it is dealt with throughout all components of the urban environment, including parking and vehicular approaches, pedestrian paths, approaches to building entrances, entrances to buildings and inside buildings. All new construction needs to adhere to accessibility standards: it will be more economical to make them barrier-free during construction than to take corrective measures afterwards.

A practical approach would be to adopt accessibility standards which have been devised for application in other parts of the region, such as in the Lebanese case described above. Legislation in general, and building regulations in particular, should have clear, in-built sections enforcing the implementation of a barrier-free environment in all new construction. There should also be provisions like minimum numbers of accessible rooms in hotels and accessible apartments in residential blocks.

Efforts should be made to influence new construction, but also to modify the great mass of existing ones.

The promotion of public awareness is important to the issue of accessibility. This, together with the vital role which local authorities and non-governmental organisations can play, should not be overlooked, especially in mobilising community action.

Financing of alterations can be supported by special grants or easy-term loans.

Requirements for the Built Environment

It is important to recognise the right of a disabled person to use and enjoy all facilities provided for the general public.

345

Table 2 Provisions for Target Groups, Gouda, The Netherlands.

Provision	Blind	Partially-sighted	Wheel-chair users	People with limited walking ability
Creation of obstacle-free route	√	√	√	√
Creation of resting places			√	
Creation of guiding lines	√	√		
Marking obstacles and crossing points	√	√		
Creation of adapted parking places		√	√	
Creation of dropped kerbs and adapted footless at crossing points		√	√	
Creation of dropped kerbs on both footless at traffic islands		√	√	
Shortening the length of crossing points on roadways	√	√	√	√
Creation of easier access to pushbutton units of traffic lights		√		
Provision of sound signal (bleeper) to indicate red/green at traffic lights	√	√		
Extension of green phase at traffic lights	√	√	√	√
Adaptation of ramps (shallower gradient)		√	√	
Adaptation of shape of handrails on bridges	√	√		√

The following points can be considered as the most important for consideration in the built environment (Tappuni, 1994):

Wheelchair users

- Even roads and surfaces with no change of level;
- Entrance to means of transport with no steps;
- The provision of sufficient space in circulation areas; and
- The positioning of equipment, switches, knobs, etc. within hand reach of a wheelchair user.

Visually impaired persons

- Pedestrian areas should be clear with no unexpected obstructions;
- Signs should be clearly displayed with sufficient lighting and at an appropriate height;

Table 3 Sample of Implementation Checklist: Signs and Signals.

Yes	No	Questions	Possible Solutions
		Are accessibility spaces identified by the international symbol of accessibility?	Mark accessible spaces with the international sign of accessibility.
		Are there directional signs indicating the location of accessible facilities?	Provide directional signs.
		Are maps, information panels and wall-mounted signs placed at a height between 0.90m–1.80m?	Adjust the height of information signs mounted too high or too low.
		Are signs clear, simple and easy to read?	Colour engraved texts. Replace signs.
		Is the colour of signs clearly distinguishable?	Use contrasting colours.
		Is the surface of the sign processed so as to prevent glare?	Provide non-gloss surface.
		Is a relief text or a text in Braille available next to information signs?	Add a text in relief or in Braille.
		Is the lettering size proportional to the reading distance?	Change the lettering size.

- Visual information like signs and texts should be supported by acoustic information; and
- Surfaces should be even with tactile direction signs.

Hearing impairments

- Segregation of vehicular from pedestrian traffic;
- Use of acoustic and visible signs;
- The installation of tele-loop amplifier systems in public gathering places; and
- Use of appropriate lighting.

The mentally retarded

- Evenly laid pavements (roads, paths, etc.); and
- Guiding directional instructions that are easily perceptible with short texts, simple symbols, etc.

Table 4 Sample of Troubleshooting Reference Tables: Wheelchair Users.

Problem	Measure	Reference Chapter
Tackling differences in levels between road and pavement	Installation of curb ramps	Curb ramps
Bridging great differences in height, usually tackled by dividing stairs	Provide ramps, wide elevator cabs or lifts	Ramps, Elevators, Lifts
Manoeuvring in tight spaces	Provide wide routes and spaces	Street furniture, pathways, parking, vestibules, corridors, rest rooms
Passing through narrow door openings and tackling high thresholds	Provide sufficiently wide door openings with no, or low-levelled, thresholds	Doors
Reaching high controls and objects	Provide low controls	Heights of selected items
Manoeuvring in rest rooms	Installation of grab bars, bath tub and shower seats	Rest rooms

BIBLIOGRAPHY

Beckman, M., 1976, **Building for Everyone: the Disabled and the Built Environment in Sweden,** Paper contributed to the United Nations Conference on Human Settlements, Ministry of Housing and Physical Planning, Stockholm.

Dajani, N., 1992, *Disabled persons in the West Bank and Gaza Strip,* in **Proceedings of the Conference on the Capabilities and Needs of Disabled Persons in the ESCWA Region,** Economic and Social Commission for Western Asia, Amman.

Department of Transport and Public Works in the Hague and the City of Gouda, May 1986, **Demonstration Project Gouda, The Netherlands: Safe Traffic Provisions for People with a Mobility Handicap.**

Diakonia, 1995, **Verbal Communication, Jerusalem.**

The Eastern Paralysed Veteran Association, 1994, **The Americans With Disabilities Act: Removing Barriers in Places of Public Accommodation.**

Gaza National Committee for Rehabilitation (GNCR) and Diakonia, 1993, **Disability and Rehabilitation Needs in the Gaza Strip: A Survey Report on Bureij and Al-Shati' Refugee Camps, Gaza City.**

Giacaman, Rita et al, March 1994, **The State of Palestine,** Centre for Engineering and Planning, Ramallah, Palestine.

Giacaman, Rita, 1994, **Health Conditions and Services in the West Bank and Gaza Strip,** September, UNCTAD/ECDC/SEU/3.

Kidd, B.J. and R. Clark, 1982, **Outdoor Access for All: a Guide to Designing Accessible Outdoor Recreation Facilities,** Department of Youth, Sport and Recreation, Melbourne.

The Northern Regional Committee for Rehabilitation, August 1994, **A Study of 22 Palestinian Villages in the Jenin District with Special Reference to the Needs of Persons with Disabilities.**

Palestine Liberation Organisation, 1984–1985, **Palestinian Statistical Abstract**, Economics Department, Central Bureau of Statistics, Damascus.

The Lebanese Company for the Development and Reconstruction of Beirut Central District (SOLIDERE) and the Economic and Social Commission for Western Asia (ESCWA), 1995, **Accessibility for the Disabled, a Design Manual for a Barrier Free Environment**, forthcoming (will be published in Beirut).

Tappuni, R., 1992, *Access for the Disabled in the Urban Environment*, in **Proceedings of the Conference on the Capabilities and Needs of Disabled Persons in the ESCWA Region**, Economic and Social Commission for Western Asia (ESCWA), Amman.

Tappuni, R., January, 1994, **Accessibility for the Disabled in the Beirut Central District**, Report prepared for The Lebanese Company for the Development and Reconstruction of Beirut Central District (SOLIDERE) and the Economic and Social Commission for Western Asia (ESCWA), Amman.

United Nations Relief and Works Agency for Palestine Refugees in the Near East (UNRWA), 5–7 December, 1990, **Report submitted to the Eighth Inter-Agency Meeting on the United Nations Decade of Disabled Persons**, Vienna.

United States Department of Agriculture (Forest Department), October 1992, **Design Guide for Universal Access to Outdoor Recreation**, Interim Draft, Washington D.C.

CODES, STANDARDS AND REGULATIONS IN PALESTINE

Mohammed M. Ziara, Rifat N. Rustom, Majed M. El-Bayya and Ahmed Amer

ABSTRACT

This paper identifies the existing codes of practice, standards and regulations (CSR) in Palestine and their inter-relationships. CSR related to rural and urban construction are emphasised. Current practices in the construction industry are also reviewed, particularly for building materials, including structural concrete.

Two case studies are discussed in detail. The first relates to regulations concerning low-rise building permits given by municipalities; the second concerns high-rise building permits supervised by the Ministry of Housing. Options and recommendations for a methodology are examined, as is criteria to adopt the CSR of the neighbouring countries. Finally, the modification or formulation of local CSR for Palestine is considered.

INTRODUCTION

CSR should be considered in order to achieve the proper design and construction of buildings. Current practice in Palestine with respect to the building industry is very heavily influenced by the education and practical experience of both engineers and workers involved in each project. In tender documents, reference is usually made to international CSR such as ACI (American Concrete Institute) and BS (British Standards) codes of practice, AASHTO (American Association of State Highways and Transportation Officials), ASTM (American Standard Testing Materials), IEEE (Institute of Electrical and Electronics Engineers) and SII (Standards Institute of Israel) standards. Regulations which are locally developed are old and usually unsuitable.

Because Palestine is being developed rapidly, CSR need to be adopted or established. New types of buildings, including multi-storey buildings, and construction techniques are becoming the main characteristics of current practice. Generally, there are no unique CSR which have been established or approved for use in Palestine. However, the Ministry of Housing in the Palestinian National Authority (PNA) has initiated a framework to prepare such requirements. Although, the process of preparation of CSR is supervised and co-ordinated by the Housing Ministry, members from all local institutions and international organisations involved in the building industry are the main contributors to the process. It is believed that issuing new CSR is both difficult and unnecessary. For this reason, some of the existing international CSR, especially those used in the region, are being assembled and studied for possible use in Palestine.

THE ISSUES: CODES, STANDARDS AND REGULATIONS

Codes of Practice

As the name implies, 'Codes' is the system of principles or rules which are meant to be used as part of legally adopted documents. As such, they differ in form and substance from documents that provide detailed specifications, recommended practice, complete design procedures or design aids. The code has no legal status unless it is adopted by government bodies having the power to regulate building design and construction.

Where the code has not been adopted, it may serve as a reference to good practice even though it has no legal status. The code provides means of establishing minimum norms for acceptance of design and construction. There are different international codes of practice that cover various fields of design and construction, e.g. structural concrete, steel structures, asphalt, water resources and distribution, etc.

Before 1967 and during the occupation, project implementation and procurement of works carried out mainly by the municipalities and a variety of United Nations agencies including the United Nations Relief and Works Agency (UNRWA), the United Nations Development Programme (UNDP) and the United Nations Children's Fund (UNICEF). municipalities in the West Bank adopted the 1954 Building Law of Jordan. In Gaza, the building laws of Egypt were implemented. The weak policy and the limited autonomy of local municipalities has caused serious problems in the utility of the building codes and most laws could not be implemented correctly.

At present, most buildings in Palestine are built using structural concrete due to the lack of any other abundant resource. Consequently, the attention of the Ministry of Housing is focused on this material. In

Palestine, different international codes are used in the design and construction of structural concrete. El-Karama Housing Project in Gaza is one of the major recent projects where ACI code has been used. The Project consists of thirteen ten-story buildings of 416 housing units.

BS code was used in the design and construction of El-Nuseirat Housing Project. It consists of four ten-story buildings of about 150 housing units. In small construction projects such as villas and small houses, codes of practice are rarely used, especially in rural areas. Moreover, these small projects are built without any supervision. At the same time, even where buildings are designed using available codes, the code often is not followed strictly and many important requirements are not considered regarding problems such as earthquakes, wind and soil exploration.

Standards

Standards are rules for measuring, or models to be followed, which provide quality assurance and comprehensive testing services during the planning, design, construction and maintenance stages. Standards and regulations also serve as a basis for government conducts in the construction industry. Standards of performance are intended for use in settling disputes between the owner, engineer, architect, contractor, material suppliers, and testing agencies. The standards for construction of buildings, roads and bridges in Palestine have been drawn extensively from the experience gained from Jordan, Egypt and other middle Eastern countries. This experience was acquainted through Palestinian engineers who worked in the aforementioned countries and also through Palestinian graduates who had their engineering degrees from the universities of these countries.

The BSI, ASTM, AASHTO, SII, and standards of regional Arab countries are commonly used in Palestine. However, there are several projects where standards are not used as contractors usually take the responsibility to carry out projects without consulting an engineer or abide by any quality control measures (e.g. construction materials testing).

The administration of standards in any country has to be an official organ for the preparation, publication and research that is necessary to develop specialised tests and to establish technical requirements to fulfil its specific needs. The Ministry of Housing is in the process of establishing and adopting standards pertinent to construction materials as an attempt to ensure quality control and better construction practices.

Regulations

Regulations deal with details of procedures issued by an executive authority of a government and having the force of law. A comprehensive

Table 1 New Regulations for Building Set-Backs.

Zone	Set back of building from base line (meters)			Maximum built-up area (%)
	Front	Sides	Back	
Houses, apartments (old city)	–	–	–	100
Houses, apartments (new city)	3	2	2	160
Beach	3	2	2	40
Industrial/ Commercial	varies	2	2	70

Source: Dahdouh and Hayek, 1975

presentation regarding the regulation of the construction of multi-storey buildings as well as low-rise buildings in Gaza are discussed in detail in the following case studies.

STRATEGIES: CASE STUDIES OF BUILDING REGULATIONS

Building regulations in the West Bank and Gaza differ in many aspects. The regulations in the West Bank are heavily influenced by Jordanian regulations; in Gaza, they are influenced by Egyptian regulations. The case studies presented here give an example of two types of regulations; namely, an old existing regulation related to low-rise buildings and a newly formulated regulation related to high-rise buildings. While the regulations for high-rise buildings are presented to show the process which was followed in developing these regulations, those of low-rise buildings are given for comparison purposes.

Case I: Low-Rise Building Regulations in Gaza

Building regulations in Gaza are divided into two categories. The first category is applied to buildings within the city limits, while the second category is applied to buildings outside these limits. In this case study, focus is placed on regulations within Gaza City.

Building Regulations Within City Limits

Because of the density of buildings within the city of Gaza, strict regulations are applied by the Planning Division at the municipality of Gaza. Since 1936, some of these regulations have been modified to cope with the increasing demand and construction of buildings.

For example, lands are allowed to be divided into lots of at least 500 square meters provided that the minimum length of the lot on the street side is 16 meters (see Zoning Law No. 28, 1936) (Dahdouh and Hayek, 1975). The built-up area is limited to 40 per cent in residential zones while in the industrial/commercial zones the build-up area is 70 per cent.

In all residential zones, the building lines should set back at least three meters (front and sides of building) and four meters (back of building) from the property lines.

For buildings along streets, at least 30 meters wide, garages or shops are permitted to be built in the front set back provided that the height of these constructions is not more than four meters. These regulations on the permitted build-up area and the set backs have been changed during the Israeli occupation. The new regulations for Gaza City are shown in Table 1.

The height of any building should not be more than twice the street width provided that the height of a house is not more than ten meters. Depending on the built-up area, parking spaces are to be provided. For a building with an area of at least 300 square meters, one parking space should be provided for each housing unit. Whenever a building is to be constructed within the city limits, the following procedure is necessary to obtain a building license:

a) The general layout of the lot with all set-backs and the percentage of built-up area is obtained from the municipality where fees are collected;
b) Detailed engineering drawings are prepared by qualified architects, civil and electrical engineers;
c) Drawings and design are checked, in general, by the Engineers Syndicate, where additional fees are collected;
d) After approval of the drawings as in part (c) above, the file is checked by the zoning department in the municipality to verify that the building regulations have been observed;
e) Once approval is obtained as in part (d), fees are paid to the municipality and the construction permit is issued;
f) Water and electricity are then provided by the municipality to the lot; and
g) The building licence will be issued once the building is constructed as shown in the approved drawings.

The fees which are collected by a municipality are usually calculated on the area and type of building. For example, the municipality of Gaza charges approximately 24 New Israeli Shekels (NIS) per square meter for residential buildings. A building permit usually takes two weeks to be issued, provided all necessary documents are available and accurate.

Building Regulations Outside City Limits

There are no restrictions on building heights in these areas. However, only one building is allowed in every 25,000 square meters of land. The building should have a maximum floor area of 180 square meters with a

Table 2 Building Fees.

Building Type	Fees per square meter (New Israeli Shekels)	
	North	South
Public buildings	1.1	0.7
Non-profit institutions	1.1	0.7
Workshop buildings	0	0
Stables	0.4	0.5
Houses above 100 square meters	18.1	16.5
Industrial buildings	1.1	0.7

maximum of two floors only. In these areas, village councils are to provide infrastructure (water, electricity and sewage) to the buildings whenever their budgets permit.

Buildings are to be licensed by the corresponding village council and two sets of license fees are collected. The first set is applied in the northern part of Gaza, including the areas of Jabalia/Nazala, Beit Lahia, Beit Hanoon and the industrial area in Airez (see the map at end). The second set is applied in the southern part, including the areas of Bani Suhila, Big Abassan, Small Abassan, Khazaa'h and Zuwaida (see the map). Table 2 presents the current fees for certain types of buildings.

The regulations currently used for low-rise buildings are adequate in general. However, there is a need to modify these regulations to reflect new forms of construction and land use criteria.

Case Study II: High-Rise Building Regulations

General Overview

After the withdrawal of Israeli forces from Gaza and the signing of the peace agreement, investment in the construction of multi-storey buildings was predominant. The Ministry of Housing launched a proposal (*High-Rise Buildings Regulation (HRBR)* (Official News Bulletin, 1995)) to formulate a regulation to control the process by which permits for high-rise buildings were to be granted by municipalities and village councils.

Scope

The existing master and structural plans imposed by the former Israeli occupation intentionally neglected the possibility that city limits could be extended horizontally and vertically. Those plans would only allow buildings up to five stories high in accordance with the zoning law.

In addition, the plans do not define any prioritised zones for high-rise buildings. This situation imposed pressure on the municipalities and village councils towards granting permits; especially, the by-laws of the

355

municipalities and village councils do not allow granting permits for buildings more than five stories high. Yet more than 70 high-rise buildings, with an average of ten stories, have been built in the past two years.

A steering committee consisting of representatives of the Ministry of Housing, the Ministry of Justice, Gaza and Rafah municipalities, the Engineers Syndicate, and other related ministries and institutions have been formed as an emergency measure to control the rapidly increasing and sporadic construction of high-rise buildings in Gaza. The steering committee formulated the *HRBR* draft. The draft was distributed to ministries, organisations, universities, the Engineers Syndicate and other organisations for review and comment; and was then initially approved by the Legal Department at the Ministry of Justice.

The regulation was approved in September 17, 1994 by the PNA and published in the *Official Newspaper* (Official News Bulletin, 1995). A special body, the '*High-Rise Buildings Committee*,' was formed with representatives from the Ministries of Housing, Local Government, Justice, Interior (Civil Defence Administration) and the Engineers Syndicate. The committee is responsible for reviewing and approving all documents, drawings, and materials related to granting a permit to a high-rise building application prior to awarding the permit by the municipalities.

The *HRBR* covered broad areas in an attempt to mainly control safety and services measures. The major areas covered are as follows:

Planning requirements:

a) Minimum set-backs and recesses required for proper ventilation and air circulation within the building itself and within the surroundings; and
b) Maximum height of the high-rise buildings.

Structural requirements:

a) Soil investigation report;
b) Structural system used with reference to resistance to wind and earthquake loads;
c) Safety margins and codes used; and
d) Report of the structural analysis and design method.

Architectural requirements:

a) Minimum ventilation and lighting spaces;
b) Minimum interior and exterior recesses; and
c) Stairs and fire escapes dimensions.

Services requirements:

a) Water supply and storage system;
b) Solid waste and public health; and
c) Elevators.

Fire safety requirements:

a) Fire escapes;
b) Civil defence; and
c) Fire resistance system.

Electrical requirements:

a) design and load criteria; and
b) construction measures.

Awarding a High-Rise Building Permit

The high-rise building permit has to go through two phases as shown in Figure 1.

Phase 1:

a) The owner solicits an engineering consulting office to carry out planning and design works;
b) The consulting engineer submits, on behalf of the owner, preliminary drawings (site plan, typical floor plan, elevation) to the municipality;
c) The municipality checks these drawings from a regulatory perspective and for general purposes;
d) The municipality will award a preliminary permit if the drawings meet the criteria and regulations of the municipality; and
e) The preliminary permit allows the owner to proceed in developing full documents; these documents should conform to the HRBR.

Phase 2:

a) The consulting engineer submits full documents (drawings, design sheets, soil investigation report and the material requested in phase 1) to the Engineers Syndicate for approval;
b) The Engineers' Syndicate Committee checks the structural safety of the building, operation, safety measures, mechanical and electrical works;
c) The consulting engineer submits the documents to the municipality

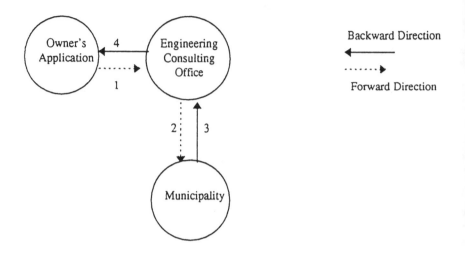

Phase I: Process for the Preliminary Check up for the High Rise Building Permit

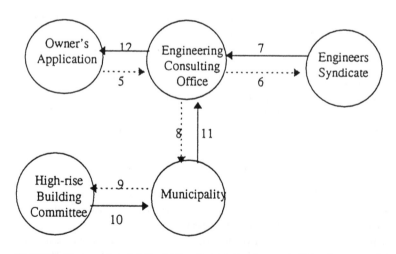

Phase II: Process for the final Check up and Approval of the Building Permit

Figure 1 Process Of Awarding A High-Rise Building Permit.

for granting a building permit. Because it is not within the municipality's legal power to approve a permit for high-rise buildings, the municipality forwards the documents to the High-Rise Building Committee;

d) Members of the High-Rise Building Committee check all the documents in their area of expertise. If the documents meet the HRBR, the committee recommends the approval of awarding a permit; and

e) The building permit is finally issued through the municipality.

Currently, there is an effort to prepare a structural plan to determine the skyline of Gaza City, and subsequently the zones where high-rise buildings will be allowed. In view of the new structural plan, the HRBR might be revised to reflect land use and urbanisation criteria.

SUMMARY AND RECOMMENDATIONS

This paper has emphasised the procedures which could be followed in obtaining CSR in Palestine. Examples and case studies were provided to show the practicability of the processes which have been followed.

The options to obtain CSR relevant to Palestine are as follows:

a) Establishment of new local CSR. This strategy consumes both time and resources;

b) Adoption, without modification, of CSR from other Arab countries in the region or those which have been established internationally; and

c) Adoption and modification of CSR from other Arab countries in the region or those which have been established internationally. The CSR which are relevant to the area would be used as a basis for modifications. This option would best suit local needs and ensure uniformity in the applicability of CSR.

Other recommendations include the following:

a) Specialised committees including representatives from all related institutions should be formed by the Ministry of Housing to collect materials, research, and the studies which would be required to prepare proposals. Priority should be given to the more demanding CSR; namely, those related to building materials;

b) A building research institute should be established to further develop adopted CSR and to monitor the implementation process; and

c) A quality control system for building materials s necessary to create a successful building industry. The Ministry of Housing has already moved quickly in this regard. Quality controls for ready-mix concrete are being prepared and should be ready to be implemented soon. This system is to be extended to other building materials such as steel bars, cement and bricks.

BIBLIOGRAPHY

Dahdouh, S. and A. Hayek, 1975, **Collection of Laws and Special Regulations of the Municipality of Gaza**, Gaza.

PNA, 1995, **Official News Bulletin**, No. 2, Legal Advisory and Legislation Council, Gaza.

Theme Four

HOUSING ALTERNATIVES AND OPTIONS FOR CONSERVATION AND RENEWAL

HOUSING ALTERNATIVES AND OPTIONS FOR CONSERVATION AND RENEWAL

Nabeel Hamdi

ABSTRACT

The overriding goal for housing will be how to ensure an adequate and sustainable supply of housing, at standards which are affordable and which fit social and political aspirations. Planning and design should respect Palestinian urban and architectural heritage and ensure historical continuity.

This paper reviews the issues at stake in meeting these objectives, and assesses the options available. Themes covered include development paradigms, new construction, housing renewal, conservation and heritage. A synthesis of the views expressed by experts in this Monograph is also presented.

INTRODUCTION

There will be severe constraints in the short-term on establishing effective policies to reduce housing deficits significantly. These constraints include the rapid increase in population (which will total an estimated 2,695,000 by the year 2000 in Gaza and the West Bank); the shortage of buildable land; the poor conditions of existing shelter; the high cost of construction materials; the poor state of infrastructure; the lack of cheap finance and reliable data; limited institutional and administrative capacity; and protracted political instability.

In discussing housing in general, it should be noted that demand in Palestine outstrips available public sector resources as it does in most other countries. Estimates for Palestine suggest an immediate housing deficit of 40,000 units and a desired increase in stock of 200,000 units to the year 2000. Criteria for counting deficits are typically ambiguous and based on standards of adequacy which are rarely affordable. Perceived deficits are often greater than actual deficits.

Housing deficits will, therefore, be difficult to predict. Estimates will need to consider: rising expectations as the peace process gathers momentum; the likely reduction in house-hold size and unpredictable patterns of migration as the economy strengthens; concealed households that come into being as soon as housing is available; the possibility of protracted political instability.

Moreover, the types of housing, their means of production and distribution, cannot be uniform. Planning will need to cater for stark variations in density (290 persons per square kilometre on average, up to 100,000 persons per square kilometre in some refugee camps); uneven demographics (50 per cent under 14 years of age, 10 per cent over 45, 4 million returnees, 35 per cent refugees in Gaza); contrasting expectations between these population groupings; and for significant variation between regions and between communities. (The proportion of the Palestinian Territories categorised according to population density, for example, varies from 43 per cent for the urban areas to a low of 5 per cent for semi-urban districts, while rural areas account for 35 per cent and the refugee camps 17 per cent).

DEVELOPMENT PARADIGMS

The search for effective ways to scale up the supply of affordable housing has polarised policy thinkers, architects, planners and others into two (potentially compatible) schools of thought, designated as *providers* and *supporters*. Each school is distinguishable by its ideals, its methods and practices, its level of centralisation of decisions, resources and production, its relative dependency on international development aid and technology transfer and in its inclusion of communities and other stakeholders in planning, design, production and management.

Key Characteristics

Key Issues

Providers

These issues cover government-provided new social housing; sites and services projects and formal privately provided new housing. They include the following considerations:

- Rationalised building based on norms and standards which facilitate mass production ignore regional and other variations;

- Large amounts of up-front capital, as well as large markets to guarantee economies of scale will be difficult to sustain;
- Preference in this approach for zoned, single function projects are out of keeping with the social and physical fabric of cities and villages in Palestine; and
- Housing types are designed to tightly defined standards of space, materials and utility, representing a careful balance of technical feasibility, building regulations and planning controls.

This renders this type of housing resource-intensive in administration, materials and money and, therefore, unaffordable to the low-income majority without heavy subsidy.

This approach also creates dependencies between recipient country and international donors and contractors, and between communities and government.

Supporters

This covers community and informally provided housing and most upgrading/improvement programmes. The following issues need consideration:

- Ensuring stakeholder participation demands effective local level organisation of non-governmental organisations and community based organisations and will vary in success, depending on the type of neighbourhoods (whether diffuse, stepping stone, transitory, etc.) and levels of patronage within communities;
- An emphasis on managing resources of land, money, materials, utilities, skills and administration, rather than on building projects demands inter-authority co-ordination and a strong institutional capability in all the above areas;
- Partnerships between formal and informal providers of housing, private enterprise and public authorities, local organisations and central administration, large-scale and small-scale producers, demand greater management capabilities within the relevant public authorities; and
- Housing is considered a non-sectoral activity, i.e. an integral part of the larger system of urban development and the urban economy. This demands greater co-ordination among government agencies, even an intersectoral agency responsible for planning and coordination.

NEW CONSTRUCTION

New construction will be an integral part of scaling up supply. The questions for policy makers will be: how much new construction (versus improvement) and of what kind? Subsequently, where will it go, who will provide and how will supply be sustained? There are three conventional providers of new housing: 1) the government (social housing and sites and services projects); 2) formal builders, private enterprise or developers; and 3) community or informal builders and organisations. Partnerships between these sectors offer opportunities for innovation.

Key Characteristics

Government-Provided, Social Housing Projects

- Characteristics follow those outlined under 'providers';
- Production economies depend on repetitive site operations. Plans are, therefore, standardised, variations in design minimised, componentisation and prefabrication maximised;
- Construction typically built to relatively high standards; and
- Rarely affordable by governments over the long term.

Government-Provided, Sites and Services Projects

- Characteristics are similar to the above, but projects involve a significant amount of self-help or aided self-help for families to design and construct their own dwellings;
- Projects are more mixed use, with incremental building. Sites consolidate over several years; and
- Ancillary programmes are common, to support and manage self-build activities, including skills training, organising credit facilities, building community development organisations and sometimes co-operative site management.

Formal, Privately Provided Housing

The private provision of housing is typically classified into four groups, each with its own distinguishable characteristics. All, however, following the characteristics outlined under *Providers*.

- Real estate speculators allied normally to urban financial institutions who, together, dominantly shape the rules by which the market operates;
- Householders and developers who typically operate in co-operation with governments and who have, in history, shaped large formal suburbs in most first world and some Third World cities;
- The construction industry, helping promote systems building and new technologies, and offering 'package deals' or turnkey schemes; and

- Private individuals who may build single houses for rent and who often operate as absentee landlords.

Community and Informally Provided Housing

Characteristics (and government roles) follow those outlined under *Supporters*. See also the section on *Upgrading*.

- Building is achieved incrementally through a series of small scale, *additive* projects, coupled with strategic level policy interventions, offering access to cheap credit, variable servicing, land and know-how;
- Linkages are encouraged between formal and informal producers, large producers and small manufacturers, and between different levels of technology;
- Multiplicity of outlets for materials, and small manufacturers – even *pavement sellers* – is encouraged, offering variety in prices and quality in goods and services and, therefore, much needed flexibility to local entrepreneurs and families;
- Standards are variable – for space, construction, material, utilities and upgradeable;
- Experts act as catalysts introducing methods, techniques and new technologies, bringing experience from outside, identifying opportunities for greater efficiency, disseminating principles, training, building institutional capabilities and removing legal, legislative and other barriers which get in the way; and
- Variety, flexibility, improvisation, incrementalism, partnerships, participation are all encouraged.

Key Issues

Government-Provided Social Housing Projects

- Issues follow those outlined under *Providers*;
- Economies of scale imply large projects and, therefore, major re-development;
- Standardisation may be based on *averages* and ignore variations in family size, income, composition and aspiration;
- Large projects often demand large vacant sites away from job markets and mostly at the expense of agricultural land;
- Design follows the *international* style with multi-storey buildings of apartments arranged in response to high land values and to achieve high densities;
- Planning typically maximises public land, placing additional burdens

on public sector maintenance and resulting in more costly infrastructure and a reduced tax base for local government; and

- Cost of construction, together with the demand for cost recovery, typically places this kind of housing out of reach of those in most need, without heavy subsidy.

Government-Provided Sites and Services Projects

- High levels of investment for infrastructure;
- Infrastructure provision could follow progressive development of building activities, and so lowering initial costs;
- Authorities often demand the compulsory use of 'permanent' materials with houses built according to a given range of designs – which raise costs;
- The price of land is often excluded from the initial cost of housing. The approach works best where a significant amount of land is already in public ownership;
- Cost recovery has generally been good, although most projects favour families with steady incomes; and
- Where housing in not the top priority for those housed in such projects – people sometimes sell out or rent and move back to inner city areas. 'Gentrification' can, therefore, follow.

Privately Provided New Housing

- House prices usually determined by the market and includes a combination of land values, construction costs, materials and finance capital;
- Private building relies heavily on established housing loans institutions and on a good supply of mortgage credit at affordable costs;
- Profit adds substantially to the final cost of housing; and
- Rarely affordable by the lowest income.

Community and Informally Provided Housing

- Issues follow those outlined under *Supporters* and under *Upgrading*;
- Programmes can be management intensive for government institutions and demand well-established community based non-government organisations;
- Building approvals procedures need to be kept procedurally simple and cost effective; and
- Results are progressive and, therefore, not quickly measurable.

HOUSING RENEWAL

Most housing improvement or renewal is typically undertaken within broader programmes or urban upgrading. Indeed, carefully targeted public investment for improving services and utilities, including roads, schools and clinics, all trigger equivalent private sector investment in housing at the community and family levels. Urban renewal is, therefore, a key component of housing renewal.

Key Characteristics

Characteristics generally follow those listed under *Supporters.*

Four key renewal activities would seem relevant to consider for Palestine: completing unfinished residential buildings; the adaptive reuse of historical buildings; repair and improvement of existing stock; and re-inhabiting villages which were abandoned during the Israeli/Palestinian conflict. Each of the renewal activities listed above will need to be considered for three main typologies of housing:

1) *Existing derelict neighbourhoods,* including slums, where housing and infrastructure have progressively deteriorated;
2) *Historic centres* and abandoned *villages* (e.g. Bit Wazan) in which buildings and utilities have deteriorated and which may be overcrowded. These areas offer opportunities for the adaptive reuse of large houses, workshops and communal buildings;
3) *Refugee camps* which have consolidated over the years and are now integral to the urban landscape (e.g. Askar or Balata). The camps are dense, with high occupancy rates and very poor sanitation, services and utilities. Improvement in this case will need to extend to infrastructure, environment, communal and recreational buildings and public open space. Other characteristics include the following:

- Selective replacement of houses which are difficult or costly to upgrade, or in order to reduce densities may be necessary;
- Physical renewal will typically be coupled with the provision of loans, the legalisation of tenure rights to land and property and the provision of community facilities (schools, clinics, community centres, etc.);
- Renewal will by necessity be intensively participatory and incremental in development (see *Community and Informally Provided Housing* above); and
- Renewal with conservation enables quick and economic ways of increasing supply, is more sensitive to existing physical and social structures, eases the pressure on land, offers local job opportunities and avoids displacing whole communities.

369

Key Issues

- Improvement is management intensive and requires a careful inventory of historic buildings (see 'Heritage') and deteriorated stock;
- Criteria need to be established for deciding minimum acceptable standards and subsequently for prioritising areas for renewal;
- Institutional and human resource capabilities need to be developed to manage land and money, promote participation, inventory buildings etc; and
- The intersectoral activities of renewal demand partnerships between institutions and between government institutions and community organisations.

CONSERVATION AND HERITAGE

Palestine's 7,000 year history has endowed it with a rich and varied of architectural heritage, much of which today belongs to the Islamic era. The *Supporters* paradigm outlined earlier, together with the preferred approach to upgrading of the existing housing and other physical fabric of towns and villages, suggests adaptive reuse as an important housing strategy for the future. Much of this is likely to involve historic buildings as well as the historic fabric of cities. Design and planning will need to be historically grounded and respectful of traditional forms.

Key Characteristics

- Palestinian architecture and urban form is attributable to the later Islamic periods, including the dynasties of the Ayyubids (1187–1250), the Bahrite Mamlukes (1250–1382), the Burjit Mamlukes (1382–1517) and the Ottomans (1517–1918);
- Palestinian architecture is strongly influenced by topography, Mediterranean climate, and is characterised by inward-looking compound type buildings, small windows, thick walls, local stone, vaults and beams, pointed arches and a variety of decorative features;
- Buildings fall into the following typologies:

  - Residential (town houses, palaces, villages);
  - Religious (mosques, madrassa, shrines, cemeteries, hospices, churches, monasteries);
  - Civil (serais, courts);
  - Military (citadels, camps, walls, gates, ports, towers); and
  - Industrial (workshops, foundries, presses).

- Architectural and urban heritage may be classified as follows:

370

- Monuments (Dome of the Rock, Al Aqsa Mosque, Church of the Nativity);
- Urban cores in old cities (Jerusalem, Hebron, Nablus, Ramallah, etc.); and
- Rural settlements (Deir Ghassaneh, Yatta, Arbas, Silwan, etc.).

Key Issues

Long periods of neglect have resulted in the destruction of numerous important buildings and the serious deterioration of others.

- Undertaking an historical typography is key to revitalisation. A national inventory of architectural heritage is urgently needed to guide adaptive reuse;
- A buildings/urban centre classification is key to assessing the suitability of buildings for housing use. A system of listing or grading could usefully be introduced;
- Criteria for listing and grading needs to be decided for both buildings and historic areas;
- A central organisation is needed (i.e. a National Council for Heritage in Palestine) in order to co-ordinate agencies' tasks and to act as a consultative body;
- New buildings and designs will need to: consider the Islamic cultural reference in architecture; avoid being revivalist; reinterpret historical precedent to fit new standards, building technologies and materials; be responsive to climate, local materials and resources; density and form (high density low rise) to the historic features of cities; and
- There is a severe shortage of skilled staff who are able to conduct detailed and systematic surveys of historic and architecturally important buildings.

SUMMARY AND RECOMMENDATIONS

There will be severe constraints in the short-term on the mobilisation of policies needed to significantly reduce housing deficits. These make it difficult to estimate demand effectively, to increase production and to manage distribution. These constraints are typical in many countries, but have been exacerbated in Palestine by the Israeli occupation.

Demand in Palestine outstrips available public sector resources, and housing deficits are therefore difficult to predict. Moreover, planning should cater for differences in density, uneven demographics, contrasting expectations of the various population groups and for variations in between regions and communities. No single response to these complex issues will satisfy all conditions.

A combined strategy of new buildings and improvement of existing stock will need to be adopted. Urban renewal, including completing unfinished houses, repairing dilapidated stock, re-occupying abandoned villages, the adaptive re-use of historic buildings, coupled with restoring of the historical fabric of inner cities is the preferred way forward. Replacement will need to be progressive and discreet, and conducted in partnership with the public authorities, between authorities and private sector enterprises, and with the full participation of communities and other stakeholders.

The informal housing sector will play a significant role in the provision of housing. It needs to be recognised and facilitated.

URBAN DEVELOPMENT: A JORDANIAN CASE STUDY

Hidaya Dajani Khairi

ABSTRACT

This paper deals mainly with the experience of the Housing and Urban Development Corporation (HUDC) in Jordan in upgrading existing low-income settlements between 1980 and 1994. The first part of the paper reviews the role of the first upgrading agency, the Urban Development Department (UDD), and explains the concept of upgrading and briefly discusses projects already executed.

The second part of the paper focuses on the HUDC's experience in community participation. The role played by local communities in upgrading sites is highlighted.

The third part of the paper discusses the importance of the studies undertaken by HUDC before, during, and after the implementation of its upgrading schemes. Finally, the need to review data obtained from a number of the studies which have already been prepared is emphasised in order to take account of the changing population conditions which have affected this area in the past five years.

INTRODUCTION

Jordan is a highly urbanised country because of high population growth and massive immigration from occupied Palestine. About 80 per cent of its population of 5.4 million is located in cities and towns.

The capital, Amman, which is also the industrial and financial centre of the country, accounts for more than 35 per cent of the population, while Irbid and Zarqa each contain 25 per cent and 15 per cent respectively.

High urban land prices, coupled with large minimum legal plot size, restrictive planning and building regulations, as well as inadequate access to established financial markets, have all combined to deny the low-income population access to reasonable housing at prices they can afford. Under such circumstances, the poor have little to do except to live in crowded, underserviced and unhygienic housing, or to squat on other people's land, and to erect illegal, rather primitive, dwellings.

Squatter areas account for about 9 per cent of the Amman/Zarqa population and about 12 per cent of that in greater Amman. It is estimated that at least 200,000 people live on these (Hujja) lands in the Amman/Zarqa area.

To address this worsening situation, the government in 1979 with the World Bank (WB) agreed to prepare the First Urban Development Project (UDP1). This involved upgrading five low-income settlements and the creation of three new sites designated for low-income families.

In 1980, a special agency called the Urban Development Department (UDD) was set up in the Municipality of Amman and given a mandate to implement the project. The Department was financially and administratively independent and directly linked to the office of the Mayor of Amman and the Municipal Council.

By 1992, the UDD had successfully completed the first urban project and had two further projects – UDP2 and UDP3 – were underway. As recommended under the National Housing Strategy (NHS), the UDD was merged with the Housing Corporation (HC), which had existed since 1966 and which mainly provided subsidised housing for government employees. The combined entity became known as the Housing and Urban Development Corporation.

HUDC currently represents the national umbrella for the housing sector. Apart from implementing new housing schemes and upgrading low-income settlements, HUDC was given the mandate to formulate national policies for the housing sector, including the implementation and updating of the NHS, which was launched in 1986.

THE URBAN DEVELOPMENT DEPARTMENT

Objectives

The main objective of the UDD was to provide adequate shelter, with security of tenure and access to essential services for the urban poor (defined as households with incomes at, or below, the 40 per cent of urban income distribution) on a full and direct cost-recovery basis.

The aim was to use a minimal cost approach to the provision of serviced land and basic infrastructure, creating conditions where individual families and the private sector could provide adequate shelter through their own effort and initiative. The stimulation of private sector participation and equity investment in the provision of shelter was central to UDD's approach.

Additional objectives included improving the educational, health, and employment conditions of low-income families, increasing productivity, the ability to pay for shelter and services, and creating an environment in which people may lead a full life in a secure community.

The secondary objectives of the UDD included the development of appropriate and effective urban planning policies and the discovery of new ways to meet the housing and related needs of low-income households.

Operation

To meet these objectives, UDD operated in the urban sector as a development agency for sites and services (S&S), housing and upgrading slum and squatter areas. Land was bought, serviced with roads, water, sewers and electricity, and divided into small plots and provided with schools, clinics and other facilities. Generally, the housing was built later by residents, although some small expandable starter accommodation was provided and some open market housing, workshops and shop units were also included. The cost of these 'site and services' schemes were recovered from beneficiaries, with, wherever necessary, mortgage and building loans arranged through the Housing Bank (HB).

The same principle was used for the second main activity – squatter area upgrading. Unserviced land occupied illegally by low-income families was purchased, properly serviced and resold to residents. UDD also undertook a range of ancillary operations in support of its projects, such as beneficiary selection, community development, property marketing, planning and construction, contract preparation and tendering and the supervision of contracts.

UDD had established arrangements with the HB (mortgage and building loans) and the City and Village Development Bank (CVDB), (cost recovery from municipalities). In addition, UDD had liaison arrangements with key service agencies, notably the Jordan Water Authority and Jordan Electric Power Company and the ministries involved, such as Education, Health, Social Development, Municipal and Rural Affairs, Environment and Planning.

UDD undertook planning and feasibility studies to identify possible projects, possible policy approaches and priorities, as well as monitoring studies of its own projects. The agency developed potential projects for appraisal (by the HB) and then proceeded to undertake detailed design and the production of tender documents. Land was acquired as necessary. Suitable contractors were prequalified and invited to bid. Following tender evaluation, construction contracts were let.

UDD undertook site supervision work and provided financial and estate management, as well as community development work in relation to its projects. Beneficiaries were selected and assisted in obtaining finance for the purchase of plots and for building. UDD also co-ordinated its activities with service agencies and local authorities concerning the approval of projects, the standards and supply of services, and operation and maintenance.

Design Principles

UDD developed a comprehensive range of design principles, performance criteria and standards. These covered land use, plot size and forms, levels of on-plot construction, layouts, roads, footpaths and parking standards, open space, education, health, and community facilities, water supply and distribution, sewerage collection and treatment, electricity supply and other related matters. In addition, a series of project acceptability criteria were prepared and used in examining whether or not a proposed project was practical, acceptable and viable.

Upgrading Concepts

The basic philosophy behind the upgrading approach is the preservation and enhancement of existing urban irregular settlements rather than clearance and replacement. This approach was envisaged as the best available solution in light of the social, environmental and economic conditions in those settlements. The philosophy aimed at creating a housing environment that is satisfactory in terms of amenity, visual appearance, shelter quality and essential services. The alternative clearance and evacuation approach is rather costly and leads to the dissolution of the social fabric of the community. To pursue this approach, UDD adopted a number of concepts, including the following.

- *Cost Recovery*

Because of Jordan's limited resources, project costs were to be recovered from beneficiaries to ensure replicability. Beneficiaries had to pay for the cost of land and on-site infrastructure while the government had to pay for the cost of community buildings and off-site infrastructure. Government subsidy also included reduced connection charges for water and electricity and exemption of building licence fees.

- *Modest Design Standard*

Project designs were prepared to the minimum acceptable and affordable standards to enable low-income beneficiaries to meet the project costs.

- *Cross-Subsidy*

Cross subsidy was adopted between project elements by using profits achieved from the sale of commercial plots to cover deficits resulting from beneficiaries' plots.

- *Self-Help*

Once the problem of land tenure was resolved and squatters become owners of the land they lived on, they were encouraged to improve their dwellings. In this regard, building loans were provided by the HB at reasonable conditions. The UDD also provided, at the beneficiaries' requests, design drawings for the improvement or extension of individual dwellings.

- *Relocation and Compensation*

Alternative affordable plots were provided to families affected by demolition due to the re-planning sites to be upgraded. Compensation for buildings demolished as a result were also made to the affected beneficiaries.

- *Community Participation in the Development Process*

In order to facilitate the physical upgrading process as well as to support welfare, organised community participation at predefined stages was undertaken involving training and livelihood programmes.

Executed Projects

Project Profiles

UDP1 1980–1987

- *Total Cost*

JD (21.73) million

- *Upgrading*

Four sites with a population of (12,790)
including (1,143) residential plots and
commercial plots, public facilities and community development.
Total Cost = JD (3.73) million

- *Site and Services*

Three sites for a population of (20,450)
including (2,777) residential plots and
commercial plots, public facilities and community development
Total Cost = JD (18) million

UDP2 1986–1991

- *Total Cost*
JD (29.16) million

- *Upgrading*
One site with a population of (1,370)
including the development of (124) residential plots and
commercial plots, public facilities and community development.
Total Cost = JD (0.73) million

- *Site and Services*
Six sites for a population of (32,920)
including (4,233) residential plots and
commercial plots, public facilities and community development
Total Cost JD (28.43) million

UDP3 1988–1994

- *Total Cost*
JD (11.42) million

- *Upgrading*
Upgrading low-income settlement with total population of (40,000)
Estimated Cost JD (8.89) million

- *Site and Services*
Land development for (15,000) persons
Estimated Cost JD (2.53) million

Financing and Cost Recovery

Finance

UDD activities have been financed through World Bank loans, central government allocations, the HB and, in later years, down payments and repayments from beneficiaries. The UDD receives its funds directly from the Ministry of Planning (MOP), the HB and the Cities and Villages Development Bank (CVDB).

Cost recovery

The UDD's cost recovery approach divided project costs into two components. The first included components recovered directly from beneficiaries, while the second included components which were paid for out of general revenue.

Recoverable Components	*Non Recoverable Components (3)*
Land acquisition (1)	Land for off-site infrastructure
On-site infrastructure (1)	Land for social facilities
Core housing (1)	Off-site infrastructure
Construction loans (2)	Social facilities
Mortgage for land purchase (2)	

1) Land, on-site infrastructure and core housing recovered from the sale of property.
2) Building and building material loans for beneficiaries directly from the HB.
3) The costs of off-site infrastructure and social facilities which are recovered through taxes and user charges.

This approach was adopted in UDP1, UDP2 and in the first site – Saladin – upgraded under UDP3. However, concerted public pressure and protest at the highly unaffordable land and development costs led to a tendency by HUDC (formerly UDD) to modify its policy and cost recovery approach in the remaining upgrading sites under UDP3.

Under this approach, beneficiaries were partly or wholly exempted from on-site infrastructure costs, keeping them in line with existing rules governing service cost recovery in other areas within municipal boundaries. Under these rules, the direct cost of infrastructural services were borne by the concerned service agency and were to be recovered through long-term general taxation.

Evaluation studies undertaken in already upgraded sites identified two important aspects as major contributions to the success of HUDC experience in upgrading. These two aspects were:

1) Community participation programmes; and
2) Studies conducted during all project stages.

COMMUNITY PARTICIPATION IN UPGRADING PROJECTS

The Issues

In the context of upgrading informal settlements, community participation may be defined as a voluntary and popular participation in the decision-making process concerning the setting of project goals, components and priorities. This participation extends throughout all stages of a project's life, i.e. from planning to completion. The participatory role assumed by local beneficiaries constitutes a core element in upgrading schemes and should be paid adequate attention by urban officials, planners and upgrading agencies.

The success of upgrading schemes may largely depend on the level of

379

participation of the concerned beneficiaries who represent the party which is well aware of conditions and problems and is most capable of prioritising and addressing them in accordance with its own needs. It is through participation that a community can approve, alter or even totally reject development proposals, an action that implies a sense of ownership, empowerment and responsibility.

It is also true to say that participation can lead to more favourable results, in terms of beneficiaries' commitments to post-development responsibilities. From experience, such commitment is a pre-requisite to the maintenance and sustainability of completed schemes and to the success of cost recovery operations.

Community participation primarily entails the mobilisation and employ-ment of all available manpower with the aim of empowering and enabling local communities to have a say in decisions related to their future. This process has involved, among other things, the formation of local organisations to act on behalf of beneficiaries. United Nations literature has also called for community involvement in the provision of shelter for all by the year 2000.

Community participation is a complex, arduous and costly process that requires special studies to ascertain its feasibility and cost effectiveness. The funding of the process of community participation also needs to be taken into consideration. Analyses of cost effectiveness must also be carried out and the result may be that some aspects of participation may simply be too costly.

Development programmes implemented during the 1990s have exhib-ited a number of interconnected aspects that need to be taken into account and which may require new paradigms.

In light of the difficulties which have occurred in government develop-ment programmes and, in contrast, the success achieved by non-governmental organisations (NGOs) in the same field, the latter can play, if supported, a more effective role in urban development projects. The envisaged role of NGOs is that of a facilitator between official and/or municipal staff on the one hand and the beneficiaries on the other. Such a role becomes more important as the work progresses and a critical stage after completion and during the maintenance the project when a new authority (usually the local municipality) takes it over from the executing agency. The presence of a third party (i.e. NGOs) at this transitional period is important and can help the local community adjust to the final development stage (i.e. to the sustainability phase).

The above review highlights the need for specialised training for all parties involved in the process of community participation. The aim of such training is to equip participants with the necessary experience to achieve project objectives; in particular, those related to comprehensive development. The empowerment of local communities to enable them to continue their activities after the development phase should be considered a strategic objective by all those concerned with development.

The Parties Involved

The two major parties concerned with community participation in the Jordanian urban project are:

1) The beneficiaries; and
2) Official staff (i.e. governmental or municipal).

The first party, i.e. the beneficiaries, should play a major role in the process of community participation because it is the user of the project and is directly effected by the outcome. The role of the second party should be confined to that of a facilitator or catalyst. The ensuing discussion deals with the beneficiaries of the project in terms of formation, origin, history and conditions.

Palestinians form the majority of residents in the informal settlements in the Amman/Zarqa area. The settlements are virtually a spillover from the existing refugee camps erected as a result of massive migration from the West Bank to the East Bank between 1948 and 1976. They were formed simply by squatting on government/or private land without prior permission and involved the erection of simple houses with poor materials (corrugated metal sheets and/or bricks). The houses were not connected to basic service networks, i.e. water, sewerage, electricity, etc. In one site in Amman for example, it was virtually impossible for any passer-by to cross the site without wetting and fouling his feet and legs with polluted water, a mixture of sewerage and surface drainage.

As for the Aqaba region, residents of squatter settlements can be divided into two distinct groups. The first consists of Jordanians who consider themselves the legitimate owners of the land due to their long history which goes back to a period prior to the establishment of the Kingdom. The second is made up of Bedouin who migrated from the Negev desert, some of whom are still leading a nomadic life. Settlements in the Aqaba area lack basic infrastructural services and the condition of houses varies from poor to good.

The above are typical examples of the different groups of people involved under urban development/upgrading projects. Various methods were devised to approach these people and to get them actively involved in the process of development.

Types, Approaches and Stages

Community participation under Jordan upgrading projects has produced a variety of features which have changed as a result of both the different political situations, i.e. more participation with the advancement of the democratisation process, and the contrasting population characteristics between upgrading sites.

To date, thirteen sites have been upgraded, including seven in Amman and six in Aqaba. All the sites have already been completed, but with varying degrees of community participation.

Projects Implemented before Democratisation

These projects include those implemented under the first Urban Development Project (East Wahdat, Jofeh, Rimam, Nuzha, Hai Amir Hassan) located in Amman, and one implemented under the third Urban Development Project (Saladin) in Aqaba. The upgrading process has involved tenure regularisation of land, site planning and the provision of all basic and social services.

The communities in the above sites did not take part in, or were not consulted, regarding the implementation of the project. Nor did they have a say in selecting development priorities. Community participation was achieved in areas of dwelling design and during physical implementation by the contractor. The carefully-planned designs of the footpaths and open spaces were conducive factors to community participation, a fact that subsequently helped to ensure the proper maintenance and sustainability of the upgraded sites.

Community centre programmes were also the focus of community participation. In fact, such participation is seen as a primary objective to strengthen local communities and enable them to take responsibilities. A further but important step in this respect was taken when residents were encouraged and assisted to establish formal associations and co-operatives.

When work began at the above sites, voices were raised against the implementation of upgrading, claiming that prices were too high. Soon after the easing of the financial burden on very poor families, opposition subsided and upgrading was successfully completed. In spite of the favourable result, it is fair to conclude that such opposition has had a negative impact on some potential upgrading sites and eventually contributed to the rejection of upgrading in some sites.

Projects Implemented after Democratisation

Projects suspended due to residents' rejection of upgrading included the following.

Hai Jann'/Zarqa

This site was selected for upgrading under the third Urban Development Project and was to include tenure regularisation and the provision of all basic services, parts of which were already, but inadequately, provided. A decision to implement the project was made without prior consultation with local residents who consequently launched a fierce battle against the project on the grounds of high development costs and the availability of infrastructural services. In fact, the cost of land in this project was relatively high because it was privately owned. Because of continued opposition to the project, the planning work was eventually stopped.

Hai Amir Ali\Russeifa

Local residents were initially contacted and were asked to express their opinions regarding upgrading their site. Although residents were illegally occupying the site and were badly in need of infrastructural services, they rejected upgrading.

They requested that the work be executed by Russeifa Municipality free of charge on an equal footing with other residents of Zarqa and Russeifa. The educated people in the site were more forthcoming in their response to the upgrading idea, but the traditional leaders – the majority of whom were old – expressed outright rejection and barred all citizens from offering any assistance to the government staff.

The head of Russeifa Municipality, although freely elected, was incapable of overriding their rejection, although he was personally in favour of upgrading. Moreover, the initial effort in this project coincided with the introduction of democracy in Jordan and with the election of members of parliament who exploited the situation, promising citizens to support their case in the parliament in order to get elected.

Previous experience with upgrading, including the negative response expressed by some localities, urged a reassessment of the already-adopted approach. Under the more flexible approach, which resulted from the reassessment, the decision to proceed with, or to cancel, a potential project rests in the hands of local residents. Residents also select their own priorities and submit a written consent form expressing a commitment to repay the cost of development.

This approach was adopted for two projects in Amman (Abu Alia and Hamlan) and for four projects in Aqaba (North and South Shallalah, and Old Town North and South).

The Amman Projects

Hai Abu Alia

Residents participated effectively in setting priorities for upgrading at this site; these priorities were confined, upon their request, to site planning and plot parcellation. They also participated in preliminary planning with respect to the definition of plot areas and footpath widths and distribution. In return, residents had to sign a written form accepting their designated plot areas and committing themselves to repay the cost of land and services provided by the developing agency. This approach proved very conducive to rapid and effective implementation of the required work.

Community participation in this site has had other important results, especially in terms of the emergence of a vitally-needed local leadership which was capable of dealing with concerned agencies. This resulted in bringing electricity to the site and in the construction of a cultural centre. Furthermore, mutual co-operation between members of the community with respect to plot allocation and meeting financial commitments was a salient feature in this site.

Hai Hamlan

The experience in this site was almost identical to that of Abu Alia, which set an example to be followed. Local leadership in this site was also instrumental in rallying support among residents and engaging them in making decisions to reblocking and replanning the site. The residents committed themselves to the upgrading costs, and the project was successfully executed.

Aqaba

In pursuit of a larger community role in decision-making, a questionnaire was circulated among local residents to identify the response to the proposed upgrading of their localities. The results were positive and encouraging in all four sites as residents expressed their approval for extensive upgrading including replanning, tenure regularisation, and provisions of all infrastructure services.

On the other hand, residents expressed reservations concerning the high land and development costs. To alleviate immediate costs on residents, bilateral agreements between service agencies and HUDC were concluded which enabled the latter to recover the cost of infrastructural services from these services agencies, which, in turn, will recover such costs from the community but over a longer period. Prolonged periods of negotiations over costs between HUDC and beneficiaries have increased costs due to accumulated interest and have increased the rate of repayment defaults.

It is relevant to mention here that a third party, namely the Aqaba Municipality and Aqaba Regional Authority, has been involved in the decision-making. Its contribution was useful in some situations but produced problems in others (e.g. pressures were exerted to modify some technical decisions concerning demolition works, road width and plot allocation).

Aqaba projects are different in some respects from those in Amman. A large proportion of beneficiaries in Aqaba do not acknowledge the fact that they are illegally occupying the land because they consider themselves the indigenous inhabitants of Aqaba. Therefore no one has the right, in their opinion, to ask them to pay for the land. Generally, however, upgrading of the four sites has been satisfactorily implemented with participation from all concerned parties.

Lessons Learned

The request by local communities that their sites be given a high priority on the list of upgrading projects is closely linked to the urgency of the needs that will be satisfied as a result of upgrading. For example, because Mahata-Amman residents (i.e. squatters) felt threatened with possible eviction by Amman Municipality, they were stimulated to co-operate closely with HUDC officials. The need for electricity also motivated Hai Abu Alia to accept and demand upgrading. On the other hand, the existence of water and electricity services in Hai Jannaa (where most houses were built of permanent materials) led the community to reject upgrading.

Defining upgrading priorities for a particular site is a fundamental step and local residents ought to be given the final say in this matter. Involvement at this stage will greatly affect residents' approval of upgrading and subsequently their financial commitment to repay the cost of development. For example, residents should be involved in the planning stage that precedes physical implementation and also during the initial surveys that will be followed by the establishment of the plot boundaries and the definition of the plot area.

The involvement of local residents in social surveys has proved feasible. Such surveys have been jointly carried out with a group of local social workers who were adequately trained to manage the activities of community centres. On the other hand, local residents were unable to participate in the physical surveys that required special technical expertise.

Existing organisations ought to be given due regard and respect. The lack of understanding and harmony between youth leaders and traditional leaders (predominantly old people) in such organisations may cause trouble and possibly lead to the failure of the upgrading projects. In addition, local women often prefer to be organised within informal local co-operatives rather than formal ones.

The local conditions, habits and traditions of residents vary from one town to another and sometimes even from one site to another in the same town. Such variations must be given due attention when planning and designing the site.

Studies have shown that the planning of footpaths, roads, pavements, semi-private open spaces and green areas can play an important role in activating social interaction between neighbours, because they form a meeting place during leisure time for people from all denominations. For example, women are upgrading areas in Amman by keeping these places clean as they use them more often than men. This is quite the opposite of the situation in Aqaba where men assume such roles due to the conservative nature of local society and also the fact that men use such places more often.

THE ROLE OF STUDIES AND RESEARCH

Procedures

Urban projects (upgrading or site and services) undertaken by HUDC are based on data provided by a series of field surveys and specialised studies. These are primarily the following:

a) Feasibility studies;
b) Registration studies – socio-economic and health surveys of target upgrading sites; and
c) Housing need studies.

Study (a) is conducted first while (b) and (c) are carried out prior to starting implementation.

In addition, other studies, including monitoring, are conducted during implementation (to follow-up work progress) and after completion to assess the effects of the project and the extent to which it has achieved its objectives.

The outcome of all the above studies constitutes the basis for defining a general framework for current and future projects which can be used by planners and executing agencies. For example, certain design and planning criteria have been reviewed and amended under the second and third urban projects based on the experience gained from the first urban project.

The studies have also played a key role in reaching the target groups (i.e. the beneficiaries) and in assessing the financial performance and viability of projects. Well-known academics and universities, both local and international, have taken part in the studies; for example, the University of Jordan and Harvard University (The study conducted jointly with the latter was entitled *Sustainable Improvement Strategies for Lower Income Urban Communities*, 1992).

Through these studies, HUDC and local staff have upgraded their capabilities and acquired considerable experience in the field. Furthermore, external funding agencies such as the World Bank were more convinced of the need to continue financing urban upgrading projects.

Types of Studies

Preliminary studies for upgrading sites

Stage I: Priority Study of Upgrading Sites

This includes:

- Initial identification of potential upgrading sites in cities and urban centres by consulting cities and villages plans and aerial photographs in addition to gathering data from concerned agencies;
- Conducting socio-economic field surveys on a typical specimen of beneficiaries living in upgrading sites to obtain data on site area, land tenure and price, house types and planning status, population density, available utilities (social and infrastructure), financial capabilities of residents and willingness to accept upgrading intervention; and
- Preparing a priority list of potential upgrading schemes, giving priority to sites with severe physical and social conditions. Recently, acceptance of upgrading by the beneficiaries has become the overriding priority.

Stage II: Site Selection Studies

This includes the following:

- Comprehensive socio-economic and health surveys of all residents living in the site to get data regarding:
  - family: name of household to whom the plot will be allocated;
  - house: to assist the replanning of the site;
  - health status: to use as a base line in follow up studies; and
  - local leadership: to co-operate with during implementation.

This data forms a reference for planners and researchers in all relevant fields.

387

- Pre-feasibility study. Costs are calculated to match the financial capabilities of beneficiaries. The site is then presented to the HUDC Board, which includes members of all the concerned agencies, for study and approval.

Stage III: Site Appraisal Study

This includes a detailed feasibility study regarding technical, social, financial and marketing factors. This study is then presented to the funding agencies (i.e. the HB for recoverable costs, and CVDB in liaison with MOP for non-recoverable costs).

After obtaining all the above approvals, the site is subjected to a detailed design.

Preliminary Studies for New Sites (S and S)

Stage I: Study on Housing Need and Demand Trends

This involves a study of housing needs, supply and demand and the financial status of residents in most urban centres. The following steps are undertaken:

1) Studying the NHS and determining the HUDC's share in housing provision;
2) Reviewing national studies on economic and social conditions of the target group;
3) Identifying the important development projects (including industry) to be implemented in the Kingdom which serve as attraction points for the target group; and
4) Informing and consulting with local municipalities regarding sites to be upgraded and the number of demolition cases to be expected as a result of replanning works.

From the results of the above, it is possible to estimate the housing needs for each city in the kingdom. Finally, the study of housing needs, supply and demand and the financial status of residents entails these additional steps:

5) Conducting specimen surveys of various cities to identify socio-economic conditions and so that they can be compared later with available data from national surveys;
6) Preparing technical studies for the planned future extension of urban areas, in terms of housing and related infrastructural services, and to identify state lands and expected prices; and

388

7) Preparing a list of alternative development sites from which sites complying with low-income housing criteria are selected.

Stage II: Site Selection Study

This includes the following selection criteria:

- Site location and availability of basic infrastructure in the vicinity of the site, including water, electricity, etc.;
- Physical conditions – topography, possible future extension, soil type and construction cost;
- Availability of health and educational facilities near the site; and the
- Site area (which should be not less than ten to 15 hectares).

A pre-feasibility study with cost estimates to assess both the financial and social suitability of the scheme to the target group is then prepared. Finally, the project is presented to the HUDC Board for study and approval.

Stage III: Final Feasibility Study

The study is prepared and presented to the funding agencies for approval as described for upgrading schemes earlier.

Monitoring and Follow-up Studies for Upgrading and S and S

These should seek to identify the following:

- The general environment of S&S or neighbourhoods to be upgraded and assessing the extent to which the project has been successful in meeting beneficiaries' needs in terms of general well-being, economy, health and environment;
- Family income and expenditure, which is then compared with the figures quoted in the affordability studies to see if any changes have occurred; and, finally,
- Cost repayment methods and welfare cases.

One example is the joint study, *Sustainable Improvement Strategies for Lower Income Urban Communities*, which was produced by HUDC and Harvard University in 1993. It covered the following subjects:

- *Uses for public open spaces.* The study highlighted the importance of such spaces, particularly for children and women. It also defined some criteria that maximise the use and benefits of these spaces; for example, giving these spaces a semi-private touch in their design, as well as concentrating relatives in adjacent zones to encourage the sharing of these spaces and their regular cleaning and maintenance;

- *Community centres* represent a preferable meeting places for children, women and particularly young girls who are shy and reluctant to stay long and meet in open space. A further attraction is the educational programmes conducted in the centres. Health and maternity centres in HUDC sites are also important for women, helping them to avoid long hours of delay at nearby hospitals, and providing them and their children with adequate health care;
- *The lack of provision of play areas* for children in HUDC sites needs further study and attention despite the extra costs that might be incurred as a result of providing such areas. Factors adding to the problem include the high percentage of youths among beneficiaries and the fact that a lot of children use roof tops as play areas.

Other monitoring studies include the following:

1) *First Urban Project: Completion Report*, 1988;
2) *Second Urban Development Project: Completion Report*, 1993; and
3) *Health and Population in Squatter Areas of Amman, A Re-assessment After Four Years of Upgrading*, 1985.

The first two studies attempted to summarise the experiences gained during project implementation and the extent to which project objectives were achieved.

Specific Short Studies

This category includes studies that must be implemented in response to needs arising during project implementation. One example is the *Community Participation Study* prepared jointly by HUDC staff and the local community (the administrative committee of the local association) in one upgrading site in Amman. The study involved some training of local staff and was aimed at assessing the local association's needs.

RECOMMENDATIONS

This paper has attempted to illustrate the dimensions of the studies undertaken for urban development projects in Jordan. The methodologies and techniques adopted during the past ten to 15 years have developed over time.

It is important to emphasise the need to review data obtained from a number of the studies already prepared in order to take account of the changing population conditions which have affected Jordan in the past five years, such as the massive influx of returnees from Kuwait as a result of the Gulf War between Iraq and Kuwait. The achievement of peace in the region could also have a major impact if hundreds of thousands of Palestinians, especially those living in irregular settlements or official refugee camps, were allowed to return home.

BIBLIOGRAPHY

Bisharat, Leila and Zagha, Hisham, 1988, **Health and Population in the Squatter Areas of Amman: A Re-assessment after Four Years of Upgrading**, Urban Development Project One: Completion Report, Municipality of Amman, Urban Development Department, Amman.

Dajani, Hidaya, 1994, **Community Participation in Upgrading Sites, Jordan Case Study**, Paper presented to the seminar on Open Cities – Community Participation For Sustainable Urban Development, United States Agency for International Development and UMP, September, Cairo.

Municipality of Amman, 1982, Urban Development Department, **A Baseline Health and Population Assessment for the Upgrading Area of Amman**, A Report to the Urban Development Department by the Population Council, Amman.

THE ROLE OF ARCHITECTURAL HERITAGE AND URBAN RECONSTRUCTION IN PALESTINE

Ihsan Fethi

ABSTRACT

Spanning more than 7,000 years, the history of Palestine has a very rich and varied architectural heritage. The prevailing architectural character today, however, is more related to the Islamic era than other historical periods.

This distinct architectural heritage, however, remains largely undocumented and has been seriously undermined by neglect, physical destruction, and insensitive modern development. With the exception of Jerusalem, perhaps, most towns and villages in Gaza and the West Bank have suffered considerable disruption in their historic physical fabric.

This paper attempts to identify the different typologies and essential characteristics of urban and rural architectural traditions in Palestine. It aims to highlight the need to conserve and enhance this heritage by proposing certain measures and policies to ensure a cultural continuity with the past.

These policies will not only cover historical cores but will also deal with modern infill within them, as well as the need to ensure that major reconstruction projects should be sensitively designed and based on Palestinian cultural tradition.

Reference shall be made to several outstanding examples in the region where architects have succeeded in reinterpreting tradition into a vivid and contemporary context.

INTRODUCTION

Palestine has been, throughout its long history, one of the major cultural and religious centres of mankind. Spanning well over 7,000 years and located in the heart of the Middle East, Palestine has been endowed with a very rich and varied cultural heritage. This includes a very significant corpus of architectural monuments and sites with ages ranging from the pre-pottery Neolithic (7,000 BC) period to the Islamic era after AD 638.

Such complexity and variety present serious, albeit interesting, challenges to any conservationist. Added to that some loaded political and historical dimensions which are bound to influence policy makers. Jerusalem is an obvious example, and monuments which are revered by both Muslims and Jews is another. However, in this paper, 'Palestine' is assumed to cover the West Bank, including East Jerusalem and Gaza.

Despite the variety of historical monuments in Palestine the prevailing architectural character today, however, is more related to the Islamic era than any other historical period. Due to long periods of political conflicts, wars, and socio-economic disruptions, this distinct architectural heritage remains largely undocumented systematically and, furthermore, has been seriously undermined by neglect, physical destruction, and insensitive modern urban development. With the exception of Jerusalem, perhaps, most towns and villages in Gaza and the West Bank have suffered considerable disruption in their historic physical fabric.

This paper attempts to identify the different typologies and essential characteristics of urban and rural architectural traditions in Palestine. It aims to highlight the need to conserve and enhance this unique heritage by proposing certain policies and measures to act as a policy framework for decision makers. The main objective is not only to conserve what remains of this heritage but also to ensure a definite cultural continuity with the past through contemporary Palestinian architecture. It is deemed here that such policies and measures should not only deal with conserving historical cores of Palestinian towns and villages but must also deal with the concomitant question of coming major reconstruction and infill projects.

Modern housing projects and public buildings should be designed to reflect the cultural and national aspirations of the newly emerging Palestinian state. Consequently, its is strongly believed, that it is imperative to examine those architectural qualities and characteristics which ensure some link with tradition and establish a certain architectural vocabulary for Palestinian identity.

It is an indisputable fact that sensitively designed projects that attempt to reflect Palestinian socio-cultural traditions would have an important impact on Palestinian society and would, almost certainly, help to generate a great sense of belonging and national pride. This, it may be argued, is the political dimension of this cultural and architectural exercise.

ARCHITECTURAL TYPOLOGIES AND CHARACTERISTICS

As was stressed earlier, the dominant architectural character of Palestine today is Islamic. Specifically, however, it is generally recognised that Palestinian architectural falls within the much broader tradition of the 'Sham' region which covers Syria, Lebanon, Palestine and Jordan.

It is proposed here, even more specifically, that the prevailing architectural character may be attributed to the latter Islamic periods from the Ayyubids (1187–1250), Bahrite Mamlukes (1250–1382) and Burjite Mamlukes (1382–1517) to the Ottoman period (1517–1918).

These historical periods, which spanned over 700 years, helped shape the essential architectural character of Palestine. Notwithstanding the stylistic variations of these periods – e.g. differing shapes of architectural elements such as arches, columns, domes, minarets, decorative treatments, etc. – building types and architectural planning remained essentially unaltered. This was due to the strong local building tradition and its momentum which naturally tended to resist typological changes but would incorporate or assimilate stylistic influences more readily. In this context, rural architecture, perhaps universally, tends to be more conservative against assimilating such changes than in major urban centres.

Apart from historical and cultural influences, Palestinian architecture was strongly influenced by geographical factors such as climate and topography. The Mediterranean climate, which is characterised by hot summers and temperate winters, clearly affected architectural planning. Thermal insulation, solar orientation, and introversion became very important considerations. Consequently, the inward-looking courtyard building type became almost a standard practice in Palestine and elsewhere in the region.

Similarly, small windows and sheltered openings within thick walls became essential architectural elements.

Consequently, in order to minimise solar exposure and provide thermal comfort, Palestinian architecture developed the vocabulary of the cubic form with solid walls pierced by small openings.

This image of 'wall architecture' or the 'solid cube' was reinforced by the widespread use of local stone. Stone construction and building techniques, a tradition in Palestine that goes back thousands of years, have obvious physical and logical implications on the architectural image. Stone gives solidity, a sense of stability and endurance. It also has a definite aesthetic appeal. For this reason, it would be difficult to imagine a so-called 'Palestinian' building without the use of stone.

While construction techniques are beyond the scope of this paper, it is important to mention here, however, that this 'solid cube' image was often tempered by the frequent use of vaults and domes. Round and pointed arches, decorative elements, and the use of alternate stone courses of differing colours (ablaq) also helped to break the rigid recti-linear geometry of traditional architecture.

Another factor which gave Palestinian architecture a dynamic interplay of form and visual perspective was topography. The vast majority of the West Bank is comprised of mountainous and hilly areas. Consequently, most villages and towns are built up undulating slopes. This topography meant that such human settlements were visually exposed more dramati-cally and one could 'read' their physical structure more easily as every individual house or building can be seen clearly within the overall fabric of the settlement. Thus, the rectilinear and cubic forms of the mass of buildings were, again, tempered by the contrasting curves of the natural environment.

The nature of this topography, together with the necessity to preserve as much land as possible for agriculture, resulted in a relatively dense building fabric composed mainly of cube-like houses stepping down the sloping hills. Important buildings or monuments, such as mosques or churches, often occupied commanding locations and their presence enhanced by their size and vertical features such as domes, minarets, or towers. Pedestrian access to the various residential quarters (mahallas) was provided by narrow alleyways running along contour lines. Steps, usually constructed in stone, ran against the slopes and provided the main pedestrian spinal pathways down to the central areas or travel routes.

Because houses were mostly built on slopes, often with relatively steep inclinations ranging from 10 per cent to 50 per cent, it became necessary for builders to establish plateaus of 'cut and fill.' This, in turn, meant the possibility of several levels in the section of each house and obviously affected its overall configuration. The occurrence of a multiplicity of levels in architecture meant a more dynamic section and more stimulating visual angles and perspectives from within.

Traditional buildings in Palestine generally follow the same typology and taxonomy of their counterparts in the Arab world. These types may be grouped under the following classifications which are based on the use of buildings:

A. *Residential*
Town House (Beit or Bayt)
Palace (Qasr)
Village House

B. *Religious*
Mosque (Masjid); Friday mosque (Jami)
School (Madrasa)
Shrines, tombs, and mausolea (Turba, Dharihs and Maqams)
Cemeteries (Maqabir)
Hospices (Takiyya [also Zawiya or Khanaqa])
Church (Kanisa)
Monastery (Deir)

C. *Commercial*
Shops (Dukans)
Markets (Suqs – [both open-air and covered])
Inns (Khans)

D. *Health*
Hospitals (Mashfa, Dour Al-Shafa')
Public baths (Hammams)

E. *Civic*
Serais (Government Centre)
Municipality (Baladiya)
Courts (Mahkama, Mahakim)

F. *Military and Communication*
Citadel (Qala'a)
Camp (Mu'askar)
Walls and gates
Bridges (Qanatir, Jissour)
Ports (Mina, Mawani')
Towers (Burj, Abraj)
Caravanserais

G. *Industrial Workshops (Mashaghil)*
Foundries (Masani')
(Soap-making – 'Masbana')Presses (Olive oil – 'Ma'sara')

It must be emphasised, however, that these typologies are broad divisions and do not, therefore, strictly apply. Traditional Islamic architecture is characterised by its adoption of a multi-functional plan with inherent flexible possibilities for change and expansion. This is particularly true of the court-yard plan type which has been employed for mosques, madrasas, khans, hospitals and houses.

With the advent of modernisation in Palestine in the 19th Century, new building types began to appear and some traditional types began to fade away. The rapid process of modernisation, which often meant Westernisation, caused fundamental changes in the socio-economic struc-ture of society and, consequently, in architectural design and typology.

The introvert courtyard plan type began to be replaced by the extrovert, closed type, with the widespread use of new building materials.

Techniques such as reinforced concrete, cement blocks, glass, and metal windows and doors, traditional typologies underwent structural changes and thereby lost their historical identity and architectural cues. However, religious buildings, being conservative in nature, resisted to some extent, these structural changes but readily adopted new technologies with obvious disregard to their associated aesthetic implications and values.

To what extent is the question of typology relevant to the issue of reconstruction in Palestine? Understanding historical typography is extremely important if traditional buildings or urban cores are to be conserved and revitalised. Preserving the architectural heritage should be regarded as one of the national priorities by the Palestinian state. These historical monuments would serve as the much needed referential anchorages for a society aspiring nation-hood. They would also serve as the inspirational fonts for contemporary Palestinian architecture.

Mass housing projects and public buildings are expected to constitute the bulk of architectural work in rural and urban reconstruction in Palestine. Traditional architecture can form the bases and lessons from which architects should develop their designs and historical references.

ARCHITECTURAL HERITAGE

The concept of 'architectural heritage' is used to include all immovable cultural property in Palestine. It is classified into the following four components:

1) Monuments or individual buildings of outstanding architectural and/ or historical interest.
   Examples: The Dome of the Rock; Al-Aqsa Mosque; the Church of the Holy Sepulchre; Ashrafiya Madrasa; Suq Al-Qattanin; the walls and gates of Jerusalem; the Church of Nativity in Bethlehem; Al-Haram Al-Ibrahimi in Hebron; and the main mosque in Nablus.
2) Urban cores, or groups, of buildings of architectural and/or historical interest.
   Examples: The old cores of the cities of Jerusalem, Hebron, Nablus, Bethlehem, Ramallah, Mar Saba, Tulkarem, Jenin and Gaza.
3) Rural settlements and villages of architectural and/or historical, scenic interest.
   Examples: Deir Ghassaneh; Yatta (near Hebron); Artas; Ebwein (near Ramallah); Ras Karkar; Abboud; Silwan (near Jerusalem); Halhul (near Hebron); and Abu Ghosh.
4) Archaeological sites and ruins.

Examples: (Urban and rural locations) Jerusalem; Jericho: Qumran; Mar Saba; Monaster; Ein Gedi; Hebron; Herodion and Bethlehem.

Published literature dealing with the architectural heritage of Palestine is surprisingly scarce. Not since the major survey of Palestine conducted by Conder and Kitchener in 1881 has there been any systematic documentation covering the West Bank and Gaza. Arab writers, geographers, and historians, have not dealt with the subject systematically. While foreign writers put more emphasis on Biblical archaeology, very little research has been carried out on the historical cores of Palestinian towns and villages.

The absence of a national inventory of architectural heritage in Palestine is a serious defect which must be addressed promptly. Some surveys have been conducted by students of architecture in Bir Zeit and Najah Universities, but they remain limited in scope and unpublished. The preparation of such an inventory should be regarded as a priority by the Palestinian authorities.

It would require several years of systematic and painstaking work by a relatively large team of technical experts. This national inventory is a fundamental step for the protection of architectural heritage.

Long periods of neglect and official disregard by local municipalities and the Israeli authorities resulted in the destruction of a significant number of important sites and monuments. Historic cores of Palestinian towns have been allowed to decay and largely abandoned by their original inhabitants (Burgoyne, 1987). Furthermore, with the absence of conservation plans and listing procedures of buildings of architectural or historic interest, these historic cores, with the exception of Jerusalem, were physically disrupted by insensitive modern development.

Numerous old houses, mosques, suqs, khans and churches were demolished and replaced by modern equivalents or commercial buildings, resulting in the destruction of the historical character of these areas. The same applies to hundreds of villages scattered throughout the West Bank and Gaza.

As for archaeological sites, those which are located in a relatively remote or inaccessible areas escaped destruction. However, other sites have been seriously damaged by modern development, or their physical context disrupted (Pearlman and Yannai, 1985).

Due to the lack of surveys and statistics, it is not exactly known how much of this architectural heritage has been lost during this century. However, it is not unreasonable to conjecture that the loss exceeds 50 per cent of the traditional fabric (Fethi, 1977). This has been the case in other Arab cities such as Cairo, Baghdad and Damascus. What remains of this heritage, therefore, should be regarded as a scarce and as an unrenewable national resource which must be safeguarded for future generations.

The preparation of a national inventory is only a first step. It must be followed quickly by listing the various components of architectural heritage. Listing or grading monuments, buildings and sites is necessary to classify cultural property according to its value. Most countries adopt listing systems in order to identify priorities for restoration and protection.

Palestinian authorities in charge of architectural heritage should adopt a simple, two-tier system based on the following categories:

Grade 1: Outstanding monuments, buildings, and sites, which possess national and/or international cultural value. Such items must not be at all changed or demolished.
Examples: The Dome of the Rock, Aqsa Mosque, the Church of the Holy Sepulchre, etc.

Grade 2: Buildings, groups of buildings, historic cores of towns and villages of architectural or historic interest. Every effort should be made to protect them, but some change and development is allowed. Some may be demolished if necessary.

Conserving the national cultural heritage requires action on a national scale.

Effective protection cannot be achieved without the necessary technical, administrative, financial and legal mechanisms. One key mechanism in this context is town planning and urban design.

In order to achieve the protection of historic cores of Palestinian towns, villages and archaeological sites, listed items of cultural property must be identified on specially prepared geographical maps. These maps should be made available to all agencies concerned with cultural resource management. Such agencies should include the Department of Antiquities, Ministries of Planning, Municipalities, Awqaf, Public Works, Communication, Agriculture, and any other official organisations which deal with large-scale projects.

In the past seven years, the Department of Antiquities in Jordan with technical assistance from the American Centre of Oriental Research (ACOR) have been developing a programme for the management of cultural resources (Palumbo et al, 1993). This included the preparation of a national survey and register of Jordan's heritage sites based on a computerised inventory of known sites called JADIS (i.e. the Jordan Archaeological Database Information System).

Hopefully, once the system is complete, it can serve as an effective tool for co-ordination between governmental and private agencies involved in development. Such a system should be initiated in Palestine because it represents the most systematic method to establish a national inventory of heritage.

When items of cultural heritage are clearly identified on geographic maps and town maps, town planners, architects, and archaeologists, would then be able to protect these items in their development maps or action plans. Otherwise, in the absence of such information these development plans would almost certainly result in the loss of heritage items.

It follows that in order to achieve effective co-ordination between different agencies based on a systematic information system a central organisational structure is needed for Palestine. It may be called the National Council of Heritage in Palestine (NCHP). It would act as the consultative and co-ordinating body for matters related to the protection of cultural heritage in Palestine.

Such national councils or commissions already exist in most countries which take their cultural resources seriously. In the United kingdom, for example, the Royal Fine Art Commission is a consultative body made of a selected number of specialists, artists, architects, and others, who consider and examine major issues and projects of art and architecture in the country and assess their environmental and aesthetic impact before implementation.

This kind of mechanism is designed to provide safeguards against decisions often made by politicians or administrators with certain political or financial interests. The cultural resources of a nation cannot be left to the mercy or whims of certain individuals with power. Local heritage societies or committees in every town and village should be set up and encouraged to play an active role in matters related to conserving the cultural property in their area. Public participation and pressure groups are an important dimension in the democratic process and in nation-building.

The criteria for listing buildings and grading them have always been controversial issues. Several Arab countries such as Iraq, Syria and Jordan set the date of AD 1700 as the listing line. This leaves all buildings between 1700 and, say, 1930 unqualified for protection unless explicitly designated as such. As a result of the laws of antiquities in these countries, numerous buildings of outstanding architectural or historic interest have been lost. Many houses and buildings built during the 1920s have significant architectural interest and, therefore, should be protected by law.

Another danger which must be pointed out is the tendency in most Arab countries to emphasis single monuments and not areas or groups of buildings. This has been the case despite the fact that Islamic historic cores (madinas) are characterised by a dense, organic structure which functions as a whole entity and not as a total of individual buildings. A similar situation exists in the old cores of the cities of Jerusalem, Hebron and Nablus. These historic areas must be protected as totalities. Planning measures and legislation should be instituted to ensure the survival of their overall historic and architectural character.

Alternatively, a 'Law of Antiquities' for Palestine should refer not only to single monuments but also to the protection, and listing, of groups of buildings and entire areas of cultural interest. Such areas may be designated 'Conservation Areas' and be clearly marked on town planning and urban design maps. Explanatory regulations must be followed in order to create the necessary mechanisms for development controls within these areas. These controls should include listed buildings and their grades, building use, materials, heights, and architectural vocabularies of building facades and character of urban elements such as alleyways, streets and squares.

Such 'infill' policies and controls of modern development within conservation areas have often helped generate positive architectural designs witch are sympathetic to the character of these areas. In Europe and elsewhere, they helped the emergence of what is now referred to as 'Regionalist Style'. For Palestine, such infill policies would hopefully not only maintain the historic character of towns, but also help to produce a Palestinian 'Regionalist' architecture.

If these historic areas are left to the mercy of developers, speculators, and whimsical architects and politicians, their character could be lost immediately. It is only through promulgating such regulations that architects and others are forced to think more sympathetically towards history and its legacy of cultural property.

Furthermore, restoration work of listed buildings or monuments within these areas would also generate and resuscitate traditional building skills and crafts now threatened by extinction. Indeed, one cannot feasibly speak of evolving a new regionalist architecture for Palestine without the availability of such skills. The establishment of a national training centre for the revival of traditional crafts of all kinds is a very important requirement for reinforcing Palestinian identity and nationhood.

CONTEMPORARY PALESTINIAN ARCHITECTURE

The quality of Palestinian architecture slumped markedly after the rapid invasion of Western building technology and the influence of the 'Modern Movement' after the 1920s. Traditional architecture suddenly, and abruptly, ended. Similar to what happened in other parts of the Arab world, it was replaced by what became known as the 'International Style,' with its familiar ideology of rejecting local particularity in favour of universality (Kroyanker, 1994).

In addition, the turbulent years that followed Arab-Israeli wars and the Israeli occupation of the West Bank and Gaza in 1967, made it almost impossible for any sort of a revival of a specifically Palestinian architecture. Most Palestinian architects who studied in Egypt or in the West did not return to work in their homeland. They preferred to work in the Gulf States, Saudi Arabia or Jordan.

Consequently, one cannot refer to any sort of distinguished architecture in Palestine today. The overwhelming majority of buildings designed and executed since the 1950s do not even qualify as architecture. Most building was done for purely commercial or utilitarian reasons. One cannot expect creative architecture to emerge under the repressive conditions of a military occupation.

Similarly, under such difficult conditions the two Palestinian schools of architecture in Nablus and Bir Zeit Universities in the West Bank could not have been expected to function properly as they were very frequently shut down by Israeli authorities.

However, it must be conceded that under such conditions one might have expected these two schools to encourage, or to emphasise, the importance of Palestinian identity in architecture. Nevertheless, there is no clear evidence that such an attempt was made.

Consequently, one can assume that a new contemporary Palestinian architecture needs to be created or re-invented.

Such an architecture, however, cannot be elaborated in steps or practical measures. It may be explained ideologically in broad terms or strategies and then left to the creative resourcefulness of Palestinian architects to formulate their own interpretations. Therefore, and in very broad terms, this new Palestinian architecture must fall within the following parameters:

- It has to be referenced to the Islamic cultural and historical heritage of Palestine;
- Such 'historicism' should be a re-interpretative and creative process and not a literal 'revivalist' one;
- This reinterpretation of history in the architectural process is positively regarded as a necessary tool for contemporaneity;
- It should deal with the prevailing climatic conditions spatially as well as materially (in this context the use of stone, even for facing, should be definitely encouraged, or even enforced in historic areas (Process Architecture, 44); and, finally,
- In housing projects, a policy of high-density, low-rise designs are adopted and encouraged.

The lack of any creative contemporary architectural examples in Palestine leads one to refer to interesting ones elsewhere in the region. Architects like Rasem Badran, Jafar Tukan and Bilal Hamad, all of whom are Palestinian in origin, have succeeded in their own way to formulate a contemporary form of identifiable Arab architecture.

Rasem Badran's examples include: workers' housing in Fuhais near

Amman (completed in 1982); a housing project for Queen Aliya Airport in Amman; a specialist hospital in Amman (completed in 1994); Abu Ghueillah housing (designed in 1979); the design for the U.A.E Embassy in Amman (1990); the winning design for Albayt Foundation (1985); and Qasr Al-Hokum Complex in Riyadh (completed in 1994).

Jafar Tukan's examples include: A Design for Albayt Foundation (1985); the winning design for the U.A.E Embassy in Amman (1990); a design for the headquarters of the organisation of Islamic Capitals and Cities in Jeddah; the Jubilee School in Amman; and S.O.S villages in Amman and Aqaba.

Bilal Hamad's examples include: Al Ribat Housing complex in Amman (completed in 1985); competition designs for pharmacists' housing in Amman; and designs for engineers' housing in Irbid, Jordan.

Noteworthy examples in Jerusalem include designs by Mills for Bab Hutta (referred to in the Harvard Jerusalem Studio conducted by the Massachusetts Institute of Technology in 1986) (Safadie, 1985).

These above-mentioned examples have been chosen to illustrate how some architects have succeeded in creating contemporary architecture based on a sensitive re-interpretation of architectural traditions. Their works could serve as an inspiration for young Palestinian architects.

Architects distinguished for their creative regional work include Rifat Chadirji, Makiya, Qahtan Awni (Iraq); Hassan Fathy, Al-Wakil, Kafrawi (Egypt), Ali Shuaibi (Saudi Arabia), Ben Miled (Tunisia) and Abdelslem Faraoui (Morocco). All of these architects have emphasised the importance of regional and historic dimensions in contemporary Arab architecture. They have developed new ways of relating the past with the present and pointed out the way for the future.

In conclusion, it must be stressed that a new Palestinian architecture cannot be created by legislation or design guidelines. Such a rebirth requires a long time of conscious experimentation and testing, based on a genuine belief in the spiritual need for cultural identity in our physical environment.

BIBLIOGRAPHY

Amiry, S. and V. Tamari, 1980, **The Palestinian Village Home**, British Museum.

Burgoyne, M., 1987, **Proposals for the Conservation of the Old City of Nablus**, Report submitted to the Nablus Municipality, The British Council.

Conder, C.R. and H. Kitchener, 1881, **The Survey of Western Palestine**, (1970 re-edition, 4 vols.), Kadem Publishing, Jerusalem.

Fethi, Ihsan, 1977, **Urban Conservation in Iraq**, 3 vols., Unpublished Ph.D diss., 3 vols., Sheffield University, U.K.

Kiraity, Josef, 1984, *In a Search for Identity*, **Process Architecture, Issue on Contemporary Israeli Architecture**, 44, pp. 8 to 9, Tokyo.

Kroyanker, David, 1944, *Affluent Arab Neighborhoods,* **Jerusalem Architecture**, pp. 101 to 167, Tauris Parke Books, London.

Levin, Michael, 1984, M*odern Architecture in Jerusalem; The Use of Stone – Tradition and Innovation,* **Process Architecture, Issue on Contemporary Architecture**, 44, pp. 10–17.

Palumbo, G. et al., November, 1993, **Cultural Resource Management (CRM) in Jordan**, Paper submitted to the Symposium on Architectural Conservation in Jordan and the Arab World, University of Jordan.

Pearlman, M. and Y. Yannai, 1985, **Historical Sites in Israel**, Chartwell Book, New Jersey.

Safadie, M., 1985, **The Harvard Jerusalem Studio**, MIT Press, Cambridge, Massachusetts.

HOUSING ALTERNATIVES: LESSONS FROM EXPERIENCE

Nabeel Hamdi

'A healthy, growing society will always have a housing problem. If I ever met a society that claimed to have solved all its housing problems, I would look at it with great suspicion and conclude that it must be in a worrying state of decline.'

Otto Koenigsberger (*Intentions of Housing Policy Alternatives*, 1987)

ABSTRACT

While the principle that the demand for affordable and socially appropriate housing should be satisfied adequately and sustainably is generally agreed, a consensus on how this should be achieved has not been reached. Instead, the debate has polarised into two schools of thought – the 'providers' and the 'supporters.'

However, other options also exist. Sites-and-services projects, which represented a watershed change in policy and which could link public housing and urban upgrading as well as acting as a bridge between 'providers' and the 'supporters,' marked the beginning of a new process aimed at involving people in producing their own housing.

Urban upgrading programmes are another alternative approach based on human need and resourcefulness, as well as local initiative, and were supported by the World Bank and other agencies in the 1970s. Such programmes today tend to be achieved incrementally through a series of small-scale projects coupled with strategic policy level interventions and the promotion of appropriate technology and local enterprise.

This paper looks at the evolution of these schools of thought and at the issues and strategies surrounding urban upgrading and improvement. An evaluation is made of the pros and cons of each approach, or combination of approaches. The importance of the neighbourhood involved – whether it is socially and politically cohesive or diffuse – is also discussed.

It is argued that the implications of an upgrading approach are pro-

405

found and that they lead to significant changes in the way architecture and planning are viewed and in the conduct of the professional involved. Finally, it is recommended that realism, based on past experience, be emphasised in the reconstruction and development of Palestine.

THE ISSUES: AFFORDABLE AND APPROPRIATE HOUSING

The evolution of housing policy has witnessed many brave attempts to satisfy adequately and sustainably the demand for affordable and socially appropriate housing. However, while agreement is common on the principle, precise definitions of what this entails in practice have varied considerably.

Debates within housing circles have examined which sectors, public or private, formal or informal, are best at delivering housing in sufficient quantity to make a difference; whether housing standards should be lowered, increased or abandoned altogether; whether the participation of communities or self-help makes any difference to productivity, user satisfaction, economies in building, or management efficiency; which of sites and services, public housing, slum upgrading, guided development or planned development are most appropriate and to whom; whether rent controls, or development controls, private ownership or co-operative ownership, partial subsidies or no subsidies have worked to control speculation, generate revenue, ensure affordability, create jobs and provide better and more housing.

Consensus has been difficult to reach. Instead, the debate has polarised into two schools of thought which can be described as 'providers' on the one hand, and 'supporters' on the other (Hamdi, 1991). These are compared in Table 1.

The first and more orthodox school promotes government and private developers as effective principal *providers* of houses. The second, alternative school of thought, recognises the important role played by communities, non-governmental organisations (NGOs) and small, informal private enterprises in housing production.

The second school promotes the management of resources (rather than the building of houses) as a key factor in reducing housing deficits and includes the proper management of land, labour, skills, services, utilities, materials and money. It also recognises the importance of partnerships between formal and informal housing markets, private enterprise and public authority, local organisations and central administration and between large-scale and small-scale producers.

Together, the two schools provide a basis for policy formulation and an agenda for action. However, each school can be distinguished by what it advocates in terms of ideals, methods and practices, the level of centralisation (of decisions, resources and production); the relative

Table 1 Theories of Practice: Key Characteristics.

Providing	Support
Objectives	
• Build houses for people	• Allocate resources for people to organise their own house building
• Use house building to fuel economy	• Use the economy to fuel house building
• Centralise resources to facilitate management and control standards	• Decentralise resources to support local enterprise and home building
• Build organisations that facilitate central initiatives	• Build regulations to support and give structure to local initiatives
• Consolidate and centralise building production	• Fragment building production and support small builders
• Sectoralise development activities for ease of management, single-function projects	• Integrate development activities and link housing to larger urban systems of employment and production
Methods	
• Build large projects to achieve scale	• Build programs and allocate resources for many small projects
• Manufacture housing to speed production	• Manage resources to increase volume
• Build fast by building instantly	• Build fast by building incrementally
• Standardise project and operations	• Promote variety, improvisation, infill, sites and services
• Tell what to do	• Tell how to find out what to do, then how to find out how to do it
Products/Component	
• Projects	• Interventions
• Behaviourally deterministic planning	• Technical aid centres
• Industrialised building systems	• Training
• Master plan	• Housing options and loan packages
	• Guidebooks, guidelines, tools and methods
	• Appropriate technologies
	• Structure plans
Key Actors	
• Consultants	• Families
• Government agencies	• Community groups, tenant organisations,
	• non-governmental organisations
• Funders	• Non-profit and voluntary organisations
• Large contractors/developers	• Government agencies
	• Small contractors
	• Funders
	• Formal and informal private community developers
	• Consultants

dependency on international development aid and technology transfer and by the extent to which it advocates involvement with communities and individual families. Each school provides opportunities as well as constraints.

The two schools also differ in the type of housing processes they promote and the products which are delivered: direct construction in the case of the first school; housing improvement or slum upgrading in the case of the second. Sites and service projects provide a bridge between the two.

Providers: The Orthodox School

In an historical perspective, it is worth remembering that few, if any, public responses to poor housing conditions have been benevolent. The provision of public housing has primarily intended to appease the poor, gain political votes, create jobs and fuel the economy. Housing policy which promoted public housing has been more an instrument of political and social reform in response to public health and public strife, than a way of increasing the supply of housing.

Historically, as well as now, these policies, while successful in isolated cases, have failed to provide adequate numbers of houses for many reasons. These include their adherence to high standards of space, construction and utilities and their consequent prohibitively high cost of production. These policies direct resources away from other sectors of industry and are difficult to maintain and administer over the long term.

Even when production was at capacity, this kind of housing fell largely into the hands of middle-income families who could afford to pay. The dilemma can be explained in various ways, not least in the tacit belief that when resources are scarce and the urgency acute, then public sector building is in itself an effective and speedy provider of houses. Various proposals are offered to support this assumption. For example, house construction can be accelerated and the volume of production increased by 'rationalising' industry and the construction process itself.

These were the ideas promoted by contractors world-wide, most of whom were in search of new markets overseas for products and services – developed mostly in northern countries. This thinking about the means of increasing production has tended to favour large contractors as well as prefabrication, systems building, and the industrial mass production of standard building components.

Typically, these processes demand large plants, sophisticated organis-ation, large amounts of up-front capital and large markets to guarantee economies of scale – none of which are available, even in the richest of developing countries. Furthermore, these processes are dominated by a professional elite of international consultants – architects, planners and engineers – whose livelihood is dependent on a flourishing 'housing problems industry' at the expense of local professionals and informal producers.

'Of the $12 billion or so which goes each year to buy advice, training and project design, over 90% is spent [by countries] on foreign consultants' (The Economist, 7 May, 1994). Their approach to problem solving is to 'bring in the consultants, establish goals, sort out priorities, put a figure and time limit to the job and then throw in the task force'.

This group of advocates prefers single function projects coupled with, preferably, lots of technology transfer to stimulate private sector investment, visibly raise public expectations for a better future, and transfer significant benefit back to the donor countries. Their spatial plans are behaviourally deterministic, i.e. they have designated areas for recreation, commerce, housing, etc. and, in compliance with orthodox development paradigms, represent 'end states.' In other words, this school advocates pre-set *goals* with targets, deadlines and completion dates rather than development *processes.*

Such rationalised housing concentrated resources in sectors of production which could be held accountable to governments and donors and from which informal production was excluded. This kind of thinking has led to types of housing which are designed according to tightly defined, preordained standards. They represent a careful balance of technical feasibility, building regulations and planning control to enable supply, quality and cost to be accurately controlled.

These are the very things which have raised costs beyond the reach of the poor majority and which have alienated public participation. They do little to improve the condition of the poor communities – indeed it has, more often, had quite the opposite effect.

Strassman (1975) pointed out, for example, that,

> 'Once construction enterprises exist, the annual volume of building depends less on a rapid rate of output from each enterprise, than on the volume of resources devoted to building . . . If dwellings are expensive and built with imported moulds and cranes as they usually are in the developing world, a country may not be able to afford to build at less volume, or to close the housing deficit very fast.'

As a result, the elimination of housing shortages quickly constitutes an economic policy question, not a technical problem. As Strassman went on to observe, 'Within a radius of about 50 kilometres of the component factory, 1,000 to 8,000 almost identical dwelling units must have a market over five years, depending on the type of Industrial Systems Building (ISB), or the investment will be a waste.'

Deficits of adequate shelter grow rather than diminish – not just because not enough houses are produced or technologies fail – but because expectations rise; because we do not allow adequately for reductions in household size; because we fail to uncover concealed households that come into being as soon as housing is available; because the age of marriage becomes unexpectedly lower; because there are more people living as independent households for a longer period; because of unpredicted migration to cities; because of political crises, natural disasters and so on.

As Koenigsberger (1987) noted,

'In the late '50s and early '60s, practically all public housing policies, whether urban or rural, ran out of steam. Except for the island city states of Singapore and Hong Kong, there was no country or city that could hope to produce public housing in sufficient numbers to cope with a steadily worsening situation.'

Supporters: The Alternative School

The alternative school of thought argues that the management of resources is critical to increasing the supply of housing. Rather than worry about the means of building production, it maintains that it may be better for governments to improve the means by which hundreds of small builders, manufacturers and suppliers, both formal and informal, gain access to land, essential building materials, cheap credit, better utilities, larger markets, and easier transportation.

For the alternative school, deciding strategic interventions is far more crucial to building projects. Building houses, whether through government or formal market channels, while arguably effective in the short term, has little to do with solving housing problems in the longer term (Hamdi, 1991).

In other words, this school feels that the large-scale production of houses can best be achieved by increasing the participation of small builders and ordinary people; by enlarging their capacity to deliver houses, services, and even some utilities located close to their market; and, in this context, by the use of what are called 'appropriate technologies.' These technologies emphasise small-scale, indigenous and locally sustainable means of production.

The emphasis here is on low capital costs, local materials, small building enterprises, collective rather than individual effort, user control and economic self-sufficiency. All this contrasts starkly with big business and with the large capital investments which support technology transfer and Western know-how.

As Ovitt (1989) has pointed out,

'The perpetuation of dependency inherent in technology transfer allows bankers, engineers and business people – the modern conquistadors – to ensure continued control of developing nations while at the same time presenting themselves as altruists. Their assistance is usually channelled through elite institutions in the underdeveloped countries, thereby creating a development bureaucracy that is narrowly controlled, urban-based and dependent.'

For the orthodox school of 'providers,' fragmentation gauges the weakness of the building industry as evidenced in both formal and informal markets in developed and developing countries. Yet others, faced with such inevitable fine-grained diversity, look upon it opportunistically as necessary to efficiency, quantity and cost-effective production, rather than its antithesis.

A fragmented, rather than consolidated, building industry is better equipped to respond to market demands and is more resilient to fluctuations in building activity (as has been the case throughout history). Rather than controlling standards or quality, or normalising production processes, the more diversity built into the system in quality and cost, the more likely it is that needs and budgets will be met. Small builders with low overheads and very little physical plant can adjust their workloads far more flexibly that can their industrialised counterparts. This level of diversity is rarely achievable at affordable costs through formal channels.

In contrast to the instant delivery of houses, scaling up the supply of housing without risking bankruptcy and without displacing entire populations means building incrementally, precisely as people in informal developments do. It means cultivating an environment in which housing, small businesses, and communities will grow, consolidate, and change and where production and building can provide opportunities for employment, for the accumulation of wealth and for improvements in health. For the alternative school, housing becomes an integral part of a larger system of urban development, not a sectorally defined activity (Hamdi, 1991).

THE OPTIONS

Sites-and-Services Projects

Sites-and-services projects represent a watershed change in policy and could form a 'bridge' between public housing and urban upgrading, as well as a link between the 'providers' and the 'supporters.' These have been coupled with various self-help and aided self-help programmes, i.e. the beginning of a formal thought process aimed at involving people producing their own housing. In sites and services projects, investments are focused on delivering land, services, utilities and housing loans.

However, these projects demand high levels of investment in infrastructure. This has been accompanied by the demand which lending agencies have placed on governments to recover their costs, and with the desire of governments to see these sites consolidated with permanent materials and in accordance with standards set by municipal authorities. As critics correctly argued, the resulting projects were in fact little more than public housing projects without the houses. Nevertheless, such sites-and-services projects did recognise, perhaps officially for the first time, that house building might better be achieved by people and small builders.

Moreover, the benefits of sites-and-services projects could not be identified confidently. Did they reach the lowest-income population? Were they cheaper to build and manage? Were they any more socially appropriate than their three-, four-, and five-storey walk-up counterparts? The World Bank's own evaluation of sites-and-services projects and upgrading is generally positive,

'The conclusions of the detailed evaluation have confirmed that the experiment embodied in the first generation of Bank-supported urban shelter projects has been remarkably successful. The validity of the progressive development model has been established.

'Self-help construction methods have been relatively efficient. The impacts of projects on the housing stock have been generally greater than anticipated. The projects have been affordable – and generally accessible – to the target populations.

'Those measurements which have been concluded indicate that the projects' impacts on the socio-economic conditions of participants have been in the directions expected. And, notably, the projects have not had negative impacts on expenditures for food and other basic necessities. Notwithstanding this general record of success, the projects have encountered some problems and produced some unexpected results. For example, most projects have experienced delays in implementation; materials and loan components have not been as successful as expected; support packages for small businesses have encountered problems; and two of the first three projects have experienced cost recovery problems.

'In addition, the use of family labour in construction has been less than expected. An analysis of projects' successes and shortcomings supports recommendations that future projects endeavour to push standards and costs still lower, include explicit provisions and opportunities for rental arrangements and incorporate credit provisions more nearly tailored to the needs of targeted families – about which we also know much more as a result of this programme (Keane and Parris, 1982).

Despite the Bank's recommendations, criticism of sites-and-services projects grew as they were completed and as their impacts were measured. Architects and planners were worried by their technically rational design emphasis and their use of co-efficients of efficiency as the sole determinants of design decisions. These projects lacked art and lacked design as an artistic endeavour. They more or less followed the international style, ignorant of context and resentful of culture.

Others argued that these projects required the same level of planning as public housing projects, that they displaced people who depended for their work on inner cities to the periphery of cities, that the cost of their administration was high, and that they would polarise classes and present far fewer economic opportunities than in the mixed economies of informal settlements (Peattie, 1982).

Families would sell out when they had finished building and would return to their shanties. There were few guarantees that people would repay their loans, and this made them unattractive to private loan institutions. In this sense, these projects favoured people with steady incomes, which most poor do not have.

In short, these projects would fail to reach those most in need unless governments continued their heavy subsidies for land and infrastructure. However, this was something governments could not afford to sustain (Hamdi, 1991).

Because they relied heavily on self-help construction, these projects were also criticised as being exploitative of labour. Some argued that the lowered housing costs made possible by self-help benefited capitalists rather than workers because it provided the opportunity to lower wages and therefore increase the extraction of surplus value (Burgess, 1982)

Urban Upgrading and Community Participation

The third and currently valued alternative to both direct construction and sites-and-services (although sometimes inclusive of both schools) falls dominantly within the paradigm of the second school of thought: that in order to increase the supply of affordable, appropriate housing, and in ways which are sustainable, governments should devise policies which manage resources to support local people and informal enterprises to enable them to provide for themselves.

This alternative approach emphasises upgrading and is based on human need and resourcefulness, dominated by local initiative rather than outside experts and industry. It is set in the context of an alternative definition of 'development,' which argues for reduced dependency relationships, for the empowerment of communities, for self-reliance and self-fulfilment.

Under this model, there are no 'front-runners' to be followed: people are not the *objects* but the *subjects* of development. International aid and co-operation, including experts and the transfer of know-how and technical assistance programmes can be a catalyst to these *endogenous* processes.

The ideas of this third, alternative 'school' have not been adopted quickly. They did become palatable, not so much because they were growing more acceptable, but rather because governments were running out of money and public confidence. At the same time, housing programmes were falling short of their targets because neither policies nor the institutions that provide houses and manage policies were effective in sustaining adequate supply.

In recognition of these changes, agencies such as the World Bank and UNDP changed their lending policies. Instead of making large transfers of financial resources to project building, the World Bank directed its funds more toward the reform of policies and institutions: to public administration, to local banks, and to providing technical assistance. Its terms of reference for borrowers encouraged programmes to be designed more on the basis of effective user demand and less on preconceived notions of adequate housing (Williams, 1984).

Upgrading was supported widely by the World Bank and others in the mid-1970s so that public authorities could 'restore formal control over land subdivision and house building processes, while seeking to mobilise the energies and resources of low-income groups for either the improvement or creation of shelter' (Global Report on Human Settlements, 1987).

Most upgrading programmes entailed the provision of loans for housing improvement, sanitation, electricity, water and drainage, the paving of streets and footpaths, the legalisation of tenure rights to land (a policy designed to control the growth of illegal settlements) and other provisions to improve community facilities such as schools, clinics, and community centres. A large number of projects involved land regularisation to establish legal boundaries to properties (as the basis for issuing titles) and to get services into these settlements.

In addition, most programmes (inevitably and out of necessity rather than desire) confronted the interests and demands of local residents. They were intensively participatory but also recognised what were often severe political constraints to empowerment. In this respect, 'all those directly responsible for implementation should be present and should freely and willingly contribute their ideas and knowledge.' (Chambers, 1993).

Current Upgrading Strategies and Prospects

While such programmes currently underway may be broad in scope, they are achieved incrementally through a series of small-scale 'additive' projects, coupled with strategic policy level interventions. Appropriate technologies and local enterprises are promoted; that is, enterprises which will not only get their materials, services and utilities from formal outlets, but which will also supply them. Therefore, linkages are established between formal and informal systems of production, between large producers and small manufacturers and between different kinds of technology.

Systems of production, purchasing and supply which link local markets with urban ones emerge. The multiplicity of large outlets, small manufacturers, and even pavement sellers offers variety in quality and in the price of goods and services. This contributes much needed flexibility to local entrepreneurs and families. All these activities stimulate productivity and employment in exactly the sector where they are most needed. Improvements to housing and small enterprises are helped by selective government interventions offering access to resources, cheap credit, variable servicing and training.

'Starting points' rather than 'end states' become the key concepts, as do *interventions* rather than *projects*. In all these respects, experts adopt a strategic role and act as catalysts, introducing the necessary methods and techniques, bringing experience from elsewhere, identifying further opportunities and possible courses of action, disseminating principles and removing barriers which get in the way of getting things done. This kind of planning is heavily reliant on local knowledge and skills in its preparation and implementation 'with preference for activities which are administration sparing rather than administration-intensive' (Chambers, 1993).

Urban upgrading is also dependent on building coalitions and fostering co-operation between government and non-government groups, between often competing government departments, between expatriate or outside experts and their local professional counterparts, and between community groups with sometimes differing vested interests, particularly early in the programme preparation. However, partnerships do not happen just because they are a good idea. Nor is it useful to talk in abstract ways about partnerships between sectors, such as private and public or formal and informal.

Usually participatory programmes happen if, and when, people and organisations are convinced that their interests will be better served with partnerships rather than without them. Many people, for example, who are accustomed to an informal way of life, may decide that co-operation with governments in formal planning will threaten their liberties and diminish their ability to act in the intuitive and spontaneous way they usually do. These issues are precisely what make improvement programmes institutionally complex and difficult to sustain.

As Lewin (1991) has pointed out,

'Continuous and prolonged participation, such as in the planning and implementations of integrated projects, the management of community facilities and services or loan and revolving funds, requires an institutional framework, voluntary and time-consuming management and solidarity or social consensus which contradict, or which are alien to, the experience horizon and informal mode of communication of the residents of squatter and other low-income settlements.'

Effective and operative partnerships begin with a discovery of common interest and subsequently with inducing a convergence of interests as a prelude to planning. Informally, these are processes that occur every day. According to McGill and Horton (1973),

'Individuals seeking information and action on their own problems converge with other individuals with similar needs for research and action ... The convergence of interest establishes a special phase of participant commitment and involvement which is continuously drawn upon and further developed as the process proceeds.'

The Issue of Neighbourhoods

In considering these issues, it may be relatively easy to mobilise interest, secure commitments, reach consensus, and involve people in neighbourhoods that are integrated or parochial. In these places, people already share a common view; there is social and political homogeneity; there are existing organisations to work with, albeit sometimes based on patronage with their own social hierarchy. Interventions in these kinds of neighbourhoods, with the potential to organise, will be in stark contrast to those that are diffuse, stepping-stones, transitory, or non-neighbourhoods, where communities may be territorially rather than socially defined.

Most new settlements, for example, are *diffuse* in the sense that they start with little or no community structure. Interventions are difficult here because initially it is not clear whose interests need to be served. In *stepping-stone communities*, planners face a different set of issues. In these places, people are transient, have no long-term commitment locally, and will probably move if dissatisfied rather than get involved.

Transitory neighbourhoods may be going through a class or ethnic turnover – from middle income to upper income, for example. There will be old-timers and newcomers, and their differences will be acute. In this context, how can differences be reconciled? Who is it one plans for?

The *non-neighbourhood* is most difficult for participatory planning and yet often in most need of collaborative action. They are often highly deprived socially, physically, and economically, devastated by new highways or recent conflict, with abandoned buildings and derelict sites, and where communication is weak and loyalty highly fragmented. Each of these differences in social and physical configurations demands methods and techniques tailored specifically to the circumstances.

These issues become even more complex when conducted in a politically volatile climate. They may be viewed with suspicion by local community leaders, who will suspect them as being set up by outsiders to expose local activists. Where project objectives do not match political ones, those who count will not get involved. This lack of proper representation can be a serious limitation to the planning process.

Sometimes, communities which feel vulnerable will be reluctant to express their concerns or to get involved for fear of reprisals or harassment. They may fall in line with the majority point of view. In these respects, the choice of appropriate technique is paramount and greater institutional control may be desirable.

In most cases, those who will be most reluctant to get involved in urban upgrading are likely to be the local professionals. This kind of work may lack the prestige and the rewards they had come to expect through their education as architects, engineers or planners. They may view this work as largely unglamorous, and unlikely to earn them a place in the annals of planning history.

They may also spend endless hours, evenings and week-ends in meetings trouble-shooting problems and negotiating alternative courses of action. Remuneration may be small, much smaller than that received by their international counterparts. Their working environment will likely be far worse than those working in offices, and some may even feel threatened working in slums and shanties.

Few projects will have conventional 'completion' dates, which will be unhelpful to conventional careers: it is not easy to compile a portfolio of projects or point to success. On top of it all, the local professionals will be under considerable peer pressure to demonstrate their creative individuality and to make good in a world that measures success in terms of professional status and prestige, usually counted in the amount of money earned, the size and location of their practice, the number of buildings built and the kind of people they know. It is unlikely that there will be much status earned, or people worth knowing, or building of architectural significance built in undertaking improvement programmes.

The implications of this approach are profound despite criticism that urban upgrading tends to serve the most able, physically and politically, and the most enterprising; that programmes are often overly planned; that their rate of cost recovery is far worse than sites-and-services projects; that they have failed to turn the tide of illegal occupations or, in fact in some cases have encouraged it. All of the established standards for design, all of the instruments of town planning, and all of the established work habits of planners, engineers and architects are brought into question. Professional freedoms that once enabled wide boulevards, housing pavilions set in wide open-spaces, garden cities and systems building are largely usurped (Hamdi, 1994).

In urban upgrading programmes, the professional becomes the 'enabler.' This new professional role demands values, methods and techniques, and training designed to serve the community as well as governments and funding agencies. Approximation and serendipity are today more the norm in this kind of work as the quest for scientific precision in modelling programmes is displaced in favour of informed intuition and in favour of getting things roughly right, or right enough to proceed.

Similarly, rapid and participatory appraisal methods displace market research and lengthy analysis. Furthermore, planning urban improvement incorporates into its processes those who are best at getting things done, and mostly without concern for a balanced or 'synchronised' programme, i.e. typically private and public sector entrepreneurs, squatters, private developers and even civil servants and public officials (Cook, 1979). Successful programmes have been small in scale, with short time horizons, where benefits can be immediately felt.

Chambers (1993) proposed several themes that are at the core of this new approach,

'The affirmation of individuals and their differences; a pluralist stance giving voice to individuals and groups so as to participate in decision making; knowledge and associated technology are seen as contextual in time and space, and so limited in their transferability; the future is recognised as uncertain and indeterminate with a sensitive dependence on current and contextual conditions.'

RECOMMENDATIONS: A NEW REALISM

These issues and lessons from experience lead us to a new realism, as summarised by Devas, Koenigsberger and others. Its relevance to Palestine needs careful consideration when making recommendations for reconstruction and development. Unless we moderate our expectations accordingly, there will be the usual disappointments and old mistakes will be repeated.

From experience, we can assume that:

• The urban population will grow inevitably;
• The form of cities will continue to be determined largely by the

decisions of individuals and private organisations rather than governments;

- There are limits on the ability of governments to intervene effectively in either housing provision or in wider urban systems, whether to regulate land development or to secure sufficient revenue through taxation or utility charges;
- Governments will continue to face resource constraints, particularly those which are in political transition or which are debt-laden or undergoing structural adjustment;
- The poor have a limited capacity to pay for services, utilities and housing, and that standards of services currently provided are therefore rarely affordable by the urban majority;
- Recovering costs from poor people often costs more than can ever be collected, and that this is one reason for the failure of revolving funds to sustain programmes, whether in housing or other sectors;
- Planning processes, for housing, infrastructure and urban improvement cannot be tidy or linear following the orthodox survey-plan-action sequence; and
- Most urban institutions, including housing authorities and local authorities, have a limited capacity to implement their plans; and that most planning authorities have an equally limited capacity to enforce regulatory systems of development control, building regulations, building permit approval, zoning ordinance and the like.

In other words, incrementalism is the way most programmes will continue to develop, whether in housing construction, housing improvement, or institution building.

Finally, as Devas points out, there will need to be realism about the nature of political agendas and political processes, recognising why proposals are so often not implemented. Equally, it needs to be recognised that politics is not an obstacle to the implementation of plans or programmes but a framework for developing a plan that can and must be implemented. This is the basis to face the challenges ahead.

BIBLIOGRAPHY

Burgess, R., 1982, **Self-Help Housing Advocacy: A Curious Form of Radicalism, Self-help Housing: A Critique**, Peter M. Ward, ed., pp. 56–95, Mansell Publishing Ltd, London.

Chambers, R., 1993, **Challenging the Professions: Frontiers for Rural Development**, Intermediate Technology Publications, London.

Cook, D.B., 1979, **City Strategies and Action Planning**, Paper presented to the Economic Development Institute, World Bank, Washington D.C.

Devas, N., 1993, **Evolving Approaches, Managing Fast Growing Cities**, N. Devas and C. Rakodi, eds., Longman Scientific and Technical, Essex, UK.

The Economist, 7 May, 1994.

Hamdi, N., 1991/1995, **Housing Without Houses**, Van Nostrand Reinhold, New York and Intermediate Technology Publications, London.

Keane, D.H. and S. Parris, 1982, **Evaluation of Shelter Programs for the Urban Poor; Principal Findings**, World Bank Staff Working Paper 547, World Bank, Washington D.C.

Koenigsberger, O., 1987, **The Intentions of Housing Policy Alternatives, Their Development and Impact in the Third World Since the 1950s**, Paper presented to the International Symposium, Development Planning Unit (DPU), University College, London, December 9 to 11.

Lewin, A.C., 1991, **Neighbourhood Participation in Urban Projects: The Role of the Donor Agencies**, Unpublished Paper presented to the GTZ Experts Conference, Dakar, Senegal.

McGill, M. and M. Horton, 1973, **Action Research Design for Training and Development**, National Training and Development Press, Washington D.C.

Ovitt, G., 1989, *Appropriate Technology: Development and Social Change*, **Monthly Review**, 40 (9), pp. 22–32.

Peattie, L.R., 1982, *Some Second Thoughts on Sites and Services*, **Habitat International**, 6 (1–2), pp. 131–139.

Strassman, W.P., 1975, *Industrialised Systems Building for Developing Countries: A Discouraging Prognosis*, **International Technical Co-operation Review**, 55 (January), pp. 99–113.

United Nations Centre for Human Settlements (HABITAT), 1986, 1987, **Global Report on Human Settlements**, Oxford University Press, New York.

DUTCH SOCIAL HOUSING POLICY IN HISTORICAL PERSPECTIVE

Gerard Milort

ABSTRACT

This paper discusses the reasons and forms of government supervision of social housing in the Netherlands, the role of housing co-operatives and the private sector. Policies regarding finance, rent and subsidies, are examined, as is the distribution of scarce resources. It examines the main features of these themes from a historical perspective, covering legislation such as the 1901 Housing Law, the Law on Town Planning, the Rent Law, the Rent Price Housing Law, the Housing Law, and the Individual Rent Subsidy Law. The question of town planning is not addressed.

INTRODUCTION

The Netherlands has extensive experience in the organised and government-supervised expansion of housing stock. Due to population growth, urbanisation, and increased concern for public health, the need arose for not only many more housing units, but also qualitatively better ones. Many working-class families lived in small slum dwellings under poor hygienic conditions, and their low wages generally made better housing unaffordable.

This provided the initial rationale for central government involvement in, and supervision of, social housing, a process in which local authorities were accorded an important role. In the first half of this century, a substantial expansion of the housing stock was achieved pursuant to the 1901 Housing Law. Government intervention during that time cannot be analysed in isolation from growing concern for the living conditions of the underclass, low-income workers, and those without either work or income.

After the Second World War, the housing stock in the Netherlands

421

expanded again, and the experiences and organisational structures which evolved before the war developed. Due to the huge scarcity of housing and low wages, much effort was devoted to the just distribution of low-cost housing and the imposition of strict rent controls. As economic growth led to greater security, it became possible to liberalise rent controls and allow rent levels to be set by the market. For those who could not afford such rents, however, individual housing allowances were provided.

THE HISTORICAL CONTEXT

Some familiarity with the historical context in which Dutch social housing policy in the Netherlands developed is essential to an understanding of current policy and legislation. Until the promulgation of the 1901 Housing Law, the role of the state in this field was extremely modest. It consisted primarily of enabling legislation concerning municipal ordinances and public health. Pursuant to the 1851 Municipal Law, municipalities were required to adopt public health ordinances. These municipal ordinances contained regulations and standards concerning matters such as the location of buildings, construction standards, fire prevention, sewage, and the like. Actual supervision of construction and existing housing stock was, however, highly inadequate.

Until this century, improvements in housing standards were almost exclusively the domain of private initiative. The involvement of wealthy citizens and government in social housing began only after several epidemics struck. A movement began which called for improvements in the working and living environment of the labouring classes through both collective measures by workers themselves (i.e. co-operatives), and state intervention.

Wealthy citizens, including factory owners, also attempted to improve the housing conditions of workers through the provision of cheap loans (3 to 4 per cent) for the construction of simple but decent housing units. The construction and development of these homes was undertaken by housing associations, which were established in the second half of the 19th Century. Within the government, voices were also raised to support construction by housing associations. The Co-operative Associations Law endowed these associations with a legal personality, which made them eligible for government support.

REGULATION AND THE MARKET

An important question was the manner in which the government could support private initiatives. It realised that it could not eliminate the consequences of poverty and poor housing overnight. It could however intervene in the market. In doing so it had several options. Light forms of supervision consist of activities which set objectives without binding the parties involved. Stronger forms of supervision consist of legal codes of conduct which must be respected by participants in the market, and general legal codes and permit systems which must be implemented by the government.

Intervention in the market also has its limitations. The government is under an obligation to provide lawful administration, and its policies must furthermore provide a credible and durable framework for other parties to operate in. Government intervention in markets can be underpinned by two main rationales. If the market is inefficient and produces poor results, supervision is required to improve its functioning. At the same time, if the market is functioning efficiently but produces unacceptable results, intervention is required to promote the achievement of desired objectives.

Social housing policy can thus be seen as the result of measures to safeguard the housing stock against external factors which disturb the operation of the market such as government policy in other sectors; and, interventions to promote desired objectives.

The measures pursued depend on the policy objectives established and the degree to which the market is able to realise them on its own.

These considerations – which remain relevant today – were also fundamental when the Dutch government first became involved in the field of social housing. The purpose of its involvement was not so much to supervise the market through detailed planning, but rather to promote its stable operation. The policy measures adopted were meant as buffer mechanisms to permit the housing market to function satisfactorily. Subsequent to lengthy discussions, these measures were laid down in the 1901 Housing Law and reflected contemporary social policies.

THE 1901 HOUSING LAW

With the adoption of the Housing Law, social housing became a recognised component of government policy. The Law has formed the basis for uninterrupted governmental and municipal responsibility for the availability of sufficient and affordable housing, and even today remains the backbone of Dutch social housing policy.

The 1901 Housing Law was saturated with the (liberal) idea that the government may intervene in society only when this is demonstrably essential, and should otherwise restrict its role to adopting legislation which regulates the conduct of market actors.

Municipal Responsibilities

The Housing Law is an enabling legislation which, in order to improve social housing, empowers municipalities to prevent and prohibit undesirable living conditions, and establishes norms for acceptable urban planning. It permits municipalities to promulgate further rules and regulations through General Administrative Measures.

The Housing Law gave municipalities a number of responsibilities and provided them with instruments to fulfil them. These were as follows:

1) Municipalities were required to adopt a **building code**, dealing not only with the quality of construction but also planning issues such as building heights. It became illegal to erect a building without a **construction permit**, which had to be denied if the building did not fulfil a set of conditions;

2) Municipalities were empowered to serve **summons**, compelling owners to improve existing houses, and through **condemnation orders** to vacate and even demolish buildings no longer fit for human habitation;

3) It became possible for municipalities to establish **zoning regulations**, which for a set period of time parcelled land within municipal boundaries for specific uses (including public space). At the time, more possibilities were created to alienate land in the public interest. This included municipal land purchases at commercially realistic rather than artificially inflated rates, which were then made available for the construction of social housing;

4) The Housing Law contained so-called **financial paragraphs**, which regulated financial support for housing construction. In this way, municipalities and recognised housing associations were able to receive financial support from the government through loans for the construction of Housing Law houses and direct subsidies which covered a portion of the operational costs; and

5) Municipalities were obliged to establish '**construction police**', responsible for issuing construction permits, summons, condemnation orders, and for investigating housing conditions within the municipality.

The role of the government was to supervise municipal policies and the activities of housing associations. For this purpose, it appointed social housing inspectors.

Eligible Institutions

Under the Housing Law, private construction companies can be considered eligible institutions, and as such make use of its provisions. However, institutions must meet a number of conditions to be considered eligible. First, they must have a legal personality in the form of a foundation or association. Second, they must operate exclusively in the interest of social housing, and their objectives in this regard must be specified in their statutes.

Such institutions are required to obey codes of conduct laid down in the Law or General Administrative Measures, and to operate as non-profit landlords. Profit as such is not prohibited, but all surpluses must be devoted to improving social housing, for example through construction, management, and maintenance. In return, eligible institutions do not pay taxes or fees. Municipalities are entrusted with the task of supervising such institutions and ensuring that they play by the rules and properly discharge their responsibilities. Eligible institutions are commonly known as housing co-operatives, and at the time of their foundation many opted for the legal personality of an association.

Between 1914 and 1922 the number of co-operatives grew from 300 to approximately 1,300. These were generally small bodies, with an average ownership of 25 housing units. Most were established by directly interested parties (e.g. workers or teachers) for the purpose of building homes for their own members.

Simply stated, a co-operative consists of two organisational components. One is the technical branch, or the actual construction company, which contains the relevant technical expertise and conducts construction and maintenance activities. The other is the leasing department, which concerns itself with questions related to rents, housing distribution, management, and other matters of concern to tenants.

Co-operatives are presided over by a board of directors, which is appointed by the management of the foundation or association. The members of the association (foundations do not have members) influence the policies of their co-operative through participation in general meetings and their votes. Internal controls are exercised by a supervisory board or board of commissioners. Financial responsibility is achieved through auditors' certificates.

Advantages of the Non-Profit Sector

Non-profit leasing is not a self-evident solution; in the absence of market pressures, it may operate less efficiently than commercial leasing. Given the social objectives social housing is meant to achieve, however, it does offer a number of advantages. For example, efficient non-profit landlords form an effective institutional basis for the provision of subsidies, because their resources do not flow away in the form of profits. More importantly, the purpose of this sector is not to achieve greater returns than alternative investments, but rather self-supporting development and durable property management.

Non-profit institutions thus form an important mechanism for the implementation of Dutch social housing policy. Financial and administrative protection makes it possible for them to operate in a segment of the market which, because of the low returns, private commercial firms have chosen to abandon.

Financing

Initially, subsidies were seen as unnecessary. Government support could take forms such as the sale of building lots at reasonable prices and the provision of sufficient financial means at moderate interest rates. However, the contributions of wealthy housing association members insufficient to stimulate construction on a sufficiently large scale.

The system whereby government loans for housing construction were made available to municipalities and eligible institutions was a breakthrough; through this method alone it was possible to prevent a situation whereby construction would stagnate on account of a lack of capital. The state was the party most able to provide low-interest loans, which were not subsidies but rather a means through which to apply economies of scale to municipalities and housing associations. By limiting loans to eligible institutions as defined under the Housing Law, the government could influence the manner in which these loans were used; loans had to be used for the construction of modest homes for tenants who could not afford to rent at commercial rates.

Municipal Housing Co-operatives

Because municipalities can also commission the construction of houses and lease them, many municipalities established municipal housing co-operatives, which exist as separate departments within the municipal apparatus. Through such co-operatives, municipalities can develop construction activities neglected by others. In a certain sense a municipal housing co-operative is also a non-profit landlord, and pursuant to the Housing Law qualifies for financial advance loans and contributions for purposes of housing construction.

RENT AND SUBSIDY POLICY

Reconstruction policy after the Second World War was geared towards the mobilisation of labour and the promotion of industrialisation. In the context of scarcity national wage and price controls were used to combat steep price increases and maintain social peace. There was great interest in both stimulating the construction of sufficient housing, and in controlling rents in a manner which made them affordable to the general population.

On the basis of previous experiences the government concluded that the best method for achieving both goals would be to pre-finance and partly subsidise the costs of new construction. Other measures were also used to protect social housing. Rent controls were needed to prevent tenants from being evicted by landlords seeking to lease houses at higher prices. Housing distribution measures were required to ensure that homes were occupied by those for whom they were intended. And preferential rights for the government in land purchases proved a useful instrument to counter the effects of land speculation and promote development in conformity with government policy.

Choices During Reconstruction

In its development of the social housing sector, the Netherlands opted for a system of cheap loans which, on the basis of the 1901 Housing Law, were provided to municipalities and eligible institutions for the construction of rental units. These loans were characterised by low rates of interest which remained fixed for long periods of time. This made it possible to realise a sustained and continual expansion of affordable housing stock, and the resultant units were known as *Housing Law houses* due to the method in which they were financed. Currently, such houses are known as rental social houses, and are intended for those with incomes below an established threshold.

The system of Housing Law loans and annual development grants is the most important factor in post-war Dutch social housing policy. It forms the basis for the current social rent sector, which is in very good shape financially as well as qualitatively. Thanks to this sector it was possible to conduct a durable, moderate rent control policy, which made housing attainable for lower income groups as well. During this period, the private sector also received governmental support for the construction and development of housing, and it was only after 1960 that unsubsidised construction for the market became significant.

A repeated point of discussion was the desired ratio of private construction to that by housing co-operatives and municipalities. In fact, the Netherlands bet on all three horses at once. Through various financing and subsidy measures appropriate to the beneficiaries concerned, housing construction by private firms, housing co-operatives, and municipalities was stimulated.

Rent Controls

Rent controls serve various objectives. During reconstruction rent policy was a component of national wage and price policy, and thereby an integral part of socio-economic policy. The objective was to keep rent levels low so as to limit wage increases and thereby improve the competitiveness of Dutch business.

The subsidy of new construction to achieve a low initial rent is not sufficient in this respect. Through rent freezes and subsequent limitations upon rent increases rapid increases can be prevented. In discussions about rent increases, the question about who would profit from eventual higher increases was always a consideration. In the Housing Law sector, higher increases result in lower operational contributions from the government. But for low income groups higher rents are problematic on account of low wages. And in the private sector higher rents result in higher profits which do not flow back to the social housing sector.

Rent controls can also contribute to efforts to stem inflation, which was an important theme in the Netherlands during reconstruction and during the 1970s. Through low rent increases the wage and price spiral is partially broken. The disadvantage of long-term rent controls with low rent increases is that rent patterns of existing housing stock over time bear less relation to quality. This is all the more the case if the costs, and therefore the rent prices, of new units do rise. Rent harmonisation, in which rent is brought into closer relation to quality, then becomes an additional objective.

The 1950 Rent Law

The 1950 Rent Law forms the context for post-war rent controls. Distinctively, this law only applied to existing stock. Rent controls concerning subsidised new construction are conducted on the basis of the subsidy regulations, and rent adjustments during the first five years. Only thereafter do such units fall under the rent adjustment regulations derived from the 1950 Rent Law. The rent levels of unsubsidised new construction was not controlled but rather left to the market.

Rent increases are determined by the Rent Law without reference to the contracting parties. In this manner the state, and specifically the parliament, has acquired a direct and significant influence over rent policy and conditions under which rents are raised. The revenues raised by rent increases are primarily intended for investment in existing stock, such as future (large-scale) maintenance and improvements.

Attempts at Liberalisation

In the 1960s the belief existed that the housing shortage would be resolved before the end of the decade, and that this would make possible a return to cost and market price rents. Attempts to liberalise rental policy and allow rent levels to be established by the market were, however, unsuccessful until the end of the 1960s. The integration of rent with wage and price policy, and controversy about the destination of money available from rent increases, had a slowing effect. A return to cost or market rents therefore lagged behind economic recovery. Because the costs of comparable houses and new construction were not the same throughout the Netherlands, housing co-operatives and municipalities demanded the introduction of objective criteria for housing value by means of a points system, which was later adopted.

Distribution

Beyond housing construction and rent policy, housing provision is in important respects a question of distribution. Can households searching for a home find living quarters appropriate to their needs without unacceptably long waiting periods? Problems in the distribution of housing are unavoidable. Households with low incomes and specific needs, such as the elderly or large families, often encounter problems. Existing stock is not always optimally utilised, and increased supply is dependent on the inclinations of tenants to move on. Houses and neighbourhoods are additionally status symbols and expressions of particular lifestyles.

Serious shortcomings in housing distribution can serve as a reason for government intervention. Such intervention will have only limited effects, because the government cannot simply eliminate the in-elasticity of supply. The government can also not neglect the heterogeneity of housing wants and needs, particularly because ensuring freedom of choice is an important policy objective.

Because of the great housing shortage in the Netherlands after the Second World War, the government felt obliged to influence the distribution process in the housing market. This entails administrative regulation of the distribution process through a permit system, whereby conditions are established regarding who may inhabit which house.

The reasons provided for this policy were as follows:

1) Under conditions of great housing scarcity, existing stock must be utilised as well and as intensively as possible. In this context, confronting speculative non-occupancy, and forced sales and leasing is considered appropriate. Excessive spatial occupancy can also be eliminated by promoting the billeting of those searching for a home in the homes of those with excessive surplus space;

2) Through physical redistribution, waiting periods are spread as fairly as possible;

3) Even in the absence of general scarcity, shortages can exist in certain sectors of the housing market. In this case, regulation and distribution are desirable;

4) It is desirable to support the target groups of such a policy, i.e. those who, without government intervention, would have much less opportunity to obtain timely and affordable housing;

5) Confronting discrimination in housing assignments through objective criteria is required; and

6) Subsidies can be optimised by ensuring that housing units built for a particular sector of the population are made available to this group.

Disadvantages were also recognised. Through regulation, the market becomes partially inoperative, freedom of choice is limited, and those seeking housing become dependent on the government for the satisfaction of their needs. Those who have easier access to the bureaucracy may thereby acquire a privileged position. As rules become more detailed, furthermore, regulation in practice becomes more difficult and evasion increases. In this case, necessary regulation in due time consequently also leads to deregulation (liberalisation).

The 1947 Housing Space Law

Great scarcity, in combination with the above mentioned rationales, led to the adoption of the Housing Space Law in 1947, which applied to the entire country. Pursuant to this Law, municipal councils were compelled to adopt housing space by-laws, prohibiting the use of an independent housing unit without the written permission of the municipal executive (the housing space permit). Such permits are in effect statements of non-objection by the executive concerning the use of a house by a specific household. The permit, incidentally, does not replace a rent contract; owner and tenant must also agree on this aspect between themselves.

The criteria for provision of such permits concern fairness and effectiveness. Fairness is protected through a priority system, established on the premise that everyone must wait approximately the same length of time for a suitable house. People can register as home-seekers and thereby acquire waiting points. Exceptional circumstances, for example homelessness or economic ties with a particular municipality, can form a justification for the provision of extra points.

Effectiveness is protected through suitability criteria. These concern both the suitability of a particular house for a particular household in terms of the size (and type) of house (i.e. optimal use of space), as they do financial suitability, so as to ensure that those with lower incomes have priority when it comes to cheap, subsidised housing units. The Law provides a number of instruments with which to ensure the fair and efficient distribution of available housing space to appropriate households.

FROM LIBERALISATION TO DECENTRALISATION

In the late 1960s and early 1970s, it became clear that the housing shortage had not been resolved to the extent hoped for. To the contrary, as a result of population growth and family dilution the demand for housing had increased significantly and a new housing shortage came into being. As a consequence, political attention shifted from rent price policy to housing construction programmes, and the achievement of construction programmes became the foundation of the new policy. Simultaneously, the 1973 oil crisis resulted in increased construction costs and inflation. This accentuated the necessity for the government to stimulate housing construction through subsidies, and after 1974 it also led to the retention of market regulation.

Multi-Year Housing Construction Programmes

To increase certainties regarding continuity in annual housing construction, multi-year housing construction programmes were established in the early 1970s. Quota restrictions and obligatory construction streams were abolished to remove limitations arising therefrom. In order to ensure that construction activities were attuned to demand, provinces and municipalities were urgently requested to carry out housing market studies.

When these studies proved to be incomparable, however, the government in 1977 decided to conduct periodic large-scale, standardised housing needs studies of its own. Municipalities were asked to complete a survey and information pamphlet, and provide a prognosis of municipal housing needs. By examining not only housing needs, but also actual achievements in recent years in the various sectors, and the effects of relocation on new housing units, the multi-year housing construction programmes can take better account of the functioning of the housing market and the wishes of inhabitants. The results of the studies are also used to determine in which sectors, and to which extent, subsidies are required to sufficiently stimulate housing construction. Since these studies were first conducted, they have been used as the basis for housing construction programmes.

Professionalisation of the Social Housing Sector

An important development in the social housing sector during this period has been the professionalisation of housing co-operatives and the expansion in the number of housing units they own. Fundamental in this respect is that eligible institutions had since the late 1960s been accorded primacy in the construction of social housing. Municipalities were not allowed to build Housing Law houses where eligible institutions within the municipality were themselves prepared to do so. Equally important was the accumulation of capital reserves by housing co-operatives, which pursuant to the Housing Law could be exclusively invested in the interests of social housing.

The Housing Law also provides for the possibility of establishing a Central Fund for Social Housing, in which co-operatives with sufficient reserves can make deposits for the benefit of co-operatives with insufficient reserves for the construction and maintenance of housing units.

SOCIAL HOUSING IN THE 1990s

In the continuing discussion on social housing concerning government regulation vs. regulation by the market, the 1990s have witnessed a number of new developments. The government has judged the time right to withdraw somewhat from social housing and leave the operation of this sector increasingly to local or regional administration or to the market itself. Due to the professionalisation of housing co-operatives during the past two decades the time has also come for the privatisation of the social housing sector, as a result of which it will be financially freer from the government.

The decentralisation of government responsibilities to lower levels of administration is also continuing. The government remains responsible for establishing the policy context and the adoption of enabling legislation. Within this framework, municipalities and provinces must manage a number of affairs according to their own insights and circumstances. Governmental finances are also largely distributed by these lower levels of administration.

CONCLUSION

The Netherlands has distinguished itself from other European countries through a large and strong social housing sector in which low-income households can find decent and affordable housing. Through eligible institutions it has been ensured that social housing stock can be durably managed and managed well. Through various financing mechanisms responsibility for the maintenance and replacement of social housing stock lies only marginally with the government.

In the Netherlands, the development of the social housing sector required almost a century. An important factor in this process was financial support. The provision of loans and subsidies for non-profit investment proved to be essential. The re-investment of revenues acquired from social housing exclusively into social housing – the *revolving fund* idea – has been an equally important factor.

Protective regulations regarding housing distribution and rent levels contributed to a fair and effective disbursement of government funds. By imposing regulations and conditions for subsidies beforehand, and through subsequent supervision, the government has retained its influence and can continue to fulfil its responsibility to ensure that sufficient housing stock is provided.

BIBLIOGRAPHY

J. van der Schaar, 1987, **Groei en bloei van het nederlandse volkshuisvestingsbeleid** [Growth and Vigour of Dutch Social Housing Policy], Delft University Press, Delft.

J. van der Schaar and A. Hereijgers, 1991, **Volkshuisvesting: een zaak van beleid** [Social Housing: A Matter of Policy], Spectrum Publishers.

URBAN AND RURAL ENVIRONMENTAL PLANNING AND MANAGEMENT

Ramzi M. Sansur

ABSTRACT

This paper deals with various issues related to environmental considerations in urban and rural planning. The current situation of planning is not very encouraging as a number of municipalities are unable to cope with the large volume of construction presently underway. Issues related to environmental protection and conservation have been largely ignored; however, it is hoped that a long-term future plan will correct this.

This paper addresses the issue of clean water and sanitation. Suggestions for regional solid waste dumps and wastewater treatment plants are offered. Recycling of as much waste as possible is recommended.

The problem of water pollution in the coastal zones is discussed and practical solutions offered. Air pollution and transportation are also addressed and suggestions to control emissions so as to reduce air pollution have been made.

Noise pollution and its effect on health is also discussed briefly. Visual pollution and zoning are emphasised, given their effect on how people relate to their cities or villages. The preservation of Palestine's many archaeological and historical sites is also discussed, as are the distinctive characteristics of the coastal zones and agricultural areas. The establishment of environmental management teams at either city governmental or regional levels is recommended. Such teams could well serve rural areas.

Other recommendations include the establishment of an intensive national programme for environmental education at all levels. A strategy for the environment is also proposed covering such issues as community participation, the community's right to know and the provision of written materials and audio-visual aids. Lastly, the greening of government policies at all levels is strongly recommended.

ISSUES: ENVIRONMENTAL PLANNING AND MANAGEMENT

It is estimated that half of the world population will be living in urban areas by the turn of the century. This trend also manifests itself in Palestine where there is gradual migration of people from rural areas toward the cities (various sources). At the same time, rural areas are being developed more and more and many are being engulfed by larger cities (WCED, 1987). This is especially true in the larger conurbations such as Nablus, Ramallah, Bethlehem and, to a certain extent, Hebron. Jerusalem has become a megacity with the incorporation of a number of villages prior to, and after, the Israeli occupation of 1967.

As far as reconstruction in Palestine is concerned, certain facts have already been established on the ground. It will be too costly to change them. Moreover, Palestine is small compared to other areas of the world and its cities and villages are close to each other. Therefore, one has to look at rural and urban development as a whole; both areas are interdependent. Environmental considerations are equal in both and the need for a clean and healthy environment also applies to both.

Historically, urban planners, even in ancient times, tried to include the provision of 'clean water supply' as part of town design. Elaborate piping and water collection systems are still seen in many places. In others, a drainage system was installed to carry sewage away. Such activities indicated a need to maintain a clean environment within urban areas. For the enjoyment of the population, parks were also created, or natural areas preserved.

In contrast, the issue of Urban and Rural Environmental Planning and Management (UEPM) is a relatively recent one. As environmental awareness increased, environmental problems began to come into focus. Planners in many developed countries started to address the issue of 'greening their urban planning' in line with the trend of environmental awareness.

The modern concept of UEPM takes the human being as the centre of such an activity and tries to plan with his or her needs in mind. Concurrently, many of the natural areas that fall within the perimeters of an urban or rural area are preserved. This could include a body of water, such as a river or a lake, or can be a forested area or even an archaeological site. The idea is to minimise human impact on nature, yet maximise human enjoyment.

Although such a concept is not easy to apply because it takes a great deal of effort and perseverance on the part of planners to put it into practice, it can be done. Because the situation in Palestine is complex, it is very difficult, now or in the future, to apply fully the concept of UEPM.

First and foremost, this concept is unknown to many planners. Second, it is costly and the limited resources available to Palestinians makes the job harder and more difficult to apply. Third, there is, and will be, many pressure groups and individuals that will oppose it, on the grounds that it is not, and will not be, a priority for many years. In the view of many planners, the immediate task is to build and to overcome the many years of Israeli neglect. This short-sightedness may continue to prevail. The bulk of the Palestinian population is environmentally illiterate, although this is not their own fault, but rather a result of their oppressive living conditions.

The situation is made more complex by the extensive and continued building of Jewish settlements in the midst of Palestinian areas. In effect, such settlements are a network of towns and villages built to modern standards linked with another network of roads and offering all the necessary services a town could offer. These built up areas have prevented the expansion of Palestinian towns and villages rendering their expansion vertical rather than horizontal and thus crowded.

The prospect of correcting such situations is currently dim. It will take monumental efforts to reverse the current trend in town planning and introduce UEPM. It has to be done on a national scale with firm laws that govern it.

Such laws have to be strictly enforced without regard to other considerations. As it stands now, builders are free to exceed their building permits and there is very little a municipality can do other than impose a ridiculously low fine. For example, there are municipal laws that regulate the construction of parking areas in high rise buildings. Many of the builders ignore this and turn underground parking garages into commercial areas, in effect causing serious environmental problems with cars being forced to move farther and farther away from congested town centres, thereby creating more pollution and noise.

Ramallah and Bethlehem are very good examples of such irregularities, with the result that the town centres are being abandoned by economically affluent people due to crowding, congestion and the inability to park. In others words, the current trend is causing towns to choke themselves, thus reducing their economic development.

The situation, though complex, may be remedied with proper investment, coupled with firm laws that make it difficult for any builder to break building or zoning laws. In this regard, laws that protect the environment and provide for a cleaner urban development must be enacted. Because urban and rural development does not start from zero, a balance must be struck between environmental considerations and the existing situation. Long-term plans should be introduced gradually to correct the situation in favour of an environmentally friendly approach.

In the following section, the main causes of environmental damage are reviewed, including air pollution, solid waste and sewage, the lack of zoning regulations, noise, urban and rural degradation and transportation. The importance of archaeological and historical sites to the environment is also discussed, as are the needs of the coastal areas.

AIR POLLUTION

Air pollution represents the most serious hazard for residents of urban areas. Sources of air pollution are varied but emission from the burning of fossil fuel in vehicles and home heating are the major sources. Other contributors to air pollution are particulate matter resulting from construction activities and the destruction of areas covered with vegetation. Particulate matter has become a serious health hazard with the infringement of metropolitan areas on agricultural land and natural areas.

Some cities in the West have been able to control, and even remedy this situation through long-term plans to reduce emissions at the source. Emissions from cars have been substantially reduced through legislation that forced auto manufacturers to increase fuel efficiency of their cars and introduce pollution control devices. Cars in Palestine are currently being imported through Israeli agents and conform to Israeli pollution control and emission standards. The most recent one is the introduction of catalytic converters and the use of unleaded gasoline, two regulations that go hand in hand. The USA was one of the first countries to introduce such laws resulting in improved emission standards and reduced air pollution. It is hoped that the Palestinian National Authority (PNA) will introduce such laws thus forcing automobile dealers to continue importing vehicles with low emissions and having pollution control devices such as catalytic converters.

The use of low sulphur fuel, also recently legislated in Israel, greatly helps in the reduction of pollution in urban areas. Home heating fuel and diesel car fuel contains a certain level of sulphur compounds that are introduced into the atmosphere causing a deterioration in air quality and resulting in health and other environmental damages. Again many cities throughout the world have improved air quality through the use of low sulphur fuel and unleaded gasoline.

Air pollution from industrial sources is currently minimal and localised. This will imply that laws have to be enacted to prevent the introduction of polluting industries into urban areas. Currently industrial zones are sitting in the middle of housing areas as residential building continues to encroach upon such areas. Industrial areas should have been placed many kilometres away from any city centre so that they remain far away from urban areas as the latter expand. As such industrial zones have to be relocated with incentives given to those that have businesses currently in them in order to reduce economic hardships. Industrial zones are important to the economy of any area and must be encouraged. With correct location and the appropriate environmental laws legislated they will pose minimal threat to urban areas.

It is worth noting here that the use of used motor oil as a source of fuel for certain industries must be discouraged and penalised. This is a wide spread phenomenon among bakeries located within metropolitan areas. Used motor oil contains many pollutants including heavy metals and organics considered dangerous for health.

In order to further reduce air pollution from within city perimeters town planning should take meteorological conditions into consideration. In Palestine prevailing winds are normally westerly with occasional easterly winds prevailing during certain seasons. Buildings and streets should take advantage of these phenomena so as to flush the city of air pollutants and keep fresh wind moving. The example of Tel Aviv, where the older buildings are constructed in a north–south direction, helps illustrate the situation. Buildings there act as barriers to westerly wind movement causing the build-up of pollutants, especially during traffic rush hours. In addition, air temperature is higher as hot air is not replaced by fresh moist air coming from the coast.

SOLID WASTE, SEWAGE AND CLEAN WATER

Solid Waste

Solid waste currently represents a serious threat to the residents of urban and rural areas. Solid waste dumps are located within many urban and rural areas. The waste is dumped in the most primitive fashion. There are no sanitary waste dumps available locally.

Open dumping is creating serious air pollution hazards as the waste is lit and a smouldering fire ensues. Smoke carrying all sorts of pollutants drifts into urban areas. Ramallah area is very well known for that. In addition solid waste is attracting vermin that find their way into towns and villages. Solid waste dumps must be located far away from metropolitan areas. It is best to recycle as much of the solid waste as possible. Through the introduction of pollution control laws recycling becomes more profitable (Sansur, 1995). Certain cities and states abroad have introduced deposits on beverage containers inducing people to return them for refunds and causing a reduction in the amount of plastics, glass and metal containers being dumped.

The trend of having solid waste dumps is an ancient phenomenon whose change is long overdue. There is practically no waste product that cannot be recycled. It may be costly, initially but will become profitable with time. Palestine is too small a country to afford having waste dumps scattered every where. It is highly advisable that multi-municipality sanitary waste dumps and land fills be created until the time when the population is ready for a more creative recycling approach.

There are many opinions as to the success of a recycling programme for Palestine. Most of the opinion centres on the low environmental awareness of the population which may result in poor participation in such a program. A programme of raising the level of environmental awareness coupled with firm laws is sure to change the current careless attitude. However, and as mentioned earlier, it may be premature to enact such laws before Palestinians take full hold of their destiny.

The system of solid waste collection leaves a lot to be desired. The current practice of placing medium and large size containers in streets for people to throw their waste in has created a health hazard and a breeding ground for insects and vermin. The majority of such containers are defective with the lids jammed in the open position and garbage ferments in them causing objectionable odours. No efforts are ever put to periodically clean or disinfect them. The perimeter of such containers is piled with garbage due to their small capacity and the carelessness of their users. A better system for households is to have the municipality distribute standard containers, for a fee of course, and have each household responsible for them.

In addition, garbage should be collected on specific days. Once a month or so should be dedicated to the collection of large items. The regulation of solid waste collection is an important consideration for urban planners and is destined to make everybody's job that much easier. A phenomenon that is on the increase is the illegal dumping of rubble from construction sites along urban and rural roads. The provision of dumping sites for such an activity with stiff fines for violators would be most welcome. Land fills must be maintained and subsidised from fees collected from users. Builders must not be allowed to leave construction material on site and on side walks after they finish the job. This phenomenon is wide spread.

Sewage

Sewage is another issue that has to be tackled in UEPM. Most municipalities have inadequate sewage collection systems and almost no sewage treatment facilities. International donors have allocated money for the larger municipalities to build new sewerage systems but the money has been trickling. In some instances such as for the municipality of Ramallah, funding of a sewage treatment plant was postponed and existing funds diverted for the creation of jobs and paying salaries due to economic hardship the Palestinians encounter during periods of Israeli closure of the territories.

Palestinian municipalities are unable to generate enough income to start major sanitation projects and are dependent on international aid. Although there is an interest in such projects by foreign donors, events on the ground and the military occupation force things otherwise. Currently the World Bank has offered a loan to the PNA to start on work sanitation and infrastructure activities.

Wastewater may divided into three types:

1) Household and Businesses;
2) Industrial; and
3) Runoff.

As with solid waste dumps, there is no sense in having each municipality construct its own wastewater treatment plant. It is preferable that regional wastewater plants be constructed. The population of even the largest towns and villages surrounding it will not exceed 200,000 individuals and therefore regional treatment plants can easily serve the purpose.

The PNA must take an active role in establishing regional wastewater treatment plants. It should not be left to foreign consultants to decide on the appropriate technology and level of treatment. Proper treatment implies the generation of safe treated wastewater appropriate for reuse in agriculture or certain industries.

It is important to emphasise the appropriate technology here. The low per capita water consumption reflects itself in high levels of biochemical oxygen demand (BOD) for sewage in the range of 700 to 900 milligrams per litre (mg/L) (Sansur, 1995). The higher the BOD level, the more taxing it is for a sewage treatment plant to bring it to acceptable levels of 30 to 50 mg/L.

In addition, the treated wastewater may be too concentrated and contain high levels of dissolved salts requiring dilution for normal long-term agricultural use. It is recommended that treatment plants be located outside municipal boundaries, preferably serving more than one urban area and designed so that they are cost effective and provide safe reusable treated wastewater. Dumping of raw sewage in wadis must be discouraged and penalised.

Industrial waste is varied in nature depending on the particular industry. It is best that such waste be treated on site at industry's own expense. When mixed with urban sewage, industrial waste could reduce the efficiency of wastewater treatment plants and in some instances cause a shutdown. Technologies are currently available to treat most industrial waste. This may result in a higher production costs, but events elsewhere have shown that industry is able to cope with such costs and even turn then to their own benefit.

Runoff refers to storm and rain water. Most sewage treatment plants are unable to cope with water from runoff during heavy rain periods. This results in the release of partially treated wastewater into designated areas. It is best that water from runoff be separated from sewers to minimise such events. Although runoff in metropolitan areas carries some pollutants with it, it should be released before entering wastewater plants during periods of heavy rain. Most Palestinian municipalities do not have provision for diverting or separating sewers from storm water.

Many households and businesses use the system of septic tanks as they have not been connected to sewerage. This is both true for urban as well as rural areas. The problem of rural areas is that there have not been serious plans to establish a sewerage system there. The incorporation of rural areas into a sewerage system should also be a priority for the PNA. More than one village may be connected to a sewage system. Villages within a reasonable distance can be connected to one of the proposed regional sewage treatment plants. Small, yet efficient sewage treatment plants can be established to serve a number of villages.

Septic tanks, which qualify more as cesspools, are scattered throughout urban and rural areas. They are, currently, the main method of disposing of sewage. Septic tanks have a short life span as drainage from them is usually poor. They fill up within a period of being constructed and leak downhill into other residential areas or open field. Emptying them has become a booming business with the wastewater being dumped into the nearest wadi or field. Not every spot is suitable for constructing a septic tank.

In other countries, no residence can be built in areas that do not have sewerage before a percolation test is done to examine the capacity of the soil to percolate waste-water. This is not followed here and the result is sewage seeping everywhere. The situation is getting more aggravated with increased construction. Septic tanks could pose a threat to some water resources. This has been evident in areas where the aquifer is shallow such as Gaza.

Clean Water

Many Palestinian municipalities suffer from water shortages year round, but they are especially likely to occur in summer. Palestinians are aware that their water resources have been diverted to the Israelis (United Nations, 1992). This situation is causing a serious health hazard to the population. The per capita water consumption for home use is in the range or 25 to 40 cubic meters per month in metropolitan areas with adequate water supplies. This is considered low and is less than one-third the consumption in Israel.

Reduced water consumption can be reflected in reduced public health. Most municipalities have old and defective water distribution networks with a high water loss. Every time there is a water shortages the distribution network is emptied of water creating a vacuum that sucks in contaminants from areas where the lines have cracks. When pumping is resumed the contaminants are distributed and pose a health hazard causing outbreak of diseases. This is a common problem in some areas and its solution lies in renewing the water network and providing a 24-hour water supply.

Water must be properly disinfected prior to distribution. Most underground water resources in the West Bank are clean but because of the poor distribution system where contamination is a real possibility disinfection becomes a must. Chlorine gas is the most widely used disinfectant. It is cheap, effective and has a residual effect which means it has a germicidal effect through out the water network. However the supply of this gas is regulated by the military authorities causing occasional shortages and leaving many areas exposed to diseases.

The provision of an adequate 24-hour water supply should be coupled with discouraging the use of storage reservoirs on roofs. Because of the interrupted water supply people are forced to install water reservoirs on the roof and the more the water shortage becomes the more such reservoirs get installed. Water reservoirs are sources of water contamination due to their exposure to the environment, especially when they lose their lids. In addition such reservoirs are eye sores.

ZONING

Zoning laws are not being adhered to. The municipalities are ineffective in enforcing zoning laws, and personal interests coupled with greed is the prevailing trend. Penalties, if imposed, are light and largely ineffective. Examples abound of infractions of such laws in each and every urban and rural areas. This situation has caused an aggravation of town planning strategies and make the job a nightmare for those involved. Lacking a Palestinian authority and the lax of the Israelis in this regards is turning towns into congested noisy and polluted entities.

Coupled with this is the presence of farm animals in the midst of towns and within residential areas. Farm animals belong in farms. Their presence in towns should not be tolerated due to the environmental and health effects they cause. Manure produced by such animals acts as a breeding ground for flies that are currently infesting each and every town especially in areas where there are chicken farms. This situation should be discouraged and must be corrected soon.

NOISE POLLUTION

It appears to a casual visitor that there are no noise control ordinances in the country. Because of the low environmental awareness among the population this issue is rarely tackled. Noise is a serious health hazard to humans. It can cause a variety of neurological and biochemical changes in the body, in addition to its damaging effect on hearing. Many of the leading industrialised nations and a good number of developing countries have enacted laws to control noise from any source. For example, noise along major routes bordering residential areas has been greatly reduced by noise absorption and reflection walls.

Noise is measured in decibels (dB). Levels above 90dB can cause serious damage to the ear, and over time, can cause permanent hearing loss. Sources of noise are varied, ranging from motorised equipment to transportation to construction activities to music and even people themselves.

Laws that govern community noise are an integral part of appropriate community development and town planning. Such laws can contribute to noise reduction. For example, the type of pavement used on roads helps reduce transportation noise. The relocation of noisy industries or the building of noise containment enclosures can benefit every body concerned. The common practice of freely using automobile or truck horns at any time of the day or night can be easily solved by the imposition of fines.

With proper education the issue of community noise can be tackled for the benefit of all. Of course certain activities, such as construction, will inevitably produce noise, but the hours of the day that it may be produced can be restricted.

VISUAL POLLUTION

Urban degradation

This is another issue that has rarely been discussed among Palestinians: the world trend toward beautifying towns. There is very little creativity in construction; most buildings are not being designed by architects.

New building codes must take this into consideration, that is to encourage the construction of beautiful buildings that offer the necessary services for their users or, in the case of residential buildings, their inhabitants. This will have a marked and positive effect on people's attitudes towards their city as opposed to the current situation of disregard.

Among the factors that degrade the looks of any urban area is the presence of TV antennas on the roofs on many residences and the presence on unauthorised commercial signs on city streets and rural areas. Graffiti is still everywhere and no serious attempts have been made by municipalities to encourage building owners to remove it.

Other important measures which would improve the appearance of our towns include laying utility infrastructure, such as electricity and telephone lines, underground. An added bonus to this is reduced power shortages and interrupted telephone services during winter. The cost of making such changes can be subsidised from special fees collected from users of such services. Loans may be available to cover the initial costs of such a change.

Parks and vegetation

Most Palestinian urban areas suffer from the lack of dedicated public parks. The few that exist have been turned into restaurants or cafes, depriving the bulk of the population from using them as recreation areas. Parks are necessary for the well being of the people. This is especially true in cities where buildings have replaced vegetation. They are necessary to humanise the cities as they contribute to a relaxed atmosphere. They are also necessary for improving urban environment by reducing the level of air pollutants.

While it is widely recognised that vegetation is an important factor in reducing pollution, it is the role of planners to dedicate areas such as green public parks for the enjoyment of the inhabitants and have them geographically distributed so as to make them accessible to the people. The upkeep for such parks can be derived from public funds, municipal taxes and income generated from renting certain concessions in them.

In addition, most pavements should have trees planted in them to provide shade, comfort, beauty and reduce pollution. A committee consisting of professionals in the field of management of public parks should be responsible for managing such facilities. Yet there are no Palestinian specialists in this field.

Foreign donors would be more than willing to train the right people for the job, because management of public parks is an important consideration in the West. Such public places can be dedicated to a variety of functions ranging from recreation areas to jogging and outdoor sports facilities to bicycling and children's entertainment facilities. Such facilities may include indoor entertainment areas for certain activities. Sports facilities can be included in the broader definition of public parks.

TRANSPORTATION

Emission from vehicles, as mentioned above, is the major contributing factor to air pollution in many metropolitan areas. In order to reduce and manage air pollution from transportation a few important factors should be considered. These are:

- Encouraging the use of public transportation;
- Importing vehicles with pollution control devices;

- Regular vehicle emission checks during and in between yearly checks;
- Imposing substantial fines on polluters;
- Using unleaded gasoline and low sulphur fuel.

In Palestine, public transportation is an important means of moving people and it offers regular service to most points, though the hours may be irregular. In addition this public transportation is private and unsubsidised. The vehicles used are often old and thus do not have any of the modern pollution control devices that are currently in use on modern vehicles. The transportation industry needs an injection of funds to modernise its fleet. These funds can come in the form of long-term loans and grants.

In addition, more taxi and bus licenses should be issued to reduce the use of unsafe private cars being used as taxis, a trend which increased under the Israeli occupation. In this regard, more licences should also be issued for the establishment of petrol stations. This will reduce the distance vehicles must drive to find a station and encourage healthy competition.

Special environmental rules apply to petrol stations, auto service stations and car wash stations. These may not necessarily be city laws, but are usually country laws. Such stations put a burden on sewage treatment plants as the waste they produce cannot be easily degraded. It is preferable that each station install waste management and control devices to minimise impact on waste treatment plants. Such devices are not necessarily costly and can be partly covered by long-term loans and grants. Waste that is produced from service stations can be easily recycled in mineral oil recycling plants. What cannot be recycled should be delivered to industrial waste treatment plants. The latter can be managed by private, municipal or central government authorities. The cost of running such plants can be partially or wholly covered by industries and facilities that produce hazardous waste.

INSECT AND VERMIN CONTROL

It has been common practice in the larger municipalities to spray pesticides and other chemicals to control flies and mosquitoes. This control has been largely ineffective due to the poor choice of strategies used. Not any chemical can work and not every pesticide is effective. Some pesticides used may pose a health as well as an environmental problem, Until a few years ago, DDT, which is banned in most countries, was still being used.

The choice of strategies to control insects must be relegated to environmental specialists which could be part of municipalities or consult for them. It is worth noting, here, that flies and mosquitoes have been on

445

the increase. The increase in flies is caused by the improper disposal of animal manure and poor garbage collection and disposal systems while the increase mosquitoes are due to the presence of stagnant water pools due to poor wastewater disposal and open water collection and storage systems.

Chemicals used for public health must be screened carefully before being selected. There are many chemicals on the market whose use has been banned or restricted in other countries, yet they continue to be imported. Preventive measures are far more effective than the use of chemicals within urban areas. Preventive measures should be adopted on a regional basis as insect and vermin control does not necessarily originate in urban areas.

There are reports in the local press of an increase in rodents. This is most probably due to improper disposal of municipal garbage. Proper disposal techniques should help alleviate this problems. Biological control for rodents works best and with the large number of stray cats around, 'rodents have very little chance of making it'. Stray dogs in many urban areas have become a menace to the public. There are reports in the local press of individuals being attacked by wild dogs. The biggest threat is from dogs that carry rabies. The encroachment of civilisation on wilderness areas is causing contact between wild animals that may carry rabies and domesticated ones. There is no easy solution to this problem other than to destroy all unlicensed and uninnoculated dogs.

ARCHAEOLOGICAL AND HISTORIC SITES

Laws are urgently needed to preserve our heritage: archaeological and historic sites as well as old buildings. With the accelerated pace of development our culture is being built over with 'modern' and largely unattractive buildings. It should be the duty of planners within a programme of urban and rural environmental planning and management to help preserve such sites.

Of particular concern are newly discovered religious sites, ancient burial places and old buildings. These are the pride of any nation and they are a tourist attraction generating income for the local population. They can be exploited in a variety of ways such as museums, restaurants, cafes and shopping areas. Such sites make a city more attractive to visitors than others.

Each of our cities and villages has a distinctive identity to offer a visitor if such sites are properly exploited. Yet planners remain oblivious to this, and only a few sites are exploited. Tourists are whisked in and out of them with the local population deriving very little benefit from them. Hotels must be built in most places of the country providing all necessary services for the visitor and the towns developed to cater for them. The tourist industry is an important source of income for Palestine and could be exploited much better. As it stands now, most tourists spend their time and money in Israel when Palestine has a lot to offer.

COASTAL ZONES

Coastal zones in Palestine refer to the coastal areas of Gaza. Urban and rural planning in such areas must take the delicate ecosystem into very serious consideration. The coastal regions have been saved from serious destructive development as the Israeli occupiers discouraged major development activities for alleged security reasons. There is talk, now, about major development activities along the coast including the building of a harbour in Gaza, oil terminals and an airport. Although such projects are needed, they should be coupled with Environmental Impact Assessments (EIA) carried out by qualified local and foreign consultants so as to minimise any damage done during development and in the future.

The construction of tourist facilities and hotels should not be allowed on the shore as the latter should be reserved for the enjoyment of the Palestinians and visitors alike. The sighting of such facilities must be preceded by a detailed EIA. One only has to recall that the coastal zone of Gaza is an important fishing ground and a source of income for many Palestinians and as thus all efforts must be put to preserve this vulnerable ecosystem.

Currently, most developed areas in Gaza are dumping raw or partially treated sewage either directly to the sea or on sand dunes. The latter is being done not out of choice but through restriction the Israelis have imposed on the dumping of sewage. It is regrettable to point out that two important sewage treatment plants that were designed by Israeli firms and executed by the UNDP in the 1980s have failed due to a multiplicity of factors. Efforts are underway to correct this situation. In addition foreign donors have brought their own consultants to Gaza to study the solid and liquid waste situation in some parts of Gaza. Regrettably such efforts are not co-ordinated with various contradictory strategies being offered while the Palestinian scientific input is minimal.

The size of Gaza, 365 square kilometres, is too small to waste on traditional solid waste dumps. There has been suggestion by foreign donors of constructing a temporary incinerator to reduce the volume of solid waste. That proposition never materialised as the amount of international aid ended it up far less than initially promised. The solution for the reduction in the volume of solid waste lies in recycling as much of it as possible and incinerating what cannot be recycled (Sansur, 1995). Gazans are active in the recycling business, especially in metals and to some extent in plastics, but their job is not easy. If laws are enacted to encourage people to separate their refuse into its various components,

447

then their job would be made much easier. Inevitably, the volume of solid waste would be reduced.

Water resources in Gaza have deteriorated to the point that salinity is on the rise, especially during the summer months (Sansur, 1995, unpublished data). Over-pumping has caused sea water intrusion into the fresh water aquifers and the only solution is the importation of fresh water from Israel or the West Bank. Other solutions of desalination are costly for a an economically depressed region such as Gaza. The provision of clean drinking water for the population is an urgent situation that must be tackled soon.

The quality of drinking water is so bad that it poses a serious health hazard for the people. Water with a total dissolved solids (TDS) content of over 500 mg/L is considered on the verge of being salty. In Gaza City, the TDS values of many of the wells exceeds 1,000 mg/L. The situation in the southern part of the Strip is far worse.

The quality of the water is not only unacceptable for health reasons, but also for most food processing and other industries. High levels of salinity result in extra costs for desalinating equipment which must be incorporated into the design of any industrial plant. Therefore, the issue of water quality is of utmost importance for the development of Gaza. Solutions are complex and costly, but feasible.

AGRICULTURE

Agricultural areas fall within the municipal boundaries of most towns in Palestine. This situation poses special problems for most planners as the rural areas are often an integral part of a city. Best examples here are the northern West Bank towns of Jenin and Tulkarem. Construction is slowly crawling into agricultural land yet is not coupled with services that are provided in towns. Agriculture is the mainstay of Palestinian economy, at least for the foreseeable future. The loss of agricultural land to housing is a world wide phenomenon whose solution is not easy. A balance must be struck between the two but should be tilted in favour of the preservation of agricultural land.

As mentioned earlier, the use of pesticides, whether in agriculture or public health is not strictly regulated. Hence residents of rural and urban areas are exposed to pesticides, either through their agricultural works or indirectly through their diets as studies have shown that pesticides have entered the Palestinian diet (Sansur et al, 1990). Thus it is important to regulate the use of agrochemicals in the country as whole to minimise undue exposure to such chemicals that pose a threat to health and alter the balance in the environment by reducing biodiversity.

RECOMMENDATIONS

The 'Polluter Pays' Principle

The 'polluter pays' principle (PPP) was first adopted in the USA as a result of the passage of legislation to curb pollution and to pay for the cost of cleanup. This principle is very simple, if an industry, a corporation, or a citizen willingly decides to break or challenge pollution control laws, the costs of the damage and any cleanup incurred are borne by the polluter. This principle should be adopted in Palestine where the absence of environmental laws and the greed of some have caused serious damage to the environment. Luckily, the damage can be corrected but the costs are high. There are two examples of this: the illegal dumping of construction rubble and the dumping of raw sewage.

A practical though costly solution, is to use the rubble to widen roads on site, and what cannot be used can be recycled into gravel for many uses, either on site or trucked to recycling centres. The Exxon Valdez incident serves as an example of the PPP. Although the ecological damage of the oil spill will take many years to recover the Company has had to pay substantial sums of money for the damage it inflicted on the environment and the people.

Environmental Management

In order to protect the environment in urban and rural areas and provide for a healthier and safer environment, a professional team should be established, preferably in each municipality. Such teams should co-ordinate their policies and operations with any environmental body created by the PNA. Rural areas that cannot afford to have a team of their own can use regional PNA environmental officials or environmental teams from nearby metropolitan areas.

The role of such teams would be to assist a municipality or a village council to manage its local environment within the guidelines that are initially set. Such guidelines should be open to the public and liable for review. People have a right the to participate in the decision-making processes relating to their environment.

Environmental Impact Assessment

Environmental Impact Assessment (EIA) is aimed at evaluating the possible environmental, social and health effects of development projects targeting land use. Development activities are bound to affect the environment. EIA studies such possible effects and produces a set of recommendations in order to minimize their impact for both the short and long term. Predicting environmental impact is crucial to better planning and improved strategies that will minimize long term negative impacts on the environment of development projects.

EIA now employs various strategies to achieve its objectives including powerful computer programs such as Geographical Information System (GIS).

Geographic Information System

Geographic Information System (GIS) have become part and parcel of environmental planning and urban and rural management. GIS has become a powerful tool for planners. Such programs use remote sensing through a variety of imaging strategies. GIS is supported by an assortment of modules such as spread sheets, data bases and decision support system. EIA and GIS should be employed in the Urban and Rural Reconstruction in Palestine.

Environmental Education

Environmental Education (EE) is not currently a part of any regular curriculum of Palestinian schools or colleges. EE is important for making the necessary future changes for the protection and defence of the environment. As mentioned earlier environmental awareness is very low among Palestinians. An intensive crash programme to initiate EE should be adopted by the PNA. EE is a national priority and should start soon especially now after the PNA has taken responsibility for education.

Such a programme can be expected to raise environmental awareness among the people and should, in the long term, result in the improvement of the environment to the benefit of all. An added benefit could be better public participation in issues related to the betterment of living conditions which would reflect itself in an improved environment.

Environmental Conservation

Some of the recommendations here apply to governments, but others should be applied by municipalities in rural and urban areas (UNCTAD/ECDC/SEU/8, 1995). They are as follows.

Community participation

Community participation is the foundation of environmental action. An environmental action plan with participation of community groups and grassroots organisations will ensure compliance.

The community's right to know

All those concerned in setting up policies at any level, whether national or municipal authorities, must promote their community's right to know on most issues, especially those relating to the environment. This policy will prevent special interest groups from passing laws that may not support policies for environmental conservation.

Publicising the environment

Be it in radio, television or the press, environmental conservation must be promoted at all levels. The provision of audio-visual and written material also helps to promote environmental awareness.

The greening of government policies

Government policies at every level should be periodically reviewed to bring them in line with modern environmental strategies. Examples abound, locally and abroad, of government policies, such as subsidised water or fuel prices, which have led to increased consumption at the expense of the environment. Such policies are unnecessary, especially for Palestine where economic resources are very limited and income generated by government is barely sufficient to cover the cost of running the country.

BIBLIOGRAPHY

Sansur, Ramzi M., 1995, **Environment and Development Prospects in the West Bank and Gaza Strip**, United Nations Conference on Trade and Development, (UNCTAD/ECDC/SEU/8), Geneva.

Sansur, Ramzi M., Kuttab, S. and Abu-Al-Haj, S., 1990, *Extent of Exposure of Farm Workers to Organophosphate Pesticides in the Jordan Valley*, **Impact of Pesticide Use on Health in Developing Countries**, Proceedings of a symposium held in Ottawa, Canada, 17–20 September.

United Nations Committee on the Exercise of the Inalienable Right of the Palestinian People, 1992, **Water Resources in the Occupied Palestinian Territory**, United Nations, New York.

WCED, 1987, **Our Common Future**, Oxford University Press, Oxford, April.

URBAN STRATEGIES FOR ECONOMIC DEVELOPMENT

Mona Serageldin and Janne Corneil

ABSTRACT

This paper focuses on housing strategies that foster development through self-reliance as a national and local objective. Two case studies are examined to illustrate policies designed to offer citizens the supportive environment they need to improve their own living conditions and pursue entrepreneurial activities.

In Taiwan, the rapid transition from a traditional agricultural society to an industrialised state has been achieved without sharp imbalances in the distribution of income. Economic growth has relied on a labour intensive, export-oriented strategy based on small and medium-sized enterprises. Effective and flexible land management and investment allocation strategies have enabled Taiwan to promote the growth of networks of small firms, foster access to land and home ownership for low and moderate income families, and control speculation in the real estate market. For more than forty years, the state has interlinked and adjusted housing and economic policies to achieve these objectives.

At the city district level in Abidjan, given the hardships caused by structural adjustment, the elected mayor of Adjamé has opted to focus on the alleviation of unemployment, poverty, and environmental degradation. Neighbourhood committees (CDQs) were established to engage the energies and resources of citizens in the development of their communities. Combining enabling frameworks, effective incentives and judicious investment strategies, he has institutionalised, nurtured and developed the CDQs, progressively building up their institutional capabilities and financial resources. CDQ activities range from environmental improvements that provide a sanitary setting for housing, to the operation of community facilities and services. By helping CDQs to expand their activities and become increasingly self-reliant, the municipality has established a sustainable, community-based development process and empowered its citizens.

The case studies selected highlight strategies which have led to remarkable achievements in two sharply contrasting situations. Palestinian public authorities at the national and local level should seek to adopt similar policies that foster sustainable economic development and enable families to pursue their own self improvement, upgrade their settlements and shape the future of their communities.

INTRODUCTION

In Palestine, pressing needs and political constraints mean that housing policy is interlinked with critical land management issues and economic development objectives. This paper focuses on housing strategies that foster development through self-reliance. The two case studies selected illustrate contrasting policies designed to offer citizens the supportive environment they need to improve their own living conditions and to pursue entrepreneurial activities.

In Taiwan, public policy has created a supportive environment enabling home-based entrepreneurs to set up flexible labour intensive manufacturing operations and to develop networks of interconnected microenterprises capable of responding to changing demand for exports and competing successfully in the international market. The linking of housing and entrepreneurship prevents marginalisation of poorer, less mobile groups and women, and establishes opportunities for their integration in the economic development process.

In Abidjan, in the face of severe hardships caused by structural adjustment and budgetary retrenchment, the mayor of Adjamé has institutionalised a sustainable community-based development process. He has created and nurtured neighbourhood committees (CDQs) to engage the energies and resources of local communities in a concerted effort to alleviate unemployment and improve environmental conditions.

CDQ activities range from environmental improvements that provide a sanitary setting for housing to community facilities operation and urban services. By building up the institutional capabilities and financial resources of the CDQs, the municipality creates an enabling environment, empowering citizens to pursue their own self-improvement and to shape the future of their neighbourhoods.

THE ISSUES: TAIWAN

Integrating Small Business in an Export-driven Economy

Taiwan's spectacular emergence as a newly industrialised economy attests to the strengths and dynamism of the policies and structures underlying its development. Gross national product (GNP) per capita rose from $400 in 1951 to $3,480 in 1986 and reached $11,604 at the end of 1994. A more impressive performance has been the ability to make the transition from a traditional agricultural society to an industrialised state and to sustain a very rapid pace of growth while avoiding sharp imbalances in the distribution of income.

Lacking natural resources, Taiwan adopted policies promoting exports of labour-intensive manufactured products to propel its economy into self-sustaining growth. Many developing nations have attempted more or less successfully to follow a similar path. What sets Taiwan apart is the nature of its production system. The economy relies on a web of small- and medium-sized industries interlinked through family-based networks and interfacing directly with the state.

Historical legacy, drawing its inspiration from the philosophy of Sun Yat Sen, emphasised the quest for affluence while avoiding social inequity. Access to land has been identified as the cornerstone of a family-based approach to development. Agrarian reform and taxation of urban land equalised land rights, enabling lower income families to own a farm or a building plot.

An array of policies promoting small business have been sustained over four decades. While the share of manufactured products in total exports rose from 8 per cent in 1953 to 94 per cent in 1992, the proportion produced by small enterprises has remained very high at 65 per cent.

The success of this model, which diverged markedly from western approaches to industrialisation, has intrigued economists. Numerous studies have analysed the prominent role of Taiwan's small and medium-sized enterprises in driving economic development. Yet, defining underlying principles that would allow the transferability of this system has thus far eluded the specialists.

While experts continue to debate the relevance and replicability of the Taiwanese model, small- and medium-sized enterprises have forged ahead, targeting markets in textiles, clothing, processed foods, chemicals, plastics and electronics. They have displayed remarkable flexibility and adaptability, constantly repositioning themselves, adjusting their targets and realigning their operations. They develop new products, adopt new technology and chart bold strategies to exploit 'niche' markets.

Palestine's situation is in many respects unique. However, there are compelling reasons for Palestine to seriously consider the Taiwan model. The stabilising impacts of small enterprise extend beyond a broad distribution of the benefits of development. Networks of small and microbusinesses allow for dispersed patterns of production linking enterprises in urban and rural locations. They generate a broad range of employment opportunities, build in the flexibility needed to respond to shifts in market demand and because they are family-based, they tend to reinforce social cohesion.

Palestinians display socio-cultural characteristics that are conducive to the development of an economic model relying primarily on the strength and dynamism of human resources. These include:

- High literacy, a skilled labour force and wide appreciation of educational achievement;
- Importance given to establishing, owning and developing a business, as well as the value placed on having a good business sense; and
- Strong family-based networks and a capacity to balance individual entrepreneurship and family obligations.

The atomistic nature of small enterprises contributes to facilitating entry by reducing the seed capital needed to establish a business. It enhances competitiveness by lowering transaction costs. Through specialisation and subcontracting, it has a built-in flexibility to target and tap markets.

High unemployment and constraints imposed by Israel on Palestinian autonomy and development have confined Palestinians to traditional activities, such as handicrafts, apparel, wood and metalworking. A lack of working capital and of land which can be used as collateral to obtain formal credit serves to deny the Palestinian entrepreneur access to technology, managerial expertise and marketing opportunities. All of these are controlled by foreign interests, and this hampers growth prospects.

Furthermore, the high import content of inputs in the production process leads to substantial leakage from the local economy, thereby depressing the multiplier effect of public and private investment. Nowhere is this more apparent than in the construction industry. Almost all building materials are imported from Israel at prices far exceeding international levels. Currently, Israel would reap 70 per cent of the economic benefits of public works and housing construction projects.

Taiwan's small enterprises certainly faced less formidable obstacles. However, in the 1950s and early 1960s, they had to fend for themselves without much support from government. Private associations were set up to mobilise capital resources by offering small depositors a higher rate of interest than formal financial institutions in order to extend credit to small entrepreneurs, albeit at a higher cost.

Support for Small Business

The small size and insular character of Taiwan dictated that government intervention be directed at protecting the operation of the market and safeguarding the entry of new entrepreneurs. Since 1968, three key programmes have been instituted to support the small business sector: These include the following:

- *The Small- and Medium-Sized Business Credit Guarantee Fund.* The fund has processed close to one million loan applications and funnelled credit to over 70,000 businesses;

- *The Small Business Integrated Assistance Centre.* This offers technical assistance and capacity building; and
- *Start-up Loans.* These are provided for entrepreneurs between the ages of 20 and 45 and have been extended to 7,600 enterprises, out of 10,500 applicants, generating over 73,000 jobs.

Administrative guidelines first issued in 1968 were reformulated no less than five times in response to the changing economic environment, domestic as well as global, but also to reflect a growing understanding of the role of the small business sector and the internal operations of microenterprises.

In the 1990s, government policy has focused on safeguarding the competitiveness of the Taiwanese small business sector in a globalised economy by improving their access to technology and helping them develop their own marketing channels. The Centre-Satellite Development, Industrial Co-ordination Centres established in 1990 to pool and co-ordinate resources among clusters of manufacturing firms and the 1991 *Statute for the Development of Medium and Small Business* reflect these new strategic objectives.

Taiwan's commitment to create an enabling environment for the small business sector has led to spectacular results. A unique blend of legislative instruments and capital allocations judiciously modulated over four decades has fostered the system's adaptation to the stringent requirements of a modern economy capable of successfully competing in an increasingly globalised marketplace.

Housing and Small Business Development

Taiwan has addressed housing as a critical component of its economic development strategy and adapted its housing programmes to the evolution of its strategic economic objectives. Government policy has protected and re-inforced the traditional system of economically productive families interlinked through community networks.

When the housing market is unconstrained by cumbersome regulatory controls on the development and use of land and buildings, low and moderate income families invest in real estate as an integral component of their self improvement strategies. Housing is viewed not only as shelter, but also as an income producing asset through commercial use and/or rental of space. As the primary locale for economic activity, the house offers readily accessible premises at an affordable cost reducing the amount of working capital needed to sustain operations.

More importantly, these savings lower dramatically seed capital requirements, thereby facilitating entry to new and young entrepreneurs. They also provide an insurance against business failure during the critical start-up period and at times of adjustment in production line and/or realignment of production and marketing processes. Indeed, in many respects, the Taiwanese shop-house has carried the concept of a productive house to its ultimate dimension.

Government intervention in the housing sector has focused on two key issues: land management and access to credit. The primary objective is to protect and encourage the owner/operator of housing and business. Land management policy emphasised three major strategies:

1) Fostering access to land for low and moderate income families in accordance with the *Equalised Land Rights* policy;
2) Control of illegal occupancy of land; and
3) Stabilising the real estate market.

Housing finance strategies focused on access to credit in order to:

• Promote ownership among low and moderate income households through subsidised loans;
• Foster small- and medium-sized firms as real estate developers and building contractors; and
• Prevent speculation and inflationary spirals in the real estate market.

From the mid-1950s to the mid-1970s, the implementation of the *Equalised Land Rights* policy was sufficient to guarantee low and moderate income families access to land. Control of illegal occupancy of land proved to be a much more difficult task. The *Procedure for Illegal Building Management* legislation, which was enacted in 1957, mandated resettlement in accordance with two guidelines: *building before demolition* and *resettling on site*. Unauthorised shelters built from 1958 on were to be demolished. A high level co-ordinating commission was established to oversee implementation in Taipei City.

The magnitude of the problem was overwhelming. In 1963, Taipei's squatter settlements accounted for 30 per cent of the city's housing stock of which 63 per cent were one room shacks lacking sanitary facilities of any kind. Over 15,000 newly built units were razed between 1964 and 1969. Resettlement initiated in 1967 affected the old stock of about 130,000 units, starting with sites needed for public projects. Squatters could opt for compensation or placement on a priority list of applicants for public housing and a market stall. The majority opted for the cash compensation alternative.

Drastic intervention of this nature dislocates entire communities, destroying their social and economic fabric. In the context of the 1960s, they were quite common in other countries in both the east and the west. Objectives ranged from removal of health hazards and urban blight to renewal of obsolete or deteriorated areas. In Taiwan, the purpose was land management; legal and regulatory controls on occupancy; valorisation and use of land; and to secure property rights.

Today, massive clearance and dislocation of citizens has become politically unfeasible. Regularisation and upgrading is a far more productive approach allowing for development of culturally sensitive solutions that can yield high economic returns.

After 1974, the real estate market overheated, driven by speculative development. The state intervened forcefully to control and deflate the escalation of land prices. Large developers were cut off from local bank credit, a ban on the construction of high-rise buildings was imposed and taxes on non-owner occupied housing were increased. Within the year, the surge in prices was brought under control and the height limits lifted. However, market demand remained weak and the real estate market stabilised.

In 1977, developers were once again allowed to access credit but on a much more limited scale. Government strategies had prevented the build-up of a dangerous real estate bubble that could derail Taiwan's progress. They also enabled small- and medium-sized family firms to continue to dominate the real estate development market. In 1983, only 2.7 per cent of Taiwan's developers had assets of more than $1.25 million, while 68.4 per cent had assets of less than $125,000.

Because of the interconnection between housing and business, private capital has provided the primary source of housing finance. The traditional rotating fund, a community-based credit mechanism is extensively used for this purpose. Unlike similar credit groups in the Middle East where participants receive the fund according to a pre-agreed sequence, Chinese participants 'bid' for the fund and the money is allocated to the highest bidder. The auction is assumed to channel resources to the entrepreneur who is able to make the most profitable use of capital while the 'bid' interest payment contributes to the fund's growth. The system favours the investment dimension of housing to the detriment of quality of the living environment.

The state housing programme, started in 1958, focused less on production than on ensuring access to credit for low and moderate income families to help them finance the construction of their own houses. Eligibility for state subsidised rental housing was consequently limited to the very poor (i.e. those below the 15th percentile). Families above the absolute poverty line but below the 70th percentile could apply for subsidised loans.

The mortgage credit finance was funded by revenue derived from a capital gains tax levied on land transactions. Mortgage regulations required applicants to acquire the building plot first, entailing that land acquisition be financed out of savings. Furthermore, houses could not be sold until the mortgage debt had been fully repaid. Such a programme clearly precluded developers from using state subsidies to boost their profits.

The programme led to a shift in housing delivery from informal to formal channels. Artisans/ contractors soon evolved into small scale developers to undertake co-operative construction relying on prefinancing of 20 to 30 per cent of the house price by prospective residents. Within its policy framework of fostering small business development, the government actively supported the small- and medium-sized construction companies. Small co-operative construction firms evolved as a consequence of the fragmented land ownership patterns resulting from land reform and the subdivision of holdings among family members.

Two types of co-operative construction prevail: the first involves an agreement between the developer and the landowner to share the finished units. The second involves prospective dwellers forming an association and initiating *entrusted construction* by retaining the contractor(s) to build the project or entrusting it to a developer in the case of larger projects.

The proportion of owner-occupied houses in the total stock increased from 40.5 per cent in 1966 to over 80 per cent in 1980 and has remained one of the highest rates in the world. Even in Taipei, housing conditions improved markedly despite congestion and high real estate prices. Habitable space per person increased from 7.2 square meters in the mid-1960s to 19.7 square meters in 1986, a remarkable achievement in less than one generation.

Investment Policy Changes

It is all the more remarkable in light of the changing emphasis of government resource allocation strategies. From 1968 on, investment priorities shifted away from *social* sectors which included housing towards directly *productive* sectors. The assisted mortgage finance programme was discontinued. Henceforth, housing finance had to rely on private capital resources. At the lower end, housing and microenterprise finance remained closely interconnected. Families invested to develop their houses and their businesses at their own pace and according to their own self improvement strategies. At the upper end, growing affluence generated demand and resources for *quality* housing.

With the take-off of the Taiwanese economy, there was no dearth of private capital to support a vigorous housing sector. Developers gradually took over the production and delivery process displacing owner/builders as the predominant suppliers of housing even for low-cost housing. Property values escalated as affluent families started to buy houses for investment rather than occupancy purposes.

Between 1978 and 1980 it is estimated that 50 to 60 per cent of housing sales in Taipei were transacted through trusts and investment companies. High production levels sustained over a decade from 1975 to 1985 eventually led to oversupply. Vacancy reached a high of 13.4 per cent in Taipei, prompting the government to intervene. On the strength of stipulations embodied in the land rights equalising act, the government declared vacant lots in inner Taipei and Kaohsung cities subject to compulsory purchase at below-market values.

Furthermore, the tax on vacant lots was raised to levels which were ten to 25 times higher than comparative rates on built-up land. Investment trusts had little choice but to valorise their holdings, adding to the glut and further depressing prices. A positive consequence of the oversupply was the opportunities created for middle income families to upgrade their housing as first-time buyers, or by trading up. The market glut in the late 1980s and early 1990s paralleled international trends.

However, the unique structure of Taiwan's economy and the government's unwavering commitment to support the family-based networks of small- and medium-sized enterprises limited the effects of speculative development to the high-end segments of the housing market. This prevented the subsequent deflation from adversely affecting moderate income families, as happened when real estate prices tumbled by ten to 30 per cent in the UK, USA, Japan and other post-industrial countries.

The major weakness of Taiwan's housing policy resulted from the government's inability to pursue land management policies capable of coping with the rapid expansion of the urbanised areas. Proactive policies are needed to guide transformation and development occurring at an astounding pace. Overwhelmed authorities could only respond through reactive tactical decisions to counteract trends judged detrimental to economic growth.

Uncontrolled development of family shops and factories was allowed to cause serious external problems, in terms of congestion, environmental pollution and inadequate public amenities. Over the past three decades, improvement in housing standards have been mitigated by the deteriorating quality of the urban environment.

Balancing between the regulatory controls needed to safeguard environmental quality and the flexibility needed to promote and integrate microenterprises as key agents of economic growth is a challenging task. The tendency to over-regulate must be checked. Cumbersome and onerous regulations stifle entrepreneurship and drive households to abandon formal processes in favour of informal modes of development.

It may very well be that Taiwan's approach to economic growth, relying on guidance and incentive at the micro level, demanded a relaxation of the quality dimension of the urban environment in the early stages of development. Environmental issues become a concern when increasing degradation impairs the functional efficiency of urban centres or starts to pose health hazards. A degree of affluence is a conditioning factor, but by no means the sole determinant of concern.

As it charts its course towards sustainable economic development, Palestine will have to determine the appropriate balance between efficiency, equity and cost that it wishes to maintain. The relationship between these three variables is bound to change over time to reflect the changing economic and social context. The starting point must be well grounded in the realities of the situation currently prevailing.

The strategic objectives should reflect a clear vision of the desired future; the short-term targets should be a sequence of pragmatic effective steps leading in this direction. However, at any point along the path, disregard of environmental and social considerations carries short- and long-term costs that should be acknowledged in order for choices to be meaningful and informed decision-making to occur.

THE ISSUES: ABIDJAN, IVORY COAST

Institutionalising Community-Based Development

In the Ivory Coast, the experience of Adjamé, one of 12 administrative jurisdictions referred to as *communes* in the city of Abidjan, demonstrates how a forward looking mayor with a clear vision and a sense of mission can create, nurture and institutionalise community-based structures to mobilise and empower residents. Adjamé's performance is all the more impressive given the context of structural adjustment, dramatic declines in income, changing political structures, and crisis management.

Decentralisation initiated in 1984, together with the transfer of administrative powers to elected mayors and municipal councils at the commune level, injected new vitality into urban management. The ability of communes to set their own priorities for capital and operating expenditures, raise their own revenues and implement projects enabled Adjamé's mayor to experiment with an innovative approach to community-based development relying on local resources and empowerment.

Adjamé is one of Abidjan's oldest urban districts and is also the city's present commercial core and its major transport node. It has the largest markets in the city, accounting for 25 per cent of all mercantile activity. Its current population is estimated at approximately 220,000, about half of whom have immigrated from neighbouring countries in search of employment within the unified regional labour and monetary market of Francophone West Africa.

During the economic boom of the 1970s, rents in Adjamé rose by a factor of six and despite the severe recession of the 80s, real estate values continue to rise and are roughly three times the Abidjan average. Along major paved roads three- to four-storey buildings are appearing with shops and offices on the lower floors and 'modern' apartments above.

The vast majority of residents still continue to purchase water from vendors and use overloaded on-site waste water disposal systems in areas where densities reach 800 to 1,000 persons per hectare. Services provided in the poorer neighbourhoods by the privately operated water supply, electricity and solid waste collection services are highly inadequate. The bulk of the refuse is not collected and ends up on the road bed or in drainage ditches.

Decentralisation allowed local urban and rural districts referred to as *communes* to set their own priorities for capital and operating expenditures to raise revenues and implement projects. But it is the transfer of administrative powers to elected municipal councils that transformed urban management by introducing new dimensions of representation and accountability in governance. In the depth of the recession, the newly elected mayors faced an increasingly critical situation as the imbalances between expanded responsibilities and budget cutbacks became untenable.

The acute shortage of public resources prompted the mayor of Adjamé to organise an action group in order to mobilise residents to actively participate in addressing urgent health and sanitation issues. The committee's most successful initiative has been the street sweeping project for the main commercial boulevard and the immediate vicinity of the central market, a major generator of garbage and trash. The sweepers are remunerated through contributions collected from about 2,000 businesses in the market area.

The committee's activities demonstrated the benefits of citizen participation. They also convinced the mayor of the need for direct outreach at the neighbourhood level. The deepening recession meant that residents had to assume primary responsibility for the improvement and management of their neighbourhoods.

STRATEGIES: THE CDQ

Concept and Organisation

Adapting the French model he observed in Marseilles to local conditions in Adjamé, the mayor in 1988 established neighbourhood committees, known as *Comités de development de quartier* (CDQs) to engage the energies of residents for the promotion of social, economic and cultural development at the community level. The strategy is to promote economic activities and provide jobs for the unemployed and to alleviate the most pressing environmental and social problems in the neighbourhood.

By 1990, eight CDQs were operational. Today, Adjamé's 19 neighbourhoods all have CDQs. The most dynamic and innovative are in the poorest districts where infrastructure is lacking, *bidonvilles* and informal settlements abound, and sanitation is a major challenge. It is not surprising that most CDQs started their activity by organising teams to undertake badly needed urban services, beginning with sanitation.

Towards Independent Neighbourhood Development Associations

The original structure of the CDQ vested decision-making in the general assembly of CDQ members, policy formulation in the council of overseers appointed by the mayor and implementation in the executive board consisting of elected and *ex officio* members.

Since 1990, the administrative structure has evolved, first in response to national political liberalisation and the institution of a multi-party system, then as a result of the mayor's forceful strategy of empowerment. Today, CDQ leadership is more representative, management is more democratic and competencies much broader. In order to be eligible to vote, residents must pay a one-time fee equivalent to 50 US cents.

There are around 7,000 active members of the CDQs in Adjamé, the majority of whom are dynamic young people. The CDQ organisation varies slightly from one neighbourhood to the other but it always includes three basic components: the president; the executive council, whose members must be residents of the area and who do not receive any compensation; and the operational units that undertake activities and whose staff is remunerated, as is the CDQ staff. Local elders, civic leaders and merchants are often included as additional members of the council. In some cases, they constitute a separate council of *wisemen*.

During his second term in office, the mayor has been restructuring the governance of the CDQs in order for them to acquire the legal status of *associations* to give them greater autonomy, including the capacity to access funding directly from central agencies, intermediary non-governmental organisations (NGOs) and other sources. Along with this evolution, the commune will provide them with technical assistance through a bureau for projects; oversee their management through a monitoring committee chaired by the mayor with membership from the CDQs and the City Council; and co-ordinate their activities through a standing committee of CDQ presidents, the communal CDQ council.

CDQ Activities and Finances

The CDQs are involved in many different activities, to varying degrees of success. These include:

• Street cleaning and garbage collection;

- Security services;
- Sanitation (pumping out septic tanks and cesspits and cleaning open drain ditches);
- Commercial enterprises, including running public fountains, stores, sports facilities, and public latrines;
- Small infrastructure improvements, such as road improvement and maintenance of drains and street lighting; and
- Social services, such as literacy campaigns, helping poor or abandoned children and the handicapped.

CDQs received seed capital from the commune to start up their operations in the form of cash contributions and physical plant. A total of 3 million CFA was allocated to the 19 CDQs to open a bank account and initiate activities. The amount of the grant depended primarily on the population of the area and its relative wealth, with larger shares allocated to the more disadvantaged neighbourhoods.

The commune also transfers to the CDQs public facilities such as public latrines and water fountains which can be operated at a profit and commercial premises they can lease. CDQs are enjoined to contract private microentrepreneurs to operate the facilities rather than attempt to do so themselves. These microenterprises retain the income generated from their operations and become self-financing. The sponsoring CDQ receives a share of net profits as working capital.

Except for the start up transfers, CDQs do not receive operating subsidies from the commune of Adjamé. Subsequent transfers are limited to providing seed capital for the launching of new activities. Having to rely on the resources they generate, the CDQs have a stake in the efficient management of their assets and in the diversification of their revenue sources. This entails expanding the scope of their activities to combine revenue from user fees for services delivered, such as security, sanitation and garbage collection with income from commercial leases and operations.

In a predominantly residential area, user fees account for over 85 per cent of CDQ revenues. In commercial or mixed use zones, total revenues are higher by a factor of two to three with user fees accounting for 65 per cent, leases for 10 to 15 per cent and permits fees for 10 per cent. Wealthy CDQ presidents and community leaders usually donate furnishings and equipment for CDQ headquarters, as well as cash contributions to cover any operating deficits.

CDQ Services

In relatively well-off residential areas, CDQs provide few services as the privately operated city services do the job. In the squatterised zones, the CDQs are unable to provide services because municipalities cannot service illegal settlements until they are regularised.

In other neighbourhoods, the CDQ will sweep the streets, collect garbage, pump out septic tanks and cesspits and clean drainage ditches. Garbage is collected from each household and brought to the collection station where the solid waste management company picks it up. Pumping trucks are supposed to empty the sludge in special dumping stations free of charge. Unfortunately, the small tanker truck operators continue to dump the contents illegally in the lagoon and the large private solid waste management contractor fails to empty the dumpsters regularly.

With the onset of the economic crisis, security has emerged as a major issue that the CDQs have felt compelled to address. Fees are collected from households and businesses and young men from the neighbourhood are hired to patrol the streets and the market area. The guards are given uniforms, a whistle, and a flashlight but are not armed. Speed bumps and moveable fences are set up to control access points in the market areas.

The street sweepers are both young men and women. They are provided with uniforms, brooms and garbage carts. Williamsville II financed its initial purchase of the equipment in a creative manner. The CDQ asked the street sweepers and the security guards to forego one-and-a-half months of their salaries, and used the fees it collected to pay for the equipment, along with some seed capital from the commune.

Fees for street sweeping, garbage collection and security services are roughly equivalent, but the security service is the most popular. CDQ presidents complain that fees have become generally harder to collect, affecting the sustainability of some activities, particularly street sweeping. The new reluctance to pay is alternatively attributed to perceptions of inadequate services or mismanagement or, paradoxically, to perceptions that conditions have improved to the point where households feel the service is no longer vital to their well-being.

CDQ Commercial Activities

The range of activities undertaken by CDQs depends on the specific assets transferred to them as well as their locational advantages. Because of the revenues they provide, commercial facilities are the CDQs' most prized possessions. The stores are leased and provide rental income, as well as a one-time fee. Two CDQs have been awarded contracts to manage the sports stadiums located in their jurisdiction. They are responsible for the management and maintenance of the facility but receive no funds from the commune. They lease out the stadiums for events and for use as an overnight parking lot. One of the two stadiums is Adjamé's sports complex.

Infrastructure Construction and Maintenance

There is a keen awareness of urban infrastructure as a valuable capital asset for the residents, the CDQs and Adjamé. There is a general consensus that infrastructure must be maintained and valorised despite the curtailment of central transfers.

The CDQ involvement ranges from pothole repair to major street repair after heavy rainfalls have eroded the compacted earth on the unpaved roadbeds. The CDQs usually purchase fill material and expect the commune to pay for the rental of machinery, particularly bulldozers and backhoes. Waste water disposal systems are often clogged, given the common practice of dumping garbage in drains. Open drain channels can be cleaned by the CDQs but underground sewers require specialised equipment that they do not have. The commune has to request service from the private water company which has been contracted to manage the waterborne sewerage system.

New CDQ Initiatives

The success of the CDQ concept has encouraged Adjamé's mayor to launch more ambitious initiatives, each with its own CDQ style administrative structure. The object of the Health initiative is to create a health centre in each of the 19 quarters which is managed by an independent CDQ structure whose executive council is to consist of an elected president, a doctor, the manager of the health centre, a representative of the local CDQ, and a representative of the mayor.

The first CDQ health centre was completed and fully operational by April, 1995. The commune paid for the renovation of an existing building, medical equipment, rent and supplies for the first six months of operation at a cost of about $20,000. Following this start-up period, the health centre is expected to be financially self-supporting. The centre will charge for the services of the doctor and paramedical staff at approximately one-tenth the rate currently charged by the government hospital under the fee structure enacted as part of the curtailment of social subsidies.

Very few private clinics in Adjamé have doctors. Most are run by paramedical staff and lack basic equipment. Even then, the fees are unaffordable to lower income residents under the fee structures enacted as part of the curtailment of subsidies.

After the first few months of operation, the CDQ board will review the fee structure, as well as the operating expenses to ensure financial viability. In the longer term, the commune expects the health centre to train its own paramedics.

Pharmaceutical supplies constitute a major bottleneck due to the delays in accessing lower priced supplies provided by the Ministry of Public Health. After waiting for almost six months, the mayor has decided to purchase supplies on the open market at much higher prices in order to operate the Centre and avoid damaging the CDQ's credibility. At this time, the commune does not have the capacity to finance health centres in other districts. Nevertheless, the mayor is already developing a long-term health strategy for Adjamé utilising the resources of all 19 centres to set up a health clinic.

The second new initiative combines micro-incubators and training programmes to encourage young Ivorians to start commercial enterprises, a sector they overlooked during the economic boom in favour of obtaining clerical jobs. In the initial phase, 40 young people are being sent to a three-month training session at the Higher Institute for Commercial Studies. A shop will be established in every neighbourhood market and will be operated by the trainees. Municipal backing has allowed the CDQ to find companies willing to supply merchandise to the store on credit.

The first has been opened and turned over to two young graduates from the Institute's Programme. The young men and women will receive fixed compensations from sales revenue for a one-year period. After a six-month start-up period, they will have to cover their own operating costs, including rent. The balance will be deposited in a savings account and used first to pay back the start-up funds granted by the commune and then to accumulate seed capital for the young entrepreneurs to start their own businesses. The CDQ store would then continue to be run by the next generation of students.

This programme is the first initiative which may entail subsidy beyond seed capital from the commune. The mayor considers it an investment in human resources that is critical to ensure the future economic development of Adjamé.

CONCLUSION

The case studies presented in this paper demonstrate strategies which have led to remarkable achievements in two sharply contrasting situations, at different geographic locations, within different institutional structures and cultural traditions.

The success of Taiwan's development policy is primarily due to the following factors:

1) Adopting strategies that build on the strengths of its social and cultural traditions;
2) Reliance on private initiative and commitment to create and maintain an enabling environment for private enterprise while providing a social safety net for the very poor;

3) Monitoring policies and adapting them to the changing structure of the global economy;

4) Implementing programmes that address the different dimensions of the strategic objectives pursued through a co-ordinated approach to land management, fiscal policy, credit availability and support services to small entrepreneurs; and

5) Avoiding partial policies and unsustainable measures that are bound to fail in the longer term and which may introduce distortions that would negatively impact macroeconomic objectives.

In the face of seemingly overwhelming obstacles, Adjamé has managed to initiate and institutionalise a sustainable community-based development process. Its success is primarily due to:

1) Fostering empowerment and accountability in local governance through the institutionalisation of community-based development;

2) Responding to the scarcity of public resources by judicious investment and leveraging in order to expand, rather than curtail, urban services to the poor;

3) Adopting strategies conducive to long-term economic viability based on sound financial management;

4) Recognising that the effectiveness of public/ private partnership rests on defining a new role for the municipality as catalyst and enabler;

5) Ensuring sustainability by providing CDQ's with seed capital for their initiatives and requiring activities to be operated on a self-supporting basis; and

6) Marshalling the higher efficiency of independent microentrepreneurs to manage and deliver urban services in the poorer districts.

Palestinians need first and foremost to establish full control over their land resources and exercise the authority to enforce property rights and enact development regulations. They also need to build up an efficient financial sector capable of financing development projects, as well as delivering credit to small entrepreneurs.

Bold and innovative strategies integrating the economic, social, and environmental dimensions of development are needed at the national, as well as the community level. Co-ordination and leveraging of public and private inputs will be required to build infrastructure and to provide urban services and access to technology.

Reliance on development assistance is not sustainable in the long-term. The development of Palestine will be achieved by the entrepreneurship and resources of its citizens. There is no substitute for representation, dedication and creativity in governance. Lack of resources should not be allowed to paralyse local authorities and lead to further impoverishment and degradation of the urban environment. Like Taiwan and Adjamé,

Palestine will need to empower its citizens by enabling them to access the resources they need to improve their economic situation, develop their communities and rebuild their devastated nation.

BIBLIOGRAPHY

Antoine, P., Dubresson, A. and Manou-Savina, A., 1987, **Abidjan 'Côté cours'; pour comprendre la question de l'habitat**, Karthala et Orston, Paris.

Atelier d'urbanisme d'Abidjan, 1984 a, **Données, statistiques et résultats, Direction et Contrôle des Grands Travaux**, Bureau central d'études techniques, Abidjan.

Atelier d'urbanisme d'Abidjan, 1984 b, **L'évolution des quartiers anciens d'Abidjan**, Direction et Contrôle des Grands Travaux (DCGTX), Bureau central d'études techniques (BCET), Abidjan.

Atelier d'urbanisme d'Abidjan, 1984 c, **Le marché immobilier d'Abidjan**, Direction et Contrôle des Grands Travaux, Bureau central d'études techniques, Abidjan.

Atelier d'urbanisme d'Abidjan, 1978, **Relevés des cours dans les quartiers évolutifs et spontanés d'Abidjan**, Working paper, Direction et Contrôle des Grands Travaux, Bureau central d'études techniques, Abidjan.

Chen, E.K.Y., Williams, Jack F. and Wong, Joseph, eds., 1991, **Taiwan: Economy, Society and History**, Centre of Asian Studies, University of Hong Kong, Hong Kong.

Chin, Pei-Hsiung, 1988, **Housing and Economic Development in Taiwan**, IURD Working Paper 483 (June), University of California, Berkeley.

Chou, Tein-Chen, 1985, *Industrial Organization in the Process of Economic Development: The Case of Taiwan 1950–1980*, **Université Catholique de Louvain**, Facultie de Sciences: Economiques, Sociales et Politiques, Nouv. Ser. No. 154, CIACO, Louvain-la-Neuve, Belgium.

Chou, Tein-Chen, 1992, *The Experience of SME's Development in Taiwan: High Export Contribution and Export Intensity*, **Rivista Internazionale di Scienze Economiche e Commerciali**, vol. 39, 12, pp. 1067–1084.

Commune d'Adjamé, Ville d'Abidjan, 1994, **Project Adjamé Santé: Resumé Synthétique des Différents Volets et Estimations Budgetaires Globales du Projet**, August, Abidjan.

Davis, D.R. and M.D. Ward, 1990, *The Entrepreneurial State: Evidence from Taiwan*, **Comparative Political Studies**, October, pp. 314–333.

Dossier pour le seminaire, Seminaire sur les comités de développement de quartiers: Thème les CDQ – un exemple développement communautaire, Bingerville, Côte d'Ivoire, April, 1993, vol. 1.

Galenson, Walter, 1992, **Labor and Economic Growth in Five Asian Countries: South Korea, Malaysia, Taiwan, Thailand, and the Philippines**, Praeger, New York.

Gold, Thomas B., 1986, **State and Society in the Taiwan Miracle**, M.E. Sharpe, Armonk, New York.

Ho, Samuel P.S., 1990, **Small Scale Enterprises in Korea and Taiwan**, World Bank Staff Working Paper 384, World Bank, Washington, D.C.

Ho, Samuel P.S., 1978, *Small Scale Industries in Two Rapidly Growing Less Developed Countries: Korea and Taiwan – A Study of their Characteristics, Competitive Bases, and Productivity*, **Study in Employment and Rural Development**, 53 (December), International Bank for Reconstruction and Development. Washington, D.C.

Institute of Strategic and International Studies, 1986, **Lessons from Taiwan: Pathways to Follow and Pitfalls to Avoid**, Kuala Lumpur.

Kao, Yueh-shi Carol and Huei-Chu Liao, 1994, *The Development of Small- and Medium-sized Enterprises in the Republic of China*, **Industry of Free China**, March, pp. 71–87.

Long, Simon, **Taiwan to 1993: Politics versus Prosperity**, Special Report No. 1159, The Economist Intelligence Unit, London.

Lotfi, Sherif, 1994, **Adjamé's CDQ, A Cost Effective Approach to Sustainable Community-Based Development**, Field report, September.

Ranis, Gustav, ed., 1992, **Taiwan: From Developing to Mature Economy**, Westview Press, Boulder, Colorado.

Research Triangle Institute and United States Agency for International Development 1994, *Municipal Development Support Project*, **The Training Project**, USAID/REDSO/WCA, August.

Serageldin, Mona, 1990 a, **Regularizing the Informal Land Development Process**, Working paper, Office of Housing and Urban Programs, United States Agency for International Development, September, Washington D.C.

Serageldin, Mona, 1990 b, **The Impact of Investments in Urban Infrastructure on Municipal Revenues and the Integration of Unformal Sector Activities: the Abidjan Experience**, Working paper, Office of Housing and Urban Programs, United States Agency for International Development, September, Washington D.C.

Serageldin, Mona, 1993, **Use of Land and Infrastructure in the Self Improvement Strategies of Urban Lower Income Families**, Working paper, Office of Housing and Urban Programs, United States Agency for International Development, May, Washington, D.C.

Serageldin, Mona, 1994, **Community-Based Development: Experiences Across Cities**, Working paper, Office of Environment and Urban Programs, Center for Environment, United States Agency for International Development, September, Washington D.C.

Serageldin, Mona and François Vigier, 1994, **Designing for Urban Growth, Abidjan, Ivory Coast, Unit for Housing and Urbanization**, Harvard University, Graduate School of Design January, Cambridge, Massachusetts, USA.

Shieh, Gwo-shyong, 1992, **Boss Island: The Subcontracting Network and Micro-Entrepreneurship in Taiwan's Development**, American University Studies, Series XI: Anthropology and Sociology, vol. 60, P. Lang, New York.

Synthèse: Rapport Général, **Seminaire sur les comités de développement de quartiers: Thème les CDQ – un exemple développement communautaire**, Bingerville, Côte d'Ivoire, April, 1993, vol. 2.

Wang, N.T., ed., 1992, **Taiwan in the Modern World**, M.E. Sharpe Inc., London.

Yu, Tzong-shian, 1985, *The Relationship Between the Government and the Private Sector in the Process of Economic Development in Taiwan, R.O.C.*, **Industry of Free China**, 64 (October), pp. 1–16.

OPTIONS FOR URBAN DEVELOPMENT IN PALESTINE

Shadia Touqan

ABSTRACT

This paper argues that the special case of Palestine requires a careful assessment of all the available options for urban development. These include new development, extensive re-development, neighbourhood renewal and conservation, as well as the adaptive re-use of historic buildings. Although the West Bank and Gaza share many of the same problems and needs, this study concentrates mainly on conditions prevailing in the West Bank, with a particular focus on the historic city of Nablus. Despite this, the proposed solutions are applicable to all urban areas in the Palestinian state.

This paper comprises three parts. The first examines the urban environment in Palestinian towns and reviews the historical and geographical context and urbanisation trends in Palestine. It also briefly describes the existing housing stock and the extent and magnitude of disrepair and decay in urban centres, in addition to examining their problems and potential for renewal and upgrading.

The second part reviews existing approaches to urban renewal policies and the international experience in public/private partnerships. It examines the existing urban design characteristics of Palestinian towns, their architectural character and recent urbanisation trends, again with Nablus servicing as the focal point for a case study. It also suggests that development for Nablus could be used as a model for integrating various development policies and the partnership approach.

The third part summarises the existing conditions and available options, as well as the need for an urban renewal policy based on a socio-economic framework and legal and institutional structures. Finally, it puts forward proposals for a broad strategic approach, including an appraisal of the requirements and priorities for local urban settlements. This approach could serve as the basis for an overall plan of implementation, and for the public and private agencies and local community groups which should work in partnership to ensure the success of both planning and implementation.

INTRODUCTION

During these early days when Palestinians partially control their land and have subsequently rushed to develop and reconstruct their shattered towns, pressure has mounted to achieve a rapid supply of badly needed infrastructure, housing and other social services. Palestinian towns and cities today suffer from multiple urban problems due to the prolonged military occupation and the harsh Israeli administration's restrictive and obstructive policies during their rule.

The question on every Palestinian's mind is, 'Where to start and what is most urgently needed?' The most frequent answer to both questions is 'housing' and/or 'infrastructure.' While the answer is valid, the question that should follow is, 'What approach, and which policies, should be followed to achieve these objectives and to begin the long-awaited process of development?'

In view of the peculiar political, legislative and administrative conditions that prevailed during the occupation, any future development plan should take into consideration the legacy of that occupation and its consequences. Furthermore, such a plan should also consider the uncertainty which will continue to prevail during the interim period with regard to the final status of land ownership, borders and the control of resources before a political settlement is reached.

EXISTING URBAN DEVELOPMENT

The Historical and Geographical Context

Major changes had been imposed by the Israeli authorities on administrative structures and jurisdictions that prevailed in various regions of the West Bank before 1967.

After the unification of Jordan with the West Bank in 1950, the Jordanian government initially maintained the structures that were established during the British Mandate. However, in 1957, it established a three-tiered administrative structure composed of districts (liwa), sub-districts (qada) and rural sub-districts (nahiyeh).

The three 'superior' districts, which were later redefined as counties (muhafatha), were: Nablus, Jerusalem and Hebron. Nablus district/county consisted of: Nablus sub-district (divided into two rural sub-districts) and sub-districts of Jenin and Tulkarm, each with its own rural sub-district (Benvinisti and Khayat, 1988).

After the occupation, the Israeli military authorities abolished the Jordanian structure and divided the West Bank into seven sub-districts, thus stripping Nablus and Hebron from their higher status. More significantly, Jerusalem was 'illegally' annexed to Israel and areas under its jurisdiction were transferred to Bethlehem and Ramallah sub-districts (Ibid.).

A dual administrative system was later developed in the Occupied Palestinian Territories (OPT) after the creation of Israeli regional councils (Military Order 848, 1979). Under the new system, a dual division of one Arab (military sub-districts) and one Jewish (regional councils) were created (Ibid.). The Arab sub-districts included Nablus, Jenin, Tulkarm, Ramallah, Bethlehem and Hebron. Jewish jurisdictional areas were mainly in Arab land brought under Israeli control by a variety of methods (Touqan, 1995) and was consequently used to establish Jewish settlements.

This ethnic division was demonstrated in separate judicial, administrative and economic systems (Benvinisti, 1988 and Touqan, 1995). However, Palestinians continued to refer to Nablus, Hebron and areas originally under their jurisdiction as 'counties or regions' in spite of major administrative changes imposed by Israeli authorities.

The pattern of urbanisation in the OPT could not be easily defined as it was difficult to distinguish between urban, semi-urban and rural communities in the absence of reliable statistics. No new municipalities were created during the occupation and the populations in some village communities exceeded those in certain cities (Benvinisti, 1988).

In many developing countries, urbanisation can be attributed to massive population movement from rural towns and villages to major cities in order to improve employment opportunities and economic and social conditions. However, due to the unique political conditions in Palestine, urbanisation has not been a result of any significant population movement, but rather as a result of the natural growth of cities and gradual transformation of smaller towns and villages into semi-urban centres.

Since this trend took place and continued without monitoring or intervention from central or local authorities, many villages and smaller towns maintained their traditional life styles in spite of acquiring more urban functions. In the absence of any central government support, such communities suffered from lack of services and utilities to enable it to carry out their new functions (Ibid.).

Palestinian sources, identified urbanisation trends by dividing the communities into four categories:

1) *Urban Communities.* These have a definite urban role with centres that perform administrative, commercial and social functions. Main urban centres in this category are Jerusalem, Nablus, and Hebron. Urban towns also considered under this category are Jenin, Tulkarm, Qalqilyah, Ramallah, El-Bireh, Bethlehem and Jericho;

2) *Semi-Urban Communities*. These include a number of rural towns and villages which acquired urban characteristics as a result of their location, increased population, changed functions, and economic activities;

3) *Rural Communities*. These include all communities predominantly active in agriculture with no significant administrative commercial or service functions; and

4) *Refugee Camps*. These include Palestinians who lost their homes in historic Palestine after the creation of Israel. Most camps are located near or within urban centres. Although communities in camps may be counted as part of the urban population, their final status can only be determined after reaching a final political solution (CEP, 1992).

Palestinian sources estimated in 1990, that around 43 per cent of the population lived in urban communities, 5 per cent in semi-urban communities, 35 per cent in rural communities and 17 per cent in refugee camps (Ibid.). In Nablus district 'county', 32 per cent lived in urban and semi-urban communities, 59 per cent in rural communities, while 9 per cent lived in refugee camps (Ibid.).

The extensive land confiscation policy and subsequent building of Jewish settlements resulted in less land available for rural development. The situation was aggravated by the fact that district and village councils which existed before 1967 were abolished. Any development in the areas outside municipal boundaries had to be approved by the Higher Planning Council, which was controlled and run by Israel.

Consequently, applications for building permits in these areas were obstructed. Furthermore, municipalities were not allowed to expand their boundaries despite the population growth and pressure for development which exaggerated the overcrowding and deteriorating conditions within the towns.

The Potential for Upgrading Housing

Three main areas in Palestinian towns have the potential for renewal and upgrading. They are existing neighbourhoods, historic centres and refugee camps.

Existing neighbourhoods

These include derelict neighbourhoods, slums and residential areas suffering from neglect, lack of maintenance and investment and general urban decay problems.

In spite of increase in investment in construction, particularly housing, since the progress in the peace process, most construction activities after 1967 were sporadic, unplanned and were carried out without compliance with building regulations, health or safety codes (Touqan, 1995).

Most of the housing built under the occupation was carried out by private, mainly personal, investors. Although a number of co-operative housing was planned only few projects were carried out. A number were abandoned before completion and most were not even started (Joint Jordanian Palestinian Committee, 1988).

However, such housing was planned for middle income groups of mainly professionals. No public housing was initiated for the lower end of the market.

Private investment in housing construction was either concentrated in the upper middle class suburbs and in individual plots in lower middle class and poorer areas many of which involved adding floors or extensions to existing buildings. Therefore, the physical condition of many neighbourhoods deteriorated over the years and suffered from overloaded services and environmental degradation.

Although such areas are densely populated and provide little space for new development, the existing buildings are in bad need for upgrading to their physical appearance and increase of service and amenity provision as well as improvement of their surroundings.

Historic centres

These are usually the historic cores and old quarters in main cities such as Nablus, Hebron and Jerusalem suffering from lack of maintenance and investment with many abandoned and under-used buildings. They also include complete historic villages such as Beit Wazan, near Nablus, and others which have been abandoned for many years.

In spite of the lack of maintenance, overcrowding, deteriorating building conditions and antiquated services historic cores provide a centrally located relatively inexpensive housing. The range of their economic activities retail, wholesale, traditional handicrafts, small scale industries is important to their population as well as their outside users. The physical structure of such areas is generally in harmony with the way the population lives. The relationship between house, street, neighbourhood and community reflects the connection between spatial organisation and social life. The mix of land uses and urban spaces and the availability of jobs that utilised a broad spectrum of skills also reflect the way people live and have lived for centuries.

Historic cores of Palestinian towns provide a good potential for residential use. Many buildings including old palaces, large houses, workshops and factories have been under-used, abandoned, vacant and partially vacant due to a variety of reasons including:

1) *Political*

   Military clashes, restriction on movement, uncertainty of the future, and absence of local or central government support;

2) *Legal*

   Absentee property laws, rent controls and restrictions imposed on development during the occupation; and

3) *Financial*

   Lack of investment due to lack of financial institutions, banks or any form of government financial help or incentives.

As most of these problems have resulted from the occupation, some of which has improved since 1993, it can be assumed that eventually the vacant, partially vacant and abandoned buildings could be targeted for adaptive re-use and residential use once legal obstacles are removed.

Refugee camps

Many of the refugee camps are located near main towns. Some of these camps, such as Askar and Balata in Nablus, became an integral part of these towns over the years as a result of expansion and urban sprawl. Most of the existing camps were established in the aftermath of the 1948 war. The majority of these camps are densely populated and suffer from multiple urban problems, although few were abandoned and became ghost towns after 1967 such as those near Jericho.

The levels of occupancy and density are very high in the camps and services and environmental conditions are extremely bad particularly in camps in Gaza. Many of the camps were built close to existing urban centre and urban sprawl over the years meant that many could not be physically separated from adjoining development such as Askar and Balata in Nablus. However, most development close to the refugee camps is also dense and suffer from poor quality construction, inadequate service provision and deteriorating environmental conditions.

The population in the refugee camps now are third and fourth generation and have a cohesive social structure which should be maintained regardless of the final political settlement. Although there is desperate need for improvement and upgrading of the physical condition of buildings, services and spaces, major redevelopment programmes will create rather than solve existing problems. Therefore, the rehabilitation of the camps should follow short term action plans based on priority identification for improvement. These should include, upgrading existing stock and infrastructure, improving surroundings, creating spaces for social, commercial and recreational activities as well as sites for new housing.

THE CHALLENGE FOR URBAN RENEWAL IN PALESTINE

The urban problems in Palestinian towns are compounded by the absence of modern institutional structures because as most public and private institutions were weakened and marginalised during the occupation. They also suffer from shortage of human, technical and financial resources. It is therefore unlikely that any single agency can be competent to deal with all aspects of existing urban problems in Palestine.

Many of the existing urban problems in Palestine is common in other developing countries including the need for institution building and land use policies. The only difference in the case of Palestine is the total absence of indigenous institutions and any plans for development during the occupation.

Options for Development

There are many options available for Palestinians today in the field of development. There is also a wealth of international experience in developed and developing countries that we can learn from and build on before we can decide on the best option that suits our needs.

Palestinians will not find one right answer for their urban dilemma, we must, therefore, continue to pick and chose among options that appear to work. These include the integration of new development, redevelopment and renewal projects planned, financed and implemented simultaneously.

There is evidence that most of small and large scale investment in Palestine is directed at new development and new construction. There is also fear that most of the financial assistance from international donor countries will be geared to mega new projects.

While Palestinians are in need of such new projects, including new schools, hospitals and factories, there is fear that existing residential areas, small businesses and commercial enterprises will be left out. This will result in further deterioration of the physical condition of buildings, services and environmental conditions of these areas. Thus aggravating their problems and increasing the gap between various sectors of the community.

Restoration and re-use of old buildings have proved viable in many cases and old cities must continue to be competitive economically if they are to emerge from their current state of physical and social deterioration. The same applies to existing run-down neighbourhoods including the refugee camps.

The basic elements of neighbourhood renewal involve improvement of the urban fabric and external envelop, improvement of internal arrange-

477

ments and amenities and improvement of the environmental and physical conditions of the surrounding areas.

Problems with housing provision and quality are generally an indicator of a wider picture of general urban decay in a particular area. They are an integral part of multiple deprivation which characterises such area. Therefore, the solutions to such problems should be based on multi-sector and multi-agency approach, in which housing initiatives relate to community regeneration in other areas such as employment, training, social and technical services and infrastructure, improvement of environmental conditions and provision of amenities. Such approach develops community confidence and encourages better social integration between various social groups.

Neighbourhoods requiring comprehensive renewal usually have very low level of economic activities. Therefore there will be need for an adequate programme and measure of subsidies. Community groups and residents should also be encouraged to carry out improvements by government provision of grants, loans and credit for renewal and upgrading projects.

The partnership approach

In the 1980s, a new trend of a partnership approach in development emerged in the UK, the US and other countries contrary to the one-agency solution to urban problems of the 1950s and 1970s. These are based on a multi agency approach which includes public and private sectors and involves the community. From European and American long experience in renewal and upgrading projects it became evident that multi sectoral partnership is needed to mobilise every possible resource, to deal with spatial, socio-economic and legal problems and to attract private resources and initiatives.

Therefore, various available agencies including public and private sectors as well as community based organisations were encouraged to become involved in identifying 'deprived' urban neighbourhoods suitable for planning, legal and fiscal intervention including social deprivation and economical inactivity in these areas.

International experience indicates that the success of urban renewal will depend on an enabling housing and neighbourhood policy at the central level, a service orientation replacing partisan ideology, continuing institutional adjustment at the local authority level and resident participation. Policies must deal with the provision of land, tenure mechanism, access to credit and other tools within control of government.

According to Carley, the partnership approach can make sense for a number of reasons:

- Multiple agencies can help each other understand the real nature of the task of urban renewal from a holistic, more accurate perspective relevant to the overall life experience of neighbourhood residents This provides the base for a more realistic policy with better prospects for successful implementation;
- The partnership approach encourages various agencies to modify their organisational culture in a more task oriented direction;
- The partnerships provide an active role for the community in a way which is impossible in the single agency approach; and
- Partnerships often represent a broad coalition among public, private and voluntary sectors. Such coalition helps various partners to develop more confidence, and command more respect and provide more resources that any agency working alone (Carley, 1990).

Partnerships: the British experience

There are generally three types of partnerships in Britain. These are the following:

- *Urban renewal partnerships.* These involve the public sector (central and local authorities), and the private sector. Such partnerships use funds obtained from; Urban Development Grant, Urban Renewal Grant, Derelict Land Grant and, lately, City Grant. These have operated mainly in areas of industrial dereliction and have little or no social housing component;
- *Housing partnerships.* These include local authorities, housing associations, building societies and private builders. A typical model is where the local authority provides land or an empty council estate on the condition that it can nominate tenants or purchasers for new refurbished homes. The housing association organises and manages the development including the tenancy mix, brings in Housing Association Grants or private finance and a private builder;
- Building societies provide working capital and may provide mortgages. The majority of schemes have been housing for outright sale or shared ownership, but there is an increasing number of innovative rental and mixed tenure developments;
- *Mixed partnerships.* Recently, a new type of partnership developed based on elements found in the above two types. Such partnerships aim to address the problems of neighbourhoods with substantial resident populations. Usually the Local Authority or a housing association is the early lead agency but with active partners from other housing associations, building societies, private builders, voluntary groups, tenant and resident groups and other levels of government; and
- These may focus on inner city neighbourhoods or peripheral estates.

479

The partnerships focus on housing refurbishment and tenure diversification as well as; employment, training, social and technical services and infrastructure and environmental improvement schemes (Ibid., 1990).

Guidelines for Evaluating Options

In conclusion, any future development policy in Palestine should examine and benefit from the available diversity of options to enable it to match the complexity of the existing problems. Some main guidelines should be taken into consideration including:

- Recognising the need for the central government to plan and implement an enabling policy for neighbourhood renewal;
- This should include the encouragement of local initiatives, involvement of voluntary organisations and local residents. Local authorities can act as a catalyst to take an over-view, to bring together the relevant partners (from housing co-operatives, community organisations and the private sector) and to direct the policy implementation;
- Integrating urban renewal as part of the overall housing policy and development plans;
- Environmental improvements should be an integral part of such policy in areas designated for renewal;
- Encouraging the private sector (formal and informal) to play a major role in the renewal/ development process; and, finally,
- Acknowledging the role of banks, financial institutions (building societies and private development companies) as important partners and benefit from them as a major source of finance and expertise.

Nablus: A Case Study

According to Palestinian sources, the region of Nablus covers more than 2,500 square kilometres. In 1990, its population was estimated at around 669,000 (CEP, 1992). The region comprises Nablus city – the regional centre – and the secondary centres of Jenin, Tulkarm, Qalqilia and Tubas. The region's population was distributed among 268 urban, semi urban and rural communities and seven refugee camps (Ibid.).

Urban design, physical characteristics and development trends

Apart from the historic core, i.e. the old city, in Nablus, other areas need upgrading and rehabilitation if they are to be used for many of the required facilities. These include residential areas in both the Eibal and Jerzim mountains, the area to the east of the centre, and (despite the political sensitivities and implications) the refugee camps. The camps grew in size and activities since they were first established as temporary accommodation for the refugees who were forced to leave their homes in Palestine in 1948 upon the creation of Israel.

The historic core in Nablus, like many historic towns in the Middle East is a mix of commercial, residential, cultural and recreational facilities. For hundreds of years and until today, the physical shape, fabric and uses in the old city did not change much. It is however important that the urban fabric, present uses and the future of the historic core in Nablus are examined in its context and in relation to the area immediately around it.

Physically, the old city blends comfortably with its surroundings as it grew organically to the north, out of the old city gates. The new development of Nablus which started in the late 1940s and early 1950s, except for few individual buildings built before, was slow, gradual and sensitive to the existing styles. In terms of their urban design and architectural styles, adjacent buildings in Ghernata and Palestine streets to the west and Commercial and Hitteen streets to the east, are simple, elegant and small scale and echo the overall style and character of many historic buildings in the old city, albeit with simpler details.

The design of the new buildings also, in line with the historic buildings, provided for commercial activities in the lower floors and residential spaces on upper floors. Socially and economically, the old city also blends with the rest as one can see from the circulation and movement in the city centre. In spite of the political conditions and restrictions, the commercial and cultural activities in the old city complement those outside its gates.

The main square in the centre acts as a hinge that connects the historic core with the rest of the city in physical, social and economic terms. Nabulsis as well as Palestinians from other towns and villages arrive at the square and conduct their business in both parts of the centre.

Although the old city today carries the scars of the long harsh years of the occupation and the military conflict, its urban fabric is still intact and its spirit alive. The city's charm, character and special personality survived hundreds of years of wars, earthquakes, Turkish occupation and finally the prolonged Israeli military occupation.

In spite of multiple urban problems in the refugee camps, these maintained a cohesive social structure over the years and some like Askar and Balata have viable markets used by residents of the main city. The population in these camps have integrated with nearby neighbourhoods and any housing or renewal strategy should take these facts into consideration.

A model for integration?

Nablus is one of the largest urban centres in Palestine. It enjoys a rich mix of historic, contemporary and modern buildings. Its cultural, educational and commercial activities attracted visitors from all over Palestine for centuries. It also has a large refugee population which have integrated with its own to a great extent. Therefore, the city of Nablus can become a model for an urban development policy based on the integration of new development, redevelopment, renewal and conservation.

Such a policy should aim to acknowledge the need for growth and change to meet the needs and aspiration of the residents; accept that the buildings, however historic or old they may be, have provided usable, useful spaces through the years; recognise that is what they were built for, and what their owners and users need them for; and ensure that the historic core continues to act as an integral part of the city centre and the business district in Nablus. With the available technology, electronic facilities and computer networks, the old city can provide space for modern uses, as well as for its own special facilities.

When restoring the physical condition of the historic city and its buildings, consideration should be taken of its settings and the area around it to ensure that the historic core is being protected, along with its environment and its social commercial and cultural activities. Accordingly, any urban renewal policy should also consider the available spaces and activities which exist in the old city. Such a policy should recognise the area's potential to play a major role in the future development process.

In addition, the policy should plan to integrate historic centres with other parts of the city. It is therefore proposed that the area immediately outside the old city, while not part of a conservation programme, be treated as an area of special character. Accordingly, urban design and architectural special guidelines for this area should be included in any conservation agenda, in terms of heights, openings details and external finishes.

This will guarantee that, aesthetically, this area continues to provide a transition between the old city and the new more modern centre. Thus presenting a suitable physical introduction to this valuable historic core and the link between the economic and social activities in the old and the new parts of the city.

The policy should also protect the social as well as the physical structure of existing neighbourhoods, including the camps, by avoiding major redevelopment schemes and focusing on upgrading, self-improvement, rehabilitation and environmental improvements. The local community should be encouraged to participate in such schemes by provision of subsidies, grants and easy credit facilities.

Finally, such a policy should ensure that planning and funding new development does not deprive existing areas from the opportunity to improve and upgrade their existing stock. New projects built near existing centres as infills or redevelopment, while providing the much needed services and spaces, should be planned and designed in harmony with the existing surroundings in terms of their style and use.

SUMMARY AND RECOMMENDATIONS

Summary

Where are we now?

In view of the current status of the peace negotiations, it can be assumed that the geographical area of the Palestinian cities are fixed for the time being and any development plan should be based on the existing size of towns. The seriousness of this problem is aggravated by the fact that there is already a severe shortage of land available for development in most towns due to the freeze imposed on their boundaries by the Israeli authorities during the occupation.

This has also resulted from the confiscation of large areas of land outside the boundaries which are still under the full control of the Israeli Higher Planning Council within the civil administration. Furthermore, land available is mainly in private ownership and part of it is also difficult to develop as a result of ownership and registration problems and, as is the case in Nablus, a result of topographical difficulties.

Other obstacles are also expected to emerge as a result of the agreement, such as an expected population increase with the return of part of the exiled Palestinians to their homeland. Moreover, an acceleration in private investment in land and property is already evident and expected to continue, before a legislative and executive structure is empowered, and building regulations and codes have been prepared and implemented.

As a consequence of this situation, a lot of development may involve reconstruction and replacement of existing buildings which may include a change in the physical appearance and in the use of these buildings or at best refurbishment to adapt them for new uses. There is danger, however, that without a clear urban renewal policy, private owners will continue a process that already started of knocking down valuable buildings, adding unsuitable extensions or converting them into inappropriate uses.

There is also the danger that most of the international aid will be directed at new projects which will have adverse effect on existing centres and historic cores, and will put more pressure on scarce land resources.

With the shortages of land and the restrictions on its use for the next few years, the increase in the pressure for development, services and housing provision, and the subsequent increase in investment, it is vital that an urban renewal and conservation policy is integrated within any development plan in Palestinian towns.

A lot of care and consideration should be taken when type, size and location of various projects are decided to ensure that while meeting the urgent needs of the present, we will not compromise our ability to meet future needs and that of future generations. It is, therefore, vital that any urban development plan should be based on the efficient use of the scarce land and natural resources available in Palestine today.

Most Palestinian urban centres have viable commercial centres albeit in bad need for repair and modernisation. Many of the towns have traditional markets which are still active and popular, existing residential neighbourhoods with varied degrees of dilapidation. Few towns also have valuable historic cores which are still active with a variety of residential, commercial and public facilities in spite of the political, economic and social problems.

It is therefore prudent that the provision of any major projects should not be made before a clear urban development and housing strategy is in place based on a careful assessment of the available human and technical resources. This should be carried out parallel to an evaluation of the existing housing stock and available space for retail, offices and recreation facilities.

Palestinians cannot afford to waste any resources now and therefore should not separate the urban renewal of their town from national development plans. Now more than ever when everybody is talking about housing provision and infrastructure it is vital that we evaluate our existing stock, and make a careful assessment of our needs based on what we have, what we can improve, upgrade, recycle and re-use before we rush to fill the already dense and scarce land resources with the obvious consequences and environmental damage it will cause.

Why urban renewal?

The advantage of an urban renewal policy is to protect, preserve and regenerate our towns socially, economically and culturally and that does not only cover historic cores but all Palestinian urban centres and neighbourhoods.

The concentration on funding and investment in new development will result in irreversible damage to the existing urban fabric, architectural heritage, environment and the social structure. The neglect of 'already derelict' stock will also result in the concentration and 'gettoisation' of the poor in less attractive areas with subsequent economic and social problems.

It is therefore proposed that the integration of urban renewal and conservation policies in urban development plans will achieve the following:

- Quick and economic supply of space for housing, retail and office facilities and recreational facilities by upgrading existing stock, utilising redundant built space within the towns and improving occupied property;
- Protection of the existing urban fabric particularly historic centres and protecting their social structure;
- A relaxation of the pressure for immediate expansion of land and infrastructure by prioritising upgrading of the existing facilities which will later be integrated in future service networks;
- The possibility of assessing available resources more clearly based on the final results of the peace negotiations and the progress in implementing the advanced stages of the interim period;
- Time for careful assessment of the needs and the existing resources based on local perceptions and priorities to enable the preparation and implementation of a local development plan instead of an imported or imposed solution;
- The provision of local job opportunities with emphasis on training; and, finally,
- An improvement in the physical appearance of the existing stock while developing a new structure which will prevent the gettoisation of historic cores and other decaying areas in Palestinian towns.

This latter point will subsequently engender a sense of belonging and create a strong local identity.

RECOMMENDATIONS

There are two main issues that should be included in any future development plans for Palestinian towns. These are the main elements of the plans, and the main players responsible for their implementation.

As described above, any development policy should integrate the new development plans with plans for upgrading and renewal of existing neighbourhoods and camps, conservation policies and adaptive re-use of existing historic centres. This will ensure that various parts of towns and society will benefit from investment, development and improvement of their living conditions.

Such development is best carried out by multi sectoral partnership which will mobilise every possible force and provide a diversity of options involving central policy, local strategy, private input and community participation.

The integration of new and renewed development and the multi agency partnership approach must be based on the following.

Survey of the existing stock

The first step that should be taken is to make a careful assessment of the existing building stock in Palestinian cities. In the case of Nablus and similar historic centres this will also include the historic cores of these cities. It is essential that the size and location of the existing buildings and their physical condition are examined before a renewal policy is determined. If the renewal policy is integrated in an overall urban development plan, the knowledge of the quality and quantity of the existing built space should precede the preparation of the plan.

The results of such survey will determine which of the existing buildings can be rehabilitated and upgraded for its present use, renovated and modified to adapt it to new use or if it is physically severely dilapidated and structurally unsound and need partial or complete replacement.

Review of relevant legislative factors

Because a legal Palestinian system is currently under preparation, it is important that a review of all legislation related to urban development such as tenure, ownership and land registration should be made a priority.

This should be made at the same time when building regulations, health and safety codes, environmental and conservation agendas are reviewed and updated. It is also important that the ownership pattern in these buildings are examined to determine which is in multiple or waqf ownership, absentees property, old or new tenancy.

As a result of the policies and practices of the occupation authorities since 1967, with regard to registration, residency permits and absentees laws, this will be slow and difficult process and it may take years to complete due to either unavailable or inaccurate data. However, a start should be made to update the official local authority's records as soon as possible.

Finance

This should be provided by the creation of public/private partnerships as discussed above. The role of central and local authorities as an enabler to various players is essential. There is need for official policies aiming at encouraging banks and building societies to facilitate loans and mortgages for upgrading and improvements of existing stock as well as new development.

To ensure the success of any urban renewal policy it is important to review the methods for encouraging owners or tenants to improve and upgrade their buildings, this could take the form of special grants, subsidies, and tax concessions for owners, security of tenure, grants and loans for tenants.

Implementation

This can best be achieved by involving a number of 'players'. The partnership may take many forms and definitions, but it can generally be defined as a partnership between the public (central and/or local government and the private sector with voluntary groups and community based organisations involvement. It could include two or more of these partners depending on the nature of the urban service it aims to provide (i.e. housing co-operatives can be involved in case of housing projects). This approach can best be used in the urban development of Palestinian towns particularly as none of the potential partners is capable on his own financially nor technically to tackle the existing urban problems.

Conservation of our historic centres and rehabilitation of existing neighbourhoods cannot be singled out as a priority, nor should it be left out as a luxury we cannot afford. Conservation integrated in an overall urban renewal policy should be an essential part of the development process of our towns and neighbourhoods. Palestinians cannot afford to waste any resources now and therefore should not separate urban renewal of their towns from their national development plans.

Now more than ever it is vital that we evaluate our existing stock, and make a careful assessment of our needs based on what we have, what we can improve, upgrade, recycle and re-use before we rush to fill the already dense and scarce land resources with the obvious consequences and environmental damage it will cause.

Conservation and urban renewal are economic, social as well as cultural necessities and leaving them out of the urban development process, is the luxury we cannot afford.

BIBLIOGRAPHY

Benvenisti, M and S. Khayat, 1988, **The West Bank Data Base Project**, The Jerusalem Post, Jerusalem.

Carley, M., 1990, **Housing and Neighbourhood Renewal**, Policy Studies Institute, London.

Centre for Engineering and Planning (CEP), 1992, **Master Planning the State of Palestine**, Palestine Studies Project, Ramallah.

Joint Jordanian Palestinian Committee, 1988, **Report on Housing Co-operatives in the Occupied Territories**, Joint Jordanian Palestinian Committee, Amman.

Touqan, S., 1995, **Urban Development under Prolonged Military Occupation**, Unpublished Ph.D. diss., University of London, London.

CONSERVATION OF CULTURAL HERITAGE: A COMMUNITY APPROACH

Mohammad Ata Yousof

ABSTRACT

In Palestine, political, social, economic and financial constraints, as well as the lack of any legislative power, have caused a crisis in the conservation of our cultural heritage. However, the history of the conservation movement elsewhere in the world shows that all decisions to conserve begin and end with cultural decisions, rather than economic ones. What matters is the strength of the social and cultural motivation to conserve cultural heritage.

A policy that delays the upgrading and preservation of our built heritage until after the economy has grown substantially would, in effect, lead to the erosion of thousands of historic buildings, if not entire historic areas. This would affect the people who live there now and in subsequent generations and might even delay the entire development programme in Palestine.

The philosophy of the conservation approach has to be 'bottom-up' rather than 'top-down.' It has to be based upon the needs, aspirations and resources of the people, upon working with communities and institutions in place and upon stimulated 'self-help' and voluntary work.

This paper will attempt to examine the development of the conservation movement in Palestine. It will highlight the reasons why we should take care of our cultural heritage and what benefits can we gain from this. It also examines the challenges facing the conservation of our cultural heritage. Finally, it concludes by providing some recommendations.

CONSERVATION IN HISTORY

Palestine's heritage covers thousands of years. Although it has a long history of statutory town planning which is almost as long as Britain's, conservation has come quite late compared to other countries (Coon, 1991, 1992).

Until World War I, construction was undertaken by the Ottoman authorities, who had little or no concept of town planning other than in military terms. However, the Turks did establish a system of building permits in urban areas (Efrat, 1984). During the height of the Ottoman Empire, prosperity existed as did a more effective administration. New roads were built and old khans repaired.

In 1542, Suleiman the Magnificent rebuilt the walls of Jerusalem that still stand today (Luke and KeithRoach, 1934; Karmon, 1971). In addition, an endowment system, *waqf*, secured the maintenance of important public buildings. When a mosque or a religious building was being funded, money was also made available to build one or several commercial establishments, such as *hammams* or shops that could be let. The revenue from the commercial establishments paid for the upkeep of the public buildings.

During this and subsequent periods until the present time, some concern has always been shown by the rulers for the large monuments, especially the great mosques. At the same time, care has been demonstrated by some wealthy families or individuals, or a group of individuals, for the repair and maintenance of religious shrines and mausoleums with the understanding that this would help them to obtain God's blessing and to access to paradise. Their maintenance has ensured their preservation as cultural symbols up to the present time.

A system of annual maintenance by tenants also existed. The frequency was a function of family size. This was a sort of collective '*dala*' (the turn), where each member of the family took part in repairing the walls and ceilings and applying a coat of lime whitewashed to interior walls. During religious feasts or when the condition of the houses required, the interiors, the courtyards and the bazaars were painted, generally a few days before the fasting month of Ramadan. The owner calculated the expense, which was then divided between the different families. However, those with very low incomes and elderly people living alone were excluded. Instead, they were asked to babysit (Based on a survey conducted by the Author in the West Bank, October, 1993 to March 1994).

A new approach to town planning was introduced after the British Mandate began in 1922. In the view of one author, 'The British, in contrast to the Turks, combined an urban culture of [the] highest standard with a romantic attachment to the Middle East' (Efrat, 1984).

Town planning during this period was regulated by the Town Planning Ordinances of 1921, 1929 and 1936 (Luke and Keith-Roach, 1934). In 1945, the Town and Country Planning Ordinance of Palestine was published (Shiber, 1968; Coon, 1992). Although this ordinance was never enacted, Article 17 of the Schemes Section, deals with *preservation of objects of archaeological interest or beauty, and buildings or places used for religious purposes or cemeteries, or concerned with religious veneration.* Article 19 deals with the control of siting, size, height, design and the external appearance of buildings.

The High Commissioner had the power to appoint a Central Commission in order to set limits to an area or district and to declare what was called a *Town Planning Area*. Local commissions, such as the Engineering Department of the Municipality, prepared schemes for the development and reconstruction of certain areas. These were based on the Central Commission's advice and consultations with the Department of Antiquities (Luke and Keith-Roach, 1934). Such schemes may have contained provisions for construction, alteration of streets, allocation of land for roads, public gardens, and the division of an area into building zones, and types of drainage, street lighting, water supply and, significantly, *the preservation of objects of historical interest and natural beauty* (Luke and Keith-Roach, 1934).

Special attention and controls were given to Jerusalem when it began to expand beyond the city walls of Suleiman. The first plan was adopted in 1918, and the last – the Kendal Plan – in 1944 (Dakkak, 1981; Efrat, 1984; Coon, 1992). The government also founded the Pro-Jerusalem Society, whose aims included the preservation of the beauty of the city and the furthering of its planning development (Efrat, 1984). Despite this Western influence, Jerusalem retained its Middle Eastern cultural and economic life. The British tried not to interfere with the management of the Moslem shrines (Benvenisti, 1976). Moreover, they sought to preserve the historical character of Jerusalem by exercising careful control over its development and by assisting its communities in necessary repair work.

According to Efrat (1984), the Mandatory government's main contribution to the development of towns was the creation of town planning commissions, whose main function was to establish the administrative machinery for building control. He adds that the control was decentralised, and exercised through local, municipal and district commissions. The legislation which gave legal authorisation to the functions of these bodies was enacted in 1936. Finally, while the government was aware of the problems relating to town planning, and knew how to develop towns according to established European practice, 'it applied this knowledge only to those areas in whose development it had a special interest' (Efrat, 1984).

Under Jordanian rule, special attention was given to the most esteemed religious monuments, such as the Dome of the Rock and Al-Aqsa Mosque. The King of Jordan contributed to their preservation from his own finances. His last contribution, $8 million, was given in 1992 for the Dome of the Rock.

The state of Jordan also played a major role in listing the buildings and walls of the Old City of Jerusalem, a move that resulted in their placement on the World Heritage list in October, 1981. The government may have been influenced by the fact that Jordan's income from tourism, which depended to a very large extent on Jerusalem and the West Bank, totalled about 11 million Jordanian dinars, or about $32 million, in 1966 (Abu-Ayyash, 1976).

After the Israeli military occupation of the West Bank and Gaza in 1967, the conservation of historical buildings and sites was completely ignored. Conservation of the national cultural heritage meant the preservation of only those sites which related to the cultural heritage of the occupier. No consideration was given to the other cultural properties in the country which had been built during the previous 20 centuries.

Even worse, Israel sought, and still seeks, to destroy Palestine's archaeological and historical heritage by all available means. In the words of one scholar, 'The links between cultural and political battle have become strong and prominent chiefly in the modern era. For those nations eager for expansion have devised effective means for destroying cultures of dominated people' (Von Grunebaum, 1962).

CONSERVATION TODAY

Several attempts at conservation have been made in the West Bank in the last 10 to 15 years, despite Israeli policy and the imposition of severe economic constraints. These attempts are clearly visible in cities like Jerusalem, Nablus, and Hebron. They can be divided into the following categories:

1) The Al-Awqaf Department (Islamic Archaeological Department) is responsible for mosques and the *waqf* donation, deriving its funds from commercial rents on premises it owns. It was also supported by Jordanian government. After September, 1994, Jordan stopped its support and placed the responsibility for funding in the hands of the new Palestine National Authority (PNA);

2) Official conservation takes place under the auspices of the municipalities, or other local bodies;

3) Private conservation is carried out by individual efforts by the owners, usually without outside help;

4) Conservation by non-governmental organisations (NGOs), such as the Centre for Development Consultancy (CDC), which support small conservation projects, but which mainly concentrate on the Old City of Jerusalem;

5) Projects carried out by departments of architecture at An-Najah National University, Bir Zeit University and Hebron Polytechnic; and

6) Personal contributions.

One example is the preservation of *Qaser Al-Qasem* (Al-Qasem Palace) in the village of *Beit Wazan,* near the city of Nablus. The owners of this building donated it to An-Najah University for preservation and use as part of the university. The building may become a Study Centre for Conservation and Reconstruction (SCCR), which is vitally needed in the West Bank. A Palestinian businessman has promised to cover the costs of the conservation work.

Another example involves the London-based Welfare Association. In 1994, it awarded a contract to the PRDU at the Institute of Advanced Architectural Studies (IAAS) at the University of York to prepare an action plan and funding proposal for the protection of the Arab and Islamic heritage of the Old City of Jerusalem (Revival, 1994). The proposal covered four main areas:

1) A priority project for restoration;
2) An emergency repair and property protection programme;
3) Preparation of a conservation plan leading to the establishment of an information system; and
4) Training, skill-building and the progressive articulation of technical standards and guidelines for restoration work.

According to *Revival* (1994), the proposal has a total value of $5,095,750 and is being financed by the Arab Fund for Social and Economic Development. The Welfare Association has started work on an executive plan.

Another active Palestinian NGO in the field of conservation is the Centre for Architectural Conservation (RIWAQ), which is based in Ramallah. The Centre works on a number of levels to protect the fabric of Palestinian cultural heritage. Among its objectives is the conservation and protection of historic towns and villages, archaeological and natural sites, monuments and buildings. RIWAQ is also concerned with the development and promotion of an indigenous Palestinian style of architecture based on firmly rooted traditions and techniques.

CHALLENGES TO CONSERVATION

The most important challenge facing conservation in Palestine is the lack of resources to finance a comprehensive programme. Conservation is not considered a top priority by people who are struggling to feed, educate and provide decent shelter for their families. Nor, perhaps, will it be a top priority for the PNA, which still exists on donations from rich countries and which is struggling to maintain the basic infrastructure needed to provide health care and to create jobs. Given the deterioration of the Palestinian infrastructure, the economic constraints and the high demand for housing, we must ask whether we can afford to allocate national funds to conservation, especially when most, if not all, the municipalities are operating with budget deficits.

The concept of conservation itself also poses a challenge. Because the concept was first brought to the West Bank by Western professionals, and then by Palestinians mainly educated in the West, it has focused primarily on the conservation of monuments. If this continues, many buildings and large historic areas will be lost.

Conservation in the West Bank is seen by the general public as being the problem of the municipalities, but the municipalities, the NGOs and local bodies at present are only responsible for safeguarding monuments. This attitude, which does not encourage public investment in conservation and repair work, has eventually led to the public neglect of properties. Like many other countries in the developing world, there is a continuing lack of respect for traditional buildings.

Moreover, modernisation, development and technological advance have greatly encouraged such neglect, particularly of the historic quarters which have undergone a drastic change in the past few decades. These quarters, which contain most of the greatest collections of national monuments as well as the finest examples of our traditional architecture, have been ruined in the cause of progress.

Problems stemming from 'development' and the lack of efficient urban design in these historic quarters have heavily overshadowed the heritage of Palestine's glorious past. They are also threatened by the shifting of social and commercial activities from them to new centres outside them. In addition, many historic structures, such as hammams, soap factories, khans and palaces, in these historic cores have been destroyed in the name of progress and modernisation. Yet these cores are considered by many to form the most attractive part of Palestine.

Another problem is the shortage of qualified staff and specialists in conservation. The field has benefited only in a very limited way from investment in education and training programmes. Not until the late 1980s did a few Palestinians started to specialise in conservation. Yet there is still no specialised organisation or institute concerned with developing conservation techniques and methods. There is an obvious lack of political will and, as a result, the commitment of finance to develop conservation through education and training, as well as by allocating money for regular maintenance and repair is missing.

Apart from a few postgraduate studies, theoretical analyses of our architectural heritage based on field studies and existing data are very scarce. Documentation and surveys which constitute the basis for any future conservation studies are also lacking. Nevertheless, the awareness of this important issue is growing. In 1994, for example, Nablus Municipality started the documentation of some monumental parts of the old town of

Nablus, and a group of concerned architects started the documentation of the old town of Hebron.

Still other challenges exit due to the total absence of any form of legislative framework for the protection of our traditional settlements and individual buildings of significant value. This can be quite a serious issue as any intervention by conservation agencies or bodies should obviously be made through a legal procedure. However, Israel froze all legislative work after 1967 and completely controlled the planning policies of the region for the benefit of the Jewish settlers. The required legislation is almost thirty years behind any other country in the region.

Because rapid economic development may occur in Palestine after peace, there is a great potential for increased stress on the traditional built environment where some of the oldest human settlements exist. Palestine is rich in cultural property which could be lost or damaged under accelerated economic development.

Another challenge stems from the fact that in Palestine, the ownership of old houses or buildings in an inherited property often belongs to a great number of individuals with the same kinship. It is rare that such property is a settled matter, entitled to one person. The multiple claims of several individuals to one property has a major impact on conservation policies.

Moreover, we cannot expect people living in very poor conditions and in places that are regarded by many as primitive, to express their desire to remain in them or even care about repairing them. Add to this, that areas of historical value are mainly occupied by poor indigenous people, as most of the rich families have left for other wealthier areas outside the historic cores, and, to a lesser extent, by migrants who have recently moved in from the rural areas and do not feel any great attachment to their houses or neighbourhoods. For them, these areas are not much better than the areas they left, so they do not express any interest in conserving them.

Finally, the common Islamic Palestinian culture is being eroded and destroyed not only by the impersonal forces of economic and cultural domination, but also by the active forces of colonial military occupation. Indeed, it may be argued that the Israeli occupying power is actively trying to destroy the Palestinian cultural identity by its policies and actions towards Palestine's traditional built environment, and that this amounts to cultural genocide against the Palestinians.

For instance, the Israeli authorities demolished three historic houses in the old town of Nablus in 1988. One of these buildings was part of one of the most significant buildings in the town, *Qasr Tuqan*, i.e. Tuqan Palace. As a result of using explosives, 61 adjacent buildings were affected. Six of them were badly damaged, forcing their occupants to leave.

The Israeli policy towards Palestinian cities in the West Bank, in particular Jerusalem, is not a purely new policy. Israel has deliberately neglected many Palestinian towns like Jaffa and Acre, forcing their inhabitants to leave and resettle outside in favour of promoting Jewish immigration with the aid of subsidised rents and tax. Today, these cities are becoming 'medieval museum' towns serving Israel's tourists.

Israeli policies in Jerusalem are creating the same effects as happened in other towns after the establishment of Israel (Abu-Shanab, 1983). As one author has expressed it, 'Apart from the two architects who built the walls for Suleiman the Magnificent, no architects have planted their legs more firmly on old Jerusalem than Safadi and Lansky' (Davey, 1978).

Matters also worsened when the military government added a bureaucratic layer with absolute power above the municipal authority, the Supreme Planning Council. Its members are appointed by the military governor and the Council controls all aspects of Palestinian development, especially outside the municipal boundaries.

As Nakhleh has written, 'Nowhere is the power of this Council more apparent than in planning, zoning, and general land use policies, particularly in decisions relating to the annexation of lands and to the proposed expansion of the corporate limits of Arab Towns. In almost every instance, the Supreme Council ruled against West Bank towns and cities in favour of the Israeli settlement policy. Furthermore, the council has the power, by military decree, to overrule or nullify any municipal decision regarding planning and zoning and forbid housing development in any area, outside the corporate limits of any town, even though that area had already been zoned residential. Such an order is usually issued in the name of military government' (1979).

Recently, the attitude towards conservation has begun to change in a positive direction. It is being included in education programmes at the university level. As a result, several academic projects have been scheduled and others carried out on the subject of conservation. Workshops and conferences are being set up to advise and encourage professionals and the general public on how best to maintain the traditional buildings and the historic quarters.

Lastly, international organisations and NGOs are playing a part in the development of conservation in Palestine. These support national and individual initiatives and encourage the official bodies to enhance their own interest in their built heritage.

CONCLUSION AND RECOMMENDATIONS

Any decision that little can be done to upgrade and preserve the existing housing stock in Palestine until the total economy grows substantially would, in effect, erode thousands of traditional historic buildings if not entire historic cores. This will not only affect the people who live there now, but subsequent generations as well and might even delay the entire developmental programme.

A solution must be found which is likely to result in substantial upgrading not for a few highly symbolic 'monuments' or religious buildings, but for thousands of humbler, but environmentally and culturally vital, buildings and historic cores, not for the future but for the immediate present. Such a solution, or programme, must be realistic in terms of the enormity of the problem, the density and rapid growth of the population, and the limited financial resources available.

With the rapidly changing circumstances and the urgent need to develop and upgrade every single sector of Palestine's infrastructure, however, it will take a longer time for the 'infant' PNA and the municipal governments to meet the physical and social needs of the historic cores. The cost of any comprehensive programme for conservation will require colossal sums of money, far more than the PNA could ever raise. Because of the magnitude of the task, large-scale upgrading projects of the existing housing stock are beyond the capacity of the PNA at this time, and most probably, for the next ten years.

Upgrading Traditional Housing

The conservation of the existing housing stock is an appropriate, practical and effective way of addressing the housing shortage. From a conservation point of view, this could be a virtue in that it controls vast developments which tend to swiftly erode the character of Palestine. Moreover, the great demand for housing at present could be well exploited to achieve the goal of conservation.

In view of such demand, the available space potential in the redundant traditional old houses could be readily exploited if people were presented with this alternative, and rehabilitation could then become the dynamic moving force for conservation. It could contribute not only to the survival of our cultural heritage for cultural, political and ideological reasons, but also for practical ones as well.

There are obvious benefits to re-using the traditional existing housing stock. The buildings themselves are unique; they are consistently better built, with craftsmanship and materials which cannot be duplicated in today's market. They were constructed with care and with good decoration seldom possible in our contemporary buildings. They have thick walls, unique window characteristics not found in new structures. They were designed to use natural light and ventilation, often being energy efficient. In summary, old buildings provide more interesting and varied environments for people to live, work, shop and eat (Fitch, 1982).

This is one of the reasons why we believe that conservation and upgrading of the existing housing stock in the historic cores is vital. In addition to the important cultural benefits, and the rationale of saving much needed land derived from the preservation and extended life of existing housing stock, houses are also repositories of large expenditures of energy and materials. The fact that their rehabilitation and upgrading is a labour intensive, rather than an energy intensive, activity, and that this will probably cost less than new work, supports the desirability of restoration for new adaptive use (Fitch, 1982).

While opponents of this view may argue that new building is cheaper than restoring old ones, it may often be more expensive to rehabilitate an old building than to construct the same building on previously unused land. Also, such costs take no account of the life support system, the infrastructure of institutions, services, and utilities without which a building could not operate at all. Moreover, such a conventional economic argument does not take into consideration such hidden costs of building new accommodation, as the loss of fertile land for agriculture; the cost of building new streets, sidewalks, street-lighting, sewer and water systems and the cost of new health, educational and municipal facilities (Fitch, 1980).

Therefore, if such hidden costs are properly taken into consideration, then the expediency of rehabilitating and preserving the existing housing stock in Palestine's historic cores, with their huge infrastructure which is already in existence and which has been paid for becomes much more attractive and practical.

On the national level, conservation projects could also create jobs for hundreds of Palestinians, as the conservation process is a labour intensive activity. These jobs could be professional or technical or as crafts-persons and general workers.

Citizen Participation and Self-Help

Any conservation project in Palestine should be designed to stimulate citizen participation and self-help activities in coping with the conditions of the historic quarters and preventing further deterioration in them, as well as in developing a sense of civic consciousness. It should be designed as a realistic and practical approach to upgrade largely through the resources most readily available – the thousands of hands and the small financial resources of the inhabitants themselves.

A start should be made with the few limited resources available, with phases and options for a more substantive wider and longer term process. A 'step by step,' carefully tailored and sensitive start with one example building in each of the historic quarters is the only tenable approach. Too much, too soon, will produce a counter reaction from the public, and be damaging to the credibility of the conservation organisations.

The programme of action would take as its reference the needs and resources of the residents as the basic criteria against which options are measured. This approach has the further possibility of satisfying needs within the potential resources and of improving the quality of living in the historic cores through economic, health and educational links.

The conservation approach should involve re-orientating the paternalistic relationship between the local authorities and residents by establishing one of co-operation and partnership, which is not limited to consultation and the physical aspects of the conservation programme but which also includes other aspects of planning, decision-making, administerial, managerial, financial and maintenance operations, and replacing the current dogmatic attitudes of meeting conservation needs by initiating small-scale pilot projects before commenting resources to larger programmes. These should be monitored and the public reaction determined to ensure the maximum acceptability of the recommended measures in the selected communities.

Establishing a community training centre to advise the local residents on how to adapt, renew and properly maintain their properties, can act as a communicative medium to pass information and encourage debate and collaboration between the experts, the local authorities and the residents. It could provide the right communicative link to pass on the local knowledge and expertise to the decision makers and the researchers. It could transmit skills from crafts-persons to local residents, thus smoothly transferring the responsibility to the community as the project becomes sustainable without outside help.

Developing an information campaign by using all available means, could provide the right climate for participation. The education of the public, especially at schools, can promote more understanding and pride in the traditional environment. The Palestinian universities should play a major role in establishing an information bank of the built heritage, as well as utilising student potential to document and maintain some of the traditional settings.

The continuous monitoring and evaluation of the conservation project are essential steps in the execution as well as in the design and implementation of future programmes. Because of the strengths or weaknesses in the programme's structure and the success or failure of its operation, it can stand as a model to followed, limited or avoided by future programmes. Monitoring and evaluation should be regarded as part of an ongoing process alongside the various stages and activities of the programme. The main purpose is to provide information concerning the impact on the intended beneficiaries of the programme and to assess the output of the programme.

Communication with, and participation by, local communities should be established. There is also an urgent need for partnerships between the various 'actors' in the conservation process (local municipalities, local experts and professionals, the educational institutions and citizens' groups) on polices and programme formulation, not only at the planning stage but also at later stages of implementation and maintenance.

Finally, as mentioned earlier, there is a great willingness to restore and conserve national monuments (single distinguished buildings such as mosques, palaces, hammams), for their prestige and to attract some international funding. However, Palestinian cultural identity is not only expressed by a group of monuments, but also by traditional small-scale buildings and areas. Therefore, any conservation decision should clearly distinguish between conserving monuments and the less dramatic, but equally important, cultural and traditional areas.

Nevertheless, if conservation is to be effective and provide the sense of continuity embodied in our traditional settings, all historic areas should be taken into consideration. It is only then that our people will realise that conservation is, first of all, for their own benefit and we can then rely on them for its success.

BIBLIOGRAPHY

Abu Ayyash, A., 1976, *Israeli Regional Planning Policy in the Arab occupied Territories*, in **Journal of Palestine Studies**, 5, 3, pp. 83–108.

Abu Shanab, B., 1983, **Jerusalem, An Islamic City: Culture and Conservation**, Unpublished dissertation, IoAAS, University of York.

Al-Quds, 1994, *Israel Expropriated 73.6 Per Cent of the West Bank's Land*, Jerusalem, 21 September (Arabic).

Appleyard, D., ed., **Conservation of European Cities**, The MIT Press, Cambridge, Massachusetts and London.

Benvenisti, M., 1976, **Jerusalem: the Torn City**, Isratyset CTD, Jerusalem.

Bianco, S. 1980, *Fez Towards the Rehabilitation of a Great City*, in **Conservation as Cultural Survival**, Proceedings of Seminar Two, Architectural Transformation in the Islamic World, The Aga Khan Award for Architecture, 26 to 28 September, Istanbul, pp. 28–41.

Coon. A., 1991, *Racial Distinctions Break on the West Bank*, **Planning**, 945, 22 November, pp. 4–15.

Coon, A., 1992, **Town Planning Under Military Occupation**, Dartmouth Publishing, England.

Dakkak, I., 1981, 'Jerusalem Via Dolorosa,' **Journal of Palestine Studies**, XI, 1, pp. 136–149.

Davey, P., 1978, *Building a New Jerusalem*, **Architects' Journal**, 29 November, pp. 1016–1018.

Efrat, E., 1984, **Urbanisation in Israel**, St. Martin's Press, New York.

Fitch, J.M., 1982, **Historic Preservation: Cultural Management of the Built World**, McGraw-Hill Book Company, New York.

Institute of Advanced Architectural Studies, 1994, *Jerusalem Revitalised: $5 Million Proposal Gets Funding Agreement*, 1 July, Revival, PRDU, University of York, UK.

Karmon, K., 1971, **Israel: a Regional Geography**, Wiley-Interscience, John Wiley and Sons, London.

Luke, S.H. and Keith-Roach, E., 1934, **The Handbook of Palestine and Transjordan**, Macmillan, London.

Nakhleh, E.A., 1979, **The West Bank and Gaza, Towards the Making of a Palestinian State**, American Enterprise Institute for Public Policy Research, Washington D.C.

Shiber, S., 1968, **Recent Arab City Growth**, Government Printing Press, Kuwait.

Von Grunebaum, G.E., 1962, **Modern Islam: The Search for Cultural Identity**, University of California, Los Angeles.

Theme Five

FINANCIAL SERVICES FOR HOUSING AND URBAN DEVELOPMENT

TOWARDS AN EFFECTIVE HOUSING FINANCE STRATEGY IN PALESTINE

Kamal Naser

ABSTRACT

The continuity and the success of housing finance policy will depend on the mobilisation of the nation's savings to attain long-term equilibrium between the supply and demand for funds. An effective housing finance strategy should begin with clear definitions of objectives about where we should be.

This paper looks at internal and external factors affecting housing finance strategies, the role of the Palestine National Authority (PNA), the legal framework and the role of the financial sector. An analysis of the various risks involved is included, and various mortgage instruments and institutions suggested.

INTRODUCTION

A distinction should be made between strategic decisions which may affect the PNA's scope of action and those which may affect the deployment of resources. These strategic decisions are influenced by internal and external factors regarding where we are at present. The gap between the long-term objectives and the current factors constitutes the basis for a housing finance strategy for the Palestinian Territories (PT) (see Figure 1).

Internal factors which need attention include the personnel of the Ministry of Housing and of the Palestinian Housing Council (PHC), their experience and the availability of resources. External factors which should be considered are the national financial sector and its investment in the housing sector, the effectiveness of the legal framework and instruments for housing finance.

Strategic objectives are used as broad concepts and encompass the

503

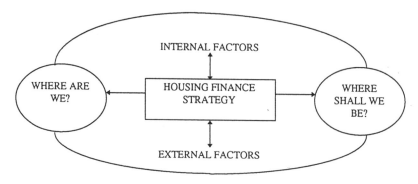

Figure 1 A Housing Finance Strategy.

statement of purpose. They also provide a specific performance-related vision and a set of strategic guidelines about how and when the PNA is expected to achieve the stated goals and objectives. The purpose of the vision forms the basis for what the PNA intends to achieve; the strategic guidance determines how the PNA's goals will determine the Authority's behaviour in meeting its strategic objectives.

The PNA needs to clearly define its vision of an effective housing finance strategy and avoid reacting to emerging housing problems. Visions and missions are likely to fail if they are not shared, or if they are generic and cannot be measured, or if they do not respond to the needs of the housing sector.

THE ROLE OF THE PNA

The Housing Ministry, in co-operation with the Ministry of Finance and the Ministry of Social Security, can work to identify the demand for housing, the distribution of per capita income, the availability of funds, and the availability of housing materials and supplies. The effectiveness of a housing finance strategy lies in its ability to ensure the flow of funds which will be necessary to meet the demand for housing. This task requires co-operation between housing developers, financial institutions and potential investors, suppliers, community representatives and lawyers.

A housing council that includes representatives from each of these organisations is vital to the success of a housing finance policy. The council should be given the responsibility of developing a housing finance policy to present to the Ministry of Housing for approval. Such a council can be accommodated within the framework of the Palestinian Housing Council (PHC). The relationship between the Housing Ministry and the PHC should be defined. The PNA can make use of the expertise gained by the PHC by delegating part of its responsibilities.

Table 1 Establishment and Branches of Banks in the PT.

Bank	Date Established	Number of Branches
Bank of Palestine	1981	8
Cairo Amman Bank	1986	15
Arab Bank	1994	5
Arab Land Bank	1994	3
Bank of Jordan	1994	5
Jordan-Gulf Bank	1994	1
Commercial Bank of Palestine	1994	1
Palestine Investment Bank	1995	1
Jordan National Bank	1995	1
ANZ Griddles	1995	1

As far as the housing finance policy is concerned, the PNA can either formulate and implement a policy that competes with the private sector (disabling strategy), or offer the private sector the required facilities necessary to operate an effective policy (enabling strategy). The former strategy can only be effective if the PNA has enough resources to meet the demand of home-buyers over a long period of time.

In reality, most countries lack such resources. In addition, intervening in the market to compete with the private sector gives the PNA a competitive advantage and makes investment in the housing sector less attractive.

Most countries opt for the enabling strategy. Under this strategy, the return on investment in the housing sector is determined by market forces. Ultimately this works to the benefit of home-buyers (i.e. the borrowers). Such a policy attracts investors to the housing sector and ensures a continuous flow of funds. Consequently, the mortgage interest rate falls.

Although the enabling strategy represents a workable option, the absence of a national social security system and an employment programme creates a gap between housing costs and affordability. This will make the implementation of the enabling strategy somewhat difficult.

To eradicate the gap between cost and affordability, the PNA can provide some form of subsidy. However, the PNA is not in a position to provide subsidies over a long period of time. Thus, a modified strategy that combines the disabling and the enabling strategies may satisfy the economic and social conditions of the PT. The PNA could take care of the low- or no-income groups and leave the responsibility for home-buyers from the middle and upper classes to the private sector.

THE LEGAL FRAMEWORK FOR HOUSING FINANCE

A housing finance policy is meaningless without a clearly defined set of rules and guidance used to organise the relationship between the home-buyers (borrowers) and investors (lenders). The legal framework should contain guidelines on the standard of construction, codes of practice and areas where housing development is allowed. The rules must protect both the borrower (from possible exploitation) and the lender (from losses by managing risk).

The legal framework must address the issue of property ownership rights (the ownership status of land jointly owned, such as *masha* land, *waqf* land and properties owned by a number of beneficiaries or heirs). In addition, a condominium law specifying property ownership rights and formal contracts between landlords and tenants must be introduced.

An appropriate property tax on unused land should be introduced to discourage speculation and encourage construction. Furthermore, regulations governing the relationship between landlords and tenants should be introduced. It is important to mention that a policy of rent control is counter productive and deters private investors from upgrading existing properties or investing in the housing sector. In addition, such a policy reduces tax revenue and creates inequalities among the population. Hence, rents should be determined by market forces and related to inflation.

THE ROLE OF THE FINANCIAL SECTOR IN HOUSING FINANCE

Although the PT have witnessed a significant increase in the number of newly established financial institutions (Table 1), their contribution to the housing sector is yet to be seen (Table 2). At present, local banks tend to transfer their deposits to foreign banks outside the country to benefit from relative political and economic stability and high interest rates offered by those banks. It is not surprising to see the banks taking such action. The main problem facing the financial institutions operating in the PT involves risk management associated with the stability, or otherwise, of macroeconomic policy.

Investors in the housing sector may face several forms of risk, such as credit, interest rate, exchange rate and political risk.

Credit risk

This is associated with repayment of the principal. It is manageable and can be minimised by:

- Rendering the loan to those home-buyers who have secure jobs; and
- Asking the home-buyer to make a significant down payment to avoid possible negative equity.

Table 2 Loans Offered by Banks Operating in the PT.

	December 1994	January 1995	February 1995	March 1995
LOANS	142,799,224	165,295,637	174,187,770	222,585,865
TERM LOANS	8,536,223	9,861,236	10,952,817	11,582,300
TOTAL ASSETS	265,668,914	345,332,359	369,242,951	451,982,335
Term Loans/Loans	0.0597	0.0596	0.063	0.052
Term Loans/Total Assets	0.538	0.479	0.472	0.493
Term Loans/Total Assets	0.031	0.029	0.030	0.026

Source: Palestinian Economic Policy Research Institute (MAS), Palestinian Banking Sector Statistical Review, June 1995.

Interest Rate Risk

This is difficult to contain since it is influenced by macroeconomic policy, particularly inflation. However, interest rate risk can be minimised by adopting the following measures or instruments:

- Mandatory long-term saving and lending;
- Mortgage-supported securities;
- Tax-exempt mortgage bonds;
- Fixed mortgage interest rates;
- Adjusted interest rate mortgages;
- Guaranteed payment mortgages;
- Price-level-adjusted mortgages;
- Blocked compensating-balance mortgages;
- Portfolio diversification; and
- Effective support facilities.

Exchange Rate Risk

This may occur as a result of the various currencies used in the PT (i.e. the US dollar, Jordanian dinar and Israeli shekel). None of the financial institutions operating in the PT is prepared to carry the risk of exchange rate fluctuations.

The foreign exchange market provides 'hedging' facilities for transferring foreign exchange risk to someone else. In addition, the exchange rate risk can be minimised by specifying a strong currency to make the periodic interest and principal repayments.

Political Risk

This reflects the political and economic uncertainties that characterise the PT. To minimise political risk, international organisations such as the World Bank can be invited to insure against it.

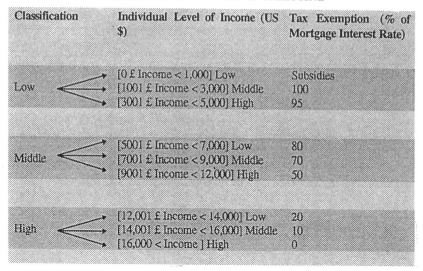

Classification	Individual Level of Income (US $)	Tax Exemption (% of Mortgage Interest Rate)
Low	[0 £ Income < 1,000] Low	Subsidies
	[1001 £ Income < 3,000] Middle	100
	[3001 £ Income < 5,000] High	95
Middle	[5001 £ Income < 7,000] Low	80
	[7001 £ Income < 9,000] Middle	70
	[9001 £ Income < 12,000] High	50
High	[12,001 £ Income < 14,000] Low	20
	[14,001 £ Income < 16,000] Middle	10
	[16,000 < Income] High	0

Figure 2 The Tax System and Home-buyer Income.

The success, or otherwise, of the housing finance policy depends on the mobilisation of the nation's savings by managing investors' risks and attracting new home-buyers (borrowers) by offering them a reasonable mortgage interest rate. To serve this purpose, the PNA should ensure that the tax system motivates both borrowers and lenders. In addition, it could limit risk to a manageable level by encouraging the use of the following measures or the establishment of certain institutions such as:

- Mandatory long-term savings;
- Share institutions/mutual institutions;
- A contract saving system;
- A mortgage bank;
- Co-operatives;
- Employees schemes; and
- Loans supported by insurance companies.

The tax system can be used effectively by classifying home-buyers into groups according to their personal income (see Figure 2).

MORTGAGE INSTRUMENTS

After mobilising the tax system and implementing measures to minimise the impact of various mortgage risks, the following mortgage instruments can be introduced:

- Fixed rate interest rate;
- Guaranteed payments mortgage;

- Adjusted mortgage rate;
- Tax-exempt housing finance;
- Step-by-step mortgage; and an
- Islamic banking mortgage.

These measures can be diversified to satisfy home-buyers' needs.

RECOMMENDATIONS

An effective housing finance strategy starts with clear definitions of objectives about where we should be. The achievement of each objective covers a relatively short period of time and as one objective is achieved, the Palestinian National Authority (PNA) should proceed to another. Otherwise, the strategy will lose its momentum.

An effective housing finance policy should begin with an intensive survey aimed at estimating the demand for housing, the funds available in both the public and the private sector for investment in the housing sector and the availability of building materials. The continuity and the success of such a policy is dependent on the ability to mobilise the nation's savings to attain long-term equilibrium between the supply and demand for funds.

Investors can be attracted to the housing sector if, and only if, they are assured that their risk is contained at a manageable level. Home-buyers, on the other hand, are prepared to borrow at a reasonable mortgage rate barring any possible exploitation. The PNA can assure both parties by adopting the following measures:

- Introducing an effective regulatory framework to protect both the borrowers and lenders;
- Combining the *enabling* and *disabling* strategies to produce a new strategy that accords with the country's needs;
- Keeping a close eye on macroeconomic policy to monitor inflation;
- Activating the tax system to reduce the mortgage interest rate; and
- Co-operating with international organisations to insure against possible apolitical risk.

In the case of the second point, combining the enabling and disabling strategies would allow the population to be classified into nine main categories so that the PNA can take care of those on the bottom of the scale and leave the responsibility of securing housing finance for the middle and upper classes to the private sector.

Finally, since neither financial institutions nor home-buyers have any experience with mortgages and mortgage instruments, a training programme should be organised for representatives from the PNA, PHC, lawyers, property developers and the financial sector.

HOUSING SECTOR PERFORMANCE AND HOUSING STRATEGY IN GAZA AND THE WEST BANK

Stephen K. Mayo

INTRODUCTION

Formulating and putting in place an effective strategy for the development of the housing sector in the Palestinian Territories will require imagination and skill, and, as importantly, thorough information about the performance of the housing sector – what works and what doesn't – and about the most appropriate ways to ensure that the sector functions well and contributes toward the attainment of social and economic objectives. This paper is a modest effort to describe a framework for both evaluating the performance of the housing sector and making choices among policies and institutions.

The general approach taken in the paper draws on a framework developed as part of the United Nations 'Global Shelter Strategy for the Year 2000', which sets out a bold design for policy reform in developing and developed countries alike based on the idea of moving from interventionist and heavily state-controlled policies toward 'enabling strategies' which require the state to play an important, but more facilitative, role than has often been the case in many of the countries in the Middle East.

An important part of deciding upon which among many 'enabling strategies' to adopt depends on having a detailed and quantitative understanding of how the housing sector is currently operating relative to that of a 'well-functioning housing sector', the properties of which can be determined, and which have, indeed, been set out in a recent World Bank housing policy paper entitled *Housing Indicators Programme* (HIP) can be used to assess the degree to which the PT housing sector meets or deviates from the goal of a well-functioning housing sector; the reasons

510

behind lagging performance of the sector; and can suggest the kinds of changes in policies, regulations, and institutions that can be instituted to improve both sectoral performance and the contribution that the housing sector makes to broader social and economic objectives.

The paper is organised as follows: Section 1 presents an overview of the stakes of good housing policy; Section 2 describes the conceptual framework used for the analysis of the PT housing sector; Section 3 presents and evaluates key indicators of housing sector performance, discusses the implications for the sector and the broader economy of the indicators, and analyses the reasons behind sector under-performance; Section 4 briefly summarises the diagnosis of sectoral performance based on the indicators; and Section 5 discusses a number of policy and institutional reforms necessary to bring about a well-functioning housing sector in PT.

The Stakes of Good Housing Policy

In most economies, the housing sector is a prominent one, accounting for from 7 to 18 per cent of Gross National Product GNP (made up of investment, which is usually from 2 to 8 per cent of GNP, and rents, which are generally from 5 to 10 per cent of GNP), 20 to 30 per cent of fixed capital formation, and 20 to 50 per cent of reproducible wealth. Some preliminary estimates have indicated that the housing, or at least the construction, sector has been one of the most prominent sectors in the PT economy within recent years, contributing, according to some estimates, in excess of 20 per cent of GNP. Moreover, the housing sector is, in general, capable of playing an important role in a country's financial affairs, with long-term loans for housing often comprising from 20 to 40 per cent of the assets of the banking system. As is discussed below, the role of formal housing finance as a contributor toward financial development has been almost completely absent in PT, to the detriment of both the housing sector and the financial system. Finally, the housing sector can comprise an important part of a country's fiscal system, serving as a source of revenue in the form of property taxation, capital gains, and other taxes, and, often, as an object of considerable subsidies. Again, in PT, the fiscal dimensions of the housing sector have been the subject of neither systematic strategic thinking nor institutional development. Fiscal policies regarding housing are at present erratic and unfocussed, diminishing the ability of the sector to contribute toward the functioning of a balanced system of taxation, subsidies, and expenditures.

Even these dimensions of the housing sector's interactions with the broader economy, however, fail to convey fully the role that housing plays in the overall performance of the economy. The housing sector is strongly linked by a number of different real, financial, and fiscal circuits to other parts of the economy such that, if the performance of the housing sector is damaged by inappropriate policies, the performance of the economy as a whole will suffer. In the United States, for example, the failure of hundreds of savings and loan institutions as a result of inadequate regulatory policies has necessitated some $300 billion in taxpayer-funded costs to compensate the depositors of failed institutions. In the United Kingdom, it has been estimated that failed housing policies have resulted in a structural increase in Britain's unemployment rate of some 2 percentage points, a major decrease in the household savings rate, increases in interest and inflation rates, and a higher balance of payments deficit. In the reforming socialist economies of Eastern Europe and the former Soviet Union, the heavy costs to their economies of low labour mobility stemming from constricted housing markets, with pervasive housing shortages and low turnover, are now a prime motivation for housing policy reform.

Getting housing policies right has the potential, therefore, not only to benefit households through safe, comfortable, and reasonably priced housing, but also by contributing to a more balanced and productive economy. Conversely, the wrong policy choices may result both in worse housing and a badly functioning economy.

The Conceptual Framework

In addressing the question of housing policy the framework used here draws heavily on the *Global Shelter Strategy for the Year 2000,* a document unanimously endorsed by the United Nations General Assembly in 1988, and which has been amplified in a recently published World Bank policy paper entitled *Housing: Enabling Markets to Work.* The Global Strategy for Shelter calls for a fundamental shift in government's role in housing. Rather than attempting to provide housing directly, a policy that has usually failed, governments are called on to play an enabling role. They should facilitate, energise, and support the activities of the private sector, both formal and informal, in housing development. This shift necessarily requires governments to obtain a broader overview of the housing sector as a whole, and to better understand the mechanisms governing housing sector performance. There is growing recognition among governments that this requires not only a more rigorous and encompassing analytical framework, but also more and better data and better, policy-oriented analysis of such data.[1]

The Housing Sector as the Product of Market Forces

In recent years market relations have been found to exist in the housing sector at all levels, from the most meagre squatter settlements to highly-regulated rent-controlled apartments. Even in centrally-planned and formerly centrally-planned economies, housing is viewed increasingly as a commodity with an exchange value, rather than as a good to be produced and allocated outside the market-place, by supply and demand, and that these forces exert powerful influences throughout all parts of the sector despite the existence of apparently distinctive submarkets.

Recognition of the pervasiveness of market forces has led to the view that although responsible housing policy must be sufficiently differentiated to deal with particular submarkets such those consisting of as high-rise condominiums, public housing rentals, and squatter settlements, it is still useful to look at the housing sector as a single market. Trends in one part of a housing market will, over time, be closely linked to those in other parts of the market. Policies designed to affect only the low, middle, or high-income submarkets will almost inevitably affect the performance of other submarkets, often in unintended or undesirable ways.

Prices, and thus housing affordability by different income, groups are determined in the market by demand and supply. Housing demand is determined by demographic conditions, such as the rate of urbanisation and new household formation, as well as macro-economic conditions affecting household incomes. It is also influenced by the system of property rights, e.g., rights to own and exchange property, and tenure security for both renters and owners; by the availability of housing finance; and by government fiscal policies, e.g., taxation, subsidies and particularly subsidies targeted to the poor.

Housing supply is affected by the availability of resource inputs, such as residential land, infrastructure and construction materials. It is also affected by the organisation of the construction industry, the availability of skilled and productive construction labour, and the dependence on imports. Both the demand and supply of housing are affected by the regulatory, institutional, and policy environment.

Housing policies and housing outcomes may in turn affect broader socio-economic conditions, such as the infant mortality rate, the rate of inflation, the household savings rate, manufacturing wage and productivity levels, capital formation, the balance of payments, and the government budget deficit. Figure 1 illustrates a simple model of the housing market.

While largely private housing markets produce most of the housing in most countries, this does not necessarily mean that these markets are either efficient or equitable. Nor does it mean that these markets completely satisfy all housing needs to help attain broader development goals. Housing sector policies must be based on a positive view of how the sector actually works in a given context, and, as well, with specific notions of how it could work better.

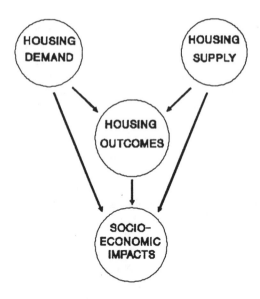

Figure 1

A Normative View of the Housing Sector

To develop a normative view of the housing sector, one must look at how the sector performs from several different perspectives. The five most important perspectives are those of housing consumers, housing producers, housing finance institutions, local governments, and central governments.[2]

Each of these perspectives focuses on different desired outcomes. Such desired outcomes, while neither universally attainable nor entirely compatible, may be expected to exert an influence both on behaviour of the key actors and on the way that they perceive the efficacy and responsiveness of government policies and programmes. The desired outcomes are as follows:

Housing Consumers

Everyone is housed, with a separate unit for every household. Housing does not take up an undue portion of household income. House prices are not subject to undue variability. Living space is adequate. Structures are safe and provide adequate protection from the elements, fire, and natural disasters. Services and amenities are available and reliable. Location provides good access to employment. Tenure is secure and protected by due process of law. Households may freely choose among different housing options and tenures (owning vs. renting). Finance is available to smooth expenses over time and allow households to save and invest. Adequate information is available to ensure efficient choice.

Housing Producers

Adequate supply of residential land is available at reasonable prices. Infrastructure networks are adequate and do not hold back residential development. Building materials and equipment and sufficient skilled labour are available at reasonable prices. Entry of new firms into the residential construction sector is not impeded. The residential construction sector is not discriminated against by special tariffs or controls. Adequate financing is available. Housing production and investment can respond to changes in demand without undue delay. Contracts are enforceable. Regulations concerning land development, land use, building, land tenure, taxation, or special programs are well defined and predictable, and government application of these is efficient, timely, and uniform. Adequate information exists to enable producers to forecast housing demand with reasonable certainty. Rates of return on all types of housing investment, including rental housing, are sufficient to maintain incentives for investment.

Housing Finance Institutions

Housing finance institutions are permitted to compete for deposits on equal terms with other financial institutions; the role of directed credit is minimised. Housing finance institutions are not forced to compete unfairly with subsidised finance. Lending is at positive real interest rates with a sufficient margin to maintain institutional health. There are sufficient deposits of an appropriate term structure for long-term mortgage lending. Mortgage lending instruments are permitted which are in demand by households, and provide adequate protection for the institution. Systems of property rights, tenure security, and foreclosure are such that the financial interests of lenders can be protected. Appropriate institutions exist that protect financial institutions against undue mortgage lending risk.

Local Governments

Housing and associated infrastructures are of adequate quality to maintain public health, safety standards, and environmental quality. Infrastructure networks and services are extended quickly to all communities. The location of new communities is close to existing main networks. Land use is productive and efficient. Sufficient land can be obtained for laying infrastructure networks and providing local amenities and public services. Housing provides a major source of municipal revenues for building and maintaining infrastructure services and neighbourhood amenities.

Central Governments

Adequate, affordable housing is available to all. Targeted subsidies are available to help households that cannot afford minimum housing. Housing sector policy is integrated into national social and economic planning. Housing sector performance is monitored regularly. The housing sector contributes toward broad social and economic objectives: 1) alleviating poverty; 2) controlling inflation; 3) generating household savings and mobilising household productive resources; 4) generating employment and income growth; 5) enabling social and spatial mobility; 6) increasing productivity; 7) generating investment growth; 8) accumulating national wealth; 9) reducing the balance of payments deficit; 10) reducing the government budget deficit; 11) developing the financial system; and 12) protecting the environment.

While the above list may be incomplete, it does provide a broad normative view of a well-functioning housing sector from the perspectives of its key actors. Needless to say, these perspectives are not necessarily mutually consistent. What may benefit one may damage another. Rent control, for example, may benefit families already housed, but may prevent further investment in rental housing and discriminate against new residents. Reducing house prices may benefit housing seekers but reduce the asset value of those owning houses. Increasing land supply may be at the expense of environmental amenities. Stronger foreclosure laws may increase mortgage financing for all at the expense of evictions for some. Resolving these incompatible interests is one of the most fundamental tasks of an effective housing policy.

These norms for a well-functioning housing sector have been taken as the basic framework for generating a comprehensive set of indicators to measure housing sector performance within the HIP, a joint programme of the United Nations Centre for Human Settlements (Habitat) and the World Bank. Indicators were designed to cover housing supply – the cost and availability of key inputs such as land, infrastructure, building materials, industrial organisation, and the regulatory environment; housing demand – demographic variables, finance, and subsidies; and housing outcomes – prices, quantities, and the qualitative features of the housing stock. All key norms for a well-functioning housing sector were translated, as far as possible, into quantitative indicators. These were then tested and collected in an 'Extensive Survey', conducted in 53 countries on all continents and at all levels of economic development. The countries covered by the Extensive Survey accounted for some 80 per cent of the world's population in 1990, and some 90 per cent of its urban population. Countries in the region which were included in the initial study were Algeria, Egypt, Israel, Jordan, Morocco, Tunisia, and Turkey.

While PT was not formally included in the initial phase of the HIP, as much housing sector data as were possible to collect from secondary sources, and drawing on the HIP format, were assembled in 1993 to facilitate a discussion of the PT housing sector in the six volume World Bank series *Investing in Peace*.[3] This discussion updates and extends that discussion, although, as noted frequently below, gaps in the data are substantial and should be remedied by a far more systematic effort to collect data based on the survey instruments used by the HIP.[4]

KEY INDICATORS OF PT HOUSING SECTOR PERFORMANCE

While a complete account of the performance of the PT housing sector would require an evaluation of housing outcomes across time and space, and for particular groups within the population, it is nevertheless useful to examine a number of key outcomes at an aggregate level. This is, in a way, analogous to the initial check-up a physician might perform upon seeing a patient for the first time. Depending on the outcome of a number of routine and universal measurements of temperature, blood pressure, etc., and a comparison of those measurements to established norms, a patient might be prescribed as either fit or in need of further tests, in order to make a diagnosis and initiate a prescriptive regime.

Within the HIP, ten key indicators of housing sector performance have been proposed for such an initial check-up. These are designed to address the concerns of the major actors within the sector that were described above, and to give a sense of key features of both housing outcomes and the functioning of key markets for housing inputs.

The ten indicators are divided into five main groups:

Price Indicators:	Indicator 1:	The House Price to Income Ratio; and
	Indicator 2:	The Rent to Income Ratio.
Quantity Indicators:	Indicator 3:	Housing Production; and
	Indicator 4:	Housing Investment.
Quality Indicators:	Indicator 5:	Floor Area Per Person;
	Indicator 6:	Permanent Structures; and
	Indicator 7:	Unauthorised Housing.
Demand-Side Indicators:	Indicator 8:	The Housing Credit Portfolio.

517

| Supply-Side Indicators: | Indicator 9: | The Land Development Multiplier; and |
| | Indicator 10: | Infrastructure Expenditures Per Capita. |

These are described below in greater detail.

These ten key indicators by themselves cannot capture all the dimensions of the housing sector. In-depth studies and sample surveys will be needed in any country to augment these measures and to monitor the effects of specific policies. Individual countries may need to supplement this basic set of indicators in line with their special concerns, particularly regarding housing outcomes for the poor, racial and ethnic groups, and for other groups with special needs.[5]

The significance of each indicator, its distribution across different levels of GNP per capita and the preliminary analysis on the results of the Extensive Survey are given below. For each indicator a graph is presented which indicates the median reported value for five different income groups of about ten countries each, and displays the highest and lowest reported value of the indicator within each income grouping. Unless otherwise noted, empirical results cited for PT are for years between 1990 and the present. Whenever possible, data for Gaza and the West Bank are reported separately, not only because of differences in housing outcomes, but also because of considerable differences in the policies and regulations which influence outcomes in each area. In some cases, it has not yet been possible to obtain data on relevant outcomes for PT. Whenever this is the case, it is noted below, and trends in the indicator in question within the region are noted, in order to illustrate the range of potential outcomes and their implications.

Interpretation of these and other indicators produces a far different picture of what constitutes the housing problem in any particular place than is commonly presented in alternative approaches such as that typified by the 'Housing Needs Assessment', which has been popularised in recent years by some bilateral assistance organisations. Not surprisingly, since the diagnostic procedure using housing indicators is different, and far more comprehensive than that used by needs assessments, the policy prescriptions likely to be forthcoming are also different. In particular, there is an almost inexorable tendency for needs assessments to prescribe the building of housing, generally at a rate well beyond that demonstrated to be within the reach of the combined public and private sectors, as the solution for 'the problem.'

But housing problems and housing's potentials, are far more profound than those indicated by sophisticated counts of households and acceptable dwellings. Not surprisingly, when the problems are examined in a

Table 1 House-Price-to-Income Ratios by Region.

Sub-Saharan Africa	2.21
South Asia	6.25
East Asia	4.15
Latin America and Caribbean	2.38
Europe, Middle East, and North Africa	6.59
Industrialised Countries	4.70

more comprehensive way, the solutions which are proposed must be equally comprehensive.

Indicator 1: The House-Price-to-Income Ratio

This is defined as the ratio of the median free-market price of a dwelling unit and the median annual household income.

Significance

If there is a single indicator that conveys the greatest amount of information on the overall performance of housing markets, it is the house price-to-income ratio. A key measure of housing affordability, when housing prices are high relative to incomes, other things being equal, a smaller fraction of the population will be able to purchase housing. As importantly, however, this indicator provides important insights into several housing market dysfunctions, indicative of a variety of policy failures. When this indicator is abnormally high, for example, it is generally a sign that the housing supply system is restricted in its ability to satisfy effective demand for housing, a feature of many housing delivery systems in both market and centrally-planned economies. In such cases, it is often found that housing quality and space are depressed below levels that are typical of countries with well-functioning and responsive housing delivery systems. When the indicator is abnormally low, it may indicate widespread insecurity of tenure, a situation which leads to reduced willingness of the population to invest in housing and to lower than necessary housing quality.

Findings

The mean reported house-price-to-income ratio is 5.0, and ranges from a low of 0.9 to a high of 14.8. The reported median increases modestly with the level of economic development. Variation among regions is slightly more pronounced, with the highest reported ratios in Europe, Middle East, and North Africa and in South Asia and the lowest in Sub-Saharan Africa and Latin America and the Caribbean. Reported ratios of house-price-to-income are particularly high in countries that have restricted private property rights and which give a prominent role to the

Table 2 House Price-to-Income Ratios in the Middle East.

	Egypt	Morocco	Jordan	Tunisia	Turkey	GWB	Algeria	Israel
GNP (1990)	600	$950	$1,240	$1,440	$1,630	$1,700	$2,060	$16,680
House price/income	6.67	7.15	3.39	6.11	5.03	6.4	11.70	5.03

public sector in the ownership of land and housing. Other countries that have particularly high house-price-to-income ratios are those with high construction costs and high land prices, caused in part by tight regulatory environments affecting land use and housing construction, with policies such as agricultural green belts and complicated and time-consuming regulations. The house-price-to-income ratio is indicative of the general level of excess demand in housing markets, and is, based on preliminary analyses, associated with reduced housing consumption (especially alternative measures of crowding and dwelling space) and reduced rates of home ownership.

In the absence of up-to-date surveys on selling prices of existing housing units, the value of the house-price-to-income ratio in PT is difficult to know with precision. Selling prices of newly built units are often on the order of a minimum of $45,000 in relation to estimated median household incomes of about $4,200,[6] which would make the ratio of *new* housing prices to income above 10, indicating that the bulk of newly built housing is only available to the upper tier of the income distribution. Existing housing, by contrast is more affordable, though there is a considerable range of uncertainty about actual prices. On average, existing housing is smaller than new housing, has fewer amenities, lower quality finish and is characterised by a greater proportion of dwellings located in refugee camps. As a rough order of magnitude, it is assumed that existing housing sells for about half of the assumed typical new housing price, $22,500, a price which corresponds to a dwelling of about 90 square metres with a price per square metre of $200, located on a plot of 250 square metres with a value of $100 per square metre.

The resulting ratio of house price-to-income, 5.4, is about average among countries in the region and among developing countries in general. On the other hand, the average value represents far from the 'best' attainable ratio – one consistent with a well-functioning housing sector. Jordan, for example (which is represented by the city of Amman) is estimated to have housing prices which are only about 3.4 times the median household income, and many developed countries have similarly low ratios. Israel, with a ratio of 5.0, is indeed an outlier among the more economically developed countries, where ratios of house price-to-income on the order of about 4 or less are typical of cities with well-functioning housing markets.

The moderately high housing prices evidenced in PT are the product, in part, of higher than necessary construction and land costs. Construction costs (per square metre) in urban areas were estimated to have been from $185 for construction with 'no finish' to $275 for 'full finish' in 1993 (CHF, 1993). Compared to other countries in the region, which use similar construction techniques, these costs appear to be quite high. Costs in Egypt, Morocco, Jordan, and Turkey, for example, were estimated to have been $90, $157, $150, and $110 per square metre respectively in 1990; while costs in Israel, were estimated to have been about $570 per square metre (HIP, 1993b). Thus the cost of 'finished' construction in PT is estimated to be only about half that of finished construction in Israel. Reasons for high unit costs of construction probably have to do with (1) the upward influence on the wage level caused by PT construction workers who work in Israel (who have made up as much as 75 per cent of construction sector employment within the past decade) and (2) dependence on Israel for building materials. While some materials are produced domestically, such as quarried stone, both wood and cement are imported either from or through Israel. In the case of cement, domestic firms producing cement products rely entirely on Israel for cement supplies, Arab investors having been repeatedly denied permission to establish a cement plant in Hebron which would satisfy all domestic needs (Bahiri 1989). A more detailed investigation of the sources of high construction costs in would appear to be a useful undertaking.

In the case of land, the price of urban land is high by international standards, and appears to have been rising rapidly. Costs per square metre of urban land suitable for residential building were estimated by the Co-operative Housing Foundation to have ranged from about $30 to $120 among different PT cities and towns in 1993, with the highest reported prices in Gaza and Nablus (CHF, p. 19). Assuming an average land cost of $60 square metre, it would take the equivalent of more than 3 years' annual income for the median household to purchase a lot of 250 square metre. Serviced land costs in Israel (Tel Aviv), by comparison, were estimated to be about $116 per square metre in 1990; there the 'typical' household would have been able to purchase a 250 square metre lot for the equivalent of only about 1 1/2 years' income. In Amman, Jordan serviced urban land was reported to be selling for about $23/ square metre in 1990; purchase of a 250 square metre lot would, similarly, have required the equivalent of about 1 1/2 years of the typical household's income.

High land prices in PT are undoubtedly a feature of a comparative scarcity of appropriately located, serviced land. Reasons for this scarcity include not only the well-known Israeli takings of land for settlements, security zones, and other purposes, but also the many restrictions imposed on Palestinian land development. Municipal boundaries have strictly defined permissible areas for land development, and, even within municipal boundaries, planning permissions have been tightly controlled. (Coon) (1992), for example has estimated that of some 2500 building permits which should be required each year to enable reconstruction in the West Bank to keep up with population increase, only about 350 per year were actually issued – a rate of one permit per 1700 persons. In other countries with similarly stringent, time-consuming, and unpredictable planning and regulatory procedures, it has been found that land and housing prices are not only structurally far higher than in places with more facilitative systems, but that prices are far more volatile – increasing more rapidly and falling more rapidly in response to shifts in demand.[7] Thus it appears, that not only are current land and housing prices higher than would be expected under a more relaxed regulatory system, but that unless actions are taken to create a far more flexible and responsive system, any surges in demand, such as those caused by an influx of 'returnees' or robust economic growth, are likely to be accompanied by rapid run-ups in land and housing prices that will inhibit further economic expansion.

A final reason behind the comparatively high housing prices in PT is the high standards of PT housing, which are often larger and better supplied with urban infrastructure than the housing stock in many other countries within the region (see the discussion below on 'Floor area per person' as well). According to the Israeli Central Bureau of Statistics, the average size of new dwellings built in PT in 1987 was 133 square metres, (Bahiri, 1989) while the 'average' unit in the stock (based on an admittedly 'cursory' analysis of 'incomplete' data) was estimated to be about 98 square metres. Based on surveys conducted in a wide variety of other countries, the median dwelling is generally from 85–90 per cent as large as the 'average' dwelling, which would suggest that a 'typical' or median unit in PT would be from 83–89 square metres. The size of new dwellings being built in PT are smaller only than the median dwelling in Australia (167 M2) and the United States (180 square metres), among all of the 53 countries represented in the Housing Indicators Program. The estimated PT median is on as par with Singapore (83 square metres) and Norway (84 square metres), and ranks behind only four countries. In determining how to reduce housing prices to a more affordable level, it is extremely important to document the degree to which such large sizes are influenced by regulations which are capable of being modified, as opposed to cultural preferences, which may not be so easily modified.

Indicator 2: The Rent-to-Income Ratio

This is defined as the ratio of the median annual rent of a dwelling unit and the median annual household income of renters.

Table 3 Rent-to-Income Ratios.

Sub-Saharan Africa	0.10
South Asia	0.19
East Asia	0.20
Latin America and Caribbean	0.20
Europe, Middle East, and North Africa	0.06
Industrialised Countries	0.18

Significance

This indicator, like House-Price-to-Income Ratio, is a key measure of housing affordability. In a well functioning housing market, housing expenditures should not take up an undue portion of household income. As with the house price-to-income ratio, this indicator conveys information on more than just affordability, however. A relatively high value for this indicator is often a sign that the supply of rental housing is failing to meet demand, and is sometimes associated with lower than necessary housing quality. A particularly low value for this indicator is a sign of the prevalence of rent control measures that result in below-market rents, but which may, in turn, depress rates of housing production and investment.

Findings

The mean reported rent-to-income ratio is 0.18, with a range of 0.03 to 0.38. In general, and consistent with previous evidence, the ratio of rent to income is low among low-income countries, rises with economic development to reach a peak in middle income developing countries, and then generally falls. Among regions, the lowest rent-to-income ratios are in Sub-Saharan Africa and in Europe, Middle East, and North Africa, which includes several countries with pervasive rent control. There is little reported variation among other regions in the median ratio of rent to income. Rents are affected both by government intervention, in the form of rent controls, and also by market factors. Countries with high demand pressure, as represented by high household formation rates, have higher ratios of rent to income; those with rent control, significantly lower ratios. Ratios of rent to income appear in turn to be associated with residential mobility and tenure choice. When rents are low, particularly in countries with pervasive rent controls, residential mobility is considerably lower than in otherwise similar countries. When ratios of rent to income are high, owning becomes more attractive than renting, with the result that home ownership rates increase.

Among the countries of the region, rents as a fraction of incomes, estimated to be from 5 to 7 per cent of household incomes, are among the lowest, the product of, at least in the West Bank, pervasive rent control which is based on the 1948–67 Jordanian law, the provisions of

Table 4 Rent-to-Income Ratio in the Middle East.

	Egypt	*Morocco*	*Jordan*	*Tunisia*	*Turkey*	*PT*	*Algeria*	*Israel*
GNP (1990)	$600	$950	$1,240	$1,440	$1,630	$1,700	$2,060	$16,680
Rent/income	0.060	0.130	0.163	0.207	0.250	0.05–	0.07	0.058

which in the West Bank have not been modified since the 1967 war. In Gaza, no such provisions apply, but rental occupancy appears to make up only from 2–4 per cent of the housing stock. Even in the West Bank, the incidence of rental housing is relatively small, about 31 per cent. The overall rate of owner occupancy of about 84 per cent (counting all occupants of refugee camps as owners) is, for the level of income of PT, the highest in the world. Typically, only about 60 per cent of the urban housing stock is occupied by owners in countries at similar income levels.

Were rents in the West Bank permitted to rise toward market levels, they would be expected to reach a level of from 19–25 per cent of median incomes – above the levels in Jordan and Tunisia, where despite a general relaxation of rent controls in recent years, the effects of early regulation still linger, and perhaps as high as the level in Turkey where there are no rent controls. Rents at such levels, which are the equivalent of from NIS 200–300 monthly for 'typical' dwellings and perhaps twice that for new dwellings are already beginning to be observed in Gaza. At such levels, rents are likely to be capable of producing a rate of return competitive with that on other investments and, as such, are capable of stimulating incentives to produce more rental housing.[8] Creation of a higher share of rental housing within the stock would appear to be consistent with a policy of encouraging greater labour mobility and hence a more flexible labour market – goals which can contribute toward the long-run goal of economic development.

Indicator 3: Housing Production

This is defined as the total number of housing units (in both the formal and informal sectors) produced last year per 1,000 population.

Significance

The indicator represents one measure of the importance of the housing sector to the broader economy, but, in combination with other data, is also important as a measure of the ability of the housing delivery system to keep pace with increasing demand for housing. As a measure of the volume of construction, it is closely related to the level of employment in residential construction, use of intermediate inputs, and, through multiplier effects, to the overall level of economic activity.[9] Housing production can also be normalised by the size of the housing stock to give

Table 5 Housing Protection Ratios by Region.

Sub-Saharan Africa	3.42
South Asia	6.05
East Asia	7.16
Latin America and Caribbean	6.01
Europe, Middle East, and North Africa	6.54
Industrialised Countries	6.12

a rate of expansion of the housing stock, which can in turn be compared with the rate of household formation, thereby indicating whether or not housing production is keeping pace with demographic change.[10]

Housing production relative to the population depends on some basic demographic characteristics of the population, particularly on household size. For a given rate of household formation, a higher rate of production of housing units relative to population will be required to accommodate a population with small households than with large households. Production, however, also depends on both supply and demand factors – each of which depend on a number of housing policies such as, for example, the availability of housing finance or the flexibility of land and building regulations.

Findings

Housing production per 1,000 population averages 6.8 for the sample. Except for the low-income countries, where production is lowest, production per 1,000 population falls modestly, though systematically, with increasing income. Among regions, rates of production are highest in East Asia and lowest in the industrialised countries. When an alternate measure of housing production is examined, the percentage rate of change of the housing stock, the trends are qualitatively identical to those for production per 1,000, but are more pronounced. Comparisons of the rate of production, as a per cent of the housing stock, with the rate of household formation indicate a vast difference in the ability of housing markets to cope with emerging housing demand. In all nine countries reporting household formation rates lower than 1 per cent, the rate of change in the housing stock is above the household formation rate. By contrast, in countries reporting household formation rates above 3 per cent, 15 of 21 (85 per cent) report that the housing stock is expanding less rapidly than the household formation rate.

Data on housing production in PT are highly uncertain as they are based on statistics from the Israeli CBS, which appear likely to systematically underestimate the role of the informal, and hence unrecorded housing sector. 'Official' statistics indicated that in 1987, some 6987 dwellings were constructed in PT, compared to an 'official' population of about 1.433 million, giving a production rate of 4.9 dwellings per 1000

Table 6 Housing Protection Ratios in the Middle East.

	Egypt	Morocco	Jordan	Tunisia	Turkey	PT	Algeria	Israel
GNP (1990)	$50	$950	$1,240	$1,440	$1,630	$1,700	$2,060	$16,680
Production per 1000	11.2	6.5	12.5	7.8	6.6	4.9–9.8	2.7	3.8

population.[11] Based on an estimated stock of dwellings of about 220,000 in 1987, such a rate of production implied that the housing stock was then expanding at a rate of about 3.2 per cent – virtually equal to the rate at which population grew during the period 1982–1991. And, given that household size remained essentially constant over this time period (see Bahiri, 1989), the housing stock was also expanding at a rate equal to the growth in the number of households.

It appears highly likely, however, that the officially recorded statistics on housing completion may substantially underestimate actual production rates. A 1992 housing strategy document (Centre for Engineering and Planning), for example estimated that only 32 per cent of all dwellings built after 1967 in the West Bank had building permits (cited in CHF, 1993). Coon estimated that as of the time of his study, there were some 13,000 families living in 1993 without permits. To the extent that official statistics are based on recorded building permits, each of these observations leaves a considerable range of doubt concerning actual production rates.

Moreover, a comparison of data on the levels of economic activity by the residential construction sector in the National Income Accounts with reported production statistics raises further questions concerning the validity of the official figures. For example, in 1990 estimated output of the residential construction sector was approximately new Israeli Shekels 380 million, out of a total of about NIS 504 million accounted for by the construction sector as a whole. In 1987, the corresponding figures were approximately NIS 349 million in residential construction and NIS 474 million in total construction. It is typical for such National Accounts data to be compiled on the basis of data on factor inputs – labour, materials, and profits rather than on the basis of output figures such as 'housing completions'. Such factor input data are often thought to be far more reliable than output data in situations where the recording of housing starts, completions, and the value of housing put in place are not commonplace. It is true by definition, however, that the 'value added' in the residential construction sector can be accounted for on the basis of either inputs or outputs. Thus with a bit of extra information, data based on one approach can be used as a check on the basis of calculations done using the other.

A simple notion of the value added through residential construction

Table 7 Annual Residential Construction Required to Produce the 1987
Residential Construction Sector Output (percentage by which 'official' output
underestimates calculated in parentheses).

Construction	Cost/square metre (1986 NIS)	Cost in 1991 $US		
		NIS 190 ($150)	NIS 230 ($185)	NIS 270 ($220)
Dwelling	90	20,409 (−66%)	16,860 (M59%)	14,362 (−51%)
Unit Size	110	16,699 (−58%)	13,794 (−49%)	11,750 (−41%)
Square	130	14,130 (−51%)	11.672 (−40%)	9,943 (−30%)
metre				
	150	12,245 (−43%)	10,116 (−31%)	8,617 (−19%)

based on an output oriented approach to national income accounting is
that it is equal to the value of construction put in place, which is in turn
equal to the number of units completed multiplied by the average cost
per unit. The average cost per unit is in turn equal to the average cost of
construction per square metre multiplied by the average size of completed
dwellings in square metres. If one has an estimate of the aggregate value
added in the sector using an input-based approach, such as that used in
the Israeli accounts, and knowing a range of construction costs and
dwelling sizes, it is possible to solve for the number of units that would
have to have been constructed to generate the volume of investment
estimated to have taken place. Table 1 presents the results of such a
calculation for the year 1987, during which NIS 349 (in 1986 NIS) were
estimated to have been invested in housing.

The range of construction costs has been chosen to represent the
range presented earlier based on the Co-operative Housing Foundation
(CHF) report for unfinished, moderately finished, and finished dwellings,
with costs deflated appropriately. Dwelling unit sizes were chosen to be
representative of the range portrayed by 'official' statistics (where, for
example, the reported 1987 average new unit was reported to have been
between 127 and 145 square metres (West Bank and Gaza respectively)
and figures that are more representative of the existing housing stock, and
which are likely to be more representative of less expensive, informal, or
unreported dwellings.

The calculations presented in the table indicate that at the 'official'
size new dwelling of about 130 square metres and 'full finish' construct-
uion costs of NIS 220 (in 1986 NIS), some 9,943 dwellings would have
been required to produce the estimated residential construction output
of NIS 349 million – indicating that official output figures are some 30
per cent below the 'required' number of units. It seems far more likely,
however, that both the costs and sizes of unreported units are smaller
than the official units. Assuming that the average unit actually built is

110 square metres and that it is produced to 'moderate' levels of finish, 'required' output is close to 14,000 units per year – roughly double the officially reported output. With either moderate finish and 90 square-metre units being the norm, or unfinished units the norm and an average size of 110 square metres, 'required' output is on the order of 17,000 units, with official output figures representing an underestimate of nearly 60 per cent.

While studies of the extent of the PT informal sector are rare, the sorts of shortfalls in official statistics suggested by the Table are common in other countries in the region. In Egypt, for example, a 1982 study found that some 64 per cent of the housing stock was 'informal', built in contravention of either zoning or building regulations, with more than 80 per cent of newly built housing falling into the 'informal' category (Mayo et al., 1982). In the case of Egypt, a principal reason for a great deal of unreported construction is that it is built incrementally, generally on the tops of existing buildings. In Cairo, for example, it was estimated that from half to two-thirds of all new residential building was taking place on the tops of existing buildings. The phenomenon of reinforcement bars pointed skyward from existing rooftops, and indicating the future course of largely undocumented expansion of the housing stock appears, based on casual observation to be nearly as prevalent in some parts of Gaza and the West Bank as has been the case in Egypt in recent years.

Were one to assume that the calculations above indicate a shortfall of roughly half in the official statistics, it implies that actual output is on the order of closer to 10 dwellings per 1,000 population rather than the 4.9 given by official statistics. Such a production rate is close to that of the highest volume producers in the region, and is, indeed, typical of economies within which housing construction is largely financed by remittance income such as Jordan and Egypt. Such a rate is also consistent with a view that the PT housing sector is capable of more than keeping up with population increases and that it has, in fact, been a major contributor to upward mobility and improvement in housing conditions.[12] A production rate of 10 dwellings per 1,000, which appears to be completely consistent with National Income Accounts data and data on unit costs and sizes, implies a rate of expansion of the housing stock of over 6 per cent – a rate capable of accommodating both natural increase of the population and a substantial share of anticipated return of Palestinian refugees.

In light of the frequent calls for massive expansion of the rate of production of housing in, it is critical that the actual rate be known with far greater certainty than is currently the case. At present, the data are highly ambiguous, and could support the notion that little more than marginal changes in the recent rate of production are called for to accommodate the needs of the population – even if the rate of return of

Table 8 Housing Investment Percentages by Region%.

Sub-Saharan Africa	0.023
South Asia	0.065
East Asia	0.052
Latin America and Caribbean	0.070
Europe, Middle East, and North Africa	0.064
Industrialised Countries	0.037

refugees accelerates considerably from current levels. In any case, as is discussed concerning the next indicator, the volume of economic activity in the sector is already well above what is typical of most well-functioning housing sectors, suggesting that premature attempts to stimulate the sector could either severely distort the economy or be unsustainable for more than a limited period.

Indicator 4: Housing Investment

This is defined as the total investment in housing (in both formal and informal sectors in the urban area), as a percentage of gross city product.

Significance

This indicator measures the proportion of overall economic activity which is accounted for by housing investment. As such, it measures directly one of the two major direct contributions the housing sector makes to the economy (the other being the production of housing services, which is reflected as 'rent' in the national income accounts).

Housing investment reflects both quantities produced and prices. Thus a given value of this indicator may reflect either high unit housing costs and low volumes or low costs and high volumes of production. Investment levels are thus likely to be affected by policies influencing both demand levels and unit costs. It is also affected by the need to rebuild housing in the aftermath of war and natural disaster. Because the indicator amalgamates both prices and quantities, it is best interpreted in relation to other data, such as housing production data and data on the physical characteristics of the housing that is being produced.

Findings

Previous studies of the determinants of housing investment have reported strong regularities in this indicator, when it is analysed at the national level. Generally speaking, housing investment as a proportion of GNP has been found to rise systematically over a broad range of economic development, to reach a peak among countries with incomes slightly below that of the lowest-income industrialised countries, and then to fall gradually with further development. Data from the Extensive Survey are

Table 9 Housing Investment Percentage In the Middle East.

	Egypt	Morocco	Jordan	Tunisia	Turkey	PT	Algeria	Israel
GNP (1990)	$600	$950	$1,240	$1,440	$1,630	$1,700	$2,060	$16,680
Housing investment/ GDP	0.023	0.024	0.100	0.070	0.077	0.134	0.086	0.037

generally consistent with previous findings, with values of the indicator lowest among countries with either very low or very high incomes and highest among countries with intermediate income levels.[13] Examples are found of countries that have high production and low costs and low production and high costs, and of countries with unusually high levels of investment because of natural disasters. Reported investment rates are lowest in Sub-Saharan Africa and industrialised countries, and highest in South Asia, Latin America and the Caribbean, and Europe, the Middle East, and North Africa.

Countries in the Middle East and North Africa are typically at a stage of economic development when housing investment is highest in relation to both Gross Fixed Capital Formation (GFCF) and Gross Domestic Product (GDP). Generally speaking, housing investment relative to GDP appears to peak at a level between $2,000 and 3,000 per capita, a level typical of many of the countries in the region. Even among the countries with high values for this indicator, PT stands out as an exception. With an estimated 13.4 per cent of GDP allocated to housing investment in 1990, PT ranks ahead of all other countries evaluated in the HIP. Housing investment as a share of GFCF in PT is, moreover, a far higher fraction (about 50 per cent) than is typical – for most countries the ratio is between 10 and 30 per cent.

The reasons behind the high ratio in PT are, by definition, straightforward and behaviourally complex. Definitionally, investment is equal to the product of production and unit costs. As noted above, both of these are higher in PT than in many other places, assuming, as suggested here that official production statistics are well below actual production figures. Behaviourally, the reasons for such a high level of investment have to do with the following: (1) high levels of income in the form of remittances rather than current income, (2) the existence of a large construction sector which while dependent on work in Israel nevertheless experiences erratic working conditions, (3) the lack of other viable investment alternatives, and (4) a tendency to invest in developing land and building housing as a way of establishing claim to the land.

Countries of the region have traditionally experienced high levels of remittances from workers abroad. Often, work is taken in the Gulf states or other countries with the explicit goal of accumulating enough resources to purchase land or materials for building a house. In Egypt in the early 1980s, remittance income made up some 15–20 per cent of GNP, and was often allocated to housebuilding (Mayo, 1982). There it was estimated that more than 70 per cent of all residential construction was being financed in whole or in part by remittances.

The construction workforce in PT has made up from 10–15 per cent of the overall workforce within the past two decades (Bahiri, 1989). Of those workers, some 70–75 per cent of them were typically employed in Israel, where they typically comprised nearly 50 per cent of the Israeli construction workforce. It would appear reasonable to assume that such a large and generally productive workforce would be not only capable but highly interested in contributing to the informal construction sector within PT, particularly during holidays and border closures.

The underdevelopment of the Palestinian financial sector is well-known (see World Bank, 1993, Vol. III). Opportunities for profitably investing savings have been limited, as development of domestic financial intermediaries has been actively suppressed. In such a circumstance, investment in land and housing represent some of the only alternatives available.

Finally, the motivations of all Palestinians to remain 'steadfast' in their territorial claims is self evident, and is undoubtedly a major motivation for high levels of housing investment.

On its surface, a rate of investment in housing typical of that in PT would appear to be unsustainable in light of international experience. Among the countries in the HIP, only Thailand (9.9 per cent) and Jordan (10 per cent), have ratios of housing investment to PT of more than 9 per cent – and the level in PT is more than 30 per cent higher as a fraction of GDP! Many of the political and economic changes that appear to be on the horizon appear to be inconsistent with a continuation of the role of the housing sector in the national economy. Each of the 'behavioural' reasons for high levels of housing investment, for example, seems likely to be diminished as a result of likely political and economic changes. Israel has, for example, begun to substitute the labour of recent Jewish immigrants for Palestinian labour. In addition, discussions of 'permanent' border closings, regardless of their long-term viability, seem certain to erode the prominent role that Palestinian labourers have played in the Israeli construction industry.

Each of these factors will diminish the magnitude of remitances and the size of the Palestinian construction industry, depressing levels of investment in the sector. As moves are made to develop the Palestinian financial sector, the prospects for expansion of housing activity could either expand or diminish. At present the level of Palestinian assets in Jordanian banks with Palestinian branches constitutes a pool of some JD500 million, which could, under a number of policy reforms and institutional developments be repatriated to be used for investments in PT rather than beyond its borders. At least some of these resources will certainly be used to expand mortgage lending for housing, possibly expanding the total level of investment in the sector. On the other hand, many macro-economic policies seem likely to focus on expanding the industrial base and the export sector, each of which could present viable investment alternatives which could compete for household savings that are currently going toward housing. Finally, with a political settlement of territorial issues the need for symbolic investments in housing may be somewhat diminished. On balance, aside from the potential role of expanded housing finance, their appears to be little to suggest that maintaining or expanding the level of housing investment will be natural or easy.

Consequently, imaginative ways to motivate continued levels of housing investment will need to be found. Some are discussed below as elements of an enabling strategy for PT.

Indicator 5: Floor Area Per Person

This is defined as the median usable living space per person (in square metres) last year.

Significance

This indicator measures the adequacy of living space in dwellings. A low value for the indicator is a sign of overcrowding. Alternate measures of crowding have been the subject of data collection and reporting in international statistical compendia. The two most common of these are Persons per Room and Households per Dwelling Unit, each of which was included among the data collected during the first phase of the HIP. Of the three measures, *floor area per person and persons per room* are highly variable among countries and are highly related to each other; either would be an acceptable measure of the adequacy of living space. The former has however, based on analysis conducted in the HIP, been shown to be the more precise and policy-sensitive measure of the two. Households per dwelling unit is only weakly related to the other two measures of crowding, does not vary nearly as much as the other measures among countries, and is subject not only to variation according to cultural preferences but also according to varying definitions of 'household' among countries.

Floor area per person is the outcome, to a considerable degree, of market forces, which are in turn shaped by a variety of housing policies.

Table 10 Median Living Space Per Person by Region (in square metres).

Sub-Saharan Africa	7.55
South Asia	7.10
East Asia	13.00
Latin America and Caribbean	15.30
Europe, Middle East, and North Africa	14.50
Industrialised Countries	31.93

Findings

The mean reported floor area per person is about 18 square metres, with a range of from 4 to 69. Floor area increases consistently with economic development, from about 6 square metres per person in low-income countries to 35 square metres per person in high income countries. Regional differences in this indicator are dominated by income differences; Sub-Saharan Africa and South Asia have the smallest amounts of floor area per person, and industrialised countries have the highest amounts.

Notwithstanding these patterns, there is still considerable variation among countries with similar incomes, much of which appears to be attributable to policy differences that have the effect of influencing land prices and construction costs. Among mid-high and high income countries, for example, the countries having the lowest amounts of floor area per person also have the highest land prices and construction costs. Preliminary multivariate analyses indicate that more than 80 per cent of the variation in this indicator can be accounted for based on three variables – GNP per capita, construction costs, and land costs. Both construction and land costs are, in turn, highly influenced by a variety of policies.

Data on floor area per person for PT housing is difficult to estimate because of the lack of data on the stock of housing. Bahiri's 'guesstimate' of about 15 square metres per person is used here, based on an estimated 'average dwelling unit' of some 98 square metres and an average household size of 6.51. Were Bahiri's figure further adjusted to produce an estimate of the median, using international experience that median dwellings are from 85–90 per cent as large as 'average' dwellings, the figure in the table would drop to from 12.8 to 13.5. Even after such an adjustment, among the countries in the region only Turkey and Israel, each of which has smaller dwellings (71 and 77 square metres, respectively) but far smaller household size than PT, have greater floor area per person.

Relative to the 'norm' for countries at its income level, the PT are about average. Similarly, reported figures for 'persons per room' somewhat above 2 (Bahiri, p. 49, reports 2.19 persons per room for PT in 1987 and CHF, p. 38, reports 2.3 and 2.6 respectively for West Bank and Gaza for 1991) are about average for countries with similar income levels

Table 11 Media Living Space Per Person in the Middle East.

	Egypt	Morocco	Jordan	Tunisia	Turkey	PT	Algeria	Israel
GNP (1990)	$600	$950	$1,240	$1,440	$1,630	$1,700	$2,060	$16,680
Floor area per person (square metres)	12.00	6.00	10.00	6.47	17.00	15.10	8.54	24.80

(see HIP, 1993, Table 5). Thus the overall impression is that overall levels of 'crowding' are about to be expected for a country of the resources of PT.

Notwithstanding its current level of 'normality', it is clear that the high level of investment in housing in PT has had a major impact on both space standards and quality levels within a relatively short period of time. In the West Bank, for example, the average number of persons per room declined from 3.2 in 1971 to 2.5 in 1985 and 2.3 in 1990. In Gaza the corresponding figures were 3.0 in 1971, 2.7 in 1985, and 2.6 in 1990 (CHF, p. 38). According to Bahiri, the number of rooms available within the housing stock expanded at twice the rate of either population or households from 1975 to 1987.

The implications of these figures on various measures of 'crowding' is that, certainly on average, it is difficult to justify the notion of a 'crowding crisis' in PT, certainly nothing that would justify extraordinary actions to expand the housing stock more rapidly than is already occurring. On the contrary, it appears that levels of crowding are quite 'ordinary' on average within PT and are, based on the amount of floor area per person, well above those of many of the countries in the region. If there is a 'crisis', it is not found in the statistical averages, but must be sought elsewhere – perhaps in the refugee camps. Here, again, the need for more and better data is apparent if policy is to be made in a way that responds to the actual, but as yet undescribed, situation.

Indicator 6: Permanent Structures

This is defined as the percentage of housing units located in structures built of permanent materials.

Significance

This indicator is one measure of the quality of housing, particularly of its durability. Very low quality housing is usually made of semi-permanent or temporary materials such as straw, cardboard or cloth, which fail to provide adequate shelter from the elements that deteriorate rapidly without frequent maintenance and repair. Permanent structures usually

Table 12 Permenent Structures.

Sub-Saharan Africa	0.793
South Asia	0.861
East Asia	0.943
Latin America and Caribbean	0.900
Europe, Middle East, and North Africa	0.967
Industrialised Countries	1.000

provide better protection from the elements, a higher standard of structural safety, and require a higher level of initial investment.

This measure is a primitive measure of 'housing adequacy,' more precise definitions of which have been reflected in the statistical procedures of many (usually industrialised) countries. Such definitions are, however, highly idiosyncratic and require data that are often unique to particular countries. As such, indicators of housing adequacy that fully reflect the nuances in definition demanded in particular countries are unusually difficult to apply in international comparisons of housing quality, and have never been regularly collected. The measure suggested here has the advantage that it is, in fact, highly variable from place to place, and therefore can distinguish easily among housing conditions in most developing countries. It is, moreover, relatively straightforward to measure. On the other hand, because the indicator attains its maximum value, 100 percent, among countries at only a modest level of GNP per capita, further exploration needs to be conducted to develop housing adequacy measures that permit distinctions to be made among countries at higher levels of economic development.

Findings

The mean reported proportion of dwellings in structures built of permanent building materials is 0.90, with a range of 0.43 to 1.0. The use of permanent building materials increases consistently with economic development, with only about two-thirds of the units in low-income cities built of permanent materials and nearly all units built of permanent materials in high-income cities. Regional variations reflect income differences, with Sub-Saharan Africa and South Asia having the least housing built of permanent materials and industrialised countries having the most.

Variation in this indicator among countries with similar incomes is considerable. Preliminary analysis suggests that both demand and supply factors are responsible for such variation. The role of rapid urban growth in creating demand pressures that cannot be instantly satisfied is apparent; cities with high growth rates have, other things being equal, lower housing quality as measured by this indicator. Cities with lower levels of residential infrastructure, as measured by either lower levels of infrastructure spending per capita or lower percentages of dwellings with

Table 13 Permanent Structures in the Middle East.

	Egypt	Morocco	Jordan	Tunisia	Turkey	PT	Algeria	Israel
GNP (1990)	$600	$950	$1,240	$1,440	$1,630	$1,700	$2,060	$16,680
Permanent structures	0.942	0.940	0.965	0.957	0.950	0.86–0.95	0.968	1.000

plot access to water also have comparatively fewer dwellings built of permanent materials. Cities in which the state has played a strong role in provision of housing generally have higher proportions of permanent housing than do otherwise similar cities.

There are no reliable statistics on the proportion of dwellings built of permanent materials in PT. A recent 'Housing Needs Assessment', after noting that 'most of the walls and roof(s) of the houses, with the exception of those in the refugee camps, are built of permanent materials' went on to note that the 'housing stock in the refugee camps ... is predominantly built with concrete block exterior walls and roofs of asbestos-cement or zinc sheets.' (CHF, 1993). The report goes on to estimate that some 60 per cent of the housing stock of the refugee camps (about 33,000 units) is 'non-upgradeable' – which could be taken to be a measure of the degree to which refugee camp dwellings are 'impermanent' and hence require replacement rather than upgrading. Were this interpretation accepted, some 14 per cent of the stock in PT would be considered 'impermanent'. Unfortunately, there is no documentation in the report as to what constitutes a 'non-upgradeable unit'. Based on the fact that even most refugee camp units have permanent walls, which was the key factor determining whether units were built of permanent materials within the HIP, the proportion of 'permanent' structures in the housing stock could easily be as high as 95 per cent.

Clearly more detailed investigation needs to be done of the structural and other conditions of housing within PT. At present, the figures presented in 'Housing Needs Assessments' must be viewed suspiciously, given the lack of observation-based data. Just as the impression of a 'crowding crisis' has been used to motivate extraordinary public or donor interventions in the PT housing sector, even as the comparative statistics fail to support a viewpoint, the 'need' to replace 'non-upgradeable' units on a crash basis has yet to be rigorously demonstrated. Indeed, many of the available figures on levels of residential amenities in refugee camps and in towns (e.g. availability of kitchens, running water, bathroom and toilet facilities, water heating facilities and electricity) suggest that differences between the camps and towns are often insignificant or diminishing over time as a result of activities of either UNRWA or the camp residents themselves (see Bahiri, Table 4.6.2).

Table 14 Unauthorised Housing % by Region.

Sub-Saharan Africa	0.667
South Asia	0.513
East Asia	0.148
Latin America and Caribbean	0.268
Europe, Middle East, and North Africa	0.149
Industrialised Countries	0.000

Indicator 7: Unauthorised Housing

This is defined as the percentage of the total housing stock in the urban area that is not in compliance with current regulations.

Significance

This indicator measures the extent to which the urban population is housed legally. It includes both squatter houses occupying land illegally, and houses constructed without the required building, land use, or land subdivision permits. A high value for this indicator is a sign that housing development is going on without enforced government controls, and that government is either tolerant of housing which does not comply with its regulations or unable to prevent trespasses.

Considerable research has suggested that tenure security associated with legal rights to own land and housing strongly influences incentives to invest in upgrading of housing and community infrastructure; affects the willingness of governments to provide water, sanitation, and other services; and greatly affects property values.

Findings

The mean reported incidence of unauthorised housing is 0.24, with a range of 0.00 to 0.78. The incidence of unauthorised housing decreases sharply with economic development, from 64 per cent in low-income cities to nil in high-income cities. Regional variation reflects income differences, with Sub-Saharan Africa and South Asia having the highest proportions of unauthorised housing and industrialised countries the lowest. Variation among countries with similar incomes, however is considerable, reflecting a wide range of market conditions and policy differences. As with other housing quality variables, cities with higher urban growth rates have proportionally more unauthorised housing than do those with lower growth rates; cities in which the state plays a greater role in the housing sector have less unauthorised housing. Latin America, where in many countries there is a well-developed tradition of squatter land invasion and subsequent consolidation, though not necessarily formal recognition of settlements, has significantly higher incidence of unauthorised housing than would be expected.

Table 15 Unauthorised Housing in the Middle East.

	Egypt	Morocco	Jordan	Tunisia	Turkey	GWB	Algeria	Israel
GNP (1990)	$600	$950	$1,240	$1,440	$1,630	$1,700	$2,060	$16,680
Unauthorised housing	0.650	0.163	0.149	0.291	0.510	(0.50)?	0.044	0.020

*Estimated

Among the countries of the region, the incidence of unauthorised housing is highly variable, from lows of 2 per cent and 4.4 per cent in Israel and Algeria respectively to highs in Turkey and Egypt of 51 per cent and 65 per cent respectively. The level in PT is not known with any confidence whatsoever, and is a priority to ascertain. Independent estimates cited above (CEP, 1992) indicate that the proportion of units built without permission since 1967 in the West Bank may have been more than two-thirds. Calculations presented above suggest that underestimates of housing construction based on official statistics may be considerable and support the Centre for Engineering and Planning (CEP) conclusion that the majority of units could be considered 'informal.'

The meaning and implications of 'informal' or even 'illegal' status is highly variable from place to place, however. In Egypt, for example, where most housing is, strictly speaking, illegal, authorities are loath to demolish illegal dwellings or even to impede the pace of construction of incomplete illegal buildings. Informal subdivision of land there has all of the physical attributes of legal subdivision, with articulated grids of streets and spaces allowed for commercial, school, and religious activities. The situation is much the same in Turkey. The difference between informal and formal areas has principally to do with (1) a slower pace of provision of infrastructure such as water, sanitation, and road paving in informal areas, and (2) a total absence of formal finance of informal housing. Each of these features contributes to a slower pace of completion of dwellings in informal areas, and, as a result, a less productive housing delivery process. At the same time, the high degree of informality creates a general sense of ambiguity concerning property rights, which makes banks reluctant to become involved in the financing of housing. Egypt and Turkey have, partly as a result, among the least developed housing finance systems among any countries at their level of economic development.

Within PT, such ambiguous property rights are caused both by the existence of housing in the refugee camps and informal housing outside the camps. For a well-functioning property market to develop and for a housing finance system to be developed which is capable of serving the needs of all parts of society, and not just purchasers of new housing (who may be among the highest income members of society), it will be

Table 16 Housing Credit Ratio by Region %.

Sub-Saharan Africa	0.053
South Asia	0.030
East Asia	0.066
Latin America and Caribbean	0.204
Europe, Middle East, and North Africa	0.095
Industrialised Countries	0.239

important to clarify existing rights and, through programs of land and property registration, dispute resolution, and issuance of titles and even title insurance. A necessary prelude to undertaking such activities is the collection of more and better data concerning the legal status of existing land and housing.

Indicator 8: The Housing Credit Portfolio

This is defined as the ratio of total mortgage loans to all outstanding loans in both commercial and government financial institutions.

Significance

The Housing Credit Portfolio is a measure of the relative size of the housing finance sector and its ability to provide households with the funds necessary to purchase housing. When housing credit forms only a small part of total credit, it is quite likely that the finance institutions face legal or institutional constraints that make it difficult for them to meet the demand for housing finance. Financial depth and strength are key elements in a well-functioning housing sector. Adequate financing should be available to smooth housing consumption over time for consumers, and to enable efficient land development and construction for producers.

This indicator is intended both to proxy access to housing finance by potential buyers of housing and to convey a sense of the importance of the housing finance system to the overall financial system. An alternate measure of access to finance was evaluated during the first phase of the HIP; the Credit-to-Value Ratio, which measures the share of annual investment in housing which is financed by long-term formal credit, was, however, found to be less well related to several qualitative and quantitative housing outcomes than was the Housing Credit Portfolio. The latter measure appears to be a better indicator of both the importance of the housing finance system to the overall financial sector and access by households to credit.

Findings

The mean reported value of the housing credit portfolio is 0.18, with a range of 0.01 to 0.44. Housing credit, as a proportion of the financial

Table 17 Housing Credit.

	Egypt	Morocco	Jordan	Tunisia	Turkey	GWB	Algeria	Israel
GNP (1990)	$600	$950	$1,240	$1,440	$1,630	$1,700	$2,060	$16,680
Housing credit portfolio (%)	0.023	0.066	0.190	0.070	0.025	0*	0.086	0.140

*Estimated

assets of a country's banking system generally increases with economic development. Only 5 per cent of outstanding credit in the low-income countries is 24 percent. Variations within and among regions in the housing credit portfolio are considerable, reflecting a variety of market, institutional, and policy influences. The prominence of housing loans in a country's banking system depends in part on institutional development in the sector; in preliminary analyses, the proportional allocation of assets toward housing loans is strongly influenced by an index that measures the depth of institutional development of housing finance, after taking account of the level of economic development and the urban growth rate. Latin America, which has a rich set of financial institutions to deal with housing finance, has an unusually high share of the assets of its banking systems allocated to housing loans, with the median reported to be 21 percent. Centrally planned economies, which have had neither market-based lending for housing nor market-oriented housing finance institutions have smaller than expected portions of their financial assets invested in mortgage portfolios.

The level of development of housing finance in countries of the region is highly variable. Egypt and Turkey, with less than 3 per cent of their banking systems' assets invested in housing are comparatively undeveloped, while Israel and Jordan, with 14 per cent and 19 per cent respectively, are comparatively well developed. In the case of Jordan, this level of development is a product both of the role of the Jordan Housing Bank and of the commercial banking system, which is heavily involved in making available housing credit.

In the case of some countries which have comparatively underdeveloped housing finance systems, the state has substituted public provision of highly subsidised rental housing for market provision and commercial credit. The proportion of public housing in the urban stock is high in countries such as Egypt (29 per cent), Algeria (25 per cent), Tunisia (15 per cent), and Morocco (15 per cent). Generally speaking the existence of large shares of heavily subsidised public housing represents a major distorting factor in urban housing markets and has led, in the case of the countries enumerated, to far higher housing prices than would be expected, lower rates of residential and labour mobility, a heavy public fiscal burden, and to comparatively underdeveloped financial systems.

In the case of PT, the proportion of bank credit allocated to housing was, during the base year for this comparison (1990), effectively equal to zero. Domestic institutions such as the Bank of Palestine have subsequently initiated modest programs of lending for housing and have agreed to act as conduits for funds provided by international donors for this purpose. Jordanian and Egyptian banks with branches in PT have, for the most part, served the function only of deposit-taking, without re-lending the savings of Palestinians back for housing or purposes other than short-term credit. Reasons for this lack of development, as well as a number of proposals for beginning a process of institutional development and policy reform capable of supporting expansion of the formal housing finance system in PT, have been discussed in CHF (1993) and in a series of papers based on World Bank missions which focused on housing finance.

In the latter, considerable emphasis is placed on the enumeration of the many diverse risks confronted by commercial banks in making housing loans in PT, and on devising policies and institutions to selectively mitigate each type of risk in order to create the conditions amenable to expansion of a commercially based housing finance system. Some of these ideas are enumerated upon below.

Indicator 9: The Land Development Multiplier

This is defined as the average ratio between the median land price of a developed plot at the urban fringe in a typical subdivision and the median price of raw, undeveloped land in an area currently being developed.

Significance

This indicator measures the premium for providing infrastructure **and** converting raw land to residential use on the urban fringe. It reflects in part the extent to which windfall profits exist in developing land for housing as the result of bottlenecks in infrastructure provision. It is thus an indirect measure of the availability of infrastructure, as well as of the complexity of the development process. It also measures indirectly the existence of monopolistic practices in residential land development. A high value for this is often a sign that there are shortages of urbanised land for housing. An additional indicator for which data were also collected during the first phase of the was the Land Conversion Multiplier, which measures the premium associated with converting land from rural to urban use by obtaining the necessary zoning and planning permits. This indicator measures the extent to which regulations restricting urban development increase land costs by restricting land supply.

While this indicator was found, during the first phase of the Housing Indicators Program, to require a great deal of care in its construction

Table 18 Land Development Multiplier by Region.

Sub-Saharan Africa	6.18
South Asia	2.90
East Asia	2.59
Latin America and Caribbean	3.43
Europe, Middle East, and North Africa	5.50
Industrialised Countries	2.50

and interpretation, it was also found to be a revealing and powerful measure of the overall performance of urban land markets.

Findings

The mean reported value of the land development multiplier is 5.2, with a range of from 1.1 to 16.6. The indicator generally declines with increasing economic development, suggesting that provision of serviced land is more responsive to demand in better-off countries. Even values of this indicator in its midrange appear to suggest that there are premia associated with the provision of serviced urban land that are considerably higher than the actual cost of land servicing. The indicator reaches its highest values in Sub-Saharan Africa, where demographic pressures of housing demand are great and infrastructure investment and housing production lag demand, and lowest in industrialised countries where demand is relatively quiescent and infrastructure supply systems are responsive to market forces. Within regions, there is considerable variability in the land development multiplier, in several instances by a factor of 6 or 7. This appears likely to be the result of differences in demand pressures on land development, in infrastructure shortfalls, in infrastructure standards, and in regulatory impediments to land development.

Countries within the region exhibit a wide range of variation on this indicator, with Egypt, Turkey, and Algeria appearing to have more distorted land markets as a result either of restricting conversion of rural to urban land or failing to provide infrastructure at a pace that is responsive to demand. In each such case it is almost certainly the case that the actual cost of providing full infrastructure services to undeveloped land is far less than the amount of premium that is represented by the price of developed land over the cost of raw land. Morocco, Tunisia, Jordan, and Israel appear, by contrast, to have done a better job of creating responsive land delivery systems. For each of them the value of the indicator is about at the norm for other countries at comparable levels of income.

Lack of data hinders calculation of the land development multiplier for PT, and the figures presented above are highly conditional. The figure at the low end of the range was derived by comparing the cost of raw

Table 19 Lord Development Multiplier in the Middle East.

	Egypt	Morocco	Jordan	Tunisia	Turkey	GWB	Algeria	Israel
GNP (1990)	$600	$950	$1,240	$1,440	$1,630	$1,700	$2,060	$16,680
Land development multiplier	10.00	5.00	4.25	3.67	10.00	4–20	11.70	2.50

land in PT cities and towns to the cost of fully serviced land based on interviews conducted by the Co-operative Housing Foundation (CHF) in 1992–93 (CHF). Such a figure is indicative of the 'infrastructure premium' only, but not any premium that is associated with conversion of non-residential to residential land. That is, the CHF figures counts as raw land that has in effect already received permission to be developed as residential land. The indicated price of raw land in ($30/sqaure metre) is, however, considerably higher than that estimated to prevail in places such as Amman ($5/square metre) or Istanbul ($10/square metre). It is, in fact, much closer to the figure provided for Tel Aviv ($50/square metre). This suggests, as both casual observation and analysis would suggest, that restrictions on conversion of rural to urban land which are imposed under various ordinances of the Israeli Civil Administration, are responsible for having caused perhaps a doubling or tripling in the cost of raw land zoned for residential use. Thus the actual Land development multiplier may be much higher – on the order of from 10 to 20, if it is assumed that under more normal conditions land prices would be closer to those in Amman or Istanbul rather than at the level that now prevails.

More information on land prices, and the current operations of land markets in PT would be extremely helpful in better identifying the causes of high land prices and the means to reduce them.

Indicator 10: Infrastructure Expenditures Per Capita

This is defined as the ratio of the total expenditures (operations, maintenance, and capital) by all levels of government on infrastructure services (roads, sewerage, drainage, water supply, electricity and garbage collection) during the current year, and the urban population.

Significance

This indicator is an indirect measure of the supply of infrastructure for residential development. When adequate budgets are available for extending urban infrastructure, the Land Development Multiplier should not be exceedingly large. Low levels of infrastructure expenditures result in land supply bottlenecks and thus in higher prices for land and housing.

543

Table 20 Infrastructure Expenditures per Capital Ratio by Region.

Sub-Saharan Africa	16.56
South Asia	15.00
East Asia	81.46
Latin America and Caribbean	30.22
Europe, Middle East, and North Africa	38.33
Industrialised Countries	620.72

They are also associated with inadequate provision of residential amenities, such as water, sewerage, drainage and electricity, and in subsequent traffic congestion, all of which affect the quality of housing.

Findings

The mean reported level of infrastructure spending per capita in $318 per annum (and with a median of $73), with a range from $0.98 to $2201.00. Spending on infrastructure not only rises consistently with economic development, but shows the greatest degree of variation across income levels of practically any other housing indicator. The median reported value of the indicator for low-income countries is $15, while for high income countries it is $814 – 54 times as high, roughly equivalent to the factor by which per capita incomes differ across income groups. Levels of infrastructure spending mirror income differences across regions, and are lowest in Sub-Saharan Africa and South Asia, and highest in industrialised countries. Preliminary analysis suggests, as expected, that the level of infrastructure spending is negatively related to the land development multiplier. Among countries with similar income levels, infrastructure spending levels are also relatively lower in centrally-planned (or formerly planned) countries.

Values for this indicator must be interpreted with a great deal of caution as data are almost universally poor and definitional problems are severe when attempting to make comparisons across countries. Taking the data as they are presented suggests that, relative to other countries in the region, Jordan and Tunisia provide relatively more generous budgets for residential infrastructure. Algeria, which during the study base period was undergoing a great deal of macroeconomic difficulty and had been experiencing declines in gross investment for some time, appears to have been considerably below the expected level of residential infrastructure expenditures.

As with many other indicators, it is difficult to come up with a reliable measure for infrastructure expenditures in PT. In general, based on the high reported gains in access to basic services reported by observers such as Bahiri (1989) and others, and evidence of high current levels of access, it is to be expected that infrastructure expenditures would be comparatively high. The figure presented $55 per year, is based on figures

Table 21 Infrastructure Expenditures Capita Ratio in the Middle East.

	Egypt	Morocco	Jordan	Tunisia	Turkey	GWB	Algeria	Israel
GNP (1990)	$600	$950	$1,240	$1,440	$1,630	$1,700	$2,060	$16,680
Infrastructure expenditures ($)	26.67	12.16	105.00	86.00	N/A	55?	13.23	N/A

contained in World Bank (1993, Volume 1, p. 10), which indicates that public sector capital expenditures in PT averaged only about 3.5 per cent of GDP over the years 1970–90, while the corresponding figure in Jordan was 9 per cent of GDP. It was assumed that in each country the same ratio would apply of infrastructure expenditures and public sector capital expenditures. PT per capital figures were then estimated using the figure for Jordan as a base. On a per capita basis, this yielded a figure for PT of $35 per capita, which was then augmented by the estimated UNRWA expenditures of approximately $20 per capita per year to give the $55 shown. While there are many uncertainties in this calculation, it appears to indicate that infrastructure expenditures in PT are only about half what they are in Jordan, despite higher GNP per capita in PT. This, by itself, appears to suggest that, despite relatively high levels of infrastructure service in PT, expenditures may be insufficient to either maintain them properly or to undertake needed expansion of services. This is obviously a question which can only be answered by more and better data collection.

A DIAGNOSTIC SUMMARY

The comparative analysis of housing sector performance presented above is highly preliminary, in light of the serious data inadequacies concerning housing in PT. On the other hand, there are a number of findings which suggest a somewhat different perception of the nature of the key sectoral issues than may be indicated by other analyses. Among the key findings are the following:

1) Housing prices are to high – the result of both construction and land costs that appear to be unnecessarily high.
2) Rent levels in the West Bank are too low – the product of unmodified rent control ordinances.
3) Housing production is highly uncertain; official statistics almost certainly underestimate the actual rate of housing production, perhaps by half or more.
4) Housing production, and hence current capacity, may be considerably higher than is believed to be the case; if so, current capacity appears to be capable of providing not only for natural population

increase but also for an accelerated rate of return of refugees living abroad.

5) Housing investment levels are higher relative to GDP than in country among the 53 studied in the Housing Indicators Program, and as such are likely to be unsustainably high. A number of factors associated with ongoing political and economic changes appear likely to put downward pressure on the housing sector over the medium to long term. This conclusion represents a qualification to that in (4) above.

6) Physical housing standards in PT are good with alternative measures of 'crowding' such as floor area per person and persons per room about normal for countries at comparable income levels, and above most other countries in the region. The large dwelling sizes in PT appear to place them in the top five cities studied in the HIP.

7) The durability of most structures appears to be good; most are built of permanent materials. Recent estimates of 'housing needs' which present undocumented figures on dwellings requiring demolition and replacement because they can not be upgraded need to be examined carefully before any such scheme is undertaken.

8) Much of the housing stock appears to have been built without the required permits and is hence 'informal' or illegal. This is likely to result in a slower pace of infrastructure servicing of such units and unavailability of housing finance.

9) The housing finance system is virtually non-existent because of repressed overall financial development and a number of specific risks associated with lending for housing.

10) Provision of serviced land for residential building appears to be inadequate as a result of restrictions on the conversion of rural to urban land, inflexible municipal boundaries, and unpredictable and time-consuming permitting procedures, as well as a lower than necessary rate of provision of urban infrastructure. This contributes toward higher prices of both land and housing.

Overall the GWB housing sector is one whose performance is mexed – in many ways it appears largely 'normal' – particularly with regard to physical characteristics of housing and, in general, concerning access to infrastructure. Distortions are apparent however in the prices of both rental and owner-occupied housing and in the components of housing cost – particularly land and construction costs. If the degree of under-reporting of housing output suggested here is substantiated, both housing output and levels of investment relative to GDP appear also to be distorted relative to expectations. While high levels of realised output and investment give some cause for optimism concerning the near-term ability of the economy to meet the needs of natural increase and return of refugees, serious doubts may be raised about either the ability to greatly increase output in the near term or to sustain the current level of economic activity in the sector.

Because of data limitations, it has not been possible to more than touch upon the needs of special groups, such as the occupants of refugee camps, or the poor. Detailed household interview surveys focusing on the social, economic and housing conditions of these and other groups is essential if a housing strategy is to be put in place which is well-targeted on the households most in need of government or donor intervention.

Notwithstanding the preliminary nature of the analysis presented here, it is possible to suggest some general directions for policy reform, institutional development, and programmatic interventions.

POLICIES FOR A WELL-FUNCTIONING HOUSING SECTOR

The analysis above has indicated many of the symptoms of a housing sector that is at present failing to contribute as effectively as possible to either social welfare or economic development. Evaluated against either the qualitative norms for a well-functioning housing sector set out in Section 2 or the quantitative norms identified within the Housing Indicators Program, there are many areas that should be the subject of policy and institutional reform efforts. Table 2 summarises the information on key sectoral performance indicators, indicating their current level and a level which might be thought of as a 'likely' outcome were the government to adopt policies designed to create a well-functioning housing sector.

Overall, the key differences between a well-functioning and a badly functioning housing sector include: (1) less distorted housing prices, with (2) lower prices for housing purchase and (3) higher prices for rents; (4) higher housing quality, (5) lower average construction costs and (6) housing investment at a sustainable level; (7) considerable reductions in the share of unauthorised housing and concomitant tenure security; (8) increases in the volume of long-term credit for housing and an (9) increase in the share of the assets of the banking system invested in housing mortgages; (10) increases in spending on infrastructure which will be reflected in (11) lower premiums for developed as compared to undeveloped land and (12) lower prices for serviced land.

Policy and institutional changes necessary to bring about a well-functioning housing sector in GWB can be specified in general terms based on a simple but powerful framework used recently in the World Bank's Housing Policy Paper (World Bank, 1993) to describe compactly the major elements of an enabling strategy for housing. In that paper, enabling strategies are described as having three major components:

Table 22 Current and Future Housing Performance Indicators.

Indicator	Current level	Direction of change	Likely future level	Comments
Key indicators				
House price-to-income ratio	5.47	Lower	3.5 – 4.5	Reflects lower land and construction costs
Rent-to-income ratio	0.05–0.07	Higher	0.19–0.25	Rent decontrol
Housing (production per 1000 people)	9.8?	Same/lower	7 – 9	Should match population change and up-grading
Housing investment/ GNP	13.4%	Lower	7–9%	Reflects housing standards reduction/ cost reduction
Floor area per person	15	Same	15	
Permanent structures	86–95%	Same/higher	95%	
Unauthorised housing	50%?	Lower	10–15%	Land registration/ titling
Housing credit/all credit	0%	Higher	10–15%	Institutional development
Land development multiplier	4–20	Lower	4	Greater infrastructure supply/less restrictive regulations
Infrastructure expenditures/person/ yr*	US$55?	Higher	$100+	Desired range uncertain

*Estimated

demand side actions, supply side action, and institutional reform, each of which, in turn, has a number of more specific elements.

On the demand side, for example, policies must be established which deal with housing finance, property rights, and subsidies/taxes. On the supply side, policies must address infrastructure provision and maintenance, regulations governing land use and housing construction, and organisation of the building industry; and in the area of institutional reform policies must deal with the co-ordination of housing sector and macroeconomic policy, poverty reduction and environmental policies, and data collection, research, and policy analysis dealing with the housing sector.

Table 23 represents a highly simplified version of the major thrust of the World Bank's housing policy paper as applied to the situation existing today in PT. The table suggests a number of 'do's' and 'don'ts' of housing policy for PT, detailed implementation of which obviously calls for a good deal more research and discussion than has been possible in the present paper. Nevertheless, were serious attention given to examining the validity of the admittedly simplified propositions contained in Table 22, and to the practical requirements of their implementation, it is likely that the debate concerning appropriate housing policies and institutions for the future would become well advanced. As a modest contribution toward such a debate, the following specific propositions are offered for consideration in debating the merits of policy and institutional reforms in each major strategic area of GWB housing policy:[14]

- Developing property rights.
  Laws and regulations clarifying rights of ownership and transfer of property, especially in multifamily buildings (e.g. condominium laws) should be established. Programs of land registration and regularisation of insecure tenure should be undertaken. Whenever possible, programs for regularising tenure should go hand-in-hand with infrastructure improvement in slum and squatter settlements, and should seek, whenever possible, to recover costs. Rent control laws should be reformed, with complete decontrol as the ultimate objective.
- Developing mortgage finance.
  Development of mortgage lending must go hand in hand with overall financial sector development. Policies and institutions must be devised which address all major elements on commercial and political risk. Financial policies should permit institutions to borrow and lend at positive real interest rates and on equal terms with other institutions. Competition should be encouraged to improve efficiency. Mortgage instrument designs should permit the interests of both borrowers and lenders to be realised through appropriate terms, especially indexing provisions. Collateral security should be fostered by well-designed and enforced systems of titling and foreclosure. Innovative institutional arrangements for promoting greater access to housing finance by the poor, such as mutual guarantees and flexible payment schedules, should be encouraged. Lending for the provision of rental housing should be facilitated. Contractual savings schemes to encourage household saving for housing should be evaluated; such schemes should also consider the possibility of targeted 'matching grants' for designated households. Government participation in retail banking for housing loans should be avoided, although some role in a 'second tier' liquidity facility should be considered.
- Rationalising subsidies.
  Governments should see subsidies as either transitional or as a last resort. They should first try other methods for improving access to housing, such as regularising insecure tenure, improving access to market-rate housing finance, removing barriers to the production of rental housing, or improving housing supply markets to reduce prices. If subsidies are necessary they must be well-targeted, measurable, and transparent, and should avoid distorting housing markets. Subsidies in the form of rent control, which have been shown to be inequitable

549

and to distort markets and reduce housing supply, should be avoided. One-time capital grants and housing allowances are usually more appropriate than rent control and production subsidies; these may be coupled with contractual savings schemes to encourage saving. Rent control regulations should be modified to foster greater competition and choice in the market place.

- Providing infrastructure for residential land development.

Continued attention should be given to both improving residential infrastructure in slum and squatter settlements and refugee camps and extending it to new areas. The agencies responsible for provision of residential infrastructure (roads, drainage, water, sewerage, and electricity) should focus less on narrow physical objectives and more on opening up urban land for residential development. This involves greater co-ordination in planning and possibly joint acquisition of rights-of-way, joint financing, and joint cost recovery. Infrastructure agencies should devote greater attention to local demand for infrastructure. Existing communities should be encouraged to participate in the process of planning and building of infrastructure projects, to ensure accountability and smooth implementation. Cost recovery mechanisms need to be improved and opportunities for privatising infrastructure provision and maintenance sought.

- Regulating land and housing development.

Regulatory environments need to provide an appropriate balance between the costs and the benefits of regulations that influence urban land and housing markets, especially land use and building. Regulations need to be established in a way that benefits rather than, as is now often the case, penalises the poor. To accomplish this, audits need to identify key urban regulations; to establish their impacts on housing demand, supply, and prices; and to establish priorities for regulatory reform. Alternative, affordable standards that do not compromise environmental, health and safety concerns should be considered. Financial regulations must be established that facilitate rather than hinder development of mortgage lending.

- Organising the building industry.

Governments should seek to create greater competition in the building industry by eliminating regulatory barriers to entry, breaking up monopolies, facilitating equal access of small firms to markets and inputs, removing constraints to the development, and use of local building materials and construction methods, and reducing trade barriers that apply to housing inputs. Access to sources of building materials other than those produced in Israel should be sought, and domestic capacity should be expanded if it is economical to do so. Direct government participation in the production and distribution of housing should be avoided.

550

Table 23 The Do's and Don'ts in Enabling Housing Markets to Work in GWB.

Instruments	Do	Don't
Developing Property Rights	• Regularise land tenure • Expand land registration • Establish condominium laws	• Institute costly titling systems • Discourage land transactions
Developing Mortgage Finance	• Allow private sector to lend • Lend at positive/market rates • Enforce foreclosure laws • Ensure prudential regulation • Introduce better loan instruments	• Allow interest-rate subsidies • Discriminate against rental housing investment • Neglect resource mobilisation • Allow high default rates
Rationalising Subsidies	• Make subsidies transparent • Target subsidies to the poor • Subsidise people, not houses • Subject subsidies to review	• Build subsidised public housing • Allow for hidden subsidies • Let subsidies distort prices • Use rent control as a subsidy
Providing Infrastructure	• Co-ordinate land development • Emphasise cost recovery • Base provision on demand • Improve slum infrastructure	• Allow bias against infrastructure investments • Use environmental concerns as reason for slum clearance
Regulating Land and Housing Development	• Reduce regulatory complexity • Assess costs of regulation • Remove price distortions • Remove artificial shortages	• Impose unaffordable standards • Maintain unenforceable rules • Design project without link to regulatory/ institutional reform
Organising the Building Industry	• Eliminate monopoly practices • Encourage small-firm entry • Encourage domestic competitors	• Allow long permit delays • Institute regulations inhibiting competition
Developing a Policy and Institutional Framework	• Balance public/private sector roles • Create a forum for managing the housing sector as a whole • Develop enabling strategies • Monitor sector performance	• Engage in direct public housing delivery • Neglect local government role

- Developing the institutional framework for managing the housing sector.

  A new institutional framework should make it possible for government, with its limited resources, to manage the housing sector in a manner that provides adequate and affordable housing for all. In most countries, an institutional mechanism for overseeing the performance of the sector as a whole, and co-ordinating the major public agencies that influence housing sector performance, is needed. Few countries now have such co-ordinating mechanisms. Institutional mechanisms should be devised to collect, analyse, interpret, and publish data on the performance of the housing sector, particularly concerning its outcomes in respect of the poor; provide an institutional linkage between housing and macro-economic planning; generate long-term plans for housing sector development in conjunction with the central planning agency; provide a forum for participation of the private sector, non-government organisation (NGOs), community-based organisations and the general public in housing policy formulation at both the national and municipal level; review the effects of regulations on housing; initiate regulatory reforms; engage in housing policy research' and influence decision makers in housing-related agencies and local counterpart institutions to improve housing sector performance.

In addition to the functions of policy formulation, co-ordination, and monitoring, other institutional responsibilities, which correspond to elements of an enabling strategy, must also be addressed by a variety of institutions. The most pressing of these functions are: (i) establishing and overseeing the regulatory framework for the delivery of housing finance by the private sector, for developing effective instruments for directing mortgage lending to the poor, and for providing an institutional linkage to the Ministry of Finance and the Monetary Authority; (ii) administering housing subsidies for the needy, focusing on beneficiaries rather than on dwelling units, to include a particular focus on reform of rent control provisions, especially as regards the treatment of old and new units, households with different needs, and ability to pay for rent increases; (iii) establishing and broadening property rights, especially through regularising tenure in squatter settlements; (iv) providing infrastructure in slums and squatter settlements; (v) bringing together infrastructure agencies to co-ordinate infrastructure provision to create an adequate supply of serviced land, and to review the impact of various regulations on the performance of the housing sector, and propose new legislation to improve sector performance.

As the paper has suggested, consideration of the benefits of these and other reforms has the potential to motivate adoption of an array of enabling policies to bring about a well-functioning housing sector, the benefits of which can far transcend their immediate impacts within the housing sector. Reform of housing policies and practices and the development of key institutions are key elements in the overall process of economic development. From the foregoing analysis it should be clear that when housing policies fail, the housing sector fails, and when the housing sector fails both society and the economy are damaged. Thus the stakes of choosing the right policies and institutional arrangements for the housing sector represent a high and demanding priority for the Palestinian people.

ENDNOTES

1) The need for better housing sector data and for operational tools to measure the performance of the housing sector led, in 1990, to the creation of the Housing Indicators Program, a joint programme of the United Nations Centre for Human Settlements (Habitat) and the World Bank. The objectives of the Programme have been to (1) provide a comprehensive conceptual and analytical framework for monitoring the performance of the housing sector, (2) create a set of practical tools for measuring the performance of the housing sector using quantitative, policy sensitive indicators and to test these tools in a broad range of countries, (3) to provide important new empirical information on the high stakes of good policy-making in the housing sector, and (4) to initiate new institutional frameworks that will be more appropriate for managing the housing sector, and for improving the formulation and implementation of housing policies. Much of the data used in this paper are from preliminary tabulations from the Extensive Survey applied in the Housing Indicators Programme in 53 cities and countries around the world.

2) Other actors may be important in different institutional settings. Among the most important of those are non-government and community-based organisations, state-owned enterprises and firms involved in real-estate brokerage. A more detailed breakdown will also need to take into account the different perspectives of specific government agencies, such as the land department or the fire department, and various agents in the formal and informal housing delivery system.

3) See Volume 5, Chapter VII, 'Housing'.

4) Discussions have been initiated between the World Bank and the Palestinian National Authority Ministry of Housing to define a component of the ongoing World Bank Technical Assistance Trust Fund addressing housing policy development, which would have as a major focus development of a data base capable of informing policy and institutional choices within the sector.

5) Preliminary analysis from the Housing Indicators Program, however, indicates that measures of overall hosing sector performance, e.g. median values of housing prices and physical outcomes, are consistently very highly correlated with outcomes throughout the income distribution.

6) This figure was estimated for 1990, and it is assumed that real incomes have not changed since then.

7) In countries such as Korea and Malaysia which have extremely rigid land regulatory systems, land prices are among the world's highest compared to

household incomes. Moreover, during years of rapid economic and demographic growth, it has been typical for land process to outpace general price increases by about 50% (Mayo and Sheppard, 1992).

8) There appears to be little information on the rental housing stock and on its economics in PT. It would be worthwhile to study the rental housing subsector in greater depth, with an eye toward creating a more level 'playing field' between rental and owner occupied housing.

9) In several developed countries, where nearly all housing is formally built, data on housing starts an alternative 'activity indicator', are easily collected and are used extensively in both popular discussion of the state of the housing sector and in sophisticated macroeconomics modelling efforts. In countries with an important informal hosing sector, where much of the housing construction activity is officially unrecorded housing starts data are difficult to collect, but housing completions can be ascertained using either sample surveys or aerial photography.

10) Data on the size of the housing stock and household formation are commonly available from censuses of population and housing, and may be combined with housing production data to produce measures of the adequacy of current production to accommodate growing populations.

11) Using somewhat different figures, Bahiri (1989) reports production rates per 1000 of 6.1 and 2.6, respectively, for the West Bank and Gaza for the period 1984–87 – and an overall figure of 4.7 per 1000.

12) See, for example, Bahiri, p. 44ff, for a discussion of the rapid rate of quality improvement of the PT housing stock in recent years.

13) See, for example, Burns and Grebler (1977).

14) For more detail on the pros and cons of each of these strategic recommendations, see World Bank, *Housing Policy Paper*, 1993, Chapter 4 and Annex 2.

BIBLIOGRAPHY

Bahiri, Simcha, 1989, **Construction and Housing in the West Bank and Gaza**, West Bank Data Project Report, Jerusalem.

Burns, Leland S. and Leo Grebler, 1977, **The Housing of Nations**, Halsted Press, John Wiley and Sons, New York.

Centre for Engineering and Planning, 1992, **Masterplanning the State of Palestine: Suggested Guidelines for Comprehensive Development**, Palestine Studies Project Report, Ramallah, March.

Coon, Anthony, 1992, **Town Planning Under Military Occupation**, Dartmouth Publishing Company, Aldershot, England.

Co-operative Housing Foundation, 1993, **Housing Needs Assessment for the West Bank and Gaza**, Co-operative Housing Foundation Report, Washington, D.C., May.

Mayo, Stephen K. et al., 1982, **Informal Housing in Egypt**, Abt Associates, Inc. Report, Cambridge, Massachusetts.

Mayo, Stephen K. and Stephen Sheppard, 1992, '**Empirical Evidence on the Effects of Development Control: Korea, Malaysia, and Thailand,**' Oberlin College Discussion Papers in Economics, Oberlin, Ohio, November.

United Nations Centre for Human Settlements, 1988, **A Global Shelter Strategy Towards the Year 2000**. Nairobi.

World Bank, 1993, **Housing: Enabling Markets to Work**, World Bank Policy Paper, Washington, D.C., 1993.

World Bank, 1993, **Developing the Occupied Territories: An Investment in Peace; Volume 2: The Economy**, Washington, D.C., September.

World Bank, 1993, **Developing the Occupied Territories: An Investment in Peace; Volume 5: Infrastructure**, Washington, D.C., September.

World Bank, 1993, **The Housing Indicators Project; Volume 1: Report of the Executive Director**, Washington, D.C.

World Bank, 1993, **The Housing Indicators Project; Volume II: Indicator Tables**, Washington, D.C.

HOUSING FINANCE POLICY IN THE PALESTINIAN TERRITORIES

Kamal Naser, Naji Mukhtar and Ayman Abdul Hadi

ABSTRACT

Following the signing of the peace treaty with Israel, Palestinians are expected to exercise control over their sectors of the economy. Housing is one of the most important sectors insofar as it employs a significant share of the national labour force and stimulates investment and economic growth. In other words, the state of the housing sector reflects, to a certain extent, the state of the economy.

Moreover, the results of housing policy will be seen as one of the most important indicators of the effectiveness of the Palestinian National Authority (PNA). The policy's success, in turn, will be measured primarily by its ability to ensure a continuous mobilisation of the nation's savings toward institutions which provide finance for housing. Consequently, any housing policy which is not supported by a considered policy regarding housing finance will be worthless.

INTRODUCTION

Housing is one of the basic needs of human beings. It is also a major determinant of health and poverty in any society. Housing will also affect any social and employment programmes initiated by the Palestinian authorities.

Housing represents a major sector in the developing countries. Previous studies have revealed that investing in housing contributes 15 to 25 per cent of the Gross Fixed Capital Formation (GFCF) and 3 to 8 per cent of the Gross National Product (GNP) (Buckly et al., 1991). The housing sector also accounts for 30 to 50 per cent of the capital stock of most of the developing countries and occupies a high proportion of the labour force.

As far as the Palestinian Territories (PT) are concerned, GFCF accounts for 27 per cent of Gross Domestic Product (GDP), of which 85 per cent is contributed by the private sector. Of this, 85 per cent is accounted for by the housing sector alone. In other words, 19.5 per cent of the PT's GNP is contributed by the housing sector. Given the restrictions imposed by the Israelis on construction and the likelihood that the responsibility for housing will be transferred to the PNA, this proportion is likely to increase.

The role of the housing sector in the economy makes it of paramount importance that the mobilisation of resources used by the housing sector, investment in these resources and their utilisation to achieve a favourable impact on the economy of the PT be monitored. Housing policy should also be reviewed to take into consideration the occasional restrictions imposed by the Israelis which prevent Palestinians from entering the Israeli labour market. The policy must accommodate these labourers to minimise dependency on the Israeli economy.

We believe that any effective housing finance policy is a product of its environment and of distinctive cultural and economic characteristics. As a result, a policy that takes these characteristics into consideration will be discussed here.

The first section of this paper reviews the financial sector in the Palestinian Territories (PT) and its contribution to housing finance. The second section considers the literature on housing development construction and costing. Housing finance institutions are discussed in the third section, while the fourth section explains risk management. Section five considers mortgage instruments and is followed by the conclusion and recommendations.

Suggestions are provided in the paper on the measures which will need to be taken to establish an effective overall policy for housing. In addition, the measures which should be employed by the PNA and by housing finance institutions to make a housing finance programme operational are outlined.

THE FINANCIAL SECTOR AND HOUSING FINANCE

The Financial Sector

Housing finance assistance is widely used to bring down the cost of borrowing to an affordable level. Although specialised housing finance institutions are established all over the world, the PT have no such facilities. The current financing system which operates in the PT is primitive due to the restrictions imposed by the Israeli occupation. The World Bank (September, 1993) described the banking system in the PT as having a "low level of measurable, formal, financial intermediation."

Before the Israeli occupation of the West Bank and Gaza in 1967, eight banks with 26 branches were operating in the West Bank. In Gaza, there were 3 banks with 4 branches (World Bank, 1993). All were closed shortly after the Israeli occupation and replaced by Israeli institutions which had 22 branches in the major cities of the PT. Following the Palestinian uprising, i.e. the *Intifada*, most of these banks were closed.

Although the Israeli banks provided high quality services and enjoyed a complete monopoly in the PT banking market, between 1977 and 1987, credit from the Israeli banks averaged just 1 per cent of GDP, compared with almost 50 per cent of Jordan's GDP shortly before the occupation. In 1966, total bank deposits in the West Bank alone reached $29 million, compared with $48 million in 1987. (This latter figure represents an all time high for the period following the Israeli occupation in 1967.) [1]

In reality, the PT have been left without a formal banking system. Instead, informal financial services are provided by money changers offering only short-term financial services. However, in 1981, the Israelis allowed the Bank of Palestine to re-open and it now operates three branches in Gaza. In 1986, the Cairo Amman Bank also re-opened; it currently operates nine branches in the West Bank. The Bank of Jordan opened in 1994, followed by the Arab Bank in 1995. There is speculation that both an investment bank and Islamic bank will open in the West Bank soon.

The operations of the Arab banks are restricted to a few services of a short-term nature. The 1993 annual reports of the Cairo Amman Bank and the Bank of Palestine showed that credit provided by the banks was less than 1 per cent of GDP. In contrast, the credit to GNP ratio, in both Jordan and Israel, was 102 per cent. Short-term deposits increased from 66 per cent in 1990 to 73 per cent in 1993. The annual reports also showed that loans provided to customers fell from 11 to 10 per cent and that investments by the banks dropped from 40 to 30 per cent in the same period.

Money Changers

The absence of an effective banking system, combined with the use of different currencies as formal intermediators, together with the high level of inflation in the Israeli economy, produced an informal banking system. This took the form of money changers. Harris (1988) indicated that the number of money changers increased from 42 in 1967 to 196 in 1986. The money changers' activities are restricted to services of a short-term nature, such as currency exchange, money transfers and the cashing of cheques.

Insurance Companies

Before September, 1994, there were only three Palestinian-owned insurance companies in the PT: the Arab Insurance Company, Al-Mashreq Insurance Company and The National Insurance Company. Of the three, only the Arab Insurance Company was established before 1967, and this was under Jordanian law. Like the banking system, the insurance sector is supervised by Jordanian as well as Israeli law.

The products of the insurance companies lack diversification; the vast majority of their transaction are related to car insurance. They also invest in the shares of some industrial companies, but their investments do not exceed 5 per cent of the capital of these companies. They also offer short-term loans up to a specified limit to well-known policy holders.

The Legal Framework for Banking

The regulations that dictate the creation and transactions of the banking system in the PT are derived from three different, sometimes conflicting, sources. The banking system in the West Bank is influenced by Jordanian Banking Law No. 94 of 1966. Although this law was replaced in 1971 by Banking Law No. 24 and amended in 1992, the outdated law is still operational in the PT. Jordan introduced a law, No. 26, to regulate the transactions of the money changers in 1992 (World Bank, 1993).

Banking operations in Gaza are influenced by the Banking Ordinance of 1941 of the British Mandate. This law was updated by Israeli military orders in 1980 and amended in 1988. The system is also influenced by the Bank of Israel law of 1954 and the Banking Licence Law of 1971, which was amended in 1988.

However, although in theory the banking system in the PT is regulated under three different jurisdictions, in realty the system is subject to 265 military orders issued to amend previous rules. As can be seen, the country lacks any sort of institutional housing finance. In addition, the West Bank and Gaza only have commercial banks which emphasise short-term credit. The PNA exercises little or no control over these banks.

Investments in Housing

Most investment in housing has been made by the private sector (see Table 1). During the period of the Israeli occupation, the construction industry alone accounted for an estimated 85 per cent of private investment. The political and economic instability, the Israeli policy pursued in confiscating Palestinian lands, and the absence of any form of publicly

Table 1 Total Investment in the PT [2].

Source	Period	Amount (US$) (millions)	Yearly Total (US$) (millions)*	Percentage (%)
Private Savings-Local and Transfers from Abroad	1967–1993	170–465		91.53
Joint Palestinian–Jordanian Committee	1979–1985	66		–
Central and Local Authorities	Yearly Average	5	6	1.18
Islamic Waqf	Yearly Average	3	3	0.59
Arab Cities Twinship programme	Yearly Average	14	14	2.76
UNRWA	Yearly Average	250	–	–
European Union	1993	50		
Non-Governmental Organisations	Yearly Average	20	20	3.94
Total			508	100

* Regular payments expected to continue in the future are used to estimate the proportion of each source to the total value of sources. The UNRWA contribution is excluded because it only covers refugee camps.

financed housing motivated private investors to put their money into housing.

Between 1979 and 1985, the Jordanian–Palestinian Joint Committee spent $66 million on housing. In 1989, the Arab Insurance Company constructed apartments for middle class groups in the West Bank with 50 per cent of the house value to be paid as a down-payment and the remainder to be amortised over five years. In 1991, the European Community (EC) provided $50 million to develop and sell low-cost houses at a low mortgage interest rate which was spread over a period of ten to 20 years.

At present, no statistics are available to estimate the demand for housing. It is estimated that an annual average of 35,000 housing units will be required in the next five years. Hence, investment in the housing sector would rise to reach $840 million per annum [3].

Actually, the current financial sector of the PT makes little, or even no contribution, to housing finance. The financial sector needs to be activated to make a better contribution to developing the housing sector. To ensure the mobilisation of savings towards the housing sector, a more specialised bank, similar to the Housing Bank operating in Jordan, needs to be established.

THE OPTIONS FOR DEVELOPMENT, CONSTRUCTION AND COSTS

In the past four decades, a variety of housing policies and programmes have been adopted to address problems facing low-income groups. Until the early 1970s, conventional public housing programmes relying heavily on state subsidies were widely used in the developing countries. The houses were built up to a high standard, thereby inflating the cost and making them unaffordable to low-income groups.

Turner (1968) argued that public housing is appropriate to middle-income groups. In an attempt to reduce inflated costs and make the price of housing affordable, governments use subsidies. This approach proved to be ineffective in solving problems of housing low-income groups due to the limited resources available to most developing countries. Rahman (1994) stated that scarce resources in the developing countries make it difficult to offer substantial subsidies for an indefinite period.

This programme is criticised by many scholars on the grounds that it is based on Western planning concepts and relies on heavily subsidised blocks of public housing (see, for example, Rackodi, 1986).

The failure of the conventional approach to providing houses for the poor gave rise to two new programmes: *the site and services programme* and *upgrading existing areas*. These programmes were adopted by the United Nations and they became important elements in the 1970s approach adopted by the World Bank for securing basic needs for low-income groups. Through these approaches, the Bank aimed to achieve afford-ability by reducing the cost of the infrastructure for an acceptable standard of house construction. Choguill (1988) pointed out that although these two programmes aimed to reduce the cost, many urban populations were still unable to contribute anything to their own housing due to their low incomes.

Although these approaches have been used throughout the developing world for many years, the problem of housing the poor still remains. Rahman (1994) revealed that in Bangladesh more than a quarter of the country's urban households are forced to live in slum areas due to financial problems. Rackodi (1991) argued that lower costs should be achieved by reducing design standards. In our opinion, in the developing countries in general and the PT in particular, lower costs can be achieved by improving the efficiency and productivity of housing developers and housing contractors.

In some countries like the PT, where there is no housing finance system, funds which individuals require for buying or building houses may be obtained from the informal sector, such as relatives and friends. Boleat (1985) showed that this approach, known as *creative financing*, was

561

used in the USA in the late 1970s and the early 1980s where the traditional housing finance system had become increasingly ineffective.

As far as the PT are concerned, the phenomenon of informal financing is evident, on a limited scale, in many parts of the country. Financing takes place at a very low cost, in many cases at zero cost, for a short period of time. Under this arrangement, the lender relies on his/her previous knowledge (i.e. close relationship) of the borrower; only in some cases will the lender demand guarantees. Land or gold can be mortgaged to ensure repayment on time.

Because housing finance is inadequate in most developing countries, housing finance systems are dominated by informal sources of finance. In this respect, Raymond and Turner (1988) asserted that although most of these countries operate formal mortgage financing systems, only ten to 20 per cent of housing production benefits from the system. Moreover, the benefit is limited to families at the top of the income distribution scale.

The most organised form of informal financing, which is used particularly by the lower income groups, is the rotating credit society by which members contribute a fixed amount each month, and each member has the right to borrow from the fund under an established procedure. Boleat (1985) stated that in Africa and the Middle East, lots are frequently drawn to decide who should have access to the funds without an interest charge. In Asia, interest is generally charged.

Components of Housing Cost

There are several different factors that should be considered in estimating housing costs, including land, building materials, labour, infrastructure, design and management costs. These components should be taken into account when seeking potential reductions in the cost of dwellings.

Land

Land is considered to be the most important factor. The cost of land constitutes the largest share of the total cost of a dwelling. In some cases, it may reach 50 per cent of the total cost [4]. Turner (1980) affirmed that unless land is available through public ownership in a large part of a city, the acquisition of land becomes a major problem. Moreover, the cost of land near places of work, in particular in inner-cities, is likely to be high. Lubell (1984) stated that during the 1960s, land prices in the major cities of the developing countries rose by ten to 20 per cent more than consumer prices indices. Mukhtar (1993) found that land price in Tripoli, Libya, increased approximately six-fold from the 1970s to the 1990s.

Consequently, low-income groups may be forced to buy plots of land in peripheral areas where land is available and cheap. However, it may not actually be a cheaper option if the relatively high servicing costs, especially for new services to be supplied to outlying areas, are taken into account. Although in some relatively wealthy countries, services and utilities can be covered by municipal budgets, the cost of the journey to work remains a big problem. Rackodi (1986) argued that the combined cost of housing and the journey to work may lead to a household abandoning the plot and moving back to slum areas near the inner-city which are closer to places of work.

To limit the effects of land speculation and to lower the price of land for the urban poor, taxation measures should be introduced. Payne (1984) pointed out that land value increment taxes and betterment taxes have been used in several countries to restrict any increase in land value due to speculation pressure and public investment. Since the PNA enjoys only limited control over the fiscal policy of the PT, this approach constitutes a weak option. Land prices could be controlled by buying large areas of peripheral land at low cost and scheduling their development strategically in relation to demand.

In addition, the PNA can keep land prices down by taking steps within its power to prevent price increases on land designated for public use and housing development. Land use must also be properly planned to avoid competing uses and wastage. For these reasons, a policy for land-use planning, including land zoning and/or sub-division regulation, is recommended.

Building materials

The high cost of building materials is another reason why housing is relatively expensive for low-income groups. Herbert (1979) showed that building materials represent about 65 per cent of total construction costs for housing in the developing countries. This is considerably higher than in most developed countries. As a result, many of the developing countries try to encourage the use of local building materials in order to reduce housing costs. In cases where individuals build their own homes, they must seek inexpensive building materials which are produced locally and also find the least costly ways to transport them to the plot. Abdul Hadi (1994) pointed out that the effective use of building materials helped to reduce building costs, provide employment opportunities and improve affordability.

A research centre to help develop low-cost building materials should be established. In the PT, most of the building materials are imported from Israel or other foreign countries, even though some of them, such as tiles, marble and some plastic products, are available in locally. Abdul

Hadi (1994) believed that the restrictions imposed by Israel on industrial development in the PT, together with excessive limits on the direct importation of building materials increased the cost of materials in the PT.

Labour

Labour is another factor that contributes to the housing costs. A shortage of skilled and semi-skilled workers and the need to pay increased wages often contribute to a rise in the cost of dwelling units. According to Abdul Hadi (1994), the labour market in the construction industries has experienced a shortage of both skilled and semi-skilled workers as a result of their migration to the neighbouring countries in search of better job opportunities. The introduction of a well-planned housing finance policy may help the indigenous construction sector to attract Palestinian labourers who have entered the Israeli construction market. This in turn could also help to contribute to the economic independence of the PT.

Infrastructure

Infrastructure is another factor which affects housing costs. The most important services which are required to operate any housing project and which, at the same time, affect the cost and affordability of individual dwelling units include access and circulation (such as roads and footpaths); storm water drainage (where rainfall is significant); water supply; sewerage; gas and electricity; street lighting and refuse collection. The cost of these depends on location and on the type of land involved.

In the urban areas of the PT, most of the required infrastructure is available, except connection to a sewage system. Instead, many homes rely on septic tanks as a method of sewage disposal. In rural areas, there is less infrastructure than in the urban areas, and a survey to classify the condition of the housing stock is needed.

Affordability

The primary approach to housing finance adopted by most developing countries is based on the principles of *affordability, accessibility and replicability*. Affordability has been described by Lee (1985, 1990) as the extent to which a household can afford to pay for specified services, based on housing costs, family income, and the propensity to pay for housing. Rackodi (1986) pointed out that the difference between the dwelling cost and the ability of the residents to pay for housing may be met by public subsidy. However, Rahman (1994) argued that not all countries, particularly in the third world, are able to provide such a subsidy for a long period of time.

To assess the level of cost for new or improved shelter, several factors should be considered. Tym (1984) limits such factors to the household life style: total earnings; security of the principal and secondary sources of income; the amount of savings and the capacity to save at all; and the spending patterns of a particular income group. Be that as it may, the relevancy of this ratio to some developing countries in general, and the PT in particular, is highly questionable. It is unrealistic to apply such a rationalisation without paying attention to the particular environment, including a country's level of personal income, family size and cost of living. In the PT, for example, only 25 per cent of the population is gainfully employed and 70 to 80 per cent of the low-income group's disposable income is spent on food.

Cost recovery leads to replicability because recovered costs will be used to produce additional housing units. Both are interrelated and a trade-off should be arranged between them to provide access for the low-income groups [5]. Mayo and Gross (1987) revealed that more than 74 per cent of the World Bank housing projects put the affordability ratio at 20 to 25 per cent of personal income.

Affordability can be improved by adopting the *housing account model* advocated by Chin-oh-Chang (1987). The model suggests that the PNA can use taxes collected from high-income home buyers to subsidise the construction of homes for low-income groups. McGee (1988) proposed another approach, the *service delivery model*, where people mobilise their resources to upgrade their environment. A further approach advocated by many researchers is *people's participation*; this suggests that people can get together to build their own homes (see, for example, Turner, 1980; Burns, 1983; Yeung, 1985; Carmon and Gavrieli, 1987).

In Burns' opinion (1983), people's participation stimulates employment and encourages national industries, thereby conserving precious foreign exchange through the use of indigenous building materials. In addition, Carmon and Gavrieli (1987) showed that people's participation gives low-income groups the opportunity to become owner-occupiers.

Turner (1980) maintained that people's participation ensures a sense of belonging and, therefore contributed to better maintenance of the services by the participants. More importantly, people's participation reduces the cost of housing and makes housing prices more affordable [6]. Angel (1983) warned that unless consensus is achieved among all the participants (such as the PNA, designers and engineers, builders and international aid agencies), the experiment stands little chance of success. On the other hand, Koenigsberger (1983) contends that people's participation might be seen as an anti-social approach since the responsibility of the PNA, to provide housing to the poor, is shifted to the participants.

Determinants of Affordability

A variety of approaches have been used to assess affordability. One approach considers *the rent/income ratio* as a co-efficient of affordability. However, this approach has been criticised on the grounds that while money spent on rent is of a short-term nature, repayment of a mortgage is of a long-term nature. Unlike the tenant, the house-buyer is expected to make a large down-payment, in addition to paying mortgage interest and saving rent over a long period of time. In other words, house buyers and tenants are not identical.

The house-buyer's affordability co-efficient includes down-payment and instalment co-efficients, while the housing consumption co-efficient is reflected in the rental value of the houses. Lee (1987) showed that the propensity to consume houses is higher for owners than for tenants. This approach may become misleading in a situation where a country's law allows what is called *rent freezing*. To protect tenants, the laws of some Middle Eastern countries set fixed rents. For these reasons, using the rent/income ratio as a predictor of affordability may distort reality.

Given that payment for housing is consumption, the economic theories of consumption can be employed to explain factors that might influence the consumption of housing.

Affordability factors are summarised in Table 2.

HOUSING FINANCE POLICY

In the preceding section, components of housing costs and predictors of affordability were investigated. In this section, the design of a housing finance policy and its implementation are examined.

A house is the largest single purchase that most Palestinians are prepared to make. Because the price of a house represents many times the individual's yearly income, a large proportion can be expected to be obtained through a loan. The owner's down payment generally represents up to 30 per cent of the purchase price [7]. Therefore, the cost and the availability of mortgage credit are important parts of the home purchase mechanism.

The main function of any housing finance system is to accumulate capital from depositors and to plough that back into the economy as housing credits. To channel housing credits to homebuyers, low down payments, long-term fixed rates and self-amortising loans need to be available. This finance system can be summarised as follows.

Attracting more savers increases the flow of funds available to lend for mortgages. Consequently, the rate of interest charges for new homebuyers falls. A successful housing finance policy is one that mobilises national

Table 2 Factors influencing affordability.

Household Source of Fund (X₁)	Household Uses of Fund (X₂)	Capital Cost (X₃)	House Features (X₄)	Affordability Household Features (X₅)	Usage (X₆)	Environment Quality (X₇)	Lagged Affordability (X₈)
* Monthly Salary	* Food	* Land	* Location	* Age	* Owner	* Infrastructure	* Affordability Y_{t-1}
* Savings	* Water	* Structure Cost	* Plot Size	* Education	* Rent	* Neighbouring	* Affordability Y_{t-1}
* Investments	* Electricity	* Services	* Design	* Skills	* Commercial	* Location (with respect to work place)	
* Remittances	* Gas & Heating		* House Size	* Family Size			
* Credit	* Telephone		* Availability of Utilities				
* Other	* Rent		* Structure Quality				
	* Transport						
	* Education						
	* Recreation						
	* Clothing						
	* Health Care						
	* Tax						
	* Maintenance						
	* Other						

Y_{t-1} and Y_{t-2} refer to previous years.

567

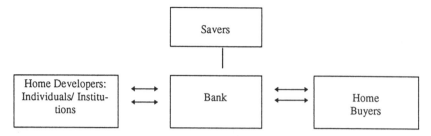

Figure 1 The Relationship between Participants in the Housing Finance Process.

savings by managing investors' risks and attracting borrowers by offering low-cost, affordable housing.

Any housing finance policy starts with a clear definition of housing policy within the boundaries of the economic development and macro-economic strategies. The PNA should spell out the objectives of its housing policy by identifying its role at the policy design stage and by specifying the relationship between the policy and the housing finance sector at the implementation phase.

The Role of the PNA

In co-operation with the economy and finance ministries, the Ministry of Housing is responsible for identifying the demand for housing, the distribution of individual income, the availability of capital, the availability of housing materials and supplies. The effectiveness of any housing finance policy depends on its ability to ensure the continuous flow of funds that will be necessary to operate the housing sector efficiently and securely. This task requires expertise from a variety of sectors, housing developers, financial institutions, potential investors, suppliers, community representatives and lawyers.

Competent, well-trained management and staff capable of addressing the daily issues relating to housing finance is vital to the success of any housing policy. A housing council that includes representatives from each of these sectors is of paramount importance. This council could recommend a housing policy to the Ministry of Housing for its approval and then be assigned the responsibility of implementing it.

The monetary authority and economic planners (i.e. from the economic and finance ministries) should work side by side to establish the basis for an effective financial sector which can be given the responsibility of transforming the housing sector. It is vital that the PNA should work on developing the financial sector in such a way that it can respond to the needs of the housing sector, especially for low-income households.

The PNA can then either exercise full control over housing finance policy and enter the market as a competitor to the private sector (i.e. what is known as the *disabling strategy*) or alternatively, provide support and facilities to the private sector to enable it to operate effectively and efficiently (i.e. an *enabling strategy*). For more details on this issue, see Christian (1991).

While the disabling strategy has some support in developing countries, the enabling strategy has gained popularity in the developed countries. The disabling strategy has been criticised on the grounds that it would give the PNA a competitive advantage over the private sector. Deciding on the number of houses to be built, the money to be lent and the mortgage interest rate makes the housing sector an unattractive investment. Investors tend to put their money in other sectors with less government intervention, it has been maintained. This would prevent a continuous flow of funds to the housing sector and ultimately increase the cost of borrowing.

The past few years have witnessed a shift in the direction of housing policy within the donor communities and in many developing countries. The trend is to move away from relying on the government for the provision of houses for the low and middle-income groups in favour of a policy which helps the private sector to build a large number of houses with minimum requirements. In this context, housing finance is viewed as a crucial factor.

Undoubtedly, market forces can ultimately work to the benefit of the homebuyers because they help to guarantee a continuous flow of funds to the housing sector, thereby resulting in low mortgage interest rates. However, in the absence of a proper social security system, and proper employment programme, the outcome of this strategy is doubtful. Thus, the PNA can use the personal level of income distribution to decide whether to implement a disabling or enabling strategy. In our opinion, the disabling strategy can be used to deal with those who earn low or no income, while the private sector is given a free hand to deal with the middle- and upper-income groups.

In this case, the PNA should provide the guidelines (i.e. a citizen's charter) on the standard of construction, code of practice, the areas where housing development is allowed and other issues. The guidelines must keep a balance between homebuyers and investors. Legislation that protects both investors by minimising their risks, and homebuyers by preventing exploitation, must be introduced by the PNA. In addition, the PNA must provide a stable macroeconomic environment in which inflation is controlled so that the interest rate risk is manageable.

Failing this, high levels of inflation will lead to high interest rates. This will make it difficult for homebuyers from low- and middle-income groups to make the inflated periodic payments which will be required and increase the likelihood of repossession.

In general, the following steps should be adopted for an effective housing finance policy:

1) Estimate the demand for housing;
2) Estimate the cost (this will be dictated by the area, the style of construction, the facilities demanded by the household);
3) Assess the capacity of the existing financial market and the percentage of this capacity that is most likely to be directed towards housing;
4) Identify the relationship between the housing sector and the financial sector;
5) Determine the difference between the cost of what is needed and what is available;
6) Attempt to bridge the gap between the cost of what is needed and what is available by either looking at possible ways to reduce the cost of construction or by investigating other sources of finance (this could be achieved by considering internal and external sources);
7) Assess a variety of combinations of possible alternatives to decide their feasibility. Economic indicators can be used to assess the feasibility of each alternative;
8) In the light of the above analysis, recommend courses of action; and
9) Follow up and report on any deviations from the stated plan.

One mechanism that can be employed to eradicate the gap between cost and affordability is to provide some sort of subsidy. However, the PNA is not in a position to offer subsides on a large scale for a long period of time. One of the policies the PNA would be advised to follow is to provide subsidies to a specific group.

Structuring Housing Finance

To structure the policy, a choice needs to be made between the public sector, private sector or a combination of the two. In the PT, the public sector can take the responsibility for housing finance through municipalities, village councils or through a national bank with nation-wide branches. The second choice is to leave the housing finance system to the private sector with a specialised housing bank with a nation-wide branches, a variety of banks and insurance companies or individual and institutional investors. Finally, the housing finance structure can be based on a combination of the public and private sectors.

As mentioned earlier, the public sector can take care of those with low incomes and leave the rest to the private sector. Encouraging private financial institutions as well as institutional investors to take part in providing finance for housing will help to integrate the housing finance system with the national financial system. This will better ensure the flow of funds to the housing sector.

However, it may be more likely that both the private and public sectors will be involved in the housing finance structure. In this case, both sectors ought to be subject to the same rules and standards. Otherwise, the public sector will enjoy a competitive advantage and this would harm the housing industry.

Institutional Forms of Housing Finance

An efficient housing sector requires capital investment to satisfy immediate demand. In order to implement an effective housing finance policy, it is vital, first of all, to determine the demand for houses, and, secondly, to identify the mortgage financing available through existing financing mechanisms.

Because the PT lack any form of institutional housing finance, the PNA can employ, or encourage the employment of, the following housing finance instruments. The Authority must bear in mind that the major objective of these instruments is to stimulate the flow of private savings to the housing sector.

Share institutions versus mutual institutions

To create a housing finance system integrated with the national financial system, publicly-owned companies (*share institutions*) could be established by issuing shares to investors seeking investment in the housing sector [8]. These companies could then build and sell houses to the public for profit. To make investment in the housing sector more attractive, tax relief can be offered to companies operating in this sector. However, with *mutual institutions* the clients are the depositors. In this case, the borrower pays interest on any loans taken out with the mutual institution and dividends are paid on deposits.

Repayment of the loan and continuous contribution by other members ensure the availability of funds for other homebuyers. The behaviour of the society's members determines the profits and losses of these institutions. This idea can then be developed to admit depositors who are unlikely to become borrowers to increase the availability of funds.

Currently, in the PT investment in shares is popular among the middle and upper classes which can afford to buy shares. As a result, share institutions can be expected to be dominated by these groups. Because the major objective of these investors is to maximise their return on investment, high house prices may result. Only a limited number of groups with relatively high incomes would benefit from such a scheme. Moreover, mutual institutions may experience insolvency problems due to the difficulty of raising the required capital.

Contract saving system

Another approach which may be appropriate in the PT is the German and French experience with a *contract saving system*. Under this system, the member makes specific annual contributions during a specified time period, after which he or she becomes entitled to a home mortgage loan equal to a multiple amount of his or her savings. Under this arrangement, the member is offered a mortgage interest rate less than the market interest rate. To motivate saving, the government offers bonuses for those who adhere to the exact contribution within the required period of time (i.e. five years).

This arrangement has the advantage that it indicates a household's ability to provide regular payments, over a specific period of time, in the savings contract. This would help to ensure that the depositors would follow the same approach when making regular payments to settle the mortgage loan.

The contract saving system may face problems in the PT in that participants may find themselves unable to complete their commitments over a set period of time. In addition, such a programme will have a limited lending capability because every successful depositor has the right to borrow after satisfying the conditions laid down by the contract. Furthermore, instability in the economy might drive up housing prices, making the borrowed amount insufficient to complete the construction of a house. Moreover, the volatility of the economy may make it difficult for depositors to meet their commitments. Nevertheless, the viability of the saving contract programme can be enhanced by integrating it with the PT's financial sector [9].

A mortgage bank

The functions and definitions of mortgage banks vary between countries. Under this system, a mortgage bank underwrites a mortgage loan at an agreed, fixed interest rate for a specified period of time. The value of the loan is not entirely given in cash. Instead, the bank provides *guaranteed notes* carrying nominal interest rates. It then becomes the borrower's responsibility to secure the cash required to build the home by selling these notes on the open market.

The borrower should agree a periodic payment (i.e. once a month) to cover the fixed mortgage interest rate. However, the borrower receives less than the principal in cash, and because the guaranteed notes can be sold at a discounted price, the borrower ends up paying a higher mortgage interest rate as well. The selling price of the guaranteed notes is determined by market forces.

The scheme provides the following advantages:

1) Because the interest rate is determined by market forces, the scheme mobilises savings and ensures a continuous flow of funds;
2) By approaching financial institutions (such as banks, insurance companies) and institutional and individual investors to cash the guaranteed notes, the scheme ensures closer integration with the national financial sector; and
3) The scheme addresses problems associated with interest rate risk management by transferring the risk from the lender to other investors who are prepared to accept higher risks.

However, although the scheme minimises interest rate risks, the lender might still experience a credit risk. When a country is experiencing a rise in interest rates, the borrower will be forced to sell the guaranteed notes at a significantly discounted price, making it difficult to secure the amount necessary to complete the housebuilding or to repay the mortgage interest. The degree of political and economical uncertainties which are to be expected in the PT could call into question the likelihood that this scheme would be successful.

Other instruments

Employees' schemes

The provision of credit to complement demotic savings is a well established mechanism in various parts of the world. A housing finance institution may introduce a financing scheme for employees whose job tenure is secure. Under this scheme, housebuilding loans are repaid over a period ranged from 20 to 25 years at a simple rate of interest. Each participating employer can devote part of the company's profit to an employees' housing scheme to be deducted from employees' salaries. Employers, whether in the private or the public sector, could be asked to top up a provident fund from their profits in exchange for tax relief.

Co-operatives

Housing co-operatives can fulfil the role of developer and financier by procuring external funds at zero, or very low, interest rates and spending them, through the co-operatives, on homes for low-income groups. Institutional organisations (such as the World Bank, United Nations Development Programme, the UK's Overseas Development Agency and others) can provide assistance to such housing programmes to help provide the necessary technical infrastructure, as well as other support systems and seed capital for housing finance institutions. Their funding may also be used to establish a special purpose housing bank.

573

Soft loans backed by insurance companies

To facilitate mortgage investment as well as the free exchange of mortgage securities in secondary markets, the PNA needs to establish a system of mortgaging which is guaranteed by insurance policies. The secondary mortgage market would supplement the PNA's allocated soft housing loans which would involve shorter amortisation periods. A housing mortgage bank would need to be introduced and funds created by selling government bonds.

Risk Management

One of the major problems facing institutional forms of housing finance involves risk management. This, in turn, is a function of the stability (or instability) of economic indicators and of macroeconomic policy [10]. Up to now, the macroeconomic policy for the PT has not been made clear, and is influenced by the policies pursued in both Jordan and Israel. This adds to the risks inherent in the housing industry because the ills in the Jordanian and Israeli economies will automatically be imported to the PT.

As far as mortgages are concerned, risk comes in two forms: *credit* and *mortgage interest rate* risk [11].

Credit Risk

Credit risk is associated with the inability of the borrower to repay the amount of principal. Unlike mortgage interest rate risk, credit risk is manageable. Loans can be issued only to those who stand a high chance of repaying the principal amount. It can also be minimised by asking the borrower to make a significant down payment (i.e. 20 to 30 per cent of the property value). The mortgage is collateralised by the property. In case of default, the lender has the right to sell the property in the open market to recover the principal.

Because the market value of the property goes up over time, the principal will always be less than the property value. The system can also be tightened by introducing an advanced insurance system to protect the borrower against any adverse eventuality (i.e. personal disability, unemployment and disasters such as death, flood, fire, etc.). In this case, credit management can be transferred from both the lender and borrower to a third party.

Interest Rate Risk

Interest rate risk is dependent upon macroeconomic policy; however, neither the lender nor the borrower can control this policy. Consequently, where lenders are offering a fixed mortgage interest rate, a rise in interest rates would their profit margin. Lenders would begin to incur a loss when the fixed mortgage interest rate became insufficient to cover the cost of servicing funds. As a result, some investors may withdraw their deposits to invest them in a more profitable sector, thereby reducing the amount of funds available for lending.

In an area like the PT, it is difficult to predict the rate of inflation, and the price of a loan should be set at a high level to account for any possible rise in prices. The following measures can also be employed to minimise interest rate risk.

Mandatory long-term saving and lending

Under this programme, savings take the form of life assurance and pension funds. These arrangements are required by law in many countries where employees make periodic contributions of a percentage of their salaries, while the employer contributes a specific percentage into a pension fund. Savings are entitled to tax relief and the amount saved can be only withdrawn on maturity or as a result of disability.

These savings, whether in the form of life assurance or pension funds, can then be mobilised in the housing sector with specific guidelines laid down by the PNA (Renaud, 1984). Because this arrangement makes both saving and lending compulsory, it may result in a low interest rate. However, the arrangement runs the risk of being perceived as a political measure in the sense that the savers could view it as another form of taxation, while the borrower may consider it a form of state subsidy.

Mortgage-supported securities

Mortgage-supported securities (MSS) consist of *bonds* and *pass-through* instruments. With bonds, the scheduled principal payment is secured by the mortgage collateral. However, under pass-through arrangements, a monthly ownership interest payment is provided from a pool of mortgages. Both investments should be backed up by PNA-insured mortgages.

MSS may attract institutional investors and would reduce geographical and institutional barriers to mortgage lending by investors outside the PT. By attracting a variety of investors to the mortgage market and by integrating the mortgage market into the traditional capital markets, the creation of MSS would ensure a flow of funds to the housing sector and stimulate the economy with little incremental cost to the PNA.

575

The PNA can then provide guarantees for the monthly payment of the principal and interest on securities issued by the private mortgage institutions. The Authority could back these securities by pools of its investments or with guaranteed mortgages. The PNA can even transfer any expected risk to insurance companies [12].

Pass-through securities appeal to pension funds and other institutional investors who do not wish to originate, or to service, mortgage loans themselves. The securities offer a safe and easily marketable investment with a long-term yield and frequent cash inflows coming from the monthly repayment of interest and principal.

Tax-exempt mortgage bonds

The use of tax-exempt securities to finance mortgage lending may attract some support. It has been maintained that programmes of tax-exempt mortgage bonds (TEMB) benefit homebuyers, the local community and the housing industry by making home ownership more affordable to more people. However, the danger is that tax exemption might exact too high a cost from the Treasury and prevent it from undertaking vital projects. In addition, the wrong people would benefit from such an exemption. For this reason, such a scheme should be introduced with strict rules to prevent possible manipulation.

Fixed-interest-rate mortgages

Market interest rates incorporate an inflation premium to compensate lenders for any expected loss in the value of their principal over the period of the life of the credit. Volatile inflation rates make fixed interest rates on long-term loans less attractive. Setting a ceiling for mortgage interest rates may backfire. When interest rates rise above the ceiling for the mortgage interest rate, savers may withdraw their deposits and invest them in unregulated financial instruments.

As a result, setting a ceiling on mortgage lending may weaken the banks' competitive advantage. Banks will compete less effectively for funds in the open market. Consequently, avoiding the use of a mortgage interest rate ceiling ensures that the bank is competing more effectively for funds in the open market to provide a more even flow of funds for home-buyers. As a consequence, the banks' average cost of funds on deposits will reflect changes in market interest rates.

Adjusted-rate mortgages

With adjusted-rate mortgages (ARM), the interest rate charges are not predetermined over the life of a mortgage and vary according to an index of various instruments. The mortgage interest rate is adjusted periodically according to agreed conditions. Any change in the cost of funds is passed to the borrower without putting any burden on the lender. All risk borne by the lender under fixed interest rate mortgage (FIRM) contracts will instead be borne by the borrower under ARM arrangements. The lender will avoid having to predict the interest rate required to assess the correct mortgage price.

Although the borrower can only benefit from the adjusted rate arrangement if the interest rate falls, such instruments tend to be risk averse by emphasising possible increases in interest rate, rather than decreases [13]. To ensure against the possibility of paying a high interest rate during the mortgage term, borrowers may be prepared to pay an extra premium for more certainty. To divide the risk between the lender and the borrower, three important options for restricting changes in the monthly mortgage payment are used:

1) Caps on the percentage change in the interest rate;
2) Caps on the adjustment period for the life of the loan; and
3) A combination of both.

It is possible to cap the monthly payments of the principal, whereas interest rates are not subject to this condition. For example, adjustments in the interest rate should not exceed 1 per cent per year, and the increase should not exceed 5 per cent over the useful life of the mortgage. As usual, no limit is placed on reductions in the interest rate. In addition, adjustments in the interest rate take place every six months, or every year.

Graduated-payment mortgages

A graduated-payment mortgage (GPM) is an adjustment payment mortgage on which the monthly mortgage payment increases according to a predetermined schedule. This arrangement is designed for young families whose income is expected to rise over time.

They start with a low monthly payment to be increased over time. At an early stage, the payment is smaller than that of the interest on the outstanding balance, and the difference is added to the outstanding principal. As the monthly payment increases, it eventually rises above the monthly mortgage interest rate and the extra amount will be used to offset part of the principal. Later payments are substantially higher than the early payments to offset the negative amortisation caused by the low early payments [14].

Although this arrangement protects lenders against any possible rise in interest rates, a sudden increase in rates during the early period of the loan could increase the risks of default.

Price-level adjustment mortgages

If inflation should soar, the mortgage instruments discussed so far, except for ARM, would require high monthly payments in relation to the borrower's income. This so-called *tilt* problem can be minimised by the use of a mortgage adjusted for price levels (PLAM), i.e. one in which the monthly payments of the mortgage are linked to price levels rather than to interest rates. Under this arrangement, the monthly payment would reflect the actual rate of inflation rather than the predicted rate (Buckly, Lipman and Persuad, 1989).

In addition to protecting lenders against unexpected increases in the rate of inflation, this type of mortgage also reduces the initial burden on borrowers. The major difference between ARM and PLAM is that while the former protects lenders against unexpected increases in interest rates regardless of the cause, the latter only protects lenders against increases in interest rate caused by inflation. Thus, ARM provides the lender with better protection against any interest rate risks.

PLAM may face three major obstacles. First, the monthly payment-income ratio of the borrower changes only when the borrower's income changes relative to a particular price index [15]. In this case, using the consumer price index might not reflect the effect of inflation on the borrower's income.

The price index could be replaced by an index of wages or salaries. However, real wages (i.e. wages adjusted for inflation) do not necessarily change in line with the average wage. Because the borrower's income is the concern in this regard, a price index that reflects income would be acceptable. The GNP deflator, rather than a price index associated with a fixed basket of goods (such as the consumer price index) would be more appropriate.

Second, PLAM might cause a liquidity problem because any increase in interest rates will be reflected fully in the cost of deposits. Consequently, *tilt* risk is transferred from borrowers to lenders. However, lenders can resist this problem by introducing *price level adjusted deposits (PLAD)*.

The third problem stems from the fact that both lenders and borrowers are subject to income tax. While the former is subject to the payment of tax, the latter expects tax relief. Moreover, the lender's after-tax income could be less than that required to maintain the purchasing power of the value of the payment. This problem can be dealt with by indexing the mortgage interest and principal payments to the price index and then adjusting for the effect of taxes.

Blocked compensating balance mortgage

Blocked compensating balance mortgages (BCBM) are relevant to those groups which earn irregular incomes, such as farmers and shopkeepers. To minimise the risk of default, lenders ask that this group participates in a BCBM scheme by making what is called a *blocked compensating balance*. This is usually equivalent to the down payment. The lender then offers a 100 per cent loan secured by the value of the property.

The blocked compensating balance will be used as a reserve to cover any irregularities in the periodic payments. Although the borrower earns the market rate interest on the balance, he or she has no access to the balance. The periodic repayments can be made under any of the above-mentioned schemes, i.e. FIRM or ARM.

Tax-exempt financing

Tax-exempt financing of home mortgages could be used to lower the cost of home construction. Under the *pass-through* tax-exempt mortgage, the PNA could issue a tax-exempt bond. Tax-exempt bonds can be sold at a lower interest rate than taxable debts. The PNA can then re-lend the proceeds from the sale of the tax exempt/bonds to investors, housing developers, home buyers or private institutional investors to make them available for the housing sector. This approach results in a substantial saving in housing costs.

In this case, the PNA lends its name to the bond issue to secure the tax exemption. However, the public issue incurs no obligation liability. This sort of mortgage can be made available for those involved in the purchase of multifamily housing and families with moderate incomes. The PNA can set the general guidelines for eligibility in such a scheme (i.e. homebuyers with an annual income less than 6,000 Jordanian dinars (JD) or families with, for example, six members and an income less than JD 10,000).

Portfolio diversification

Interest rate risk can be minimised through *portfolio diversification*. Under this scheme, part of the mortgage loan portfolio is converted into short-term loans and issued to housing developers and material suppliers. The ability, or otherwise, of the lender to issue short-term loans depends on the *gap ratio* [16]. The gap represents the degree of risk associated with the mortgage interest rate (i.e. one minus the gap ratio). Lending capacity also depends on the *sensitivity of the deposits*. While some investors retain their savings regardless of any fluctuations in interest rates (*insensitive deposits*), others tend to withdraw their savings as changes in interest rates occur (*sensitive deposits*).

Effective support facilities

The following support facilities should be introduced to minimise the need for risk management.

1) *An effective legal regulatory system*

   The regulatory system must ensure the continuous development of the housing sector and provide adequate guidelines for an effective housing finance system. Protection of both lenders and borrowers, in terms of risk management, and maintaining the flow of funds to the housing sector should be the ultimate goal of the regulators. Rules need to be tight enough to ensure confidence in the system.

   An effective mechanism needs to be worked out to enforce law through close supervision. Guidelines covering licensing, capital requirements, supervision, staffing and transactions verification and financial disclosure should be spelled out clearly to avoid any financial crises.

2) *Guarantees*

   The PNA may provide guarantees that cover *mortgages* and *deposits.*
   Mortgage Guarantees: The PNA may guarantee the repayment of mortgages for low income groups.
   Deposits Guarantees: To reassure depositors, the PNA may offer guarantees to compensate depositors in case of losses up to a specific percentage of their deposits.

3) *An effective information system*

   A system which gathers information on the borrower's ability to repay his or her loans, including information on personal income, spending, credit history and other factors, should be introduced. Such a system could be sponsored by the private sector's financial institutions with help from the PNA. The system could be linked to those who sponsor the project.

MORTGAGE INSTRUMENTS

There are several mortgage instruments which could be adopted by financial institutions in the PT. They are not mutually exclusive, and one or more could be employed simultaneously. Alternative mortgage instruments are designed to accommodate the needs of residential mortgage borrowers and mortgage lenders. To integrate the mortgage market with the traditional capital market, a variety of mortgage instruments need to be developed.

A successful mortgage instrument is one that attracts borrowers and appeals to investors. These include the following instruments (the applications of the models below are available from the author upon request).

1) *Fixed rate amortising mortgage*
   With a fixed rate amortising mortgage (FRAM), the borrower makes repayments to cover the mortgage interest rate and the principal. The borrower accumulates equity in the property over the useful life of the loan. This guarantees repayment of the debt over the term of the loan.

$$P_R = B_A \, / \, P_{n \rceil} \, I$$

Where:

P_R = Periodic Repayment
B_A = Borrowed Amount

$$P_{n \rceil} I = \sum_{t=1}^{n} 1 / (1+i)$$

i = Interest Rate
t = Period of Time

2) *Graduated-payment mortgage (GPM)*
   This scheme starts with low periodic payments to be increased over time. The difference between the periodic repayment and the effective mortgage interest rate is added to the principal.

3) *Adjusted mortgage rate (AMR)*
   Unlike an FMR, where interest rate risk is borne by the lender, with an AMR the risk is transferred to the borrower. Consequently, the lender can offer an affordable mortgage interest rate. Where the lender divides the risk with the borrower, caps may be put on either the percentage change in the interest rate or on the adjustment period during the life of the loan, or on both. It is possible to cap the monthly repayments of the principal, whereas interest rate payments are not capped.

$$P_R = B_A \, / \, P_{n \rceil}^{a} i^{a}$$

Where:

P_R = Periodic Repayment
B_A = Borrowed Amount

$$P_{n\urcorner}i^a = \sum_{t=1}^{n} 1/ (1+i \pm \blacktriangle i)^t$$

i = Interest Rate

$\blacktriangle$i = Change Increase or decrease) in i.

t = Period of Time

4) *Tax-exempted housing finance*

Under this arrangement, the population would be divided into various income groups. The classification of the income groups must reflect the standard of living in the PT.

Group	Classification	Annual Income	Tax Exemption
	(US$)	(%)	
	Upper A_1	Income>40,000	-0-
High	Middle A_2	30,000<Income≤40,000	10
Income	Low A_3	25,000<Income≤30,000	20
	Upper B_1	20,000<Income≤25,000	50
Middle	Middle B_2	15,000<Income≤20,000	70
Income	Low B3	10,000<Income≤15,000	80
	Upper C_1	5,000<Income≤10,000	95
Low	Middle C_2	2,500<Income≤5,000	100
Income	Low C_3	Income<2,500	Subsidies

Model 1 can then be rearranged to take into consideration a group's income as follows.

$$P_R = B_A/P_{m\urcorner}i - [P_R * T_R * E_R] \ldots$$

Where:

T_R = Income tax rate

E_R = Exempted rate

5) *Step By Step Mortgage (SSM) [17]*

This scheme is suitable for low-income groups undertaking incremental housing construction. The homeowner can start with a service site and a core unit and add to them over time. Financial institutions provide funds for the acquisition of the site and services and for the core of the house. It is then the homeowner's responsibility to decide on future additions to the house, for which a loan could be secured.

The loans are either short- or medium-term. Loans given to the homeowner are similar to those provided to housing developers, in the sense that developers also apply for loans as the construction work progresses. The renewal of the loan depends on three main factors: the lender's past experience of the borrower, the borrower's income and the value of the property.

6) *Islamic Banking Instruments*
Islamic banks offer an *ijara* contract which is similar to a mortgage in the West. There are two forms of Islamic mortgage.

- *Ijara (repayment mortgage)*
This instrument provides no option of ownership for the client. The bank purchases the property and lets it to the client for an agreed monthly rent. (This scheme is similar to the mortgage down-payment policy employed by Western financial institutions. However, while rent is charged by the Islamic bank, its counterpart, interest, is charged in the West.)
- *Ijara wa-iktina (endowment mortgage)*
Here the buyer has an option to eventually own a property. (This scheme is similar to the repayment policy employed by financial institutions in the West, with rent payments being replaced by interest payments.)

Before finalising contracts related to *ijara wa-iktina*, specific conditions need to be met. The bank should make sure that the property will not be used for purposes that would violate Islamic law (i.e. producing or selling alcohol, rearing pigs or selling pork, installing or selling gambling machines). In addition, the rent must be defined and pre-agreed to avoid any form of speculation. Furthermore, the mortgage must not be based on any form of interest.

The *ijara wa-iktina* can be operative as *murabaha* or as *musharaka*. With a *murabaha* instrument, the bank purchases the property on behalf of the client and then sells it to the client in instalments at an agreed price over an agreed period of time.

With *musharaka*, the bank agrees to purchase a property which a client cannot afford to buy, but allows it to be used exclusively by the client. The property value is then divided into units to be paid at an agreed monthly rent. The unit is determined by dividing the value of the mortgage by the agreed period of time over which the mortgage is expected to be paid, usually 12 months.

$$U = MV \ / \ [U/n]$$

Where:

U = Unit
MV = Mortgage Value
L = Useful Life of the Mortgage
n = Period of Time (usually 12 months).

In addition to the monthly unit, the client is required to make periodic repayments (usually monthly) made up of investments. The bank invests the monthly unit and shares any profit accruing from these investments with the client. The amount (unit plus profit) will accumulate until it reaches the purchase price of the asset, after which the asset becomes the client's property.

RECOMMENDATIONS

It is evident that the financial sector of the PT is still in its infant stage with little, involvement in housing finance. More work should be done by both the PNA and the financial sector to create and activate a housing finance system. Incentives should be given to the financial sector to involve it more in housing finance. To achieve this, the PNA could undertake the following steps:

1) Introduce an effective regulatory framework which provides protection for both lenders and borrowers;
2) Classify house-buyers into nine main categories according to their level of personal income. The PNA can restrict its involvement to those classified at the bottom of the scale (i.e. the low-income groups) and give a free hand to the private sector to deal with the middle- and high-income groups;
3) The PNA can use the tax regime to reduce the cost of borrowing and to attract more investors to the housing sector;
4) Different housing design standards, local developers and local building materials can be used to reduce the housing unit cost;
5) In order to introduce different housing design standards and develop local building materials, a centre for building construction materials needs to be established; and
6) To protect borrowers, the operations of the financial institutions need to be regulated and scrutinised by an observing body. The qualifications of the managers and their competence in handling housing finance transactions should be emphasised. Regulation should be extended to include financial institutions' credit policy, assets, reserves and the disclosure of specific financial information.

An effective housing finance institution starts with competent management. Management ought to be not only well qualified but also experienced, honest and trustworthy. Any housing finance policy depends on the degree of commitment which managers of the housing financial institutions have towards such a policy. Because the PT have little experience in the housing finance area, training programmes sponsored by outside contributors need to be introduced. Seminars should be arranged regularly to ensure management competency.

The institutions should adopt an intensive advertising campaign to inform borrowers' about their services. Moreover, because the ability of housing finance institutions to provide a wide range of products is also crucial to the success of the institutions themselves, products suitable to various groups in the PT should be introduced. Finally, the housing finance institutions can stay in touch with their customers by establishing a research and development unit to investigate consumer behaviour in response to fluctuations in the economy.

ENDNOTES

1) These statistics were obtained from different sources including: Israeli Central Bureau Statistics, *National Accounts for Judea, Samaria and Gaza District, 1968–1986*; Israeli Central Bureau Statistics, *National Accounts for Judea, Samaria and Gaza District, 1983–1990*; Bank of Israel, Supervisor of Banks, *Annual Statistics of Israeli's Banking System*; Central Bank of Jordan, Annual Report, 1968.

2) See Note 1.

3) This estimate takes into consideration the growing demand for housing supplies among young families, the average annual population growth, the average size of the Palestinian family, the upgrading of refugees camps, the replacement of old housing units, the returnees and the released detainees.

4) After the Israelis and the Palestinians signed the declaration of principles in Oslo in 1993, land prices in some areas went up more than 10 times.

5) Since the recovered costs will be used to produce additional housing units, cost recovery leads to replicability.

6) Since conscription into military service will not be in use in the foreseeable future in the PT, the idea of volunteer work employed by local universities can be generalised to include secondary schools and all national universities to help in constructing the country. New graduates can also be incorporated in the process.

7) This percentage is used as an insurance policy against possible risk. The main thrust of down-payment is to ensure that the property value is higher than the borrowed amount and in case of default the lender can recover the principal. In a case where the borrower has secured job, the lender may be prepared to offer a 100 per cent mortgage. Hence, the value of the down-payment varies among borrowers.

8) The system can increase its lending capacity by connecting it with commercial banks, institutional investors, insurance companies or with some arrangements with the National Authority to issue secured bonds restricted to saving contracts members.

9) Instability in the macroeconomic policy results in high levels of inflation and this will affect the mortgage interest rate.

10) The PT lacks an independent monetary policy and hence macroeconomic policy. In addition, the dependence of the OT's economy on both the Jordanian and the Israeli economies makes it less protected against any inflationary pressures.

11) Since the country does not have its own currency and many currencies are in use, financial institutions should account for possible exchange rate risk.

Political instability is another sort of risk to account for. However, this sort of risk can be insured by some international bodies i.e. the World Bank.

12) The National Authority can introduce effective rules to protect insurance companies and borrowers. Otherwise, insurance companies will be reluctant to take such a risk.

13) It is well recognised, however, that the average income of the individual borrower is likely to increase as the interest rate rises to incorporate premium for expected inflation.

14) To avoid negative amortisation, the monthly payment of the principal needs to be reviewed every 5 years to ensure the payment of the principal at the maturity date of the mortgage.

15) However, inflows from PLAM will only reflect the real inflation rate.

16) Gap ratio equals (short-term assets, minus short-term liabilities, divided by short-term liabilities. Short-term here means the period of time required to adjust the loan interest rate.

17) The same principle can be applied on cases where housing upgrading takes place.

BIBLIOGRAPHY

Abdul Hadi, R., 1994, **Construction and Housing in the West Bank and the Gaza Strip**, United Nations Conference on Trade and Development (UNCTAD), EEDC/SEU/4 (17 October).

Angel, S., 1983, *Upgrading Slum Infrastructure*, **Third World Planning Review**, V, 1, (February), pp. 5–22.

Boleat, M., 1985, **National Housing Finance System: A Comparative Study**, Croom Helm, London.

Buckly, R., B. Lipman and T. Persuad, 1989, **Mortgage Design Under Inflation and Real Wage Uncertainty: The Use of Dual Indexed Instruments**, World Bank Discussion Paper, Washington DC.

Burns, L.S., 1983, *Self-help Housing: Evaluation of Outcomes*, **Urban Studies**, 20, 3 (August), pp. 299–309.

Carmon, N. and T. Gavrieli, 1987, *Improving Housing by Conventional Versus Self-help Methods: Evidence from Israel*, **Urban Studies**, 24, 4 (August), p. 325.

Chin-ho-Chang, 1987, **The Housing Account Model: An Alternative for Low-Income Housing Policy**, Paper presented to the international seminar on 'Income and Housing in Third World Development,' 30 November–4 December, New Delhi, pp. 1–23.

Choguill, C., 1988, *Problems in Providing Low-Income Urban Housing in Bangladesh*, **Habitat International**, 12, 3, pp. 29–39.

Christian, J.W., 1991, *Designing the Housing Finance System*, **Housing Finance International Journal**, Part II (September), pp. 2–26.

Harris, L., 1988, *Money and Finance with Underdeveloped Banking in the Occupied Territories*, ed. G.T. Abed, **The Palestinian Economy: Studies in Development under Prolonged Occupation**, Routledge, New York.

Herbert, J.D., 1979, **Urban Development in the Third World**, Praeger Publishers, New York.

International Monetary Fund, 1994, **International Financial Statistics**, 12 vols., Washington, D.C.

Koenigsberger, O.H., 1983, *The Role of the Planner in a Poor (and in a Not so Poor) Country*, **Habitat International**, 7, 1–2, pp. 49–55.

Lee, M., 1985, *Myths of Affordability*, **Third World Planning Review**, 7, 2, pp. 131–142.

Lee, M., 1990, *The Affordability Criterion: Inefficient, Inequitable and Immoral?*, eds., R. Malkh and N. Peter, **Income and Housing in Third World Development**, Aspect Publishing, London.

Lubell, H., 1984, *Third World Urbanisation and International Assistance*, **Urban Studies**, 21, 1, pp. 113.

Mayo, S.K. and D.J. Gross, 1987, *Sites and Services and Subsidies: The Economic of Law Cost Housing in Developing Countries*, **The World Bank Economic Review**, 1, 2, pp. 320.

McGee, T.G., 1988, *Metropolitan Governments, Urban Planning and the Urban Poor in Asia: Lessons from the Past and Present, Paper presented to the 'Expert Group Meeting on Increasing the Absorptive Capacity* of Metropolitan Economies in Asia,' **UNCRD**, Nagoya, Japan, 11–14 January, p. 19.

Mukhtar, N.A., 1993, *Development Planning and Population Distribution in Libya*, Unpublished M. Phil thesis, UWCC.

Payne, G.K., 1984, **Low Income Housing in the Developing World**, John Wiley and Sons, Chichester, U.K.

Rackodi, C.,1986, *Housing and Urban Development in Lusaka*, Unpublished Ph.D. thesis, UMIST, Manchester, UK.

Rackodi, C.,1991, *Developing Institutional Capacity to Meet Housing of the Urban Poor*, **Cities**, August, pp. 228–243.

Rahman, M.M., 1994, *A Review of Institutional Housing Finance in the Urban Areas of Bangladesh*, **Third World Planning**, February, pp. 71–85.

Raymond, J.S. and M.A. Tuner, 1988, *Creating Housing Finance Strategies in Developing Countries*, **Housing Finance International**, August, pp. 4–13.

Renaud, B., 1984, *Housing and Financial Institutions in Developing Countries*, **International Union of Building Societies and Saving Associations**, Chicago.

The World Bank Report, 1993, *Private Sector Development*, **Developing the Occupied Territories: An Investment in Peace**, 3 (September), Washington, D.C.

Turner, A., ed., 1980, **The Cities of The Poor, Settlement Planning in Developing Countries**, Croom Helm, London.

Turner, J.C., 1968, *Housing Priorities, Settlement Patterns and Urban Development in Modernising Countries*, **Journal of the American Institute of Planners**, 34, pp. 354–363.

Tym, R., 1984, *Finance and Affordability*, ed. G. Payne, **Low Income Housing in the Developing World**, John Wiley and Sons, Chichester, U.K.

Yeung, Y., 1985, *Provision of Urban Services in Asia: The Role of People-Based Mechanisms*, **Regional Development Dialogue**, 6, 2 (Autumn), pp. 48.

587

HOUSING CO-OPERATIVES IN THE WEST BANK AND GAZA

Ishaq Yacoub Al-Qutub

ABSTRACT

Housing co-operatives are socio-economic institutions which play a vital role in servicing middle and limited income social strata and in achieving social welfare and an economic balance in both rural and urban societies. This study analyses the development of co-operative housing in the West Bank and Gaza, the fundamentals on which this type of co-operatives is premised, as well as the role which these co-operatives could play in solving housing problems.

In addition, this paper examines the contribution of housing co-operatives to socio-economic development, including their promotion of public participation and the development of a democratic system and local leadership. It concludes with a series of observations and recommendations regarding the future development of housing co-operatives and the requirements of relevant legislation, government policies, research and administrative structures.

INTRODUCTION

Co-operatives were first established in Palestine during the British mandate in 1920, when labour (for agricultural workers) co-operatives were set up. Arab co-operative activity developed later in several cities and villages, and by 1941 there were a total of 244 co-operatives of various kinds. It should be noted, however, that no housing co-operatives were actually registered during this formative period. In 1948, co-operative activity in Palestine came to a halt with the outbreak of the first Arab-Israeli war.

Despite the fact that Gaza remains one of the most densely populated areas in the world, with a population of 2,100 per square kilometre, not one single housing co-operative existed in Gaza until 1994, although a total of 88 co-operatives of various types did exist in that period. Gaza is faced with several impediments to the development of co-operatives, such as the absence of an adequate sewage system and of portable water, as well as the problem of random and unorganised housing and refugee camps which lack basic essential services.

All these conditions underline the dire need for the introduction of a new experiment in housing co-operatives as an effective tool of development and for addressing the housing crisis and ensuring popular participation in confronting environmental challenges.

As for the West Bank, the first Jordanian law on co-operative work was enacted in 1952 and was later amended in accordance with law 17 for 1956. The *Law on Housing Co-operatives* (No. 42), which was enacted in 1959, regulated the relationship between co-operatives and their membership. Co-operatives of various types in the West Bank reached a total of 858 by 1967, in addition to 250 others of the school type. Many of these co-operatives (of the agricultural, housing, crafts and professional types) ceased to exist in the aftermath of the 1967 Israeli occupation of the West Bank.

The following analysis will examine the qualitative and quantitative development of co-operatives in the West Bank and Gaza within the framework of the general socio-economic understanding of the concept of co-operatives.

CO-OPERATIVES AFTER 1967

A total of 855 co-operatives exist in the West Bank and Gaza combined, with a total membership of 56,000 members (43,000 in the West Bank and 13,000 in Gaza) [1].

A study prepared by Daoud Istanbouli and Adnan Obeidat (1995) revealed the following facts:

1) Of the 855 total, 402 are active co-operatives, and 182 are housing co-operatives;
2) Membership in these co-operatives totals 95,942 members of both sexes;
3) The assets of all co-operatives totalled 4.41 million Jordanian dinars (JD), approximately $8.53 million, with housing co-operatives owning about JD 3.1 million in assets, or approximately $7.27 million, equivalent to one-half of the net assets of co-operatives of all kinds;
4) The assets of co-operatives in general consist of olive oil presses, barley factories, wells and water systems, already built housing, heavy machinery and tools for multiple purposes, generators and electricity networks;
5) The cash flow of these co-operatives amounted to JD 5.17

(approximately $6.7), equivalent to 43 per cent of the net assets, which effectively means that co-operative members subsidise the assets of the co-operative movement;

6) Loans and grants received by the co-operative movement since 1967 can be estimated at JD 2.16 million, approximately $2.8 million, equivalent to 44 per cent of the net assets of co-operatives combined. In other words, co-operatives have contributed a little less than one-half of their net assets. This indicates that conditions under the Israeli occupation have increased the reliance on loans and grants, thus weakening the development and movement of the co-operatives' own resources;

7) The assets of the housing co-operative sector have netted more than 50 per cent of the total assets of the co-operative movement combined;

8) Agricultural co-operatives (productive, service and marketing) constitute more than 35 per cent of the total number of active co-operatives;

9) Housing co-operatives in the West Bank and Gaza constitute approximately 5.12 per cent of the aggregate number of similar co-operatives in the Arab world which have reached a total of 1,459 co-operatives that combine a total membership of approximately 5.1 million. Housing co-operatives in the Arab world have built approximately one million housing units and 2,020 housing projects, in addition to eight tourist villages (Arab Labour Organisation, 1995); and

10) Housing co-operatives in the Arab world constitute approximately 6.5 per cent of the total number of co-operatives of various types.

HOUSING CO-OPERATIVES IN THE WEST BANK

A total of twelve housing co-operatives, or what is equivalent to five per cent of the total number of co-operatives of various types, was registered in the West Bank prior to 1967. Only two co-operatives were able to purchase land for the purpose of building housing units; the co-operative of the Post Office Quarters (1959), which was able to build 40 housing units along the Jerusalem/Ramallah road; and the Jericho Housing Co-operative which managed to build a total of 72 housing units in 1960.

Generally speaking, the co-operative housing sector in the West Bank and Gaza suffered a recession in the post-1967 period as a direct result of the political situation. Sources of income diminished significantly in the period between 1967 and 1978 under Israeli occupation. Housing co-operatives were especially affected by the military occupation policies which combined the application of the Jordanian co-operatives law and the restriction of the freedoms of co-operatives in selecting sites for construction, purchasing land, and building housing units both vertically and horizontally.

The occupation authorities have resorted to a myriad of justifications and excuses for this policy, some relating to the confiscation or designation of certain lands as closed military or agricultural areas, or for the construction of Israeli settlements, of roads leading to them, or of financial institutions (especially in the Jerusalem area).

Other Israeli justifications sought to limit construction activity within current municipal limits or within boundaries amended to accommodate the expansion of settlement activity rather than the needs of the Palestinian population. The Israeli occupation authorities, nevertheless, did initially grant a building permit to the housing project by the co-operative of Jerusalem teachers in Bir Nabala/Jerusalem, only to revoke it later once construction began in 1979 (Obeidat, 1995).

The Beneficiaries

One of the most important events which affected the development of co-operative housing in the West Bank and Gaza was the 1978 Arab Summit in Baghdad which approved a package of financial assistance programmes of which the housing sector was allocated $70 million for housing projects. Consequently, a total of $70.27 million was spent on housing co-operatives, with each co-operative receiving approximately $20,000 on the condition that it was matched by a similar amount of the co-operative's own resources to build collective or individual units, depending on the nature of the project itself.

Residents of Jerusalem received an additional $3,000 to cover costs accruing from licensing fees and other infrastructural expenses. Conditions stipulated by the Joint Jordanian-Palestinian Committee included the availability of a piece of land registered in the name of the loan recipient or in the name of the co-operative and of a construction permit, in addition to the beneficiary of the loan being a permanent resident of the occupied territories and a supporter of a family with a proven capability to repay the loan. The loan itself was dispensed in accordance with the progress of construction. In addition to the above, beneficiaries from housing loans were individuals who met the conditions set forth in Table 1.

It is evident from the table that the financial assistance that accrued to co-operative members amounted to about 36 per cent of the total assistance package, which was valued at $70 million, while co-operatives themselves were allocated 39 per cent of the above amount. The average size of a loan received by a co-operative member stood at $20,000 and $8,170 for those who were not members. The circle of beneficiaries

Table 1 The Distribution of Beneficiaries from Housing Loans According to Areas, Membership and Allocations.

Location	Co-operatives Number of Beneficiaries		Allocations In Thousands	
Jerusalem	299	1,012	1,839	5,400
Ramallah	437	366	2,571	2,278
Bethlehem	63	241	753	1,526
Hebron	118	435	724	2,784
Nablus	285	6,200	1,985	1,358
Tulkarm	35	71	245	463
Jenin	178	56	1,246	361
Jericho	–	113	–	–
Total	1,415	2,500	9,543	14,800

Source: Bseiso, Fouad, 1987. The statistics appeared in **Developmental Affairs**, 1992, p. 20.

expanded to northern areas of the West Bank and south to the Jordan Valley area.

Despite the availability of loans, the process of developing co-operative housing nevertheless lacked the administrative organisation, the proper training on the management of co-operative work, and the co-ordination and complementary with other types of co-operatives and socio-economic institutions in urban areas. Consequently, housing co-operatives in the West Bank and Gaza experienced serious impediments, some relating to membership problems, supervision and following up on procedure with an indifferent Israeli military occupation.

Other obstacles were directly linked to limited financial resources, high land prices and difficulty in obtaining permits from the Israeli authorities to build outside the boundaries of municipalities. Difficulties faced by housing co-operatives were further compounded by a lack of adequate expertise that is needed for the success collective co-operative projects and of local Arab lending institutions (the rate of interest charged by Israeli lending banks stands at about 22 per cent), as well as the inability of borrowers to repay the loan, hence effectively limiting the ability to pump these funds into new projects to secure housing for other sectors of society.

Given that the majority of loans extended by the Joint Jordanian-Palestinian Committee were on individual basis, collective co-operative activity and co-ordination suffered greatly as a result, and so did adherence to appropriate building codes (Adnan Obeidat, 1995). Until 1991, the rate of occupancy of these units reached 56 per cent of all units with complete structures. At the end of 1992, European community member countries announced the allocation of $37 million for the construction of housing co-operatives, which effectively reactivated the registration activity for the establishment housing co-operatives.

The Organisational Structure

Prior to 1967, the organisational structure of housing co-operatives in the West Bank was closely tied to that of sister co-operatives in Jordan, as both Palestinian and Jordanian co-operatives fell under the jurisdiction of the Department of Co-operatives at the Ministry of Social Affairs, and were closely affiliated with the Co-operative Institute and the Audit Bureau. In the post-1967 period, the Israeli occupation authorities took over the supervision of the organisational structure of co-operatives, while allowing these co-operatives to co-ordinate activities with Jordan as far as financing and salaries were concerned. Gradually, however, co-operatives came under closer Israeli supervision from new offices in Nablus, Ramallah, Bethlehem, Hebron and Gaza.

The Israeli occupation authorities, however, prevented the establishment of any other co-operative organisation, such as the general or qualitative co-operatives, while at the same time separating the West Bank and Gaza administratively by placing the individual areas under a civil administration supervised by a military governor. At the same time, the Israeli authorities allowed co-operatives to maintain their registration with the Jordanian authorities.

Organisations related to and affiliated with housing co-operatives, as earlier noted, were multiple prior to the Israeli occupation. After the Israeli occupation, the relationship between these organisations and co-operatives was restricted to direct contacts established by individual co-operatives with donor organisations, both regional and international, American assistance programmes included, in the areas of financing, training or marketing and exchange of information.

On the whole, co-operatives were, however, unable to establish a functional relationship with Arab and non-Arab co-operatives and organisations, with the exception of sporadic invitations to conferences or lectures on co-operative work and activities. The Israeli authorities did, on the other hand, hold a series of lectures and training sessions for the staff of co-operative organisations for the purpose of steering the activities and administrative organisation of these co-operatives in a manner that served Israeli occupation policies.

The Palestinian National Authority (PNA) has completed preparation for legislation on co-operative activity which is based on the establishment of new qualitative unions both at the regional and national levels, as in, for example, co-operatives in the Nablus area establishing a general union for the Nablus region, while regional unions coming together under the umbrella of a general union for housing co-operatives for the entire area of the West Bank and Gaza.

These unions would in turn be subsumed under a larger federation of all co-operatives irrespective of their purpose. Such structural arrangement would consolidate the overall organisational structure of co-operatives, while enhancing a bottom-up popular representation, and allowing housing co-operatives to develop and upscale intra-co-operative co-ordination.

LEGISLATION

Legislation guiding and directing the activities of housing co-operatives in the West Bank and Gaza derives from the Jordanian *Law on Co-operatives* (No. 17) of 1956. The new Palestinian legislation, on the other hand, distinguishes itself from the Jordanian law in that it outlines the duties and commitments of housing co-operatives within the larger framework of legislation on co-operatives in general. Co-operatives of various types are paid special attention in the new Palestinian legislation, while, at the same time, housing co-operatives are allowed to maintain a distinctive character in Palestinian society. The new legislation also gives housing co-operatives a greater opportunity to compete with the private sector on fair grounds, while still maintaining their complete independence.

Until such time that the new Palestinian legislation on co-operatives is issued, housing co-operatives in the West Bank and Gaza will continue to fall under the jurisdiction of the Jordanian *Law on Housing Co-operatives* (No. 42). The projected Palestinian legislation on co-operative activity includes special provisions for the protection of housing co-operatives and their membership, as well as other articles on financial dealings, membership regulations and conditions, rules on leasing and purchasing housing units, and guidelines for administering, expanding and liquidating the assets of housing co-operatives.

The Israeli civil administration authorities have relied throughout the years of occupation on the Jordanian legislation on co-operative activity, and accepted the application by Palestinian co-operatives of the Jordanian law governing the internal organisational activity of co-operatives, even though this legislation varied dramatically from the law governing co-operative activity in Israel. At the same time, however, the Israeli authorities ensured that all Palestinian co-operatives registered and obtained a license from Israel, while limiting their activities, financing and administration in a fashion tailored to fulfil Israeli regulations and objectives that ultimately served Israel's national security.

The legislation on co-operative housing paved the road for treating housing co-operatives as organisations with a distinctive character and special privileges as far as contracting financial and commercial agreements and consolidating ties with other socio-economic institutions on behalf of their membership, both at the national and international levels. Furthermore, the legislation set the guidelines according to which co-operatives could obtain loans from a variety of sources against the mortgage of their own assets and could provide social and economic protection for their members.

At the Arab level, legislation governing the activities of co-operatives varies from one Arab country to another as far as the usage of specific terminology, the administrative structure overseeing the activities of co-operatives, and as far as the tools and means of implementation. All these factors combined control the scope of co-operative activity and transactions, whether with national, Arab or international organisations.

The legal framework governing the activities of co-operatives is of vital importance to the functioning of co-operatives and is necessary for defining group ownership of land, obtaining funding for construction and outlining the rights and obligations of members and financing parties alike. A co-operative should be recognised as a registered institution in order fulfil its obligations toward its members and for members to be legally bound by the rules of the co-operative.

Legislative laws governing the activities of co-operatives include special provisions on the goals and objectives, membership requirements, the rights and obligations of members, funding, means of conducting financial transactions, the rules of accounting and on committees or organisations affiliated with membership.

As far as objectives are concerned, co-operatives usually aim to assist members in securing housing or improving housing units through obtaining loans, encouraging saving, securing technical assistance and searching for suitable land for construction, in addition to providing services and co-operative assistance. Membership requirements stress age, profession, income, and housing and residential needs in a certain location. Usually a co-operative stipulates conditions for the transfer of ownership to new members once construction is completed, as well as guidelines for settling rights in advance of the transfer of ownership to new members.

As far as the rights and duties of members are concerned, the by-laws of co-operatives cover the various aspects of ownership, amount of instalments, retrieval of loans and payment of fees, payments, maintenance, environmental protection, organisation of public facilities relating to housing projects, as well as internal elections and the responsibilities of the board of directors and of the co-operative's sub-committees.

With regard to financing, the by-laws of a co-operative cover rules relating to stock shares, fees, savings, fees for services, interest rates, means and mode of loan repayment, as well as clear provisions on the relationship between the funding and borrowing parties and the co-operative as a responsible party on the one hand, and between the co-operative and its members on the other hand.

FUNDING

Ownership and controls go hand in hand, i.e. member beneficiaries bear the primary responsibility for securing the necessary funding for a co-operative project. The availability of additional sources of funding undoubtedly strengthens a co-operative's ability to organise and conduct its activities. A primary characteristic of co-operative work is the application of the principle of proportionality as far as stock shares owned by members are concerned.

Housing co-operatives provide services to members at cost prices. Co-operatives are only a means to an end and not an end in themselves. Members have the right to decide on the admission of new members into co-operatives and on the sale or lease of their homes. The financial contribution of members is generally directed toward the improvement of services, rather than to secure a return on investment. Co-operatives need funding to carry out day to day activities, such as securing offices and public services, purchasing tools for maintenance, covering operational costs and commercial expenses from salaries, transportation and taxes, and saving for emergency situations (Abrahamsen, 1976).

The extent of interest members take in the success of their co-operative is reflected in the investment in co-operative housing itself, the amount of funds owned by members and the savings or emergency account, as well as the availability of additional funds. Capital could be of two types: an investment type where funding is drawn from membership fees; and an accumulative type where capital is secured through the co-operative's activities themselves such as the provision of services to members at market price, or from the lease of facilities and spaces in housing projects.

The amount of capital drawn from investment could be determined from the contribution of members either through shares or stocks, in addition to membership dues and fees for services provided by the co-operative and to other sources such as borrowing from housing banks or other local or international lending institutions according to specific terms. Studies are currently underway to establish a housing bank in the West Bank and Gaza. Other local lending institutions from whom co-operatives could borrow funds against the mortgage of their assets include The Palestinian Council for Housing and commercial banks which provide banking services and lend money to individuals.

Sources of Funding

Although a multiplicity of sources of funding for co-operatives in the West Bank and Gaza has been available, these sources, nevertheless, have generally lacked the complementary, co-ordination and clear guidelines that are essential for the growth and development of co-operatives.

Some of the primary sources of funding for co-operative housing in the West Bank and Gaza which have already been mentioned were the Joint Jordanian-Palestinian Committee and the Co-operative Organisation. The former provided individual loans on a continuous basis, whereas the latter financed the salaries of the bulk of employees in the co-operative field throughout the occupation years until 1988 when Jordan severed its legal and administrative ties with the West Bank.

As far commercial banks and insurance companies are concerned, their role was generally limited until the 1970s when some banks opened branches in the West Bank. These institutions, however, provided individual loans on a very narrow scale in the light of the difficulty involved in the implementation of the rules of collecting loans and of obtaining guarantees from borrowers for loan repayment.

The Palestinian Housing Council (PHC) was established in 1991 as a non-profit organisation registered in Jerusalem for the purpose of building housing projects in the West Bank and Gaza. The Council received a total of 5,600 competitive applications for 1,400 housing units which were planned upon the receipt of a grant of $80 million from the European Community and the United States Agency for International Development (USAID). The size of these housing projects varies from 30 to 460 units.

The Council favours the establishment of individual co-operatives for each project with a membership that includes all beneficiaries, while an elected board of directors supervises the local affairs of the new housing community in accordance with a signed agreement with the PHC on the payment of monthly instalments, and on the process of buying and leasing the units. The co-operative, furthermore, places conditions for the compliance and co-operation of its members in protecting the environment, securing maintenance, as well as in providing the necessary services for adults and children of both sexes.

Other sources of funding came from organisations such as The Agency for Near East Refugee Assistance (ANERA) and other non-governmental organisations (NGOs) which provide unorganised and sporadic assistance that did not fall within a comprehensive policy nor a set programme.

Additionally, it should be noted that efforts are currently underway by the PNA to establish a housing bank in the West Bank and Gaza along the lines of the Housing Bank in Jordan.

A study by the PHC in 1995 has revealed that 33 housing co-operatives obtained loans from the Joint Jordanian-Palestinian Committee. One-half of these co-operatives were registered in the Ramallah area. Five co-operatives managed to secure loans from a variety of other sources, some European, others Arab and Palestinian or mixed.

From the foregoing, it is evident that sources of funding for co-operative housing have never been organised by any party, nor has there ever been a Palestinian organisation to follow up on and oversee co-operative housing activity. Furthermore, it should be noted that the bulk of assistance received by the co-operative housing sector came as a reaction to deteriorating political conditions in the West Bank and Gaza and in order to counter the Israeli occupation practices and bolster the steadfastness of the Palestinian people in those areas at any cost and by all means possible (Department of Planning and Research, 1995).

CHARACTERISTICS OF CO-OPERATIVE HOUSING

Co-operatives can practice internal restrictions to prevent violations which could take place in relation to an illegal sale of housing units, or the transfer of ownership or lease of units without the prior consent of the board of directors of the housing co-operative.

The chances of a member withdrawing from a co-operative or violating its regulations are greatly reduced as the board of directors becomes more active in securing an atmosphere of harmony and stability, and services to members. Additionally, the co-operative plays a role in securing opportunities for funding from members, housing units, as well as ensuring the repayment of loans, and the maintenance of housing units while minimising the costs of preventive services and operations.

Moreover, the co-operative performs the tasks of administration, drawing up a plan for the growth and development of a project and following up on the day-to-day management of activities. These tasks fall within the larger framework of training members and the board of directors and providing them with the required expertise, skills, and information to administer co-operative affairs in accordance with the co-operative's by-laws.

A main characteristic of co-operative housing is the ability to create local urban communities and to develop a mechanism for self-service and a dynamic for collective work. Co-operatives in themselves need not alter or replace traditional institutions; rather they provide a sense of security and stability as well as social welfare services to the community through joint co-operation in thick and thin, and in social and festive occasions.

Additionally, co-operatives contribute to economic and social development and to the betterment of the socio-economic conditions under which members live through the provision of health, education, employment opportunities and better services for members and their families old and young alike, as well as through catering to members with special needs.

Types of Housing Co-operatives

Generally speaking, there are three different types of housing co-operatives. The first type consists of co-operatives that help members in the purchase or rent of a home of their own by drawing on the latter's savings or on loans, whose responsibility ends when members repay their financial obligations.

Building co-operatives form the second type. These secure land for members and contribute in the construction of housing units, as well as in drawing the design, administration and maintenance of housing units. The activities of the third type of co-operatives are limited to the construction of collective housing units, which are made available to members within the framework of collective housing.

Co-operatives as Socio-Economic Institutions

Co-operatives in themselves could be regarded as distinctive socio-economic institutions which meet the requirements of what constitutes a system. At the same time, however, co-operatives are also both directly and indirectly linked to the community and to the local and national economic systems.

Co-operatives in general have become especially important in the West Bank and Gaza in the aftermath of the Israeli occupation. The sharp increase in land prices and construction costs, the increasing difficulty in transportation between the various areas, the sharp discrepancy in the levels of income of the various socio-economic classes, the stringent Israeli policy in granting housing permits and the strangulation of individual construction initiatives and projects have all resulted in a stronger dependence on co-operative housing projects as a means to achieve and fulfil social and economic objectives.

From a social perspective, it has traditionally been the case that population groups in the main cities sharing one or similar professions who establish housing co-operatives as a means to secure a degree of social harmony, coexistence and co-operation. These groups work together to build appropriate homes in terms of size, location, infrastructure and facilities, and to determine the desired building code that meets appropriate sanitary conditions and secures a degree of social cohesion and interaction in accordance with the social values commonly accepted by participants. They further attempt to co-operatively achieve a set of security and social controls to regulate the rules of interaction between members of the group and to set a standard for a socially acceptable code of behaviour.

Within this social framework, roles, duties and positions for running a co-operative housing project are set, and so are the fundamentals of decision-making, responsibility and duty sharing as well as the penalties and rewards for the purpose of maintaining the freedom and dynamism of the local community and its cohesion.

The principle of religious, political and racial neutrality in the membership requirements of co-operatives and in the organisation of activities protects members and the social environment against ideological, spiritual and racial strife that could undermine the social fabric and threaten the spirit of neighbourly relations and co-operation. Additionally, the nature of open membership to all those who meet membership conditions is in itself a guarantee for democratic practices and a continued co-operative expansion.

As far as financial issues are concerned, housing co-operatives are special in that they offer members the opportunity to participate in a housing project as owners, founders, and supervisors on the conduct of the purchase and investment, as well as on savings and borrowing, the facilitation of all financial dealings within the framework of instant and long-term reaching collective well being.

The primary function of co-operative housing is to build or secure homes for members. Once this objective is achieved, co-operatives attend to the business of financing loans, taking care of changes and building annexes, in addition to developing services and facilities for members.

Housing co-operatives are registered in accordance with special laws and regulations premised on co-operative principles. The administration of co-operatives is conducted by a board of directors elected by members with common interests on the basis of the one-person one-vote formula, irrespective of stock holdings which ceiling is set by the general secretariat. Additionally, the board oversees the co-operative's financial affairs, from collecting membership dues and increments, savings, as well as investment, savings and distribution of profits on the basis of membership priority, and setting the limits on stock holdings.

As socio-economic institutions, housing co-operatives play an important role in achieving a balance among the rich and the poor, in protecting members against being used by merchants or large establishments, and in making available the tools and instruments needed for construction at an acceptable price and quality on conditions that are in accordance with the goals, aspirations and financial means of the co-operative group. Simultaneously, housing co-operatives form a purchasing and productive power unit, in the sense that they perform marketing, purchasing and productive services for members within the framework of the housing community or related institutions on acceptable terms and conditions.

Housing co-operatives are an effective tool for the formation of small local communities and securing of housing and services for members. Additionally, they play an important role in the development of social relations and economic, recreational and consumer activities and the establishment of an efficient socio-economic system.

Housing co-operatives are also a social system that incorporates a number of families who reach an agreement among themselves to form a local community within the framework of a housing project to satisfy the social and economic needs and services which cannot be individually met and achieved. The real value of co-operatives lies in their ability to realise and absorb the idea and ideology of co-operative ventures which carry socio-economic dimensions.

Furthermore, housing co-operatives contribute to the alleviation of housing problems, as they constitute dynamic social units that are self-administered and with both the capacity and capability to find the means to organise activities and administer day-to-day affairs of members, and to affect their socio-economic and educational environment.

Housing co-operatives protect urban and rural communities alike against social disintegration, the collapse of the social system and relations, as they are established within the framework of a set of laws and regulations that are recognised by the state as an integral part of society that enjoys a distinctive system. This system is interconnected with other socio-economic, spiritual, health, and cultural systems as well as the national and regional environment.

Law and legislation organise the relationship of the individual with the co-operative and that of the co-operative with funding agencies and other societal organisations and bodies. If a co-operative body lacks the understanding for the principles, concepts and values of co-operative work that bind members to the co-operative, the co-operative itself becomes susceptible to internal feuding and abuse of power and position.

CO-OPERATIVE HOUSING IN THE 1990s

There has been an marked increase in the reliance on co-operative housing by many social groups in the West Bank and Gaza, such as engineers, teachers, health care and banking employees, as well as by the employees of the United Nations Refugee and Works Agency (UNRWA) and by other groups with intermediate and limited levels of income, especially at a time when land prices and rents have consistently risen.

The following table illustrates the distribution of housing co-operatives in the West Bank and Gaza according to the size of membership:

The above table indicates that there exists in the West Bank and Gaza a total of 160 housing co-operatives with a membership ranging from 51 to 99 members. Only ten co-operatives have a membership exceeding one hundred. If we assume that a member is the head of a household averaging 6.2 members, then the total number of members in all co-operatives combined can be estimated at over 6,000.

Table 2 The Distribution of Housing Co-operatives According to Size of Membership and Areas.

Number	Jerusalem	Ramallah	Nablus	Jenin	Tulkarm	Hebron	Bethlehem	Total
10–20	10	26	5	2	5	8	6	62
20–30	9	24	7	4	3	6	2	55
30–40	–	8	2	8	5	–	5	28
50–60	2	3	3	2	1	2	2	15
60–80	–	–	1	–	–	3	1	5
80–100	–	1	–	–	–	–	1	2
100–200	–	2	1	2	–	2	1	8
200+	–	–	1	1	–	–	–	2

Source: Palestinian Housing Council.

The above study conducted by the PHC has indicated that there are 54 co-operatives with a membership of from 100 to 200 individuals, while there are 12 co-operatives comprised of 201 to 400 individuals, and 16 others with a membership of 400 to 1,000 members and above [2].

THE INFRASTRUCTURE FOR CO-OPERATIVE HOUSING

Housing co-operatives in the West Bank and Gaza lack the primary infrastructural institutions usually set up within the more comprehensive framework of development. They are rather a response to changing unstable conditions or to an event that necessitate the setting up of housing co-operatives, or a reflection of a policy imposed by the Israeli occupation authorities toward land and housing. They have also been highly dependent on the flow of foreign aid to the occupied territories.

The study conducted by the PHC on housing in the occupied territories has revealed that a total of 56 housing co-operatives has purchased the land on which projects were built, while 26 others have obtained the land through the power of attorney. Nine other co-operatives took possession of the land through a court order against an Israeli military measures to seize the land owned by the co-operative, while four co-operatives leased the land on which the project was constructed.

As for the area of the land owned by housing co-operatives, the study indicated that the land ownership of 38 co-operatives ranged between one and ten dunums, and of 29 others between ten and 20 dunums. The land area owned by 16 other co-operatives ranged between 20 to 40 dunums, while the land holding of four others ranged between 6–10 dunums. These lands are located either within the limits of major cities and municipalities (53 co-operatives), or outside city limits (29 co-operatives), or in villages (9 co-operatives). Seventy-nine housing co-operatives managed to obtain landscaping maps, while seven others failed to obtain these maps.

A total of 67 co-operatives received construction designs, while 19 others could neither obtain the designs nor the landscaping maps until the present. Thirty-five co-operatives managed to obtain building permits from the Israeli military administration, while 46 others received licensing from municipalities headed by civilian representatives of the military authorities.

As far as the nature of the housing project itself, the above study indicated that members of 45 co-operatives opted for separate individual units, while members of 22 others chose a continuous style of housing complexes. Sixteen co-operatives built housing units in four-story apartment buildings, while twelve others decided on five- to six-storey apartment buildings, with only three co-operatives building apartment complexes of seven to ten stories.

Additionally, 28 co-operatives reported that completing housing projects with ten to 40 units, while six others finished from 41 to 80 housing units and above. As for the phases of the construction process, 14 co-operatives managed to lay the foundation stone, while 15 others completed the structure, with nine others fully completing the construction. Thirty-two co-operatives indicated that the number of units occupied by members ranged between one and 40 units.

THE COST OF CONSTRUCTION

Construction costs of housing units is dependent on a number of factors, such as the area of the unit and its market value, as well as the costs of the infrastructure, building technology, the grade of the finishing, the fees of the contractor and the prices of the building material. The above study has indicated that the average cost of the individual unit in the West Bank varies from one area to another, with 13 co-operatives listing the total cost of a housing unit (with an average area of 120 square metres) as ranging between JD 10,000 and JD 20,000, and 28 others putting the average cost at JD 10,000 to JD 20,000. Thirty-four co-operatives estimated the cost of building an independent house at between JD 31,000 and JD 40,000, or above.

Housing co-operatives in the West Bank play a vital role in forming viable local socio-economic communities and in urban development, despite the formidable tasks they have had to face under the conditions of Israeli occupation. It is unlikely that a fundamental change in the progress of co-operatives would be achieved until after the transfer of authority to the Palestinian Authority is completed, and only after the latter begins to exercise its new authorities. Obviously, there is a dire need for lending and funding institutions as well as for the facilitation of procedures related to registration, organisation, administration, training, and the development of relations and activities in local communities.

CONCLUSION AND RECOMMENDATIONS

The future development of housing co-operatives in the cities, municipalities, and villages of the West Bank and Gaza is linked to a number of factors and political, economic and social indictors relating to the beneficiaries from co-operative housing projects, and the new co-operative legislation and its applications.

An analysis of the current and future needs of housing in the West Bank and Gaza requires a compilation of the main socio-economic indicators by which socio-economic figures needed for measuring progress of housing co-operatives could be gauged. Housing co-operatives are economic units that rise, develop and expand successfully only when in accordance with general economic requisites, as well as with the need for social organisation and sound democratic administration.

Co-operative legislation and laws should be responsive to co-operative principles and should determine the duties, rights and obligations of members of the board of directors and the general secretariat. Furthermore, co-operative legislation should outline the social and financial principles which regulate the relationship between co-operatives with other local and regional institutions as well as services rendered to members.

The role housing co-operatives play in urban development is still marginal and could be further enhanced if the proper conditions and means of operation are made available, such as the encouragement by the PNA of such a housing pattern, the availability of land at reasonable prices as well as of lending institution and the technological infrastructure which would enable co-operatives to confront future challenges presented by the peace process.

The importance of housing co-operatives is far more important than ever, as the need to secure proper quality housing at an affordable price intensifies in the wake of attempts to confront the challenges of natural population growth and rising levels of rural migration as well as the influx of thousands of returnees from abroad within the framework of the peace process.

There is a clear demand for several studies and extensive scientific research to lay the required foundations for housing co-operatives and to help them develop their capabilities and contributions, especially in the area of providing proper housing for limited income groups and for developing a healthy environment. There is also a need for future investigation in order to create cohesive local housing communities and to develop a mechanism for self-administration, and projects in which members could contribute their own resources and raise consciousness about co-operative housing and the requirements for its success.

There is also a need for close co-ordination between housing co-operatives and both governmental and non-governmental institutions, local and international alike, in the areas of policy-making on housing and population that contribute to organised urban and rural development within the framework of a planned scheme so that co-operative housing occupies its proper position in the process of urban development. Co-ordination should be in the areas of funding, lending, legislation and the economics of construction as well as the development of productive co-operatives of the service and consumption types which complement the role of housing co-operatives in general.

ENDNOTES

1) A detailed distribution of co-operatives in the West Bank according to socio-economic indicators can be obtained from the author.
2) Further details regarding the membership of co-operatives can be obtained from the author.

BIBLIOGRAPHY

Abrahamsen, M., 1976, **Co-operative Business Enterprise**, McGraw Hill, New York.

Arab Labour Organisation, 1995, *Co-operatives and Development,* **Annual Year Book**, p. 33 (in Arabic).

Bseiso, Fouad, 1992, *Statistics,* **Developmental Affairs**, p. 20.

Department of Planning and Research, 1995, **Current Conditions of Housing Co-operatives in the West Bank**, Palestinian Housing Council, Jerusalem.

Lewin, A.C., 1981, **Housing Co-operatives in Developing Countries: A Manual for Self-Help in Low-Cost Housing Schemes**, John Wiley and Sons, New York.

Obeidat, Adnan, *The Practical Experience of Housing Co-operatives in the Occupied Territories,* **Developmental Affairs**, p. 20.

Preuss, W., 1967, **Co-operation in Israel and the World**, Rubin Mass, Jerusalem.

Qutub, I., 1966, *Impact of Rural Credit and Thrift Co-operative Societies in Jordan: A Study of Three Villages,* Ph.D. Dissertation, Michigan State University, East Lansing, USA.

Roy, E., 1964, **Co-operatives Today and Tomorrow**, The Interstate Printers, Danville, Illinois, USA.

FINANCING PRIVATE HOUSING

Nidal Rashid Sabri

ABSTRACT

This paper aims to increase private investment in housing in the Palestinian Territories (PT). Investment in the private housing sector has increased significantly in the past three years, but still falls far short of meeting the increased demand.

This paper seeks to 1) disclose the economic, financial, legal and other constraints affecting the private housing sector; 2) indicate the size of investments and the role of private business in developing the housing sector; 3) explore the sources of private financing for housing and trends in investment regarding the provision of credit for housing; and 4) analyse the rate of return on various kinds of private housing finance.

Two major recommendations to facilitate investment and the expansion of the private housing sector are made. First, a credit plan is needed for the private sector to increase the supply of housing which is properly priced and in good condition. Second, legal and other problems facing the development of the private housing sector must be resolved.

INTRODUCTION

In most countries, the financing system plays a vital role in housing supply (Fair, 1972) and explains housing marketing equilibrium (Gerber, 1985). In addition, the correlation between the cost of financing and the housing supply is very high (Alrcelus and Melters, 1973). However, the role of the financial system in the developing countries is less important in determining the size of housing supply than in the developed countries: credits to finance housing forms 85 per cent of the total investment in the housing sectors of developed countries compared to 16 per cent in the developing countries (Buckley, 1994). This paper seeks to analyse the financing aspects of private housing and the major features of this sector in the PT in order to find ways of increasing the supply of private housing.

There needs to be an investigation of the best ways to increase the supply of private housing and to encourage speculative builders and investors to invest in it. In addition, it is important to determine whether housing shortages are related mainly to a lack of existing financing instruments, or are caused by other related obstacles. Various studies (Sabri, 1991 and 1995 a and Biasucci, 1992) indicated that financing is part of the problem of housing shortages.

ISSUES: PRIVATE HOUSING FINANCE

Financial Obstacles

The major features and shortcomings of the private housing sector in the PT are as follows:

- The cost of building housing according to the traditional ways of building in Palestine is very high. A substantial share of residential private housing consists of luxury units. About 45 per cent of the housing units in the West Bank are built of stone. which costs far more than houses built of concrete or blocks (ICBS, 1993). The average size of a housing unit built in the PT is increasing (from 120 square metres on average during the period from 1968 to 1990 to 140 square metres in 1992);
- The area used to build on a lot is 500 square metres compared to 96 square metres – the median for ten other similar countries. The average cost per square metre is about $300 compared to $212 – the median for ten other similar countries (World Bank, 1994). This situation decreases the rate of return in case of renting or reselling housing units; and
- The decreasing number of speculators who build for renting. The rent control, or protection of renter, law prevents owners from increasing the rent regardless of the inflation rate and this has led to a decrease in the number of speculators who build for family rentals. The size of rental units in the PT is less than ten other similar countries, such as Jordan, Turkey, Chile, Poland, Mexico, Malaysia, Tunisia and Algeria (World Bank, 1994). In addition, the proportion of rented units in Gaza has decreased from 6.4 per cent of the total in 1981 to 2.1 per cent in 1992 and from 13.5 per cent to 10.2 per cent in the West Bank during the same period (ICBS, 1993).

Other legal, administrative and general obstacles which impede the improvement of housing are the following:

1) The lack of laws or tax policies to encourage or support investment in housing (like the measures which exist in the developed and unde-

veloped countries to help low-income families) in the PT (Segal and Bird, 1988);

2) The limited areas allocated for building housing in cities and villages;

3) The difficulty of obtaining licenses for building outside the cities unless approved by the military authority;

4) Problems in transferring ownership and registering land and problems in registering an apartment (Sabri, 1991); and

5) The lack of planning and the shortages of public utilities, including limited resources of water, electricity, public safety services and sewerage (Abu-Eisheh, 1994).

Increased housing expenditure in Palestinian family budgets is another problem. Despite the fact that the majority of the Palestinians live in houses which they own, rather than in rented houses, the average cost of housing is high. A recent study indicated that the average non-refugee family spends about 7.2 per cent of its total budget on housing. Including families living in owned and rented houses, this ratio increases to 18.2 per cent when utilities such as light, fuel and water are considered. In addition, families who reside in rented houses in the main cities spend on average 20 per cent to 35 per cent of their budgets on housing (Sabri and Jabr, 1992).

Yet another obstacle stems from the minimal contribution of the public sector to private housing. There were no contributions whatsoever from either central and/or local (municipalities) budgets to private housing during the period from 1967 to 1994 (Sabri, 1995 b). However, there was a limited contribution from other public parties. These included the following:

1) In 1993, the European Commission allocated a grant of $50 million to support housing through the Palestinian Housing Council (PHC). The project aims to build 1,000 multi-family units in the urban areas;

2) The United Nations Relief and Works Agency (UNRWA) contributed a very limited amount during the period 1967 to 1992. UNRWA is responsible for the housing sector inside refugee camps. It increased from 1970 to 1994 by just 15 per cent, while the population of refugees increased by more than 100 per cent. Only an average of $250,000 a year was allocated to improve existing housing in the refugee camps (UNRWA, 1970 to 1992);

3) The Islamic *Waqf* department allocated an annual budget for private co-operative and commercial housing totalling $1 million to $2 million during the period 1968 to 1992;

4) The Jordanian-Palestinian Committee offered a loan of $20,000 for each of the 1,400 members of 42 co-operative housing societies, located primarily in the district of Ramallah, through the Jordanian

608

co-operative bank (HABITAT, 1987). However, 70 per cent of the units cost between $45,000 and $75,000;

5) Accordingly, the loans contributed to just 30 per cent – on average – of the total co-operative housing unit costs. In some co-operatives, the ratio was only about 10 to 15 per cent. Because of this, the majority of these co-operative housing units have not yet been completed; and

6) Another 2,159 loans of $20,000 each were granted to individuals directly by the Jordanian-Palestinian Joint Committee. This bought the total amount distributed to co-operatives and individuals to $66 million during the period 1979 to 1985 (Jordanian-Palestinian Joint Committee, 1987).

The Role of the Financial System

The official financial system has played no role in housing investment in the PT to date. Twenty-seven branches which had operated in the territories were closed after the Israeli occupation authorities in 1967. Until 1986, when the military authorities allowed the Cairo-Amman Bank in the West Bank to re-open, there were no commercial banks other than the Palestine Bank in Gaza.

Specialised housing institutions do not exist, while the six newly re-opened commercial banks operate under severe restrictions. In the past, these have included limits on the volume of deposits accepted from customers; limits on capital/deposit ratios; and certain requirements regarding the transfer of funds to the Bank of Israel where they must be deposited without any interest (Jabr, 1993).

Mutual funds (unit trusts), investment companies and real estate investment trusts do not operate in the PT; nor are there any financial intermediaries. There is also no correlation between interest rates and the supply of housing, such as exists in the developed countries.

Although the PT in 1989 had a Gross National Product (GNP) of about $2.5 million, a Gross Domestic Product (GDP) of about $1.55 million and total consumption of about $2.1 million as in 1989 (Sabri, 1995 b), the existing commercial banks offered only about $65 million in short-term credit between 1986 and April, 1995. Of this amount, not one long-term loan had been issued to finance a housing project by April, 1995.

Table 1 presents a summary of the present commercial bank credit operations, based on data collected by the author. It indicates that most credit was granted for an average of 18 months, primarily for commercial and personal reasons. The interest rate was between 9 per cent and 13 per cent in the case of Jordanian dinars (JD) and between 21 per cent and 24 per cent for New Israeli Shekels (NIS).

As far as the unofficial financial system (including money changers, for

Table 1 Summary of Banking Credit in the PT 1986 to April, 1995.

Banks	Interest Rates (%)	Maximum Credit Period	Purposes	Total Credi	Investment in housing
Arab Bank	–	20 Months	Personal & Commercial		Nil
Amman-Cairo Bank	–	48 Months	Personal & Commercial		Nil
Jordan Bank	–	20 Months	Personal & Commercial		Nil
Ottoman Bank	–	N/A			Nil
Gulf Bank	–	36 Months	Personal & Commercial		Nil
Palestine Bank	–	N/A			
Commercial Palestine Bank	–	24 Months	Personal & Commercial		Nil
Total Credit Granted by Banks 1986–1994	JD 9–13 NIS 21–24 $8–11	20 to 48 months	Personal & Commercial	$65 Million	Nil

JD = Jordanian dinars; NIS = New Israeli shekels; $ = US dollars.
Source: Data Collected by the Author. N/A = Not Available.

example) is concerned, no long-term loans have been granted for housing, except for a few which were based on personal connections or issued for joint ventures. Altogether, the credit system in the PT contributed about 1 per cent of the total private investment in housing during the period from 1967 to 1995. This consisted of about $115 million offered by both the Joint Committee and the PHC, rather than by any professional financial body.

Private Investment

Investment in private housing in the PT during the period from 1971 to 1994 was acceptable by international standards except between 1967 and 1972 and between 1987 to 1990 (the years of the *Intifada*) despite the non-existence of financing instruments. This may be related to the following reasons:

1) The contribution of Palestinians working outside the PT (i.e. in the Arabian Gulf and USA). Most investment in private housing and commercial building complexes came from transfers made by Palestinians. These formed 80 per cent of the investments in commercial housing between 1989 to 1994, according to the author's estimate;

2) For local residents building a house is the safest venture during occu-

Table 2 Investments in Housing 1968 to 1994.

Years	Annual Building ('000 square metres)	Average Cost per square metres ($)	Values thousand ($)
1968	35.3	45	1,590
1970	110.0	60	6,600
1972	242.9	90	21,860
1974	477.3	115	54,890
1978	896.8	140	125,550
1980	1,041.6	150	156,240
1982	1,063.2	160	170,110
1984	978.1	190	185,840
1986	1,131.4	230	260,220
1987	1,180.2	250	295,050
1988	1,010.0	260	262,600
1989	1,100.0	260	286,000
1991	1,200.0	290	348,000
1992	1,610.0	295	474,950
1993	2,020.0	300	606,000
1994	2,260.0	310	678,000

Sources: Calculated by author based on ICBS, 1970–1994; Data collected concerning the years 1988 to 1994.

pation, curfews and sieges. The price of property is always increasing, therefore it is the best investment because the value of the property appreciates;
3) Given the lack of banks and financial institutions, building a house becomes a way of saving and sometimes is the only investment opportunity a Palestinian may have; and
4) Taxes, including the property and education taxes imposed by the municipalities on housing, are moderate, except in East Jerusalem.

As a result, the Palestinians living inside and outside the PT continued to invest in the private housing sector during the period, but to a differing extent (See Table 2). After 1992, it increased dramatically.

Table 3, based on records from Al-Bireh municipality for the last eight years, indicates the extent of this rapid increase during the last four years. It shows that the average building of private housing increased four times in the period from 1987 to 1990 to the period 1991 to 1994. It increased from 5,974 square metres in 1987 to 80,452 square metres in 1992 and then to 153,545 square metres in 1994.

Of the total built housing, 99 per cent is related to private family and/ or business purposes. Commercial housing (for business and industrial purposes) formed 8 per cent of the total investment in housing during the period 1992 to 1994. The total investment in private housing amounted to $45 million in 1994 in Al-Bireh city alone.

Table 3 Annual Housing Building in Al-Bireh Municipality.

Years	Total	Family Housing	Commercial	Public
1994	153,545	141,950	11,488	107
1993	106,967	95,628	10,145	1,194
1992	80,542	73,770	5,591	1,187
1991	39,640			
1990	29,697			
1989	24,456		–N/A–	
1988	26,467			
1987	5,974			

Source: Collected data from the records of Al-Bireh municipality, January, 1995.
N/A = Not Available.

OPTIONS: SOURCES OF INVESTMENTS

The private supply of housing units in the PT results from the following factors:

- Households which arrange the construction of family housing units for their own use. This category represents the largest supply of housing units in the PT;
- Households which arrange the construction of their own family housing units to rent them for temporary periods, to be used later on by a member of their families;
- Households and speculative builders who build single and multi-family units to be rented as an investment project. These groups work only in the major cities, not in villages or refugees camps. Only 2 per cent of total private housing units in Gaza and 10 per cent of the total housing in West Bank were rented in 1992. The total investment in rented private housing units in the PT was estimated to be $150 million in 1992. According to the author's calculations, this would represent annual gross revenues of about $7.2 million in the West Bank and $500,000 in Gaza;
- Members who are organised in co-operatives to build their own houses;
- Other public and non-profit parties such as UNRWA and the PHC; and
- Speculators who build multi-family units for reselling.

Table 4 summarises the sources of housing investment and the major type of housing projects and purposes of each source from 1968 to 1995. Individuals and companies are the two most important categories of contributors to housing investment.

Table 4 Sources of Private Housing Investments 1968 to 1995.

Initiators	Sources of Funds	Purposes
Households construct their own family housing units to rent	Private local savings	Family and commercial housing
	Transfers from individuals abroad	
Households construct their own family housing units to live in	Private local savings	Private family units
	Transfers from individuals abroad	
Building their own housing through co-operative projects	Credit granted from the Joint Committee	Private family Co-operative housing
	Private local savings	
Speculator builders build multi-family housing units for selling cash or on instalments.	Collected advanced Instalments from customers	Multi-housing family units
	Invested capital	
Public contributions	UNRWA Investments	Refugees housing
	EC through National Housing Council	Private family housing
	Al-Waqf Investments	Commercial housing

Source: Collected data compiled by the author.

Individuals

Individuals may build their housing to live in, to rent for temporary periods, or as an investment project for permanent rent using their own savings collected locally or through transfers from abroad. In the absence of a financial system to support house building, the only way of financing private investment is through private savings, either those of existing residents or of Palestinians living abroad.

Accordingly, the size of newly added housing units is correlated to the total private savings of Palestinians in both the PT and abroad. The rate of saving, and the amount of money held by residents in the PT, is low compared to the levels which prevail in other economies with a similar level of development (Harris, 1988).

This is due to the fact that many Palestinian residents hold their saving outside the PT – in Jordan and in the West, for example. However, the situation has changed since 1994, when it was estimated that $100 million had been deposited by Palestinians in newly re-opened banks in the PT. There is still no exact figure concerning the marginal propensity to save (MPS), a figure which is needed to estimate the amount of potential savings. Some estimates ranged between 15 per cent and 28.3 per cent

613

of GDP, including transferred savings from abroad (Sadler, Kazi, and Jabr, 1984; UNCTAD, 1989).

The official data indicates that total private investment was about $475 million in 1987. It was estimated at much less by Harris' study – about $50 million in 1987, $54 million in 1988, and $57 million in 1989 (ICBS, 1990 and Harris, 1988). The savings fund is the only main source available at present to finance housing. While this does not mean that all investments are directed to the housing sector, this is the only way for families who are looking for affordable houses.

Companies

The second most important category of contributors to private housing investment consists of companies which build houses for rent or for sale. There are many new speculative property firms which have started to build multi-housing units for rent or for sale to individuals for cash or for instalment payments. There are three types of such businesses:

- speculative corporations which work in various business activities in addition to developing and/or building multi-housing units;
- joint-venture firms; and
- private and public corporations which are established and work exclusively to build for renting and/or selling family housing units.

Concerning the general business corporations, there are few corporations which deal with land and housing as a matter of extra-business activities, and/or as a way of investing their retained earnings. One example is the Massayf company in Ramallah, which built three commercial buildings for rent, and one single housing project for selling which included 30 units. All the units were sold for about $100,000. The company's total assets were $1,894,500; its capital amounted to $1,482,600 (Massayf, 1991).

The second type of housing firm is the joint-venture firm which usually begins by carrying out a special project such as multi-housing units. They are organised as partnerships between groups of speculators, such as contractors, civil engineers and investors. Some of these firms engage in only one project, while others may continue in the business but not on a continuous basis. The number of these firms is now increasing. The average housing units per project ranged between eight and 30.

The third type of housing firm is the corporation which works exclusively as a developer and/or a builder of housing projects. The number of corporations working on housing projects exclusively had increased to more than 25 by April, 1995. Most of these are private corporations with a capital of around $1 million or less. The number of housing units built ranged from 10 to 50 a year. The housing corporations are concerned

Table 5 Balance Sheet of An Average Corporation Working in Building
Housing for Sale 1994.

Assets	Ratio (%)	Liabilities	Ratio (%)
Cash and Bank	6	Accounts Payable	12
Accounts Receivable (Instalments)	14	Other Accounts	2
Construction & lands	64	Receivable Amounts in Advanced	45
Fixed Cost	9	Reserves	11
Other Accounts	7	Capital	30
Total Assets	100	Total Capital and Liabilities	100

Source: Data collected from some housing corporations.

primarily with luxury projects to sell because their target is high income
buyers who can pay a large down payment.

Table 5 analyses the financial position of a model for such corporations
and presents the assets and liabilities of an average housing corporation
based on data collected by the author from various corporations.
Table 5 shows that buildings and land form about 64 per cent of total
assets, while account receivables form only 14 per cent of the total. This
means that the credit granted to customers is less than the advance
payments collected, which form about 45 per cent of total liabilities.

The balance sheet shows no long-term loans, and operations are
financed from the capital, reserves and advance payments from customers. Only a very small part of credit is granted from suppliers of
building materials, not from banks. The housing corporations may use
only overdrafts on their current accounts, which forms the maximum
extent of commercial bank involvement in the housing sector in the PT.

The primary sources of finance for operating housing projects in most
of these corporations comes from the payments advanced by buyers,
which are usually collected one year before starting the project. This is
known as selling on maps, which means that the customers finance the
project, not the corporation, and the housing corporation acts as little
more than an organiser who invests the funds of the registered buyers,
using the owner's share as working capital. The down payments range
from 30 to 80 per cent, the higher down payment the lower the selling
price will be. The monthly instalments are distributed from two to six
years maximum.

The future instalments are covered and financed from the down
payment collected for other new projects. Table 6 presents an example
of an instalment system used by housing corporations in the first half of
the 1990s.

Table 6 An Instalment System for Housing Corporations 1990 to 1994.

Years	Selling Price per Apartment 100–130 square metres	131–160 square metres	Maximum Period of Instalments	Down Payments ($)
1990	53,000	60,000	1–2 Years	15,000
1991	61,000	65,000	2–4	20,000
1992	65,000	72,000	2–4	25,000
1993	68,000	85,000	2–5	30,000
1994	75,000	100,000	2–6	40,000

Source: Average actual prices of sold apartments in selected projects in the West Bank.

Financial Analysis

The above findings indicate that the major sources of finance for housing are local savings and transfers from abroad and the smaller funds provided by speculators working as joint ventures and corporations. The commercial banking system is not involved. However, these sources are far from matching the increasing demand for family housing units. The issue here is to determine the best way to encourage other speculators and companies to contribute more in this regard. However, neither group can be expected to enter the business of house building without assurances of a reasonable rate of return on their investments.

An examination of the profitability of the main business sectors working in private housing is needed to guide new investors toward such activities. These include those sectors of private housing where profit is sought through renting or selling a single or multi-unit and covers housing units for rent, commercial buildings for rent and housing units for sale.

Housing Units for Rent

In order to determine the rate of return for renting family housing units in the PT, the following elements need to be assessed.

- *The cost of building a housing unit:* this increased by 400 per cent between 1967 to 1994. This means that there is an increase of 15 per cent annually on average. The cost of a unit in the PT is three times higher, compared to the average in the ten other similar countries mentioned above. In addition, because of the political situation, the time needed to finish building a housing unit is 30 per cent longer than the average time in the ten similar counties (World Bank, 1994). The average cost of construction of an apartment built of stone includes:

Price of land	20%
Maps and licenses expenses	10%
Skeleton – Materials	18%
Skeleton – Labour	7%

| Finishing | 42% |
| Connecting of utilities | 3% |

However, these ratios may be different from one location to another and from one housing project to another. Table 7 shows that the average cost of building a housing unit of 130 square metres ranged from $8,200 in 1966 to $25,000 in 1976, $51,000 in 1991 and $62,000 in 1994.

- *The annual revenues:* the average monthly rent per apartment was about $35 in the West Bank and $30 in Gaza up to 1993 (ICBS, 1993). The average rent of an apartment between 1993 to 1995 increased to $120. By April, 1995. the average rent rate of an apartment in the major cites had reached $200. However, the rent may not increase in line with the inflation rates in the future, due to the protected rent law.

  The high rents now will decrease in real terms after years when they have been rising in line with inflation (Inflation rates were as follows: 1986 – 50 per cent; 1987 and 1988 – 11 per cent; 1989 – 16 per cent; 1990 – 17 per cent; 1991 – 7 per cent; 1992 – 14 per cent). The rent law aims to protect the lessee, rather than the lessor. However, to encourage business activity in rented housing, a law that is balanced between both should be applied.

- *The operation cost and annual taxes:* This includes a property tax rate of 18 per cent of the value of the rent and an annual maintenance cost. It does not include the education tax which is supposed to be paid by the renter. However, in many cases, owners pay the education tax, which is 7 per cent of the rent value. Revenue from rents is not yet subject to income tax.

Based on the above three elements, the annual rate of return on investment in renting family housing units has been calculated and presented in Table 7. It shows that the rate is very low, ranging from 2 to 5.1 per cent during the period from 1966 to 1995. It was less than 5 per cent after 1968, but it has started to increase gradually since 1992.

However, the rate does not include the salvage value of the assets, i.e. the value of the land when the house needs to be rebuilt or renovated. The rate of return for renting housing may be increased significantly if new low-cost construction methods, involving rationalisation processes and repetitive mass production, are adopted (Jabaji, 1985).

Commercial Buildings Including Stores and Offices for Rent

Commercial house building including stores and offices has increased rapidly in the past four years. Commercial rent has advantages over family housing rent: first, it obtains a much higher rate per square metre; second, it includes key money as a lump sum revenue at the beginning

Table 7 Return on Investment (ROI) for Housing Rental Units (1966 to 1994).

Years	Cost[1] per apartment ($)	Annual Rent[2] per apartment ($)	Annual Cost[3] per apartment ($)	Annual net profit[4] ($)	Return on Investment (%)
1966	8,200	540	124	416	5.1
1969	14,200	400	92	308	2.2
1976	25,000	1,300	299	1,001	4.0
1987	42,000	1,600	368	1,232	2.9
1989	43,000	1,700	391	1,311	3.0
1991	51,000	2,000	430	1,570	3.1
1993	56,000	2,800	469	2,331	4.0
1994	62,000	3,400	586	2,814	4.5

1) Cost of construction an apartment, it includes the price of land and licenses expenses and connecting of water and electricity to the unit.
2) It includes property tax rate of 18 per cent of the rent value, and maintenance cost.
3) The annual net profit for renter of an apartment of an average of 130 square metres calculated by deducting rent revenue from annual cost.
4) Calculated by dividing net profit over the cost of construction of the housing unit. The ROI does not include the salvage value.

Source: Data collected and compiled by the author.

of the rent; and third, the cost of construction, especially for finishing, is lower than in family housing.

However, the cost of land for commercial building is much higher because of their locations. Nevertheless, the total cost of commercial building per square metre is lower than that for family housing by about 5 to 15 per cent. The distribution of the costs of a commercial building may be estimated as follows:

Price of land	32%
Maps and licences expenses	11%
Skeleton – Materials	18%
Skeleton – Labour	7%
Finishing	30%
Connection of utilities	2%

Table 8 presents the estimated rate of return for investments in renting commercial buildings from 1966 to 1995. It shows that the average rent per square metre increased from $3 to $15 in the two-year period from 1980 to 1981, to $40 in the period 1989 to 1990 and to $55 by April, 1995.

The data of commercial renting was determined based on the actual average cost and revenues for stores and offices in selected cities. The annual revenues are estimated based on the average rate of renting per

Table 8 Return on Investment (ROI) for Commercial Housing (1966 to 1990).

Years	Cost[1] per square metre ($)	Rent[2] per square metre ($)	Key Money[3] per square metre ($)	Revenue[4] per square metre ($)	R O I per square metre (%)
1966–1967	30	3	–	3	10
1979–1970	45	3	–	3	7
1973–1974	70	6	20	8	11
1976–1977	90	9	40	13	14
1980–1981	110	15	45	19.5	18
1984–1985	130	16	50	21	16
1987–1988	145	16	20	18	12
1989–1990	170	17	40	21	12
1990–1991	200	25	85	33.5	17
1992–1993	250	35	110	46	18
1993–1994	270	50	150	65	24
1994–1995	290	55	200	75	26

1) Average construction cost per square metres including land.
2) Average rent per square metres for a store or an office in the major cities after deducting taxes and maintenance.
3) A lump sum to be collected one time from the renter.
4) Annual revenues = annual rent plus 10% of key money.

Source: Compiled by the author.

square metre plus 10 per cent of the collected key money. The key money is collected once at the beginning of the rent period, and it is generally amortised over ten years as revenues received in advance.

Table 8 also shows that renting commercial housing is now prospering. Returns have ranged between 17 and 26 per cent in the last five years, primarily as a result of the increased key money.

Housing Units for Sale

The experience of building housing for sale is very limited. As a result, many ventures have faced problems and encountered financial losses, while others produced promising returns. The main problem is the increase in raw material prices, in addition to the number of idle days in implementing long-term projects due to the political situation. Moreover, the cost of connecting utilities to large building complexes is high. General expenses, especially for selling and promotion, are also high.

The estimated rate of return on investments in selling housing units is based on several assumptions, including the following:

1) An apartment with an average size of 130 square metres;
2) per cent of the selling price is a down payment and the remainder is to be paid in 24 monthly instalments;

Table 9 Rates of Return On the Sale of an Apartment (130 square metres.)

Year	Price[1] a unit ($)	Cost[2] per unit ($)	General[3] Expenses ($)	Net Profit Per Unit ($)	Invested[4] Capital ($)	Rate of Return[5] (%)
1990	53,000	45,000	3,000	5,000	22,500	22
1991	61,000	51,000	3,400	6,600	27,500	24
1992	65,000	55,000	3,500	6,500	30,000	22
1993	68,000	56,000	3,800	8,200	34,000	24
1994	75,000	62,000	4,000	9,000	37,500	24

1) Based on 35 per cent down payment and 24 instalments to be paid in two years.
2) Includes the price of land and licence expenses and connecting of water and electricity.
3) Include administration and selling expenses of the corporation.
4) Invested capital is 50 per cent of the total operation of a project.
5) Rate of return per project, while the annual rate of return is between 11 per cent to 12 per cent.

3) Costs include land, licence expenses and the cost of water and electricity connections;
4) General expenses include administration and selling expenses of the corporation;
5) Invested capital is 50 per cent of the total cost, with the other 50 per cent covered by buyers' payments and credits granted by suppliers of building materials; and
6) Prices and costs are average and are estimated based on data collected in the last five years from a sample of corporations.

Based on the data collected by the author, Table 9 presents the average estimated rates of return on the sale of housing units during the last five years.

These figures are averages and they change from one project or corporation to another. The rate of return per project ranged from 22 to 24 per cent during the last five years. Because each apartment (as part of the project) needs an average of two years to be completed, the annual rate of return should be divided by two; therefore, the rate of return ranges from 11 to 12 per cent a year.

SUMMARY, CONCLUSION AND RECOMMENDATIONS

The findings of this study may be summarised as follows:

• There has been a significant increase in investment in the private housing sector in the last three years, but the increase falls far short of matching the increased demand for housing which has accompanied the current political settlement and which has raised apartment rents in some cities by 300 per cent in the last two years;

- Credit finances just 1 per cent of private housing in the PT, compared to 86 per cent of total housing investment in the developed countries and 16 per cent in the developing countries;
- No credit has been granted in the form of long-term loans for housing from either official or unofficial financing systems, except for a few cases which were based on personal connections or which were financed through joint ventures; and
- Annual investment in housing has ranged from \$125.55 million in 1978, to \$295.05 million in 1987, to \$474.95 million in 1992 and \$678 million in 1994. This means that investment in housing has increased dramatically since 1992.

The annual rate of return on investment in family housing units to rent is very low, i.e. ranging from 2 to 5.1 per cent during the period from 1966 to 1995. However, this is expected to increase substantially in the next few years.

The annual rate of return for corporations building housing to sell ranges from 11 to 12 per cent. The rate of return of renting commercial housing has ranged from 17 to 26 per cent during the last five years. Both housing sectors are profitable and use the funds collected from instalments paid in advance and from key money collected from commercial renters to finance a substantial share of the construction.

Based on the above findings, two major recommendations may be provided to expand private investment in housing. Because of the failure of the new re-opened commercial banks to play a role in the housing sector, a national credit plan is needed to address the issue of shortages in the housing supply in a serious and comprehensive way. The credit plan should indicate the mechanisms and the procedures to be followed in carrying out special housing projects, either on a commercial or subsidised basis.

The credit plan should be based on accurate data concerning the anticipated level of housing shortages. Its framework would include the following.

1) *Stating the target population.* While the rented commercial housing companies and corporations building luxury housing for sale may finance their activities through allocated capital investments and advanced payments from buyers and renters, individuals building houses to live in for family rentals as well as speculators who plan to build low income housing units to sell, need to be supported financially through the provision of long-term loans with low interest rates.
2) *Sources of funds.* Both commercial and public specialised financial institutions should participate in financing the national housing plan.

3) *Beneficiaries.* These should be middle- and low- income groups, distributed over different districts. However, different groups of individuals and institutions working in the housing sector may need different credit lines and approaches.

4) *Payments and repayments.* A variety of these may be used, including various timetables for the repayment of the interest and the principal on loans.

5) *Financial instruments.* Housing banks, co-operative banks, land development institutes, public and private construction institutions may be used to implement the national plan.

6) *The type of collateral.* This should be stated, such as personal or property guarantees or postponing the registration in case of selling on an instalment basis.

7) *The discount rate and cost of capital.* This needs to be determined for the various financial instruments.

The second recommendation is that other problems which have been reported need to be solved. These deal with reforming the rent law, the property rights system and related laws on taxation to encourage building for low-income families. Other needed reforms concern measures to facilitate the registration of an apartment; to expand the zoned and development areas of cities; to ease procedures for obtaining building licences; to transfer land ownership and to develop and adapt new construction methods for low-cost construction, as well as laws to encourage investment in housing and to remove restrictions imposed on the new commercial banks and on the transfer of funds.

BIBLIOGRAPHY

Abdulhadi, Rami, 1994, **Construction and Housing in the West Bank and Gaza Strip**, United Nations Commission on Trade and Development, Geneva.

Abu-Eisheh, Sameer, 1994, **Public Utilities in the West Bank and Gaza Strip**, United Nations Commission on Trade and Development, October, Geneva.

Abu Kishk, Bakir, 1985, **The Contribution of the Housing Sector to the Economy of the Occupied Territories**, Unpublished paper, United Nations Centre for Human Settlements (HABITAT), p. 13.

Al-Bireh Municipality, 1995, **Official Record**, Unpublished Data, April, Al-Bireh.

Alrcelus, F. and Meltzer, A.H., 1973, *The Markets for Housing and Housing Services*, **Journal of Money, Credit and Banking**, February.

Biasucci, John W., 1983, **Housing Finance Report for the West Bank and Gaza Strip**, Unpublished report, The Co-operative Housing Foundation.

Buckley, Robert M., 1994, Housing Finance in Developing Countries: The Role of Credible Contracts, **Economic Development and Cultural Change**, XLII, 2, January, pp. 317–332.

Fair, R.C., 1972, *Disequilibrium in Housing Models*, **Journal of Finance**, May.

Gerber, S, 1995, *Existence and Description of Housing Market Equilibrium*, **Regional Science and Urban Economics**, XX, pp. 7–56.

United Nations Centre for Human Settlements (HABITAT), 1987, **Study on the Institutions and Instruments Needed for Financing and Implementing a Housing Programme in the Occupied Palestinian Territories**, HS/C/10/3.

Harris, Laurence, 1988, *Money and Finance with Undeveloped Banking in the Occupied Territories*, **The Palestinian Economy**, ed. by George T. Abed, Routledge, New York.

Israeli Central Bureau of Statistics, 1968–1993, **Administrative Territories Statistical Quarterly**, Jerusalem.

Israeli Central Bureau of Statistics, 1968–1993, **Judaea, Samaria and Gaza Area Statistics**, Jerusalem.

Israeli Central Bureau of Statistics, 1972–1994, **Statistical Abstract of Israel, Nos. 23–44**, Jerusalem.

Jabaji, Daud, 1985, **The Applicability of Building System V for Housing Low-Income Groups**, Unpublished paper, United Nations Centre for Human Settlements (HABITAT).

Jabr, M. Hisham, 1993, **Financial and Banking Policies in the Occupied West Bank**, The An-Najah National University Publishing Centre.

Jordanian-Palestinian Joint Committee, 1987, **Financial Statistics**, Technical Bureau, Amman.

Massayf Company of Ramallah, 1991, **Report of the Board of Directors**, Ramallah.

Palestinian Central Bureau of Statistics, 1995, **Survey of Institutions**, Statement No. 1, Unpublished report, April.

Sabri, Nidal Rashid, 1978, **Housing Problems in the West Bank**, Birzeit University and the Union of Engineering Professionals, Birzeit, West Bank.

Sabri, Nidal Rashid, 1991, *Subsidized Housing Channels in the Occupied Palestinian Territories*, **Journal of Palestine Studies**, Spring, pp. 222–224.

Sabri, Nidal Rashid and Jabr, M. Hisham, 1992, *Budget Analysis of a Palestinian Family*, **Arab Studies Quarterly**, Winter, pp. 35–44.

Sabri, Nidal Rashid, 1993, **The Financing Potentialities and Obstacles of Housing in the Occupied Palestinian Territories**, Unpublished manuscript.

Sabri, Nidal Rashid, 1995 a, **Changing the Role of the State in Subsidized Housing: The Case of a Developing Environment**, The Economic Research Forum Publication.

Sabri, Nidal Rashid, 1995 b, **Public Finance in West Bank and the Gaza Strip**, United Nations Commission on Trade and Development, Geneva.

Sadler, P. G. and Abu Kishk, Bakir, 1981, **Human Settlement Problems and Social Dimension in the West Bank and Gaza Strip**, United Nations Commission for Western Asia, Beirut.

Sadler, P. G., Kazi, U. and Jaber, H., 1984, **Survey of Manufacturing Industry in the West Bank and Gaza Strip**, United Nations Industrial Development Organisation, June, Vienna.

Segal, M.A. and Bird, B.M., 1988, *The New Low-Income Housing Credit*, **The Tax Adviser**, July, pp. 507–519.

United Nations Commission for Trade and Development, 1989, **The Palestinian Financial Sector under Israeli Occupation**, New York.

United Nations Relief and Works Agency, 1970 to 1992, **Internal Financial Statements for West Bank and Gaza Strip**, Unpublished reports, Jerusalem.

World Bank, 1994, World Development Report, **Infrastructure for Development**, Oxford University Press, Oxford.

World Bank, *Housing*, 1994, **Developing the Occupied Territories: Infrastructure**, Chapter 7, Washington, D. C.

World Bank, 1994, **Emergency Assistance Programme for the Occupied Territories**, Washington, D. C., April.

HOUSING FINANCE IN JORDAN: SOURCES AND CONSTRAINTS

Magdy Tewfik

ABSTRACT

Prior to 1964, housing finance was almost non-existent in Jordan. A major breakthrough occurred in 1974 when the Housing Bank (HB) was established. Today, the country has well developed institutions to provide finance for housing, including conventional banks, mortgage banks and Islamic financial houses as well as the HB.

The first part of this paper provides an overview of Jordan's housing strategy, its objectives and challenges. The second part examines housing needs and housing delivery systems briefly. Housing finance, eligibility and affordability are discussed in the third part, and this is followed by an investigation of how this is relevant to the West Bank and Gaza. Finally, recommendations are made regarding financial institutions and their operations and actions which could contribute to an expansion of competition in terms of mortgage finance.

INTRODUCTION

The success of any housing project is largely dependent on effective planning and financing. In most cases, limited income households do not possess adequate financial resources to cover the cost of the down payment or the monthly instalments required to purchase a house.

In developing countries, the ability to borrow funds to finance housing investment is a key determinant of whether a family can afford to become a homeowner and whether it occupies a unit of minimal acceptable quality. Formal housing finance has an extremely important role to play in generating housing demand. Without financing, the household must wait to purchase its own home until it has amassed sufficient savings by itself, or obtained a loan from members of the extended family, friends or, less frequently, informal lenders. The problem with these 'auxiliary'

625

sources is that not everyone has access to these sources, and sometimes the cost of funds may be high, particularly when provided by an informal lender (Jordanian Ministry of Planning, 1987d).

However, very few of the developing countries have well-established, formal housing institutions such as those in Jordan and some of the Latin American countries. Economic and political circumstances often lead to the failure of many housing finance systems. High interest rates, soaring inflation, unsafe risks on long-term mortgage loans and awkward financial systems imposed by government programmes leave a narrow margin for the financing institutions, in developing nations, to mobilise adequate resources for housing finance (Bottom, 1989).

It is noteworthy that during the period 1983 to 1988, the World Bank (WB) has contributed generous funds to finance housing projects afford-able to lower income groups in many of the developing countries. In 1988, some $680 million which represented or 34 per cent of the total urban loan was generated by the WB to provide shelter for the urban poor. This amount has much exceeded that which has been contributed to the development of agricultural schemes badly needed in many of the less developed countries. The year 1972 though, marked the first housing project financed and built by the WB (Beckley, 1989). The WB, however, has limited its 'soft loans' to finance part of the on site infrastructure costs for lower income housing in developing countries, and Jordan is one of the recipients.

In response to the rapid changes in urbanisation and demand, substantial achievements in Jordan's housing sector have been carried out during the past two decades by both the private and public sectors. Housing finance through formal institutions has contributed to many housing starts. However, despite this success, there are questions that need to be addressed concerning who actually received formal sector loans and which income groups were favoured, as well as the issue of how the receipt of formal finance interacts with the use of funds from other sources. Yet the phrase, 'a house for each household,' expresses a national objective which the government is striving to achieve.

HOUSING STRATEGY IN JORDAN

The National Housing Strategy (NHS) of Jordan was approved on December 27, 1988. Ironically, the official endorsement has not been complemented with the necessary legislative and constitutional procedures which would have maintained the jurisdictional power of the Strategy. Several major studies were conducted as part of the preparation of the Strategy. These covered: housing delivery systems; residential land analysis; housing vacancies; landlord-tenant legislation; housing finance; land and housing taxation; housing and infrastructure subsidies; rural housing; construction costs and technologies; and the impact of housing on the economy. Twenty-two technical reports have been carefully reviewed by four senior committees representing the relevant private and public sectors to check the validity of the recommendations of the various components of the housing sector.

The NHS has considered the wide range of national development inter-sectoral and sectoral goals for the 1986–1990 National Plan and beyond. It has, simultaneously, developed certain objectives which are capable of being measured and tested through the achievement of policies and investment programmes. The objectives of the NHS are:

- To provide adequate, affordable housing for all income groups with minimum resourse to direct or indirect subsidies;
- To develop a precisely targeted programme for serving the minimum shelter needs of lower income groups through formal and informal channels;
- To improve the efficiency of urban land markets in each major town so that land ceases to be a constraint to lower income households wishing to build the first stage of a complete house;
- To maximise the efficient use of existing capacity in the housing and residential land sector, regarding:

  1) Physical capacity (Government and individual affordability); and
  2) Technical capacity (Public and private sector mechanisms for providing housing).

- To develop a capacity for the substantial delivery of housing based on economic efficiency through private sector initiatives;
- To develop housing investment programmes in the private or public sector which produce maximum benefits to national and local economies;
- To maximise use of indigenous building materials and construction techniques while minimising overall construction costs at each income group level;
- To develop a NHS which can be implemented with a minimum requirement for:

  1) New planning and/or implementing organisations, and for
  2) Controls on land use and construction; and

- To develop a NHS which can be easily modified as the macro-economic situation and/or regional development emphasis changes (Jordanian Ministry of Planning, 1987f).

The NHS has clearly specified that the shortage of housing for low-income groups is basically due to both the lack of land at an affordable price and accessibility to finance. In effect, the Strategy has culminated in three alternatives based on the realities of housing actors' behaviour in Jordan as well as certain future social and economic parameters. The three alternatives can be summarised as follows:

1) *Existing Trends Continued.* In this alternative the past performance of the housing sector and government policies are assumed to be maintained throughout the Plan period 1986–1990 and through 2001. Thus the share for owner-builders dominates at 86 per cent, while developers have 4 per cent, public housing 6 per cent, and the Urban Development Department (UDD) 4 per cent;

2) *Strong Public Housing Programmes.* In this alternative, it is assumed that the government wants to reach the maximum housing unit production levels. To do so, the government should embark on an ambitious public housing programme to build some 6,800 public housing units (i.e. lower cost) annually. It is assumed that policies influencing the private sector should remain unchanged as under alternative 1; and

3) *Guided Private Sector.* This alternative assumes that the government will rely primarily on owner-builders and private housing to produce appropriate, affordable target units in the required numbers (Jordanian Ministry of Planning, 1987f).

Of course, Alternative 3 has been favoured as it involves the reduction of government intervention in housing production. Nevertheless, the NHS has recommended that incentives should be put into place to encourage private developers to implement 'sites and services' and core house type projects for lower income families. A package of incentives could include tax exemptions, lower standards, the possibility of a finer mix of plot sizes permitting cross subsidies, and zoning variances allowing small commercial areas to be included in the project that would make it more profitable.

In order to follow up the strategic recommended policies of the NHS, the Directorate of Housing Planning was established under the umbrella of the Housing and Urban Development Corporation (HUDC). This directorate has been assigned the task of supervising the implementation stages of the Strategy and making the necessary evaluation and review. Notwithstanding its slow implementation, the process has already encountered a number of obstacles. Among these are:

• The Strategy did not include detailed action plans, nor did it provide a workable mechanism for the implementation of its recommendations;
• There is little commitment to the recommended policies of the NHS from the concerned public agencies. They seem to have their reservations and uncertainties, especially in the absence of high level political back up. As far as the Strategy is concerned, very little attention is given by the public sector in terms of co-operation and co-

ordination with the HUDC. Some public officials disregarded the recommendations concerning the provision of land and housing for low-income families on the grounds that such action would adversely affect the urban image and increase the number of slum areas in cities;

• Successive organisational and administrative changes at public housing institutions have occurred. For example, in 1992 the HUDC was created as a quasi-independent entity under the jurisdiction of the Ministry of Public Works and Housing by merging the former UDD and the Housing Corporation (HC), two entities with dissimilar, and often conflicting characters (World Bank, 1994). However, the limited administrative experience and meagre financial resources of the HUDC make it extremely difficult to cope with the Strategy and its implementation policies on the national level (Basbous, 1995);

• Other extraneous factors had adverse effects, including a sharp devaluation of the Jordanian dinar (JD), substantial reductions in the flow of remittances by Jordanians working abroad, and the precipitous decline of the local economy during and after the war between the Allies and Iraq. Moreover, the speculative boom in the construction industry in 1991 exacerbated an already precarious situation by directing resources into a more lucrative area;

• The unprecedented influx of 300,000 returnees from the Gulf states, together with a sharp escalation of building costs, has multiplied the number of low-income households which are unable to enter the housing market. Consequently, the economic crisis has seriously reduced private savings and left no chance for the private sector to be an active producer of appropriate, affordable target units as it was envisaged by Alternative 3 of the NHS; and

• To solve the magnitude problem of housing the low-income families, the Strategy has solely recommended the system of private ownership without considering other alternatives such as rental systems which would appear to be more realistic for the very poor.

HOUSING IN JORDAN

Housing Needs

The quality of housing available to most households in developing countries is a major problem that each of these nations is being forced to address. Nation after nation is trying to find approaches that will yield substantial gains within a few years. Often, however, these efforts are being expended without a complete and realistic definition of the task at hand. This can and does lead to putative solutions which are inappropriate, and extremely costly 'false starts' are sometimes the consequence (Jordanian Ministry of Planning, 1987a).

Housing constitutes the most important sector in the Jordanian economy in terms of its share of gross fixed capital formation (20 to 30 per cent in period 1975–1985). During 1992, residential construction formed about 9 per cent of the gross national product (GNP) (Jordanian Ministry of Planning, 1993). Jordan has the highest proportion of investment in housing among the Arab countries (Al-Tawil, 1992). The housing stock of conventional units consisting of 353,865 units in 1979 has increased to 831,107 units by 1994, making a growth rate of 235 per cent in less than 15 years. However, housing shortages still exist throughout the country, particularly in Amman and Zarqa where the population reached 2.2 million in 1994 (Jordanian Department of Statistics, 1995).

Room overcrowding in sub-standard older units is perhaps the most serious problem and one which will be expensive to remedy. Forty-six per cent of the population is living at two to three persons per room, and 18 per cent at four or more persons per room (Jordanian Ministry of Planning, 1987e). Based on the estimated housing needs and the assumed cost levels and affordability, the total yearly housing investment required to meet targets in the 1993–1997 National Plan would be around JD 150 million (in 1993 prices), of which JD 72.5 million would be needed to provide new units, upgrading and replacement of old ones in Amman (ESCWA, 1993). On the other hand, some 68 per cent of the estimated annual housing investment is required by lower income groups, who still have limited access to finance and credit facilities that would enable them to build their own houses (Al-Tawil, 1992).

The main issues facing the supply of housing can be summarised as follows:

- The escalation of construction costs *vis-a-vis* the regular income particularly of low income families;
- A shortage of access to finance and credit facilities that can be more affordable for households with median incomes and below (Jordanian Ministry of Planning, 1987c);
- A lack of reliable data on the existing housing situation which is essential for analysis and evaluation;
- The high cost of land in urban areas remains a major barrier to many low- and moderate-income families, preventing them from obtaining a legal and affordable plot on which to build. The share for land in urban areas is generally around 40 per cent of the total cost of a housing unit. In contrast, the cost of land in rural areas is not a major factor in total housing costs; and
- Large deficits accrue from inefficient zoning policies and under-utilisation of the available infrastructure in urban areas. Diseconomy is mainly attributable to the random expansion of municipal master plan areas and the large proportion of serviced urban land which continues

to be vacant (Tewfik, 1989). Much urban housing has taken the form of sprawling, scattered developments on large plots. This has resulted in excessive infrastructure costs and a shortage of affordable housing for low-income groups.

Housing Delivery Systems

The housing delivery systems in Jordan is essentially characterised by private sector and individual housing construction. An estimated 108,000 housing units were built during the period from 1980 to 1985 at a rate of 18,000 units per year. Of this total, 11,200 units, or 10.4 per cent, were built by the public sector, 1.9 per cent by co-operatives and 2 per cent by corporate real estate developers. The remainder, 87.7 per cent, were built by small scale contractor/developers and individual owner-builders.

Based on the results from the 1986 National Housing Survey and other available data, it is estimated that 67,350 housing units were built in Greater Amman and other urban areas during the period from 1980 to 1985. This formed 62.4 per cent of the total estimated number of units built during the period (Jordanian Ministry of Planning, 1987b).

The public sector plays a limited though important role in providing housing of specific target groups. These include low-income families in both urban and rural areas, government employees, and military personnel. However, for the 1993–1997 National Plan period, it has been estimated that housing needs averaged 25,000 new dwelling units per year to meet the growing demand (Jordanian Ministry of Planning, 1993). Nevertheless, the former (HC), private corporate developers and housing co-operatives are all involved in producing housing for households with median incomes which have been able to build their own dwellings as owner-builders.

HOUSING FINANCE, ELIGIBILITY AND AFFORDABILITY

In Jordan, approximately 50 to 70 per cent of owner occupied houses and apartments in urban areas are inherited or built on previously owned land. This percentage rises to 80 per cent in rural areas. Individual housing construction is financed from a number of sources predominantly from family savings and sales of property and other assets. Whilst, informal finance sources are mainly loans from relatives and/or friends (Jordanian Ministry of Planning, 1987d).

Prior to 1964, housing finance was almost non-existent in Jordan. A major breakthrough occurred in 1974 when the Housing Bank (HB) was established. Now the country has well developed formal housing finance institutions (see Table 1).

Formal finance sources are a heterogeneous lot. However, loans from

Table 1 Institutions and Funds Providing Housing Finance in Jordan 1980–1985.

Institution or Fund	Number of Loans	Loan Amounts (JD)	Number of Units	Average Loan Amount (JD)	Average Units Per Loan	Average Amount of Loan Per Unit (JD)
PUBLIC SECTOR						
Housing Corporation						
• Persons	–	–	–	–	–	–
• Corporation	1,577	19,023,839	1,577	12,063	1.00	12,063
Subtotal	1,577	19,023,839	1,577	12,063	1.00	12,063
Military Housing Corporation						
• Officers housing fund	300	15,410,510	690	51,368	2.30	22,334
• Soldiers housing fund	6,595	19,830,090	6,595	3,007	1.00	3,007
Subtotal	6,895	35,240,600	7,285	5,111	1.06	4,837
Total public sector	8,472	54,264,439	8,862	6,405	1.05	6,123
PRIVATE SECTOR						
Housing Bank	17,081	216,303,878	35,918	12,663	2.10	6,022
Corporate developers						
• REFCO	1,306	22,130,175	1,306	16,945	1.00	16,945
• DARCO	155	1,155,188	115	10,045	1.00	10,045
• ACARCO	59	1,710,000	59	28,983	1.00	28,983
• Islamic Investment House	326	6,334,000	326	19,429	1.00	19,429
Subtotal	1,806	31,329,363	1,806	17,347	1.00	17,347
PRIVATE HOUSING FUNDS						
• Petroleum Refinery Company	107	1,408,240	107	13,161	1.00	13,161
• Jordanian Co-operative Organisation	75	4,200,000	106	56,000	1.41	39,623
• Teachers housing funds	378	3,620,974	378	9,579	1.00	9,579
• Jordan University housing	317	3,172,960	317	10,009	1.00	10,009
• Jordan elected employees	198	2,573,256	198	12,996	1.00	12,996
Social Security employees fund	168	1,896,953	168	11,291	1.00	11,291
Subtotal	1,243	16,872,383	1,274	13,574	1.02	13,244
Total private sector	20,130	264,505,624	38,998	13,140	1.94	6,783
Total public and private sector	28,602	318,770,063	47,860	11,145	1.67	6,660

Source: Jordan Ministry of Planning, National Housing Strategy, Technical Memorandum No. 14, February 1987.
Note: The list only includes those funds for which information was available for the number of housing units financed.

banks, financing companies, real estate developers, military housing funds and employees funds play a small role in financing in urban areas and almost none in rural areas. In the case of housing constructed on previously owned land, in urban areas, loans from banks are significant.

The Housing Bank

Being the largest depository institution in Jordan, the HB generates the largest amount of loanable funds (JD 816.9 million deposits at end 1994), with branch offices throughout the country. Since its establishment, the Bank contributed to over 129,000 housing starts with a total built area of 18.1 million square metres. The HB makes loans for a variety of purposes such as construction or purchase of a new house, expansion or completion of an existing unit, and home maintenance.

The HB's individual loan programme sets a number of conditions and requirements for granting loans. They include one loan per citizen, and applicants should have title to a plot of land, a building licence for a house 200 square metres or less, and a statement of the borrower's income showing a monthly income of JD 375 or less. Loan amounts are limited to 27 times the borrower's monthly income, JD 10,000 or 75 per cent of the cost, whichever is lower. Repayment (in monthly instalments) should not exceed 30 per cent of household income. Loans are granted at a 7 per cent interest rate for a maximum of 15 years (Mahmoud and Akkawi, 1995), as the Bank cannot safely lengthen this period further without violating the rule of an Ottoman Law (*murabaha*).

This law stipulates that interest payments on a loan should not exceed the principal repayments. The HB also operates on a commercial basis and makes loans for middle and higher income families to built houses. It acts as a major instrument of government housing policy through the provision of loans for housing purposes to individuals, real estate agencies and public corporations.

Nevertheless, there are questions that need to be addressed concerning who has actually received formal sector loans. Apart from official pronouncements about lending policies, underwriting standards, and social objectives, what is the profile of recent mortgage borrowers and how does it compare with that for other recent home purchasers? How important is the type of unit proposed for purchase? How does the receipt of formal finance interact with the use of funds from other sources?

Several factors are assumed to be key determinants of who obtains formal financing. These include economic resources (e.g. income and assets), type of employment and occupation, characteristics of the property being purchased, and other sources of funds available to the household. It goes without saying that the higher the level of income the better the household's ability to repay a given loan. However, formal

Table 2 Loans Extended by the Jordan Housing Bank (1974–1994).

Lending Activities	1974–1991 Millions of JD	1992 Millions of JD	1993 Millions of JD	1994 Millions of JD	Total Millions of JD
Housing loans	602.9	92.0	78.7	120.4	894.0
Credit facilities	408.2	63.8	82.8	91.1	645.9
Development loans	194.5	14.3	25.8	25.7	262.0
Total	1205.6	170.1	189.0	237.2	1801.9

Source: Housing Bank, Amman 1995.

institutions are more willing to lend salaried persons, since their incomes are regular, easily verified, and more easily attached if necessary. It is worth mentioning that in rural areas formal financing is by far the weakest compared with any urban location in the country. This reflects in part the low incidence of rural home purchasers obtaining formal finance, which in turn points to the lack of outreach by housing lenders to these areas (Jordanian Ministry of Planning, 1987d).

While the HB appears to have ample funds to lend in total, its emphasis has been moving away from mortgage lending to commercial loans (e.g. to develop tourist facilities, shops and home construction exceeding the individual loan amount), thus providing for only a minority of housing finance for lower income households (see Table 2). On the other hand, government employees and members of the military are no more likely than others to obtain loans from formal sources. This result raises the question of whether the special programmes for these groups which involved substantial subsidy are really allowing more of them to become home owners than might otherwise be the case.

Islamic Financing Institutions

A discussion of the *riba* or usury versus *mudharaba* or risk-sharing in Islamic finance is beyond the scope of this paper (Qutub, 1971 and Al-Qurtubi, 1987). Islamic financing institutions emerged during the 1980s to deal with most banking practices in a manner described as non-usurious, which is rather different from normal banking practice, and is in conformity with Islamic principles. For example, repayments on a loan to purchase a house are made through a system of rental payments which are shared with the bank, or the investment company, on a prorated basis. Depositors, however, receive dividends based on the earnings of the institution.

Given the potential for this form of loan and the possible increase in borrowing according to Islamic banking rules, there would seem to be a good reason for other banks to introduce more competitive terms for such loans while at the same time arranging repayment of loans in conformity with Islam. In Egypt, for example, many banks have extended special branches to deal with customers who favour Islamic banking practices.

The most notable existing example is the Jordan Islamic Bank, which had deposits totalling JD 462 million at the end of 1994. Founded in 1979, it began its housing finance programme in the mid-1980s. The Bank sponsors the construction, selling and financing of housing schemes and provides loans to supply beneficiaries with building materials. The maximum amount of an individual loan is JD 5,000, which is repaid by monthly instalments over a period of five years with a profit rate of 6.5 per cent (Shehadeh, 1989).

However, the Bank can also extend much larger loans, depending on the status of the borrower. Since its establishment, the Bank has contributed to more than 45,138 housing starts with a total investment of JD 138.2 million by the end of 1994 (Shaheen, 1995). The profit on loans issued by Islamic funding institutions is normally higher than those of the banks operating in accordance with conventional banking practices. However, the monthly payments agreed in accordance with Islamic banking practices do not oblige the borrower to bear any additional charge if the repayment is extended for certain reasons beyond the agreed five-year period.

The Relevance of the Jordanian Experience

Unlike the West Bank and Gaza, Jordan is a relatively prosperous country and its housing problems are not as severe as in the Palestinian Territories (PT). Furthermore, Jordan has developed institutions and legislation in the housing field, including mortgage banks, corporate developers, a functioning land registration system, municipal control of building permits and construction inspections.

Following the Israeli occupation, the housing situation constitutes one of the most serious economic and social problems confronting the Palestinian people in the West Bank and Gaza. Housing requirements in the PT have been identified. Some attempts have even been made to estimate projected demand (UNCTAD, 1994). However, a housing strategy, as an integral part of a national economic and social development programme, has not yet been formulated (UNCTAD, 1994).

It can be argued that because Jordanian banks operated branches in the West Bank before the Israeli occupation in 1967 and because of the strong historical and cultural ties existing between the two nations, the continuity of effective economic ties between Jordan and its future neighbouring state could be justified. Similar banking systems and finance mechanisms are expected to be established in liberated Palestine. Some of the Jordanian commercial banks have already re-opened in the main cities of the West Bank, and the HB will soon extend its operations there. The Bank of Palestine and some Egyptian commercial banks are operating in Gaza.

HOUSING FINANCE IN PALESTINE

Under the Israeli occupation, investment in construction sector has generally been private. Traditionally, construction of individual housing units constitutes the bulk of private investment in the West Bank and Gaza, particularly in rural and semi-urban communities.

During the period 1980 to 1987, the contribution of the housing sector to gross domestic capital formation in the PT rose from around $224 million to $360 million, representing an average of around 69 per cent of total gross domestic capital formation. After 1987, the construction sector experienced a sharp decline in output because of Israeli restrictions, the disruption of the socio-economic life of people in the PT and a decline in remittances and private transfers (UNCTAD, 1994).

Owing to the constrained financial situation prevailing is most of the rural communities in the West Bank and urban refugee communities in Gaza, it is common practice to live in buildings which are not completely finished. Additional rooms or entire floors are then completed while the building is in use (UNCTAD, 1994). Isolated 'pillars of hope' have been built on rooftops of buildings awaiting the completion of an additional floor, forming a common urban feature in towns and villages of the PT.

During the period from 1979 to 1986, the Joint Palestinian–Jordanian Committee extended 2,762 individual housing loans totalling about $47.5 million. The West Bank received 2,500 individual housing loans and Gaza the remaining 262 (UNCTAD, 1994). Other sources involved in housing delivery include real estate development companies, local business developers, housing co-operatives and professional associations funds. Unfortunately, most of these contributors are poorly equipped to engage in effective housing.

Since 1967, the absence of formal Palestinian credit facilities, coupled with Israeli restrictions on land use and the confiscation of lands owned by Arabs in the PT has imposed major constraints on development activities in general, and housing in particular. This situation was partially addressed through the housing loan programme implemented by the Joint Committee during the period from 1979 to 1986, as mentioned above. Despite the reopening of some Jordanian commercial banks in 1986, there has been no finance, credit or mortgage facilities for housing.

Israeli banks offer prohibitive credit programmes to Palestinians in Jerusalem. The absence of local Palestinian financial institutions, capable of extending credit for housing purposes, continues to represent a major obstacle to the development of the construction and housing sector, especially for low-income community groups (UNCTAD, 1994).

However, a recent programme adopted by the Arab Bank encourages Palestinian customers to establish saving accounts for the purchase of new houses. The scheme involves a nominal, fixed, monthly contribution into a homebuyer's savings account. The monthly instalment is determined on the basis of the monthly income of the prospective homebuyer.

This monthly savings contribution has no upper or lower limit, but an incentive is established to encourage savers to maximise their monthly payments. The savings mechanism operates for a minimum of three years. At any point after this three-year period, the beneficiary is entitled to receive a loan up to three times the amount saved in the homebuyer's savings account. Thus, higher monthly savings contributions will result in a higher three-year savings total and hence a higher loan may be issued to cover, in part or in full, the down-payment cost for a new house. This will also enable the homebuyer to obtain financing for the remaining cost of the new house.

RECOMMENDATIONS AND CONCLUSIONS

In this review of housing finance in Jordan, the following conclusions can be drawn, and recommendations made:

1) The Jordan Central Bank (JCB) regulates the monetary system in the country. This system is conservative and biased toward the HB at the expense of the other banks and financial institutions. This needs to be corrected. Imaginative and innovative thinking in new housing finance mechanisms should be promoted actively to increase loans to households at the lowest end of the income scale. If subsidies are required so that those on lower incomes can afford a basic unit, they should be provided up front. Measures are needed urgently to tighten loopholes and the leakage of subsidies given to non-target households;

2) The Ottoman Law (*murabaha*) should be reconsidered with regard to interest repayment concerning low income borrowers. By extending repayment periods, the payments would be lowered in effect, thus making certain loans more affordable to these families. What is needed is a system whereby the government insures, and if necessary, buys down or subsidises interest rates to mortgage-issuing institutions to make their operating procedures more responsive to lower-income borrowers. However, the NHS has recommended that the government should institute a mortgage default insurance programme (Jordanian Ministry of Planning, 1987d);

3) It is, by all means, not justifiable that the HB remains the only institution in the local market which enjoys privileged incentives from

the government, such as tax advantages and financial guarantees, in recognition of its mandate to assist low-income households. The government should allow other financing institutions to compete with the HB on an equal footing. This would tend to eliminate challenging requirements and provide competitive terms to obtain long-term mortgages or loans from a formal financing source. Banks should also more actively foster the provision of loans for building materials, especially for small owner-builders;

4) Profit on loans charged by Islamic financial institutions should be kept equal to those of the banks operating with conventional banking practices. This might convince more borrowers to benefit from non-usurious financial facilities; and

5) Although it is relatively recent, Jordan's experience in the housing field, should be considered by the PNA. The future state requires the formulation of a workable housing strategy, codes, standards and regulations of housing, and the provision of optimum methods of housing finance in order to cope with the acute shortage of housing in the PT.

BIBLIOGRAPHY

Al-Qurtubi, Abdullah and M.A. Al-Ansari, 1987, **Al-Jami Li-*Ahkam*, Al-Quraan**, Dar Al-Fikr Lil-Tiba'a Wal-Nashr Wal-Tawzie, Beirut, 1st Edition, Part III, pp. 347–376 (in Arabic).

Al-Tawil, Nabil, 1992, *Housing Finance in the ESCWA Region: Institutions and Procedures*, **Proceedings of the Symposium on Low-Cost Housing in the Arab Region**, Sana'a, 24–28 October 1992.

Basbous, Adel, 1995, *Evaluation of the Jordan National Strategy*, Paper presented to the Symposium on the Role of Legislation in Housing Affordability, Amman, 5–6 April 1995 (in Arabic).

Beckley, Robert, 1989, *Global Trends in Housing: Subsidising Credit or Mobilising Savings*, **Proceedings of the Regional Conference on Housing Finance**, Amman, 25–29 June.

Bottom, Dale, 1989, *Global Trends in Housing Finance*, **Proceedings of the Regional Conference on Housing Finance**, Amman, 25–29 June 1989.

Government of Jordan, Department of Statistics, 1995, **Preliminary Results of the Population and Housing Census 1994**, January.

Government of Jordan, Ministry of Planning, 1987a, *Revised Housing Needs and Associated Investment in Jordan, 1986–2006*, **National Housing Strategy**, Technical Memorandum, No. 5, January.

Government of Jordan, Ministry of Planning, 1987b, *Housing Delivery Systems in Jordan*, **National Housing Strategy**, Technical Memorandum, No. 8, February.

Government of Jordan, Ministry of Planning, 1987c, *Housing and Housing Land Affordability*, **National Housing Strategy**, Technical Memorandum No. 13, February.

Government of Jordan, Ministry of Planning, 1987d, *Housing Finance in Jordan*, **National Housing Strategy**, Technical Memorandum No. 14, February.

Government of Jordan, Ministry of Planning, 1987e, *Main Issues,* **National Housing Strategy**, Technical Memorandum No. 20, April.

Government of Jordan, Ministry of Planning, 1987f, *Draft Final Report: Executive Summary,* **National Housing Strategy**.

Government of Jordan, Ministry of Planning, 1993, *Economic and Social Development,* **The National Development Plan 1993–1997**.

Mahmoud, Ezzat and Hussam Akkawi, 1995, *Subsidy Policies in the Housing Sector,* Paper presented to the Symposium on The Role of Legislation in Housing Affordability, Amman, 5–6 April, 1995 (in Arabic).

Qutub, Sayyed, 1971, *Fi Zilal Al-Quraan,* Dar Ihiaa Al-Turath Al-Arabi, Beirut, Part III, 7th Edition, pp. 465–490, (in Arabic).

Shaheen, S., 1995, *The Experience of the Jordan Islamic Bank,* Paper presented to the Symposium on The Role of Legislation in Housing Affordability, Amman, 5–6 April 1995 (in Arabic).

Shehadeh, M.A., 1989, *The Experience of Islamic Banks and Finance Institutions in the Housing Field in Jordan,* **Proceedings of the Regional Conference on Housing Finance**, Amman, 25–29 June.

Tewfik, Magdy, 1989, *Urban Land in Jordan: Issues and Policies,* **Cities**, 6:2, pp. 119–136, May.

The World Bank, 1994. **Project Completion Report: Second Urban Development Project**, Washington D.C., June

United Nations Conference on Trade and Development (UNCTAD), 1994, **Construction and Housing in the West Bank and Gaza**, Study prepared by Rami Abdul Hadi, 17 October.

United Nations, Economic and Social Commission for Western Asia (ESCWA), 1993, *Housing and Basic Services in Rapid Changing Urban Areas: Crisis Housing,* Chapter 3: **Housing Situation in Four Fast Growing Arab Capitals**; Amman, November (in Arabic).

Theme Six

THE CONSTRUCTION INDUSTRY

THE CONSTRUCTION INDUSTRY

Jan Söderberg

ABSTRACT

The construction industry is the tool through which a society achieves its goals of urban and rural development. Obviously, there are many ways of achieving these objectives, and some are more efficient and constructive than others.

The purpose of this paper is to focus attention on the ways and means through which one can achieve these objectives in a manner consistent with a sound economy and at the lowest cost to the consumer. It also looks at ways which would contribute to the technological advancement of Palestine and the development of an export-oriented construction industry.

An overview analyses the construction process, drawing on experience in Sweden. This is followed by a discussion of its advantages and disadvantages and suggestions for improvements.

The main body of the paper examines how the construction process could be developed in Palestine and includes topics such as the cost of construction, forms of procurement, the role of consultants and of contractors, the identification of supplies, the importance of the labour force, codes and standards, information technology and renovation. Finally, it emphasises the importance of research and development and of training.

INTRODUCTION

Palestinians have been committed to construction. It is almost as if being unable to build their own country, they have opted to become involved in construction everywhere else. Palestinians have excelled in many areas of both consulting and contracting. This positive attitude to construction and to engineering is also deeply rooted in the culture of Palestine: witness the enormous range of classical structures that enhance both the urban and rural landscape. Today's Palestinians are keeping faith with their traditions when they promote all aspects of this vital industry.

If building expenditures are spent within a country's national economy, the construction industry can become the locomotive of that country's economy. The multiplier effect determines the extent of self-reliance. When the engineering, labour, materials and equipment are provided from within the local economy, there is an associated multiplier factor of three to four.

At present, Palestinians produce only a limited amount of the inputs required for construction. This is a very serious challenge, and consequently Palestinians must pay very special attention to developing a sustainable economic base for their construction industry. Palestinians need not produce all the inputs which they require, but they must export construction supplies and services to pay for the importation of construction services, equipment and supplies.

The truncated Palestine which is slowly and painfully emerging is too precious to allow the atmosphere to be polluted by burning emissions from cement plants. Furthermore, a technologically dependent cement industry, such as those which exist in Jordan, Syria and the other Arab countries, requires tariff protection to survive economically. This increases the cost of cement for the consumer. Moreover, the return on capital invested in these plants is low. One Arab country which invested $600 million in two cement plants manages to earn only $1 million of profit in a good year. And this is after taxing the population heavily by forcing them to pay high prices for their cement.

Obviously, Palestinians have to identify those products and services which have high value added and for which they have a comparative advantage. Fortunately, there are a number of such products and services which can be considered.

THE CONSTRUCTION PROCESS IN SWEDEN

The construction process is very complicated. A lot of interested parties are involved, including clients, users, designers, officials, contractors, suppliers and others. The design of the product takes place far away from the building site. The distance is both geographically and mentally very great.

In addition, the various designers involved (such as architects, structural engineers and others) mostly work in separate offices. Meanwhile, those involved in production are normally not involved in the design. The same applies to those who manage the facility, such as real estate agents.

To achieve a beneficial result from this complicated process, it is important to look at the process as a whole. Because the construction industry in Palestine has evolved in very bad conditions, it is important to learn from other countries' failures, as well as their successes. One common failure is that there are imbalances in the industry: some interested parties dominate it, while others are neglected.

The Swedish Example

This analysis is based on my own practical experience from working in construction, on research carried out by myself and others, and on discussions held with various people in the industry over a long period of time. In real life, there are, of course, many deviations from my description of the construction process. However, the reason for presenting these points of view is to spark off discussion.

So far, I have not received any objections to my description, but rather a lot of expressions of agreement. I am still interested in receiving constructive comments which could help to increase the positive factors and reduce the negative ones. It is also important to underline the fact that most criticisms of the Swedish construction process also apply to other countries.

The Positive Factors

First of all, these include the fact that project work forms a daily routine for builders, especially when compared to other industries. They can start on empty ground in February and complete the building in December in the same year.

Secondly, delegation to craftsmen is a tradition which is being reinforced in Sweden. The craftsmen are taking part in the planning of production on site more and more.

Thirdly, the craftsmen are trained to a level which is only two years short of being accepted to university. The training of engineers and architects is also on a high level.

Finally, there is the reliability of the Swedish industry. Although sometimes Swedes are considered a little boring in the way they keeping promises, for example, the people who do business with them appreciate their reliability.

The Negative Factors

One of the most negative aspects of the Swedish industry is that the construction process is, in effect, conducted like a relay race, but one in which the baton is passed very poorly. First the architect receives it, then the structural engineer, then the installation designers, then the production people, then (when the building project is complete) the facility (or real estate) manager.

The building process also encourages the development of opponents rather than team players, and pits clients against contractors, contractors against sub-contractors, architects against contractors, building project managers against architects and contractors against building project managers. In addition, education in schools of architecture competes against education in schools of civil engineering.

Other negative factors include the fact that there is too little analysis in the early stages of the process, particularly at the design stage where there is also insufficient economic control. No bills of quantities are provided in the documentation for invitations to tender, and there are no architects on the building site. There is also little feedback from experience, insufficient and unclear information to future users, and only a small amount of prefabrication.

Production planning often takes place only in 'the head' of the site manager, and computer support is lacking. Wage and material distribution systems often do not work, there is a resistance to improvements and very few women are employed in the building process. Finally, quality assurance is often neglected, as is the science of building installations.

Suggestions for Improvements

The process in Sweden could be improved by increasing co-operation and reducing antagonism. Various interested parties could be taken into the process at an early stage and individuals could be motivated to do better work.

The economics of a building project should be controlled from the start to finish of the design stage and, of course, during the production stage. Quantities be estimated successively and used in the purchasing contracts. Such control should also include assessments of annual costs (i.e. *life cycle costing*).

The production and the facility of the building project should be planned at the design stage. Quality assurance work should also be a natural and dominant part of the planning and the information needed for decisions should be understood by all those concerned. In addition, the design process should facilitate the use of alternative thinking to the greatest possible extent, so that, for example, changes in the documentation of the building can be made quickly and easily without any mistakes appearing in various parts of the project, such as in its installations.

Information technology should become a part of the construction process and designers should be given an opportunity to make use of their experience. New forms of co-operation and purchasing should be created, and prefabrication should be increased. Finally, women should be allowed to take part in the building process.

A Vision of the Future

The suggestions for improvement can provide a vision of the future construction process. The examples below are taken from the design stage.

The architect sits in front of his computer, using computer-aided-design (CAD) software, and selects an outer wall for the office building he is planning. He retrieves a brick wall (OW101) from his own library in the computer, and then enters the number in the appropriate place.

If he desires, he can obtain additional information on the screen about the various properties of the wall, such as a picture of its design or information indicating that this kind of wall must have certain foundations.

At the same time, he asks the person responsible for production and economy in the project to examine the wall from a productive and economical point of view. This person can then analyse these conditions for the building section, including the appropriate quantities, presented to him without any 'interfering' information.

Using this, he can both check the budget as regards investment and annual costs and carry on working with the production schedule which he is gradually building up using previous experience in the form of production data and preparations for work which are stored in his own computerised library and connected to the technical solution. The planner can also check, for example, with the supplier of any bricks that may be used in the building regarding prices and delivery times and – if considered necessary – make a preliminary booking for the bricks.

The architect, the structural engineer and the installation consultants meet regularly and co-ordinate the various designs and installations. This is done with a large screen on the wall, on which the various building elements, rooms and parts of the installations are shown in both two and three dimensions.

The same project can be examined from another viewpoint by, for example, the client and the users to check functions and the environment, using animated computer graphics. From yet another point of view, the property manager can obtain information on the life of the selected building materials and their other long-term properties.

Both the cost estimates and the production data will be given, showing likely spreads in the confidence ranges. The total uncertainty in costs and time can be stated successively and improved to the desired degree. This means, for example, concentrating first on the factors which give the greatest total spread.

The quantities of the various building elements and installations are estimated successively and automatically throughout the design period and constitute the documentation of the agreements with the sub-contractors. Throughout the design stage, quality assurance forms a continuing and natural part of the process.

When the design stage is completed, the production plans – or at least very good documentation which can be taken over by the production group responsible for carrying out the construction – is ready. This might also include documentation for planning the management of the building. It is also possible to visualise both the production and the completed building.

The production plans will, of course, be gradually revised and improved during production, with ongoing planning in intense co-operation between the various interested parties. This mode of operation will require new forms of procurement, with early co-operation between the various participants, from the client and the architect to the building contractor and the facility (i.e. property) manager.

THE PALESTINIAN CONSTRUCTION PROCESS

To develop the construction process in Palestine, the following steps should be taken:

- Decide the state-of-the-art in construction today;
- Find out how things should be in co-operation with the people involved; then make recommendations; and, finally
- Make the changes.

It is very important to look at the process as a whole, starting with effective management in the briefing stage of the process and all the way through the production stage. A lot of this development work should be done in co-operation with researchers and people from the industry (see below). A training programme could be an important (see below) part of the developing of the Palestinian Construction Industry.

Construction Costs

Admittedly, data on construction in Palestine is limited. Nevertheless, Stephen Mayo has been able to estimate that the cost of construction per square metre in Palestine is double the cost in Jordan. It should be possible to improve the efficiency of construction through the adaptation of modern management, better building techniques, higher labour productivity, better use of materials, and a greater use of local inputs. The aim throughout is to reduce the cost of construction.

Many actions need to be undertaken. Many parties are expected to be interested in cost reductions, including the clients, the consumers, the Ministry of Housing (which would like to reduce the burden for the consumer), the Ministry of Economy, the Ministry of Finance (which should want to make the Palestinian economy more efficient), the contractors (who will be able to increase their margin of profit and serve their clients better), and the engineers' association (which would like to project a good image and achieve a higher level of social responsibility).

Reducing the costs to consumers may be accompanied by higher margins of profit for consultants and contractors. The challenge is to reduce the costs of the construction projects by finding more effective ways to deal with:

- Materials (through a greater use of local inputs);
- Land (by focusing on rural areas);
- Equipment (by establishing equipment-leasing companies);
- Contracting (by better training, research and development and the use of better management, etc.); and finally, by
- Financing the contractors.

The costs of the project must be controlled throughout the entire process, including both the design and production stages. Cost controls must include annual costs (i.e. life-cycle costs) in order to get a balanced building with acceptable running and maintenance costs.

To be able to manage this type of cost control, a lot of data concerning costs must be collected. This should cover the following costs:

- Investment costs;
- Land;
- Fees to authorities;
- Fees to consultants;
- Financial costs during project time;
- Materials (including transport costs);
- Craftsmen's' man-hours for various activities;
- Craftsmen's wages;
- Special contractors (for flooring, painting etc.);
- Contractor's equipment;
- Contractor's staff;
- Contractor's over head and profit annually;
- Capital costs; and
- Running costs (including cleaning, heating/cooling, electricity; etc.).

In addition, data must be obtained on the cost of maintenance (i.e. *life-cycle cost*). Estimating methods must be devised for these various types of costs. It is also important to decide the rules for estimating the various quantities related to the costs.

649

Forms of Procurement

It is important to find easy, clear and competitive forms of procurement at all stages of the construction process and especially when it comes to contracts between clients and consultants and between clients and contractors.

Different forms of contracting – the standard approach, the divided contract approach, the design-and-build approach, etc. – should be analysed and forms of contract decided. It is also necessary to have a set of *General Conditions* which are accepted by all the parties involved.

Consultants

It is very important to promote the development of consulting firms in Palestine. The firms should be organised with modern management ideas (such as that of delegating responsibility) and with information technology as soon as possible. Some important parts to develop are:

- The organisation of the firm, its management and leadership;
- Economic controls;
- The financial services to the firm;
- Insurance and risk cover;
- Project management;
- Quality management;
- Information technology;
- Procurement;
- Cost estimating; and
- Training.

Contractors

The main issue in the Palestinian construction industry is to develop effective, well-managed, competitive firms of contractors. Some important parts to develop are:

- The organisation of the firm, its management and leadership;
- Economic controls;
- The financial services to the firm;
- Insurance and risk cover;
- Cost estimating;
- Procurement;
- Project management, especially on the sites;
- Quality management;
- Production planning;
- Material administration (logistics);

- Production methods;
- Equipment;
- Information technology;
- Training; and
- Research and development.

Construction Supplies

It is important to identify a large range of products and services which, if produced locally, could fulfil the local needs and even be exported. The analysis and development of the building materials industry must also deal with logistics in order to obtain an effective transport system.

The Labour Force

To enhance labour productivity, it is important to start training programs for craftsmen and women.

Codes, Standards and Modular Construction

The construction process needs codes and standards to provide effective communication among all the interested parties. Modular construction is an important tool in the struggle for low costs in the construction industry; otherwise, it is very difficult to create an effective industrial approach to the design of buildings. Cupboards, windows, doors, gypsum boards are all examples of products which need to be designed in a modular system.

Information Services and Information Technology

Thanks to the rapid development of information technology (IT), there are good opportunities to establish an effective information service for the construction process and industry. However, it is essential that the users are capable of defining the demands to be made on IT tools; otherwise, it is easy to be overwhelmed by the hardware and software people.

Renovation

The renovation of old cities and buildings must be carried out with careful, as well as effective, methods in order to maintain cultural values. This should also make it possible for normal consumers to afford to live in renovated buildings.

Other Subjects

Of course, there are many more subjects to discuss concerning the construction industry than the ones mentioned here. Discussion can provide more ideas. Some examples of these other subjects are:

- Prefabrication;
- Testing facilities and laboratories;
- Co-operation with established firms (consultants, contractors, suppliers) from other countries; and
- Co-operation with other research and development institutions from other countries.

RESEARCH AND DEVELOPMENT SERVICES

It is very important to create first class research and development in the construction industry as soon as possible. Research institutions in Palestine should play a key role. The first step should be to decide the state of the art in various areas of the construction process, then to analyse how things should be. This should be followed by recommendations, together with measures concerning the people involved in the process. Finally, research and development should evaluate the changes made in the industry.

TRAINING

A training programme for people involved in different parts of the process could follow a similar pattern as the work of research and development. This means that training programmes should involve the following two stages.

1) Introduction with good and bad examples from various countries. All the participants should be given homework to investigate the state of the art in some important areas in his/her own firm/organisation, i.e. how the planning of the site-works are made. The time should about one week. After about four weeks, it is time for the next stage.
2) Reports from the participants about the state of the art should follow the first stage, along with lectures and seminars showing good examples, and discussions about how things should be. Homework should involve discussions with the people at the firm about how things should be. The time for this seminar should be about one week. After about four weeks, it is time for the next step, and so on.

The advantage of this type of training is that people get involved in a process of change concerning their own firm or organisation instead of just joining a course without any connection to daily work. This also provides strong support for making the necessary changes in the organisation.

THE PALESTINIAN ENGINEER AND THE GENERAL UNION OF PALESTINIAN ENGINEERS

Marwan Abdul-Hameed

ABSTRACT

It is estimated that there are about 56,000 Palestinian engineers, of whom 8 per cent are inside Palestine itself. This paper looks at the organisation of Palestinian engineers, beginning in 1935 when the first society was formed in Jaffa. Societies existing in various Arab countries formed by Palestinians in exile after the beginning of the contemporary Palestinian revolution are also discussed, as is the formation of the General Union of Palestinian Engineers (GUPE) in Baghdad in 1973.

The structure of the Union is explained, as are its activities at the Arab and international levels, its aims and its branches. The paper then discusses relations with the Engineering Society in Gaza and with the Engineers' Syndicate in the West Bank as a prelude to examining the engineering abilities of Palestinians, including those in the diaspora.

The recommendations of a series of meetings in Tunis in January, 1994 are given in detail concerning the future of Palestine regarding its housing policy, consultative work, contractural deals, the financing of sovereign projects and industrial policy.

Subsequent meetings of Palestinian contractors and consultants are described, including the conclusions reached, particularly with regard to the encouragement of Arab consolidation with Palestinian engineers and contractors, the importance of design, and the obstacles facing consulting bureaus and contractors. Finally, the paper provides recommendations for removing the difficulties facing both consultants and contractors.

INTRODUCTION

The Palestinian people have a high percentage of educated individuals and, in particular, of engineers. Despite the lack of a proper census, the number of Palestinian engineers in all branches, including agricultural engineering, is estimated to total 56,000. They are scattered all over the world. Inside Palestine, they constitute 8 per cent of the total. To make this army of engineers effective, it was necessary to establish an institution that would provide them with both a framework and an organisation.

HISTORICAL BACKGROUND

The first move was in 1935 when a society of Palestinian engineers was formed in Jaffa, followed by other engineering societies in Jerusalem and Gaza. The emergence of these societies encouraged the Palestinian Engineering Corporation to take part in the Arab meeting of engineers held in Alexandria in 1935, and in which Engineer Rasheed al-Hussaini represented Palestine. That meeting was the first step towards the creation of the Arab Engineers Union which later came to include at least half a million Arab engineers. However, the Zionist invasion of Palestine in 1948 made it impossible to create a unified organisation for Palestinian engineers because of the dispersion and geographical distribution of Palestinian Arabs throughout the world.

With the onset of the contemporary Palestinian revolution in 1965, Palestinian engineers once more called for the creation of some sort of union. Groups of engineers in exile were created in Algeria, Syria, Iraq, Kuwait and Libya. These five organisations agreed to form a constituent committee of nine of their engineers to initiate the second stage of organising Palestinian engineers. The committee's efforts led to the meeting of the Union's constituent conference in Baghdad on 6 December, 1973, a meeting attended by many representatives of Arab and international engineering associations.

The Union became one of the Palestinian professional organisations under the umbrella of the Palestine Liberation Organisation (PLO). According to its constituent regulations, the Union holds general national conferences once every four years attended by representatives of branches elected to membership of the conferences.

STRUCTURE, ACTIVITIES AND AIMS

Structure

The Plenary Conference constitutes the highest level of the Union and consists of:

- Members of the High Council elected by the last conference held;
- Members of the administrative organs of branches; and

- Elected members of each branch according to quotas stipulated in basic regulations.

The *High Council*, which is the highest authority in the Union during its sessions and in the absence of the plenary conference. It consists of:

- Chairmen of all administrative organs; and
- Twenty-two members elected by the plenary conference.

The *General Secretariat* is the executive organ elected by the High Council. It consists of nine members who elect the secretary-general of the Union from themselves.

The Union is regarded as one of the Palestinian professional and popular organisations and as part of the PLO. In this capacity, the Union participates in the work of the following Palestinian institutions:

- The Palestinian National Council (with 8 members);
- The Palestinian Central Council (with the secretary-general in his legal capacity); and
- The Palestinian Central Council for Palestinian popular organisations.

At the Arab level, the Union is:

- An active member of the Arab Union of Engineers which represents half a million Arab engineers. The Palestinian member served as the Arab Union's chairman for two terms;
- A member of the Arab Union of Agricultural Engineers;
- A member of councils of scientific research; and
- A member of the Arab Chamber of Arbitration for disputes in contractual and building affairs;

The Union also represents the PLO in the Council of Arab Ministers of Housing and in the Council of Arab Ministers of Agriculture.

At the international level, the Union is:

- A member in the World Federation of Engineering Organisations;
- Chairman of the International Committee for the Development;
- Creation of Engineering Syndicates in Developing Countries;
- Deputy chairman of the World Federation, 1993–97;
- A member of the International Union of Architects;
- A member of the International Union for Workers in the Scientific Field; and
- Representative of the PLO at ministerial level in the United Nations Committee for Human Settlements (Habitat).

The Union joined the Arab Engineers' Association as an active member in 1974. With the support of Arab brothers and friends all over the world, the Union, after a long struggle in the general assembly of the World

Federation of Engineering Organisations held in Tunisia in 1975, was able to join the World Federation as an active member. The majority voted for the Union's membership and the vote led to the resignation of the British secretary-general on the grounds that Palestine was not a state and that, according to its Constitution, only states had the right to have their engineering associations join the federation.

The voting had a decisive effect on the work of Palestinian engineers. As the World Federation consists of all the world's engineering associations totaling 89, and as it enjoys the recognition of the UN and of UNESCO, Palestine thus regained its natural status among the international engineering family.

Branches

The Union has branches in Algeria, Iraq, Syria, Lebanon, Yemen, Tunisia, Libya, Egypt, Kuwait, Qatar, Saudi Arabia and Germany. There are also preparatory committees in the USA (where there is an important group of 6,000 engineers), Greece, Italy, Britain and France.

Aims

The Union aims to uphold the engineering profession and to raise its scientific standards in order to promote an Arab renaissance. In addition, its aims include the following:

1) Raising the social and moral standards of engineers as well as their scientific and professional efficiency;
2) Bringing together Palestinian engineering skills and to help provide its members with jobs as well as protecting their interests;
3) Providing for missions and seminars in Arab and foreign countries aimed at increasing efficiency among Palestinian engineers;
4) Establishing a social security fund for Palestinian engineers;
5) Carrying out projects to serve the aims of the Palestinian revolution and to develop the Union's resources;
6) Pooling the skills of Palestinian engineers and focussing their efforts to serve the Palestinian revolution;
7) Contributing to the consolidation of the PLO, the sole legitimate representative of the Palestinian people;
8) Emphasising the scientific method in the struggle of the Palestinian revolution;
9) Co-operating with other popular Palestinian organisations to bring about the creation of a central council for Palestinian popular organisations;
10) Consolidating co-operation and links with all engineering syndicates

and popular organisations in Arab countries, and participating actively in their activities;

11) Supporting the Arab engineering movement and mobilising its efforts to serve Arab society, and participating in Arab engineers' seminars and conferences;

12) Strengthening the Union's relations with national and international syndicates and engineering organisations, and taking part in international seminars and conferences; and, finally

13) Asserting the Palestinian personality in international gatherings and informing the world's engineers of the truth of the Palestinian cause.

RELATIONS WITH ORGANISATIONS IN GAZA AND THE WEST BANK

The General Union of Palestinian Engineers is the legitimate representative of all engineers wherever they live, and represents them in all Palestinian, Arab or international gatherings. It also serves to provide a scientific base for the PLO. It has branches in all countries where Palestinian engineers live.

The Engineering Society in Gaza and the Engineers' Syndicate in the West Bank are natural extensions of the Union in the fatherland. The fact that they were not amalgamated in the Union was due to the Israeli occupation and to concern that they might be closed down or their work obstructed.

The Engineering Society in Gaza was established in accordance with the Ottoman law of societies. It is independent and has its own legal status. The Engineers' Syndicate in the West Bank, both before the Israeli occupation and now, is a branch of the Jordanian Syndicate of Engineers. The General Union agreed to this status in order to ensure the continuity of professional work in a manner that would not cause it to be a target of abuse by the occupying authorities.

In April, 1993, the Jordanian Syndicate of Engineers invited the General Secretariat of the Union, the Syndicate's Council in the West Bank and the Board of Directors of the Engineering Society in Gaza to a meeting in Amman. The participants agreed to form one Palestinian engineering body; however, they also decided to maintain the existing organisations until suitable circumstances for their integration arose.

After the creation of the Palestinian National Authority (PNA), a committee was formed by the general secretariat to prepare for a conference which is to constitute the official launch of an independent Palestinian Engineering Syndicate. Today, it performs its functions at the general secretariat, which has moved from Algiers to Gaza, and holds occasional meetings dealing with professional affairs to maintain the primary role of engineers in the construction process at the professional level.

Both the Syndicate in the West Bank and the Society in Gaza provide significant contributions at the professional level, including holding specialised seminars on a variety of topics such as environment, energy, water resources, industrialisation, housing, etc. They also issue regulations regarding the practice of the profession, endorse consultative studies in Gaza and the West Bank and codes in various fields. In addition, they prepared drafts for specifications and have studied the viability of creating a Palestinian centre, or institute, to deal with issues of quality, specifications and laboratory research.

PALESTINIAN ENGINEERING ABILITIES

The figure of 56,000 Palestinian engineers in the world includes architects, geologists and agriculturalists, even though some countries have unions or syndicates for each of these specialisations. This conforms with the practice of the Arab Engineering Union's Committee for Engineering Education.

During 27 years of Israeli occupation, no developmental, structural or infrastructural projects were carried out in the Palestinian Territories (PT). This led to unemployment among engineers, and they often had to take jobs that had little to do with their specialisations. As a result, they could not gain the experience they needed and lost touch with scientific developments in various fields of engineering.

Abroad, work conditions and the chances of gaining knowledge and experience have been quite different. Palestinian engineers found themselves facing the challenge of survival and work in an atmosphere of unequal opportunity in foreign lands. For this reason, Palestinian engineers tended to work hard in order to gain by the experience and technology they needed.

In the diaspora, Palestinian engineers worked in important and huge development projects and in a variety of specialised fields, as well as in construction. They were able to become familiar with the latest developments in science and technology in their fields. This created a gap in experience between engineers working abroad and those within the PT which needs to be remedied immediately through integration, solidarity and friendliness (see below).

The largest number of engineers are civil engineers, followed by electrical and mechanic engineers. This is due to the law of supply and demand, the nature of projects during the economic boom, the rise of oil prices and the absorption of a great number of engineers in the field of building and construction. Many engineers have managed to set up consulting offices abroad and at home, the standard of which varies from poor to high, i.e. meeting international requirements. Other engineers have preferred to establish contracting companies, some of which are very large and operate worldwide (i.e. the Athens-based Consolidated Contractors Company).

Most engineers work as employees in firms and government offices in a variety of countries, although some have chosen an academic route, working with universities or in vocational education.

Dispersion led Palestinians to enter universities and various higher institutes of learning in a number of countries. Many engineers graduated from universities or institutes in formerly socialist countries which offered scholarships or which enrolled them at a financial cost less than that charged by similar universities in the West.

Others could afford to be taught in Western countries, especially the USA where the number of Palestinian engineers still there exceeds 6,000. They work in all fields, including university teaching, research centres and big companies. Still other Palestinian engineers were educated in Germany, Britain and France, or in Asian countries such as India, Pakistan and the Philippines. Today, this variety of universities and countries is an asset thanks to the direct contacts it provides Palestinians with differing cultures and civilisations, technologies and sciences.

After the signing of an agreement between the PLO and Israel became a reality, the general secretariat of the Union felt that a new phase of the conflict has begun, and that armed conflict turned into an economic, cultural and technological struggle. In the coming phase, the tools differ from previous periods. Today, the development of an independent state needs the best modern methods, up-to-date technology, good management, efficiency, and requires the pooling all Palestinian experience and skills if the possibilities ahead are to be realised.

During the first week of January, 1994, the general secretariat invited a number of Palestinian engineers (not more than 50) who possessed rare capabilities and long, successful and prominent expertise in their fields of specialisations to meet for three days in Tunis. This was three months after the signing of the Declaration of Principles. The general secretariat presented a working paper for the meeting with five basic themes on which participants were asked to offer their views and recommendations. The leadership of the PLO participated in the meeting, gave its blessing to the initiative and Chairman Yasser Arafat took part in most of the sessions.

The working paper and organisation of the meeting stressed the following themes:

1) The national policy of housing;
2) Consultative work in Palestine;
3) Contractual deals in Palestine;
4) Financing sovereign strategic projects; and
5) National policy in industry.

Although only a limited number of engineers were invited and had to pay their own traveling and accommodation expenses, we were surprised by the hundreds of applications made by engineers to take part in the meeting. This demonstrates how keen they were to express their views on the process of reconstruction and on the establishment of a Palestine worthy of its people and capable of surviving competition and of facing the challenges ahead.

This enthusiasm proved that the engineers are well aware of their basic role in that process, the success of which depends on efficiency, ability and expertise in the struggle which is to prove whether we are worthy of a state. For three days, the meetings went on with the participation of 80 Palestinian engineers and several leaders of the PLO who are interested in the subject. The atmosphere was friendly and the discussions frank and direct.

Recommendations of the Tunis Meeting

The meeting drew up a number of recommendations, some of which were general, while others concerned specific subjects such as finance, infrastructure, planning, social services, housing, transport and communications, industry, agriculture and water, as well as consultancy. These recommendations are as follows.

General

1) That the PNA and the Economic Council make use of skilled andprominent Palestinians who are loyal to the fatherland concerning the direction and control of development and reconstruction in the PT.

2) That the general secretariat of the Union of Palestinian Engineers hold, during the next two years, seasonal meetings consisting of a select number of engineers covering all specialisations, to ensure that the recommendations of the Tunis meeting are followed up and to discuss other topics that will require other recommendations.

3) That the general secretariat of the Union set up a committee of experts from different engineering specialisations which, in turn, would be divided into special consultative committees for the Union and for the PNA.

4) That the general secretariat of the Union collect data on Palestinian engineering expertise everywhere, for all specialisations, whether individuals or institutions, during a period not longer than a year and that it submit at every session a report on what has been achieved in this regard.

5) That the PNA and the general secretariat of the Union provide a databank of statistics, reports, maps and other information necessary

661

for development and that they use such information to serve those dealing with development and construction.

6) That the PNA and the Economic Council mobilise Palestinian human resources, local resources and Palestinian institutions and classify and train them and that they co-operate with foreign companies in the field of advanced technology, giving Israeli firms no chance to control Arab and national companies.

7) That the PNA concentrate on Palestinian self-financing through the public savings of the Palestinian people and by encouraging Palestinian capital abroad to invest in the homeland.

8) That the PNA set up systems that would ensure the contribution of all Palestinian institutions in training technical and administrative cadres, at their own expense.

9) That the PNA pass legislation to protect the environment.

10) That advanced technology be used and adapted to Palestinian society and that bilateral relations be employed in this respect, bearing in mind the fact that human resources are the prime factor in the process of transferring and adapting technology.

Finance

1) That the political leadership establish a financial council and draw up financial policies for Palestine.

2) That infrastructural projects and public amenities be financed with regard to priorities requested by local committees of cities, villages and local government institutions.

3) That economic and financial policies be drawn up in a way that would provide a balance between the need of an independent state to create work opportunities to alleviate the present high rate of unemployment (which amounts to more than 58 per cent) and the need to carry out comprehensive development while avoiding accumulating debt that could lead to high interest payments and a consequent doubling of debt.

Infrastructure, City Planning and Amenities

1) That a council for comprehensive national planning be established to set forth a general policy for the utilisation of Palestinian land.

2) That the process of transferring the functions of the Higher Co-ordination Council in the occupied territories to the PNA and subsequently to provincial committees be escalated. (This implies the achievement of sovereignty in the PT.

3) That a council for provincial planning be created to prepare a working

provincial strategy for all the PT and to re-evaluate previous structural strategies.

4) That provincial and local committees be entrusted with the preparation of structural and detailed plans for cities and villages according to regulations, laws and legislations enacted by the PNA.

5) That land surveys as well as land, air, sea, and geological photographs be prepared with specific timetables, taking into consideration that specifications should be numerical to provide for the needs of planning (The survey required for this, and the collection of available data, should help fulfill strategic requirements).

6) That geographical data systems' technology be used in drawing up maps at all levels.

7) That policies required for administering basic services such as water, sewage and electricity as well as other amenities be adopted.

8) That the sites of public amenities be fixed in urban plans and decided regarding either direct purchase or expropriation so that engineering plans for general amenities can be prepared and budgets for this drawn up.

Hospitals, Institutes and Schools

1) That special attention be given to health and education, and that an emergency plan be drawn up to raise their standards.

2) That new institutes in technical, specialised and agricultural fields be established and existing ones developed.

3) That suitable programmes to rehabilitate and improve the living conditions of those harmed during the 'struggle', specially prisoners, the wounded, families of those killed, and the needy be developed.

4) That the establishment of health-care centres and laboratories be expanded to cover the needs of villages and townships and that modern systems of hospital administration be introduced.

5) That a scientific research council be established to encourage, support and develop scientific research work.

Housing

1) That the PNA pay special attention to Jerusalem and its buildings, and to the maintenance of its architectural and cultural identity in order to prevent the disintegration or decline of the Palestinian presence there.

2) That existing Palestinian institutions working in construction and housing, especially the Palestine Housing Council, be supported through the establishment of active relationships with other concerned institutions such as the Co-ordination Authority, Statistics Department,

Social Affairs and Labour Departments, townships, provincial planning bodies, the Union of Palestinian Engineers and contractors.

3) That attention be paid to the architectural patterns of our heritage when drawing up plans, that shanty buildings not be allowed to be introduced, and that respect for structural and detailed plans, as well as licensing and building regulations be respected.

4) That the participation of technical and engineering experts in setting up a system for Palestinian specifications and measurements to control quality be ensured and that different environmental conditions be taken into consideration.

5) That open competitive methods be adopted in carrying out housing projects in conformity with the engineering competition system set up by the Union of Palestinian Engineers with specialised vocational arbitration.

6) That a housing bank to provide housing loans at suitable and easy terms be created to encourage savings and the provision of houses for each profession in all production and services projects.

7) That new cities and suburbs be built to link dense areas of population and to enhance the establishment of amenities and services while protecting agricultural land.

Transport and Communications

1) That Palestinian control of communication systems, networks and information be assured. This requires the immediate preparation of studies and plans for communications including their administrative, technical and temporal planning and implementation according to international specifications.

2) That the development of maintenance be emphasised and the efficiency of relevant workers be increased, technical cadres be trained, institutes be supported and specialised teaching be modernised, along with methods of information and communication systems, and that instruments and apparatus that require maintenance at lower costs be introduced.

3) That plans for seaports and airports as a symbol of national sovereignty be considered with a preference for the political over the economic dimension. This should help to support the political leadership in this field.

4) That existing runways be modernised and that control of Jerusalem airport be sought along with its expansion and modernisation as well as the expedition of construction and equipping of a permanent airport in Gaza and of a temporary one in Jericho (However, the special requirements of the Jericho airport, because of its geographical site, should be taken into consideration).

5) That the need for a political decision to expedite work on the Gaza seaport be emphasised with due regard to the necessary technical considerations.

6) That the PNA create its own mechanism, as quickly as possible, to execute plans for airports and seaports, given that these require a long period of planning, drawing and execution and that both field studies required for drawing up special plans based on data gathered and a timetable for the execution of plans be prepared.

Industry, Energy, Agriculture and Water

1) That new industrial cities be created according to a plan drawn up by the Industrial Cities Establishment, in accordance with the comprehensive national plan.

2) That the importance of an investment law to open doors for marketing Palestinian industrial and agricultural goods be emphasised.

3) That industries of advanced technology, such as electronics, visual instruments, lenses, solar batteries and genetic engineering be encouraged and supported because there are many Palestinian experts in these fields.

4) That water be treated to protect the environment, using the most modern, suitable and inexpensive technical methods.

5) That Palestine be self-reliant in generating electrical energy to avoid political and economic dependence on neighbouring countries and the negative effects this would have on cost and surpluses. Electricity links should also be set up between Gaza and the West Bank.

6) That scientific studies and researches be directed and supported to benefit from various energy resources, such as wind, sun and nuclear energy.

7) That a centre for earthquake observation and a meteorological station be established.

8) That the economic feasibility of making desalinated seawater available for urgent needs be studied. Available water resources are scarce, yet the demand for their use in all fields is increasing, so it will necessary to adopt a national water policy that can raise the standard of exploiting water resources and provide advice for domestic water use and in industry and agriculture. Palestinian water rights should also be kept in mind in political negotiations.

9) That the creation of a national industrial authority be urged. It would aim to list and classify small and average-sized industries and to call on the private sector to engage in these activities.

10) That two banks to finance industry and agriculture with low-cost loans be established.

Consulting Bureaus and Contracts

1) That the creation of official governmental institutions to provide policies and legislation and to supervise the activities of consulting bureaus and contractors in construction be expedited. They should start functioning immediately within the framework of regulations and laws concerning the engineering profession.

2) That the general secretariat be asked to start lay the general basis for organising the profession at once and decide the technical specifications for construction projects and all matters regarding planning and execution of construction in Palestine.

3) That the Union's general secretariat be asked to embark immediately on making arrangements necessary for ensuring close co-operation with Palestinian vocational institutions in consulting and contractual work inside and outside Palestine, together with training and follow-up, and that the secretariat be asked to hold two conferences for consulting bureaus, contractors and people interested in these fields. This should be done within a period two months after the Tunis meeting.

4) That the political leadership be urged to advise the legal committees working on a Palestinian constitution and future legislation to produce regulations and laws to organise engineering activities.

5) That the political leadership be asked to establish a free zone (in at least one city) to encourage investment and export industries, including those that require either high tech or competition.

Meetings

At the recommendation of the Tunis meeting, the Union's general secretariat called for two other meetings in Tunis to prepare for a conference. The schedule included an initial meeting for Palestinian contractors; a second meeting for Palestinian consultants and advisors; and a conference for contractors.

The conference was attended by 120 contractors who reviewed the work of the preparatory committee and endorsed the basic statutes of the established Union for Palestinian Contractors and the drawing up of regulations, rules and contracts concerning the profession in Palestine. The conference was attended and supervised by Chairman Arafat and representatives of the World Bank, donor countries and international associations. It elected a bureau for the Union headed by a contractor, Dawood al-Zir. It is due to prepare another conference to be held within a year.

The conference noted the wide gap between contractors at home and abroad, and advised that it should be filled with the support of contractors abroad for their colleagues at home to improve their performance and integrate their actions. Any conflict or strife between contractors would lead to the penetration of Western companies. It called for policies to uphold the Arab existence in Palestine and to encourage Arab support for the Palestinians in carrying out large projects and ensuring their success. This would also ensure that Palestinian engineers and contractors participate in the proportion fixed by regulations regarding foreign companies.

The meeting of Palestinian consultants was attended by 90 representatives from consulting bureaus located both abroad and at home. It lasted for two days during which participants reviewed ways of organising the profession. They put forward their recommendations, formed their advisory committee and framed regulations and a future strategy for the Consulting Bureaus' Association, which is headed by engineer Ibrahim Abu Ayyash, under the umbrella of the General Union of Palestinian Engineers.

The most noteworthy remark was that whoever controls design controls the project specifications and the entire operation. Thus it is vital that Palestinian consultants have the principal role in design and rely on bureaus at home which are supported and integrated with Palestinian and Arab bureaus abroad. It is also vital that Palestinian engineers, wherever they live, participate in building their country. The PNA endorsed the contractors' conference, its structure and regulations, as well as the association of consulting bureaus.

CONSULTING BUREAUS

There are a large number of consulting bureaus registered in Gaza and the West Bank. The Consulting Bureaus' Association, through the Engineering Society in Gaza and the Engineers' Syndicate in the West Bank, has started to apply professional practices and to re-register and classify engineering bureaus in Palestine in accordance with the regulations, laws and systems endorsed by the Engineering Bureaus' Association in Tunis, as well as by the PNA. This initiated the classification process for engineering bureaus and engineering advisors according to specialisation, size and number. Foundations were laid for relationships with bureaus abroad and in the homeland, as well as for ways of benefitting from the support of bureaus abroad through solidarity and co-operation.

The real problem affecting Palestinian engineering expertise is that able engineers who wish to return to their homeland are barred from entry in line with Israel's position in the Israeli-Palestinian Agreement. This in effect limits the number of people allowed to return until the conclusion of a final peace settlement that might remove this barrier.

The consulting bureaus have already absorbed all architects and civil engineers who were previously unemployed, while others are still without work because of the scarcity of their specialisations, such as textile engineering. This is a result of the emergency programme which is currently being operated by PECDAR and of some small projects, especially in the construction field, in which the private sector is active due to the urgency of needs and to increasing demand.

OBSTACLES AND DIFFICULTIES

Consultants

Consulting bureaus suffer a number of circumstances and from the lack of big projects. The obstacles may be summed up as follows:

1) A lack of data to use in designing;
2) The inadequacy of designing complicated plans;
3) The preference for designing building projects; and
4) The inadequacy of repair operations in general.

Contractors

As with consultants, the Union of Palestinian Contractors began by counting, registering and classifying contractors. This led to a considerable sifting of the contractors' ranks. They were authorised to work and to compete and bid after their enrollment and classification by the relevant authorities and by PECDAR. This sector flourished noticeably when the PNA and PECDAR arranged for bids in the emergency programme, which, though limited, were welcomed by local contracting firms.

Palestinian contractors at home have been occupied with very small projects which do not need extensive skills or complex administration. The obstacles they have faced are financial, professional and political.

Financial Obstacles

Contractors lack the financial resources necessary for keeping up with work requirements, such as securities. Most contractors cannot pay the security currently required. This may lead to the non-payment of bills on time and/or to the posting of security in the following ways:

1) A per cent of the project costs to ensure quality of execution;
2) A per cent of the loan offered;
3) A per cent retained by banks; and
4) Mortgage of land to banks at a rate of interest ranging from 10 to 13 per cent to guarantee the repayment of loans.

Professional Obstacles

These include the following:

- A lack of administrative efficiency;
- The absence of computers for administration;
- Inefficiency in construction management;
- Ignorance of the system of claims;
- Poor standards in designing; and
- Chaotic pricing.

Political Obstacles

These include the following:

- The repeated closure of frontiers by the occupying authorities which leads to the late delivery of supplies and equipment; and
- Restrictions on the importation of goods from abroad.

RECOMMENDATIONS

Obstacles and difficulties facing contractors and consultants need to be removed. This could be done by agreeing the following objectives:

1) Encourage partnerships between Palestinian contracting companies at home and abroad;
2) Encourage solidarity between consultant bureaus;
3) Provide local contractors with expertise and information in fields mentioned above;
4) Arrange for periods of training at home for Palestinian, Arab and foreign experts;
5) Provide local contractors and consultant bureaus with engineering, administrative and modern financing information in order to raise the standard of their performance; and
6) Establish in Palestine a centre providing advice and expertise in all engineering, consultative and contractual fields.

This centre could be financed by the private sector, arrange for seminars and study periods, set up training courses, provide analysis in order to boost the building sector and the transfer of expertise, advise the PNA and provide the contracting and consulting sectors with free services. Companies in the diaspora interested in contributing to the building up of the state could also help create this centre.

In summary, the technical abilities of Palestinians constitute a huge store of treasure for the population. Real investment should concentrate on the construction industry in Palestine in order to create strong Palestinian institutions capable of exporting their work, in addition to their achievements at home. Attention to this is absolutely vital due to the lack of economically important natural resources in Palestine, and to the development programmes which are expected in the region as a whole.

The region's need for such institutions for contractors and consulting bureaus should be met by those working abroad and at home until the time when the Palestinian people regain their sovereignty and achieve complete independence.

The fact that nearly half the number of engineers of Palestinian origin are in Jordan makes it absolutely necessary – besides relying on the Arab dimension – that our colleagues, the Jordanian engineers, are given a prominent role in the reconstruction of Palestine and in the process of creating institutions and useful partnerships.

TRANSPORTATION PLANNING IN PALESTINE

Sameer Abu-Eisheh

ABSTRACT

The transportation sector in the Palestinian Territories (PT) has suffered considerably from the Israeli occupation due to the constraints imposed on its development. For more than 28 years, transportation planning by the Israelis was directed toward the needs of Israeli settlement and Israel's alleged security requirements, rather than toward satisfying the development needs of Palestinians.

Palestinians must build a capability to plan transportation for both urban and rural development and to establish appropriate transportation planning methodologies to examine and evaluate development scenarios and alternative plans. Such methodologies would assist in the arrival at the most appropriate plans regarding the provision of transportation facilities and services aimed at promoting social and economic development.

Emergency rehabilitation programmes and corrective policies and measures should be considered in order to assist the transportation sector in satisfying immediate mobility and accessibility requirements.

This paper looks at the state of the transportation system, including the road network, level of motorisation, and road conditions, and the role of transportation planning in urban and rural development in the PT. Transportation practices are reviewed, as is road planning under Israeli occupation and by Palestinians themselves.

The state of the transportation system is presented first, followed by a review of transportation planning practices according to the Israeli plans and then by the Palestinians. The need for appropriate transportation planning is discussed.

Next, a modelling framework is suggested for transportation planning process. Finally, examples of issues, strategies and policies to be considered in transportation planning for urban and rural development are presented, including scenarios for growth, demographic and socio-economic variables, land use, the size and spatial distribution of Palestinian communities and planning for sustainable and balanced development. The paper ends with conclusions and recommendations.

TRANSPORTATION IN PALESTINE

The existing underdeveloped transportation systems and poor services in the PT are inadequate to satisfy the increasing demand for transportation and to facilitate and induce socio-economic development. The transportation sector in the West Bank and Gaza, like other sectors, suffered from the constraints imposed by the Israeli authorities on its development since occupation in 1967. There has been no systematic transportation planning, nor investment in the transportation infrastructure.

The roadway network forms the backbone of the transportation system in the PT. After the Israeli occupation of the West Bank and Gaza in 1967, non-ground transportation services were halted. The Israelis controlled Qalandia Airport, north of Jerusalem, and did not allow the Palestinians to operate it, and stopped operations at the small seaport in Gaza. The Israeli authorities controlled the passageways which connect the West Bank and Gaza with the rest of the world. Railway service, which extended to parts of the northern West Bank and along Gaza, was halted after 1948.

The Extent of the Road Network

Roads in Palestine had evolved from old footpaths to a primitive network of paved roads during the late Ottoman rule and the British mandate. The network was expanded during Jordanian rule in the West Bank and Egyptian rule in Gaza. The existing structure did not change considerably after the Israeli occupation in 1967.

The national road network has a total length of 2,040 kilometres, including 1,862 kilometres in the West Bank and 178 kilometres in Gaza. These roads are classified into major, regional and local roads, but do not include urban roads and agricultural roads. The national road network connects the Palestinian urban and rural communities together within the West Bank and Gaza, and with other communities across the borders. Figure 1 shows the existing road network in the West Bank and Gaza.

The major roads connect the large urban areas, while the regional roads serve the smaller towns. These roads are paved and most of them are two lane roads, with widths of four to seven metres. Two segments of the major road network are four-lane divided highways, including one segment between Jerusalem and Ramallah, and another as part of road no. 4 running along Gaza. The major and regional roads are either north-to-south or east-to-west roads, based on the nature of the terrain in the country and the transportation patterns. Most local roads which link the villages or which connect with major and regional roads are one-lane paved roads, with a width not exceeding three metres. However, there were about 70 kilometres of unpaved local roads in 1990 in the West Bank, serving about 60 rural communities which had a total population of about 23,000 Palestinians.

Roadway facilities connect the PT with the outside world. Two passage-ways connect the West Bank with Jordan via Damiah and Allenby bridges across the River Jordan, and a third connects Gaza with Egypt through Rafah passageway.

The overall density of roads reached 9.7 kilometres per 10,000 population in 1991. This density is less than that of any other country in the region except Egypt. For example, in 1990 road density reached 27.5 kilometres per 10,000 population in Israel. The indicates how poor road network serviceability is in the PT; road construction has not kept pace with the increase in population and their mobility requirements. Density of roads with respect to the total area of the PT reached 0.35 kilometres per square kilometre in 1991. The indicates poor road network coverage and accessibility.

Motorisation Levels

The total number of registered vehicles has increased dramatically over the last few decades, reaching about 100,000 in 1991. In the West Bank, the total number of vehicles (excluding those for Palestinians in Jeru-salem which are not distinguished in Israeli statistics) reached about 76,000, representing a 19-fold increase over the 1967 figure. Private cars formed 67 per cent of all registered vehicles.

In Gaza, the total number of registered vehicles reached about 24,000 in 1991, representing an eightfold increase compared to 1967. Private cars formed 76 per cent of all registered vehicles. The average annual rate of increase in the number of vehicles in the West Bank is almost twice that of Gaza. In 1991, motorisation levels reached 792 registered vehicles in the West Bank and 359 in Gaza per 10,000 population.

Urban Road Networks

Urban road networks provide services to the built areas within the bound-aries of the cities and towns in the West Bank and Gaza. Most of the towns in the PT were built centuries ago, their old quarters forming the centre of these towns today. Old and narrow roads form the heart of the road networks in the urban areas.

The high rates of motorisation levels in the West Bank and Gaza

673

generate higher traffic volumes, especially in urban areas. No major capacities were added to urban roads and streets after occupation in 1967. Therefore, the relatively narrow urban streets with limited capacities are currently oversaturated. Traffic volumes reach, or exceed capacities, especially during peak periods, producing severe traffic congestion.

Road Conditions

In general, the conditions of the road network are poor. About 942 kilometres of roads in the West Bank, which represent more than 50 per cent of the total road length, can be described as severely to moderately deteriorated. Similar conditions exist in Gaza.

The nature of the terrain in the PT, especially in the mountainous areas of the West Bank where more than 80 per cent of the total road length is located, forced the use of successive curved segments with various radii. The vertical slopes of roads in these areas frequently exceeds 10 per cent. This causes reductions in design and operating speeds, and consequently limits the capacity of roads in these areas.

TRANSPORTATION PLANNING PRACTICES

Planning Under Israeli Occupation

After the occupation of the West Bank and Gaza, the Israeli authorities began preparing a number of roadway planning schemes. These schemes were oriented towards the fulfilment of the Israeli goals and objectives, regardless of the development needs of the Palestinians.

The first plan was prepared just after occupation and was called the National Highway Master Plan, or $T/M/A/3$. A number of highways were planned and built, especially in the West Bank, to meet Israel's accessibility requirements for settlement and its alleged security needs.

After 1977, Israeli strategies regarding highway planning in the occupied PT reflected the new policies of a government which was led by the rightist Likud party. These strategies considered the promotion of Jewish settlements in all parts of the occupied PT the main priority. Highway planning aimed to fully integrate the road network in the West Bank with the Israeli transportation system. These objectives were stated in the 1983–1986 plan prepared by the World Zionist Organisation.

A regional master plan for roads in the West Bank was prepared by a number of Israeli ministries and bodies, including the Ministry of Defence, the Higher Planning Council and the Civil Administration. The plan, published in 1984 under order number 50, was based on the $T/M/A/3$ and the World Zionist Organisation plans. The estimated total length of roads according to the plan was 1,873 kilometres, classified into four types: express, major, regional and local. Not all local roads appear in the maps attached to the plan, as the total length of roads includes segments of roads connecting new settlements which were to be built.

Most of the roads in the plan bypass the Palestinian urban and rural communities, and in many cases these roads effectively isolated Palestinian villages by disconnecting their access roads and by failing to provide links with the new roads. The plan identifies extraordinary road and right-of-way widths. The width of the roads ranges from 40 to 120 metres, while the width of the right-of-way reaches 300 metres. This resulted in a total area of 367 square kilometres of roads and right-of-way widths that were to be confiscated, forming 6.7 per cent of the total area of the West Bank. Many segments of the plan were built or are currently being implemented.

As far as urban planning in the West Bank and Gaza is concerned, the Israelis prevented the Palestinian municipalities from developing their physical and transportation plans. Many of the long-term urban physical plans for these municipalities were prepared by Israeli consultants in order to facilitate their approval. The Israeli Higher Planning Council, the dominant authority in planning-related matters, has not yet approved the plans submitted years ago by Palestinian municipalities, except for a few towns such as Beit Jala and Jenin.

Short-term transportation plans, which include suggestions to improve traffic flow conditions within the urban areas – such as changes in traffic circulation directions or in the installation of traffic signals, have to be approved by the Israeli authorities as well, although each municipality should have the responsibility and authority to do so within its own jurisdiction. Most of these plans, which were submitted by the municipalities, such as those of Nablus and Ramallah, were not approved by the Israeli authorities.

Planning by Palestinians

The Israelis did not allow the Palestinians to plan for themselves, especially on the national and regional levels. Nevertheless, Palestinians recently have begun to prepare development plans for their future state. The first transportation plan prepared by Palestinians followed a request from the United Nations General Assembly (Resolution 42/190) in 1987 for the preparation of an in-depth study on future transportation infrastructure needs. A study was prepared and submitted to the United Nations Centre for Human Settlements (UNCHS), entitled *Future Transportation Infrastructure Needs for the Palestinian People in the West Bank and Gaza* (Abu-Eisheh et al., 1989).

This was followed by another study entitled *Local Village Access Roads in the West Bank and Gaza: Masterplan for Future Development* which was sub-

675

mitted to the United Nations Centre for Human Settlements (Abu-Eisheh et al., 1990). It considered the long-term development requirements for a more detailed network to serve rural communities.

These two studies resulted in a proposed plan for a multi-modal transportation system for the year 2010. The basic assumptions considered included two scenarios. One was based on the assumption that the natural growth of the present Palestinian population would continue and that growth trends in the economy would increase; the other assumed that in addition to the natural population growth, 1.5 million Palestinians would return from abroad and that there would be a more rapid increase in economic growth.

The main objectives considered in developing these plans emphasised the anticipated role of transportation in unification and integration between the two parts of the Palestinian state, i.e. the West Bank and Gaza, in facilitating mobility and accessibility, and in the promotion of socio-economic development.

A short-term transportation plan for the West Bank and Gaza was prepared later upon the request of the Department of Economic Affairs and Planning of the PLO (Abu-Eisheh, 1991). The study was published later as part of the *Programme for the Development of the Palestinian National Economy 1994–2000* (PLO, 1993). The study assumed a two-year transitional period, followed by a five-year period preceding the emergence of a Palestinian entity having full control. The study assumed a natural growth of the present Palestinian population, in addition to the return of 0.4 million Palestinians from abroad, as well as a rapid increase in economic growth. The objectives considered in developing the plan included similar objectives to those set for the long-term plan, as presented above. The plan resulted in a more detailed scheme for an integrated multi-modal transportation system.

As a result of the recent changes in the political situation and the transfer of power to the Palestinians in the West Bank and Gaza, development plans are being prepared. Currently, the Palestinian Ministry of Planning and International Co-operation is preparing a physical plan for the PT under the *Institution Building Capacity for Physical Planning in Palestine* project, which is planned to be ready in 1997.

As part of the project, a unit concerned with land-use/transportation planning is being created and is intended to deal with all planning levels, but with priorities geared towards the national and regional levels. A master transportation plan is expected to be one of the major outputs of the project. Under the same project, pilot physical plans for Gaza, Jericho and Ramallah/Al-Bireh urban areas will be prepared, which will consider developing the proper transportation plans. This will be followed by the preparation of physical plans for other urban areas in the PT.

The Palestinian Ministry of Transport, in co-operation with the Technical Assistance and Training unit of the Palestinian Economic Council for Reconstruction and Development (PECDAR), will supervise projects for developing short-range transportation plans for the urban areas of Gaza, Ramallah/Al-Bireh, Bethlehem and Nablus. These projects, which will start very soon, would result in transportation system management (TSM) plans oriented towards the relief of traffic congestion in these areas.

TRANSPORTATION PLANNING

Appropriate transportation planning plays a basic role in the provision of proper transportation facilities and services to facilitate and encourage socio-economic development. The lack of proper facilities and poor services are barriers to agriculture, industry and trade and may hinder the entire development effort because transportation development helps to achieve an efficient distribution of population, industry and income (Queiroz and Gautam, 1992). While the provision of the transportation system by itself is insufficient to induce development, it is an essential pre-requisite for development.

Proper transportation plans for the PT must be developed to remedy the negative impact on the transportation sector caused by the constraints imposed during the Israeli occupation. The present conditions of the sector are regarded as inadequate to provide cost-effective services and to support future Palestinian economic development (World Bank, 1993).

The Palestinians should develop appropriate transportation plans based on sound planning methodologies. The most appropriate planning model which is capable of simulating existing transportation patterns and of predicting future demand for transportation is needed. The model should be able to evaluate possible land-use and growth scenarios, to predict their traffic-related impacts, and to test alternative transportation plans. As a result, decision-makers will be provided with the proper tools and the necessary information required for the proper allocation of transportation funds.

A FRAMEWORK FOR TRANSPORTATION PLANNING

The Planning Process

Transportation planning is a process which enables the modelling of demand for transportation and the forecasting of traffic flow patterns. Traditionally, long-term land-use/transportation planning studies have been divided into two phases: the calibration phase, where the models are built and tested utilising the base-year data; and the projection phase, where the developed models are utilised in forecasting future demand for transportation based on projections of socio-economic variables for the design year.

The modern approach to the key tasks of the long-term transportation planning process involves modelling of the traveler's trip-making process and the simulation of traffic flows in transportation networks. The approach is known as the four-step transportation planning procedure and includes models representing trip generation, trip distribution, mode split and traffic assignment (see below).

Planning Levels

In order to develop a comprehensive transportation plan for the PT, analysis needs to be carried out on a three-level hierarchical transportation network. The first is the national level, the second is the regional level and the third is the urban level. The national level should consider representative links connecting the 30 urban areas of the West Bank and Gaza and their ties to the outside world (i.e. the international dimension). All transportation systems (land, air and sea) should be considered at this level.

The regional level should consider a more detailed network, including links connecting the more than 400 rural communities in the PT. The urban level should consider the links and nodes of the roadway networks inside the urban areas.

The consideration of a hierarchical road network structure is related to the above mentioned future transportation studies (Abu-Eisheh et al.,1989,1990). For each level, passenger transportation should be analysed, but for the first two levels freight transportation should be studied as well.

Limitations on Planning

The appropriate transportation planning methodology used in the case of Palestine should consider simpler, cheaper and transparent techniques because of the present limitations related to the availability of travel data and information, the institutional structure, and the lack of well-trained expertise and capital.

For example, data which can be classified into demand-oriented and supply-related should be collected to build and calibrate the transportation planning models. However, due to limitations regarding the availability of data, the proposed modelling techniques for utilisation should be modified and adjusted to suit conditions in the PT where detailed socio-economic data are lacking. In addition, it is extremely difficult, expensive and time consuming to collect extensive travel

678

behavior data by conducting large-scale household or road-side travel surveys.

The International Experience

The Institute of Transportation Engineers recommended the development and utilisaation of transportation planning approaches appropriate to different contexts in developing countries (Institute of Transportation Engineers, 1986). A number of transportation planning studies in developing countries utilised transportation planning methodologies which were originally developed in the more advanced countries. These applications have produced only limited, or sometimes no, success (See, for example, Ueberschaer, 1976 and Khisty, 1985).

The construction of the origin-destination trip matrix, which expresses trip distribution, is a very essential and basic step in the transportation planning process for all planning levels. Usually the matrix is constructed based on the estimation of trip generation and distribution models, which require so much data. As an alternate to this modelling procedure, the estimation of the matrix was performed directly from traffic volume counts. Many studies have suggested the estimation of the origin-destination matrix from traffic counts, which considerably require less data (See, for example, Evans and Kirby, 1973, Leblanc and Farhangian, 1982 and Ratnajake, 1988).

This alternate modelling procedure in constructing the origin-destination matrix was successfully utilised in a number of countries, including some developing countries. The framework applied by Ratnajake is unique in developing the matrix on a nationwide level for a developing country, i.e. Sri Lanka (Ratnajake, 1988). The model was analysed, modified and tested regarding its applicability for an urban area – Nablus – in the PT (Abu-Eisheh, 1992). The analysis demonstrated the model's simplicity and low cost and its limited data requirements, yet also showed a sound theoretical basis. The detailed technical specifications and issues of the original work and its modification for use in the Palestinian case can be found elsewhere (Ratnajake, 1988 and Abu-Eisheh, 1992).

The Modelling Approach

In the development of the modelling system, modelling techniques which have been successfully applied in transportation planning studies in many countries, including developing countries, should be utilised. The modelling approach should follow the methodology which considers the four-step transportation planning procedure, as indicated earlier, after careful modifications and adjustments to suit the case of the PT. Although these techniques utilise computer-based models, they require limited data and only reasonable computer expertise.

The general methodology which should be adopted is outlined below. Minor methodological variations must be considered depending on the level of analysis (i.e. whether national, regional or urban) and on whether the analysis is for passenger travel or freight traffic. Before analysis, and for each level, network links and nodes need to be identified and traffic zones defined. The necessary data must be collected, including traffic volumes and data concerning demographic, socio-economic and land-use characteristics. Limited travel surveys are to be conducted.

Trip Generation

Trip generation rates are suggested to be derived from respective values based on rates for other countries with similar conditions. These rates should be studies and modified in order to arrive at proper trip generation estimates which suite the Palestinian case. These rates can be calibrated using the results of limited travel surveys. Passenger trip generation will be modeled considering three general trip purpose categories: work and business, social, and educational/religious/cultural/recreational trips. Similarly, trip attraction rates are to be estimated.

Trip Distribution

Evaluation of the most appropriate trip distribution model for use in the study needs to be carried out, with special attention given to testing the possibility of using the gravity model. Taking into account the limited ability to collect detailed origin-destination data, techniques to estimate origin-destination matrices from traffic volume counts collected from representative links in the network should be considered the most appropriate trip distribution model for the calibration phase, regardless of whether passenger travel or freight movement is involved. It is suggested that the framework discussed above (in the international experience section) be used. A form of the gravity model should be drawn up for each trip purpose.

Mode Split

Modal split of passenger travel into the proper modes, including private auto, bus and shared taxi needs to be modelled using simplistic statistical methods. However, for the national level, which takes into consideration international travel, other relevant modes should be considered, such as the air transportation mode. Regarding freight traffic, all possible modes for use are to be considered including those for air and sea transportation. For other planning levels, the appropriate modes of transportation need to be considered.

Traffic Assignment

Modelling of network traffic flow patterns should be performed using standard traffic assignment techniques. Special attention should be given to evaluate the possible use of capacity-restraint traffic assignment techniques, especially in the calibration phase. In urban areas, where congestion is noticed, equilibrium techniques could be used. Testing the resulting model flow patterns and comparing them with existing traffic volume counts should be performed, and therefore, calibrations need to be carried out. The calibrated traffic flow pattern will provide a basis for comparison with other flow patterns for future plans/scenarios.

Future Plans/Scenarios

Based on future projections of demographic/socio-economic/land-use variables, trip generation, trip distribution, mode split and traffic assignment can be estimated for the design year. Evaluation of suggested future land-use patterns and alternative transportation plans should be made. Each of these should be quantified, coded and modelled using the suggested procedure. This would result in the possibility of comparing such scenarios or plans with each other in order to recommend the most suitable policy.

ISSUES, STRATEGIES AND POLICIES

The estimated transportation planning models, which represent the transportation demand and the transportation networks flow patterns, can be utilised to evaluate the impact of any number of nationwide or regional planning strategies and policies concerning urban and rural development. These may include the size and distribution of Palestinian communities and planning for sustainable and balanced development.

Scenarios for Growth

Due to various possible political, demographic and economic conditions in the PT, a number of expected scenarios for growth must be considered and analysed. Low, medium and high population and economic growth scenarios should be modelled. Each scenario can be identified as a set of demographic and socio-economic variables and land-use patterns and tested for a given transportation system. Alternatively, for each defined scenario, a number of suggested transportation plans could be evaluated and compared to arrive at the most suitable and sound plan. The use of the calibrated models, as described above, would result in more realistic results than using simplistic trend analysis methods.

Demographic and Socio-Economic Variables

The future demographic and socio-economic conditions of the PT will affect the demand for transportation greatly. Demographic conditions which should be taken into consideration include natural growth and the expected return of hundreds of thousands of Palestinians to the West Bank and Gaza. The number of Palestinian returnees may vary from less than 100,000 to more than one million in the coming decade. Many factors, including political, economic and stability-related factors will have an impact on the figure. Therefore, possible variations in future demographic conditions should be considered.

Future socio-economic variables should be projected and considered in the analysis because they will affect transportation demand in the PT. Their impact needs to be investigated, especially concerning the motorization level and the rates and purposes of generated or attracted trips. The social variables that should be considered include household size and family type and age and sex distributions. The economic variables that should be considered consist of aggregate and disaggregate indicators.

The aggregate indicators would give an overview of the general economic conditions including gross domestic product, gross national product, employment and taxation. The disaggregate indicators include the household, per capita and disposable income. For each future socio-economic scenario, these conditions should be modelled through trip generation and attraction models and later evaluated using the traffic assignment model.

Land Use

Future land-use patterns affect trip generation rates and trip distribution patterns greatly . Therefore, planned land uses, according to future development and physical plans for the PT, form major inputs to the transportation demand models, whether related to the national, regional or urban levels. One suggested future nationwide land-use plan, for example, is illustrated in Figure 2 (Abu-Eisheh et al., 1989).

Planned new urban or rural communities, planned locations of newly developed agricultural land, industrial zones and touristic sites in the PT give very clear examples of new land uses which will affect the national and regional planning levels. Future land-use plans on the urban level should indicate, for example, the possible zoning and spatial distribution of commercial complexes, residential neighbourhoods, industrial zones and new major educational, health and cultural institutions.

All the above mentioned changes in land-use patterns can be transferred into dependant variables of land-use models which would represent, in the case of the urban planning level, variables such as the increase in residential units and the increase in commercial, industrial and retail built up areas. These would cause an increase in trip generation and attraction rates (and alter trip distribution patterns), representing induced and developed traffic and resulting in projections of future traffic in the transportation network. Consequently, the effects these may have on the transportation system can be evaluated and compared.

This would require the identification of a number of relevant indicators, which should be based on thorough planning studies. These might be considered as independent variables, including, for example, intensity of land use, amount of land for different uses, net development density per year and employment by land-use type.

Size and Distribution of Palestinian Communities

Strategies regarding the possible establishment of new towns and villages in the PT and their suggested spatial distribution and sizes or those regarding the development of existing urban and rural areas, should be based on a number of considerations, including the distribution of the existing urban and rural communities, the land-use patterns on the national and regional levels, relationships between new and existing communities and development opportunities. Some tudies have made suggestions for the establishment of new Palestinian population centres in various regions such as the Jordan Valley (Centre for Engineering and Planning, 1992).

Scenarios which anticipate the return of hundreds of thousands of Palestinians from abroad suggest that most of them may choose to settle in existing or new urban areas due to the presence of employment or business opportunities. Other relevant strategies may include the designation of specific Palestinian urban and rural areas as developing zones. These may include a number of big villages which will eventually turn into small towns.

The impact of any strategy regarding the spatial distribution and size of Palestinian communities on the transportation system can be evaluated for both the national and regional planning levels. Consequently, the required improvements in the transportation facilities and services to cope with these developments can be planned. Alternatively, the model can assist in recommending the optimum size of new communities and their best location, so as to minimise the impact on the transportation networks or to minimise the associated investment in the transportation system.

Planning for Sustainable Development

Transportation planning for the future should consider planning for sustainable development. Attention should be given to building Palestinian transportation planning capabilities (for both institutional infrastructure and human resources), as well as to the formulation of transportation plans for national, regional and urban planning levels so that changing conditions can be taken into account.

Sustainable planning for the future should consider the specialisation and integration of the various regions of the PT. Planning for transportation systems should take into account the preservation of local materials, energy and natural resources, which are already scarce. In addition, special attention in planning new transportation facilities or in improving existing facilities should be given to satisfy the aim of preserving the environment in Palestine.

In this regard, examples of related policies include supporting the public transport rather than private transport, designing roadway facilities which minimise damage to nature and which have the least consumption of resources, and suggesting transportation plans and traffic control measures which minimise pollution. All these policies could be defined, tested and evaluated using the proposed model, and the results can help to identify the best plans and courses of action to facilitate planning for sustainable development.

Planning for Balanced Development

An important objective of development strategies for the PT is the promotion and sustaining of an equitable distribution of national income between the various population groups, with due consideration to regional balance (Centre for Engineering and Planning, 1992). This objective should be considered in developing future development plans in general, and transportation plans in particular.

Transportation planning should consider the objective of balanced development in Palestine. This should aim to produce equitable development for both the West Bank and Gaza regions, and within the various parts of each of these regions. Transportation planning should attempt to achieve a balance among geographical locations and different income classes for both urban and rural communities. However, more attention should be paid to underdeveloped and remote areas to make them more accessible and to assist in their socio-economic development. Alternative plans which aim to achieve these policies can be tested using the suggested model to examine and compare their effects.

CONCLUSIONS AND RECOMMENDATIONS

Future transportation planning for the PT should focus on building Palestinian transportation planning capabilities (for both related institutional infrastructure and human resources) and the choice of appropriate transportation planning methodologies, rather than the formulation of transportation plans for national, regional and urban planning levels in order to establish the mechanism for proper planning and to better respond to changing conditions. Appropriate transportation planning would result in modelling demand for transportation and the flow patterns on the transportation networks for any number of development scenarios or alternate transportation plans. This would provide decision-makers with the necessary tools and information they need to allocate transportation funds properly.

The provision of transportation facilities and services would assist in inducing and promoting socio-economic development for the PT. The lack of such facilities and poor services are barriers to agriculture, industry and trade and this could adversely affect the entire development effort. Proper transportation planning for the PT is greatly needed and should be a priority in order to remedy the negative effects on the transportation sector due to the constraints imposed on development under the Israeli occupation. The present conditions of the sector are inadequate to provide cost-effective services and to support future Palestinian economic development.

Despite the need for long-term transportation planning for the PT, immediate actions should be taken in order to rehabilitate the deteriorated highway network, to extend roadways to communities not served by paved roads, to reduce congestion in urban areas, to link the West Bank with Gaza, and to enhance transportation links with the rest of the world. Finally, appropriate transportation planning methodologies should consider the current limitations of the PT, especially those related to the availability of detailed data and statistics.

BIBLIOGRAPHY

Abu-Eisheh, S., 1994, **The Israeli Transportation Planning Policies in the West Bank**, Paper presented to the Conservation in the West Bank Seminar, July, University of York, York, UK.

Abu-Eisheh, S., 1992, **The Adaptation of Appropriate Transportation Planning Methodologies for Developing Countries**, Proceedings of the Jordanian Conference on Civil Engineering, University of Jordan, Amman.

Abu-Eisheh, S., 1991, **The Suggested Development Plan for the Transportation**

Sector, Paper submitted to Department of Economic Affairs and Planning, Palestine Liberation Organisation, Tunis (Arabic).

Abu-Eisheh, S. et al., 1990, **Local Village Access Roads in the West Bank and Gaza: Masterplan for Future Development**, Paper submitted through the Centre for Engineering and Planning to the United Nations Centre for Human Settlements (UNCHS).

Abu-Eisheh, S. et al., 1989, **Future Transportation Infrastructure Needs for the Palestinians People in the West Bank and Gaza**, Paper submitted through the Centre for Engineering and Planning to the United Nations Centre for Human Settlements (UNCHS).

Benvenisti, M. and S. Khayat, 1988, *The West Bank and Gaza Atlas*, **The Jerusalem Post**, Jerusalem.

Centre for Engineering and Planning, 1992, **Masterplanning the State of Palestine: Suggested Guidelines for Comprehensive Development**, Ramallah.

Coon, A., 1995, **Urban Planning in the West Bank Under Military Occupation: An Examination of the Law and Practice of Town Panning in the Occupied West Bank**, Institute for Palestine Studies, Beirut (in Arabic).

Evans, S. and H. Kirby, 1973, *A Three Dimensional Furness Procedure for Calibrating Gravity Models*, **Transportation Research**, 8, pp. 105–122.

Grossman, D. and A. Derman, 1989, *The Impact of Regional Road Construction on Land Use in the West Bank*, **The Jerusalem Post**, Jerusalem.

The Institute of Transportation Engineers, Technical Committee 6F–30, 1986, *Research Needs for Transportation Planning for Developing Countries*, **Institute of Transportation Engineers (ITE) Journal**, April.

Israel Central Bureau of Statistics, **Statistical Abstracts of Israel**, Jerusalem, various editions.

Khisty, C., 1985, **Research on Appropriate Planning Methodologies for Developing Countries**, Paper presented to the 64th Annual Meeting of the Transportation Research Board, Washington, D.C.

LeBlanc, L., and K. Farhangian, 1982, *Selection of Trip Table which Reproduces Link Flows*, **Transportation Research**, vol. 16B, pp. 83–88.

Meyer, M.D. and E.J Miller, 1984, **Urban Transportation Planning: A Decision-Oriented Approach**, McGraw-Hill, New York.

Palestine Liberation Organisation, 1993, **Programme for Development of the Palestinian National Economy for the Years 1994–2000**, Tunis.

Policy Research Inc., 1992, **Development Opportunities in the Occupied Territories: Infrastructure**, Report for USAID, Clarksville, Maryland.

Queiroz, C., and Gautam, S., 1992, **Road Infrastructure and Economic Development: Some Diagnostic Indicators**, World Bank, Washington, D.C.

Ratnayake, L., 1988, *Estimating Origin-Destination Matrices from Link Volume Counts: A Simple Intercity Auto Travel Demand Model for Sri Lanka*, **Transportation Planning and Technology**, vol. 12, pp. 263–271.

Ueberschaer, M., 1976, *Problems of Long-Term Travel Behaviour Forecasts in Developing Countries*, in **Transportation Planning for Better Environment**, ed. by Stinger, P. and Wenzel, H., Plenium Press, New York, pp.69–81.

World Bank, 1993, *Developing the Occupied Territories: An Investment in Peace*, **Infrastructure**, vol. 5.

Wright, P., and Ashford, N., 1989, **Transportation Engineering: Planning and Design**, 3rd edition, John Wiley and Sons, New York.

CONSTRUCTION IN PALESTINE

Abdelfattah Abu-Shokor

ABSTRACT

This paper investigates the condition of the Palestinian construction sector as well as developments that have taken place in the West Bank and Gaza. The paper focuses on the most important changes in the sector and on its problems. It aims to identify the measures that must be taken by the Palestinian National Authority (PNA) concerning the sector in Palestine so that it can play a leading and important role in the reconstruction and development of the Palestine economy.

Subjects covered include ground transportation (roads), sea ports, airports and railways, as well as construction in the hotel sector and industry, agriculture and commerce. The paper illustrates the important role of the private sector in the field of construction for housing purposes. On the other hand, the paper shows the marginal role of the public sector in the field of construction in the Palestinian Territories (PT).

This study aimed to determine the domestic capital formation of investments in construction and to determine sources for these investments. It found that the construction sector has always been a leading one in the Palestinian economy in terms of its growth rates and contribution to the generation of local production, domestic capital formation, creation of job opportunities and multiplier effects for construction related industries.

This paper also examined the problems and obstacles that have beset the Palestinian construction sector. Finally, it examines the new horizons that have emerged for this sector in the wake of the peace process.

INTRODUCTION

Because the construction sector is one of the most important sectors in the building of a country's economy, it has always received special attention due to the mutual and interdependent influence that this sector has

687

on the other economic sectors in the country, especially in view of the fact that this sector is closely related to population growth.

The construction sector plays an important role in building installations for the purposes of housing, industry, agriculture and commerce, in addition to health, education, cultural and sports facilities and other public services. Road construction is vital for transportation, and construction in general takes on an economic importance because of its role in providing job opportunities, and therefore local income generation and local production.

In the occupied PT, the construction sector was one of the leading sectors that achieved higher rates of growth in the 1970s and in the mid-1980s. The contribution of this sector has increased in terms of providing job opportunities for the Palestinian labour force and the generation of local production in the PT. However, this sector has been subject to many setbacks which have decreased its role in building the Palestinian economy in contrast with its counterparts in many developing and neighbouring countries.

Construction in the occupied PT was limited to housing financed by personal savings and external remittances sent by Palestinian employees working abroad. In contrast, the Israeli occupation authorities have encouraged the construction sector in Palestinian lands to serve the Jewish settlement of the occupied areas. Thus one might talk of the development of a dualism in the construction sector, with the result that there is one modern sector for Jewish settlements and another traditional sector for local Palestinian citizens.

DEVELOPMENT OF THE CONSTRUCTION SECTOR

Construction

The construction sector usually includes ground transportation network, sea ports and airports. The transportation network also includes postage, ground roads and railway network.

There is no railway network in the PT, and its only airport, Jerusalem (Qalandiya) Airport has been closed by the Israeli military occupation authorities since 1967. Palestinians have been barred from using it. For sometime, the airport has been used by the Israeli civil aviation authority for local flights. The only port in Gaza has also been closed by the Israeli occupation authorities since 1967, so the Palestinians have not been able to use it as an outlet to the sea. Therefore, this study of the Palestinian construction sector will be limited to ground transportation, especially road building.

By 1947, there were some 656 kilometres of paved roads. In the wake of the Israeli occupation in 1967, there were 1,332 kilometres of asphalted roads [1]. The main direction of these roads was from north to south passing through the West Bank and linking the towns of Nablus, Jerusalem and Hebron. However, there were other secondary roads linking Palestinian villages with West Bank cities. By the end of 1993, the length of paved roads in the West Bank had risen to 1,760.3 kilometres [2], an increase of 428.3 kilometres (33.2 per cent). However, most of this increase was to serve Israeli settlement activities in the West Bank rather than to serve Palestinian interests and their need for development and growth.

The road network in the West Bank is weak and insufficient to serve economic development. The roads are not wide enough to accommodate the traffic flow. There are also no highways like those in Jordan and Israel.

When comparing population to the available roads, one finds that the rate is lowest in the West Bank. This rate reaches 1.2 kilometres per thousand residents. In contrast, this figure in Israel amounts to about 2.75 kilometres per thousand. In Syria, the rate was 2 kilometres per thousand, while in Jordan the rate was 1.4 kilometres per thousand persons [3].

In Gaza, the ground transportation is also in poor shape. By the end of 1993, there were 168 kilometres of paved roads [4], linking the strip from north to south. There are also some roads linking the villages and refugee camps with the main roads. This is in addition to internal roads in major cities.

In other words, the condition of roads in Gaza is similar to that in the West Bank. All existing road networks are in need of modernisation and expansion to encourage economic growth and development. Some $500 million is needed to finance this in the West Bank and Gaza as well as to develop Qalandiya Airport in Jerusalem.

Buildings

Buildings are distributed according to their uses, i.e. for housing, tourism, industry and agricultural use, as well as for public services. These four types account for a variety of shares in the Palestinian building sector as a whole. Tables 1 and 2 illustrate the development of building by area, ownership and purpose.

The Palestinian construction sector doubled in size every year between 1968 and 1977. The area which was built rose from 82,200 square metres in 1968, it rose to 213,000 square metres in 1971, and in 1973 it increased to 364,200 square metres. In 1977, the area exceeded 842,900 square metres. However, between 1978 and 1983, the Palestinian building sector witnessed only slight increases in terms of the built area.

Between 1984 and 1986, the built area declined to the level reached

Table 1 The Projects in Gaza.

Types of Projects	No. of Studied Projects	Owner	Donors	Contracts Value U.S. $	Implementing Agency
Schools	25	• UNRWA	• Saudi Arabia • US AID • EC • Others	500,000–1,000,000	Local Contractors
Housing	19	• PHC • Local Investor	• EC • US AID • Private	1,000,000–2,000,000	Local Contractors
Roads	12	• PECDAR	• World Bank	800,000–2,000,000	Local Contractors
Water Networks and Wells	14	• PECDAR	• World Bank	120,000–1,500,000	Local Contractors

Table 2 Gross Domestic Production and Construction (1972 to 1992).

Years	Gaza GDP Millions ($)	Construction %	West Bank GPD Millions ($)	Construction %	Gaza and West Bank GDP Millions ($)	Construction %
1972	77.6	10	198.6	9	276.2	9
1974	153.4	15	395.3	11	548.7	12
1976	195.6	20	454.9	14	650.5	16
1978	196.9	21	498.5	14	695.4	16
1980	287.7	21	756.3	14	1,044.0	16
1982	291.4	23	710.6	17	1,002.0	19
1984	261.4	22	727.4	16	988.8	18
1986	347.6	22	1,189.0	15	15,367.0	16
1988	444.5	22	1,345.4	15	1,789.9	16.7
1990	545.6	18.5	1,674.4	22.6	220.0	21.6
1991	538.8	18.5	1,513.3	27.7	2,052.1	25.3
1992	645.6	21.4	1,841.0	22.8	2,486.6	22.4

in 1980. This was due to a fall in the size of remittances and financial assistance from Palestinian expatriates and from Arab countries. In 1987, the built area in the PT slightly exceeded the level reached in 1982.

Data for the total area built in the PT from 1988 onwards exists. The only available figures are those provided by the Israeli Bureau of Statistics for Gaza in 1988 and 1989. Although the area in Gaza increased in 1988 compared with 1987, the rise was only slight. One can assume that the area of building in the West Bank did not witness a higher increase during the *Intifada*, compared with that in Gaza.

In general, one notices a considerable increase in building activities in the PT since the signing of the Declaration of Principles agreement in Washington in 1993 between the PLO and Israel. However, there are no available reliable data about building activity. One can assume that this has increased greatly in terms of area and number of buildings, i.e. it may have risen several fold in comparison to previous years.

Table 1 indicates clearly that the private sector has always played the leading role in construction in the PT and that the role for the public or governmental sector is marginal.

The public sector had a higher built area only in 1971, when the built area rose above 52,000 square metres (i.e. 24.41 per cent of the total built area). By 1980, after a fall in the area built annually by the public sector, only 4,700 square metres were completed by the public sector (i.e. 0.46 per cent of the total building area in the same year).

Housing

The amount of built area allocated for housing in the PT ranged between 28,600 square metres in 1978 to 1,197,500 square metres in 1987. Perhaps the most important development was the continuous increase in the share taken by the much larger apartments, as shown in Table 2. The table also shows that building for housing occupied the largest share of the built area completed each year in the PT. This exceeded 80 per cent generally, and in some years was even higher, i.e. in 1981 when the built area rose to 85 per cent of the total.

There was also another important development in buildings for housing purposes in terms of the continuous increase in the share taken by much larger housing. A big fall occurred in the percentage of small apartments compared to a high increase in the percentage of larger apartments. Until 1980, activity was mainly focused on two- or three-bedroom apartments at the expense of one bedroom apartments. After that, the share of four- or five-bedroom apartments began to increase. In 1987, these large apartments took some 50 per cent of all completed apartments in the West Bank, compared to 60 per cent of all those completed in Gaza. This indicates a qualitative charge toward an increase in the average dimension of completed apartments.

One may conclude that there was a drop in the share of housing units consisting of one bedroom in both the West Bank and Gaza. In 1978, there were 157 one-bedroom apartments as compared to 45 in 1984. This increased to 103 in 1987, but never again reached the level of 1978.

In Gaza, there was also a drop in the number of one-bedroom apartments built every year. In 1978, there were 109 new apartments compared to just 28 apartments in 1987.

To conclude, one notices that the development of much larger apartments did not lead to a similar improvement in housing quality in terms of the individual's share of the living and building area. The average number of persons living in a one-bedroom apartment reached 2.5 in 1985; this fell to 2.3 persons per one-bedroom in 1993. In Gaza, the average was 2.6 persons in 1993[6]. All this indicates a large fall in the number of rooms and housing apartments in the PT in general In contrast, the average number of persons for each one-bedroom apartment in Israel in 1993 was 1,047 [7].

Hotels

Buildings in the hotel sector occupied a decreasing status in the total area of buildings annually. By 1964, there were 59 hotels of various tourist grades in the West Bank. Two-thirds of these hotels were located in East Jerusalem [8].

In Gaza before 1967, there were only ten hotels, five of which met international tourist standards, with the remainder only meeting local ratings. However, in the last three years of the Israeli occupation, the number of hotels in the West Bank (excluding East Jerusalem) increased considerably. In 1970, the number of hotels rose to 29. After that, the number of hotels in the West Bank dropped to 15 by 1980. This number increased to 17 in 1985 and to 18 in 1986. But in 1991, the number dropped to four.

This fall was accompanied by a decline in the number of rooms in hotels. In 1970, there were 342 rooms compared to 174 rooms in 1991. Moreover, the percentage of room occupancy dropped from 26.7 per cent in 1970 to 7.2 per cent in 1991. This clearly shows the low activity of the Palestinian tourism sector.

In East Jerusalem, the number of hotels was subject to fluctuation. In 1972, there were 34 hotels compared to 40 hotels in 1984. This number fell to 39 in 1985 and to 34 in 1990 [10].

The number of rooms also fell from 2,359 in 1984 to 2,085 in 1990 [11]. The room-occupancy rate dropped as well, falling from 45.2 per cent in 1982 to 30.6 per cent in 1988 [12]. Since the signing of the Declaration of Principles agreement between the PLO and Israel in 1993, the tourism sector has restored its activity, particularly in East Jerusalem. The number of hotels and room-occupancy rates are expected to increase and to bring more business for hotel owners and more jobs for people employed in the sector. In Gaza, the number of hotels has not changed since the Israeli occupation in 1967.

Regarding the quality of Palestinian hotels and their room distribution, the share of rooms in five-star hotels was 402 rooms in 1974 in East Jerusalem, i.e. 22.3 per cent of the total number of rooms in the same year. But the share of this five-star hotel category dropped in 1990. Due to the drop in the number of five-star hotels, from three in 1994 to two in 1990, the number of rooms in this category fell to 344 rooms [13]. In the West Bank, there were only two five-star hotels in 1990, and the number of rooms in this category amounted to 344 [14]. In contrast, the number of five-star hotels in Israel in 1990 was 22, and the number of rooms in these hotels was 5,433 [15].

Industry, Agriculture and Commerce

Unfortunately, there has been no information about the dimensions of premises allocated for industrial of agricultural purposes in the PT. However, I believe their share was very low. This can be proved by the weakness and backwardness of the industrial zones in, both the West Bank and Gaza. This can also be generalised about building activities in the agriculture sector.

Construction for commercial purposes occupies the largest share after construction for housing. This can be seen in the huge expansion of building projects for office and various commercial purposes. The Palestinian private sector needs primarily buildings for commercial purposes. A sizeable number of these commercial buildings are also used for industrial purposes.

CONSTRUCTION IN THE PALESTINIAN ECONOMY

Investment

In terms of the economic growth rate and total investment, the Palestinian construction sector is considered to be the leading economic sector in the PT. Gross domestic capital formation in the PT rose from $10.8 million to $520.3 million dollars (i.e. by 4,717.6 per cent) between 1968–1987, i.e. by an annual average of some 248.3 per cent. This was primarily attributable to the contribution of the construction sector, which ranged between 43 and 82 per cent during the period.

The second half of the 1970s and the first half of the 1980s witnessed huge investments in the Palestinian construction sector. These came primarily from remittances sent by Palestinian expatriates abroad, from financial assistance given the PT by foreign and Arab countries. Most of these funds were directed toward the building sector.

Private investment represented between some 55.3 per cent and 88.2 per cent of gross domestic capital formation between 1968 and 1987. This indicates the minor role played by the public sector in construction compared to the private sector. Private sector investment in the construction sector represented from 60 to 85.8 per cent of total investment in the sector, most of which was directed into housing.

Capital formation and investment in construction in the West Bank is double that for Gaza. Gross domestic capital formation in the West Bank rose from \$7.1 million to \$371.4 million between 1968 and 1987. The share of this accounted for by investment in construction increased from 40 per cent in 1968 to 85.9 per cent in 1981.

Private investment in the domestic capital formation in the West Bank rose from 39.4 per cent in 1968 to 88.2 per cent in 1987. Investment in construction accounted for the largest share of total private investment, ranging from 69.42 per cent in 1972 to 85.2 per cent in 1976. After 1972, the percentage began to fluctuate, but it only fell to 77.89 per cent. In Gaza, construction also accounted for the largest share of the of gross capital formation and of private capital formation.

Construction's increased role in private capital formation occurred during the so-called oil era when Palestinian employees in the Arab Gulf countries sent back remittances to the West Bank and Gaza. Arab financial aid was also provided to the territories as a result of a plan to support financially the steadfastness of the Palestinian people. This plan was adopted by the Arab countries in the Arab summit held in Baghdad in 1978.

Between 1972 and 1975, the growth rate in the construction sector in the West Bank amounted to 46.6 per cent, compared with 39.4 per cent in Gaza. This was actually the highest rate of growth among the various sectors in the PT. Between 1981–1987, these rates were only 10.9 per cent and 5.3 per cent respectively [16].

Since the outbreak of the Palestinian *Intifada* in 1987, until the signing of Declaration of Principles agreement between the PLO and Israel in Washington in September, 1993, the construction sector in the PT witnessed a recession and depression in investment in this sector. For example, the rate of growth in this sector was negative in both the West Bank and Gaza, amounting to –24 per cent and –20 per cent respectively [17].

After the signing of the Declaration in Washington, the Palestinian construction sector began to witness a noticeable improvement in activity. This was due to the optimistic atmosphere fostered by the peace process which attracted the interest of private Palestinian investors both inside and outside the PT. Despite the lack of information about the sector during this period, observers of economic developments estimate that activities in the construction sector doubled.

Construction and Employment

Undoubtedly, the construction sector plays a distinguished role in the absorption of Palestinian labour force as opposed to both industry and agriculture sectors. The construction sector's share in the employment of

Table 3 Size of Employment in the Building Sector Inside the PT (thousands).

Years	West Bank		Gaza		West Bank and Gaza	
	Number	%	Number	%	Number	%
1970	8.38	8.4	4.49	8.5	12.87	8.4
1975	7.72	8.4	2.38	5.1	10.10	7.3
1980	10.09	10.7	3.38	7.3	13.47	9.6
1985	12.87	12.4	4.10	8.4	16.97	11.1
1990	13.95	10.9	6.74	11.0	20.69	11.0
1991	12.99	10.5	6.59	10.0	19.58	10.4
1992	14.13	10.17	8.87	12.4	23.0	11.3
1993	21.56	14.6	12.99	15.4	36.96	14.9

the Palestinian labour force has increased continuously a large number of Palestinian workers got engaged in this sector either working in building and construction in the PT of in Israel proper. The volume of Palestinian work force working in the construction sector, in the PT and Israel increased from a 23,900 workers in 1970 to some 97,900 workers in 1993 (see Table 1).

The Palestinian work force in the construction sector in 1993 comprised some 13 per cent of the total volume of the Palestinian labour force in the same year [18].

The largest part of the Palestinian labour force in the construction sector worked in the Israeli construction sector. The volume of Palestinian workers in the Israeli sector rose from 11,900 workers in 1970 to 60,941 in 1993, when they represented 62.25 per cent of the total Palestinian labour force working in the construction.

The Palestinian work force employed in construction in the West Bank and Gaza, also increased during the same period. The size of the work force rose from 12,800 in 1970 to 36,960 in 1993. The share of construction sector workers in the total Palestinian labour force in the West Bank and Gaza rose from 8.4 per cent in 1970 to 14.9 per cent in 1993.

In 1970, there were 8,380 workers in the West Bank's construction sector compared to 21,560 in 1993. This represented an increase in the share of construction relative to the total labour force in the West Bank from 8.4 per cent in 1970 to 14.6 per cent in 1993.

A similar trend existed in Gaza. The size of the labour force employed in construction rose from 4,490 workers in 1970 to some 13,000 workers in 1993. The share of the construction sector in the employment of new workers in Gaza increased from 8.5 per cent to 15.4 per cent during the same period.

Construction and Production

In the 1970s and the first half of the 1980s, the construction sector was the leading economic sector in achieving economic growth in the PT. The sector is expected to play the same role at present due to the positive atmosphere to investment in the wake of the Oslo Agreement and the Palestinians self-autonomy between the PLO and Israel.

Data cited in Table 2 shows that the construction sector increased its contribution to GDP from $24.8 million in 1972 to $556.9 million in 1992. The sector also increased relative to other economic sectors: its share of GDP rose from 9 per cent in 1972 to 22.4 per cent in 1992.

At the same time, there has been stagnation in the percentage of the industrial sector's contribution and a drop in the contribution of the agricultural sector in the Palestinian GDP. The share of industry in GDP never surpassed 9 per cent between 1972 and 1992, while the share for agriculture declined from 36 per cent in 1972 to 19.2 per cent in 1992.

In addition to the construction sector, one also finds that the service, tourism and commerce sectors have achieved absolute and relative increases in their share of GDP. This is attributable to the remittances transferred by Palestinian expatriates abroad as well as to the wages earned by Palestinian workers in Israel. This was in addition to flow of financial aid from Arab and foreign countries, part of which was invested in the construction sector as well as in commerce and services.

Construction and Related Industries

One question that can be raised in this respect is the following: has the growth achieved by the Palestinian construction sector created a backward or forward effect on the development of related industries in the PT? When examining the industrial sector since the Israeli occupation in 1967, one finds the prosperity of construction sector-related industries, particularly the huge expansion of the marble and stone extraction workshops. This building related industry has prospered partly due to local demand and partly due to an increase in demand for these products in the oil-rich economies of the Gulf states and in the Israeli market as well.

In the West Bank, marble and stone cutting workshops represented some 33 per cent of all industrial plants employing less than eight workers, compared to 20 per cent of all industrial concerns employing eight workers or more. Of 425 industrial plants employing eight workers or more, there were 88 involved in marble and stone cutting.

Furthermore, there has also been the development of manufacturing concrete products, such as mixed cement, brick making, tiles, ceramics (i.e. Chinese tile) in addition to other metal industries such as aluminium making for construction purposes. Factories employing more than eight workers include an aluminium plant, 31 blacksmithing workshops for construction purposes, and 32 industrial plants for mixed cement making, bricks and ceramics.

In industrial plants employing less than eight workers, plants producing concrete products, bricks, Chinese tile and ceramics represented 48 per cent of the total. Local production of these products does not meet the needs of the local market, and huge quantities must be imported from Israel.

In Gaza, there were some 93 construction and building-related industries, representing about 17 per cent of the total local industrial plants. Most produced glass products and construction materials.

It appears that there has been a lack of industrial development for certain building materials such as cement, iron, Chinese tile, ceramics, aluminium and wood fabrications required in construction. All these products are imported from Israel. These imported materials represent some 60 per cent of total cost of building materials [22]. This clearly indicates the weakness of investment in the Palestinian construction sector.

PROBLEMS IN THE CONSTRUCTION SECTOR

Despite the substantial success achieved by the construction sector in the PT, in terms of rates of economic growth and its contribution to the local produce, employment or new workers and meeting partially the local needs of the Palestinian society, this sector has suffered from a number of problems that have prevented it from assuming its big role in the Palestinian economy as is the situation in neighbouring and developing countries. However, this sector remains a leading economic sector that has taken the lion's share in the domestic capital formation.

Of the salient problems facing the Palestinian construction sector, the confiscation of Palestinian lands in the West Bank and Gaza by the Israeli occupiers is the most important. The Israeli authorities have prevented Palestinians from building on these lands and allocated all these lands for Jewish settlement purposes.

As a result, Palestinian building work has been forcibly limited. At the same time, there has been an expansion of Israeli settlements in the PT. All Palestinian lands have been confiscated, seized or expropriated by the Israeli authorities. By the end of 1991, Israel had confiscated some 67 per cent of the land in the West Bank and 40 per cent of that in Gaza. Of this land, 65 per cent has been allocated for settlement purposes; the remaining areas have been declared closed military zones that cannot be used or entered into by Palestinians [23]. By the end of 1994, the amount of confiscated land in the West Bank had risen to some 74 per cent of the total [24].

Another problem facing the Palestinian construction sector has been the severe restrictions on building, particularly in villages and cities. Building inside cities and villages borders has been restricted though many military orders regardless of whether the building was for housing or for public purposes.

Because of these military orders, many of the municipality and village council powers have been usurped. A Higher Planning Committee, consisting only of Israeli officers, has taken over these powers. The authority of these councils and municipalities has also been restricted in terms of giving building permits within the borders of municipalities. The power to change, cancel or suspend the implementations of a building permit or plan within city limits has also been in the control of the Committee.

In addition, the Palestinian construction sector suffered from severe restrictions on the transfer of remittances from Palestinian expatriates abroad. The money would usually flow to the construction sector. The Israeli occupation authorities have also prevented the development of a financial infrastructure that would support the construction sector. All banks operating in the West Bank and Gaza before 1967 have been closed for more than 25 years.

The Israeli authorities allowed the Cairo Amman Bank to re-open in the West Bank in the late 1980s, but have prevented it from giving loans of more than 15,000 Jordanian Dinars without the permission of the Israeli occupation authorities. These restrictions have also prevented the development of a Palestinian housing bank specialised in giving loans for housing projects in the PT. It is worth mentioning here that the Israeli authorities agreed to ease some of these financial restrictions only after the Oslo and autonomy agreements.

One final obstacle facing the Palestinian construction sector has been the lack of Palestinian physical and regional planning to counter Israeli housing plans in the PT. Such Palestinian planning would have met Palestinian needs and their growth requirements regarding population increases and development. Moreover, there has been no general body specialised in planning for housing, particularly for social housing for poor and low-income families in the PT. The limited financial resources available to the Palestinian Housing Council prevent it from assuming its important role in housing development.

FUTURE DEVELOPMENT

After surveying the obstacles and problems facing the Palestinian construction sector, it has become crystal clear that the Palestinians have been usurped of their power of decision making regarding the use of land and any constructions on it. All these powers have been in the hands of the Higher Planning Committee established by the Israeli military authorities whose interests have always been to facilitate and intensify Israeli settlement in the PT while severely restricting Palestinian construction.

Therefore, the development of the Palestinian construction sector depends on the ability of the Palestinians to restore planning and to have use of occupied Palestinian land. In the wake of the Palestinian–Israeli agreement signed in Oslo in 1993, the Palestinians have partially restored their powers within municipality and village council borders. Outside these borders, the land has remained under Israeli control.

The partial restoration of authority to plan and decide land use within municipal and village council limits will open great avenues for the construction sector to develop and prosper. This will enable the Palestinian authorities to open new roads and widen them and to establish industrial zones, schools, hospitals and other public institutions as well as to expand Palestinian universities and to set up social housing projects. Building licenses would then be granted without restrictions. This will also give the Palestinians the opportunity to set up city and village master plans.

The positive atmosphere generated by the Israeli-Palestinian agreements will give the Palestinians the opportunity to explore other avenues to develop the construction sector in terms of investment. These agreements have encouraged the private sector to invest particularly in construction and, as a result, building activity has increased in all the towns of the West Bank and Gaza for housing, industrial, commercial and other purposes.

Finally, investment in the construction sector is expected to rise significantly in the future as a result of the possibility of developing related industries for building materials, especially those industries which would allow the substitution of building materials currently imported from Israel.

SUMMARY AND RECOMMENDATIONS

Although the construction sector occupies an important role in building a country's economy, its importance has been taken for granted in the PT. It should be given particular attention because of the influence it has on the various other economic sectors of the economy.

As explained, the Palestinian construction sector has been one of the leading economic sectors in terms of growth rates. This sector was the main factor and incentive behind the achievement of higher economic growth rates in the Palestinian economy in the 1970s and first-half of the 1980s.

The growth achieved by the construction sector is attributable mainly to the huge investments it received increasingly from the Palestinian private sector. Most of these investments were used for housing purposes. On the other hand, the role of the public sector (i.e. the Israeli occupation authorities) in construction for Palestinians was minimal, and it decreased continuously. The role of the public sector under the Israelis was restricted to the building of an infrastructure for Jewish settlements in the PT.

At the same time, the Israeli occupation authorities neglected the infrastructure of the PT and the Palestinian population was left to take care of itself. Palestinians roads were totally neglected. Moreover, the Israeli authorities never thought of developing airport or railway facilities, let alone sea ports for Palestinians. On the contrary, the authorities closed down the ones that existed prior to the occupation or restricted their use to Israelis only.

The only significant development in the Palestinian construction sector was restricted to housing. This has been solely done by the Palestinian private sector. This kind of building accounted for about 80 per cent of the total area built each year. There was also trend toward building larger apartments. Despite this, the supply of buildings for housing did not meet the burgeoning demand, mainly due to the population increase in the PT.

Hotel construction underwent a recession as well as a drastic drop in growth and development. This has been due to intense competition from the Israeli tourist hotels. Building for commercial, industrial and agricultural purposes suffered a similar fate as construction in the hotel sector.

The positive atmosphere created by the peace process led to an increase in private sector investment in construction particularly for housing and commercial purposes.

It should also be stated that the construction sector has been one of the outstanding Palestinian economic sectors in terms of volume of investment and its big role in the formation of domestic capital and the generation of the GDP in addition to the creation of job opportunities and the establishment of building-related industries. Investment in the construction sector increased from 23 per cent of domestic capital formation to 82 per cent. The construction sector also increased its contribution of GDP to 22.4 per cent, and has even surpassed the agricultural sector. Construction has also played a very important role in creating job opportunities for new Palestinian entrants to the labour force. The contribution of the building sector in new employment rose from 8.4 per cent in 1970 to 14.9 per cent in 1993.

Furthermore, the burgeoning investment in the Palestinian construction sector has led to the development of a number of related industries: quarries, stone cutting workshops, brick making, tile, and ceramics, blacksmithing workshops, aluminium, glass-making, furniture and wood.

However, the multiplier effect of investment in the building sector is still weak, and more than 60 per cent of the value of building materials and products used in construction is currently imported from Israel.

Despite its success compared with the other economic sectors, particularly the industry and agriculture sectors, the Palestinian construction sector has not assumed a full role similar to its counterparts elsewhere in the neighbouring countries due to the many obstacles and problems it has been encountered. These obstacles and problems include the confiscation of Palestinian lands and the severe restrictions imposed by the Israeli occupation authorities regarding the powers of villages and city hall councils to grant building licenses. The Israeli authorities have withdrawn many of these councils' powers particularly in the infrastructural development of roads, schools and industrial zones.

The building sector is also suffering from the lack of Palestinian regional planning and, at the same time, from Israeli plans aimed at speeding up Jewish settlement activities in the PT and at limiting Palestinian urban expansion. There is also no Palestinian authority in charge of housing, planning and the building of apartments for low-income families.

The recovery of planning authority and controls regarding land use from the Israelis will help greatly to provide avenues for the development of Palestinian construction, particularly within the village and city limits once these areas are relinquished by the Israeli military authorities and planning powers are transferred to the PNA. To make use of these new avenues or opportunities, the PNA must take several measures to develop the construction sector, including the following:

- Set up a Palestinian housing strategy and master plan for new cities to absorb the returnees;
- Make a regional plan for the whole PT regardless of the authority in charge of planning and land use in the territories;
- Establish Palestinian institutions in housing, particularly for low-income families;
- Encourage the establishment of building-related industries in order to reduce the deficit in the balance of payments, create new job opportunities, and achieve an increase in the GDP. This should be in addition to doubling the multiplier effect of investments in construction;
- Increase the supply of apartments and give the private sector a leading role in providing financial facilities and easy loans for these; and
- Set up and implement a plan to renovate old quarters in Palestinian towns and villages to help protect Palestinian heritage.

BIBLIOGRAPHY

Abu-Shokor, Abdelfattah et al, 1991, **Industrialisation in the West Bank**, An-Najah University, Documentation and Transcript Centre, Nablus.

Abu-Shokor, Abdelfattah, 1995, **The Palestinian Arab Economy Under the Israeli Occupation** from 1948–1994, Arab language forum, University of Jordan, Amman.

Benvenisti, M. and S. Khayat, 1988, **The West Bank and Gaza Atlas**, Jerusalem.

Government of Israel, Central Bureau of Statistics, 1993 and 1994, **Statistical Abstract of Israel**, Jerusalem.

Okasha, Mahmoud and Sami Abu-Zafereh, 1992, **Industrialisation Determinants and Perspectives in the Gaza Strip**, Jerusalem.

United Nations Committee on Trade and Development, 1994, **Prospects for Sustained Development of the Palestinian Economy in the West Bank and Gaza Strip, 1990 to 2010: A Quantitative Framework**, Geneva.

United Nations Committee on Trade and Development, 1994, **The Tourism Sector in the Occupied Territories**, Geneva.

World Bank, 1993, **Developing the Occupied Territories, An Investment in Peace**, Washington, D.C., September.

CONSTRUCTION PROJECT DELAYS IN GAZA

Adnan Enshassi

ABSTRACT

Delays in construction projects are a major concern for all the contracting parties. A number of reports have been written in recent years stressing the importance of recognising and documenting both the reasons for, and costs of, such delays.

This paper seeks to define and analyse construction delays in Gaza. Data for this study was obtained from 70 different projects, including schools, housing, roads and water networks in the territory.

After examining the possible causes of delays and the nature of the contract system in civil engineering, the paper discusses the provisions of a contract and methods of documenting and recording delays. The results of the study in Gaza are summarised and recommendations made to minimise such delays.

INTRODUCTION

Changed conditions occur when the work encountered on a construction project is significantly different from that described in the contract documents. Change orders, which are directives from the owner or his agent, can alter the terms and conditions of the contract, i.e. to add extra work, delete work and change the standard of the contract. The impact of changes on any project differs depending on the nature and the specification of the contract. If there is a quantity variation in the case of a unit-price contract, the price schedule determines the changes. However, in a lump-sum contract, an overrun is likely to result in a claim. The project manager should be able to evaluate both the direct costs and the effect of the costs of the change, as well as allocating these between the contract parties.

An important factor of project cost control is scheduling contractors

703

to avoid interference, delays and other detrimental effects of one contractor's operations upon another's. Contracts normally contemplate that there will be delays throughout the course of construction. Where delays affect a small part of the overall project, normal change and extra work provisions of the contract can usually be followed.

This paper will begin by presenting the methodology of the study, prior to examining the contract system in civil engineering and problems causing delays in project implementation.

METHODOLOGY

Data for this study was obtained by means of site visits by the author to a number of projects in Gaza. These projects cover several sectors, such as schools, housing, roads, and water networks.

The sample of the study consisted of 70 projects distributed in several locations in Gaza. They were owned by several institutions, such as the United Nations Relief and Works Agency (UNRWA), PHC, and the Palestinian Economic Council for Reconstruction and Development (PECDAR), as well as local investors. These projects are being implemented by local contractors with some assistance from foreign managerial consulting firms. The works ranged in value from about $500,000 to more than $2 million (see Table 1).

THE CONTRACT SYSTEM IN CIVIL ENGINEERING

The execution of a civil engineering project requires that its purpose should first be identified. Then the project has to be carefully planned and implemented. The planning and organising systems used for any project will depend primarily on its complexity; however, its ultimate realisation requires the co-ordination of the contract parties, i.e. the promoter, the engineer and the contractor. The creation of a contract requires the responsibilities, obligations and duties of these parties to be defined clearly and set out in such a system that the project is brought to reality.

A contract is essentially an agreement between two or more parties to do or refrain from doing something. Civil engineering contracts are invariably formed when a process of offer is made by a contractor to an employer to carry out the works set out in contract documents. This is normally in the form of a tender. A simple contract is formed when a tender submitted by a tenderer is accepted by the employer.

Table 1 The Projects in Gaza.

Types of Projects	No. of Studied Projects	Owner	Donors	Contracts Value U.S. $	Implementing Agency
Schools	25	• UNRWA	• Saudi Arabia • US AID • EC • Others	500,000–1,000,000	Local Contractors
Housing	19	• PHC • Local Investor	• EC • US AID • Private	1,000,000–2,000,000	Local Contractors
Roads	12	• PECDAR	• World Bank	800,000–2,000,000	Local Contractors
Water Networks and Wells	14	• PECDAR	• World Bank	120,000–1,500,000	Local Contractors

CONTRACT PROVISIONS

When a delay arises on a construction project, all contract provisions relating to delays should be located and separated out of the contract documents. A delay may be stated as a period during which a contractor is unable to deploy labour and equipment in a manner to achieve the intended output or progress of work. In this case, a liquidated damage clause is usually included in the contract (Haswell and de Silva, 1982).

When the owner is held responsible for the delay, the main contractor may be entitled to a time extension and also monetary compensation. In most cases, delays will lead to additional expenses incurred by the contractor. These expenses occur due to accelerating the job, reallocation work forces, storing extra materials on the job site, or loss of productivity of workers due to reassignment, among other reasons (Ahuja, 1980).

The contract documents should determine whether a delay is excusable, non-excusable or compensable. Excusable delays are not caused by the contractor. In this case, the contractor is entitled to an extension of time under the contract documents. This kind of project delay covers both unforeseen conditions stated in the delay clauses of the contract. Delays are caused by events beyond the control of the contractor.

In order to justify an extension of contract time, the activities delayed must be critical to the project. Nonexcusable delays which are caused by the contractor could lead to actual or liquidated damages for the owner, or to additional costs for accelerating the project.

In extreme cases, excessive delays could lead to termination of the contract by the owner. Compensable delays are caused by the owner's actions or various omissions from the contract documents. In such instances the main contractor will be entitled to additional costs incurred unless there is a valid contract clause stating otherwise (Gay, 1974).

Delays in the implementation of projects can be identified in every stage of the project cycle, from the concept and initial planning through to the completion of the project. There are a number of factors and/or problems which can cause a delay in project implementation (O'Brien, 1976). These are:

- Inadequate planning infrastructure development;
- Problems in financing a project;
- Inadequate assessment of technology;
- Delays in various approvals and consequent changes in the basic assumptions made;
- Lack of expertise in project appraisal;
- Absence of human resource planning;
- Weakness in the process of equipment procurement;
- Ambiguity in the relationship between various agencies involved in the project;
- Delayed drawings and instructions;
- Adverse physical conditions;
- Work suspensions;
- Failure to give possession of the site at the agreed date (I.C.E., 1979); and
- Civil unrest.

The most common sources of delay are 1) unforeseen conditions; 2) the owner; 3) the engineer and 4) the contractor.

DOCUMENTING AND RECORDING DELAYS

Recording delays is an important procedure for all contracting parties concerned. There are several means of documenting and recording the detailed facts surrounding the different types of delays that are encountered in the construction environment.

Any factor which may affect the cost of performing a contract must be well documented, regardless of whether the parties involved foresee a claim or a change of situation. In many cases, a variance in the original plan appears to be a minor one and all parties seem to be in a agreement; nevertheless, at a latter date, the minor problem may have grown into a major one and no one seems to know anything about an agreement (McClellan, 1982).

Methods of documentation include schedule charts and graphs. These are the most widely used and accepted way of documenting the time impact of delays through. By comparing as-build schedules with the originally planned schedule, a determination can be made concerning the amount of time overrun that has occurred on the project due to specific delays encountered.

Accurate daily inspection reports should be maintained by the site engineer. These reports should indicate the areas in which work was performed, any type of problems which were faced, and any instances of lost time or inefficiencies. Particular emphasis should be placed on the areas which may be subject to a delay claim later.

Minutes of all project meetings should be maintained. These meetings should include possible pre-bid meetings, pre-construction meetings, change order or modification meetings and project schedule meetings. The minutes of these meetings should normally be signed by the parties represented at the meetings to indicate concurrence with the approved minutes.

Other important documents and records to be preserved are all original contract documents, including the invitation to bid, specifications, plans, addenda, etc. Any job diaries maintained by office or field supervisors, all shop drawings which have been submitted for approval, all periodic progress payment estimates and daily weather reports should also be retained (Sweet, 1977).

RESULTS

Most of the projects were found to be behind schedule. Closure of the borders was the primary reason for delays in project implementation. This constituted a severe problem for the local contractors and prevented them from purchasing the materials required to execute their projects from Israel. Delays are often caused by confusion at the critical stages.

Other factors are problems of project financing and delay in the issue of drawings and instructions. Delays in the awarding of contracts were responsible for 30 per cent of the projects in this sample falling behind schedule. Another problem stemmed from the fact that a large number of project managers in Gaza do not have not enough experience to manage projects effectively. Table 2 highlights the causes of delay and percentage of projects delayed, as well as the measures needed to minimise the delays.

CONCLUSION AND RECOMMENDATIONS

The economy in Gaza is currently in turmoil. The construction industry contributes 12 per cent of gross domestic product (GDP). Therefore, it is imperative to minimise the problems causing delays in construction in order to improve the performance and productivity.

Delays in construction projects are a major concern to project man-

Table 2 Causes of Delay, Percentage of Projects Delayed and Measures to be Taken.

Causes behind delays	Percentage of projects delayed	Measures to be taken
Border closure	100%	• Improve political situation
Poor management practice	64%	• Improve management procedures • Training
Financial problems	52%	• Owners should send all instalments to contractors on time
Delays in the award of contracts	30%	• Owners should award the contracts on time
Confusion due to inadequate specifications	25%	• Specifications should be clearly and correctly written

agers. There are a number of problems causing delays; of these, the most common are inadequate project formulation, lack of proper implementation and poor management practice. In Gaza, the major problem that causes delay in construction projects is the closure of borders and civil unrest. Both are very difficult to overcome, and both depend on the political situation. Accurate scheduling of materials to programmed delivery dates and their linkage to the actual site layout and storage arrangements is highly desirable.

In general, to minimise delays in projects, scientific project management, rigorous monitoring and detailed pre-construction planning based on a realistic assessment of resources should be used. Analyses of projects that suffered time and cost over runs show that the main reason is the inability to make the use of right management techniques, or failure to apply this in implementation. In order to maintain a project schedule, it must be possible to detect any divergence quickly through a system of progress reporting that makes prompt identification of schedule deviations possible. This requires that actual progress be compared with that which was planned. For this reason, effective training programmes are needed to improve engineering practices and procedures in Gaza.

BIBLIOGRAPHY

Ahuja, H. N., 1980, **Successful Construction Cost Control**, John Wiley & Sons, New York.

Civil Engineering Procedure, I.C.E, 1979.

Conditions of Contract, 5th Edition, I.C.E. 1973.

Gay, O.M., 1974, **Factual Networks and Construction Delays**, Report to School of Civil Engineering, Georgia Institute of Technology.

Haswell, C.K, and D.S. de Silva, 1982, **Civil Engineering Contracts**, Butterworth, London.

McClellan, Van, J., 1982, **Construction Contracts**, General Services Administration, Washington D.C.

O'Brien, J., 1976, **Construction Delay: Responsibilities, Risks and Litigation**, Books International, Boston, Massachusetts.

Sweet, J., 1977, **Legal Aspects of Architecture Engineering and the Construction Process**, West Publishing Co., St. Paul, Minnesota.

ECONOMICS OF THE
CONSTRUCTION INDUSTRY:
BUILDING MATERIALS

Falak Halim Sarraf

ABSTRACT

Until 1967, the economy of the West Bank and Gaza was based on agriculture. Although the potential to establish an industrial sector based on the country's natural and human resources existed, industrial growth has suffered as a result of the cumulative effect of Israeli regulations issued during the 27 years it occupied both these territories.

At present, the building materials sector is limited to stone-based industries utilising limestone and marble which are abundantly available in the West Bank. However, non-metallic building materials such as cement, gypsum, lime, glass and ceramics can be produced from local resources in the future. Geological studies indicate the presence of clay, gypsum, glass sand, dolomite, limestone and soda ash.

Developing new building materials industries will greatly assist efforts to provide the required infrastructure and hundreds of thousands of housing units which are urgently needed.

This paper recommends that a field survey be undertaken with respect to the construction materials industry in the West Bank and Gaza. This survey should provide up-to-date data which could become the basis for further development programmes. Other recommendations include the establishment of adequate infrastructure facilities for research and development; educational and training institutions; a natural resources authority; an organisation for national standards and specifications, and a data bank for industrial technology.

BUILDING MATERIALS IN PALESTINE

The building materials industry in the West Bank and Gaza produces minimally processed mineral building materials (such as stone, marble,

Table 1 Geographic Distribution of Stone-Quarries in the West Bank in 1988.

Area	Stone-Quarries Number	Per Cent (%)
Nablus	54	37.24
Ramallah	8	5.52
Bethlehem	1	0.69
Hebron*	82	56.55
Total	145	100.00

*These quarries are marble-quarries.
Source: E/ESCWA/1D/89/4, 1989.

aggregates, gravel and sand) and concrete products (such as concrete blocks and terrazzo tiles).

Raw materials required for the first category are abundantly available. Those required for the second category are also available, except for the cement, which is currently imported from the Nesher factory in Israel.

Minimally Processed Mineral Building Materials

This category, which includes natural building stone, marble and natural aggregates, is characterised by its basic dependence on the availability of non-metallic minerals and by its low added value.

Building stone

The available building stone in the West Bank is well known for its hardness and durability. It is abundant in the areas of Kabatia, Nablus, Qalqilia and Jenin.

Kabatia and Jamma'in stone is the most commonly used, not only in Palestine but also in Jordan and some other Arab countries. These limestones range in colour between white and the pink found in the area around Bethlehem.

There are around 145 building stone quarries in the West Bank. Their geographic distribution is given in Table 1.

The production rate of the stone quarries varies from one to another, depending on the nature of the rock, the geographic location, and quarry accessibility. Such data reveals that the production rate of one quarry in the area of Hebron is higher than that of another quarry in the Nablus area. Table 2 gives the production rates for each area.

Natural building stone quarrying and processing began as a small-scale enterprise employing basic machinery and requiring intensive labour. In 1973, the industry moved from the traditional and almost manual phase into a more technological one, where machinery to break rocks, such as mechanical jack hammers, air-compressed breakers, loaders, and lorries,

711

Table 2 Production Rates of Stone Quarries in 1988.

Area	Number of Stone Quarries	Average Daily Production (m3/ one quarry)	Average Annual Production* (m3)	Per Cent
Nablus	54	5	64,800	19.43
Ramallah	8	4	7,680	2.30
Bethlehem	1	5	1,200	0.40
Hebron*	82	12	236,160	77.87
Total	145	–	309,840	100.00

*Working days during one year equals 240 days.
Source: E/ESCWA/ID/89/4, 1989.

Table 3 Geographic Distribution of Stone-Cutting Plants in 1988.

Area	Stone-Cutting Plant Number	Per Cent (%)
Nablus & Tulkarm	43	33.1
Ramallah & El-Beera	19	14.6
Bethlehem & Beit Jala	23	17.7
Hebron*	45	34.6
Total	130	100.00

*These are cutting-marble plants.
Source: ESCWA, E/ESCWA/ID/89/4, 1989.

were introduced. This modernisation was carried out in order to fulfil the continuous increase in market demand. As a result, the production rate increased nearly tenfold, and the industry's dependence on intensive labour was reduced.

Natural building stone, after being quarried, needs to be trimmed to obtain ashler stone (the squared stone used in building or for facing walls). The ashler is manually shaped using special tools, such as hammers and chisels. In the early 1970s as a result of the boom in the construction industry, electrical saws to cut the stone were introduced. As with machinery to break rocks, this increased the production rate and decreased the labour input.

Results of a field survey conducted by the Economic and Social Commission for West Asia indicate that until 1986 around 130 stone-cutting plants are available in the West Bank. All of these were established after 1973 (ESCWA, 1989). Table 3 shows the geographic distribution of stone-cutting plants in 1988.

Table 4 gives the daily production at that time. It ranged between 150 and 2,800 linear meters. The capital invested in these plants ranged from 10,000 Jordanian Dinars (JD) to JD 1 million. Most of this was invested in the machinery needed, the lorries for transporting the stone. In a study conducted by the United Nations Commission for Trade and Development (UNCTAD), the number of quarries and of plants for cutting

Table 4 Daily Production of Stone-Cutting Plants in 1988.

Daily Production (Linear Meter)	Stone-Cutting Plants (Per Cent)
150–200	15
201–300	40
301–400	25
401–500	15
>1000	5
Total	100

Source: E/ESCWA/ID/89/4, 1989.

either marble or stone was estimated to amount to about 200 and 350 respectively (UNCTAD, 1989).

Building stone is sold in three main markets: the West Bank, Israel, Jordan and other Arab countries through Jordan. The sudden construction boom that occurred in Jordan during 1973; the consent of the Israeli authorities to let Palestinians export building stone to Jordan; and the consent of Jordanian authorities to let their production enter the country were the real factors behind the usage of electrical stone-saws, and, accordingly, behind the progress of the entire stone industry.

The ESCWA survey also indicated that around 55 per cent of stone production in 1988 was exported to Jordan, compared to 24 per cent and 21 per cent exported to the West Bank and to Israel respectively.

Marble

Marble is another inorganic, non-metallic mineral which is processed and used in the West Bank. Marble is a dense, hard and highly polished stone which is employed in construction as wall and floor tiles as well as for decoration.

Marble processing is similar to stone processing, including quarrying and cutting. However, marble is also subjected to a polishing process. Good reserves of marble are available around the city of Hebron. The number of marble quarries, their production rates and the number of marble-cutting plants are given in Tables 1, 2 and 3 respectively under the heading 'Hebron.'

The development of the marble industry, including the introduction of electrical saws, and the purchasing power of the relevant markets is similar to that of the building stone industry.

Aggregates

The construction industry consumes a large amount of aggregates, either for buildings or for roads. The traditional aggregates used in the West Bank are crushed limestones. The aggregate-production plants sector is another mining industry which is based on limestone quarries, in addition to industrial scale crushers. Around 15 aggregate-production plants are available in the West Bank; nine are located in the Ramallah area, and six in the Nablus area (ESCWA, 1989). Unlike stone-cutting plants, aggregate-production plants require large areas of land, ranging from 25 to 240 dunums (1 dunum = 1,000 square meters).

In most cases, the plants own at least 70 per cent of the land and rent the remainder. This adds to the capital needed for such investments, in addition to the investment required for the crushers and other machinery.

The aggregate-production plants witnessed remarkable growth in 1973, and this was reflected in the development and modernisation of their machinery.

Production varied between 300 and 2,000 tons a day in 1989. This was sufficient to satisfy local demand. The West Bank consumed around 64 per cent, while Israel and Gaza consumed 24 per cent and 12 per cent respectively (ESCWA, 1989).

Concrete Products

Concrete blocks and terrazzo tiles are the two concrete industries available in the West Bank and Gaza. As mentioned earlier, the raw materials required for such products are available, except the cement which is imported from Israel.

Blocks

Concrete blocks are used in buildings for partition walls, but since the early 1970s they have been used to build external walls as well. This was due to the sharp increase in the price of building stone - the traditional material used to build external walls. Another factor has been the violation of municipal laws requiring the use of natural stone to build the external walls of buildings.

As a result of the sudden increase in demand in the early 1970s, the technology employed to produce concrete blocks developed from manual brick-making machines, producing 500 blocks/day, to automatic ones that produce around 6,500 blocks/day.

Concrete block plants in the West Bank use local coarse aggregate (crushed limestone), fine aggregate (sand), and ordinary Portland cement. Sand and cement are imported from Israel. There are around 65 block-making plants in the West Bank which employ some 360 labourers, and 87 plants in Gaza employing 480 workers (Urttani & Habash, 1983).

Blocks are produced in different sizes. The length and height are constant; that is, 400 and 200 millimetres (mm) respectively, while the

Table 5 Numbers and Types of Terrazzo Tiles Factories in West Bank.

Year	Terrazzo Tiles Factories Modern	Average	Traditional	Total
1979	–	35	60	95
1980	4	28	54	86
1981	5	25	54	84
1982	5	25	50	80

Source: Urttani & Habash, 1983.

width varies from 40 to 200 mm. Concrete blocks for roofs are also produced.

Tiles

The production of terrazzo tiles increased noticeably during 1973 in order to satisfy local demand. Israel consumed about 60 per cent of the production at the time. Later on, when Israel established a modern competitive tile industry (such as the Nemleet Factory), the export rate of West Bank tile plants declined to 20 per cent. West Bank sales also fell due to the better quality of Israeli tiles available in the local market. These two factors continued to affect the tile industry adversely in the 1980s, as did the stagnation of the construction sector in general.

This is reflected in the reduction in the total number of tile factories from 95 in 1979 to 80 in 1982 (Table 5). Most of the reduction occurred in the traditional and average factories; these fell by 20 as a result of the establishment of modern factories which had higher production rates and better quality (Urttani & Habash, 1983). The number of factories in the West Bank dropped to 58 in 1984 with 400 employees. In Gaza during the same year, there were 50 tile factories with 250 workers (Samed al-Iqtisadi, 1988).

Terrazzo tile factories in the West Bank and Gaza use local crushed limestone aggregate and marble chips from the Nablus and Hebron areas. In addition to sand, ordinary and white cement are imported from Israel (Urttani & Habash, 1983).

BUILDING MATERIALS AND THE CONSTRUCTION INDUSTRY

The Role of Building Materials

The building materials and construction sectors play a significant role in the economic and social development process. Because of this, governments pay close attention to these activities and they receive a great deal of support in terms of funding and public policies.

Valuewise, some two per cent of the world's production originates in the building materials industry. In global trade, building materials account for approximately three per cent of the total value. The import shares of the developing countries are three to four times those of their exports of building materials. Imports account for roughly one-fifth of the developing countries' consumption of building materials (UNIDO/Sectoral Studies Series No. 39, 1987).

Building materials are produced by a number of industry branches, the unifying element being that they constitute inputs to the construction sector. However, the products from these industries are also used for purposes other than construction. Thus, while it is perfectly possible to speak about the production of building materials, it becomes much more difficult to define in operational terms a building materials industry. In examining the building materials sector in the West Bank and Gaza, the following difficulties were encountered.

- Very few statistical data considered building materials as a separate sector. Data was classified under a variety of sectors such as industry, housing, labour force and construction.
- Very little statistical data was based on field surveys. The majority was based on statistics released by the Israeli Central Bureau of Statistics (CBS). Moreover, East Jerusalem is not treated by the CBS as part of the Palestinian Territories, but as part of Israel.
- Reliable statistical data for the years after the *Intifada* has been difficult to obtain, especially for the years following 1990, and in particular for Gaza.

Costs and Prices

The cost of building materials is a major component of any construction project. Up-to-date prices for locally produced building materials in the West Bank and Gaza are given in Table 6 below.

Obstacles Facing the Building Materials Industry

The building materials industry in the West Bank and Gaza faces multiple, interrelated problems. Some of these are related to the industrial sector in general, while some others affect the building materials industry primarily.

Palestinian industry in general faces the following difficulties.

1) Unequal competition with Israeli products. Israeli practices have aggravated the already existing difficulties inherent in competing

716

Table 6 Cost of Building Materials produced in West Bank and Gaza.

Building Material		Characteristics	Unit	Shekels*
Stone	Building Stone	First Grade Jamma'in	Linear meter	17.8–18.9
Based	Marble	–	600×400×30mm	75.0
Industry	Aggregate	Coarse (Follia) (20mm)	m3	33–36
		Med. (Adassia) (12mm)	m3	33–36
		Fine (Semsemia) (7mm)	m3	44.0
		Fine (sand)	m3	36.0
	Concrete	400×200×100mm	One block	1.0
Concrete	Blocks	400×200×150mm	One block	1.5
		400×200×200mm	One block	1.8
Products				
	Terrazzo	300×300mm		
	Tiles	Indigenous Marble Chips	m2	18–20
		Italian Marble Chips	m2	28–30

*One Jordanian Dinar = 4.45 Israeli Shekels.
Source: The Author's Search, May 1995.

with the relatively better quality and lower-priced Israeli manufacturers, which benefit from unrestricted access to local Palestinian markets.

2) Restrictive practices by Israeli authorities, including delay or obstacles in issuing building or operating permits for enterprises which are considered to compete with existing Israeli industries, and/or which represent a basic industry such as cement.

3) The Israeli domination of the Palestinian external trade sector.

4) A small restricted market. A lot of external markets were lost due to the Arab-Israeli Boycott.

5) Factories and plants are subjected to tax rates and assessments which far exceed those applied prior to occupation. Such taxes include Value Added Tax (VAT), production tax, customs tariff, Tamah tax, import tariffs and others.

6) The lack of an adequate and efficient banking system. The absence of normal credit services represents a serious constraint for those aiming to expand successful operations, and deprives producers of the means to modernise production facilities.

7) Raw materials and machinery required for the production process within the factories can only be imported by Israeli authorities.

8) Palestinian manufacturers are prevented from building the infrastructure required for their plants, such as roads, electricity and water.

9) A low level of technical expertise. All firms with sophisticated

machinery suffer from a serious lack of qualified maintenance and repair technicians.

10) The lack of an industrial data bank and of programmes for research and development, studies, and technical assistance.

The following problems relate to the building materials industry in particular.

1) The variable restraints placed by the occupation authorities on the construction sector, causing a reduction in local demand for building materials. A large number of the plants which produce these products are, at present, working with reduced capacities. This in turn causes an increase in production costs, and consequently higher selling prices.

2) The lack of an indigenous cement industry leaves the supply and price of this vital material in total control of the Israeli authorities. This affects adversely cement-dependent building industries such as those producing concrete blocks and tiles.

3) Increased fuel prices have had a direct negative effect on mining because this industry requires large amounts of fuel. Most stone, marble and aggregate production plants are located in areas which lack electricity supplies.

4) The flooding of the West Bank and Gaza with Israeli terrazzo tile production which is of good quality and which has lower prices.

5) Poor maintenance of equipment, lack of spare parts, and working with salvaged machinery and equipment. This reflects adversely on the quality and quantity of production of blocks and tiles in particular.

6) Electricity power supplies to local stone-cutting and aggregate-production plants are frequently shut down. Consequently, supply and production rates are irregular.

FUTURE PLANNING

Production and Trade

In a study conducted by United Nations Industrial Development Organisation (UNIDO), six main types of building materials were differentiated (UNIDO, 1987). They are as follows:

1) Non-metallic building materials (cement, lime, asbestos, clay, glass, blocks, electrical insulation and sanitary and plumbing fixtures);

2) Primary metal building materials (metal bars, rods, sections, tubes, pipes, and rails, screws);

3) Finished metal products (finished metal structural parts, hard tools, boilers, stones, locks, hinges, valves, fixtures and fittings);

718

4) Wooden building materials (lumber, veneers, wood-based panels, and builders' woodwork);
5) Chemical building materials (pitch, tar, bitumen, paints, varnishes, plastics, and glues); and
6) Minimally processed mineral building materials (such as stone, sand, gravel, and aggregates).

As mentioned, building materials currently manufactured in the West Bank and Gaza are almost totally limited to minimally processed mineral building materials, and to the blocks and tiles included in the category of non-metallic building materials. This situation is similar to that which prevails in many developing countries.

The most significant gains made by the developing countries have been in the largest group of building materials, namely non-metallic mineral products. In the developed countries, the relatively largest gain in production has been in finished metals and in chemical building materials.

While non-metallic products are the most extensively produced building materials, primary metal products are the most widely traded. Owing to their low value-to-weight ratio and their universal availability, the minimally processed materials are barely traded at all.

Consumption, Construction and Population

The growth in the consumption of building materials in the developing countries is faster than in either construction or population. In contrast, in the developed countries the annual growth in population, construction and building materials have kept pace with each other.

In the West Bank and Gaza, this correlation between population, construction and building materials is distorted due to the following factors:

- A very high population growth rate, which amounts to 3.6 per cent and 3.8 per cent for the West Bank and Gaza respectively;
- A relatively low construction growth rate, which remained constant for the years 1980 to 1986; and
- A restricted building materials industry. Low production rates for building materials will be reflected in consequent low consumption rates.

Recommended Building Materials Industries

Non-metallic building materials are the largest group of building materials, and at the same time, those most employed in construction. This group of materials is basic to any construction industry. It includes the following:

719

- Cementitious (binding) materials such as cement, lime and gypsum;
- Building components such as blocks and bricks (concrete, clay, sand-lime), tiles (concrete, clay), drainage and sewage pipes (concrete, clay), kerbstone, and gypsum tiles and boards; and, finally
- Glass and ceramics (floor and wall tiles and sanitary ware).

Primary metal building materials are another necessary item for buildings, especially for structural elements in construction where steel bars are required for reinforced concrete.

The following groups of building materials have been investigated considering the availability of their raw materials, of the labour force and related technology in relation to the needs of the construction industry. They are recommended for future implementation.

Cement

The West Bank and Gaza procure all their cement supply from Nesher, which is Israel's monopoly cement manufacturer. A survey dated 1985 put consumption of cement at some 460,000 tons (UNCTAD, 1989; *Samed al-Iqtisadi*, 1988). Because of inadequate local supplies in Israel, the quantity of cement channelled to the Palestinian Territories is often considerably less than the volume of effective demand.

In 1978, a group of entrepreneurs from the West Bank and Gaza sought to establish a local cement factory. A permit from the Israeli authorities for the plant was given in 1994 (Abu Own, 1994). The factory is clearly viable economically and, in addition, would achieve other objectives, including the following:

- It could reduce dependence on Israel for a strategic commodity which the Israeli authorities may decide to withhold from the Palestinian Territories;
- It could help reduce the cost of imports from Israel;
- By making cement more readily available and possibly at lower prices, Palestinians could expand their construction activity and reduce population congestion;
- By making cement more available and possibly at lower prices, other cement-based building materials industries such as blocks and tiles would be enhanced; and
- Such an industry would provide a lot of work opportunities for Palestinian labourers.

In early 1979, the founding committee of the cement project succeeded in having the firm registered under the name of the Arab Cement Company (ACC). The Board of ACC commissioned a German firm to conduct exploratory surveys and formulate implementation plans. The initial results were very encouraging, as raw materials were found in abundant quantities in a number of locations.

Suitable limestones, clays, marly clays, and gypsum are available in the Hebron area (Yatta, Bani-Naim, and Beit-Ainoun), Nablus area (Silat Edh Dhahr), as well as in North Jerusalem (Jaber, 1981).

The location of the factory is planned to be near Hebron; production capacity would amount to 1,500 to 3,000 tons a day (As'ad, 1994) (Utaili, 1993).

Cement demand in the West Bank and Gaza is estimated to amount to about 200,000 tons a year (As'ad, 1994) (Utaili, 1993).

Although, the Israeli authorities agreed to the registration of ACC, they subsequently obstructed the implementation of the project itself, prior to the granting of a permit in 1994. This was done by rejecting ACC's request for prescribed mining permits, claiming that the project was not economically viable. Israeli opposition may have reflected protectionist motives.

Lime

A hydraulic lime industry is recommended since the raw materials required are available. The industry is based only on limestone having a high percentage of calcium carbonate. Large quantities of limestone deposits having such specifications are available in the Nablus area, Western area of Dead Sea, and in Gaza (Hardan, 1983) (Utaili, 1993).

The calcination process (transferring calcium carbonate to calcium oxide at around 1,000 to 1,200 degrees Centigrade) does not involve high degree of technology, and does not require highly trained labour.

The industry requires energy for the calcination process. The final products – quicklime and slaked lime are used in a number of other industries such as paints, building plasters, water treatment and agriculture.

Gypsum

A gypsum industry is highly recommended since gypsum is an essential ingredient in the cement industry. It is added to cement clinker to retard the hardening process in order to obtain a setting time practical for field applications.

Building gypsum, which is also known as Plaster of Paris, is obtained by heating the gypsum ore to about 150 to 200 degrees Centigrade. The production technology is similar to that of the lime industry; it is not complicated, but requires energy. The required labour is available.

Natural gypsum ores are available in the West Bank. The best quality ore, which has a high percentage of calcium sulphate), is located to the west of Dead Sea (*Samed al-Iqtisadi*, 1988). Gypsum is also available in Gaza and in the El-Nabi Mussa area (Utaili, 1993).

Plaster of Paris is the basic material for other gypsum products such as gypsum plasters, gypsum boards and gypsum forceiling tiles (for acoustic insulation). It is also used for interior building decorations, for moulds required by several industries (such as ceramic sanitary ware), for school chalk, for jewellery crafts and other products.

Ceramics

Ceramic floor and wall tiles are essential components of buildings in addition to sanitary ware, ceramic tiles are mostly produced by a semi-dry pressing method, prior to pouring on a layer of glaze.

Although the production process is an automatic one, skilled labour is needed to watch the production line. Tunnel-kilns are used to fire the tiles and all conditions of the firing stage (maximum temperatures, the rate of heating, etc.) are electrically controlled. However, technical staff should be able to set these conditions according to the variations in raw materials and their proportions.

Raw materials required are kaolinitic clays, glass-sand and limestone. These are available in the West Bank and Gaza, where traditional pottery and ceramic crafts for tourism have always been known and produced.

Kaolinitic clays are largely available in the Jerusalem district, Gaza, Nablus, Jenin, and Hebron. Glass-sand is available in Hebron, and limestone in several locations (*Samed al-Iqtisadi*, 1988) (Utaili, 1993) (Abu Own, 1994) (Hardan, 1983).

Glaze materials consisting of more refined clays (ball-clay or china-clay) may need to be imported, as is the case with Jordanian ceramic industries. Oil-fired kilns should be used for economy.

Sanitary ware is another recommended industry. Sanitary ware such as sinks, wash basins and closets are produced by the slip-casting method, and glazing is applied by either dipping or spraying. The raw materials batch mainly consists of kaoline, ball-clay or china-clay, quartz and feldspar, which means that some will be imported. Regarding feldspar, geological references do not mention it, but it does not mean that it is not available. A geological investigation should be performed along with a feasibility study for this industry.

Glass

Sheet glass is a fundamental component in buildings. The raw materials required for the industry are almost all available: glass sand from the Hebron area, limestone and soda ash from Dead Sea area (*Samed al-Iqtisadi*, 1988) (Utaili, 1993). The supply of feldspar needs to be investigated regarding possible locations, properties and suitability for the industry. However, ornamental glass items and household glass pieces have always been a traditional craft production in the city of Hebron.

This industry requires high technology, large invested, capital, technical staff, and trained labour. External markets should also be considered in addition to the domestic demand for such an industry.

Concrete Reinforcing Steel Bars

Steel reinforcement bars for reinforced concrete structures are as essential as cement in the construction industry. Concrete reinforcement steel bars used by the construction industry in the West Bank and Gaza are imported from Israel.

Iron ore is available to the east of the city of Nablus In 1955, investigations proved that the discovered deposit near Nablus is in fact a natural continuation of the iron mines already utilised by Israel in the middle district of Palestine. These ores contain around 28 per cent iron (Hardan, 1983).

A steel bars industry requires a high degree of scientific and technological know-how, and a large capital investment. As indicated by a proposed steel bar project (*Samed al-Iqtisadi*, 1990), the total value of produced bars is estimated at $36 million. This represents the previously imported value. The investment recovery value is estimated to reach 43.3 per cent.

Steel Pipes

Steel pipes are widely used in two main economic sectors, namely agriculture and construction. At, present such pipes are imported from Israel. Iron ores are available near Nablus. In a proposed steel pipes project (*Samed al-Iqtisadi*, 1990), the value of the production is estimated to total $4.7 million U.S. dollars. The estimated recovery investment value is around 20.4 per cent.

Ready-Mixed Concrete

Ready-mixed contributes to better quality concreting, reduced machinery, shorter-time durations and more practical field conditions. The raw materials needed for such an industry in the West Bank and Gaza are available, except for the cement which is imported from Israel. In this case, most of the expected gain for such an industry is related to the enhancement of the concreting process. On the other hand, if the cement can be produced locally, as suggested strongly, the benefits of this industry would be enhanced.

Other Concrete Products

Concrete products, other than blocks and tiles, are also required for construction works. Concrete pipes for water drainage and sewage are recommended as future supplementary products. Moreover, the production of kerbstone, which is used to build street edges, is also recommended. Raw materials (except cement) and labour requirements for these products are available in the West Bank and Gaza.

Paints

Paint products are widely used in the construction industry. They are used not only in the construction stage but also afterwards for maintenance purposes.

Main raw materials for this industry such as limestones, glass sand and iron oxides are all available in the West Bank and Gaza (Utaili, 1993).

RECOMMENDATIONS

The establishment of a national building materials industry which can operate independently and effectively requires a number of measures. These include the following:

- A comprehensive field survey in respect of construction materials industries is highly recommended. This survey should cover the different aspects of the industries, including their numbers, locations, technologies employed, production rates, raw materials availability, marketing, labour force, problems encountered, and quality control programmes;
- Education systems including universities and polytechnics which provide qualified human resources;
- Scientific research institutions to promote research and development;
- A national authority to exploit natural resources for local needs. This would help to develop the raw materials required by the building materials industry;
- A national institution dealing with standards and meteorology. This would help quality control programmes to be implemented to assure standard specifications for locally produced building materials;
- Provision of governmental local technological laboratories to perform quality control tests on local building materials; and
- A national data bank to provide access to scientific and technical information related to building materials and to the construction industry.

BIBLIOGRAPHY

Abdullah, S., 1987, *Effect of Occupation on the Development of Palestinian Building Construction and Housing*, **Samed al-Iqtisadi**, IX, 69–70, pp. 76–81, Arabic.

Abu Shukker, A., 1990, *Industry Status in The Palestinian Occupied Lands*, **Samed al-Iqtisadi**, XII, 81, pp. 15–29, Arabic.

Abu Kushq, B., 1981, **Arab Industry in The Occupied Lands**, Paper presented to Development for Sustenance Conference, Jerusalem.

Abu Own, J., 1994, *Development of Housing Sector in the Occupied Lands*, **Samed al-Iqtisadi**, XVI, 95, pp. 136–167, Arabic.

Al-Jundi, I., 1986, **Industry in Palestine During the British Mandate**, Dar El-Karmel, Samed, Amman, Arabic.

Al-Utaili, S., 1993, *Utilisation of Raw Materials in the Palestinian State*, **Samed al-Iqtisadi**, XV, 93, pp. 9–19, Arabic.

Arab Industrial Development Organisation, 1984, **Industrial Development in Palestine** (West Bank and Gaza), AIDO–02–013–001, AIDO Publications, Baghdad, Arabic.

As'ad, A., 1994, *Status and Horizon of Industrial Sector Development*, **Samed al-Iqtisadi**, XVI, 95, pp. 99–109, Arabic.

Cement Industry in the Occupied Land, 1988, **Samed al-Iqtisadi**, X, 72, pp. 171–174, Arabic.

Economic and Social Commission for Western Asia (ESCWA), 1989, **Industrial Development in Palestine**, E/ESCWA/ID/89/4, United Nations Publications, Amman, Arabic.

Hardan, T., 1983, *Industry and Future Development in Occupied West Bank and Gaza*, **Samed al-Iqtisadi**, XV, 45, pp. 5–30, Arabic.

Investment Opportunities in the Occupied Palestinian Land, 1990, **Samed al-Iqtisadi**, XII, 81, pp. 65–83, Arabic.

Jaber, H., 1981, **Cement Issues in The Occupied West Bank**, Paper presented to Development for Sustenance Conference, Jerusalem.

Tayeim, S., 1985, *Small-Scale Traditional Industries in the Occupied Lands and their Development*, **Samed al-Iqtisadi**, VII, 53, pp. 99–104, Arabic.

The Industrial Sector in the Palestinian Occupied Land, 1988, **Samed al-Iqtisadi**, X, 72, pp. 19–52, Arabic.

Ukasha, M., 1993, *Industrial Sectors and the Extent of Development in the Gaza Strip*, **Samed al-Iqtisadi**, XV, 94, pp. 140–173, Arabic.

United Nations Conference on Trade and Development (UNCTAD), 1989, **Palestinian External Trade Under Israeli Occupation**, UNCTAD/RDP/SEU/1, United Nations Publications, Geneva.

United Nations Conference on Trade and Development (UNCTAD), 1994, **Main Features of Domestic and External Merchandise Trade of the West Bank and Gaza**, UNCTAD/ECDC/SEU/5, United Nations Publications, Geneva.

United Nations Conference on Trade and Development (UNCTAD), 1994, **Prospects for Sustained Development of the Palestinian Economy in the West Bank and Gaza, 1990–2010: A Quantitative Framework**, UNCTAD/ECDC/SEU/6, United Nations Publications, Geneva.

United Nations Conference on Trade and Development (UNCTAD), 1994, **Public Utilities in The West Bank and Gaza**, UNCTAD/ECDC/SEU/2, United Nations Publications, Geneva.

United Nations Industrial Development Organisation (UNIDO), 1987, **The**

Building Materials Industry: Its Role in Low-Cost Shelter Programmes, Sectoral Studies Series No.39, Limited Distribution, Vienna.

Urttani, M. and W. Habash, 1983, **Construction and Related Industries in the West Bank**, Arabic.